T0211124

Lecture Notes in Computer Science 13598

More information about this series at https://link.springer.com/bookseries/558

George Bebis · Bo Li · Angela Yao · Yang Liu ·
Ye Duan · Manfred Lau · Rajiv Khadka ·
Ana Crisan · Remco Chang (Eds.)

Advances in Visual Computing

17th International Symposium, ISVC 2022
San Diego, CA, USA, October 3–5, 2022
Proceedings, Part I

Editors
George Bebis
University of Nevada
Reno, NV, USA

Bo Li
University of Illinois Urbana-Champaign
Urbana, IL, USA

Angela Yao
National University of Singapore
Singapore, Singapore

Yang Liu
Microsoft Research Asia
Beijing, China

Ye Duan
University of Missouri
Columbia, MO, USA

Manfred Lau
City University of Hong Kong
Kowloon, Hong Kong

Rajiv Khadka
Idaho National Laboratory
Idaho Falls, ID, USA

Ana Crisan
Salesforce
Seattle, WA, USA

Remco Chang
Tufts University
Medford, MA, USA

ISSN 0302-9743 ISSN 1611-3349 (electronic)
Lecture Notes in Computer Science
ISBN 978-3-031-20712-9 ISBN 978-3-031-20713-6 (eBook)
https://doi.org/10.1007/978-3-031-20713-6

This Springer imprint is published by the registered company Springer Nature Switzerland AG
The registered company address is: Gewerbestrasse 11, 6330 Cham, Switzerland

Preface

It is with great pleasure that we welcome you to the proceedings of the 17th International Symposium on Visual Computing (ISVC 2022), which was held in San Diego, USA, during October 3–5, 2022. ISVC provides a common umbrella for the four main areas of visual computing including vision, graphics, visualization, and virtual reality. The goal is to provide a forum for researchers, scientists, engineers, and practitioners throughout the world to present their latest research findings, ideas, developments, and applications in the broader area of visual computing.

This year, the program consisted of six keynote presentations, nine oral sessions, one poster session, two special tracks, and one tutorial. We received close to 110 submissions for the main symposium from which we accepted 45 papers for oral presentation and 16 papers for poster presentation. A total of eight papers were accepted for oral presentation in the special tracks from 14 submissions.

All papers were reviewed with an emphasis on the potential to contribute to the state of the art in the field. Selection criteria included accuracy and originality of ideas, clarity and significance of results, and presentation quality. The review process was quite rigorous, involving three independent double-blind reviews followed by several days of discussion. During the discussion period we tried to correct anomalies and errors that might have existed in the initial reviews. Despite our efforts, we recognize that some papers worthy of inclusion may have not been included in the program. We offer our sincere apologies to authors whose contributions might have been overlooked.

We wish to thank everybody who submitted their work to ISVC 2022 for review. It was because of their contributions that we succeeded in having a technical program of high scientific quality. In particular, we would like to thank the keynote speakers, the program chairs, the steering committee, the international Program Committee, the special track organizers, the tutorial organizers, the reviewers, the sponsors, and especially, the authors who contributed their work to the symposium. We would like to express our appreciation to Springer for sponsoring the "best" paper award again this year.

We sincerely hope that ISVC 2022 offered participants opportunities for professional growth.

September 2022

George Bebis
Bo Li
Angela Yao
Yang Liu
Ye Duan
Manfred Lau
Rajiv Khadka
Ana Crisan
Remco Chang

Organization

Steering Committee

George Bebis (Chair)	University of Nevada, Reno, USA
Sabine Coquillart	Inria, France
James Klosowski	AT&T Labs Research, USA
Yoshinori Kuno	Saitama University, Japan
Steve Lin	Microsoft, China
Peter Lindstrom	Lawrence Livermore National Laboratory, USA
Kenneth Moreland	Oak Ridge National Laboratory, USA
Ara Nefian	NASA Ames Research Center, USA
Ahmad P. Tafti	University of Southern Maine, USA

Computer Vision Chairs

Li, Bo	University of Illinois Urbana-Champaign, USA
Yao, Angela	National University of Singapore, Singapore

Computer Graphics Chairs

Liu Yang	Microsoft Research Asia, China
Duan Ye	University of Missouri, USA

Virtual Reality Chairs

Lau Manfred	City University of Hong Kong, Hong Kong
Khadka Rajiv	Idaho National Laboratory, USA

Visualization Chairs

Crisan Ana	Tableau Research, USA
Chang Remco	Tufts University, USA

Publicity

Erol Ali	Eksperta Software, Turkey
Loss Leandro	Quantaverse LLC, USA

Tutorials and Special Tracks

Hand Emily	University of Nevada, Reno, USA
Tavakkoli Alireza	University of Nevada, Reno, USA

Awards

Sun Zehang	Apple, USA
Amayeh Gholamreza	Tesla, USA

Web Master

Adhanom, Berhe Isayas	University of Nevada, Reno, USA

Program Committee

Adamo-Villani, Nicoletta	Purdue University, USA
Agu, Emmanuel	Worcester Polytechnic Institute, USA
Ahmad, Touqeer	University of Colorado Colorado Springs, USA
Alderighi, Thomas	ISTI-CNR, Italy
Alim, Usman	University of Calgary, Canada
Amayeh, Gholamreza	Tesla, USA
Ambardekar, Amol	Microsoft, USA
Ammi, Mehdi	LIMSI-CNRS, France
Angara, Naga Surya Sandeep	National Institute of Health, USA
Anvari, Zahra	University of Texas at Arlington, USA
Apperley, Mark	University of Waikato, New Zealand
Argyros, Antonis	Foundation for Research and Technology – Hellas, Greece
Asari, Vijayan K.	University of Dayton, USA
Asesh, Aishwarya	Adobe, USA
Athitsos, Vassilis	University of Texas at Arlington, USA
Averkiou, Melinos	University of Cyprus, Cyprus
Baciu, George	The Hong Kong Polytechnic University, Hong Kong
Bais, Abdul	University of Regina, Canada
Bajpayee, Abhishek	Massachusetts Institute of Technology, USA
Balazs, Peter	University of Szeged, Hungary
Balcisoy, Selim	Sabanci University, Turkey
Barneva, Reneta	SUNY Fredonia, USA
Barzel, Ronen	Independent Consultant, UK
Bashiri, Fereshteh S.	UW-Madison, USA
Basu, Aryabrata	Emory University, USA

Batmaz, Anil Ufuk	Concordia University, Turkey
Behrisch, Michael	Utrecht University, Netherlands
Bender, Jan	RWTH Aachen University, Germany
Benes, Bedrich	Purdue University, USA
Bhargava, Ayush	Facebook, USA
Bhatia, Harsh	Lawrence Livermore National Laboratory, USA
Bhatia, Sanjiv	University of Missouri - St. Louis, USA
Bist, Ankur	Govind Ballabh Pant University of Agriculture and Technology, India
Biswas, Ayan	Los Alamos National Laboratory, USA
Borges, Dibio	Universidade de Brasília, Brazil
Borland, David	University of North Carolina at Chapel Hill, USA
Bouguila, Nizar	Concordia University, Canada
Braz Pereira, Jose	EST Setúbal/IPS, Portugal
Brimkov, Valentin	Buffalo State College, USA
Broll, Wolfgang	Ilmenau University of Technology, Germany
Bruder, Gerd	University of Central Florida, USA
Bryan, Chris	Arizona State University, USA
Capin, Tolga	TED University, Turkey
Chai, Sek	SRI International, USA
Chang, Jian	Bournemouth University, UK
Chatzis, Sotirios	Cyprus University of Technology, Cyprus
Chen, Cunjian	Michigan State University, USA
Chen, Zhonggui	Xiamen University, China
Chiang, Yi-Jen	New York University, USA
Cho, Isaac	Utah State University, USA
Chourasia, Amit	University of California, San Diego, USA
Dang, Tommy	Texas Tech University, USA
Dasgupta, Aritra	New York UniversityUSA
Dequidt, Jeremie	University of Lille, France
Dhillon, Daljit Singh	Clemson University, USA
Diamantas, Sotirios	Tarleton State University, USA
Diehl, Alexandra	University of Konstanz, Germany
Dingliana, John	Trinity College Dublin, Ireland
Doerner, Ralf	RheinMain University of Applied Sciences, Germany
Doretto, Gianfranco	West Virginia University, USA
Doulamis, Anastasios	Technical University of Crete, Greece
Du, Shengzhi	Tshwane University of Technology, South Africa
Dutta, Soumya	Los Alamos National Laboratory, USA
Ebert, Achim	University of Kaiserslautern, Germany
Egbert, Parris	Brigham Young University, USA

El Ansari, Mohamed	University of Ibn Zohr, Morocco
El-Alfy, El-Sayed M.	King Fahd University of Petroleum and Minerals, Saudi Arabia
Emami Gohari, Ebrahim	LinkedIn, USA
Entezari, Alireza	University of Florida, USA
Erol, Ali	Sigun Information Technologies, Turkey
Eslami, Mohammad	Technical University of Munich, Germany
Ferrara, Matteo	University of Bologna, Italy
Ferreira, Nivan	Universidade Federal de Pernambuco, Brazil
Ferrise, Francesco	Politecnico di Milano, Italy
Fierrez, Julian	Universidad Autonoma de Madrid, Spain
Fisher, Robert	University of Edinburgh, UK
Foresti, Gian Luca	University of Udine, Italy
Frey, Steffen	University of Groningen, Netherlands
Fudos, Ioannis	University of Ioannina, Greece
Fujishiro, Issei	Keio University, Japan
Fusek, Radovan	VŠB-Technical University of Ostrava, Czech Republic
Gavrilova, Marina	University of Calgary, Canada
Gdawiec, Krzysztof	University of Silesia, Poland
Geist, Robert	Clemson University, USA
Geng, Zhenglin	Epic Games Inc., USA
Giorgi, Daniela	ISTI-CNR, Italy
Girish, Deeptha	University of Cincinnati, USA
Goh, Wooi-Boon	Nanyang Technological University, Singapore
Grisoni, Laurent	University of Lille, France
Gustafson, David	Kansas State University, USA
Hamza-Lup, Felix	Georgia Southern University, USA
Hand, Emily	University of Nevada, Reno, USA
Haworth, Brandon	University of Victoria, Canada
Hazarika, Subhashis	Palo Alto Research Center, USA
Hodgson, Eric	Miami University, USA
Holmberg Bahnsen, Chris	Aalborg University, Denmark
Hua, Jing	Wayne State University, USA
Hussain, Muhammad	King Saud University, Saudi Arabia
Imiya, Atsushi	Chiba University, Japan
Iwasaki, Kei	Wakayama University, Japan
Jenkin, Michael	York University, Canada
Jeschke, Stefan	NVIDIA, Austria
Jiang, Ming	Lawrence Livermore National Laboratory, USA
Jung, Sungchul	Kennesaw State University, USA

Kam, Ho Chuen	The Chinese University of Hong Kong, Hong Kong
Kanai, Takashi	University of Tokyo, Japan
Kenyon, Garrett	Los Alamos National Laboratory, USA
Kim, Edward	Drexel University, USA
Kim, Hyungseok	Konkuk University, South Korea
Klosowski, James	AT&T Labs, USA
Kollias, Stefanos	National Technical University of Athens, Greece
Komuro, Takashi	Saitama University, Japan
Kosmopoulos, Dimitrios	University of Patras, Greece
Krone, Michael	University of Tübingen, Germany
Kuijper, Arjan	TU Darmstadt, Germany
Kuno, Yoshinori	Saitama University, Japan
La, Hung	University of Nevada, Reno, USA
Lai, Yu-Kun	Cardiff University, UK
Laramee, Robert S.	Swansea University, UK
Lee, D. J.	Brigham Young University, USA
Lewis, Robert R.	Washington State University, USA
Li, Frederick	University of Durham, UK
Li, Xin	Texas A&M University, USA
Lien, Kuo-Chin	XMotors.ai, USA
Lin, Chun-Cheng	National Yang Ming Chiao Tung University, Taiwan
Lin, Stephen	Microsoft, China
Lindstrom, Peter	Lawrence Livermore National Laboratory, USA
Linsen, Lars	Westfälische Wilhelms-Universität Münster, Germany
Liu, Shiguang	Tianjin University, China
Loaiza, Manuel	Universidad Católica San Pablo, Peru
Loss, Leandro	QuantaVerse LLC,USA
Loviscach, Joern	Fachhochschule Bielefeld, Germany
Lu, Aidong	UNC Charlotte, USA
Macdonald, Brendan	NIOSH, USA
Makrogiannis, Sokratis	Delaware State University, USA
Mansoor, Hamid	Worcester Polytechnic Institute, USA
Martins, Rafael M.	Linnaeus University, Växjö, Sweden
Masutani, Yoshitaka	Hiroshima City University, Japan
Mathews, Sherin	University of Delaware, USA
Matkovic, Kresimir	VRVis Research Center, Austria
Mcgraw, Tim	Purdue University, USA
McNamara, Ann	Texas A&M University, USA
Mestre, Daniel	Aix-Marseille University, France

Meunier, Jean	University of Montreal, Canada
Miao, Xikui	Brigham Young University, USA
Mistelbauer, Gabriel	Stanford University School of Medicine, USA
Moreland, Kenneth	Oak Ridge National Laboratory, USA
Morishima, Shigeo	Waseda University, Japan
Morris, Brendan	University of Nevada, Las Vegas, USA
Moujahdi, Chouaib	Mohammed V University in Rabat, Morocco
Mousas, Christos	Purdue University, USA
Musse, Soraia	Pontificia Universidade Catolica do Roi Grande do Sul, Brazil
Nazemi, Kawa	Darmstadt University of Applied Sciences, Germany
Nguyen, Quang Vinh	Western Sydney University, Australia
Nicolescu, Mircea	University of Nevada, Reno, USA
Nikou, Christophoros	University of Ioannina, Greece
Noh, Junyong	Korea Advanced Institute of Science and Technology, South Korea
Ntalianis, Klimis	University of West Attica, Greece
Nykl, Scott	Air Force Institute of Technology, USA
Okada, Yoshihiro	Kyushu University, Japan
Olague, Gustavo	CICESE, Mexico
Olano, Marc	University of Maryland, Baltimore County, USA
Oshita, Masaki	Kyushu Institute of Technology, Japan
Paelke, Volker	Hochschule Bremen, Germany
Palagyi, Kalman	University of Szeged, Hungary
Papagiannakis, George	University of Crete, Greece
Papakostas, George	Eastern Macedonia and Thrace Institute of Technology, Greece
Papka, Michael	Argonne National Laboratory and Northern Illinois University, USA
Patanè, Giuseppe	CNR-IMATI, Italy
Patrignani, Maurizio	Roma Tre University, Italy
Payandeh, Shahram	Simon Fraser University, Canada
Pedrini, Helio	University of Campinas, Brazil
Petrakis, Euripides	Technical University of Crete, Greece
Placidi, Giuseppe	University of L'Aquila, Italy
Ponnusamy, Vijayakumar	SRM University, India
Ponto, Kevin	University of Wisconsin-Madison, USA
Poovvancheri, Jiju	University of Victoria, Canada
Pronost, Nicolas	Université Claude Bernard Lyon 1, France
Qi, Lei	Iowa State University, USA
Qin, Hong	Stony Brook University, USA

Rasmussen, Christopher   University of Delaware, USA
Regentova, Emma   University of Nevada, Las Vegas, USA
Reina, Guido   University of Stuttgart, Germany
Reinhard, Erik   InterDigital, France
Rekabdar, Banafsheh   Portland State University, USA
Ren, Hongliang   National University of Singapore, Singapore
Rhyne, Theresa-Marie   Independent Consultant, USA
Ribeiro, Eraldo   Florida Institute of Technology, USA
Rodgers, Peter   University of Kent, UK
Roy, Sudipta   Jio Institute, India
Rudomin, Isaac   BSC, Spain
Sadlo, Filip   Heidelberg University, Germany
Saha, Punam   University of Iowa, USA
Sakamoto, Naohisa   Kobe University, Japan
Sandberg, Kristian   Computational Solutions, Inc., USA
Santamaria, Pang Alberto   Microsoft Health AI, USA
Sapidis, Nickolas S.   University of Western Macedonia, Greece
Sarfraz, Muhammad   Kuwait University, Kuwait
Scalzo, Fabien   University of California, Los Angeles, USA
Schultz, Thomas   University of Bonn, Germany
Schulze, Jurgen   University of California, San Diego, USA
Sharma, Puneet   UiT-The Arctic University of Norway, Norway
Shead, Timothy   Sandia National Laboratories, USA
Shehata, Mohamed   Memorial University, Canada
Shi, Yifei   NUDT, China
Singh, Gurjot   Fairleigh Dickinson University, USA
Singh, Vineeta   University of Cincinnati, USA
Skurikhin, Alexei   Los Alamos National Laboratory, USA
Slavik, Pavel   Czech Technical University in Prague,
                                  Czech Republic
Snoeyink, Jack   University of North Carolina at Chapel Hill, USA
Solari, Fabio   University of Genoa, Italy
Spagnolo, Paolo   National Research Council, Italy
Sreevalsan-Nair, Jaya   IIIT Bangalore, India
Su, Chung-Yen   National Taiwan Normal University, Taiwan
Sugimoto, Maki   Keio University, Japan
Sun, Changming   CSIRO, Australia
Sun, Guodao   Zhejiang University of Technology, China
Sun, Zehang   Apple Inc., USA
Séquin, Carlo H.   University of California, Berkeley, USA
Tapamo, Jules-Raymond   University of KwaZulu-Natal, South Africa
Tavares, João Manuel R. S.   FEUP and INEGI, Portugal

Thalmann, Daniel   Ecole Polytechnique Fédérale de Lausanne,
                            Switzerland
Theisel, Holger   Otto-von-Guericke University, Germany
Tian, Yuan   InnoPeak Technology, Inc., USA
Tong, Yan   University of South Carolina, USA
Tozal, Mehmet Engin   University of Louisiana at Lafayette, USA
Tubaro, Stefano   Politecnico di Milano, Italy
Umlauf, Georg   Constance University of Applied Sciences,
                            Germany
Valkov, Dimitar   Saarland University and DFKI, Germany
Viriri, Serestina   University of KwaZulu-Natal, South Africa
Voulodimos, Athanasios   University of West Attica, Greece
Wang, Chaoli   University of Notre Dame, USA
Wang, Cuilan   Georgia Gwinnett College, USA
Watkins, Yijing   Pacific Northwest National Laboratory, USA
Wiebel, Alexander   Worms University of Applied Sciences, Germany
Wischgoll, Thomas   Wright State University, USA
Wong, Kin Hong   The Chinese University of Hong Kong,
                            Hong Kong
Wong, Tien-Tsin   The Chinese University of Hong Kong,
                            Hong Kong
Wu, Kui   Massachusetts Institute of Technology, USA
Xu, Wei   Brookhaven National Laboratory, USA
Yamamoto, Goshiro   Kyoto University, Japan
Yanagida, Yasuyuki   Meijo University, Japan
Yang, Xiaosong   Bournemouth University, UK
Yang, Yueming   Baldwin Wallace University, USA
Yen, Hsu-Chun   National Taiwan University, Taiwan
Yi, Hong   Renaissance Computing Institute, USA
Yu, Zeyun   University of Wisconsin-Milwaukee, USA
Yuan, Xiaoru   Peking University, China
Zabulis, Xenophon   FORTH, Greece
Zara, Jiri   Czech Technical University in Prague,
                            Czech Republic
Zeng, Wei   Xi'an Jiaotong University, China
Zhang, Jian   Bournemouth University, UK
Zhao, Mengyang   Dartmouth College, USA
Zheng, Jianmin   Nanyang Technological University, Singapore
Zheng, Yuanjie   Shandong Normal University, China
Zhu, Chenyang   Simon Fraser University, Canada
Zhu, Ying   Georgia State University, USA

Keynote Talks

Towards Scaling Up GANs

Eli Shechtman

Adobe Research, USA

Abstract. Generative adversarial networks (GANs) have progressed tremendously since their introduction in 2014. They can generate high-quality imagery and their latent space lends itself to editing real images in an intuitive and controllable way. However, they are known to have limitations related to their scalability. They work well when trained on datasets of a single object category, but struggle with more complex scenes. GANs are also limited in the resolution of images they can generate and train on, typically showing results up to 1K pixel resolution that push the current hardware to the limits in memory and training time. To address these, I will first describe a mid-level image representation for a generative model of scenes. The representation is mid-level in that it is neither per-pixel nor per-image; rather, scenes are modeled as a collection of spatial, depth-ordered "blobs" of features. When trained on scenes, our model learns to associate different blobs with different entities in the scene and to arrange these blobs to capture scene layout. We demonstrate this emergent behavior by showing that, despite training without any supervision, our method enables applications such as easy manipulation of objects within a scene and scales well to a diverse dataset of multiple scene categories. I will then describe 'any-resolution' training of GANs that can exploit the variety of image resolutions available in the wild, learning from pixels that are usually discarded, to enable high- and continuously-variable resolution synthesis. We achieve this by switching from the common fixed-resolution thinking, to a novel 'any-resolution' approach, where the original size of each training image is preserved. We introduce a new class of generators that can learn from this multi-resolution signal to synthesize images at any resolution, and show how to train them by sampling patches at multiple scales. Our experiments show generated images from several categories with both coherent global layouts and realistic local details, going beyond 2K and up to 8K resolution. Finally, I will relate these scalability efforts to other recent large-scale generative models (such as Dall-E 2, Imagen and others).

Sensible Machine Learning for Geometry

Justin Solomon

MIT, USA

Abstract. From 3D modeling to autonomous driving, a variety of applications can benefit from data-driven reasoning about geometric problems. The available data and preferred shape representation, however, varies widely from one application to the next. Indeed, the one commonality among most of these settings is that they are not easily approached using data-driven methods that have become de rigueur in other branches of computer vision and machine learning. In this talk, I will summarize recent efforts in my group to develop learning architectures and methodologies paired to specific applications, from point cloud processing to mesh and implicit surface modeling. In each case, we will see how mathematical structures and application-specific demands drive our design of the learning methodology, rather than bending application details or eliding geometric details to apply a standard data analysis technique.

Designing Augmented Reality for the Future of Work

Doug Bowman

Virginia Tech, USA

Abstract. Augmented Reality (AR) technology has improved significantly in recent years, to the point where it is expected that major technology companies will release consumer-focused AR glasses in the near future. Technical challenges in optics, power, and tracking remain, but are solvable. But what will we use these AR glasses for, and how will they provide value? In this talk, I will argue that some of the most impactful applications of future AR glasses will be those that transform the way we work. Using examples from my research on AR for knowledge work and intelligent AR for construction work, I will explain why user experience considerations are crucial to the adoption of AR for future work. Studying the design of these applications today will lead to guidelines that can help ensure the success of AR for the future of work tomorrow.

The Future of Visual Computing via Foundation Models (Banquet Keynote Talk)

Ce Liu

Azure Cognitive Services, Microsoft, USA

Abstract. Thanks to big data, computing power and modern network architecture, we are seeing a wave of continuous breakthroughs find their way into people's everyday lives. While modern AI has reached human parity on a few well-defined research benchmarks, a rapidly growing number of disjointed AI tasks are needed to mimic human intelligence in understanding the open and complex world. As each AI task is often defined by the statistics manifested from large amounts of task-specific data, we end up building expensive silos without a synergistic way of knowledge sharing and transferring among the different AI tasks. In this keynote I will share the future of visual computing via large-scale image-language foundation models, such as CLIP and Florence (image to text) and Dall-E (text to image), as a new AI paradigm to integrate fragmented tasks. Empowered by a semantic layer learned from the latest transformers, these foundation models have demonstrated not only unprecedented capabilities in zero-shot and few-shot transfer learning for new tasks in the wild, but also fascinating potentials to unify common visual computing tasks such as recognition, detection, segmentation, captioning and image editing. I will also discuss how the research communities can develop disruptive and creative AI systems using foundation models of various modalities.

3D Reconstruction: Leveraging Synthetic Data for Lightweight Reconstruction

David Jacobs

University of Maryland, USA

Abstract. Reconstruction and regression tasks are central problems in computer vision. We consider, for example, using a single image to recover the 3D structure of an indoor or outdoor scene, or of a human face or body, or recovering the reflectance properties of surfaces or the lighting in a scene. However, in such tasks it is challenging to obtain large amounts of accurately labeled real training data; it's easy to label an image by saying: "this is a picture of a dog", but much harder to label the shape of an object or its reflectance properties, or the lighting in a scene. In many cases, computer graphics provides access to large quantities of labeled data, but there is a domain gap between real images and images generated by graphics. I'll discuss a series of works that address the challenge of using labeled synthetic data to infer properties of the world from real images. I'll discuss methods that are lightweight, in the sense of requiring only a single image or a few easily acquired images.

Human-AI Interaction in Visual Analytics: Designing for the "Two Black Boxes" Problem

Chris North

Virginia Tech, USA

Abstract. Human-AI interaction plays a crucial role in visual analytics, enabling analysts to use AI to help analyze data. In support of this goal, explainable-AI visualizations seek to unmask the underlying details of black box AI learning algorithms, enabling human analysts to understand algorithmic state and results. However, to truly enable human-AI interaction, we will argue that there exists a second black box representing the cognitive process of the user, containing information which must be communicated to the algorithm. Using this "Two Black Boxes" problem as motivation, we propose a design philosophy for human-AI interaction. We discuss usability challenges associated with each phase of communication between the pair of cooperatively-learning entities and the benefits that emerge from opening the black boxes of human and AI for data analysis tasks.

Contents – Part I

Object Detection and Recognition

Deep Learning II

Video Analysis and Event Recognition

Computer Graphics

ST: Biomedical Imaging Techniques for Cancer Detection, Diagnosis and Management

Contents – Part II

Segmentation and Tracking

Virtual Reality

Posters

Deep Learning I

Unsupervised Structure-Consistent Image-to-Image Translation

Shima Shahfar[ID] and Charalambos Poullis[✉][ID]

Immersive and Creative Technologies Lab, Department of Computer Science and
Software Engineering, Concordia University, Montreal, QC, Canada
shimashahfar@gmail.com, charalambos@poullis.org

Abstract. The Swapping Autoencoder achieved state-of-the-art performance in deep image manipulation and image-to-image translation. We
improve this work by introducing a simple yet effective auxiliary module based on gradient reversal layers. The auxiliary module's loss forces
the generator to learn to reconstruct an image with an all-zero texture
code, encouraging better disentanglement between the structure and texture information. The proposed attribute-based transfer method enables
refined control in style transfer while preserving structural information
without using a semantic mask. To manipulate an image, we encode both
the geometry of the objects and the general style of the input images into
two latent codes with an additional constraint that enforces structure
consistency. Moreover, due to the auxiliary loss, training time is significantly reduced. The superiority of the proposed model is demonstrated
in complex domains such as satellite images where state-of-the-art are
known to fail. Lastly, we show that our model improves the quality metrics for a wide range of datasets while achieving comparable results with
multi-modal image generation techniques.

Keywords: Structure-consistent image-to-image translation · Style
transfer · Training class imbalance

1 Introduction

Image-to-image translation and image manipulation techniques attracted much
attention [10,20,24,26,28,37,38,54,58,67] recently as they can have a significant effect on many different tasks. Of particular interest is creating realistic
synthetic training datasets to improve models' performance and generalization.
One example that demonstrates the use of a synthetic dataset in the training
of networks is presented in [65] where the authors introduce a semi-supervised
approach to generate datasets for semantic segmentation.

There are a plethora of works [27,28,32] which report that for images containing single objects such as faces, or for images having the same semantic layout such as building facades, deep image manipulation techniques can produce

---

Supplementary Information The online version contains supplementary material
available at https://doi.org/10.1007/978-3-031-20713-6_1.

realistic synthetic images. However, generating natural scenes or more visually complex images remains a challenge due to differences in the semantic layouts of the input images.

The challenge of deep image manipulation state-of-the-art with complex scenes is recognizing and learning essential features and characteristics from the input image. Structural information is typically shared or has common characteristics across different images in a dataset. On the other hand, the texture appears entangled with intrinsic image features. The standard approach to preserving the structural information is to condition the generation process on the input semantic mask using conditional image synthesis frameworks. However, that approach is not practical for image manipulation since the assumption of having access to semantic masks does not hold in most cases. Researchers explored different methods such as [37,48], but in this work, we assume that image representations can be disentangled into the content/structure and texture/style.

Fig. 1. Our method learns structure-consistent image-to-image translation *without* requiring a semantic mask. We learn to disentangle structure and texture for applications such as style transfer and image editing tasks. The first (left) image shows the first input image, and the other images show the generated images in which the structure is retained from the first input image and the texture from the second, third, and fourth input images, respectively, shown in the inset images. Note that the tree's structure is preserved, and its texture -in this case, the foliage's colour and density-changes according to the texture of the second input image in the inset. Our model was not trained on any season transfer dataset.

To address this problem, we propose an auxiliary module that enforces the separation of structure from texture. This branch promotes the disentanglement of structure and texture by suppressing texture-related information in the structure code by applying a gradient reversal layer. Additionally, it encourages the emergence of deep features that are highly important for image editing tasks. Better structure preservation can also impact many applications ranging from creating a 3D synthetic simulation world, image editing, semantic image synthesis, and style transfer. More importantly, the proposed technique can remove biases from training datasets caused by class imbalances. Many benchmark datasets introduce bias [7,40] that can limit the generalization capability of any network trained on them and significantly limit the impact of networks trained on these datasets in real-world scenarios.

This paper pursues three main objectives: 1) consistent and accurate structure preservation, 2) diverse, and 3) realistic image synthesis. Our goal is to learn multi-modal structure-consistent image-to-image translation in a fully unsupervised approach without requiring semantic segmentation masks. Our technical contributions can be summarized as follows:

- A new approach for a structure-consistent image-to-image translation that does not rely on prior knowledge on the scene geometry.
- An auxiliary module that enforces the disentanglement between the structure and texture information with an explicit loss term for penalizing the synthesis of realistic images when no texture information is provided.
- An extension of the Swapping Autoencoder model with our auxiliary module. We quantitatively and qualitatively demonstrate that our method generates synthetic images structurally consistent with the source input image.

We present experiments on several datasets, simple datasets with minimal variations in the semantic information of the training examples such as CelebA-MaskHQ [34] Fig. 2b, and complex datasets where the semantic information varies drastically such as the LSUN Church [59] Fig. 1, and Cityscapes [7] Fig. 4b. Our results demonstrate that the proposed method improves the performance at a fraction of the training time required by state-of-the-art.

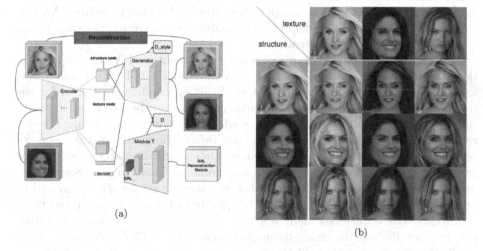

(a)   (b)

Fig. 2. (a) **Overview.** The geometry of the objects and the general style of the input images are encoded into two latent codes with an additional constraint that enforces structure consistency. We introduce a new module that encourages better disentanglement between the structure and the style, based on gradient reversal layers. This results in an attribute-based transfer that allows for a finer style transfer control while preserving structural information without requiring a semantic mask. (b) **Performance on CelebAMask-HQ:** Our model generates structure-consistent samples while transferring style from one image to another. Unlike most models that fail to preserve small structural details, our approach is able to preserve fine details such as earrings (see last row).

2 Background and Related Work

This section provides an overview of the most relevant state-of-the-art, grouped according to their methodology.

Generative Models. Generative Adversarial Networks (GANs) [14] introduced an adversarial process to train a generative model. The problem is formulated as a zero-sum game between a generator and discriminator where the optimal solution is to find a Nash equilibrium. Ian J. Goodfellow refers to this framework as a minimax two-player game in which generator G tries to minimize the probability of the discriminator D to recognize the fake samples, and D tries to maximize the probability of assigning the correct label. The objective function is given by,

$$\min_{G} \max_{D} V(D, G) = E_{x \sim p_{data}(x)}[\log D(x)] + E_{z \sim p_z(z)}[\log(1 - D(G(z)))] \quad (1)$$

GANs have proven to be very successful [4,27,28,66] compared to other common approaches such as [19,43,46,52,53]. Both GANs and Variational Autoencoders (VAEs) [31] contain an encoder and a decoder; however, they differ in a sense that GAN is a framework for estimating data distribution. On the other hand, VAEs learn the stochasticity within the data using the encoder's latent code to match the Gaussian distribution by reparameterizing the latent distribution and maximizing the log-likelihood function. Some methods [2,68] combine GAN and VAE or GAN and Autoencoders in their models to achieve multi-modal image generation and prevent mode collapse.

Conditional generative models such as conditional VAEs [49], conditional GANs [42], conditional autoregressive methods [15,43], to name a few, have shown promising results [67] but we focus on conditional GANs for the rest of this section. Generative adversarial networks can be extended to conditional generative models [42] by feeding additional information c into the discriminator and generator. This c can be any information such as edge mask for semantic segmentation task or class labels for classification. By doing so, the generator can use prior noise $p_z(z)$ and additional information c to create a hidden representation and the discriminator will use the information provided as an input for a better discrimination. The quality of the results generated using conditional GANs inspired many applications employing this method, including, but not limited to, image-to-image translation [26,38,54,58], image editing [5,16], image inpainting [39,50,57], text-to-image [56,62], photo colorization [36,47,61,64], conditional domain adaptation [3,5,6,60], super resolution [25,33], style transfer [12,21,25,27,28,55]. Our work extends the image-to-image translation framework with a focus on image manipulation and style transfer.

Image-to-image translation is a framework to transfer an input image into a synthesized output image while preserving some information from the input. There are many methods designed for different applications. The main difference is in the information they preserve from the input image, which depends on the application. Image-to-image translation showed promise [10,20,24,67], however, as stated in [68], the quality improvement may come with the cost of losing multi-modality. Recent works show that it is possible to prevent losing multi-modality and use this method for multi-domain scenarios [22,35,68].

Unsupervised disentanglement aims to model the variations in data. It has been the focus of several pioneer works such as [4,18,48]. InfoGAN [4], for example, achieves this by maximizing the mutual information between latent variables and input data, whereas [29,35,45,68] disentangle input information to structure and texture codes. Our work builds on the same principles to disentangle structure and texture in a completely unsupervised approach. However, we go one step further and aim for better disentanglement by introducing a new module to enforce better separation between the two. We show that our approach can achieve the desired disentanglement and generate realistic and diverse images while disentangling structure from style better than previous methods.

Multi-modal image synthesis overcomes the limitation of conditional GANs ignoring the latent code, also known as mode collapse. The idea behind the multi-modal image-to-image translation is to learn a conditional distribution while generating diverse images. Early works on conditional image-to-image translation were mostly focused on producing deterministic outputs [24,38], which limits their applicability. In Sect. 4, we show that our method can synthesize comparable results with the current state-of-the-art [68,69].

Style transfer also known as texture transfer, can be defined as the problem of synthesizing an image with style extracted from the source image while preserving the semantics of the content image. Recent style transfer methods [27,28] proposed the use of conditional normalization layers such as Conditional Instance Normalization [9] and Adaptive Instance Normalization [21] as a practical approach to transfer the global style. Normalization layers used in most style transfer methods diminish semantic information. Spatially-Adaptive Normalization [44] was introduced as a way to avoid semantic-level information loss. We propose a closely related method for preserving semantic information without having access to a segmentation mask.

3 Method

Deep image manipulation requires an architecture with excellent feature extraction capabilities that allows for better disentanglement of texture from structure later on. Using an encoder, our goal is to disentangle the structure from the texture for both input images to our model. When swapping the texture or structure codes between the two randomly sampled input images $x_1, x_2 \in \mathbb{R}^{H \times W \times 3}$, our model can synthesize an image with the same structural information as to its content reference, but having the visual appearance or texture of the style reference image. Thus, we aim to generate realistic synthesized images where the structure for the first image is preserved while transferring the style from the second image.

Our solution comprises three key modules with two discriminators namely D and D_{style} as shown in Fig. 2a: an encoder E, a generator G, and a disentanglement module T which enforces better disentanglement of the structure from the style. The encoder learns how to encode visual information into two latent codes. Similar to [45], we enforce a mapping from any combination of the two latent codes to a realistic image by training an autoencoder. The generator synthesizes realistic images using the two extracted latent codes. The disentanglement module is designed to enforce the separation of the structure from the texture. We present the details of the objective function in the subsequent sections.

3.1 Encoder

The encoder E learns a mapping from the input image to two latent codes corresponding to the structure and the texture. We use a traditional autoencoder training process. We employ a reconstruction loss to measure the difference between the original image and the synthesized version with an additional non-saturating adversarial loss [14] to enforce realistic image generation, and is defined as,

$$L_{enc}(x_1, \hat{x_1}) = L_{rec}(E, G) + L_{adv}(E, G, D) = \|x_1 - G(E(x_1))\|_1 - \log(D(G(E(x_1)))) \tag{2}$$

3.2 Generator

Assuming we have already learned how to disentangle the structure from the texture, we can pass two images x_1, x_2 to the encoder and get the latent codes z_1, z_2 where $z_1 = (z_s^1, z_t^1)$ and $z_2 = (z_s^2, z_t^2)$. We assume z_s is the encoded structure and z_t is the texture of an input image and $\hat{x_1}$ is the reconstructed image. The generator conditioned on the latent structure code learns to map the extracted structure and texture codes to an image. The texture code will be added through weight modulation/demodulation introduced in [28]. Swapping the two texture codes before passing them to the generator is a common method to transfer style from one image to another. To ensure that the generated image is realistic, an additional non-saturating adversarial loss [14] is added, given by,

$$L_{swap}(E, G, D) = -\log(D(G(z_s^1, z_t^2))) \tag{3}$$

3.3 Structure and Texture Disentanglement

The latent codes must represent the structure and texture. However, this cannot be achieved in our current setting without additional constraints to encourage consistent structure and texture disentanglement. The approach used for learning consistent texture codes is to enforce all the patches sampled from the image generated in the previous step by swapping the textures to be visually similar to patches extracted from the texture reference image [45]. We achieve this using the following loss:

$$L_{style}(E, G, D_{style}) = -\log(D_{style}(C(G(z_s^1, z_t^2)), C(x^2))) \tag{4}$$

where C is a random crop of size in the range $[\frac{1}{8}, \frac{1}{4}]$. This formulation results in learning a more consistent style transfer. Experiments have shown that this term is not enough and that better disentanglement can be achieved by enforcing the structure code not to contain texture-related information. In order to enforce structure consistency, we introduce an extra module with a gradient reversal layer as its first layer followed by a generator. Gradient reversal layer act as an identity function during forward but during backward it multiplies the gradients with -1. This new generator has the same architecture as the original generator, but it reconstructs an image with an all-zero texture code that is theoretically impossible. Our analysis of previous works shows that structure code contains spatial information and includes style-related information. An inconsistent encoding will cause the network to generate odd samples that do not follow the algorithms and cannot be interpreted. We train this module using a reconstruction loss and a non-saturating adversarial loss [14].

$$L_{aux}(x_1, \hat{x_1}) = L_{rec}(E, T) + L_{adv}(E, T, D) = \|x_1 - T(E(x_1))\|_1 - \log(D(T(E(x_1)))) \tag{5}$$

Adding the gradient reversal layer, as shown in [11], forces the encoder to suppress any style-related information in the structure code. It also proved to be useful in cross domain disentanglement [13]. The auxiliary loss from this branch would help the encoder to disentangle structure from texture better.

3.4   Objective Function

We jointly train the encoder, generators and discriminators to optimize the final objective, which is the weighted sum of previously mentioned loss functions and is given by,

$$L_{total} = \lambda_{rec}L_{enc} + \lambda_{swap}L_{swap} + \lambda_{style}L_{style} + \lambda_{aux}L_{aux} \tag{6}$$

where $\lambda_{rec}, \lambda_{swap}, \lambda_{style}, \lambda_{aux}$ are weights that control the importance of each term. The optimal values used for each term are discussed in Sect. 4.

Table 1. Quantitative comparison of FID and training time/number of iterations on the validation set with state-of-the-art methods. Our proposed method achieves comparable performance while it converges significantly faster.

Method	LSUN Church	#iterations
StyleGAN2 [28]	57.54	48 M
Swapping [45]	52.34	14 days × 4 V100 GPUs
Ours (validation)	51.42	5 M

4   Experiments

Implementation Details. In all reported experiments, we randomly crop and resize the input images to 256×256 resolution. We use the Adam optimizer [30] with $\beta_1 = 0.0$, $\beta_2 = 0.99$. All reported results are computed on 4 NVIDIA TESLA P100 GPUs. The discriminator D is based on StyleGAN 2 [28] and D_{style} is based on Swapping autoencoder [45]. We experimented with different hyper-parameters for $\lambda_{rec}, \lambda_{swap}, \lambda_{style}, \lambda_{aux}$ but in this version we simply set the loss weights to be all 1.0.

Datasets. We evaluate our method on four benchmark datasets curated for scene understanding and semantic segmentation.

– CelebAMask-HQ [34] has 30,000 face images collected from the CelebA [40] dataset. CelebAMask-HQ contains annotations for 19 classes. However, we do not use masks in our training pipeline.
– LSUN church [59] is a subset of the Large-scale Scene Understanding (LSUN) dataset. The training set contains 126,227 images. It is a challenging dataset if no preprocessing is applied due to the diversity of the images.
– Cityscapes [7] is a street view dataset collected from 50 cities across Germany. The training set contains 3000 images with fine annotations, and the test set contains 500 images. It is considered a challenging dataset for image-to-image translation because each scene may contain up to 30 classes.

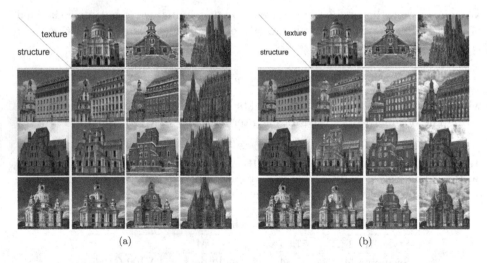

(a)   (b)

Fig. 3. Left: Results from Swapping Autoencoder [45] on LSUN Church. Right: Our results on the same images. As evident, our model achieves better feature embedding and can retain the structural information of the input image while swapping only the texture with that of a second input image. Finer-level details such as spires and buildings outline are also retained. Most notably, our model was trained for a fraction of iterations compared to [45].

– Inria [41] is an aerial imagery dataset designed for semantic segmentation of building footprints. The training set contains 180 images with 5000 × 5000 resolution from 5 cities. Each image covers an area of approximately 1500 m × 1500 m. The test set contains 180 images of the same size collected from 5 cities that are not part of the training set.

Baselines. We compare our approach to a number of image-to-image translation, style transfer and multi-modal image synthesis methods including Swapping Autoencoder [45], StyleGAN2 [28] and BicycleGAN [68]. We either use the results published by authors or generated using their official source code for all comparisons.

Performance Metrics. We use Fréchet Inception Distance (FID) [17] to measure the quality of generated images and LPIPS [63] to compare the similarity of reconstructed images. FID calculates the difference between the real and the generated data distributions using the Inception network to extract the features while LPIPS calculates the perceptual similarity of the input with the reconstructed version. Additionally, in the supplementary material, we report on the SIFID metric on the LSUN church dataset for the training and testing sets, and include additional comparisons and use-cases.

Structure-Consistent Style Transfer. This section evaluates the quality of our generated images on style transfer and compares them to state-of-the-art. In Fig. 3, we provide a qualitative comparison of our synthesized images with our baselines. We find that our method produces comparable results with [45] and [28] on LSUN Church dataset. A significant advantage of our approach is that it required only 5M iterations for training which demonstrates that not only is our approach significantly faster than our predecessors, but it surpasses their performance in terms of FID on the validation set, as shown in Table 1. Figure 3 shows that our method can generate samples with high visual quality on style transfer while preserving structure. Furthermore, structure similarity across generated samples supports the idea behind our auxiliary branch.

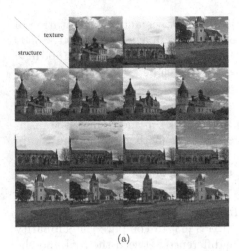 

(a)   (b)

Fig. 4. (a) **Image translation on LSUN Church.** Each column corresponds to a particular texture extracted form the images on first row, respectively, each row contain the generated images with shared structure embedding. (b) **Image translation on Cityscapes.** The left column shows the input images from Cityscapes, the second column are reconstruction of input images. We provide a visualization of structure latent codes in the third column after applying PCA and then resizing it to 256 × 256 for the purpose of visualization. The last column shows our generated images by swapping the texture between first and third row and between second and fourth row. As it can be seen the lightning information, asphalt texture and coloring of the facades are the main information that transferred by swapping the texture codes.

Realism of Reconstruction. The diagonals of Fig. 2b, 5a and 4a show the quality of our method on image reconstruction task from the learned feature embedding. Our method preserves windows, doorways, trees, spires and generally the geometry of the objects as well as finer details such as earrings and tank top strap in Fig. 2b (second row). We report quantitative comparison using the LPIPS [63] to compare the similarity of reconstructed images.

Disentanglement of Structure and Texture. Accurately disentangling structure and texture is an important task both for style transfer and image manipulation. Given that this disentanglement is performed entirely unsupervised, we can evaluate the effectiveness of our new module by comparing the performance of our method with previous works on style transfer from existing images. Better disentanglement of structure and texture leads to a finer manipulation, resulting in significantly more realistic images. Figure 3 (left) shows the results from Swapping Autoencoder [45] on LSUN Church. Our results, shown on the right, demonstrate that our model achieves better feature embedding and generates images that retain the structural information of the input image while transferring only the texture from the second input image. Finer-level details such as spires and buildings' outlines are also preserved.

Texture Code Normalization. We evaluated the effect of normalization on the texture latent code and found that applying $\mathcal{L}_2$-norm results in faster convergence and more realistic synthesis. In this work we do not employ normalization in the generator, as in [23,51], and similar to [45].

Contexts. In Fig. 4b, we show examples from LSUN Church [59] that showcase the applicability of our method to other contexts. The bottom row shows a concrete example of how our technique preserves structures while transferring fine details. As it is evident, the building's structure is preserved while the texture is replaced. Similarly, the tree's structure is preserved, and its texture -in this case, the foliage's colour and density- changes according to each of the source images appearing in the top row. It should be noted that the model was not trained on any season transfer dataset. Semantic image synthesis is one of the critical tasks in designing 3D environments, image colorization, and image editing, but it requires semantic masks and corresponding input images for training a model. This poses a limitation for many real-world applications where it is not simple to produce segmentation masks to train a conditional generative model in a supervised setting, but they need accurate semantic consistency. Our method can perfectly adopt for semantically multi-modal image synthesis in an unsupervised setting.

(a)   (b)

Fig. 5. (a) **Style transfer on CelebAMask-HQ.** The first row shows the texture input image. The other rows show the results using the structure image in the first column. On the second row, the specular highlight on the face is embedded as a structure and is retained. (b) **Performance on Inria dataset.** Left-to-right: first input x_1, second input x_2, reconstruction of x_1, our generated sample using structure of x_1 and texture of x_2. The semantic mask of x_1, if available, can be transferred to the synthetic image therefore increasing the labeled images in the training set that exhibit the textural characteristics of x_2.

4.1   Comparison to State-of-the-Art

Figure 9a, 9b, and 8 shows additional qualitative results on both reconstruction and style transfer tasks. The tables in Fig. 6a and 6b present a quantitative comparison of our method with that of Swapping Autoencoder [45], StyleGAN2 [28], MaskGAN [34], and BicycleGAN [68].

Method	LSUN Church	CelebAMask-HQ	Cityscapes
Ours	51.42	29.69	162.46
Swapping [45]	52.34	32.83	182.5
StyleGAN2 [28]	57.54	-	-
MaskGAN [34]	-	46.84	-
BicycleGAN [68]	-	-	87.74

(a)

Method	LSUN Church
StyleGAN2 [28]	0.377
Image2StyleGAN [1]	0.186
Swapping [45]	0.227
Ours	0.203

(b)

Fig. 6. (a) Quantitative comparison of FID on style transfer with some label-to-image translation work that are known for multimodal image synthesis and Swapping Autoencoder. In cases that we didn't have access to metric values calculated by the author, we trained their model for the same number of iterations as our network. Our method can achieve better results on CelebAMask-HQ and comparable results on LSUN Church trained for only 1.2M and 5M images. (b) Comparison of reconstructed image quality using LPIPS [63] on LSUN Church. Our method focus on preserving structural details and can produce high quality results. Given the fact that our model have only been trained on 5M images which reduce the training time by a great factor, our method can reconstruct input images better than StyleGAN2 [45].

5   Applications

As stated earlier, an important motivation of our work is to remove biases from training datasets caused by class imbalances. Benchmark datasets such as [7, 40] have inherent biases that adversely affect the network's generalization and significantly limit the effectiveness of networks used in real-world scenarios.

In this section, we present results on two unique applications employing the proposed technique:

- The first application addresses bias in training datasets and demonstrates how our method contributes to overcoming this issue.
- The second application addresses the cost-effective generation of training datasets for the task of semantic segmentation in satellite images without incurring additional labelling costs.

Furthermore, we present additional comparisons with state-of-the-art and quantitative results on the datasets LSUN Church [59], CelebAMask-HQ [34], Inria [41]. We conclude with a discussion on the limitations of our technique.

5.1   Addressing Bias in Training Datasets

Often we talk about biases in different datasets as an issue that needs to be addressed while designing the method, and we observe some generalization issues caused mainly due to imbalances in class distributions. A different approach is to adjust or expand our existing datasets to overcome this issue. Our method can preserve fine details; for example, in face datasets, these often imbalanced features can be gender, age, skin colour, hair colour, and accessories such as earrings, eyeglasses, hats, etc. Using our method allows us to balance the dataset by generating synthetic images with under-represented features. Furthermore, in cases where labels are available for the source image, these will also be the same for the generated images since our method preserves the same structure as the source image and only changes the appearance, as shown in Fig. 7.

5.2   Training Datasets for Semantic Segmentation of Satellite Images

Collecting satellite imagery for semantic segmentation is known to be an expensive and challenging task. The process of capturing images is expensive, but it may also contain inaccuracies due to the dynamic environment, e.g. a new

Fig. 7. The first (left) image shows the first input image, and the second/third/fourth images show the generated image where the structure is retained from the first input image and the texture from the second/third/fourth input image, which appear in the inset images.

Fig. 8. This figure provide an example of how our method can preserve the geometry of objects and semantic details while transferring the style. This would allow us to generate multiple samples with no extra labeling cost.

building may appear that was not present at the time of acquisition of the satellite images. Another common issue is that the data collected from one city/continent cannot be easily generalized for a different city/continent. Considering all the challenges mentioned above, deploying a semantic segmentation network for aerial imagery can be challenging. Our structure-consistent network is designed to help overcome these challenges by generating realistic samples for different cities and weather conditions and generally creating datasets by style transfer. Our approach significantly reduces the time needed to process the data since we can expand any existing dataset to the desired style by only having a few images from the new city without requiring semantic labels Fig. 8. Moreover, it can also be extremely useful for editing or expanding already existing datasets by changing the learned structure embedding.

6   Discussion and Limitations

Our method is superior to state-of-the-art unsupervised approaches and gives comparable results to supervised techniques for image manipulation and image-to-image translation. We showed that incorporating the proposed auxiliary module as part of the training encourages better disentanglement of the structure from the texture and better feature embedding. This opens up new applications for image editing and style transfer, such as balancing existing datasets by generating images from underrepresented classes, expanding semantic segmentation datasets, creating multi-view datasets, etc. Previous works [8] explored the effect of combining multiple loss functions with different weights in a single model using [18] to achieve better optimization. We believe the same can be applied as a future step on our pipeline for image manipulation. The importance of structure versus texture may differ from one application to another. By designing an architecture in which one can specify the percentage of structure versus texture for image generation, our method can address even broader range of challenges.

The proposed method works best when both structure and texture reference images contain the same object classes. Otherwise, the model's behaviour is not entirely predictable. An example of this limitation is where the texture reference image does not have vegetation, but the structure reference image contains a tree. In this scenario, the network may choose to copy the original texture. Additionally, in some cases, our network will generate an image with very little change to the structure image or replace some objects due to inconsistency between represented classes in the structure and texture reference images. We have not removed such cases during training. Ignoring them can be a reasonable next step for style transfer tasks until we better understand the underlying meaning of learned texture embedding.

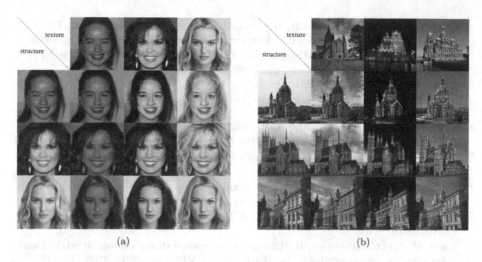

(a)   (b)

Fig. 9. (a) Examples of style transfer on CelebAMask-HQ using our learned embedding. (b) Image translation on LSUN Church showing the quality of our method in different lightning and weather.

7 Conclusions

We presented an end-to-end process for training a structure-consistent image manipulation of existing images. We showed that our approach could disentangle structure and texture with higher accuracy while preserving finer details than state-of-the-art. We have extensively tested our method and showed that it could consistently transfer texture to the correct parts and preserve structural information without requiring a semantic mask. Most notably, this is achieved while also reducing the computational time needed for training such a network to a fraction of the time needed for the current state-of-the-art. Although our method outperforms much state-of-the-art in the image-to-image translation task, defining and disentangling structure from texture in multi-object scenarios such as Cityscapes remains challenging due to the diversity of the objects and complexity of the scene. In the future, we plan to explore the knowledge embedded in latent codes for different datasets and extend this framework to other domains as discussed in Sect. 4.

References

1. Abdal, R., Qin, Y., Wonka, P.: Image2StyleGAN: how to embed images into the StyleGAN latent space? In: Proceedings of the IEEE/CVF International Conference on Computer Vision (ICCV) (2019)
2. Bao, J., Chen, D., Wen, F., Li, H., Hua, G.: CVAE-GAN: fine-grained image generation through asymmetric training. In: IEEE/CVF CVPR, pp. 2745–2754 (2017)
3. Bousmalis, K., Silberman, N., Dohan, D., Erhan, D., Krishnan, D.: Unsupervised pixel-level domain adaptation with generative adversarial networks. In: IEEE/CVF CVPR (2017)

4. Chen, X., Duan, Y., Houthooft, R., Schulman, J., Sutskever, I., Abbeel, P.: Info-GAN: interpretable representation learning by information maximizing generative adversarial nets. In: Proceedings of the 30th International Conference on Neural Information Processing Systems, pp. 2180–2188 (2016)
5. Choi, Y., Choi, M., Kim, M., Ha, J.W., Kim, S., Choo, J.: StarGAN: unified generative adversarial networks for multi-domain image-to-image translation. In: IEEE/CVF CVPR (2018)
6. Choi, Y., Uh, Y., Yoo, J., Ha, J.W.: StarGAN V2: diverse image synthesis for multiple domains. In: IEEE/CVF CVPR (2020)
7. Cordts, M., et al.: The cityscapes dataset for semantic urban scene understanding. In: IEEE/CVF CVPR (2016)
8. Dosovitskiy, A., Djolonga, J.: You only train once: loss-conditional training of deep networks. In: International Conference on Learning Representations (2020)
9. Dumoulin, V., Shlens, J., Kudlur, M.: A learned representation for artistic style. CoRR (2016)
10. Esser, P., Haux, J., Ommer, B.: Unsupervised robust disentangling of latent characteristics for image synthesis. In: IEEE/CVF CVPR, pp. 2699–2709 (2019)
11. Ganin, Y., Lempitsky, V.: Unsupervised domain adaptation by backpropagation. In: International Conference on Machine Learning, pp. 1180–1189. PMLR (2015)
12. Gatys, L.A., Ecker, A.S., Bethge, M.: Image style transfer using convolutional neural networks. In: 2016 IEEE CVF/CVPR, pp. 2414–2423 (2016)
13. Gonzalez-Garcia, A., Van De Weijer, J., Bengio, Y.: Image-to-image translation for cross-domain disentanglement. arXiv preprint arXiv:1805.09730 (2018)
14. Goodfellow, I., et al.: Generative adversarial nets. In: NeurIPS, vol. 27 (2014)
15. Guadarrama, S., Dahl, R., Bieber, D., Norouzi, M., Shlens, J., Murphy, K.: Pix-Color: pixel recursive colorization. arXiv preprint arXiv:1705.07208 (2017)
16. He, Z., Zuo, W., Kan, M., Shan, S., Chen, X.: AttGAN: facial attribute editing by only changing what you want. IEEE TIP **28**(11), 5464–5478 (2019)
17. Heusel, M., Ramsauer, H., Unterthiner, T., Nessler, B., Hochreiter, S.: GANs trained by a two time-scale update rule converge to a local nash equilibrium. In: NeurIPS, vol. 30 (2017)
18. Higgins, I., et al.: beta-VAE: learning basic visual concepts with a constrained variational framework. In: ICLR (2017)
19. Hinton, G.E., Salakhutdinov, R.R.: Reducing the dimensionality of data with neural networks. Science **313**(5786), 504–507 (2006)
20. Hu, Q., Szabó, A., Portenier, T., Favaro, P., Zwicker, M.: Disentangling factors of variation by mixing them. In: IEEE/CVF CVPR, pp. 3399–3407 (2018)
21. Huang, X., Belongie, S.: Arbitrary style transfer in real-time with adaptive instance normalization. In: ICCV (2017)
22. Huang, X., Liu, M.-Y., Belongie, S., Kautz, J.: Multimodal unsupervised image-to-image translation. In: Ferrari, V., Hebert, M., Sminchisescu, C., Weiss, Y. (eds.) ECCV 2018. LNCS, vol. 11207, pp. 179–196. Springer, Cham (2018). https://doi.org/10.1007/978-3-030-01219-9_11
23. Ioffe, S., Szegedy, C.: Batch normalization: Accelerating deep network training by reducing internal covariate shift. In: Bach, F., Blei, D. (eds.) Proceedings of the 32nd International Conference on Machine Learning. Proceedings of Machine Learning Research, vol. 37, pp. 448–456. PMLR, Lille, France, 07–09 July 2015
24. Isola, P., Zhu, J.Y., Zhou, T., Efros, A.A.: Image-to-image translation with conditional adversarial networks. In: IEEE/CVF CVPR, pp. 1125–1134 (2017)

25. Johnson, J., Alahi, A., Fei-Fei, L.: Perceptual losses for real-time style transfer and super-resolution. In: Leibe, B., Matas, J., Sebe, N., Welling, M. (eds.) ECCV 2016. LNCS, vol. 9906, pp. 694–711. Springer, Cham (2016). https://doi.org/10.1007/978-3-319-46475-6_43
26. Kaneko, T., Hiramatsu, K., Kashino, K.: Generative attribute controller with conditional filtered generative adversarial networks. In: IEEE CVF/CVPR, pp. 7006–7015 (2017)
27. Karras, T., Laine, S., Aila, T.: A style-based generator architecture for generative adversarial networks. In: IEEE/CVF CVPR, pp. 4401–4410 (2019)
28. Karras, T., Laine, S., Aittala, M., Hellsten, J., Lehtinen, J., Aila, T.: Analyzing and improving the image quality of StyleGAN. In: Proceedings of the IEEE CVF/CVPR, pp. 8110–8119 (2020)
29. Kazemi, H., Iranmanesh, S.M., Nasrabadi, N.: Style and content disentanglement in generative adversarial networks. In: 2019 IEEE WACV, pp. 848–856. IEEE (2019)
30. Kingma, D.P., Ba, J.: Adam: a method for stochastic optimization. preprint arXiv:1412.6980 (2014)
31. Kingma, D.P., Welling, M.: Auto-encoding variational bayes. arXiv preprint arXiv:1312.6114 (2013)
32. Kotovenko, D., Sanakoyeu, A., Lang, S., Ommer, B.: Content and style disentanglement for artistic style transfer. In: ICCV (2019)
33. Ledig, C., et al.: Photo-realistic single image super-resolution using a generative adversarial network. In: IEEE/CVF CVPR, pp. 4681–4690 (2017)
34. Lee, C.H., Liu, Z., Wu, L., Luo, P.: MaskGAN: towards diverse and interactive facial image manipulation. In: IEEE CVF/CVPR (2020)
35. Lee, H.-Y., Tseng, H.-Y., Huang, J.-B., Singh, M., Yang, M.-H.: Diverse image-to-image translation via disentangled representations. In: Ferrari, V., Hebert, M., Sminchisescu, C., Weiss, Y. (eds.) ECCV 2018. LNCS, vol. 11205, pp. 36–52. Springer, Cham (2018). https://doi.org/10.1007/978-3-030-01246-5_3
36. Lee, J., Kim, E., Lee, Y., Kim, D., Chang, J., Choo, J.: Reference-based sketch image colorization using augmented-self reference and dense semantic correspondence. In: IEEE/CVF CVPR (2020)
37. Li, Y., Singh, K.K., Ojha, U., Lee, Y.J.: MixNMatch: multifactor disentanglement and encoding for conditional image generation. In: IEEE/CVF CVPR (2020)
38. Liu, M.Y., Breuel, T., Kautz, J.: Unsupervised image-to-image translation networks. In: Guyon, I., et al. (eds.) NeurIPS, vol. 30. Curran Associates, Inc. (2017)
39. Liu, M.Y., et al.: Few-shot unsupervised image-to-image translation. In: IEEE/CVF CVPR (2019)
40. Liu, Z., Luo, P., Wang, X., Tang, X.: Deep learning face attributes in the wild. In: ICCV (2015)
41. Maggiori, E., Tarabalka, Y., Charpiat, G., Alliez, P.: Can semantic labeling methods generalize to any city? The INRIA aerial image labeling benchmark. In: IEEE International Geoscience and Remote Sensing Symposium (IGARSS). IEEE (2017)
42. Mirza, M., Osindero, S.: Conditional generative adversarial nets. arXiv preprint arXiv:1411.1784 (2014)
43. van den Oord, A., Kalchbrenner, N., Espeholt, L., Kavukcuoglu, K., Vinyals, O., Graves, A.: Conditional image generation with PixelCNN decoders. In: NIPS (2016)
44. Park, T., Liu, M.Y., Wang, T.C., Zhu, J.Y.: Semantic image synthesis with spatially-adaptive normalization. In: IEEE/CVF CVPR (2019)
45. Park, T., et al.: Swapping autoencoder for deep image manipulation. In: NeurIPS (2020)

46. Salimans, T., Karpathy, A., Chen, X., Kingma, D.P.: PixelCNN++: improving the PixelCNN with discretized logistic mixture likelihood and other modifications. arXiv preprint arXiv:1701.05517 (2017)
47. Sangkloy, P., Lu, J., Fang, C., Yu, F., Hays, J.: Scribbler: controlling deep image synthesis with sketch and color. In: IEEE/CVF CVPR (2017)
48. Singh, K.K., Ojha, U., Lee, Y.J.: FineGAN: unsupervised hierarchical disentanglement for fine-grained object generation and discovery. In: IEEE/CVF CVPR (2019)
49. Sohn, K., Lee, H., Yan, X.: Learning structured output representation using deep conditional generative models. In: NeurIPS, vol. 28, pp. 3483–3491 (2015)
50. Song, Y., Yang, C., Lin, Z., Li, H., Huang, Q., Kuo, C.C.J.: Image inpainting using multi-scale feature image translation. arXiv preprint arXiv:1711.08590 (2017)
51. Ulyanov, D., Vedaldi, A., Lempitsky, V.S.: Instance normalization: the missing ingredient for fast stylization. CoRR abs/1607.08022 (2016)
52. Van Oord, A., Kalchbrenner, N., Kavukcuoglu, K.: Pixel recurrent neural networks. In: International Conference on Machine Learning, pp. 1747–1756. PMLR (2016)
53. Vincent, P., Larochelle, H., Bengio, Y., Manzagol, P.A.: Extracting and composing robust features with denoising autoencoders. In: Proceedings of the 25th International Conference on Machine Learning, ICML 2008, pp. 1096–1103. Association for Computing Machinery, New York (2008)
54. Wang, T.C., Liu, M.Y., Zhu, J.Y., Tao, A., Kautz, J., Catanzaro, B.: High-resolution image synthesis and semantic manipulation with conditional GANs. In: Proceedings of the IEEE CVF/CVPR (2018)
55. Xian, W., et al.: TextureGAN: controlling deep image synthesis with texture patches. In: IEEE/CVF CVPR (2018)
56. Xu, T., et al.: AttnGAN: fine-grained text to image generation with attentional generative adversarial networks. In: IEEE/CVF CVPR (2018)
57. Yeh, R., Chen, C., Lim, T.Y., Hasegawa-Johnson, M., Do, M.N.: Semantic image inpainting with perceptual and contextual losses. arXiv preprint arXiv:1607.07539 **2**(3) (2016)
58. Yi, Z., Zhang, H., Tan, P., Gong, M.: DualGAN: unsupervised dual learning for image-to-image translation. In: ICCV (2017)
59. Yu, F., Zhang, Y., Song, S., Seff, A., Xiao, J.: LSUN: construction of a large-scale image dataset using deep learning with humans in the loop. arXiv preprint arXiv:1506.03365 (2015)
60. Yu, X., Chen, Y., Liu, S., Li, T., Li, G.: Multi-mapping image-to-image translation via learning disentanglement. In: NeurIPS (2019)
61. Zhang, B., et al.: Deep exemplar-based video colorization (2019)
62. Zhang, H., et al.: StackGAN: text to photo-realistic image synthesis with stacked generative adversarial networks. In: ICCV (2017)
63. Zhang, R., Isola, P., Efros, A.A., Shechtman, E., Wang, O.: The unreasonable effectiveness of deep features as a perceptual metric. In: IEEE/CVF CVPR (2018)
64. Zhang, R., et al.: Real-time user-guided image colorization with learned deep priors. ACM Trans. Graph. (TOG) **36**(4), 1–11 (2017). ACM New York, NY, USA
65. Zhang, Y., et al.: DatasetGAN: efficient labeled data factory with minimal human effort. In: CVPR (2021)
66. Zhu, J.-Y., Krähenbühl, P., Shechtman, E., Efros, A.A.: Generative visual manipulation on the natural image manifold. In: Leibe, B., Matas, J., Sebe, N., Welling, M. (eds.) ECCV 2016. LNCS, vol. 9909, pp. 597–613. Springer, Cham (2016). https://doi.org/10.1007/978-3-319-46454-1_36

67. Zhu, J.Y., Park, T., Isola, P., Efros, A.A.: Unpaired image-to-image translation using cycle-consistent adversarial networks. In: ICCV (2017)
68. Zhu, J.Y., et al.: Multimodal image-to-image translation by enforcing bi-cycle consistency. In: NeurIPS, pp. 465–476 (2017)
69. Zhu, Z., Xu, Z., You, A., Bai, X.: Semantically multi-modal image synthesis. In: IEEE/CVF CVPR (2020)

Learning Representations for Masked Facial Recovery

Zaigham A. Randhawa[ID], Shivang Patel[ID], Donald A. Adjeroh[ID],
and Gianfranco Doretto[(✉)][ID]

West Virginia University, Morgantown, WV 26506, USA
{zar00002,sap00008,daadjeroh,gidoretto}@mix.wvu.edu

Abstract. The pandemic of these very recent years has led to a dramatic increase in people wearing protective masks in public venues. This poses obvious challenges to the pervasive use of face recognition technology that now is suffering a decline in performance. One way to address the problem is to revert to face recovery methods as a preprocessing step. Current approaches to face reconstruction and manipulation leverage the ability to model the face manifold, but tend to be generic. We introduce a method that is specific for the recovery of the face image from an image of the same individual wearing a mask. We do so by designing a specialized GAN inversion method, based on an appropriate set of losses for learning an unmasking encoder. With extensive experiments, we show that the approach is effective at unmasking face images. In addition, we also show that the identity information is preserved sufficiently well to improve face verification performance based on several face recognition benchmark datasets.

Keywords: Face unmasking · GAN inversion · Face verification

1 Introduction

Face recognition in unconstrained environments is still a challenging problem, despite the impressive progress of recent approaches based on deep learning [8, 43]. A major factor affecting performance is the presence of occluded parts of the face. Although face recognition under occlusions is not a new problem [53], its relevance has been refreshed in light of the COVID-19 pandemic, which has led to a dramatic increase of people wearing protective masks of various kinds in public venues. This new *status quo* is posing challenges to the pervasive use of face recognition technology, leading to government institutions initiating studies to better evaluate the effects of face masks on current approaches [36].

There is more than one way to mitigate the loss of performance of face matchers dealing with face images wearing masks [53], and one of them is to attempt to reconstruct the face appearance on the occluded region. The main advantage of this approach is that it can be used to potentially improve the performance of any face matcher.

G. Bebis et al. (Eds.): ISVC 2022, LNCS 13598, pp. 22–35, 2022.
https://doi.org/10.1007/978-3-031-20713-6_2

Recent approaches for face reconstruction and manipulation based on deep learning [11,40,41] leverage the extraordinary generative power of these methods in capturing the statistics of the face manifold [24]. In this work we plan to harness that capability even further. Differently than previous approaches, which aim at generic face manipulations, we develop a method that is specifically focussed on unmasking images of faces wearing masks. Our method does not involve the detection or segmentation of face masks, and can be used as a preprocessing step to unmask a face image, which can then be fed to a face matcher.

We frame the problem as a special instance of a GAN inversion [7,42], where the GAN network is a StyleGAN2 architecture [24]. We do so by designing a set of losses and a training procedure for learning an encoder network that maps the input image of a face wearing a mask onto an appropriate code space of faces not wearing masks. This is meant to be the input space of the generator network that will then reproduce the face image without mask.

Ultimately, the challenge is to generate face images that preserve the identity of the input in order to improve face recognition performance. This is why we test our approach with several face recognition datasets. In particular, we show that it can produce compelling face reconstructions with competitive image quality metrics. In addition, we evaluate extensively how our method works for improving face verification under several face masking conditions.

2 Relevant Works

Image Recovery Under Occlusion and Recognition. Our work can be considered as a type of occlusion recovery which coud be used for face recognition [53]. A lot of works treat occlusions as noise and compress the occluded images/faces down to a lower resolution or latent space. This helps to filter out the noise and reconstruct the images back at a higher resolution. Some of these approaches employ more traditional methods like sparse representations [12,22,22,25,28,32,45,56] and PCA [9,32,38], while others rely on neural networks [13,17,26,50] to accomplish this task. Our approach is more similar to the latter. Additionally, some of these methods are occlusion aware and rely on occlusion segmentation or contours to help with the image recovery process [2,5,10,47,51,52]. Therefore, occlusion map prediction is part of their model. On the other hand, we do not require any kind of occlusion information. Additionally, some works try to make occlusion neutral feature-extractors/encoders [6,30] or train the face matching networks to adapt to occlusions [46]. In that sense, our method is not occlusion neutral, and although we do employ ArcFace [8] and FaceNet [43] to help with the training and facial verification tasks, at no point do we train these matchers.

GAN Inversion. A lot of approaches used local discriminators and global discriminators and trained GANs from scratch to reproduce faces/images free of occlusions [14,21,27]. Some others used variations of cyclic losses for image/facial deocclusion [19,29]. We decided to use a pretrained StyleGAN2 [24] as our generator. As stated in [1,57], real life face reconstruction via StyleGAN based on the original $\mathcal{W}$ space is a very hard task. Some approaches have extended the $\mathcal{W}$ space to new ones, named $\mathcal{W}+$ [41,49], $\mathcal{W}*$ [44], p [57] etc, while others have trained the decoders with various losses to achieve exact facial GAN inversion [7,16,42]. We decided to build our approach based on the $\mathcal{W}+$ space via the pSp model [41] and keep the generator fixed. Additionally, related to us, a couple of works employ ℓ-norm losses in the latent space of their StyleGAN architectures [16,37,40]. However, none of them use the latent space loss for image recovery or inpainting with StyleGAN.

We also report that [27,39,49] employed face parser losses in the output space while training for GAN inversion/facial reconstruction). However, our work does not use such a loss. Perceptual losses like LPIPS were also used by us and other works [33,49,51]. ID losses based on Facenet, ArcFace, LightCNN etc. were also used while training for GAN inversion/face unmasking [14,33,37,49,51,55]. Just like [27,29,33,34,49], we also employed an ℓ-norm loss on the output image space to help with image reconstruction.

3   Method

Given an image M of a face wearing a mask, we are interested in developing an approach for face unmasking, which is the task of mapping M onto a new image U, depicting the same person in M, only without the mask. We assume that the unmasking process can be modeled by the relationship $U = g \circ f(M)$, where f maps M onto a representation w, and g generates U from the representation. We do not make assumptions about the specific type of face mask, nor do we require a mask detection or segmentation process to be involved in the unmasking task. We do however, require the face in M to be aligned in terms of 2D position, 2D orientation and scale with the nominal alignment of the dataset used for training the model $g \circ f$.

3.1   Baseline Model

In the case when the face in the image M was not wearing a mask, since no mask needs to be removed, we would expect this condition to be true: $U = M$. Also, let us indicate with $T \doteq U = M$ the image of the face without mask. Therefore, the model $g \circ f_0$ should behave like a face autoencoder, where the encoder in this particular case is indicated with f_0. While there are several implementations of face autoencoders [11,40,41], since we are ultimately interested in evaluating how the approach would improve the performance of face recognition, we want one that executes face autoencodings that are photorealistic, and that can maintain face identity. The state-of-the art in that category is the pSp model [41], where the generator g is a StyleGAN2 network [24], and the encoder f is based on a feature pyramid model built on top of a ResNet backbone, and followed by a mapping to a set of 18 *styles*. The styles capture different levels of image detail, roughly divided in three groups, coarse, medium, and fine. Every style is a 512-dimensional vector. The collection of the 18 style vectors constitutes the representation w, which is an element of the space referred to as $\mathcal{W}+$ in [41].

The training of the pSp model is approached as a "GAN inversion" task, meaning that the generator network is trained offline (i.e., StyleGAN2), and is kept locked while only the encoder f_0 is being trained, with the task of "learning to invert" the operation of the generator. This approach is mainly due to the success of StyleGAN2 in modelling the face space, and also due to the difficulty in designing and training such kind of models.

In order to train the encoder f_0, the pSp model combines a number of losses. The fist one is a reconstruction loss based on the ℓ_2-norm

$$\mathcal{L}_R(T) = \|T - g \circ f_0(T)\|_2. \tag{1}$$

The second aims at maintaining the perceptual similarity between input and reconstructions, and is based on the LPIPS metric $P(\cdot)$ [54]

$$\mathcal{L}_{LPIPS}(T) = \|P(T) - P(g \circ f_0(T))\|_2. \tag{2}$$

In order to preserve the face identity of the input in the reconstructions, an identity preserving loss is used to maximize the cosine similarity between the normalized ArcFace [8] representations $AF(\cdot)$ of the input image and the reconstruction

$$\mathcal{L}_{ID}(T) = 1 - AF(T) \cdot AF(g \circ f_0(T)). \tag{3}$$

The encoder f_0, which we refer to as the *baseline encoder*, is then trained by minimizing this loss, which is written on a per-image basis as

$$\mathcal{L}_0(T) = \mathcal{L}_R(T) + \alpha\mathcal{L}_{LPIPS}(T) + \beta\mathcal{L}_{ID}(T), \tag{4}$$

where α, and β are hyperparameters striking a balance between the loss terms.

3.2   Unmasking Model

Given an image M with a masked face, we can still make the assumption that in our original model $g \circ f$, g is a face image generator, modeled with StyleGAN2, and that we keep it fixed. Therefore, training the encoder f becomes a specialized GAN inversion problem. If T is an image of a face not wearing a mask, we make the assumption that T is identical to M, except for the area of M corresponding to the pixels on the face mask.

To train the encoder f we combine several losses, most of which are a modification of those used to train the baseline model f_0. See Fig. 1. Specifically, we require the autoencoding of M (i.e., U) to be close to T in the ℓ_2-norm sense

$$\mathcal{L}_R(T, M) = \|T - g \circ f(M)\|_2. \tag{5}$$

We also want the autoencoding of M to be perceptually similar to T according to the LPIPS metric $P(\cdot)$ by minimizing

$$\mathcal{L}_{LPIPS}(T, M) = \|P(T) - P(g \circ f(M))\|_2. \tag{6}$$

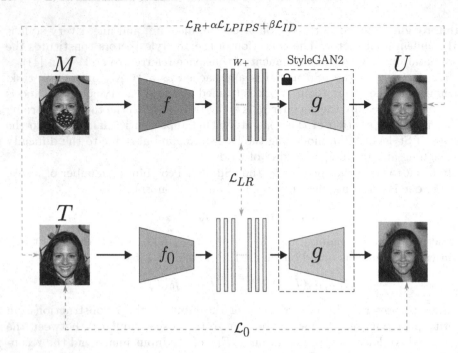

Fig. 1. Unmasking architecture. Overview of the architecture and the losses used to train the baseline encoder f_0, and the unmasking encoder f. The generator g is kept fixed at all times. T is a face image. M is the same face image wearing a mask. U is the autoencoded version of M.

In addition, the identity of the autoencoding of M should be as close to the identity of T as possible, and for that we maximise the similarity between the respective normalized ArcFace representations $AF(\cdot)$ by minimizing

$$\mathcal{L}_{ID}(T, M) = 1 - AF(T) \cdot AF(g \circ f(M)). \qquad (7)$$

We also observe that ideally, the baseline model should be such that $T = g \circ f_0(T)$. Therefore, we would want as much as possible that $g \circ f_0(T) = g \circ f(M)$, but this could be achieved by simply having $f_0(T) = f(M)$. So, we encourage that with the loss

$$\mathcal{L}_{LR}(T, M) = \|f_0(T) - f(M)\|_2, \qquad (8)$$

which we name *latent reconstruction loss*. Finally, the encoder f, which we refer to as the *unmasking encoder*, is trained by minimizing this combined *unmasking loss*, which is written on a per-image basis as

$$\mathcal{L}_{UM}(T, M) = \mathcal{L}_R(T, M) + \alpha \mathcal{L}_{LPIPS}(T, M) + \beta \mathcal{L}_{ID}(T, M) + \gamma \mathcal{L}_{LR}(T, M), \qquad (9)$$

where α, β, and γ are hyperparameters striking a balance between the loss terms.

Table 1. Datasets. Quantitative summary of the datasets used.

Name	Original # of images	Total # of masked images	# of train, test IDs	# of train, test images
FFHQ	70000	69794	—,—	55811, 13593
CelebA	202599	196999	8141, 2036	157597, 39402
LFW	13233	13168	4754, 1144	10794, 2374
RMFRD	2118 M + 90468	806	218, 64	597, 209

3.3 Datasets

Because of the pandemic, there is a number of datasets and tools to add masks to face images. For instance, Masked-FaceNet is a dataset with faces from the FFHQ dataset wearing masks correctly and incorrectly [4], RMFD is a collection of real world masked faces, including also face images with same identity not wearing masks [48], and so is DS-IMF [35]. The MAFA dataset [15] has a lot of real world masked images, but neither with identification information nor with corresponding identities without wearing masks. In our experiments we used the FFHQ dataset [23], CelebA [31], and LFW [20], and we used the MasktheFace toolkit [3] to create the pairs of face images (T, M), where M is a version of T with a synthetic mask added. Note that the MasktheFace toolkit failed to mask faces of certain images and those were not included in further training and testing of the models. In addition, we used a subsection of RFRD called RMFRD, which has real life masks only. Table 1 gives details on the size of the datasets used.

3.4 Implementation Details

For training our approach, we assume that a StyleGAN2 generator model g is given to us and is kept locked. Then, we train the baseline encoder f_0 with the loss (4). Subsequently, we use f_0 to initialize the unmasking encoder f, and we train it with the loss (9). Also, we conduct the experiments by first learning the model for the dataset with higher resolution, and then we use the baseline model to initialize the baseline model of the dataset with the immediate smaller resolution. So, we start from the FFHQ dataset [23], then we process CelebA [31], then LFW [20], and finally RMFRD [48].

The generator g based on StyleGAN2 allows to generate images at 1024×1024 resolution with an architecture based on 18 layers. It is also possible to use only the first 14 layers of StyleGAN2 and work with a model that generates images at 256×256 resolution [41], which is also much faster to train. We verified, as reported in Sect. 4, that working with the smaller network does not affect face verification results significantly, since the images are downscaled before feeding them to the face matcher. Therefore, unless otherwise stated, we always use the model with the smaller 14 layers generator architecture.

The approach we use assumes that the input images have faces that are sufficiently aligned. This is the case for FFHQ and CelebA. For LFW, we used the deep funneled images [20], which correct for the orientation of the faces and properly align them. We also crop a 150×150 region out of the original 250×250 images to leave out image areas containing significant background clutter that were making the training difficult to converge. Note also that the cropped images were then resized up to 256×256 prior to be used.

Additionally, RMFRD has very low quality images and a very variable resolution, and it is in general a very challenging dataset. Because of this, we used OpenCV to only keep faces where we could detect both eyes, and we rotated the faces to make the eyes horizontal, and resize them to 256×256. Moreover, this dataset has faces wearing real masks as M images, and there are no identical images with faces without masks as T images. Therefore, the training is approached in two phases. First, we used the unmasked faces in the training set to train the baseline and the unmasking models just like we did for the other datasets. Second, we fine-tune the model with the images with real masks as follows. The losses (5) and (6) are computed based only on the periorbital region of the face because it is visible, which is identified automatically from the position of the eyes. The loss (7), instead, uses as T, an image with the same identity and that is not wearing a mask. Finally, in the loss (8) T is replaced with an estimate $\hat{T}$ of a face image without mask, generated by g to have the same periorbital region of the masked face in the M image according to the ℓ_2-norm.

4   Experimental Results

We evaluate our unmasking model extensively, by providing results pertaining the unmasking of face images wearing masks, the image quality metrics of those images, and we evaluate to what extent the unmasking process might help improving the performance of a face matcher. We use four datasets, FFHQ [23], CelebA [31], and LFW [20], and RMFRD [48], and two face matchers, ArcFace [8] and FaceNet [43].

Face Verification Notation. The face verification experiments are conducted with different unmasking settings. The notation used to indicate these settings is defined as follows. MM indicates when both the probe and the gallery face images are masked. MT indicates when the probe image is masked and gallery images are not. UU indicates that both probe and gallery images were originally masked but they were both unmasked by our approach before verification. UT indicates that the probe was originally masked but was unmasked by our approach before verification and the gallery images were not masked. TT indicates when the probe and the gallery images were not masked. This is expected to provide the upper bound results.

18 Layers vs 14 Layers Architecture. We compared the two generator architectures based on 14 and 18 layers in terms of face verification performance as well as image quality of the unmasked images. A key difference between the

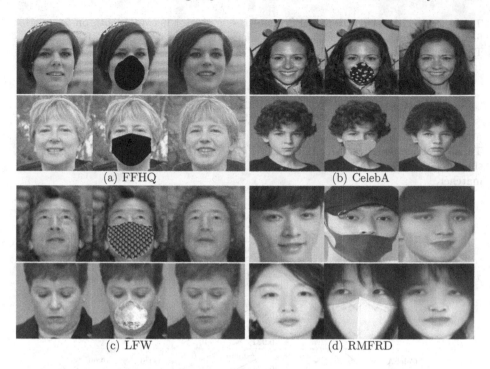

(a) FFHQ   (b) CelebA

(c) LFW   (d) RMFRD

Fig. 2. Face unmasking. Qualitative face unmasking results on various datasets. For each row we have original face image (T), masked image (M), and unmasked image (U).

architectures is that the 14 layers provides 256×256 images and the 18 layers provides 1024×1024 images. Table 2 shows the results on CelebA. The metrics used are area under curve (AUC) for face verification, and peak signal to noise ratio (PSNR) and structural similarity index measure (SSIM) for image quality [18]. The main conclusion is that the difference between architectures is not significant. For AUC purposes, this is not surprising because the images are downsampled to 112×112 for the face matchers. Also, the pSp framework only accepts input at a resolution of 256×256. Therefore when calculating SSIM and PSNR, the 1024×1024 images are downsized to 256×256 for the model input and the resulting output quality is very similar to that of the 14 layers model. The 18 layer model has slightly better facial verification AUCs because it has more expressive power. On the other hand, the 14 layer model has marginally better SSIM and PSNR values because it has to produce images at a lower scale. Therefore, in the remaining experiments we used the 14 layered architecture, which also allows for a faster training time.

Face Unmasking. We conducted face unmasking experiments with the four datasets FFHQ, CelebA, LFW, and RMFRD. Qualitative unmasking results can be seen in Fig. 2. The unmasked images have resolution 256×256. For FFHQ the mask was simply black, for CelebA and LFW we show the case of different

Table 2. Architecture depth. Effects of the generator network depth on face verification in terms of AUC, and unmasking image quality in terms of PSNR and SSIM. The dataset used is CelebA.

Architecture	UU	UT	PSNR	SSIM
14-layer	0.9590	0.9422	19.00	0.75891
18-layer	0.9596	0.9440	18.51	0.75568

Table 3. Face verification. AUC, SSIM, and PSNR values of an ablation study of the unmasking loss for different face verification settings. ArcFace was used as face matcher.

Dataset	$\mathcal{L}_R$	$\mathcal{L}_{LPIPS}$	$\mathcal{L}_{ID}$	$\mathcal{L}_{LR}$	UU / MM	UT / MT	TT	SSIM	PSNR
FFHQ	✓	✓	✓	✓				0.69450	17.92
CelebA	✓				0.750 / 0.825	0.750 / 0.824	0.891		
CelebA				✓	0.833 / 0.825	0.840 / 0.824	0.891	0.72905	18.30
CelebA	✓	✓	✓		0.952 / 0.931	0.964 / 0.940	0.984		
CelebA		✓	✓	✓	0.947 / 0.931	0.962 / 0.940	0.984		
CelebA	✓	✓	✓	✓	0.959 / 0.931	0.971 / 0.940	0.984	0.75891	19.00
LFW	✓	✓	✓		0.944 / 0.952	0.958 / 0.958	0.990		
LFW	✓	✓	✓	✓	0.957 / 0.952	0.968 / 0.958	0.990	0.67737	17.04
RMFRD	✓	✓	✓	✓		0.609 / 0.602			

shape and color masks added, and the masks in RMFRD are real masks worn by the subjects.

Ablation of the Unmasking Loss. In Table 3 we report an ablation study where in the unmasking loss (9) we include only the components indicated. We do so for a face verification experiment using the CelebA, LFW, and RMFRD datasets. The AUC values highlight the contribution coming from using only $\mathcal{L}_R$, only $\mathcal{L}_{LR}$, and how much performance deteriorates when each of them is removed from the full model.

The first two experiments in Table 3 concentrate on the cases when the model is only trained with either $\mathcal{L}_R$ or $\mathcal{L}_{LR}$. The facial verification results for these two models only use 3000 images from the test dataset (the rest of the models use the entirety of the test dataset). Please note that $\mathcal{L}_R$ is not enough to learn a model where the UU case is better than the MM, or the UT case is better than the MT, highlighting the fact that adding the $\mathcal{L}_{LPIPS}$ and $\mathcal{L}_{ID}$ is important for $\mathcal{L}_R$. For CelebA, a model with only $\mathcal{L}_{LR}$ allows the UU and UT cases to outperform the MM and MT cases respectively, but adding the rest of the losses

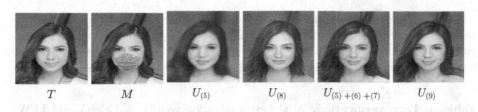

T $\qquad$ M $\qquad$ $U_{(5)}$ $\qquad$ $U_{(8)}$ $\qquad$ $U_{(5)+(6)+(7)}$ $\qquad$ $U_{(9)}$

Fig. 3. Ablation of face unmasking. Left two images: original face image (T) and same image with mask (M). The right four images are unmasked versions of M obtained with different models.

further increases the facial verification AUCs by a large margin. Additionally, for LFW, which is a lower resolution dataset, removing $\mathcal{L}_{LR}$ causes UU and UT to not outperform MM and MT respectively, further highlighting its importance. The final takeaway is that the full model allows for UU and UT to surpass MM and MT, respectively, and allows to approach the upper bound set by the TT scenario.

Also, Table 3 summarizes the results on image quality metrics such as SSIM and PSNR. LFW has lower metrics than the other datasets because it has the lowest quality images, especially due to the aforementioned cropping of the T, and M images from a size of 250×250 to 150×150 followed by an upsampling to 256×256. Additionally, FFHQ also performs worse than CelebA because the comparison between U and T is done at a resolution of 256×256, for which the T has to be downsampled, which detrimentally affects the SSIM and PSNR metrics. CelebA images, instead, are three times more than FFHQ for training, and are upsampled from 178×218 to 256×256, suffering the least amount of distortion. Finally, the CelebA model with only $\mathcal{L}_{LR}$ performs worse than the full model in terms of both SSIM and PSNR. This is because the latter has more constraints to satisfy, which gives better GAN-inversion results. More qualitative results can be seen in Fig. 3, which follows similar trends.

Figure 3, instead, shows a qualitative ablation of the unmasking results, obtained by progressively adding more components in the unmasking loss (9). From the left, we have the original face image (T), and the version wearing the mask (M), followed by an unmasked face (U) with a model trained only with $\mathcal{L}_{R}$, which is rather blurry, despite the fact that the generator is a StyleGAN2 network that produces sharp face images. Then, fourth from the left, the unmasked face was obtained with a model trained only with $\mathcal{L}_{LR}$, which is relatively sharp, but the identity drift is noticeable. Second from the right, the unmasked face was obtained with a model without only $\mathcal{L}_{LR}$, whereas the last image was unmasked by the full model.

Face Verification with FaceNet. In Table 4 we report face verification results on CelebA and LFW based on FaceNet [43] as the face matcher. The train/test split used are the same as those used in the complete $\mathcal{L}_{UM}$ models in Table 3. Note that the results establish the same relationships between the various settings as those deductible from Table 3. This is relevant because now we have trained the unmasking models with one face matcher (i.e., ArcFace), while we have tested them with another one (i.e., FaceNet), confirming that even the previous results were not subject to strong biases, since models were trained and tested with the same face matcher, since ArcFace is used in the loss (7).

Table 4. Face verification. AUC face verification results on CelebA and LFW. FaceNet was used as face matcher during testing.

Dataset	$\mathcal{L}_R$	$\mathcal{L}_{LPIPS}$	$\mathcal{L}_{ID}$	$\mathcal{L}_{LR}$	UU / MM	UT / MT
CelebA	✓	✓	✓	✓	0.868 / 0.832	0.867 / 0.814
LFW	✓	✓	✓	✓	0.9833 / 0.9834	0.9845 / 0.9844

5 Conclusions

In this work we have proposed a method for unmasking the face image of a subject wearing a mask. We formulate the problem as a GAN inversion, because we leverage the generative modeling of the face manifold of current methods. We designed a set of losses to learn an unmasking encoder that enables mapping the input image onto a new face image. Our set of experiments show that the unmasking process recovers compelling face images, with competitive image quality metrics. In addition, by testing the unmasking process with two face matchers, our set of results on face verification confirms that the identity is preserved sufficiently well to provide a consistent significant improvement on three commonly used face recognition benchmarks.

Acknowledgements. This material is based upon work supported in part by the Center for Identification Technology Research and the National Science Foundation under Grants No. 1650474 and No. 1920920.

References

1. Abdal, R., Qin, Y., Wonka, P.: Image2StyleGAN: how to embed images into the styleGAN latent space? In: IEEE ICCV, pp. 4432–4441 (2019)
2. Abdal, R., Zhu, P., Mitra, N.J., Wonka, P.: Labels4Free: unsupervised segmentation using StyleGAN. In: IEEE ICCV, pp. 13970–13979 (2021)
3. Anwar, A., Raychowdhury, A.: Masked face recognition for secure authentication. arXiv preprint arXiv:2008.11104 (2020)
4. Cabani, A., Hammoudi, K., Benhabiles, H., Melkemi, M.: MaskedFace-Net-a dataset of correctly/incorrectly masked face images in the context of COVID-19. Smart Health **19**, 100144 (2021)
5. Chen, Y.A., Chen, W.C., Wei, C.P., Wang, Y.C.F.: Occlusion-aware face inpainting via generative adversarial networks. In: IEEE ICIP, pp. 1202–1206. IEEE (2017)

6. Cheng, L., Wang, J., Gong, Y., Hou, Q.: Robust deep auto-encoder for occluded face recognition. In: ACM International Conference on Multimedia, pp. 1099–1102 (2015)
7. Daras, G., Dean, J., Jalal, A., Dimakis, A.G.: Intermediate layer optimization for inverse problems using deep generative models. arXiv preprint arXiv:2102.07364 (2021)
8. Deng, J., Guo, J., Xue, N., Zafeiriou, S.: ArcFace: additive angular margin loss for deep face recognition. In: IEEE CVPR, pp. 4690–4699 (2019)
9. Deng, Y., Dai, Q., Zhang, Z.: Graph Laplace for occluded face completion and recognition. IEEE TIP **20**(8), 2329–2338 (2011)
10. Din, N.U., Javed, K., Bae, S., Yi, J.: A novel GAN-based network for unmasking of masked face. IEEE Access **8**, 44276–44287 (2020)
11. Donahue, J., Krähenbühl, P., Darrell, T.: Adversarial feature learning. arXiv preprint arXiv:1605.09782 (2016)
12. Fidler, S., Skocaj, D., Leonardis, A.: Combining reconstructive and discriminative subspace methods for robust classification and regression by subsampling. IEEE PAMI **28**(3), 337–350 (2006)
13. Gao, R., Grauman, K.: From one-trick ponies to all-rounders: on-demand learning for image restoration. arXiv preprint arXiv:1612.01380 (2016)
14. Ge, S., Li, C., Zhao, S., Zeng, D.: Occluded face recognition in the wild by identity-diversity inpainting. IEEE T-CSVT **30**(10), 3387–3397 (2020)
15. Ge, S., Li, J., Ye, Q., Luo, Z.: Detecting masked faces in the wild with LLE-CNNs. In: IEEE CVPR, pp. 2682–2690 (2017)
16. Ghosh, P., Zietlow, D., Black, M.J., Davis, L.S., Hu, X.: InvGAN: invertable GANs. arXiv preprint arXiv:2112.04598 (2021)
17. He, Z., Zuo, W., Kan, M., Shan, S., Chen, X.: AttGan: facial attribute editing by only changing what you want. IEEE TIP **28**(11), 5464–5478 (2019)
18. Horé, A., Ziou, D.: Image quality metrics: PSNR vs. SSIM. In: ICPR, pp. 2366–2369 (2010)
19. Hu, B., Zheng, Z., Liu, P., Yang, W., Ren, M.: Unsupervised eyeglasses removal in the wild. IEEE Trans. Cybern. **51**(9), 4373–4385 (2020)
20. Huang, G.B., Mattar, M., Lee, H., Learned-Miller, E.: Learning to align from scratch. In: NIPS (2012)
21. Iizuka, S., Simo-Serra, E., Ishikawa, H.: Globally and locally consistent image completion. ACM Trans. Graph. (ToG) **36**(4), 1–14 (2017)
22. Iliadis, M., Wang, H., Molina, R., Katsaggelos, A.K.: Robust and low-rank representation for fast face identification with occlusions. IEEE TIP **26**(5), 2203–2218 (2017)
23. Karras, T., Laine, S., Aila, T.: A style-based generator architecture for generative adversarial networks. In: IEEE CVPR, pp. 4401–4410 (2019)
24. Karras, T., Laine, S., Aittala, M., Hellsten, J., Lehtinen, J., Aila, T.: Analyzing and improving the image quality of StyleGAN. In: IEEE CVPR, pp. 8110–8119 (2020)
25. Leonardis, A., Bischof, H.: Robust recognition using eigenimages. Comput. Vis. Image Underst. **78**(1), 99–118 (2000)
26. Li, C., Ge, S., Zhang, D., Li, J.: Look through masks: towards masked face recognition with de-occlusion distillation. In: Proceedings of the 28th ACM International Conference on Multimedia, pp. 3016–3024 (2020)
27. Li, Y., Liu, S., Yang, J., Yang, M.H.: Generative face completion. In: IEEE CVPR, pp. 3911–3919 (2017)

28. Li, Y., Feng, J.: Reconstruction based face occlusion elimination for recognition. Neurocomputing **101**, 68–72 (2013)
29. Li, Z., Hu, Y., He, R., Sun, Z.: Learning disentangling and fusing networks for face completion under structured occlusions. Pattern Recogn. **99**, 107073 (2020)
30. Liu, G., Reda, F.A., Shih, K.J., Wang, T.C., Tao, A., Catanzaro, B.: Image inpainting for irregular holes using partial convolutions. In: ECCV 2018, pp. 85–100 (2018)
31. Liu, Z., Luo, P., Wang, X., Tang, X.: Deep learning face attributes in the wild. In: Proceedings of the IEEE ICCV, pp. 3730–3738 (2015)
32. Luan, X., Fang, B., Liu, L., Yang, W., Qian, J.: Extracting sparse error of robust PCA for face recognition in the presence of varying illumination and occlusion. Pattern Recogn. **47**(2), 495–508 (2014)
33. Ma, X., Zhou, X., Huang, H., Jia, G., Chai, Z., Wei, X.: Contrastive attention network with dense field estimation for face completion. Pattern Recogn. **124**, 108465 (2022)
34. Menon, S., Damian, A., Hu, S., Ravi, N., Rudin, C.: Pulse: self-supervised photo upsampling via latent space exploration of generative models. In: IEEE CVPR, pp. 2437–2445 (2020)
35. Mishra, S., Majumdar, P., Dosi, M., Vatsa, M., Singh, R.: Dual sensor Indian masked face dataset. In: IEEE International Conference on Automatic Face and Gesture Recognition (FG 2021), pp. 1–8. IEEE (2021)
36. Ngan, M., Grother, P., Hanaoka, K.: Ongoing face recognition vendor test (FRVT) part 6a: face recognition accuracy with masks using pre-COVID-19 algorithms. Technical report, NIST (2020)
37. Nitzan, Y., Bermano, A., Li, Y., Cohen-Or, D.: Face identity disentanglement via latent space mapping. arXiv preprint arXiv:2005.07728 (2020)
38. Park, J.S., Oh, Y.H., Ahn, S.C., Lee, S.W.: Glasses removal from facial image using recursive error compensation. IEEE PAMI **27**(5), 805–811 (2005)
39. Pernuš, M., Štruc, V., Dobrišek, S.: High resolution face editing with masked GAN latent code optimization. arXiv preprint arXiv:2103.11135 (2021)
40. Pidhorskyi, S., Adjeroh, D.A., Doretto, G.: Adversarial latent autoencoders. In: IEEE CVPR, pp. 14104–14113 (2020)
41. Richardson, E., et al.: Encoding in style: a StyleGAN encoder for image-to-image translation. In: IEEE CVPR, pp. 2287–2296 (2021)
42. Roich, D., Mokady, R., Bermano, A.H., Cohen-Or, D.: Pivotal tuning for latent-based editing of real images. arXiv preprint arXiv:2106.05744 (2021)
43. Schroff, F., Kalenichenko, D., Philbin, J.: FaceNet: a unified embedding for face recognition and clustering. In: IEEE CVPR, pp. 815–823 (2015)
44. Shukor, M., Yao, X., Damodaran, B.B., Hellier, P.: Semantic and geometric unfolding of StyleGAN latent space. arXiv preprint arXiv:2107.04481 (2021)
45. Su, Y., Yang, Y., Guo, Z., Yang, W.: Face recognition with occlusion. In: IAPR Asian Conference on Pattern Recognition (ACPR), pp. 670–674. IEEE (2015)
46. Trigueros, D.S., Meng, L., Hartnett, M.: Enhancing convolutional neural networks for face recognition with occlusion maps and batch triplet loss. Image Vis. Comput. **79**, 99–108 (2018)
47. Wang, M., Hu, Z., Sun, Z., Zhao, S., Sun, M.: Varying face occlusion detection and iterative recovery for face recognition. J. Electron. Imaging **26**(3), 033009 (2017)
48. Wang, Z., et al.: Masked face recognition dataset and application. arXiv preprint arXiv:2003.09093 (2020)
49. Wei, T., et al.: A simple baseline for StyleGAN inversion. arXiv preprint arXiv:2104.07661 (2021)

50. Xie, J., Xu, L., Chen, E.: Image denoising and inpainting with deep neural networks. In: Advances in Neural Information Processing Systems, vol. 25 (2012)
51. Xinyi, Z., Runqing, J., Tianxiang, H., Hao, Y.: Identity preserving face completion with landmark based generative adversarial network (2021)
52. Xiong, W., et al.: Foreground-aware image inpainting. In: IEEE CVPR, pp. 5840–5848 (2019)
53. Zeng, D., Veldhuis, R., Spreeuwers, L.: A survey of face recognition techniques under occlusion. IET Biometrics **10**(6), 581–606 (2021)
54. Zhang, R., Isola, P., Efros, A.A., Shechtman, E., Wang, O.: The unreasonable effectiveness of deep features as a perceptual metric. In: IEEE CVPR, pp. 586–595 (2018)
55. Zhao, F., Feng, J., Zhao, J., Yang, W., Yan, S.: Robust LSTM-autoencoders for face de-occlusion in the wild. IEEE TIP **27**, 778–790 (2016)
56. Zhao, S., Hu, Z.P.: A modular weighted sparse representation based on fisher discriminant and sparse residual for face recognition with occlusion. Inf. Proc. Lett. **115**(9), 677–683 (2015)
57. Zhu, P., Abdal, R., Qin, Y., Femiani, J., Wonka, P.: Improved StyleGAN embedding: where are the good Latents? arXiv preprint arXiv:2012.09036 (2020)

Deep Learning Based Shrimp Classification

Patricia L. Suárez[1(✉)], Angel Sappa[1,2], Dario Carpio[1], Henry Velesaca[1], Francisca Burgos[1], and Patricia Urdiales[1]

[1] ESPOL Polytechnic University, FIEC, CIDIS, Guayaquil, Ecuador
{plsuarez,asappa,dncarpio,hvelesac,faburgo,purdiale}@espol.edu.ec
[2] Computer Vision Center, Bellaterra, 08193 Barcelona, Spain
asappa@cvc.uab.es

Abstract. This work proposes a novel approach based on deep learning to address the classification of shrimp (Pennaeus vannamei) into two classes, according to their level of pigmentation accepted by shrimp commerce. The main goal of this actual study is to support the shrimp industry in terms of price and process. An efficient CNN architecture is proposed to perform image classification through a program that could be set other in mobile devices or in fixed support in the shrimp supply chain. The proposed approach is a lightweight model that uses HSV color space shrimp images. A simple pipeline shows the most important stages performed to determine a pattern that identifies the class to which they belong based on their pigmentation. For the experiments, a database acquired with mobile devices of various brands and models has been used to capture images of shrimp. The results obtained with the images in the RGB and HSV color space allow for testing the effectiveness of the proposed model.

Keywords: Pigmentation · Color space · Light weight network

1 Introduction

The actual report on shrimp export shows that Ecuador in the last 3 years has become the main supplier of shrimp in the world. By 2022, 209 million pounds were exported representing USD 599 million dollars. It represents of 37% compared with the same period (cited from National Chamber of Aquaculture, 2022). The shrimp industry has evolved in the last two decades, which leads to the mandatory automation of manual processes in any of its production stages. Therefore, technology has become the best ally to improve productivity and quality control. Especially, in those countries where this industry has become one of the pillars of the gross domestic product, reaching export levels that place them as the first in the world. Following the importance of this industry, the use of technology based on computer vision nowadays has been developing very fast to support the automation of critical processes from the farm to the processor. In particular, those most susceptible to human error for quality control or classification of subtypes for dealing with the right price between the farmer and processors, as well, an efficient packaging and distribution processes. One of the most failure-prone processes visually evaluated the shrimp based in color (varies farm to farm) and the manual shrimp class classification made by a specialist. This task has always been tedious and time-consuming, dependent on the specialists who perform it, and prone to human error. These tasks become more complex when the objects to be classified are aquatic species that are susceptible to rapid deterioration due to high temperatures or constant handling. Provide the right deal price and final market is base in score visually and hand made set.

A special case of the object is the shrimp which, being a product of mass consumption in many countries, has become crucial to have automated processes with the least incidence of manual activities to classify them. Therefore, in this work, it is proposed to implement algorithms based on computer vision and deep learning to classify shrimp (Pennaeus vannamei) more quickly, efficiently, and with fewer incidents or failures. With this proposal, a classification method is developed that allows determining, based on a trained model, the type of shrimp according to its pigmentation. These processes are intended to reduce the time and costs of the shrimp at packaging process. Since shrimp industries have evolved last decade, there are various techniques based on computer vision to identify, classify and segment shrimp. For example, in [13], a method is proposed to detect the freshness of shrimp captured by mobile devices, using a deep learning architecture. Another approach that discriminates shelled shrimp (Metapenaeus ensis) by their status between fresh, frozen-thawed, and cold stored using hyperspectral imaging applying successive projections algorithm (SPA) is presented in [9]. Similarly, in Liu et al. [5] the authors propose a shrimp recognition based on a computer vision approach to determine the freshness of shrimp before shipment to distribution centers for human consumption.

In the current work, a novel computer vision-based approach is proposed for shrimp class classification. In this approach, we explore the use of color space imaging to train our model to determine if working in another color space other than the RGB one can improve the results obtained in the validation of the model. We have trained our model using images from the RGB and HSV color spaces. The core idea is to validate the effectiveness of the classification results on each color space image dataset. Additionally, in our research, we have generated our own set of good-quality images of shrimp in the same packaging line and shrimp harvested at the farm. To fulfill this task, we have used a set of cameras from mobile devices to capture the images of the shrimp with different lighting level that considerably increase the shadows in the shots and not facilitates the focus of the shrimp in the images. Likewise, the shrimp images have been captured in different environments or scenarios.

The proposed pipeline consists of firstly capturing shrimp images, then images are labeled by experts, and these images are used then for training the proposed architecture. We propose a lightweight network that classifies the

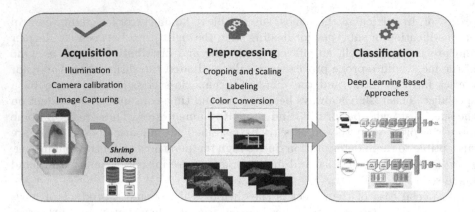

Fig. 1. Pipeline for shrimp classification.

shrimps into two out of the four classes according to their pigmentation. Due to the imbalance present in the data set, where the samples of one of the classes are almost 30% larger, we augment the dataset with less samples and undersample the larger class. Another limitation is the similarity that the shrimp samples of categories present to each other. Those limitations can lead to the network failing to learn in its early stages and thus minimizing the performance of the resulting trained model. In the architecture, to reduce the problem caused by the discarding of negative information, it is proposed to use the Leaky ReLu activation function, which allows the information to maintain the necessary variability in the outputs of the model layers so that they remain differentiable and the model can continue learning. The main contributions in the paper are summarized as follows:

– A dataset with labeled images have been generated; it contains high-quality data to be used for training deep learning-based approaches. This dataset contains images from different points of view, illumination, and backgrounds. The dataset corresponds to a variety of shrimp species named Penaeus vannamei. This dataset will be available for the computer vision community.
– A lightweight CNN architecture is proposed, to support the automation of the shrimp classification for a massive distribution market. The model is trained using our dataset and it achieves better results compared with other models of state of the art.

The manuscript is organized as follows. Section 2 presents works related to the classification problem, which serve as the baseline to design our image acquisition system, the image preprocessing, and the proposed architecture presented on the pipeline. Section 3 presents the proposed shrimp classification architecture. Experimental results and comparisons with different implementations are given in Sect. 4. Finally, conclusions are presented in Sect. 5.

2   Related Work

As described above, this paper presents an approach to perform shrimp classification according to their pigmentation. To define the best architecture design, different approaches have been reviewed in the literature for shrimp classification. Some of these techniques are based on color information, and patterns detected, among others. In this section, some relevant techniques related to this topic have been summarized.

Most of the techniques are based on deep learning, however, some approaches are proposed using classical computer vision techniques or machine learning models. One of the approaches based on machine learning is presented in [8] where the authors propose a method to detect the freshness of shrimp. The method is based on the use of labels that change their color depending on the state of the freshness of the shrimp. The label detects the high content of flavonoids present in shrimp. With the collected information, the authors have implemented an algorithm based on the near neighbors model of machine learning to perform the classification and quantization of the sensed colors. Additionally, another machine learning-based approach was proposed by Carbajal et al. [1], where the authors propose a fuzzy logic inference system based on an abstract to classify shrimps' habitat quality to solve a biological problem.

Another approach based on the use of CNN and logistic regression has been presented in [11]. It uses visible and near-infrared hyperspectral imaging techniques to discriminate the freshness of shrimp while frozen. Shrimps have been classified into two classes according to their freshness grades (fresh and stale). Each grade is defined based on its volatile basic nitrogen level. A similar approach is presented in [12] where the authors propose a hyperspectral imaging algorithm that combines machine and deep learning techniques to extract spectral features. This proposed approach can estimate the total volatile basic nitrogen (TVB-N) existing on Pacific white shrimps'. On the other hand, in [3], a CNN approach called ShrimpNet is proposed to classify six types of shrimp categories. This architecture can perform shrimp recognition to support the sources of animal protein available for human consumption. Instead, for shrimp quality control, in [4] the authors propose a CNN model that detects the presence of soft-shell on the body of shrimp and determines its level of deterioration. The called Deep-ShrimpCL proposed network introduces combined self-learned features in each layer of the model to optimize local receptive fields. Following the line of classification of shrimp characteristics, in Ma et al. [6], the authors have designed a deep learning network. This network allows monitoring the freshness of the shrimp by recognizing the fingerprint of the smell. This model has used the Wide-Slice Residual Network for food Recognition 50 (WISeR50) [7].

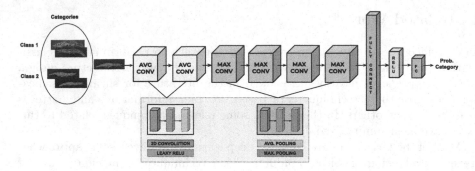

Fig. 2. Shrimp classification architecture using HSV dataset

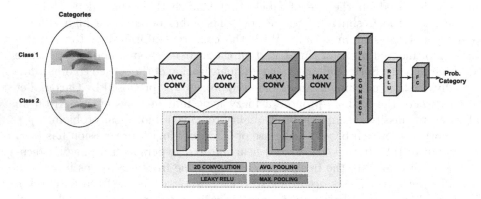

Fig. 3. Shrimp classification architecture using RGB dataset

3   Proposed Approach

3.1   Acquisition

To carry out the generation of the dataset, different models of smartphones with different image resolutions, heights and perspectives were used. To facilitate the task of labeling by the experts, physical labels were placed with the name of the category to which each photographed shrimp belonged. Figure 4 shows some examples of the images captured from smartphones. Since the images of each shrimp also contain the category label they belong to, a simple pre-processing has been done to leave only the shrimp in the image and later use these images for training the neural networks. To carry out this task, a script written in Python was used that semi-automatically selects the area where the shrimp is, cuts the image, and saves it in PNG format in a folder where they were organized by category.

Class: 1   **Class: 2**

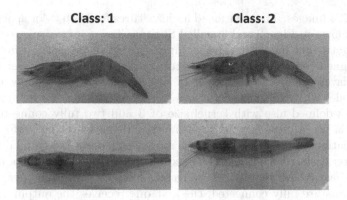

Fig. 4. Some illustration of different point of views of the acquired dataset

3.2 Preprocessing

Once the shrimp dataset has been correctly labeled according to its pigmentation categories, it proceeds with the preprocessing before model training. To carry out the classification of shrimp, a set of experiments has been prepared to perform the classification designing a model with a lightweight parameters. Only two of the four categories has been considered in this study, considering the class of shrimp required by the market and final product. The data set has a great similarity in its identifying characteristics. Also as mentioned before, our dataset is not balanced, there are more samples in one category than the other category which makes it more difficult to generalize the model. To overcome this limitation we have proposed training not only with RGB color space images, but HSV color spaces. We have included images converted to the HSV color space to improve the extraction of relevant shrimp features and facilitate the classification process. Also we have reduced our dataset samples to balanced both categories, introducing a more challenging problem. Also, we have applied data augmentation to increase the amount of data available for training, to reduce overfitting, and finally for improving the generalization of the model.

3.3 Classification

A novel-lightweight network has been designed to classify shrimp according to their pigmentation. This deep learning based network has been designed to differentiate the pattern of the two categories of shrimp using both color spaces (RGB-HSV). In order to speed up the training time and overcome the unbalanced dataset size we have applied fine tunning by using the weights of deep networks, such as VGG [10] or ResNet [2]. As mentioned above, we have defined the use of the data set in the HSV color space, since during the experiments, training took less time and better classification efficiency metrics were obtained. The proposed networks have fewer parameters compared to state-of-the-art models that use RGB images. The mentioned architectures for both color spaces (RGB, HSV) are shown in Figs. 2 and 3, called ShrimpCL.

Both lightweight models receive as input the set of categorized images. The model designed for RGB image classification consists of five layers: four convolutional layers defined with kernels of size 3 and two fully connected layers. For the model with HSV images, it has been built with 7 layers: six convolutional layers defined also with kernel size of 3 and two fully connected layers. Both models use a cross-entropy loss function to measure the performance of the classification model. In addition, the model includes a LeakyRelu activation function after each convolution and a maximum grouping operation of maximum group layer features to summarize the results of the convolution operation. The last two layers are fully connected, the first one receives the output of the last convolutional layer, which allows connecting all the outputs of the convolution operation, as it was done in the multilayer perceptron technique.

For the classification model with RGB images, the first fully connected layer consists of 512 nodes, while for the HSV model it consists of 1024 nodes. The last fully connected layer in both models (RGB and HSV) enables class scoring using the softmax activation function, to obtain the probability distribution corresponding to each class type. The models support multiclass classification, in our case only two classes are needed. If it is required to modify the number of classes, it is only necessary to modify the number of nodes of the last fully connected layer of the proposed models. To extract the pattern able to differentiate the categories of shrimps', in our architectures, we have applied a large receptive field in each layer and also, we have applied Leaky relu, reducing the slope during training for negative values resulting in the convolutional operations.

ShrimpCL networks for each color space have been trained from scratch using the Nesterov ADAM (NADAM) optimizer with a learning rate of 0.00027, which provides faster model convergence and generalization. The following section shows the results obtained from each of the experiments carried out and the corresponding comparisons are made to validate the efficiency of the designed models and determine which one presents the best results. The obtained results are presented in the next section.

4 Experimental Results

This section presents the obtained results with the classification networks designed to identify two categories of shrimp according to their pigmentation. The architectures have been designed to receive shrimp samples from each category labeled as input based on the color spaces of the images used. These architectures have been evaluated with images of different color spaces, that is, they have been evaluated in two scenarios: *i*) classification problem of two classes of shrimp samples of RGB color space, and *ii*) problem classification of two classes with shrimp samples of the HSV color space. In addition, as previously indicated, two representative state-of-the-art architectures (i.e., VGG16

[10] and ResNet50 [2]) have been fine-tuned and it has been possible to determine which network obtains the best metrics. The results obtained are used to make the corresponding quantitative comparisons.

The two-class classification approach was trained using a set of 1,300 images (800 images for training, 300 images for testing, and 200 images to validate the trained model).

It is important to mention that in order to select the best architecture, not only the quantitative values of efficiency for each category of shrimp have been considered, but also the average efficiency of the model and the number of parameters of the proposed architecture. As mentioned above, according to the obtained results, the model proposed for the images of the HSV color space is the one that has obtained the best quantitative metrics. In particular, the values are higher for the case of one of the classes (Class 1) and remain the same in the other class (Class 2), when compared to the model evaluated with images of the RGB color space.

The proposed architecture using HSV images is lighter than the shrimp classification architecture using RGB images. Since this model has fewer parameters, it is trained in less time, without affecting the efficiency of the classification. The results of the proposed lightweight network, ShrimpCL for HSV images, can be seen in Table 1, for the two-class classification problem. The table also shows, the results of the first classification model using RGB images designed for the experiments, but later improved with a lighter architecture. Also, include the state-of-the-art models, such as VGG-16 [10], ResNet-50 [2] and ShrimpCL for RGB images evaluated in this paper. As can be seen, the proposed lightweight architecture using the HSV color space images shows better quantitative results than all previous approaches. Furthermore, it should be noted that the proposed HSV architecture requires fewer parameters than our approach using the RGB color space and more than two hundred times fewer parameters than the VGG architecture.

Table 1. Results of shrimp classification

Network architecture	Categories		Metrics	
	Class 1	Class 2	Avg. acc	# of net. param.
VGG16-RGB	0.960	0.968	0.964	134268 K
RESNET50-RGB	0.890	0.946	0.918	23591 K
ShrimpCL for RGB	0.963	0.950	0.956	1646 K
ShrimpCL for RGB-Ligth-Weight	0.972	0.965	0.968	593 K
ShrimpCL for HSV-Light-Weight	**0.981**	**0.973**	**0.977**	**473 K**

5 Conclusions

This work tackles the challenging problem of classifying shrimp based on their pigmentation. Taking into account that the pigmentation characteristics between the defined classes are similar in some cases of the samples of the data set, as well as the number of samples for each class, it is not necessarily balanced, which complicates the design of the proposed solution. This lightweight CNN classification model has been validated using shrimp images in the HSV color space. The results prove that using this color space reduces the complexity of the problem. This is because the characteristics detected in the images become more distinguishable. Therefore, the efficiency in the classification of shrimp based on their pigmentation is improved. Model validation could be extended with other shrimp categories and explore the use of other color spaces or spectra to identify patterns presented in the shrimp images.

Acknowledgements. This work has been partially supported by the ESPOL Polytechnic University; and the "CERCA Programme/Generalitat de Catalunya". The authors gratefully acknowledge the NVIDIA Corporation for the donation of a Titan Xp GPU used for this research.

References

1. Carbajal, J., Sánchez, L.: Classification based on fuzzy inference systems for artificial habitat quality in shrimp farming. In: 2008 Seventh Mexican International Conference on Artificial Intelligence, pp. 388–392. IEEE (2008)
2. He, K., Zhang, X., Ren, S., Sun, J.: Deep residual learning for image recognition. In: Proceedings of the IEEE Conference on Computer Vision and Pattern Recognition, pp. 770–778 (2016)
3. Hu, W.C., Wu, H.T., Zhang, Y.F., Zhang, S.H., Lo, C.H.: Shrimp recognition using ShrimpNet based on convolutional neural network. J. Ambient Intell. Human. Comput. 1–8 (2020)
4. Liu, Z.: Soft-shell shrimp recognition based on an improved AlexNet for quality evaluations. J. Food Eng. **266**, 109698 (2020)
5. Liu, Z., Jia, X., Xu, X.: Study of shrimp recognition methods using smart networks. Comput. Electron. Agric. **165**, 104926 (2019)
6. Ma, P., et al.: Integrated portable shrimp-freshness prediction platform based on ice-templated metal-organic framework colorimetric combinatorics and deep convolutional neural networks. ACS Sustain. Chem. Eng. **9**(50), 16926–16936 (2021)
7. Martinel, N., Foresti, G.L., Micheloni, C.: Wide-slice residual networks for food recognition. In: 2018 IEEE Winter conference on applications of computer vision (WACV), pp. 567–576. IEEE (2018)
8. Noor, A., Evi, J., Safitri, A.D., Mustari, M., Tiandho, Y., et al.: Melastoma malabathricum l. Extracts-based indicator for monitoring shrimp freshness integrated with classification technology using nearest neighbours algorithm. SINERGI **25**(1), 69–74 (2021)
9. Qu, J.H., Cheng, J.H., Sun, D.W., Pu, H., Wang, Q.J., Ma, J.: Discrimination of shelled shrimp (metapenaeus ensis) among fresh, frozen-thawed and cold-stored by hyperspectral imaging technique. LWT-Food Sci. Technol. **62**(1), 202–209 (2015)

10. Simonyan, K., Zisserman, A.: Very deep convolutional networks for large-scale image recognition. arXiv preprint arXiv:1409.1556 (2014)
11. Yu, X., Tang, L., Wu, X., Lu, H.: Nondestructive freshness discriminating of shrimp using visible/near-infrared hyperspectral imaging technique and deep learning algorithm. Food Anal. Methods **11**(3), 768–780 (2018)
12. Yu, X., Wang, J., Wen, S., Yang, J., Zhang, F.: A deep learning based feature extraction method on hyperspectral images for nondestructive prediction of TVB-N content in pacific white shrimp (Litopenaeus vannamei). Biosys. Eng. **178**, 244–255 (2019)
13. Zhang, Y., Wei, C., Zhong, Y., Wang, H., Luo, H., Weng, Z.: Deep learning detection of shrimp freshness via smartphone pictures. J. Food Meas. Characterization 1–9 (2022)

Gait Emotion Recognition Using a Bi-modal Deep Neural Network

Yajurv Bhatia$^{(\boxtimes)}$ (ID), A. S. M. Hossain Bari (ID), and Marina Gavrilova (ID)

Department of Computer Science, University of Calgary, Calgary, Canada
yajurv.bhatia@ucalgary.ca
https://science.ucalgary.ca/computer-science

Abstract. Gait Emotion Recognition is an emerging research domain that focuses on the automatic detection of emotions from a person's manner of walking. Deep learning-based methodologies have been proven highly effective for computer vision tasks. This paper provides a powerful deep-learning architecture for emotion recognition from gait by introducing the fusion of domain-specific discriminative features with latent deep features. The proposed Bi-Modal Deep Neural Network (BMDNN) combines salient features extracted from a deep neural network with highly-discriminating handcrafted features. The proposed architecture outperforms state-of-the-art methods in all emotional classes on the Edinburgh Locomotion MoCap Dataset.

Keywords: Human motion · Deep learning · Long short-term memory · Gait · Emotion recognition · Laban movement analysis

1 Introduction

Gait Emotion Recognition (GER) is defined as the inference of human emotions by analyzing a person's manner of walking. It is an emerging domain of research, significant for computer vision applications, namely gaming, virtual reality, and human-robot interactions. The data collection for GER systems does not require the subject's cooperation. Recognition can be performed from a distance, and is non-intrusive [1]. Furthermore, it can be adopted for a wide range of applications, such as fall prevention in smart homes [2], disaster management [3], medical diagnostics [4], and emotionally aware robot design [5].

Gait analysis requires coordinates of body joints over time collected using motion capture systems [6], depth-based sensors [7], or extracted from videos of people walking using pose-estimation [8]. The data can then be categorized into emotions. Two popular emotion representation models are: the Distinct Categories (DC) model and the Pleasure Dominance Arousal (PDA) model [9]. The DC model considers mutually exclusive emotion classes, while the PDA model presents a continuous three-dimensional space where Pleasure, Dominance, and Arousal are the axes. The Distinct Categories model is adopted in our research.

Preliminary works on GER were based on traditional Machine Learning (ML) methodologies [10,11]; however, those approaches only explored a handful of

G. Bebis et al. (Eds.): ISVC 2022, LNCS 13598, pp. 46–60, 2022.
https://doi.org/10.1007/978-3-031-20713-6_4

specific features, which resulted in average performance. Incorporating Deep Learning (DL) techniques to produce and exploit larger feature sets have only recently started to be investigated [5]. Graph and pseudo-image based methodologies benefit from inherent structural information of the human body, but fail to explore low-level features between distant vertices. Works based on Recurrent Neural Networks (RNN) process gaits as sequences to explore all dependencies, but use ineffective training methodologies or a sub-optimal network. Furthermore, DL methods generally require substantial amounts of data to perform well. Subsequently, the lack of large datasets for GER resulted in researchers relying on synthetic gaits or mixed datasets [12]. Therefore, a powerful neural network that processes gaits sequentially and is trained on real gaits for emotion recognition, is required to address the above mentioned research gaps.

This paper answers the following research questions:

1. Can domain-specific handcrafted features be fused with latent deep features to improve gait emotion recognition performance?
2. Can the gait emotion recognition performance be enhanced by combining and processing handcrafted features with raw gait data?
3. Can handcrafted features be used to make a deep learning model resilient to class imbalance in the dataset?
4. How Laban Movement Analysis feature groups affect the performance of a sequential neural network?

In this research, for the first time domain-specific handcrafted features based on Laban Movement Analysis (LMA) are combined with latent features extracted from a Deep Neural Network (DNN). A sequential neural network based on Long Short Term Memory (LSTM), and Multi Layered Perceptrons (MLP) is proposed to facilitate feature fusion. Unlike prior research, the fused feature set is processed further to extract information-rich high-level features before classification. Furthermore, L2 regularizers are employed to ensure a high performance across all emotion classes. Additionally, the effects of various LMA-based feature groups on GER performance are studied. The contributions of this research are:

1. A novel fusion of robust LMA-based domain-specific handcrafted features with latent features extracted from a deep neural network is proposed.
2. A powerful Bi-Modal Deep Neural Network (BMDNN) to facilitate the combination and processing of the handcrafted features with deep latent features is introduced.
3. A comprehensive analysis of GER performance with respect to different LMA-based feature groups is conducted.
4. An ablation study of the proposed deep learning architecture is performed to validate the performance on imbalanced dataset of real gait samples and the importance of the introduced feature fusion.

The performance of the proposed methodology is evaluated on the Edinburgh Locomotive MoCap Dataset [13] by performing comparison with most recent state-of-the-art methods. The results show that the proposed model outperforms all recent methods with the highest class and mean Average Precision.

2   Related Works

The research conducted on GER can be broadly classified into: classical ML-based and DL-based approaches.

Most ML works in GER were focused on producing an information-rich feature vector to classify emotions. One of the earliest work was published by Janssen et al. in 2008 [14] to measure the force applied by the subjects during emotional walks. In 2010, Karg et al. [10] used two feature sets based on statistical parameters and eigen-postures to train Naïve Bayes (NB), Nearest Neighbour and Support Vector Machine (SVM) classifiers. Venture et al. [15] used a similarity index-based classification for a feature vector based on auto-correlation matrices of degrees of freedom of body joints. In 2016, Li et al. [16] applied Discrete Fourier Transform to identify key frequencies in gait trajectories to build a feature set. The domain witnessed other interesting works on accelerometer-based GER [17]. In 2018, Ahmed et al. [18] refined ten gait feature groups by Analysis of Variance (ANOVA) and Multivariate ANOVA to achieve better GER performance. However, the reliance on domain-specific handcrafted features did not ensure optimal results. Therefore, the recent works explored automatic feature extraction using data-centric DL algorithms.

Using DL methods for GER recognition is the latest development in this domain. The first methodology proposed by researchers for GER was based on Graph Neural Networks (GNNs). In 2018, Yan et al. [19] devised a graph-based representation that utilized temporal connections between corresponding body joints. This Spatial-Temporal Graph Convolution Network (STGCN) was extended by adding an average pooling and a 2D convolution layer to extract deep features in [12]. However, the training data was not representative of the gait data collected in the real world and resulted in low performance.

In 2019, Randhavane et al. [20] proposed a LSTM-based network to produce deep features to fuse with affected features. Similar to [12], the limitation of dataset size was addressed by synthetically generating gaits. The method, however, had an ineffective LSTM and classification module, and did not demonstrate good emotion classification performance. In 2020, the same authors [5] represented gaits as pseudo-images and processed them using a Convolutional Neural Network (CNN). In 2020, Bhattacharya et al. [21] proposed hierarchical processing of gaits using Gaited Recurrent Units, which offer less control over the memory cell when compared to LSTMs.

All DL approaches required substantial data to train a neural network. Paired with a lack of gait datasets for emotion classification, some authors resorted to train models on artificially produced gaits [12,20,21]. Hence, their training data was either non-representative of real gaits or had too much variation. Some methods relied on adding affective features to improve the robustness [12,20]; however, the feature sets were limited. Moreover, the features were introduced directly to the classifier, hence the assessments were made using low-level information. Graph and pseudo-image based methods [5,12] processed gaits structurally to benefit from skeletal dependencies of the human body. Actions occurring in different localities of the skeleton can indicate the same emotion. However, due to a rigid structure used in graph-based methods, such low-level features were not explored. On the other hand, RNNs processed gait data sequentially to exploit all possible joint dependencies. Regardless, the only works based on sequential networks used ineffective feature extraction module [20] or a training methodology that was not aligned with emotion classification [21].

Laban Movement Analysis (LMA) [22] has been effective at discriminating emotions from body movements [23]. However, no prior DL work combined the powerful LMA-based handcrafted features with features extracted using a DNN. The domain has also not seen works that process handcrafted and deep features together to derive more information-rich features. Additionally, the sensitivity of DL models toward the data distribution was not studied. These gaps are addressed in the proposed research.

3 Methodology

This paper proposes a novel fusion of deep features extracted using a sequential neural network and robust domain-specific handcrafted features (see Fig. 1) to address the limitations mentioned in Sect. 2. The proposed architecture employs LSTM units to extract sequential and temporal gait features for emotion recognition by exploiting the dependencies among all body joints. Moreover, robust handcrafted features: Joint Relative Distances (JRD) and Joint Relative Angles (JRA) [1], are included to determine the relative geometric motions and directions of body joints and are inputted into the first module. All possible relative angles and distances are considered in the proposed method to overcome the limitation of favouring only a few body joints. The stability and recognition performance are further improved by incorporating domain-specific LMA features to capture the dynamic structural properties of a subject's body while walking. Information-rich LMA-based features are fed to the MLP subnetwork to fuse with deep features which results in robustness and resilience to the imbalanced dataset. The proposed method achieves remarkable precision scores across all emotion classes and outperforms all recent state-of-the-art methods.

The entire DNN has an attenuated design where each layer comprises lesser or equal number of units than the previous one. This ensures that the information is condensed towards the end of the network. The Bi-Modal Deep Neural Network (BMDNN) consists of two modules; the LSTM-based feature extraction module sequentially processes gait data to produce a rich feature vector. The second module, the MLP-based decision module is responsible for combining and condensing the information extracted by the LSTM subnetwork and the features calculated using LMA, and to map to the four emotion classes. Moreover, the batch normalization layer in the MLP module ensures lower loss during training with fast and smooth parameter updates.

The input to the first module is a concatenated vector of size $[T, (N*C)+F]$, where T is the number of frames of each gait sequence, N is the number of body joints, C is the number of coordinates for each body joint, and F is the combined size of the angle and distance-based handcrafted features (JRAs and JRDs),

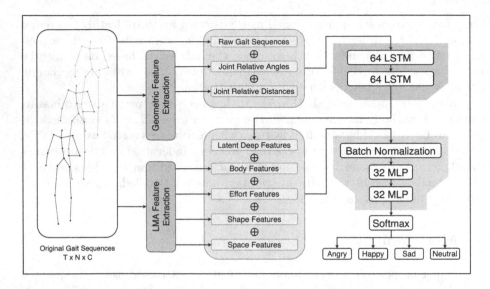

Fig. 1. The architecture of the proposed GER deep learning method

described later. The input to the second module consists of the latent deep features of size 64, extracted from the first module, concatenated with the robust domain-specific LMA features. If the inputs are not normalized, optimization of the model is skewed and produces too large or too small gradient values, restricting optimal parameter updates. Moreover, since the input to the first module is gait data, normalizing it through conventional pre-processing methods would distort the structure of the gait sequences. Hence, the combined feature vector from both inputs is normalized by the network via the batch normalization layer in the beginning of the MLP module.

The first half of the network has two LSTM layers, each with 64 units, a Hyperbolic Tangent (Tanh) activation, and a L2 regularizer with a penalty of 0.01. The regularizers penalizes high weights, hence preventing overfitting. The Tanh activation, ensures that the negative values from the inputs are not ignored while producing the activations.

The second half of the architecture contains a batch normalization layer before two MLP layers. Each layer has 32 units with Tanh activations to ensure an overall tapered design for refining features. The second subnetwork combines the information from the features extracted by the LSTM subnetwork with the LMA-based handcrafted features, to produce high-level features. These high-level features are mapped to the four emotion classes using a Softmax activation.

The model is optimized using a RMSprop optimizer with a momentum of 0.5, a rho of 0.3, and an epsilon of $1e-7$ for 400 epochs. Furthermore, the training is performed using a batch size of 64 and categorical cross-entropy loss function.

DNN-based approaches are sensitive to the composition of the training data and might result in low performance for under-represented emotion classes.

Therefore to introduce more robustness, we propose a novel hybrid architecture that integrates the domain-specific features.

The *handcrafted geometric features*, JRAs and JRDs, are processed by the sequential feature extracting module alongside the raw gait sequences to produce deep information-rich feature sets of size 64. Since the LSTM network processes sequential data, the JRA and JRD features are calculated frame-wise. The additional information encapsulated by JRDs and JRAs, contributes to the high performance of the model.

JRAs describe the motions of the body by calculating the angles formed by any two body joints, $A(x_1, y_1, z_1)$ and $B(x_2, y_2, z_2)$, on the mid spine body joint $S(x_0, y_0, z_0)$, thus consisting of $\binom{N-1}{2}$ angles, where N is the number of body joints. The calculation for JRAs is described in Eq. (1) where $\|\vec{SA}\|$ and $\|\vec{SB}\|$ are the norms of vectors $\vec{SA}$ and $\vec{SB}$, respectively.

$$\theta = \cos^{-1}\left(\frac{\vec{SA} \cdot \vec{SB}}{\|\vec{SA}\| \, \|\vec{SB}\|}\right) \tag{1}$$

The JRDs, as defined in Eq. (2), are Euclidean Distance (ED) measures between two body joints $A(x_1, y_1, z_1)$ and $B(x_2, y_2, z_2)$. They encode the relative movement of various body joints in terms of the distance between them, which is beneficial for emotion recognition [1].

$$ED(A, B) = \sqrt{(x_2 - x_1)^2 + (y_2 - y_1)^2 + (z_2 - z_1)^2} \tag{2}$$

To improve the performance of the model for emotion classes with low data representation, the proposed method employs statistically cumulated handcrafted features resilient to unbalanced datasets. These handcrafted features are based on the Laban Movement Analysis (LMA) [22] which provides a structural description of the movement of a subject's body using four groups: *body, effort, shape, and space*. These groups comprise of 17 features calculated in the temporal domain, i.e. the features are calculated for each time frame of the gait sequence and have a combined size of $(17, T)$. However, the LMA features must be converted to a one-dimensional vector to make it compatible for the MLP subnetwork. This flattening of the features is performed by calculating histogram values on 100 bins, thus making the final feature set of shape $(1700, 1)$. The final feature set is concatenated with the latent deep features extracted from the LSTM subnetwork $(64, 1)$ to form the input vector for the MLP subnetwork.

The *body feature group* (Head Inclination Angle, Flex Angle, Abduction Angle, Knee Angle, Stride Angle, Knee Stride Length, Foot Stride Length) describes the physical and structural characteristics of the body using seven angle and distance measures. These features capture the information about the connections of the body as it moves.

The *effort features* (Kinetic Energy, Knee Average Velocity, Heel Average Velocity, Elbow Average Velocity, Wrist Average Velocity) encapsulate the subtle intent behind the motion of a body by measuring the energy/force put into the motion. This feature group describes the amount of expression [23]. The velocity of a particular joint at a time frame i can be calculated as the difference between the joint's position at the ith frame and the joint's position at the $i+1^{th}$ frame, described in Eq. (3). Additionally, the Kinetic Energy at a given time frame i is calculated using Eq. (3), where m is the mass of the joint ($m = 1$), v is the velocity of the kth joint and N is the total number of the body joints.

$$KE^i = \frac{1}{2N} \sum_{k=1}^{N} m.v_k^{i^2} \; ; \quad V_A^i = A^{i+1} - A^i \tag{3}$$

The next movement component, *shape*, contains a single feature: density index, which captures the progression of the body's shape change with respect to time. The metric represents the variation of the body shape throughout the gait, which indicates how smooth/uneven the movements are. To determine the Density Index , the centroid C of the body for each frame i is calculated according to Eq. (4), where J_k is the vector containing the $x, y,$ and z coordinates of the kth body joint, and N is the total number of body joints. Finally, the Density Index (DI) is calculated as described in (4), where J_{kx} is the x coordinate of the kth body joint.

$$DI^i = \frac{1}{N} \sum_{k=1}^{N} \sqrt{(C_x^i - J_{kx}^i)^2 + (C_y^i - J_{ky}^i)^2 + (C_z^i - J_{kz}^i)^2} \; ; \quad C^i = \frac{1}{N} \sum_{k=1}^{N} J_k \tag{4}$$

The fourth category in LMA is *space* (Whole Body Bounding Volume, Upper Body Bounding Volume, Lower Body Bounding Volume, Spatial Symmetry Index), which delineates the way a subject makes use of the surrounding space during a gait. The Spatial Symmetry Index is indicative of relaxation [24]. The Bounding Volume (BV) is the product of d_x, d_y and d_z (Eq. (6)), which are distances calculated in Eq. (5). Lastly, the spatial symmetry is calculated by computing the barycenter of the skeletal body for each frame, and then using it to calculate the symmetric indices for each axis. The Symmetric Index (SI) at a given time frame i for an axis w is defined in Eq. (7), where LW, RW, and BC represent the coordinates of the left wrist joint, the right wrist joint and the barycenter of the body. Subsequently, the overall symmetry index is calculated according to Eq. (7).

$$d_x = max_{k \in K} J_{kx} - min_{k \in K} J_{kx}; \quad d_y = max_{k \in K} J_{ky} - min_{k \in K} J_{ky}$$
$$d_z = max_{k \in K} J_{kz} - min_{k \in K} J_{kz} \tag{5}$$

$$Bounding\ Volume = d_x \times d_y \times d_z \tag{6}$$

$$SI^i = \sqrt{(SI_x^i)^2 + (SI_y^i)^2 + (SI_z^i)^2} \; ; \quad SI_w^i = \frac{(LW_w^i - BC_w^i) - (RW_w^i - BC_w^i)}{(LW_w^i - BC_w^i) + (RW_w^i - BC_w^i)} \tag{7}$$

4   Experimental Results

The proposed method uses a subset of the Edinburgh Locomotive MoCap Dataset (ELMD) [13] containing 1855 gait sequences, recorded for four seconds at 60 Hz. Hence, each sequence has 240 frames. Each frame contains 3D coordinates for 21 body joints. A study [20] used a crowd sourced platform to assign emotion labels to 1835 gaits. These samples contain 1048 Angry, 454 Happy, 254 Sad and 79 Neutral gaits and are used for training, validation and testing with a 80:10:10 stratified data split.

The proposed neural network was trained and tested on a set of values of learning rates, batch sizes, different activation functions, and using different feature fusion techniques. This section also includes ablation studies to validate the necessity and impact of the key components of the methodology. The proposed method is evaluated using: the Average Precision (AP) for each emotion class, and micro and macro mean Average Precision (mAP) scores. To ensure optimal training of the DL model, experiments for various hyperparameters and their respective values were performed.

Optimizers: The proposed method was trained with three popular optimizers to identify which one ensures the lowest loss and hence, better learning. Stochastic Gradient Descent (SGD) was found to produce steep and smooth loss curves; however it could not facilitate the network to reach low loss values (see Fig. 2d). SGD also caused the network to be susceptible to the data composition of the dataset shown in Table 1. On the other hand, Adam optimizer resulted in a significantly lower loss value (see Fig. 2e). However, Root Mean Squared propagation (RMSprop) produced the smoothest loss graphs (shown in Fig. 2f) indicating an optimal learning and achieved the lowest loss out of all the optimizers. The model also produced the most precise predictions with RMSprop optimizer mentioned in Table 1.

Table 1. Performance comparison of the proposed model for different optimizers

Optimizers	Class AP angry	Class AP happy	Class AP sad	Class AP neutral	Micro mAP	Macro mAP
SGD	0.94	0.58	0.23	0.08	0.58	0.46
Adam	0.99	0.93	0.95	0.91	0.97	0.94
RMSprop	**0.99**	**0.95**	**0.97**	**0.91**	**0.98**	**0.96**

Batch Sizes: The proposed architecture was trained with a range of batch sizes: 16, 32, 64, and 128. All batch sizes resulted in an effective learning that can be observed through the smooth loss graphs produced during training. Based on Table 2 results, the batch size of 64 was chosen for the proposed model.

Learning Rates: The learning rate of the model regulates the magnitude of the weight updates and therefore, how fast the model converges. To determine

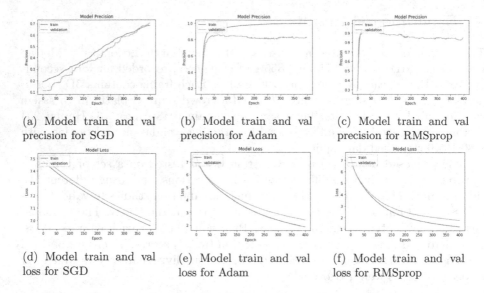

(a) Model train and val precision for SGD

(b) Model train and val precision for Adam

(c) Model train and val precision for RMSprop

(d) Model train and val loss for SGD

(e) Model train and val loss for Adam

(f) Model train and val loss for RMSprop

Fig. 2. Precisions and losses of model over 400 epochs for various optimizers

an optimal learning rate for the proposed architecture, the model was trained on learning rates from $4e-6$ to $4e-5$. As seen in Table 3, the learning rate of $1e-5$ results in the best precision of the model and hence was selected.

Feature Fusion Experiments: Two experiments were performed to find the best way to fuse the domain-specific features with deep features. First, the LMA features were calculated for each frame of the gait sequence and concatenated to the input of the LSTM subnetwork. Second, the calculated LMA features were flattened to be combined with the input of the MLP subnetwork. When the LMA features are fused with the deep features and provided to MLP subnetwork, the performance increases and the skewness of the performance towards highly representative emotion classes is eliminated (Table 4).

Table 2. Performance of the model for different batch sizes

Batch size	Class AP angry	Class AP happy	Class AP sad	Class AP neutral	Micro mAP	Macro mAP
16	0.99	0.92	0.95	0.91	0.97	0.94
32	0.99	0.94	0.96	0.89	0.98	0.95
64	**0.99**	**0.95**	**0.97**	**0.91**	**0.98**	**0.96**
128	0.99	0.94	0.96	0.83	0.98	0.93

Table 3. Performance of the model for different learning rates

Learning rate	Class AP angry	Class AP happy	Class AP sad	Class AP neutral	Micro mAP	Macro mAP
4e−6	0.99	0.93	0.95	0.87	0.97	0.94
8e−6	0.99	0.96	0.94	0.81	0.98	0.93
1e−5	**0.99**	**0.95**	**0.97**	**0.91**	**0.98**	**0.96**
2e−5	0.99	0.90	0.94	0.87	0.97	0.93
4e−5	0.99	0.93	0.95	0.81	0.97	0.92

Table 4. Performance of the model for different fused feature sets

Feature fusion method	Class AP angry	Class AP happy	Class AP sad	Class AP neutral	Micro mAP	Macro mAP
LMA w/LSTM input	0.99	0.87	0.64	0.41	0.95	0.73
LMA w/MLP input	**0.99**	**0.95**	**0.97**	**0.91**	**0.98**	**0.96**

Number of Epochs: The number of epochs determine how many iterations the model is trained for. If the model is trained for only a few epochs, the model exhibits suboptimal performance whereas the model overfits if the training goes on for too long. Thus, to determine the optimal number of epochs the network was trained for 1000 epochs and the training and validation losses were monitored. The model shows convergence shortly before the 400th epoch as seen in Fig. 3. Thus, the number of epochs was set to 400.

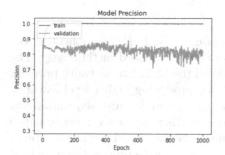

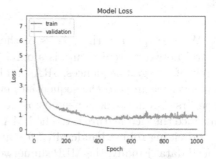

(a) Training and validation precision of the model for 1000 epochs

(b) Training and validation loss of the model for 1000 epochs

Fig. 3. Precisions and losses of model over 1000 epochs on the ELMD dataset

Table 5. Ablation Study for the various components of the proposed methodology

Architecture		Class AP angry	Class AP happy	Class AP sad	Class AP neutral	Micro mAP	Macro mAP
LSTM subnetwork	✓	0.98	0.60	0.45	0.17	0.88	0.55
Geometric features	×						
MLP subnetwork	×						
LMA features	×						
LSTM subnetwork	✓	0.98	0.67	0.50	0.26	0.89	0.60
Geometric features	×						
MLP subnetwork	✓						
LMA features	×						
LSTM subnetwork	✓	0.99	0.87	0.82	0.61	0.95	0.82
Geometric features	✓						
MLP subnetwork	×						
LMA features	×						
LSTM subnetwork	×	0.99	0.93	0.97	0.86	0.98	0.94
Geometric features	×						
MLP subnetwork	✓						
LMA features	✓						
LSTM subnetwork	✓	0.99	0.88	0.86	0.52	0.95	0.81
Geometric features	✓						
MLP subnetwork	✓						
LMA features	×						
LSTM subnetwork	✓	0.99	0.93	0.97	0.85	0.97	0.94
Geometric features	×						
MLP subnetwork	✓						
LMA features	✓						
LSTM subnetwork	✓	0.99	0.95	0.97	0.91	0.98	0.96
Geometric features	✓						
MLP subnetwork	✓						
LMA features	✓						

We now present the results of the ablation study. Each component of the neural network architecture is a crucial part of the proposed methodology. The input of raw gait sequences, JRAs, and JRDs to the LSTM subnetwork provides low-level features to the sequential network for producing higher-level features. The first subnetwork is responsible for condensing gait features sequentially to produce the rich feature set. The LMA features further enhance the performance by providing robust handcrafted features that make the model resilient to unbalanced data. Finally, the MLP subnetwork is responsible to process the combined features from the deep extracted features and the LMA-based handcrafted features, to produce high-level features for emotion recognition.

Effectiveness of Geometric Features: The geometric features introduce all possible angle and distance measures between two joints. Deep features are formed using the combined information from body joints and geometric features for each time frame. On removing the geometric features from the input of the LSTM module, the overall performance of the model decreases (Table 5).

Effectiveness of LMA Features: The handcrafted features using Laban Movement Analysis provide robustness and result in a well regularized model. Each of the feature groups contribute distinct information to the proposed architecture. As seen in Table 5, on excluding LMA feature groups a drastic decrease in the model precision for most emotions, as well as the model's resilience towards data imbalance is reduced. Performance of the model for emotion classes with lower data representation are affected strongly.

Effectiveness of LSTM and MLP Subnetworks: The LSTM and MLP subnetworks are crucial building blocks of the proposed methodology. The main function of the LSTM module is to produce information-rich deep features from which further high-level features are extracted by the MLP module for classification. The MLP subnetwork also facilitates the fusion of deep features and LMA features. As shown in Table 5, on removing the LSTM module from the network, the model precision value decreases by 0.02 for the Happy class and by 0.05 for Neutral class. The effect is stronger with the removal of the MLP module from the network. The precision values across all emotion classes except Angry decrease significantly and result in a macro mAP of 0.82.

Importance of Each LMA Feature Group: The proposed method was trained and tested with different LMA feature groups to identify their impact on overall model performance. Though all the features were necessary to achieve the highest performance, some feature groups were crucial for identifying certain emotions. As seen from Table 6, the most contributing feature groups for the identification of Happy and Neutral gaits were Body and Space features which contain angular, distance, and volumetric measures. This indicates that Happy and Neutral gaits contained in the dataset can be distinguished from other emotional gaits by geometric body positions and the space occupied by the subject during the gait. In contrast, Effort features proved to be important for recognizing Sad gaits because kinetic energies and velocities of various joints effectively capture the slower body movement of Sad emotions in comparison to other emotional gait. Another interesting observation is that the model precision for the neutral class is 0.46 with just shape features (density of the body joints); however, the model achieves a 0.91 precision with all the features combined, which is much higher than any individual feature group's precision. This indicates that Shape feature group contributes unique information.

Table 6. Model performance with various LMA feature groups

Feature group used with BMDNN	Class AP angry	Class AP happy	Class AP sad	Class AP neutral	Micro mAP	Macro mAP
No LMA features used	0.99	0.88	0.86	0.52	0.95	0.81
Body features	0.99	0.94	0.88	0.87	0.97	0.92
Effort features	0.99	0.88	0.90	0.80	0.96	0.90
Shape features	0.99	0.89	0.80	0.46	0.95	0.78
Space features	0.99	0.90	0.88	0.87	0.97	0.91
All LMA features	**0.99**	**0.95**	**0.97**	**0.91**	**0.98**	**0.96**

Table 7. Comparison of the proposed method with state-of-the-art methods

Methods	Class AP angry	Class AP happy	Class AP sad	Class AP neutral	Micro mAP	Macro mAP
STEP (2020) [12]	0.22	0.52	0.30	0.12	0.29	0.27
ADF (2019) [20]	0.22	0.59	0.30	0.12	0.31	0.27
STGCN (2018) [19]	0.06	0.97	0.20	0.01	0.34	0.41
HAPAM (2020) [21]	0.97	0.66	0.40	0.18	0.60	0.88
ProxEmo (2020) [5]	0.90	0.92	0.94	0.94	0.92	0.93
BMSNN (2022) [25]	0.99	0.91	0.90	0.65	0.97	0.86
Proposed BMDNN	**0.99**	**0.95**	**0.97**	**0.91**	**0.98**	**0.96**

Comparison with State-of-the-Art: The best configuration of the proposed architecture was compared with the most recent state-of-the-art methods. The performances of STGCN [19], ADF [20], STEP [12], HAPAM [21], ProxEmo [5], and BMSNN [25] were compared with the proposed method. Most of the methods mentioned earlier were unable to train on small datasets like ELMD. Table 7 shows that the proposed architecture outperforms all other methods across all classes. In comparison to the best prior method, BMSNN [25], the proposed BMDNN architecture achieves an increase in the Average Precision by 4.4% for the Happy class, by 7.7% for the Sad class, and by 28.6% for the Neutral class. Furthermore, the micro and mean Average Precision scores of 0.98 and 0.96 respectively, are also observed to be superior. Hence, the proposed BMDNN architecture outperforms the state-of-the-art methodologies in terms of overall precision, while maintaining high performance in all emotion classes.

The highest scores achieved by the proposed BMDNN architecture are attributed to the powerful LSTM and the MLP subnetworks. The high performance is also a result of the overall attenuated design of the neural network, the normalization techniques, and the regularization techniques employed. Another major contributing factor is the information-rich handcrafted features exploited by the DNN architecture.

5 Conclusion and Future Work

This paper proposes a unique approach of fusing latent features with the robust domain-specific handcrafted features for recognizing four classes of emotions from human gait sequences. The proposed architecture uses delineating handcrafted features based on the four components of human motion: Body, Effort, Shape, and Space, based on the Laban Movement Analysis. The LMA features are fused in a way that achieves the best performance mitigating the performance drop for under-represented classes. The proposed architecture achieves a micro mean Average Precision of 0.98, and a macro mAP of 0.96 that outperforms all recent state-of-the-art methods on the ELMD dataset.

Recent advances in deep learning have shown transformer networks to be proficient for sequential processing. Hence, architectures based on such networks can be explored in the future. The research on emotion recognition from gait opens new avenues for its utilization in smart homes, human-computer interaction, robotics, virtual reality, and gaming.

Acknowledgment. The authors acknowledge the Natural Sciences and Engineering Research Council (NSERC) Discovery Grant funding, as well as the NSERC Strategic Partnership Grant (SPG) and the Innovation for Defense Excellence and Security Network (IDEaS) for the partial funding of this project.

References

1. Ahmed, F., Paul, P.P., Gavrilova, M.L.: DTW-based kernel and rank-level fusion for 3D gait recognition using Kinect. Vis. Comput. **31**(6), 915–924 (2015)
2. Meyer, B.M., et al.: Wearables and deep learning classify fall risk from gait in multiple sclerosis. J. Biomed. Health Inform. **25**(5), 1824–1831 (2020)
3. Gavrilova, M.L., et al.: Multi-modal motion-capture-based biometric systems for emergency response and patient rehabilitation. In: Research Anthology on Rehabilitation Practices and Therapy, pp. 653–678. IGI Global, USA (2021)
4. Zhuang, J.R., Wu, G.Y., Lee, H.H., Tanaka, E.: Applying the Interaction of Walking-Emotion to an Assistive Device for Rehabilitation and Exercise. In: IROS, pp. 6489–6494. IEEE, China (2019)
5. Narayanan, V., Manoghar, B.M., Dorbala, V.S., Manocha, D., Bera, A.: ProxEmo: gait-based emotion learning and multi-view proxemic fusion for socially-aware robot navigation. In: IROS, pp. 8200–8207. IEEE, USA (2020)
6. Menolotto, M., Komaris, D.S., Tedesco, S., O'Flynn, B., Walsh, M.: Motion capture technology in industrial applications: a systematic review. Sensors **20**(19), 5687 (2020)
7. Bari, H., Gavrilova, M.: Artificial neural network based gait recognition using kinect sensor. IEEE Access **7**(1), 162708–162722 (2019)

8. Artacho, B., Savakis, A.: OmniPose: a multi-scale framework for multi-person pose estimation. arXiv preprint (2021)
9. Xu, S., et al.: emotion recognition from gait analyses: current research and future directions. arXiv preprint (2020)
10. Karg, M., Kühnlenz, K., Buss, M.: Recognition of affect based on gait patterns. IEEE Trans. Syst. Man Cybern. Part B **40**(4), 1050–1061 (2010)
11. Talebi, H., Hoang, W., Gavrilova, M.L.: Multi-scale foreign exchange rates ensemble for classification of trends in forex market. Proc. Comput. Sci. **29**, 2065–2075 (2014)
12. Bhattacharya, U., Mittal, T., Chandra, R., Randhavane, T., Bera, A., Manocha, D.: STEP: spatial temporal graph convolutional networks for emotion perception from gaits. In: AAAI, pp. 1342–1350. AAAI, USA (2020)
13. Habibie, I., Holden, D., Schwarz, J., Yearsley, J., Komura, T.: A recurrent variational autoencoder for human motion synthesis. In: 28th British Machine Vision Conference, pp. 1–11. BMVC, UK (2017)
14. Janssen, D., Schöllhorn, W.I., Lubienetzki, J., Fölling, K., Kokenge, H., Davids, K.: Recognition of emotions in gait patterns by means of artificial neural nets. J. Nonverbal Behav. **32**(2), 79–92 (2008)
15. Venture, G., Kadone, H., Zhang, T., Grèzes, J., Berthoz, A., Hicheur, H.: Recognizing emotions conveyed by human gait. Int. J. Soc. Robot. **6**(4), 621–632 (2014)
16. Li, S., Cui, L., Zhu, C., Li, B., Zhao, N., Zhu, T.: Emotion recognition using Kinect motion capture data of human gaits. PeerJ **4**, e2364 (2016)
17. Zhang, Z., Song, Y., Cui, L., Liu, X., Zhu, T.: Emotion recognition based on customized smart bracelet with built-in accelerometer. PeerJ **4**, e2258 (2016)
18. Ahmed, F., Sieu, B., Gavrilova, M.L.: Score and rank-level fusion for emotion recognition using genetic algorithm. In: ICCI*CC, pp. 46–53. IEEE, USA (2018)
19. Yan, S., Xiong, Y., Lin, D.: Spatial temporal graph convolutional networks for skeleton-based action recognition. In: AAAI Conference on Artificial Intelligence, USA, pp. 1–9 (2018)
20. Randhavane, T., Bhattacharya, U., Kapsaskis, K., Gray, K., Bera, A., Manocha, D.: Identifying emotions from walking using affective and deep features. arXiv preprint (2019)
21. Bhattacharya, U., et al.: Take an emotion walk: perceiving emotions from gaits using hierarchical attention pooling and affective mapping. In: Vedaldi, A., Bischof, H., Brox, T., Frahm, J.-M. (eds.) ECCV 2020. LNCS, vol. 12355, pp. 145–163. Springer, Cham (2020). https://doi.org/10.1007/978-3-030-58607-2_9
22. Laban, R.V.: The Mastery of Movement. 3rd edn. (1971)
23. Levy, J.A., Duke, M.P.: The use of Laban movement analysis in the study of personality, emotional state and movement style: an exploratory investigation of the veridicality of "body language". Individ. Differ. Res. **1**(1), 39–63 (2003)
24. Albert, M.: Nonverbal Communication. Routledge, UK (2017)
25. Bhatia, Y., Bari, A.S.M.H., Hsu, G.S.J., Gavrilova, M.: Motion capture sensor-based emotion recognition using a bi-modular sequential neural network. Sensors **22**(1), 403–423 (2022)

Attacking Frequency Information with Enhanced Adversarial Networks to Generate Adversarial Samples

Jue Ding[✉], Jun Yin, Jingyu Dun, Wanwan Zhang, and Yayun Wang

ZheJiang Dahua Technology Co., Ltd., Hangzhou 310053, China
ding_jue@dahuatech.com

Abstract. In recent years, convolutional neural networks (CNNs) are widely used in various computer vision tasks with advanced performance. However, adversarial samples which add small-magnitude perturbation to images or videos are seriously threatening the application of CNNs. Some existing attack methods pay attention to the time domain information of the inputs, while the information in frequency domain is usually ignored. Others attack frequency domain by massive queries or significantly perceivable perturbation. In this paper, we propose a new method to attack the frequency information. The frequency information is combined with the Generative Adversarial Network (GAN) to design a novel algorithm called Frequency Attack Framework (FAF), which can attack the high-frequency information and the low-frequency information. Double discriminators are constructed on the GAN architecture to make attack more efficient in different frequency bands. The proposed algorithm generates optimal perturbation, resulting in adversarial samples with high attack transferability and quality. Several well-trained CNNs are fooled by FAF, and all of them have high error rates. Even when CNNs add defenses, our algorithm has a good performance.

Keywords: Adversarial attack · Generative adversarial network · Frequency information · Transferability

1 Introduction

With the wide application of convolutional neural networks (CNNs) in various fields [1], the vulnerability of them has become a problem that researchers are concerned about [2]. Adversarial samples [3], which are difficult to distinguish from clean ones by naked eyes, can mislead CNNs to make incorrect predictions with high probability. At present, various adversarial attack methods have been proposed, which can be divided into white-box attacks [4] and black-box attacks [5]. In the white-box attacks, parameters of the target model are known, and attackers can easily cheat CNNs. Instead, black-box attackers do not know the parameters of the target model, and in some cases, they do not even know the output of the model. Therefor the implementation of black-box attacks becomes more difficult [6]. There are three common branches in black-box attacks, including gradient-based attack methods [7], optimization-based attack methods [8],

G. Bebis et al. (Eds.): ISVC 2022, LNCS 13598, pp. 61–73, 2022.
https://doi.org/10.1007/978-3-031-20713-6_5

and GAN-based attack methods [9]. Although various black-box attack methods have been proposed, there are still many problems which have not been solved. Gradient-based attack methods like FGSM [7], BIM [10] and PGD [11] constantly modify local pixels of the input through gradient information until the end of the attack. Their transferability is good, but they usually need more iterative attack times, and the perturbation is easy to perceive by human vision. Optimization-based attack methods like C&W [12] can fool the source model with minimum perturbation, but suffer from weak transferability. GAN-based attack methods like advGAN [13] utilize a generator G to output the adversarial perturbation, which is added to clean images to generate adversarial samples. The discriminator D tries to distinguish between clean samples and adversarial samples. AdvGAN has a good performance on MNIST [14] and CIFAR-10 [15] datasets, but its transferability decreases on complex high-resolution datasets such as ImageNet [16].

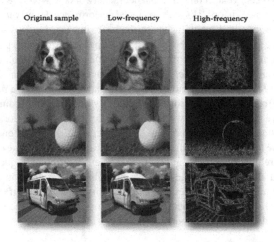

Fig. 1. Low-frequency information and high-frequency information of images

In our work, we propose a novel frequency attack framework (FAF) focusing on attacking frequency [17] information in order to generate adversarial samples with high transferability and perceptual quality on complex high-resolution datasets. Other attack methods based on GAN can be easily integrated into our framework. Frequency information of images is important for the training of CNNs, even if the structure and parameters of models are different. The high-frequency information almost imperceptible to humans is exploited by CNNs to trade robustness for accuracy [18]. Meanwhile the low-frequency information is the basis for CNNs to obtain recognition ability during the training time. Based on this, we design a GAN structure, which contains double discriminators to attack the high-frequency information and low-frequency information respectively. Moreover, our loss function is the combination of three different losses which help to guide the training process. In the experiment, our algorithm can generate the minimum perturbation with high transferability, and various well-trained CNNs produce incorrect predictions with high confidence. Compared with several efficient black-box attack methods [11] [13] [23], FAF achieves a better performance. Adversarial samples generated by FAF have high transferability even when attacking CNNs with defenses.

In summary, our contributions are listed as follows:

1. We propose a frequency attack framework, which focuses on attacking the frequency information. Our method can fool CNNs with optimal perturbation. To the best of our knowledge, we are the first to explore the method using frequency information in the GAN-based attacks.
2. We use double discriminators in GAN structure to attack the high-frequency information and the low-frequency information respectively, and design special loss functions to optimize the training process. Our algorithm framework is robust and efficient.
3. Our frequency attack framework can integrate existing GAN-based attacks easily, and generate adversarial samples with high transferability.

2 Related Work

2.1 Adversarial Samples

Adversarial attacks are aimed to make CNNs confused by disturbing the input. Generally speaking, the adversarial sample is composed of the source image and a special perturbation. This small change is difficult to detect, but can fool well-trained models to output false predictions with high confidence. The adversarial attack can be expressed by following equations:

$$
\begin{aligned}
&\text{find } Z \\
&\text{s.t } F(X) \neq F(X + Z) \\
&\|Z\| \leq \varepsilon,
\end{aligned}
\tag{1}
$$

where a CNN F predicts differently on the original sample and the adversarial sample, and these samples are very similar. The restriction of Z is measured by $\| \cdot \|$, which could be the L_1, L_2, L_∞ norm or other metrics.

2.2 Black-Box Attacks

In reality, it is almost impossible for attackers to obtain the parameter information of the attacked model, so black-box attacks are more challenging than white-box attacks. Existing popular black-box attacks mainly depend on the transferability of perturbation. GoodFellow et al. [7] develop an effective method for generating adversarial perturbation, which is called as fast gradient sign method (FGSM). This algorithm uses the gradient information of the model and attacks only once with high efficiency. Kurakin et al. [10] propose an optimization method for FGSM, which uses the category with the lowest probability in model output as the target class, and turns the original sample into an adversarial sample. Finally, the target model is guided to output the target class.

Carlini et al. [12] propose an optimization-based attack method, which makes the perturbation invisible. Moosavi et al. [19] generate the minimum perturbation through iterative calculation, and gradually change pixels of images until a misclassification occurs. Xiao et al. [13] propose a GAN-based method called advGAN, which conducts adversarial training through three parts: generator, discriminator and surrogate model. The generator can output the perturbation, and discriminator tries to distinguish between the original sample and the adversarial sample.

2.3 Frequency Features and Attacks

When we try to make judgments based on our visual system, the low-frequency information in images dominates our perceived information. The information in high-frequency components is usually ignored due to the unperceivable characteristic of these components. Instead, CNNs can both perceive high-frequency information and low-frequency information in images. Recent studies [18] have found that high and low frequency both play important roles in training and application of CNNs. At the beginning of training, CNNs use low-frequency information to optimize the weights to minimize training loss [20]. With the increase of training iterations, high-frequency information is captured to further optimize the capacity of CNNs. Well-trained CNNs often use the high-frequency information as a supplement on the basis of fully learning the low-frequency information.

Prior to our work, several frequency-domain attacks have been adopted to generate the adversarial perturbation. Li et al. [21] propose the F-mixup algorithm to mixup two inputs in frequency-domain to achieve attacks. The attacker optimizes the adversarial perturbation by making queries to probe top-1 label. Sharma et al. [22] prove that it is particularly effective for low frequency attack models with defenses or not. Guo et al. [23] show that using exclusively low frequency perturbation can make CNNs output wrong results. Deng et al. [24] develop a frequency-tuned universal attack method to improve the universal attack performance. This approach is adaptively bounded in the frequency-domain and generates robust adversarial perturbation.

3   Our Frequency Attack Approach

3.1 Separate High and Low Frequency Information

In order to attack the high frequency and low frequency separately, we need to separate them from images. Fourier transform, wavelet transform and other methods can be used to achieve this mission. From the perspective of efficiency, our algorithm utilizes Fourier transform function and inverse Fourier transform function to separate the frequency information. Specifically, we use Fourier transform function FFT($\cdot$) to transform the image from time-domain to frequency-domain. A circle C($\cdot$) centered in the frequency-domain image is used to segment the information. The information in the circle is transformed into low-frequency information by inverse Fourier transform IFFT($\cdot$), and the rest is used as high-frequency information. Figure 1 shows the result. The whole information separation process can be expressed by following equations:

$$V = \text{FFT}(X)$$
$$V_L = \begin{cases} V(i,j), & \text{if}\,(i,j) \in C(r) \\ 0, & \text{otherwise} \end{cases}$$
$$V_H = \begin{cases} V(i,j), & \text{if}\,(i,j) \notin C(r) \\ 0, & \text{otherwise} \end{cases} \qquad (2)$$
$$X_L = \text{IFFT}(V_L)$$
$$X_H = \text{IFFT}(V_H),$$

where r is the radius of the circle, which is set as 78 in this paper.

3.2 Dual Discriminators Support Attack

[25] has proved that dual discriminators can effectively avoid the mode collapse problem. Inspired by this, we design dual discriminators together with a generator to make a minimax game. When a generator outputs adversarial perturbation, a discriminator rewards high scores for high frequency information whilst another discriminator, conversely, favoring low frequency information. And the generator must optimize adversarial samples to fool these discriminators. Further, the complementary characteristics of two discriminators can improve the performance of adversarial perturbation.

3.3 Frequency Attack Framework

The overall structure of FAF is illustrated in Fig. 2. In order to improve the stability of the training process and the effectiveness of the attack, the high and low frequency information of images are shared by double discriminators. FAF mainly consists of four components: a generator G, a high-frequency discriminator D_1, a low-frequency discriminator D_2, and a surrogate model F. In the training phase, we input the source sample X into the generator G, and the generator outputs the complete frequency perturbation Z. We use Fourier transform function to separate the high-frequency components X_H and low-frequency components X_L of the sample. Similarly, the perturbation Z is also separated into high-frequency perturbation Z_H and low-frequency perturbation Z_L. Then $X_L + Z_L$ is sent into low-frequency discriminator D_2, which is used to distinguish the difference between $X_L + Z_L$ and X_L. Next, we input Z_H into the high-frequency discriminator D_1, which is used to distinguish the difference between Z_H and X_H. In order to make the effect of the algorithm better, there is a pre-trained model to serve as the surrogate model F. We take $X + Z$ and Z_H as the input of the surrogate model. By constantly attacking the surrogate model during the training process, the transferability of adversarial samples can be increased. In the test phase, the trained generator G generates an adversarial perturbation Z by inputting a clean sample. The final adversarial sample is $X_{adv} = X_L + Z_L + 2 * Z_H$. The high-frequency information in the source sample is replaced by the perturbation Z_H, since the high-frequency perturbation is similar to the high-frequency feature, but can disturb the output of CNNs.

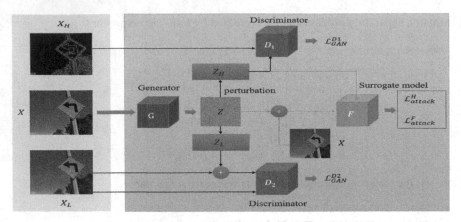

Fig. 2. Overview of FAF.

3.4 Network Architecture

The proposed model is composed of a generator and double discriminators, and they are constructed a similar architecture as image super-resolution [26]. The generator is modified by using three $3*3$ convolutions to replace the final $9*9$ convolution, so that it has more powerful abilities of feature extraction and expression to generate high quality adversarial perturbation. For adversarial attacks, every down-sampling process will drop out some detail information in source samples, which is important for generating the perturbation. Therefor the generator architecture does not contain pooling or deconvolution layers. The high-frequency discriminator and the low-frequency discriminator are designed as the same architecture. Both generator and discriminator networks can be regarded as fully convolutional networks, which are robust to different size of inputs.

3.5 Loss Function

Our FAF mainly includes three loss functions: GAN loss, attack loss and norm loss.

Firstly, we introduce the GAN loss function, which consists of generator loss and discriminator loss. They are aimed to make FAF attack low-frequency information and high-frequency information effectively. Inspired by [27], the least squares objective functions can stabilize the training process to achieve better results. Specifically, generator loss is defined as follows:

$$\mathcal{L}_{GAN}^{G} = \sum_x \left[(D_1(G(x_H)) - a)^2 \right] + \sum_x \left[(D_2(G(x_L) + x_L) - a)^2 \right], \quad (3)$$

where the parameter a is a random number ranged from 0.7 to 1.2.

The discriminators in FAF, D_1 and D_2, play a role of discriminating between the clean sample and the adversarial sample. The discriminator losses are defined as follows:

$$\mathcal{L}_{GAN}^{D1} = \sum_x \left[(D_1(x_H) - b)^2 \right] + \sum_x \left[(D_1(G(x_H)) - c)^2 \right], \quad (4)$$

$$\mathcal{L}_{GAN}^{D2} = \sum_x \left[(D_2(x_L) - b)^2 \right] + \sum_x \left[(D_2(G(x_L) + x_L) - c)^2 \right], \quad (5)$$

where the parameter b is a random number ranged from 0.7 to 1.2, and the parameter c is a random number ranged from 0 to 0.3. They are soft labels.

Then we introduce the attack loss. Attack loss is mainly composed of $\mathcal{L}_{attack}^{F}$ and $\mathcal{L}_{attack}^{H}$, which aims to fool the surrogate model F and increases the transferability of adversarial samples.

The $\mathcal{L}_{attack}^{F}$ is defined as follows:

$$\mathcal{L}_{attack}^{F} = max(max_{i \neq t} F(x)_i - F(x)_t, k), \tag{6}$$

where the threshold k is set to 0, $F(x)_t$ is the probability of the ground truth class, and $max_{i \neq t} F(x)_i$ is the probability of a class with highest probability except the ground truth one.

Since the high-frequency information of inputs contains some irrelevant noise and almost imperceptible, the cross-entropy loss is used to increase the transferability of high-frequency perturbation:

$$\mathcal{L}_{attack}^{H} = \mathcal{L}_{ce}(F(x_H), t), \tag{7}$$

where t stands for the second largest probability of the input.

And the norm loss $\mathcal{L}_{norm}$ is used to limit the magnitude of the perturbation. We use a soft hinge loss as same as [13].

Finally, the total loss is expressed as follows:

$$\mathcal{L}_{total} = \mathcal{L}_{GAN} + \alpha \mathcal{L}_{attack}^{F} + \lambda \mathcal{L}_{attack}^{H} + \mathcal{L}_{norm}, \tag{8}$$

where the weight parameters of $\alpha = 10$ and $\lambda = 10$ are used to control the tradeoffs among different losses.

4 Experiments

In this section, we evaluate the performance of Frequency Attack Framework, both quantitatively and qualitatively. We further test the FAF in different cases and find that FAF has a better performance than other popular methods. In the experiments, we select 2348 images from ImageNet [16] validation sets, which can be classified correctly by several different well-trained CNNs, including ResNet152 [28], VGG19 [29], DenseNet121 [30], ResNext101 [31], ResNet50 [28] and MNASNet [32]. For preprocessing, the input is resized to $3 * 256 * 256$ and normalized to the range between 0 and 1. During the training process, the Adam optimizer with learning rate 0.001 is used for optimizing the generator and discriminators. The experiments are implemented in PyTorch with 4 NVIDIA GeForce RTX 2080Ti GPUs.

Fig. 3. Adversarial samples generated by FAF. The samples on the left are original samples from ImageNet. The samples on the right are adversarial samples generated by FAF.

4.1 Evaluation Metric

For the attack performance, it is important to keep high attack rates while maintaining good perceptual quality. The Fréchet perception distance (FID) is used as the metric of image quality, and its calculation formula is the same as that in [33]. Inspired by the adversarial attack competition[1], we normalize it to the range between 0 and 1 to facilitate the comparison of experimental results. Typically, higher S_{F_norm} score enjoys better image quality. The S_{F_norm} is defined as follows:

$$S_{F\_norm} = \frac{\sum \sqrt{1 - \frac{\min(FID(X, X_{adv}), \beta)}{\beta}}}{N}, \tag{9}$$

where X is the original sample, X_{adv} is the adversarial sample and N standards the number of images we use. β stands for a threshold set to 200. It means that the similarity between original samples and adversarial samples is very low when $FID(X, X_{adv})$ exceeds the threshold.

4.2 Ablation Study

To prove the high transferability of FAF, we analyze the following aspects of our FAF, and conduct a series of experiments: 1) the adversarial perturbation of different frequency bands including high frequency (H-FAF), low frequency (L-FAF) and full frequency (F-FAF), 2) the $\mathcal{L}_{attack}^{H}$.

Firstly, we compare the adversarial perturbation generated from low, high and full frequency attack. Experiments are repeated five times, the average S_{FID_norm} score and the average error rate are reported in Table 1. In this table, RN152, RNext101, DN121, RN50 and MNAS stand for ResNet152, ResNext101, DenseNet121, ResNet50 and MNASNet respectively.

---

[1] https://tianchi.aliyun.com/competition/entrance/531853/information.

Table 1. Ablation of different frequency bands attacks (ResNet50 as the target model)

Method	S_{F_norn}	RN152	VGG19	RNext101	DN121	RN50	MNAS
L-FAF	0.75	79.75%	91.21%	79.39%	63.92%	96.99%	92.61%
H-FAF	0.75	65.07%	92.74%	73.19%	56.81%	92.92%	**94.81%**
F-FAF	**0.75**	**83.94%**	**93.47%**	**79.97%**	**72.34%**	**98.58%**	94.10%

According to Table 1, neither attacking the high-frequency information nor low-frequency information is as good as attacking the full frequency, when the quality of adversarial samples is similar.

Table 2 shows the impact of $\mathcal{L}_{attack}^{H}$ on the adversarial sample. When we utilize $\mathcal{L}_{attack}^{H}$, it is good at enhancing the transferability of adversarial samples.

Table 2. Ablation of different attack losses (ResNet50 as the target model)

Method	S_{F_norn}	RN152	VGG19	RNext101	DN121	RN50	MNAS
$\mathcal{L}_{attack}^{H}$	**0.75**	**83.94%**	**93.47%**	**79.97%**	**72.34%**	**98.58%**	**94.10%**
w/o-$\mathcal{L}_{attack}^{H}$	0.75	78.69%	92.79%	78.78%	65.43%	98.58%	93.99%

Without this loss, attack algorithm may lack attention to the important information of high frequency. It is a common property in different CNNs, which makes adversarial perturbation transferable.

4.3 Transferability of FAF

We compare FAF with well-known attacks advGAN [13], LF-BA [23] and PGD [11]. In order to ensure the fairness of experiments, all algorithms are evaluated the attack capability on the basis of similar S_{F_norm}. PGD is implemented by foolbox [34], and parameters are not changed. LF-BA and advGAN are used parameters as same as [23] and [13]. We use FAF, advGAN, LF-BA and PGD to attack five neural networks, and then feed the generated adversarial samples to six other models. Experiments are repeated five times. The average S_{F_norm} score and the average error rate of models are reported in Table 3. FAF, advGAN and PGD all have a high white-box attack success rate, in which PGD has the highest performance since transfer-based methods generate adversarial samples by making dozens of attacks on each clean sample. On the contrary, GAN-based methods focus on finding the optimal perturbation of the whole datasets and attack only once. Meanwhile the transfer performance varies a lot, in situations of different surrogate models and victim models, FAF achieves the best black-box attack performance. The transferability of FAF is about 6% to 20% higher than other attack methods. In Fig. 3, we show several adversarial samples generated by FAF.

4.4 Attack Under Defenses

In this experiment, we apply PGD, advGAN, LF-BA and FAF to attack ResNet50. Different from the last experiment, victim models are added different defense methods to enhance the robustness. JPEG Compression [35], Median Smoothing [36], and Pixel Squeezing [37] are used, which have been verified effective on ImageNet. These defense methods are used with provided parameters. Table 4 shows the comprehensive black-box attack performance of different attack methods against ResNet50 under defenses. Generally speaking, the defenses can decrease the average error rate but FAF still maintains the highest transferability. In this work, Pixel Squeezing does not seem to work well, since the performance of PGD is enhanced. But FAF still has a better performance than PGD in this case.

Table 3. Average error rate (Top-1) of different attack methods.

Surrogate	Method	S_{F_norm}	RN152	VGG19	RNext101	DN121	RN50	MNAS
RN152	advGAN	0.67	88.60%	88.97%	70.24%	55.39%	86.10%	93.54%
	PGD	0.71	**99.95%**	82.90%	67.83%	63.48%	86.50%	84.35%
	LF-BA	0.71	68.06%	87.33%	67.42%	58.73%	86.93%	90.20%
	FAF	**0.71**	98.68%	**89.20%**	**85.10%**	**73.26%**	**88.68%**	**93.79%**
VGG19	advGAN	0.63	35.67%	99.98%	42.51%	27.42%	70.46%	85.00%
	PGD	0.66	52.64%	**100%**	47.09%	60.06%	79.44%	91.82%
	LF-BA	0.68	65.72%	92.93%	70.53%	61.75%	83.37%	90.20%
	FAF	**0.68**	**66.60%**	99.44%	**72.96%**	**66.47%**	**83.85%**	**95.73%**
DN121	advGAN	0.67	55.35%	91.63%	61.70%	80.02%	82.91%	93.53%
	PGD	0.70	63.30%	85.83%	57.35%	**99.99%**	83.53%	86.74%
	LF-BA	0.70	66.70%	92.59%	69.89%	63.50%	88.71%	90.97%
	FAF	**0.70**	**85.29%**	**94.11%**	**81.83%**	98.14%	**92.67%**	**95.43%**
RNext101	advGAN	0.72	67.79%	86.66%	93.61%	56.71%	79.80%	94.61%
	PGD	0.75	65.22%	80.26%	**99.73%**	54.76%	75.98%	80.76%
	LF-BA	0.73	62.52%	90.12%	65.67%	53.53%	84.07%	88.25%
	FAF	**0.75**	**83.42%**	**93.57%**	98.53%	**61.95%**	**93.17%**	**96.93%**
RN50	advGAN	0.72	63.90%	91.69%	60.87%	50.41%	97.86%	93.73%
	PGD	0.75	60.56%	81.84%	49.00%	53.39%	**99.98%**	80.82%
	LF-BA	0.75	59.75%	89.35%	60.56%	51.58%	84.24%	86.29%
	FAF	**0.75**	**83.94%**	**93.47%**	**79.97%**	**72.34%**	98.58%	**94.10%**

Table 4. Average error rate (Top-1) under defenses (ResNet50 as the surrogate model).

Victim	Method	None	Smooth [36]	Pixel [37]	JPEG [35]
RN152	advGAN	63.90%	18.63%	58.73%	49.05%
	PGD	60.56%	43.66%	61.12%	46.06%
	LF-BA	59.75%	19.59%	28.24%	22.32%
	FAF	**83.94%**	**54.58%**	**68.98%**	**70.66%**
VGG19	advGAN	91.69%	63.14%	94.65%	74.32%
	PGD	81.84%	80.89%	94.33%	77.37%
	LF-BA	89.35%	59.97%	80.15%	53.41%
	FAF	**93.47%**	**84.67%**	**95.94%**	**80.11%**
DN121	advGAN	50.41%	23.10%	61.19%	36.35%
	PGD	53.39%	48.83%	61.64%	48.37%
	LF-BA	51.58%	18.99%	20.44%	16.06%
	FAF	**72.34%**	**49.01%**	**66.64%**	**51.70%**
RNext101	advGAN	60.87%	17.68%	59.35%	48.67%
	PGD	49.00%	38.73%	60.42%	44.05%
	LF-BA	60.56%	20.66%	26.92%	25.98%
	FAF	**79.97%**	**51.82%**	**67.02%**	**68.93%**
MNAS	advGAN	93.73%	61.09%	91.46%	83.80%
	PGD	80.82%	71.69%	92.13%	80.14%
	LF-BA	86.29%	47.61%	68.82%	46.08%
	FAF	**94.10%**	**82.62%**	**94.02%**	**89.31%**

5 Conclusion

In our work, we propose a Frequency Attack Framework (FAF), which can effectively generate adversarial samples on complex high-resolution images and achieve a high transferability on the black-box attack. Our method is the first to attack on frequency information by GAN structure. Our algorithm is robust and efficient when attacking frequency information. FAF enjoys a significant attack to frequency-domain when double discriminators are constructed. Compared with some popular attack methods, the perturbation generated by FAF can be less perceptible while maintaining a high transferability. When increasing the robustness of CNNs by defense methods, FAF still outperformances others. Since FAF alters the domain of attacked information only, existing GAN-based attack methods can be integrated to it easily.

References

1. Zou, Z., et al.: Object Detection in 20 Years: A Survey (2019). arXiv:1905.05055

2. Qiu, S., et al.: Review of artificial intelligence adversarial attack and defense technologies. Appl. Sci. **9**(5), 2076–3417 (2019)
3. Akhtar, N., et al.: Threat of adversarial attacks on deep learning in computer vision: a survey. IEEE Access **6**, 14410–14430 (2018)
4. Tramer, F., et al.: On Adaptive Attacks to Adversarial Example Defenses (2020). arXiv:2002.08347
5. Papernot, N., et al.: Transferability in Machine Learning: from Phenomena to Black-Box Attacks using Adversarial Samples (2016). arXiv:1605.07277
6. Brendel, W., et al.: Decision-Based Adversarial Attacks: Reliable Attacks Against Black-Box Machine Learning Models (2018). arXiv:1712.04248
7. Goodfellow, I.J., et al.: Explaining and Harnessing Adversarial Examples (2015). arXiv:1412.6572
8. Szegedy, C., et al.: Intriguing properties of neural networks. In: ICLR (2014)
9. Hu, W., et al.: Generating adversarial malware examples for black-box attacks based on GAN (2017). arXiv:1702.05983
10. Kurakin, A., et al.: Adversarial examples in the physical world. In: ICLR (2017)
11. Madry, A., et al.: Towards deep learning models resistant to adversarial attacks. In: ICLR (2018)
12. Carlini, N., et al.: Towards evaluating the robustness of neural networks. In: IEEE Symposium on Security and Privacy (2017)
13. Xiao, C., et al.: Generating adversarial examples with adversarial networks. In: IJCAI (2018)
14. Yann, L., et al.: The MNIST database of handwritten digits (1998)
15. Krizhevsky, A., et al.: Learning multiple layers of features from tiny images. Handbook of Systemic Autoimmune Diseases **1**(4), (2009)
16. Jia, D., et al.: Imagenet: a large-scale hierarchical image database. In: CVPR (2009)
17. Awasthi, B., et al.: Faster, stronger, lateralized: low spatial frequency information supports face processing. Neuropsychologia **49**(13), 3583–3590 (2011)
18. Wang, H., et al.: High-frequency component helps explain the generalization of convolutional neural networks. In: CVPR (2020)
19. Moosavi, D., et al.: deepfool: a simple and accurate method to fool deep neural networks. In: CVPR (2016)
20. Geirhos, R., et al.: Imagenet-trained CNNs are biased towards texture; increasing shape bias improves accuracy and robustness. In: ICLR (2019)
21. Li, X.C., et al.: F-mixup: attack CNNs from fourier perspective. In: ICPR (2020)
22. Sharma, Y., et al.: On the effectiveness of low frequency perturbations. In: ICJAI (2019)
23. Guo, C., et al.: Low frequency adversarial perturbation. In: UAI (2019)
24. Deng, Y., et al.: Frequency-tuned universal adversarial attacks. In: ECCVW (2020)
25. Nguyen, T., et al.: Dual discriminator generative adversarial nets. In: NIPS (2017)
26. Ledig, C., et al.: Photo-realistic single image super-resolution using a generative adversarial network. In: IEEE Computer Society (2016)
27. Mao, X., et al.: Least squares generative adversarial networks. In: ICCV (2017)
28. He, K., et al.: Deep residual learning for image recognition. In: CVPR (2016)
29. Simonyan, K., et al.: Very deep convolutional networks for large-scale image recognition. In: ICLR (2015)
30. Huang, G., et al.: Densely connected convolutional networks. In: CVPR (2017)
31. Xie, S., et al.: Aggregated residual transformations for deep neural networks. In: CVPR (2017)
32. Tan, M., et al.: MnasNet: platform-aware neural architecture search for mobile. In: CVPR (2019)
33. Heusel, M., et al.: GANs trained by a two time-scale update rule converge to a local nash equilibrium. In: NIPS (2017)

34. Rauber, J., et al.: Foolbox v0.8.0: A Python toolbox to benchmark the robustness of machine learning models (2017). arXiv:1707.04131
35. Dziugaite, G., et al.: A study of the effect of jpg compression on adversarial images (2016). arXiv:1608.00853
36. Cohen, J., et al.: Certified adversarial robustness via randomized smoothing. In: ICML (2019)
37. Xu, W., et al.: Feature squeezing: detecting adversarial examples in deep neural networks (2017). arXiv:1704.01155

Visualization

Explainable Interactive Projections for Image Data

Huimin Han, Rebecca Faust(✉), Brian Felipe Keith Norambuena, Ritvik Prabhu,
Timothy Smith, Song Li, and Chris North

Virginia Tech, Blacksburg, VA 24061, USA
{huimin,rfaust,briankeithn,ritvikp,tim23,songli,north}@vt.edu

Abstract. Making sense of large collections of images is difficult. Dimension
reductions (DR) assist by organizing images in a 2D space based on similarities, but provide little support for explaining why images were placed together
or apart in the 2D space. Additionally, they do not provide support for modifying and updating the 2D space to explore new relationships and organizations
of images. To address these problems, we present an interactive DR method for
images that uses visual features extracted by a deep neural network to project
the images into 2D space and provides visual explanations of image features that
contributed to the 2D location. In addition, it allows people to directly manipulate the 2D projection space to define alternative relationships and explore subsequent projections of the images. With an iterative cycle of semantic interaction
and explainable-AI feedback, people can explore complex visual relationships in
image data. Our approach to human-AI interaction integrates visual knowledge
from both human mental models and pre-trained deep neural models to explore
image data. We demonstrate our method through examples with collaborators in
agricultural science.

Keywords: Interactive dimension reduction · Semantic interaction ·
Explainable AI · Image data

1 Introduction

People commonly use dimension reduction (DR) methods to explore data for sensemaking tasks [8]. DR methods excel at mapping high-dimensional data to a low-dimensional
space (typically 2D) while preserving meaningful structure and relationships. Several
methods add interaction to enable exploration, modification and understanding of the
2D space. For example, some systems incorporate semantic interactions which couple
cognitive and computational processes by inferring meaning behind interactions and
updating the model accordingly [12].

However, most of interactive DR methods have limited support for image data, often
representing images as arrays of pixels and treating them the same as tabular data. This
not only limits the DR's ability to determine similarities between images, but also often
inhibits interaction methods for understanding the 2D space. For example, Self et al.'s
Andromeda uses Weighted Multidimensional Scaling (WMDS) to create an interactive
DR that supports semantic interaction for exploring and understanding 2D projection
spaces via model steering [29]. After an interaction, the model learns new weights on

G. Bebis et al. (Eds.): ISVC 2022, LNCS 13598, pp. 77–90, 2022.
https://doi.org/10.1007/978-3-031-20713-6_6

the input dimensions that infer meaning from the interaction and explain the information learned by the projection. However, when a dataset does not have interpretable dimensions, these explanations become meaningless. What's more, because a single pixel has an arbitrary meaning across all images, weighting the same pixel in each image does not have a uniform effect on all of the images. Thus it does not make sense to directly project images from pixel arrays.

We know from past research that deep neural networks excel at extracting meaningful features from images and embedding them into a new representation [7]. Classifiers commonly use these embeddings, achieving high accuracy which indicates that the embeddings must be well suited for finding similarities between images. The question then remains, how can we use these feature embeddings to create more meaningful projections of image data and capture human feedback?

In this paper, we present an interactive DR method, built from Self et al.'s Andromeda, that supports semantic interaction for exploring projections of image data. Our method leverages the feature embeddings extracted from a convolutional neural network to project image data to a low-dimensional space using WMDS, while supporting semantic interaction to enable people to explore and update the projection space. Our method enables people to directly manipulate the 2D locations of images to define new pairwise relationships in the 2D space and then learns new projection weights that best respect those relationships. Using these weights to re-project the images, people can observe impact of those relationships on the projection space. Each dimension now represents some feature of the images, rather than an arbitrary pixel, but are still not directly interpretable. Increasing the weight on a feature increases its importance in the projection but still does not provide any insight into the information learned. Thus, while updating the weights now has inherent meaning, people have no real understanding of this meaning. That brings us to our second question: how can we translate the learned weights back to the image space?

In addition to providing an interactive DR, our approach provides explanations of features of importance in the 2D space through the use of a weighted backpropagation algorithm. We adapt a traditional visual backpropagation method for generating saliency maps [4] to apply the feature weights from the projection. Doing so creates saliency maps that emphasize the image features most influential to the projection's placement of the image. Thus, we are able to push the information learned from the human interaction back through the network to the image space, where people can interpret it.

Our method helps people explore multiple projections of their image data through semantic interactions and explain the effects of these interactions on the placement of images through saliency maps. Figure 1 presents an example using our method.

The contributions of this paper include:

- An interactive-AI method for dimension reduction that semi-automatically projects images based on visual knowledge from both pre-trained neural models and human feedback.
- An explainable-AI method for saliency mapping through weighted backpropagation that explains important image features.
- A usage scenario, built from our collaboration with agriculture sciences, illustrating a real world example of image exploration tasks supported by our methods.

Projection Plots

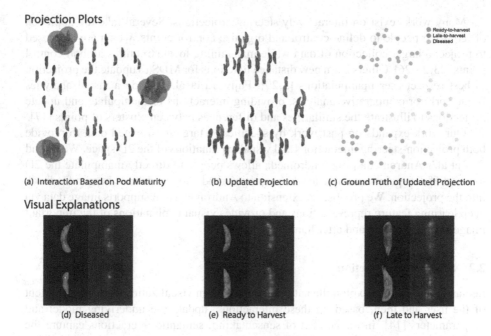

(a) Interaction Based on Pod Maturity   (b) Updated Projection   (c) Ground Truth of Updated Projection

Visual Explanations

(d) Diseased   (e) Ready to Harvest   (f) Late to Harvest

Fig. 1. Interactions to explore maturity level in edamame pod images. (a), shows user manipulations based on maturity level. (b) shows the updated projection while (c) shows the ground truth maturity level. (d)–(f) shows the explanations of important image features for each maturity level.

2 Related Work

Our work draws elements from interactive dimensionality reduction techniques, semantic interaction methods, and explainability in deep learning. In this section, we start by discussing related works from the interactive dimensionality reduction literature. Next, we focus on semantic interaction and its applications in sensemaking. Finally, we discuss explainability techniques for deep learning methods in the context of image data.

2.1 Interactive Dimensionality Reduction

Dimensionality reduction techniques are commonly employed to analyze and visualize high-dimensional data by projecting it onto a 2D or 3D space [31]. Alone, DR algorithms typically produce a static projection space with no means for exploration or manipulation. Thus, many scholars sought to develop *interactive* DR techniques capable of capturing user feedback and subsequently modifying the projection.

Some interactive DR methods create a bi-directional workflow where people can alter data in the high dimensional space to see the effect on the 2D location and vice versa [6,22]. Other works explore the idea of backwards (or inverse) projections that allow people to select locations in the 2D space and generate corresponding high-dimensional representations [16,28]. PEx-Image specifically targets image data, providing interactions for exploratory tasks, such as zooming into specific projection regions, displacing points to resolve overlapping and displaying nearest neighbors of selected images [11].

Many works exist on interactively steering projections. Several take the approach of requiring people to define control and organize control points, which are then used to project a larger collection of data while maintaining local structures around control points [23,25,26]. Others learn new distance functions for MDS to update the projection to best respect user manipulations [5,29]. Fujiwara et al. provide a visual analytics framework for comparative analysis, providing interactions to manipulate and update projections to illustrate the similarities and differences between clusters of points [17].

Our work expands on past work by specifically targeting imaged data to provide both projection-steering interactions and visual explanations of the 2D space. We extend Self et al.'s Andromeda [29]. Andromeda allows people to directly manipulate the 2D location of data points and updates the projection model to incorporate human feedback into the projection. We propose an extension to Andromeda that supports image data via deep learning feature representations and provides visual explanations of the important image features, before and after human feedback.

2.2 Semantic Interaction

Semantic interactions exploit the natural interactions in visualizations to learn the intent of the user and then, based on these interactions, update the underlying model and its parameters [14]. In the context of sensemaking, semantic interactions capture the analytical reasoning of the users [13], and support analysts throughout the sensemaking process [10].

Most semantic interaction systems work using a dimensionality reduction model, similar to the interactive dimensionality reduction methods described in the previous section. Semantic interaction is a bidirectional pipeline [9] and requires capturing the changes in the visualization and turning them into changes to the model. In the dimensionality reduction case, this is usually done through the use of an inverse transformation (e.g., inverse WMDS) [33]. There are several models that can be used to solve the bi-directional transforms required to implement semantic interactions, such as Observation-Level Interaction [15], Bayesian Visual Analytics [21], and Visual to Parametric Interaction [24].

Previous work has also shown how to integrate deep learning models with semantic interaction techniques. Bian and North [1] developed a semantic interaction model for text analytics integrating traditional dimensionality reduction techniques with a BERT neural network as its core component. Bian et al. [2] continued the development of these semantic interaction models and designed an explainable AI framework based on counterfactuals that help users understand the generated projection.

2.3 Explainability in Deep Learning

Scholars have proposed several explainability methods for convolutional neural network (CNN) models, the backbone of most image-based deep learning applications. Bojarski et al. [4] proposed a visualization method that shows which pixels of an input image contribute the most towards the predictions of a CNN model. In particular, their technique allows debugging CNN-based systems by highlighting the regions of the input image that have the highest influence on the output of the model. Zeiler and Fergus [35] developed a novel visualization technique that provides insight into the intermediate feature layers of a CNN in a classification task. Zhou et al. [36] use a global average pooling layer to shed light on how this layer enables CNN models to localize objects in images. In particular, their approach generates a Class Activation Map (CAM) using global pooling. However, while these explanation techniques are powerful, they are designed for specific CNN-based models. To address this weakness, researchers have proposed visual explanation techniques for a large class of CNN-based models. For example, Selvaraju et al. [30] generated CAMs based on gradient information of target concepts (Grad-CAM). Grad-CAM provides fine-grained explanations of the CNN predictions, but suffers from performance issues with multiple occurrences and single-object images.

Despite the recent advances in explainable deep learning for image data, there is a dearth of studies exploiting explainable deep learning techniques for interactive DR in the context of image analysis. Thus, our work seeks to fill this gap and combine interactive DR for images with explainable deep learning techniques. In particular, we base our work on the method of Bojarski et al. [4], as visual backpropagation provides an efficient way to generate explanations of relevant image features for the users by pushing the weights obtained in the interactive DR loop through the backpropagation process.

3   Tasks

Before discussing the details of our method, we first must discuss the sensemaking tasks of someone using our tool. Pirolli and Card described the sensemaking process as having two primary loops: the foraging loop and the sensemaking loop [27]. The foraging loop focuses on searching and filtering information and extracting evidence. The sensemaking loop then uses this information to iteratively construct representational schemas as well as generate and test hypotheses about the data.

In the context of image data, simply looking at every image does not provide sufficient information to make sense of the data. The foraging loop requires filtering and extracting sets of images relevant to the task at hand. Then, those images must be organized into a schema that provides a structured representation for consuming the image data and testing hypotheses. The process of generating and refining the schema typically requires several iterations of foraging for information under the current schema, updating the schema based on the new information, and evaluating how the schema fits the task at hand to determine if it requires further refinement.

Our method supports this schematization step through iterative exploration of the images and refinement of the 2D representation to reflect prior knowledge of the analysis task. Through discussions with collaborators in the plant sciences, we identified the following tasks to support this iterative process: (1) Define custom similarities based on prior knowledge and (2) link human and machine defined similarities

These tasks create a synergy between the machine and the human where they work together as a team, teaching each other what they have independently learned from the data. In the end, we create an analysis pipeline where the human perceives the data, conveys their knowledge to the machine, and the machine then re-organizes the data based on this information, while providing explanations of its reasoning. The remainder of this section discusses these tasks in greater detail.

3.1   Define Custom Similarities Based on Prior Knowledge

When analyzing data, people typically have some prior knowledge about the data, such as what categories of or similarities between images they expect to exist within the data. For example, in a set of edamame pod images, the analyst may expect images of healthy pods and diseased pods. Static dimension reduction plots, may or may not adequately reflect this prior knowledge. In the previous example, the person analyzing may want to inspect healthy vs diseased pods, but the model may not naturally recognize these differences. Furthermore, static projections do not enable people to explore different projections defined under different guidelines. To enable hypothesis testing, people must be able to steer the projection to define similarities in the data in a way that reflects their prior knowledge. With our method, people directly manipulate the 2D location of images to define new relationships within the data that the model then learns and uses to re-project the images accordingly.

3.2   Link Human and Machine Defined Similarities

The previous task focuses on teaching the projection model to incorporate human knowledge. However, while it helps the model learn human knowledge, it does not help people understand the model's knowledge. People need ways to inspect the image features most important to the 2D projection. This helps them not only understand the 2D space, but also validate the models perception of their knowledge and potentially identify other image similarities/differences beyond the knowledge they taught the model. Our method provides saliency maps that illustrate the features of the image that the projection most heavily used to place the image. Viewing the explanations of multiple images provides insight into why the model placed them near or far from each other and provides a means for understanding the 2D space.

4   Workflow and Methodology

In this section, we describe the expected user workflow and interactions, as well as the underlying methodology. Figure 2 gives an overview of the workflow while Fig. 1 presents an example of using this workflow.

4.1   Initial State

Upon loading the data, our method extracts image features to project. It then uses Weighted Multidimensional Scaling (WMDS) to project the features into 2D which provides the initial view of the data and a starting point for the exploratory analysis. We chose WMDS because it uses pairwise similarities as the input for projection and thus changes in the 2D similarities conceptually map directly back to the input space.

Feature Extraction. Recently, deep learning models have become popular for feature extraction in images [18]. In particular, Convolutional Neural Networks (CNN) have shown great power in image-related tasks and as a result using CNNs has become the standard in feature extraction [32]. For our research, we use pre-trained ResNet18 [20] as a fixed feature extractor to generate features vectors from images.

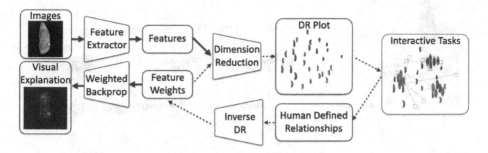

Fig. 2. An overview of our workflow. First, we extract image features using a deep learning feature extractor which we then pass to an interactive DR method (WMDS) that facilitates semantic interactions. After interactions, we pass the newly defined relationships to the inverse DR where it learns new projection parameters that best respect them and re-projects the images.

Given an image dataset $\mathscr{D}$, we forward propagate the images through the network with the fully connected layer removed. The final representations are denoted as $\mathscr{X} = ResNet_{\mathrm{pre-trained}}(\mathscr{D})$. The feature space $\mathscr{X}$ is a 512-dimensional space used to represent the images. Each image representation ($x_i \in \mathscr{X}$) is the output of applying average pooling to the final feature map of the network. We use $\mathscr{X}$ as the input to the interactive dimension reduction loop.

Weighted Multidimensional Scaling. Using the features extracted from the images ($\mathscr{X}$) as input, we perform MDS on a weighted data space to project the images to 2D, using the following function:

$$y = \operatorname*{arg\,min}_{y_1,\ldots,y_n} \sqrt{\sum_{i<j\leq N} (dist_L(y_i, y_j) - dist_H(w, x_i, x_j))^2} \qquad (1)$$

where N is the number of points in the dataset, $dist_L(y_i, y_j)$ is the low-dimensional distance between y_i and y_j and $dist_H(w, x_i, x_j)$ is the weighted high dimensional distance between the feature representations x_i and x_j, given the dimension weights w.

For the initial projection, we initialize w with equal weights for every dimension, relying solely on the raw image features to organize the images.

4.2   Interactions and Inverse Projection

After the initial projection, our method allows people to directly manipulate the projection plot, dragging points into new positions in the 2D space. Manipulated points define new pairwise relationships for the projection model to learn during the inverse projection. Once the analyst completes their interaction, the model uses these relationships to optimize the projection weights to create a layout that best respects the defined relationships.

Interactive Dimension Reduction. To facilitate interactive dimension reduction, we use inverse WMDS (WMDS^{-1}) to update the projection after semantic interactions, as originally described in Andromeda [29].

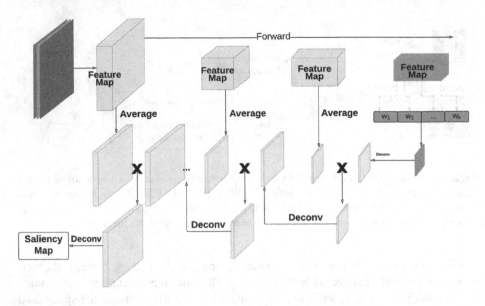

Fig. 3. Weighted visual backpropagation process

After a person re-positions a subset of the points, y^*, we perform WMDS^{-1} to calculate new weights optimal for maintaining the specified relationships, thus capturing human feedback. WMDS^{-1} uses the following equation to update the weights:

$$w = \underset{w_1,\dots w_d}{\arg\min} \sqrt{\frac{(\sum_{i<j\leq N}(dist_L(y_i^*,y_j^*) - dist_H(w,x_i,x_j))^2}{\sum_{i<j\leq N} dist_H(w,x_i,x_j)^2}} \tag{2}$$

This equation produces a vector of dimension weights that best respects the 2D pairwise similarities specified through the interactions. We normalize the weight vector to sum to 1, so as to normalize the HD distances to a roughly constant sized space. We then re-project the images using Eq. 1 with the updated weights to create a layout that incorporates human feedback.

4.3   Visual Explanations

Our method also provides visual explanations in the form of saliency maps that highlight the important features for projecting a given image, shown in Fig. 1(d)–(f). In these maps, the brighter pixels correspond to features of greater importance.

In the initial view, before semantic interactions, these explanations indicate the features of importance identified by the feature extractor that the projection model then uses to place the images. After an interaction, the optimized parameters are pushed backwards through the feature extractor, using weighted backpropagation, to generate new saliency maps that emphasize the features learned by the projection model. By inspecting the differences between the original saliency map and the post-interaction map, people can understand what features the projection learned from their interaction.

Weighted Visual Backpropagation. Figure 3 illustrates our weighted visual backpropagation method. We base our proposed method on the visual backpropagation method proposed by Bojarski et al. [4]. This method computes the actual contribution of neurons to the feature representation, making the backpropagation fast and efficient. We make this method projection-aware by applying the projection weights to the backpropagation.

To implement our method, we utilize the feature maps after each ReLU layer. For the feature map of the last convolutional layer, we conduct channel-wise multiplication with the weights w obtained from the interactive DR loop to back-propagate the user's intent. We then average the other feature maps to get a single feature map per layer. The deepest single feature map, highlighted in green in Fig. 3, is deconvolved with the same filter size and stride as the convolutional layer immediately preceding it. This scales the feature map to match the size of the map in the previous layer. Then we point-wise multiply the deconvolved feature map by the averaged single feature map of the previous layer. This process is repeated until we reach the input image.

We keep our notation consistent with Bojarski et al. [4]. Note, we will only describe our modification to their method. For full details, please refer to Bojarski et al. Consider a convolutional neural network $\mathcal{N}$ with n convolutional layers. Let $\gamma(i)$ denote the value of pixel i of the input image and v represent a neuron. e represents an edge from some other neuron v' to v and a_e denotes the activation of v ($a_e = a(v)$). $\mathcal{P}$ denotes a family of paths. The contribution of the input pixel i, calculated by the original Visual Backpropagation method, is defined as:

$$\theta_{VBP}^{\mathcal{N}}(i) = c * \gamma(i) \sum_{P \in \mathcal{P}} \prod_{e \in P} a_e \tag{3}$$

To back-propagate the weighted feature map, we conduct channel-wise multiplication for the last feature map with weights gained from the interactive DR loop. We denote et as the edge that connects nodes from the layer $(t-1)$ to the layer t. Let k denote the kernels for each layer. The contribution of the input pixel i calculated by our Weighted Visual Backpropagation method is defined as

$$\theta_{WVBP}^{\mathcal{N}}(i) = c * \gamma(i) \sum_{P \in \mathcal{P}} \prod_{e \in P} a_{et} \tag{4}$$

where

$$a_{et} = \begin{cases} a(v) & \text{if } t \neq n, \\ a(v) * w_k & \text{if } t = n. \end{cases}$$

and w_k is the weight from the inverse projection corresponding to channel k of the feature map in the final layer.

5 Usage Scenario: Edamame Pods

We developed this usage scenario with our collaborators in the plant sciences department [19]. Our collaborators identified the need for incorporating human perception into model development for identifying plant features. Initially, they wanted to organize images of edamame pods based on maturity level. However, when sorting the images they also discovered that the pods contained varying numbers of seeds, which often correlates to the consumers' perception of quality. They envisioned that a method like ours would help them re-organize the images based on this newly identified feature and allow them to reuse the original model. In the remainder of this section, we discuss two scenarios for organizing images of edamame pods. For our example, we use a subset of their edamame pod dataset containing 60 images, with 20 images per maturity stage.

Maturity Stage. The maturity stage of each pod is defined as either diseased, late-to-harvest, or ready-to-harvest. Here, we test if our method can sort the images according to these phenotypes and whether the features captured by the model to separate the images are related to the underlying phenotypes, illustrated in Fig. 1. First, we project the edamame pods to 2D. Then, we observe the visual phenotypes for maturity and interactively drag a subset of pods (highlighted in green) in order to group them into 3 clusters according to the desired phenotype categories, shown in Fig. 1(a). We hypothesized that, through this interaction, the underlying model would learn new weights for the feature space that satisfy the newly defined projection and properly capture the user's mental model of pod maturity.

Figure 1(b) shows the updated projection (generated after approximately 25 s), which produced three main clusters of pods according to their maturity stage. Figure 1(c) shows the ground truth of the images. This indicates that the desired phenotypes were effectively captured by the weighted features and represented in the updated model.

The explainable feature visualizations of specific pods depict the most important visual features learned by the interactive model. In Fig. 1(d) we see that one of the important visual features learned by the model to determine the disease phenotype is a salient discolored spot. Similarly, in Fig. 1(e,f), the model focuses on image areas correlated to important features of each pod. This provides insight into that parts of the pod are important for visually discerning the maturity stage. Furthermore, these results provide a link between human perception and machine learning.

Number of Pods. For the same pods dataset, we also want to explore a different visual phenotype: number of seeds per pod. However, the images were not originally collected to determine the number of seeds. Thus, the number of seeds is a novel visual feature that can be observed directly by the end users but is not initially used to cluster images in the default projection. As before, the images of edamame pods are displayed in the 2D plot. We then interactively drag pods (highlighted in green) to group them into 3 clusters according to the number of seeds (1, 2 or 3), as shown in Fig. 4(a). We hypothesize that by dragging a subset of the images, the underlying model will learn the weights for the feature spaces that satisfy the user-defined projection based on the number of seeds.

Figure 4(b) shows the updated projection. We find that the projection model captures "number of seeds" phenotype. Figure 4(c) shows the ground truth of the updated projection, instead of well-separated groups, the updated projection shows a linear relationship. We notice that there are two "three-seed" pods projected closer to the "two-seeds" pods. To learn more about why these two pods are mis-projected, we explore

Projection Plots

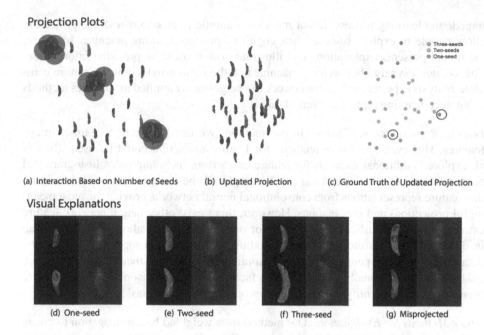

(a) Interaction Based on Number of Seeds   (b) Updated Projection   (c) Ground Truth of Updated Projection

Visual Explanations

(d) One-seed   (e) Two-seed   (f) Three-seed   (g) Misprojected

Fig. 4. Interactions to explore images based on the number of seeds. (a) shows the interaction based on seed count. (b) shows the updated projection while (c) shows the ground truth seed count. (d)–(f) shows the explanations of important image features for each seed count while (g) shows the explanations of two misprojected images.

the visual feature explanations for each group. Figure 4(d, e, f) shows the saliency map for the three groups accordingly. We find that the most important CNN features mainly capture the overall shape of the pod, as well as the position and the "raised" area of the seeds to differentiate pods with different numbers of seeds. Yet for those two misprojected pods, they are either dominated by the disease spot or do not have the obvious shape of three seeded pods, as shown by Fig. 4(g).

6 Discussion

General Framework for Analysis Using Deep Learning Features. One of the central problems with using deep learning feature representations in data analysis is the loss of access to the original data features. Typically, people must sacrifice analysis transparency for performance. However, our method presents a framework in which we maintain access to the original data features by leveraging the underlying deep learning model to create explanations from the underlying data features. Through the use of weighted backpropagation, we push the information learned by the projection model back through the neural network to generate explanations relative to the underlying data features. In doing so, we take a step towards solving the "two black boxes" problem, as defined by Wenskovitch and North [34]. The "two black boxes" problem identifies both the deep learning algorithm and the human cognitive process as black boxes that impede the learning process. In our method, semantic interactions with the projection allow people to express some of their cognitive processes to the machine. In return, the model presents explanations that illustrate how it uses the provided information. This creates a synergy between the machine and the human and facilitates a more complete analysis experience. This framework can be generally applied to analytics methods using deep learning representations of data.

Feature Representation Choice. In our method, we use ResNet18 to extract image features. However, alternative methods for feature extraction could be used. Bian et al. explored additional methods for feature extraction, including color histogram and Scale-Invariant Feature Transform [3]. We explored these methods as well but found that feature representations from convolutional neural networks provide the most meaningful projections and explanations. However, there exist other neural network feature extractors besides ResNet18. The design of our method easily allows people to swap in different CNN feature extractors, including those designed for specific tasks and datasets. This allows people to further customize projections of their data for the given analysis task. Additionally, our method can facilitate the comparison of different feature representations to identify the one most appropriate for a given task.

Other Methods for Explanation. Our method uses weighted backpropagation to create explanations of the effects of semantic interactions. However, this method is only one candidate for creating explanations of interactions. There exist other methods for generating feature explanations that we can adapt to our method. For example, we also adapted Grad-CAM to consider the weights from the projection model to generate explanations [30]. We found that Grad-CAM excels when images contained multiple entities, however, it falls flat when searching for specific image features. As our method benefits from finer-grained explanations, Grad-CAM was not a suitable method. Adapting other methods for creating model explanations remains to be explored in future work.

7   Conclusion

In this paper, we presented an interactive dimension reduction method for exploring image data using deep learning representations of images. Our method provides semantic interactions that allow people to incorporate their prior knowledge into the projection model. It uses custom-defined relationships to learn new projection weights optimal for respecting these relationships. Additionally, our method provides visual explanations of the effects of semantic interactions on the projections placement of images. These explanations illustrate the image features most important for projecting the images and illustrate the effects of interactions. We provide a real world usage scenario to demonstrate the method's effectiveness at organizing data from human-defined similarities. Overall, we found that our method was able to capture human feedback and incorporate it into the model. Our visual explanations help bridge the gap between the feature space and the original images to illustrate the knowledge learned by the model, creating a synergy between human and machine that facilitates a more complete analysis experience.

Acknowledgements. This material is based upon work supported by the National Science Foundation under Grant # 2127309 to the Computing Research Association for the CIFellows 2021 Project. This project was funded, in part, with an integrated internal competitive grant from the College of Agriculture and Life Sciences at Virginia Tech.

References

1. Bian, Y., North, C.: DeepSI: interactive deep learning for semantic interaction. In: 26th International Conference on Intelligent User Interfaces, pp. 197–207 (2021)
2. Bian, Y., North, C., Krokos, E., Joseph, S.: Semantic explanation of interactive dimensionality reduction. In: 2021 IEEE Visualization Conference (VIS), pp. 26–30. IEEE (2021)
3. Bian, Y., Wenskovitch, J., North, C.: DeepVA: bridging cognition and computation through semantic interaction and deep learning. arXiv preprint arXiv:2007.15800 (2020)
4. Bojarski, M., et al.: VisualBackProp: efficient visualization of CNNs. arXiv preprint arXiv:1611.05418 (2016)
5. Brown, E.T., Liu, J., Brodley, C.E., Chang, R.: Dis-function: learning distance functions interactively. In: 2012 IEEE Conference on Visual Analytics Science and Technology, pp. 83–92. IEEE (2012)
6. Cavallo, M., Demiralp, Ç.: A visual interaction framework for dimensionality reduction based data exploration. In: Proceedings of the 2018 CHI Conference on Human Factors in Computing Systems, pp. 1–13 (2018)
7. Cheng, T.Y., Huertas-Company, M., Conselice, C.J., Aragon-Salamanca, A., Robertson, B.E., Ramachandra, N.: Beyond the hubble sequence-exploring galaxy morphology with unsupervised machine learning. Mon. Not. R. Astron. Soc. **503**(3), 4446–4465 (2021)
8. Cunningham, P.: Dimension reduction. In: Cord, M., Cunningham, P. (eds.) Machine Learning Techniques for Multimedia. Cognitive Technologies, pp. 91–112. Springer, Heidelberg (2008). https://doi.org/10.1007/978-3-540-75171-7_4
9. Dowling, M., Wenskovitch, J., Hauck, P., Binford, A., Polys, N., North, C.: A bidirectional pipeline for semantic interaction. In: Proceedings of Workshop on Machine Learning from User Interaction for Visualization and Analytics (at IEEE VIS 2018), vol. 11, p. 74 (2018)
10. Dowling, M., et al.: Interactive visual analytics for sensemaking with big text. Big Data Res. **16**, 49–58 (2019)
11. Eler, D.M., et al.: Visual analysis of image collections. Vis. Comput. **25**(10), 923–937 (2009)
12. Endert, A., Chang, R., North, C., Zhou, M.: Semantic interaction: coupling cognition and computation through usable interactive analytics. IEEE Comput. Graph. Appl. **35**(4), 94–99 (2015)
13. Endert, A., Fiaux, P., North, C.: Semantic interaction for sensemaking: inferring analytical reasoning for model steering. IEEE Trans. Visual Comput. Graph. **18**(12), 2879–2888 (2012)
14. Endert, A., Fiaux, P., North, C.: Semantic interaction for visual text analytics. In: Proceedings of the SIGCHI Conference on Human Factors in Computing Systems, CHI 2012, pp. 473–482. ACM, New York (2012). https://doi.org/10.1145/2207676.2207741
15. Endert, A., Han, C., Maiti, D., House, L., North, C.: Observation-level interaction with statistical models for visual analytics. In: 2011 IEEE Conference on Visual Analytics Science and Technology, pp. 121–130. IEEE (2011)
16. Espadoto, M., et al.: Unprojection: Leveraging inverse-projections for visual analytics of high-dimensional data. IEEE Trans. Vis. Comput. Graph. (2021)
17. Fujiwara, T., Wei, X., Zhao, J., Ma, K.L.: Interactive dimensionality reduction for comparative analysis. IEEE Trans. Visual Comput. Graph. **28**(1), 758–768 (2022). https://doi.org/10.1109/TVCG.2021.3114807

18. Ghosh, S.K., Biswas, B., Ghosh, A.: A novel noise removal technique influenced by deep convolutional autoencoders on mammograms. In: Acharjya, D.P., Mitra, A., Zaman, N. (eds.) Deep Learning in Data Analytics. SBD, vol. 91, pp. 25–43. Springer, Cham (2022). https://doi.org/10.1007/978-3-030-75855-4_2

19. Han, H., et al.: Interactive deep learning for exploratory sorting of plantimages by visual phenotypes (2022)

20. He, K., Zhang, X., Ren, S., Sun, J.: Deep residual learning for image recognition. In: Proceedings of the IEEE Conference on Computer Vision and Pattern Recognition, pp. 770–778 (2016)

21. House, L., Leman, S., Han, C.: Bayesian visual analytics: BaVA. Stat. Anal. Data Min.: ASA Data Sci. J. 8(1), 1–13 (2015)

22. Jeong, D.H., Ziemkiewicz, C., Fisher, B., Ribarsky, W., Chang, R.: iPCA: an interactive system for PCA-based visual analytics. In: Computer Graphics Forum, vol. 28, pp. 767–774. Wiley Online Library (2009)

23. Joia, P., Coimbra, D., Cuminato, J.A., Paulovich, F.V., Nonato, L.G.: Local affine multidimensional projection. IEEE Trans. Visual Comput. Graph. 17(12), 2563–2571 (2011)

24. Leman, S.C., House, L., Maiti, D., Endert, A., North, C.: Visual to parametric interaction (v2pi). PLoS One 8(3), e50474 (2013)

25. Mamani, G.M., Fatore, F.M., Nonato, L.G., Paulovich, F.V.: User-driven feature space transformation. In: Computer Graphics Forum, vol. 32, pp. 291–299. Wiley Online Library (2013)

26. Paulovich, F.V., Eler, D.M., Poco, J., Botha, C.P., Minghim, R., Nonato, L.G.: Piece wise Laplacian-based projection for interactive data exploration and organization. In: Computer Graphics Forum, vol. 30, pp. 1091–1100. Wiley Online Library (2011)

27. Pirolli, P., Card, S.: The sensemaking process and leverage points for analyst technology as identified through cognitive task analysis. In: Proceedings of International Conference on Intelligence Analysis, McLean, VA, USA, vol. 5, pp. 2–4 (2005)

28. dos Santos Amorim, E.P., Brazil, E.V., Daniels, J., Joia, P., Nonato, L.G., Sousa, M.C.: iLAMP: exploring high-dimensional spacing through backward multidimensional projection. In: 2012 IEEE Conference on Visual Analytics Science and Technology, pp. 53–62. IEEE (2012)

29. Self, J.Z., Dowling, M., Wenskovitch, J., Crandell, I., Wang, M., House, L., Leman, S., North, C.: Observation-level and parametric interaction for high-dimensional data analysis. ACM Trans. Interact. Intell. Syst. (TiiS) 8(2), 1–36 (2018)

30. Selvaraju, R.R., Cogswell, M., Das, A., Vedantam, R., Parikh, D., Batra, D.: Grad-CAM: visual explanations from deep networks via gradient-based localization. In: Proceedings of the IEEE International Conference on Computer Vision, pp. 618–626 (2017)

31. Tukey, J.W., Wilk, M.B.: Data analysis and statistics: an expository overview. In: Proceedings of the 7–10 November 1966, Fall Joint Computer Conference, pp. 695–709 (1966)

32. Villaret, M., et al.: Affective state-based framework for e-learning systems. In: Artificial Intelligence Research and Development: Proceedings of the 23rd International Conference of the Catalan Association for Artificial Intelligence, vol. 339, p. 357. IOS Press (2021)

33. Wang, M., Wenskovitch, J., House, L., Polys, N., North, C.: Bridging cognitive gaps between user and model in interactive dimension reduction. Visual Inform. 5(2), 13–25 (2021)

34. Wenskovitch, J., North, C.: Interactive AI: designing for the 'two black boxes' problem. In: Hybrid Human-Artificial Intelligence Special Issue, pp. 1–10. IEEE Computer Society, Washington (2020)

35. Zeiler, M.D., Fergus, R.: Visualizing and understanding convolutional networks. In: Fleet, D., Pajdla, T., Schiele, B., Tuytelaars, T. (eds.) ECCV 2014. LNCS, vol. 8689, pp. 818–833. Springer, Cham (2014). https://doi.org/10.1007/978-3-319-10590-1_53

36. Zhou, B., Khosla, A., Lapedriza, A., Oliva, A., Torralba, A.: Learning deep features for discriminative localization. In: Proceedings of the IEEE Conference on Computer Vision and Pattern Recognition, pp. 2921–2929 (2016)

MultiProjector: Temporal Projection for Multivariates Time Series

Tommy Dang[✉] and Ngan V. T. Nguyen

Texas Tech University, Lubbock, TX 79409, USA
{tommy.dang,ngan.v.t.nguyen}@ttu.edu

Abstract. This paper applies the recent advances of visual analytics, which combine computers' and humans' strengths to the data exploration process, to alleviate the scalability and overplotting issues of dimensional projection techniques for high-dimensional temporal datasets. Our approach first uses clustering algorithms to select the representative data points at each time step for each data profile. We then apply dimension reduction techniques to visualize the temporal relationships via connecting lines. Finally, we propose a couple of different underlying models to treat time steps and the time dimension to mitigate the final projections' visual clutter. We built a web-based prototype, called *MultiProjector*, to integrate these components into a unified data exploration process. The prototype is validated on several high-dimensional temporal datasets in various application domains to demonstrate our approach's benefits.

Keywords: HPC monitoring · Projections · Graph visualization

1 Introduction

Temporal datasets are increasing in size and complexity due to the growth of many fields such as scientific applications, economics, and finance. A time series is a chronological collection of observations throughout time [10]. Temporal datasets may have one variable (univariate time series) or many variables (multivariate time series). The latter is more complicated in terms of the analysis as relations between variables play a fundamental role in analyzing this type of time series [27]. An example of the multivariate time series is the US employment data. The monthly statistics of employees in various economic sectors (such as Education, Finance, or Construction) form a multivariate time series collection. In this example, each sector is a variable, and the state is an individual observation. In this paper, we consider the temporal dependencies between variables and inter-relationships between individuals over time.

There are many efforts to integrate temporal information into common visual presentations of cross-sectional datasets, or high-dimensional non-temporal datasets, such as parallel coordinates [8,14], radar charts [26], and hierarchical layouts [13]. Ali et al. [2] introduce the application of sliding window and dimension reduction techniques in visualizing long multivariate time series. Their approach helps to display the similarity of chronological sliding windows of the

G. Bebis et al. (Eds.): ISVC 2022, LNCS 13598, pp. 91–102, 2022.
https://doi.org/10.1007/978-3-031-20713-6_7

multivariate time series, enabling the detections of repetitive patterns or interesting anomalies. This paper considers each instance in the multivariate time series as a data point in the high-dimensional space. Similar data points are grouped based on their multivariate values to provide a compressed summary of the data profile. The projected positions of the remaining data points represent the interrelationships of individuals and the evolution of these individuals via connecting lines. By marrying clustering methods and dimension reduction techniques into a unified framework, we provide scalable multidimensional projections for large temporal data. The contribution of this paper is listed as the following.

- We discuss, compare and summarize the pros and cons of various dimensional reduction techniques in the context of temporal data.
- We propose a couple of different underlying models to treat time steps and the time dimension to reduce the number of projected data points without affecting the global structure and mitigate the final projections' overplotting issues.
- We implement an interactive web-based prototype to visualize high-dimensional temporal datasets. Our approach and prototype are demonstrated on real-world datasets in various domains to illustrate its benefits.

2   Related Work

2.1   Visualizing High Dimensional Temporal Datasets

Many works have been carried out to provide visualizations for high-dimensional time series. Specifically, there are many efforts to add time dimensions into common visual presentations of cross-sectional datasets, or high-dimensional non-temporal datasets, such as matrix [3], parallel coordinates [5], and circular layouts [9]. We firstly consider the temporal extension of the scatterplot. Time-Seer [6] transforms the collection of time series in the datasets into time series of Scagnostics, which are metrics for visual features of the scatterplots for each pair of variables. It uses these Scagnostics as a signal to identify unusual events. Congnostics [22] proposes a list of eight metrics for connected scatterplots' visual features and helps to visualize the dynamic correlation between variables of an individual.

TimeCluster [2] proposes the use of dimension reduction techniques to visualize long multivariate time series. It considers each sliding window as a point in a high-dimensional space, whose number of dimensions equals the time series values in the window. For example, an individual has three variables, and the sliding window has a size of sixty. In this case, the high-dimensional space has 180 dimensions. After reducing the dimensions by deep convolutional auto-encoder, the authors continue to apply other dimension reduction methods such as PCA [31], t-SNE [19], and UMAP [20]. Their approach helps to reconstruct the whole temporal dataset to only one view to observe some interesting patterns like clusters or abnormalities.

2.2 Dimension Reduction

Principal Component Analysis, or PCA, is one of the most popular linear dimension reduction techniques. It projects the original data to a lower-dimensional space, such that the variance of the projected data is maximized [31]. In addition to the linear projections, many nonlinear dimension reduction techniques have been developed. The t-Distributed Stochastic Neighbor Embedding, or t-SNE, is a frequently used nonlinear projection. It computes the similarities between data in the high-dimensional space by Gaussian distribution before reconstructing these similarities by Student t-distribution in a low dimensional space [19]. This method requires both time and memory complexity up to $O(N^2)$, which may not be efficient for large datasets. The acceleration of this technique using the Barnes-Hut algorithm can reduce the time complexity to $O(Nlog(N))$ and the memory complexity to $O(N)$ [29]. Uniform Manifold Approximation and Projection, or UMAP, is recently introduced to the literature [20]. It has been proved to be comparable to t-SNE in the visualization of large datasets. Becht et al. [4] provide a comparison for the running times of some popular projection methods, including t-SNE and UMAP. To stabilize the projection results for streaming multidimensional data, Fujiwara et al. [12] propose geometric transformation and animation methods. However, the approach does not aim to resolve the scalability issues of the multidimensional projection techniques [11]. This paper utilizes and expands the three projection methods mentioned in this section to various multivariate temporal datasets. We will discuss in detail our visual methodology in the next section.

3   Methodology

Our research problem is projected onto the three dimensions: individual data entries, variables of these individuals, and time. An example of this data structure is the monthly US employment rates. This dataset has 53 states and territories in the US as 53 individuals. Each state has many economic sectors such as Good Producing, Manufacturing, Financial Activities, etc., and they are considered the variables of each individual. The net change in the number of employees per month of a specific sector of a particular state form a time series in this collection. Before any computations and visualizations, we apply the min-max normalization for every variable in the dataset to scale them to the unit range.

3.1   Clusterings

To handle large multivariate time series, not all data points join the dimension reduction computation. Instead, we first perform clustering across all snapshots to abstract a large number of data points into the major groups and focus on data instances at the group changes. Our approach is based on the observation that stable profiles may not contain much insight when analyzing time series, but they consume the computational resources for rendering the projections and causing overplotting issues. In particular, our *MultiProjector* web-based proto-type supports two clustering algorithms: *k-means* and *leader bin*. The former requires a given number of groups and a convergence criterion such as the min-imal decrease in squared error [15]. Users can also set the maximum number of iterations to stop the *k-means* computation. The latter allows a flexible range of leaders with a consideration: it is inefficient if there are too many leaders, while it tends to over-summarize the dataset if there are too few ones [7]. *MultiProjector* uses *leader bin* as the default multivariate clustering method since it provides the representative instances (leaders) and more stable clustering outcomes.

3.2   Multidimensional Projections

We consider three popular classes: PCA, t-SNE, and UMAP. PCA projects data points into a few orthogonal or uncorrelated principal components, which retain the whole data maximum variance. Usually, the first two components retain most information about the dataset, so it is reasonable to use PCA to project the data points in high-dimensional space to two-dimensional space. However, this method has two main disadvantages [30]. The first one is that it is inappro-priate for embedding extremely high-dimensional space due to the overlapping problem or the curse of dimensionality. The second drawback is that it favors the large pairwise distances, not the small ones. The nonlinear methods (t-SNE vs. UMAP) can avoid the overlapping issue of distinct clusters. While t-SNE focuses on preserving the local structure of the dataset, UMAP can reconstruct the global structure.

3.3   Visualizing the Time Dimension

A straightforward approach for plotting temporal domain is using the connected lines. To enforce the time dimension in the computation, we integrate time as a new dimension (increasing from min to max) along with variables for computing the projection. This method allows time to contribute to the projection of data points and to distinguish any individual at different time points. Additionally, we introduce the use of the third axis along with the 2D space to display time. In other words, this approach projects all individuals at the same time point into a 2D layer before aligning them onto the layers in chronological order on the third axis to illustrate the temporal evolution. This third dimension enforces the contribution of time to the final projection of the dataset. The summary of the idea of integrating the time domain into the 2D projection is depicted in Fig. 1.

3.4   Multivariate Representations

Each individual at a specific time point is defined by its multivariate metrics. As we aim to plot the multivariate metrics directly on the projected space, circular representations are more appropriate for a large number of variables [21]. An intuitive presentation for an individual at a time point is a radar chart that

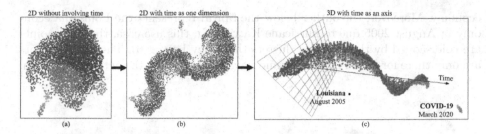

Fig. 1. Visualizing the US monthly employment data in 22 years: (a) 2D UMAP projection (b) 2D UPMAP projection considering time as an additional variable in the multidimensional project, and (c) Integrating the time domain into the 3D projection.

shows its multivariate values [17]. The position of each data point is determined by its multivariate values. Then, the Euclidean distance between any pair of data points measures how similar they are. Before applying projections, we reduce the number of input data points by compressing similar timestamps of the same data profile together. In other words, we care about the changes while discarding the static points in the high-dimensional time series data.

4   Use Cases

4.1   Use Case 1: Monthly US Employment Rate

The US employment dataset contains 53 states and territories [1]. Each state is considered as an individual profile that is recorded on 15 economic sectors. In particular, the monthly net change of the number of employees in every economic sector of each state is retrieved from January 1999 to May 2020. Totally, there are 12,495 data points in this dataset to be considered in the final projection.

In this use case, we focus on the 2D UMAP projection and its 3D variances, as depicted in Fig. 1. Different from the incremental approach discussed by Fujiwara et al. [12], we consider data points in all time steps as a whole in the projection. This allows us to avoid the unstable layouts (such as flipped or rotated) generated by independent projections for each time step. Figure 1(b) depicts the chronological sequence when we consider time as an additional variable for the UMAP projection. In Fig. 1(c), time is used as the third axis (from left to right), the 53 multivariate data points representing the economic status of states and territories in a given month are scattered on a plane orthogonal to the time axis. We can easily notice the interesting spiral pattern from the point of view of how the points are arranged throughout the 3D space in Fig. 1(c). This can be explained as the US economy is completing a circle after the 2008 Great recession. The orange points at the rear of the spiral region are states in March 2020. These points are most dissimilar to most of the points in the spiral region, which means the US experienced a significant drop in the number of employees in March 2020 when Covid-19 started wreaking havoc on the US economy. Moreover, the outlier below the Spiral represents the Louisiana economy in August 2005 due to hurricane Katrina. In this use case, the data points are color-coded by the k-means clusters that they belong to. The cluster colors are only there for visual inspection and have no impact on the actual projection.

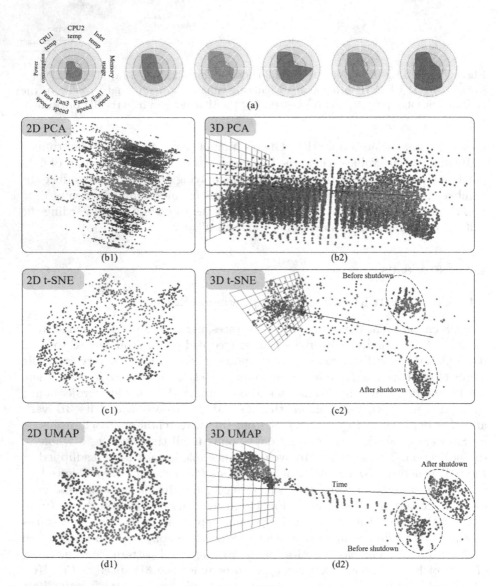

Fig. 2. Multidimensional projections of the computer health metrics: (a) The multivariate data is first classified into six groups. (b) PCA projection of 12,609 operating statuses, (c) t-SNE, and (d) UMAP projection of 1,225 operating statuses. The data points are colored by their multivariate statuses as defined in (a) (Color figure online).

4.2   Use Case 2: Monitoring Computer Metrics

The second use case considers the health metrics of a High-Performance Computing system at a university [28]. The system has 467 nodes, and thus they are 467 individuals in the high dimensional time series associating to nine health metrics, such as CPU temperatures, fans speeds, memory usage, and power consumption [18]. In other words, they are nine variables in the temporal dataset. The metrics are recorded at 5 min frequency. In particular, the dataset that we use in this use case is on March 21, 2019.

The multivariate operating statuses of computing nodes in the High-Performance Computing system are first classified into six major groups using the k-means algorithm. Users can select different clustering methods as well as the number of clusters on their choices. As depicted in Fig. 2(a), radar charts are used to represent the multivariate status of the computing nodes as they can quickly capture the *morphology* of the computing statuses [17]. The PCA projection in Fig. 2(b) takes 876 ms. The PCA projections are pretty uniform, and no visual pattern can be easily discerned.

Based on the observation that system administrators care more about the significant changes rather than the static computing nodes [23], we propose to reduce the number of static operating statuses and only focus on the dynamic behaviors of the system (when the group switchings happen). Therefore, we reduce the number of multivariate data points ten times from 12,609 down to 1,225. This allows our approach scaling well with the large time-dependent multivariate datasets. Figure 2(c) shows 2D t-SNE projection and our modified 3D temporal projection. Notice that the 3D projection, with time as the third axis, displays the three dense regions at the beginning and the end of the observed period. The first region on the grids is the first time step, and therefore, the operating statuses of all 476 computing nodes are recorded. The middle region is sparse since we only plot the significant changes on the metrics, such as CPU and memory usage, most probably associating to the HPC scheduler events (a new user is allocated the computing resources or a new job is dispatched). Toward the end of the observed period, there are separated into two groups: green and red vs. orange and blue. As shown in the radars in Fig. 2(a), the green and red groups have high *CPU temperatures* and high *fan speeds* while the orange and blue groups are normal operating statuses. In particular, the chill water for the HPC center was accidentally disconnected at around 2 pm on March 21, 2019, leading to the overheat issues on all computing nodes (green and red nodes). At 4 pm, the system had been automatically shut down and then returned to the normal operations (orange and blue groups). Regarding UMAP in Fig. 2(d), the 2D projection is quite uniform and has no visible cluster or outlier. In the 3D UMAP projection, the similar dynamic behaviors of the system are also captured on the temporal domain. We can also notice that our data reduction technique has also mitigated the serious overplotting issues in Fig. 2(b2). Our *MultiProjector* also supports embedding the multidimensional representation of computing nodes directly in the projection for visual inspections.

Our *MultiProjector* also supports embedding the multidimensional representation of computing nodes directly in the projection for visual inspections. Figure 3 depicts the same example in Fig. 2(d1) in a compressed honeycomb layout. In particular, *MultiProjector* initializes a force layout from the UMAP configuration. The data points automatically resolve collisions before projected onto a regular honeycomb layout. Specifically, each bee cell in Fig. 3 contains a representative operating status of a node. The saturation of the radar indicates how long the computing node stays on that status (no significant changes on the health metrics). In this example, we draw a trajectory of a sample profile, *compute-3-41*. We can visualize the chill water impacts on this computing node: The node started with the normal operating status at 14:00, then traveled through overheat states in green and red at 15:45 and 15:50, and finally ended up with a blue state after the HPC system reset at 16:00.

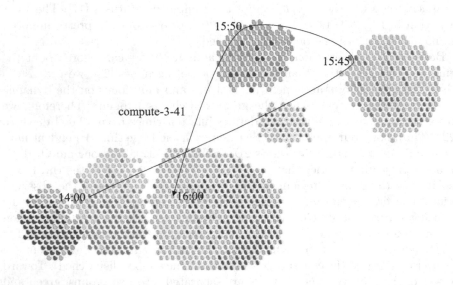

Fig. 3. Visualizing 1,225 operating statuses in our non-overlapped honeycomb layout: The six color-coded clusters are produced by the k-means algorithm on nine health metrics, such as *CPU temperatures*, *memory usage*, and *fan speeds*. The arrow connects various operational status of compute-3-41 in 2 h.

4.3   Use Case 3: Plant Genetics

In this use case, we target the visual clutter issue of multidimensional projections. The data was retrieved from the *Center for Functional Genomics of Abiotic Stress* [16]. In particular, we need to consider 20,450 plant genes experimented under 12 tested conditions, with *STOP1* mutant for the last 6 conditions. These experimented conditions are abbreviated as *wt* for wild type, *stop1* for knock-out mutant background for the transcription factor, *hp* for high phosphate supply (1 mM), *lp* for low phosphate supply (0 mM), *Al* for Al stress pH 5, and *Fe* for Fe excess supplied to the medium pH 5. For example, nametags for the conditions composed as *wthp6* means wild-type/high Pi supply/pH 6 and *s1hp6* means stop1 ko/high Pi supply/pH 6. *Al* and *Fe* are only tested conditions under low Pi and pH 5, and hence there are two library replicates for Al and Fe for each genotype and toxicity. In the input data, the first column contains gene names, and the next six columns are the wild type conditions, including the base condition, *wthp6*. The last six columns are the corresponding *STOP1* mutant conditions.

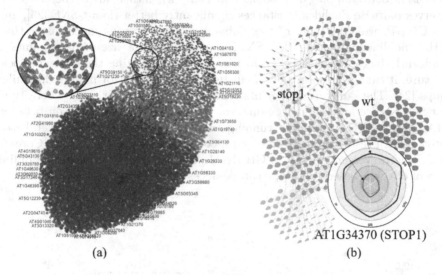

(a)   (b)

Fig. 4. Visualizing gene expressions using our *MultiProjector* prototype: (a) 20,450 plant genes (b) 210 transcription factors (Color figure online).

Figure 4 shows the expression levels of 20,450 genes under six controlled conditions through two time steps: before and after the application of *STOP1* mutant. Therefore, we have 40,900 data points in this projection. Figure 4(a) shows overplotting issue of 2D UMAP projection. Notice that low expressed genes tend to locate on the top while highly-expressed genes flow down the bottom (the blue region). To alleviate the visual clutter issue, we first reduce the number of projected genes by focusing on transcription factors (the genes that change their expression behaviors significantly), which are identified by the Euclidean distance of the multivariate values before vs. after the injection of *STOP1* mutant. Figure 4(b) shows our non-overlapped honeycomb layout of the 210 transcription factors. The arrows in the background highlight the group transitions of these 210 genes. We can notice the major group changes are between green to yellow and purple to orange. We have annotated the special gene *STOP1* and its rare transition from the most active group (blue) to an inactive one (green), as depicted in the enlarged radar view. In this example, *MultiProjector* provided a compressed projection view of gene expression data that allows biologists to visualize and identify the behaviors of the leading factors under the tested conditions. This type of analysis is important for plant treatments and drug designs.

4.4 Discussion

PCA is a linear projection and hence is the fastest method with about one second for thousands of data points in the web-based environment. However, it has an issue of overlapping data points, especially when there are outliers. UMAP preserves pairwise Euclidean distances significantly better than t-SNE [25], and thus UMAP preserves more of the global structure. It runs much faster than another nonlinear method, the t-SNE, especially as the size of data points is significantly large. Because t-SNE focuses on reconstructing the dataset's local structure, it cannot perform well in clustering data points for finding dissimilar groups [24]. The same groups' points tend to pull each other, so the density of the t-SNE projection may not be uniform. Figure 5 gives a comparison between UMAP and t-SNE in terms of running time (in *log* scale) via our web-based prototype. All tests were performed on a computer with 2.9 GHz Intel Core i5, macOS Sierra Version 10.12.1, 8 GB RAM. The introduction video and online demo of our web-based prototype can be accessed at https://git.io/JLppG.

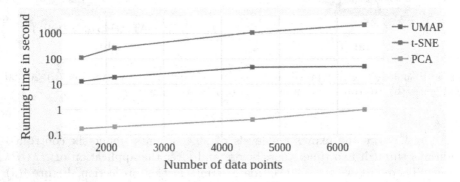

Fig. 5. Running time comparisons of PCA, UMAP, and t-SNE in our web-based application using Google Chrome.

5   Conclusion

Multidimensional projections are popular methods for reducing high-dimensional data onto lower-dimensional planes. However, the importance of the time element is not always considered properly. In this paper, we investigate the temporal domain as one of the dimensions in multidimensional projections. This allows us to impose the temporal changes onto the lower-dimensional space (such as 2D or 3D). We project different time steps as a whole and align them over the 3rd axis in order to keep the spatial coherence between them. To project a large number of input data points, we focused on the significant time steps for each data profile where multivariate variances occur. Our temporal data reduction technique also helps to mitigate the overplotting issues generated by multidimensional projections. We experiment our approach on various existing dimensional reduction methods and demonstrate them on different domains.

References

1. U.S. bureau of labor statistics databases. http://www.bls.gov/data/. Accessed 08 Jan 2021
2. Ali, M., Jones, M.W., Xie, X., Williams, M.: TimeCluster: dimension reduction applied to temporal data for visual analytics. Vis. Comput. **35**(6), 1013–1026 (2019). https://doi.org/10.1007/s00371-019-01673-y
3. Bach, B., Pietriga, E., Fekete, J.D.: Visualizing dynamic networks with matrix cubes. In: Proceedings of ACM Conference on Human Factors in Computing Systems, pp. 877–886 (2014)
4. Becht, E., et al.: Dimensionality reduction for visualizing single-cell data using UMAP (2019)
5. Burch, M., Vehlow, C., Beck, F., Diehl, S., Weiskopf, D.: Parallel edge splatting for scalable dynamic graph visualization (2011). https://doi.org/10.1109/TVCG. 2011.226
6. Dang, T.N., Anand, A., Wilkinson, L.: Timeseer: scagnostics for high-dimensional time series (2012)
7. Dang, T.N., Wilkinson, L.: ScagExplorer: exploring scatterplots by their scagnostics (2014). https://doi.org/10.1109/PacificVis.2014.42
8. Dasgupta, A., Kosara, R., Gosink, L.: Meta parallel coordinates for visualizing features in large, high-dimensional, time-varying data. In: IEEE Symposium on Large Data Analysis and Visualization (LDAV), pp. 85–89. IEEE (2012)
9. Fischer, F., Fuchs, J., Mansmann, F.: ClockMap: enhancing circular treemaps with temporal glyphs for time-series data. In: Meyer, M., Weinkaufs, T. (eds.) EuroVis - Short Papers (2012). https://doi.org/10.2312/PE/EuroVisShort/ EuroVisShort2012/097-101
10. Fu, T.C.: A review on time series data mining (2011)
11. Fujiwara, T., Kwon, O.H., Ma, K.L.: Supporting analysis of dimensionality reduction results with contrastive learning (2020). https://doi.org/10.1109/TVCG.2019. 2934251
12. Fujiwara, T., Chou, J.K., Shilpika, Xu, P., Ren, L., Ma, K.L.: An incremental dimensionality reduction method for visualizing streaming multidimensional data (2020). https://doi.org/10.1109/tvcg.2019.2934433
13. Greilich, M., Burch, M., Diehl, S.: Visualizing the evolution of compound digraphs with timearctrees. In: Proceedings of Eurographics Conference on Visualization, pp. 975–990 (2009). https://doi.org/10.1111/j.1467-8659.2009.01451.x
14. Gruendl, H., Riehmann, P., Pausch, Y., Froehlich, B.: Time-series plots integrated in parallel-coordinates displays. In: Computer Graphics Forum, vol. 35, pp. 321–330. Wiley Online Library (2016)
15. Hartigan, J.A.: Clustering Algorithms, 99th edn. Wiley, New York (1975)
16. Herrera-Estrella, L.: My journey into the birth of plant transgenesis and its impact on modern plant biology (2020). https://doi.org/10.1111/pbi.13319,, https:// onlinelibrary.wiley.com/doi/abs/10.1111/pbi.13319

17. Kammer, D., et al.: Glyphboard: visual exploration of high-dimensional data combining glyphs with dimensionality reduction (2020). https://doi.org/10.1109/TVCG.2020.2969060
18. Li, J., et al.: Monster: an out-of-the-box monitoring tool for high performance computing systems. In: 2020 IEEE International Conference on Cluster Computing (CLUSTER), pp. 119–129 (2020). https://doi.org/10.1109/CLUSTER49012.2020.00022
19. Maaten, L.v.d., Hinton, G.: Visualizing data using t-SNE (2008)
20. McInnes, L., Healy, J., Melville, J.: UMAP: uniform manifold approximation and projection for dimension reduction (2018)
21. Meyer, M., Munzner, T., Pfister, H.: MizBee: a multiscale synteny browser (2009)
22. Nguyen, B.D.Q., Hewett, R., Dang, T.: Congnostics: visual features for doubly time series plots. In: Turkay, C., Vrotsou, K. (eds.) EuroVis Workshop on Visual Analytics (EuroVA). The Eurographics Association (2020). https://doi.org/10.2312/eurova.20201086
23. Nguyen, N., Hass, J., Chen, Y., Li, J., Sill, A., Dang, T.: Radarviewer: visualizing the dynamics of multivariate data. In: Practice and Experience in Advanced Research Computing, pp. 555–556. PEARC 2020, Association for Computing Machinery, New York, NY, USA (2020). https://doi.org/10.1145/3311790.3404538
24. Nguyen, N.V.T., Dang, T.: Ant-SNE: tracking community evolution via animated t-SNE. In: Bebis, G., et al. (eds.) ISVC 2019. LNCS, vol. 11844, pp. 330–341. Springer, Cham (2019). https://doi.org/10.1007/978-3-030-33720-9_25
25. Oskolkov, N.: tSNE vs. UMAP: global structure. http://towardsdatascience.com/tsne-vs-umap-global-structure-4d8045acba17. Accessed 08 Jan 2021
26. Pham, V., Nguyen, N., Li, J., Hass, J., Chen, Y., Dang, T.: MTSAD: multivariate time series abnormality detection and visualization. In: 2019 IEEE International Conference on Big Data (Big Data), pp. 3267–3276 (2019)
27. Tsay, R.S.: Multivariate Time Series Analysis: With R and Financial Applications. Wiley, Hoboken (2013)
28. TTU: high performance computing center (HPCC) at Texas tech university. website (2020). https://www.depts.ttu.edu/hpcc/ Accessed 6 July 2020
29. Van Der Maaten, L.: Accelerating t-SNE using tree-based algorithms (2014)
30. Van Der Maaten, L., Postma, E., Van den Herik, J.: Dimensionality reduction: a comparative (2009)
31. Wold, S., Esbensen, K., Geladi, P.: Principal component analysis (1987)

Deep Learning Based Super-Resolution for Medical Volume Visualization with Direct Volume Rendering

Sudarshan Devkota$^{(\boxtimes)}$ and Sumanta Pattanaik

University of Central Florida, Orlando, FL, USA
`sudarshan.devkota93@knights.ucf.edu`, `sumant@cs.ucf.edu`

Abstract. Modern-day display systems demand high-quality rendering. However, rendering at higher resolution requires a large number of data samples and is computationally expensive. Recent advances in deep learning-based image and video super-resolution techniques motivate us to investigate such networks for high fidelity upscaling of frames rendered at a lower resolution to a higher resolution. While our work focuses on super-resolution of medical volume visualization performed with direct volume rendering, it is also applicable for volume visualization with other rendering techniques. We propose a learning-based technique where our proposed system uses color information along with other supplementary features gathered from our volume renderer to learn efficient upscaling of a low resolution rendering to a higher resolution space. Furthermore, to improve temporal stability, we also implement the temporal reprojection technique for accumulating history samples in volumetric rendering. Our method allows high-quality reconstruction of images from highly aliased input as shown in Fig. 1.

Keywords: Super-resolution · Volume rendering · Medical imaging

1 Introduction

With recent advancements in imaging technology, medical volume data, such as computed tomography (CT) scans and Magnetic Resonance Imaging (MRI) images, are readily available. The rendering performed with these 3D data for visualization of anatomical structures plays a significant role in today's clinical applications. The quality of the 3D volume data, as well as the visual fidelity of the rendered content, directly affects the diagnosis accuracy in clinical medicine. For larger volume data, the traversal of the volume becomes increasingly costly and can negatively affect the frame rate for high resolution rendering.

In recent years, several works have addressed the goal of resolution augmentation in the medical imaging sector as a software based post-processing technique rather than an engineering-hardware issue. Such software based techniques have a variety of use cases. For instance, in cases of remote visualizations, high-resolution rendering from supercomputers can only be saved or streamed at a

© The Author(s), under exclusive license to Springer Nature Switzerland AG 2022
G. Bebis et al. (Eds.): ISVC 2022, LNCS 13598, pp. 103–114, 2022.
https://doi.org/10.1007/978-3-031-20713-6_8

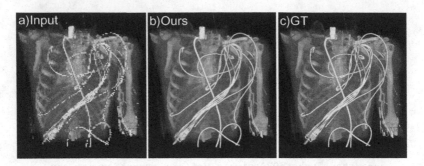

Fig. 1. Results of our super-resolution network for volumetric rendering with a) input rendering at a low resolution of 240×240 which is upscaled by a factor of 8×8 to obtain the high-resolution output b) at 1920×1920. c) is ground truth image.

compressed lower resolution state due to storage and bandwidth limitations. This data, when streamed to the client-side, needs to be decompressed and upscaled in such a way that the reconstruction error is kept as low as possible. Moreover, high-resolution displays in modern-day mobile and Virtual Reality (VR) systems demand high-resolution and high-quality rendering.

A variety of high quality image reconstruction techniques have been proposed to address this issue. Recent works in deep learning have demonstrated that learning-based image and video super-resolution methods can efficiently upscale inputs to a higher resolution when the network is trained on low and high-resolution pairs of images [4]. In image and video super-resolution literature, super-resolution is generally studied as a deblurring problem. However, unlike photographic images, each pixel sample in a rendering is a point sample in space and time which makes the final rendering to have aliasing artifacts typically at lower resolution. Thus, upscaling rendered content is considered as an anti-aliasing and interpolation problem [21].

In our work, we investigate a deep learning based super-resolution approach for direct volume rendering (DVR) of 3D medical data. Leveraging prior works on image and video super-resolution architectures, we present a rendering pipeline that includes an artificial neural network to perform upscaling of a ray-casted visualization of medical volumetric data. Motivated by a recent work on super-sampling of surface-only rendered content [21], we plan to use the neural super-sampling architecture as a basis and extend it for volumetric rendering. Our proposed pipeline consists of a volume renderer that outputs a low-resolution rendering of medical volume data along with a number of supplementary features which enables the super-resolution network to make sensible interpretations of these features for generating a high-resolution representation of the input. Furthermore, in order to improve the temporal stability and to aid in information refill, we implement a simple, yet effective way to perform temporal reprojection for volumetric cases. This allows our network to effectively propagate and aggregate samples from neighboring frames to the current frame.

We summarize our technical contributions as follows:

- We demonstrate a learning-based technique that performs up to 8×8 upsampling of highly aliased volumetric rendering with improved visual fidelity and temporal stability.
- We experimentally verify the effectiveness of supplementing the network with additional features to improve the quality of reconstructed image.
- We implement an effective temporal reprojection technique for the accumulation of history samples in volumetric rendering.

2   Related Work

2.1   Image and Video Super-resolution

Deep learning-based super-resolution techniques started to gain popularity since the initial works by [4] where they used deep convolutional neural networks (CNN) to learn end-to-end mapping between low/high-resolution images. Several other CNN-based models have been proposed since then to improve upon the network architecture. Instead of learning the direct mapping between input and output, Kim *et al.* [12] proposed to learn the residual between the two images by introducing a very deep network. After the introduction of residual network [7], Zhang *et al.* [22] and Lim *et al.* [16] applied residual blocks to further improve the performance of the network. To improve upon the perceptual quality of the reconstructed photo-realistic images, Ledig *et al.* [15] incorporated generative adversarial networks [6] and proposed to use a combination of loss functions including perceptual loss [11] and adversarial loss [6].

Video super-resolution (VSR) is more challenging compared to single image super-resolution in that one needs to gather auxiliary information across misaligned neighboring frames in a video sequence for restoration. In some recent works, recurrent networks have been widely used in video super-resolution architectures [2,9] which naturally allows for gathering information across multiple frames. Another group of networks uses motion estimation between frames to fuse multiframe information and to improve temporal coherence. Jo *et al.* [10] proposed to use dynamic upsampling filters for implicit motion compensation while Kim *et al.* [13] used a spatio-temporal transformer network for multiple frame motion estimation and warping.

2.2   Resolution Enhancement for Rendered Content

Several methods have been proposed to improve the visual fidelity of rendered content or to upsample a rendering performed at a lower resolution. Weiss *et al.* [20] used a deep learning-based architecture to upscale the resolution for iso-surface rendering. Nvidia recently introduced a super-sampling technique that uses a deep neural network and temporal history to accumulate samples [5]. Similarly, Xiao *et al.* [21] demonstrated up to 4×4 upsampling of highly aliased input. These methods, however, perform image reconstruction for surface-only rendered content. In our work, we focus on performing up to 8×8 super-resolution of volumetric visualization with high visual and temporal fidelity. Furthermore, most of these above methods propose to use motion information between frames to use temporal history, however, computing screen space motion information for volumetric rendering is not straightforward.

3   Methodology

In this section, we describe the overall framework of our system.

3.1   Direct Volume Rendering Framework

In our DVR framework, we cast rays from the camera through pixels of the viewport. When the ray reaches the volume contained in an axis-aligned bounding box, the ray is sampled via ray marching, i.e., stepped along at equal distances. At every step of the ray, a transfer function maps the interpolated intensity value at that position to an RGBA vector. As the ray steps through the volume, a local gradient is combined with a local illumination model to provide realistic shading of the object. The final pixel value is computed using front-to-back compositing of the acquired color and alpha (opacity) values along the ray. The ray is terminated early if either the accumulated opacity reaches close to 1 or the ray leaves the volume.

The issue with high-quality super-resolution for rendered content is that the information at the to-be-interpolated pixels at the target resolution is completely missing and since pixels are point-sampled, they are extremely aliased at geometry edges, especially at low resolution. An effective way to handle these aliasing artifacts is temporal anti-aliasing (TAA) which attempts to gather multiple samples per pixel by distributing the computations across multiple frames. Motivated by this, we implement a similar technique to perform super-resolution i.e., compute and gather multiple sub-pixel samples across frames and feed this information to our super-resolution network to upscale the low-resolution rendering. However, for volumetric rendering, accumulating samples from previous frames presents a few challenges which we discuss in the sections below.

3.1.1   Motion Vector and Depth In rendering, a motion vector defines an analytically computed screen-space location where a 3D point that is visible at the current frame i would appear in the previous frame $i-1$. The main principle of temporal methods to perform either anti-aliasing or upsampling is to compute multiple sub-pixel samples across frames, and then combine those together for the current frame. The samples from the previous frame are reprojected using the motion vector to the current frame. The input to our renderer is static volumetric data without any motion of its own, so performing reprojection using the motion vector depends entirely on the camera transformation matrices and depth information. Unfortunately for direct volume rendering, we lack this depth information since we are not looking at a single position in the world space but a

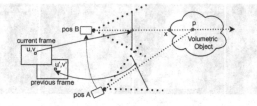

Fig. 2. Camera movement around a volumetric object from *posA* to *posB*. Point x is the first hit point on the volumetric object when the ray passes through the volume for the current camera position, while p is a point inside the volume where the alpha value is maximum along the ray.

number of points in the volume along the ray. Hence, computing motion vectors to perform reprojection is challenging.

To overcome this, we implement a naive approach where we use the point of maximum alpha along the ray to perform reprojection. Since this position will have the maximum contribution to the final accumulated sample, we found that this quasi-depth information computed using this heuristic gives an acceptable approximation for the estimation of motion vector. We start from the current frame coordinate u, v as shown in Fig. 2. Once we have the world space position for the point p in space where we have maximum alpha along the ray, we can use previous camera transformation matrices to reproject this position back to previous frame coordinates u', v'. The difference between the two frame coordinates gives us the screen space motion vector due to camera movement.

3.1.2 Disocclusion and Ghosting

Once we have the motion vector between two consecutive frames, we additionally incorporate temporal anti-aliasing to our final rendering with an additional compute shader call, thus adding a post-processing pass to our DVR pipeline. We utilize the history color buffer and motion vector to gather samples from the previous frame and combine them with the samples in the current frame. History samples can sometimes be invalid. Trivially accepting all of the history samples causes ghosting artifacts in the final rendered image because of disocclusion. As we move the camera, regions of the volume that were not previously visible may come into view. To address this issue, similar to [17,18], we resort to using neighborhood clamping which makes the assumption that colors within the neighborhood of the current sample are valid contributions to the accumulation process. Specifically, we implemented 3*3 neighborhood clamping which produced reasonably effective results for our volume rendering case.

3.1.3 Supplementary Features

Previous works on reconstruction networks for surface data [14,21] have shown that supplementing a network with additional features improves the overall performance of the network. This motivates us to opt for a few supplementary features adapted to our volumetric case. Xiao *et al.*

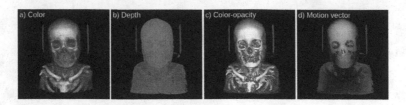

Fig. 3. Input feature images from the training dataset. From left to right: a) Final rendered color image with 3 channels RGB, b) Depth with a single channel and c) color-opacity vector (opacity is not shown) with 4 channels RGBA at the position where alpha is maximum along the ray; d) Example Motion vector image with 2 channels.

[21] showed that the reconstruction network benefits with depth as an additional input to the network, but as discussed in Sect. 3.1.1, depth information is not well defined for the volumetric case, so we resort to using the depth at the point of maximum alpha value along the ray since the final rendering will have more contribution from this point. Additionally, we also save color and opacity values at this point. When adding them as input, we are able to obtain additional gains with our network (Sect. 5.1).

In addition to feeding the network with rendered frames and supplementary features from the current and the previous time steps, we also provide a screen space 2D motion vector which is used to warp the previous frames to the current frame. Using optical flow or motion estimation is common in the video super-resolution literature (Sect. 2) to capture the temporal dependency between successive frames and to reduce the complexity of the network. Figure 3 shows all types of inputs that our network receives.

3.2   Network Architecture

Figure 4 depicts the data flow through our network. The overall network architecture has been inspired from Xiao *et al.* [21] with a number of modifications to suit our needs. We implement residual blocks to extract features from the input since they are easier to train and allow a better flow of information due to the presence of shortcut connections [7]. For our reconstruction network, we adopt a similar autoencoder architecture by Hofmann *et al.* [8] which has been successfully applied to volumetric data. For the loss formulation, we implement Charbonnier loss because of its benefits mentioned in Sect. 3.2.5.

3.2.1   Residual Block
The first component of the network is a residual block which is used to extract features from the input frames, where by 'input frames', we mean all the rendered color images from current and previous frames with their supplementary features excluding motion vector. The residual block we use in our network (Fig. 5) has two 3×3 convolutional layers. Each convolutional layer is followed by a rectified linear unit (ReLU) activation function. After the second convolutional layer, the output from the layer is added together with the

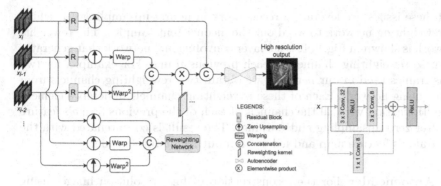

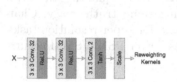

Fig. 4. Overall network architecture with components inspired from Xiao *et al.* [21] and Hofmann *et al.* [8]

Fig. 5. Residual block

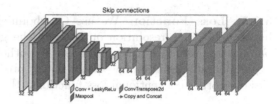

Fig. 6. Reweighting network

Fig. 7. Autoencoder for reconstruction of high resolution image

input to the residual block, before sending it to the final ReLU activation function. To transform the input into the desired shape for the addition operation, we introduce an additional 1×1 convolutional layer in the skip connection.

3.2.2 Zero Upsample and Warping We implement zero upsampling technique [21] to upscale the low-resolution input to the target resolution. In zero upsampling, every pixel in the low-resolution space is upsampled to be surrounded by pixels with zero values in high-resolution space. Once all the input frames and the feature maps (extracted from the residual block) are upsampled to target resolution, the previous frames and the corresponding feature maps are processed further with the warping module, where they are backward warped to align with the current frame with the help of motion vectors. All input frames (after zero upsampling and warping) are then concatenated and fed to a reweighting network as shown in Fig. 4.

3.2.3 Reweighting Network As discussed in Sect. 3.1.2, there are a few limitations associated with using motion vectors that prevent its direct use for accumulating history samples. In addition to disocclusion and ghosting, motion vectors do not reflect shading and lighting changes between two frames. To address these issues, we leverage a recent work in neural upsampling [21] which uses a reweighting network to weed out the inconsistent samples. The reweighting network is shown in Fig. 6. It is a 3 layer convolutional network that generates a pixel-wise reweighting channel for each previous frame. For example, for two previous frames used in our network, we obtain two reweighting channels from the reweighting network. Each of these reweighting channels undergoes elementwise multiplication with all the channels of each of the previous frame's feature maps (after zero upsampling and warping). The result is concatenated with the current frame's feature map and fed as an input to an autoencoder.

3.2.4 Autoencoder For the reconstruction of high-resolution images using the concatenated result from Sect. 3.2.3, we adopt a similar autoencoder network from Hofmann *et al.* [8]. It uses a fully convolutional encoder and decoder hierarchy with skip connections as shown in Fig. 7.

3.2.5 Loss Function We use Charbonnier loss [3] to quantify the error between the high-resolution output and the given ground truth image. Charbonnier loss is known to be insensitive to outliers and for super-resolution tasks, experimental evaluation has shown that it provides better PSNR/SSIM accuracies over other conventional loss functions [1].

$$L = \frac{1}{N} \sum_{i=0}^{N} \rho(y_i - z_i), \tag{1}$$

where, $\rho(x) = \sqrt{x^2 + \epsilon^2}, \epsilon = 1 \times 10^{-8}, z_i$ denotes the ground truth high resolution frame, and N denotes the number of pixels.

4   Dataset

In order to generate a high quality dataset, we incorporate 3 different volumetric data (CTA-Cardio: $512 \times 512 \times 321$, Manix: $512 \times 512 \times 460$, CTA Abdomen Panoramix: $441 \times 321 \times 215$) with different transfer functions. We render 36 videos from each volume data and each video contains 100 frames. Each of these videos start from a random camera position in the scene that is selected from a large candidate pool. We split the dataset generated from each scene into 3 sets: training (80%), validation (10%), and test (10%).

For ground truth high-resolution images, we render the volume data at 1920×1920 resolution with temporal anti-aliasing turned on. For low-resolution input, the temporal anti-aliasing feature is turned off and the images are rendered at varying resolutions: 480×480, 240×240, and 120×120. In image and video super-resolution literature, it is common practice to use blurred and downscaled versions of the original high-resolution image as low-resolution input to the network. In contrast, our low-resolution input is directly generated from our volume renderer. We train different networks to perform 4×4, 8×8, and up to 16×16 super-resolution with the respective combination of low and high-resolution images.

Table 1. Quantitative comparison between two networks: with and without the use of additional RGBA information from the point of maximum alpha

	With additional information		Without additional information	
Volume dataset	PSNR(dB)	SSIM	PSNR(dB)	SSIM
CTA-Cardio	38.09	0.9705	37.07	0.9683
Manix	37.92	0.9651	36.96	0.9631
CTA-Abdomen	31.89	0.9560	31.44	0.9557

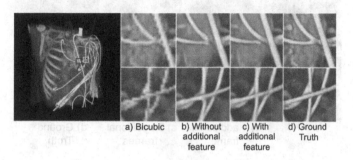

a) Bicubic   b) Without additional feature   c) With additional feature   d) Ground Truth

Fig. 8. Visual comparison for 8×8 upscaling with different techniques on the CTA-Cardio dataset. Images on the top and bottom row (enlarged sections of the blue and yellow boxes respectively) are from two different sections of CTA-Chest. a) represents input upscaled with bicubic interpolation. Comparing b) and c), we notice improved edges and details in the upscaled image when the super-resolution network is supplemented with additional RGBA information from the point of highest contribution

5 Evaluation

For the evaluation, we compare the performance of different variants of our network on Peak Signal To Noise Ratio (PSNR) and Structural Similarity Index (SSIM). The reported results are observed on the validation set.

5.1 Performance Gain with Additional Feature at the Input

As discussed in Sect. 3.1.3, including auxiliary features at the input generally benefits the network to achieve additional performance gain. In Table 1, we compare the observed performance metrics for all the three datasets when we include an additional feature at the input. The additional feature is the RGBA information obtained from the point of highest contribution along the ray. In addition to quantitative improvement in both PSNR and SSIM, we also observe improved edges and details in the reconstructed images as shown in Fig. 8.

5.2 Performance Gain with Additional Previous Frames

In Table 2, we report the quantitative evaluation of three different networks, each of which takes a different number of previous frames. We are able to make addi-

Table 2. Performance gain achieved with additional previous frames on CTA-Abdomen(table on the left) and CTA-cardio (table on the right) Dataset for 4×4 upsampling. N denotes the number of previous frames.

N	1	2	3	N	1	2	3
PSNR (dB)	31.86	32.60	32.98	PSNR (dB)	39.35	39.94	40.49
SSIM	0.9552	0.9606	0.9638	SSIM	0.9690	0.9755	0.9783

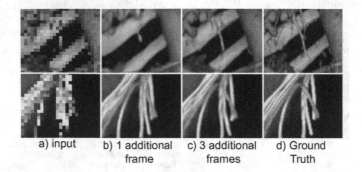

a) input   b) 1 additional   c) 3 additional   d) Ground
frame   frames   Truth

Fig. 9. Visual comparison for 4×4 upsampling on CTA-Abdomen and CTA-Cardio. a) is the input to two different networks: one takes a single previous frame whose output is in b), and the other takes up to 3 previous frames whose output is in c).

tional gains on both PSNR and SSIM with additional previous frames supplied to the network. In addition to improvements in the quality of the reconstructed image (Fig. 9), incorporating additional frames also improved the temporal stability of the reconstructed video sequence (video: youtu.be/1FZCQG0SBac).

Table 3. Quantitative comparison for various upsampling ratios on the Manix dataset

Upsampling ratio	4×4	8×8	16×16
PSNR(dB)	42.37	37.92	33.65
SSIM	0.9787	0.9651	0.9471

5.3   Upsampling Ratio

To test the limits of our super-resolution network, we take it one step further and perform up to $16 \times$ super-resolution. The observed PSNR and SSIM metrics are shown in Table 3. The target resolution for all the upsampling ratios was the same 1920×1920, while the input resolution varied according to the upsampling ratio. As the upsampling ratio increases, the quality of the reconstructed images steadily deteriorates and the network is unable to reconstruct the low-level features which are also evident from the images shown in Fig. 10.

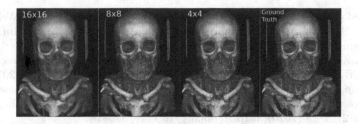

Fig. 10. Visual comparison for various upscaling ratios on the Manix dataset. For all images, target resolution was 1920 × 1920.

6   Conclusion and Future Work

In our work, we introduced a new pipeline to perform super-resolution for medical volume visualization. Our approach includes several adjustments tailored to the volumetric nature of the data. Despite our improvements, there are numerous future works that could be performed from here. Currently, all of our volumetric datasets are static volumetric data without any motion of their own. The introduction of dynamic volume will add more challenges to the system. Another future extension could be supplementing our network with additional volumetric features from multiple depths inside the volume. We believe this can further improve the reconstruction ability of the super-resolution network.

Furthermore, it should be noted that our system was designed for offline application and less importance was given to run-time performance. The current implementation of our network is able to perform super-resolution at an interactive frame rate of 10 fps (0.1018 s per frame). With run-time optimizations and integration of TensorRT, which can provide up to 6x faster accelerated inference [19], our system has the potential to achieve real-time frame-rate.

References

1. Anagun, Y., Isik, S., Seke, E.: Srlibrary: comparing different loss functions for super-resolution over various convolutional architectures. J. Vis. Commun. Image Represent. **61**, 178–187 (2019). https://doi.org/10.1016/j.jvcir.2019.03.027
2. Chan, K.C.K., Wang, X., Yu, K., Dong, C., Loy, C.C.: BasicVSR: the search for essential components in video super-resolution and beyond. CoRR abs/2012.02181 (2020). https://arxiv.org/abs/2012.02181
3. Charbonnier, P., Blanc-Feraud, L., Aubert, G., Barlaud, M.: Two deterministic half-quadratic regularization algorithms for computed imaging. In: Proceedings of 1st International Conference on Image Processing, vol. 2, pp. 168–172 (1994). https://doi.org/10.1109/ICIP.1994.413553
4. Dong, C., Loy, C.C., He, K., Tang, X.: Image super-resolution using deep convolutional networks. IEEE Trans. Pattern Anal. Mach. Intell. **38**(2), 295–307 (2016). https://doi.org/10.1109/TPAMI.2015.2439281
5. Edelsten, A., Jukarainen, P., Patney, A.: Truly next-gen: adding deep learning to games and graphics. In: NVIDIA Sponsored Sessions (Game Dev Conference) (2019)

6. Goodfellow, I., et al.: Generative adversarial nets. In: Ghahramani, Z., Welling, M., Cortes, C., Lawrence, N., Weinberger, K. (eds.) Advances in Neural Information Processing Systems. vol. 27. Curran Associates, Inc (2014)

7. He, K., Zhang, X., Ren, S., Sun, J.: Deep residual learning for image recognition. In: IEEE CVPR, pp. 770–778 (2016). https://doi.org/10.1109/CVPR.2016.90

8. Hofmann, N., Martschinke, J., Engel, K., Stamminger, M.: Neural denoising for path tracing of medical volumetric data. Proc. ACM Comput. Graph. Interact. Tech. **3**(2), 1–18 (2020). https://doi.org/10.1145/3406181

9. Isobe, T., Jia, X., Gu, S., Li, S., Wang, S., Tian, Q.: Video super-resolution with recurrent structure-detail network. ArXiv abs/2008.00455 (2020)

10. Jo, Y., Oh, S.W., Kang, J., Kim, S.J.: Deep video super-resolution network using dynamic upsampling filters without explicit motion compensation. In: IEEE CVPR, pp. 3224–3232 (2018). https://doi.org/10.1109/CVPR.2018.00340

11. Johnson, J., Alahi, A., Fei-Fei, L.: Perceptual losses for real-time style transfer and super-resolution. In: Leibe, B., Matas, J., Sebe, N., Welling, M. (eds.) ECCV 2016. LNCS, vol. 9906, pp. 694–711. Springer, Cham (2016). https://doi.org/10.1007/978-3-319-46475-6_43

12. Kim, J., Lee, J.K., Lee, K.M.: Accurate image super-resolution using very deep convolutional networks. In: IEEE CVPR, pp. 1646–1654 (2016). https://doi.org/10.1109/CVPR.2016.182

13. Kim, T.H., Sajjadi, M.S.M., Hirsch, M., Schölkopf, B.: Spatio-temporal transformer network for video restoration. In: ECCV (2018)

14. Koskela, M., et al.: Blockwise multi-order feature regression for real-time path-tracing reconstruction. ACM Trans. Graph. **38**(5), 1–14 (2019). https://doi.org/10.1145/3269978

15. Ledig, C., et al.: Photo-realistic single image super-resolution using a generative adversarial network. In: CVPR, pp. 105–114 (07 2017). https://doi.org/10.1109/CVPR.2017.19

16. Lim, B., Son, S., Kim, H., Nah, S., Lee, K.M.: Enhanced deep residual networks for single image super-resolution. In: IEEE CVPR Workshops, pp. 1132–1140 (2017). https://doi.org/10.1109/CVPRW.2017.151

17. Lottes, T.: TSSAA temporal super sampling AA (2011). https://timothylottes.blogspot.com/2011/04/tssaa-temporal-super-sampling-aa.html

18. Pedersen, L.J.F.P.: Temporal reprojection anti-aliasing in inside (2018). https://s3.amazonaws.com/arena-attachments/655504/c5c71c5507f0f8bf344252958254fb7d.pdf?1468341463

19. Sardana, A.: Accelerating inference up to 6x faster in pytorch with torch-tensorrt (2021). https://developer.nvidia.com/blog/accelerating-inference-up-to-6x-faster-in-pytorch-with-torch-tensorrt/

20. Weiss, S., Chu, M., Thuerey, N., Westermann, R.: Volumetric isosurface rendering with deep learning-based super-resolution. IEEE Trans. Vis. Comput. Graph. **27**(6), 3064–3078 (2021). https://doi.org/10.1109/TVCG.2019.2956697

21. Xiao, L., Nouri, S., Chapman, M., Fix, A., Lanman, D., Kaplanyan, A.: Neural supersampling for real-time rendering. ACM Trans. Graph. **39**(4), 142:1–142:2 (2020). https://doi.org/10.1145/3386569.3392376

22. Zhang, Y., Tian, Y., Kong, Y., Zhong, B., Fu, Y.: Residual dense network for image super-resolution. In: IEEE CVPR, pp. 2472–2481 (2018). https://doi.org/10.1109/CVPR.2018.00262

Interactive Virtual Reality Exploration of Large-Scale Datasets Using Omnidirectional Stereo Images

Thomas Marrinan[1,2]([✉]), Jifu Tan[3], Joseph A. Insley[2,3], Alina Kanayinkal[1], and Michael E. Papka[2,4]

[1] University of St. Thomas, St. Paul, MN 55105, USA
tmarrinan@stthomas.edu
[2] Argonne National Laboratory, Lemont, IL 60439, USA
[3] Northern Illinois University, DeKalb, IL 60115, USA
[4] University of Illinois Chicago, Chicago, IL 60607, USA

Abstract. Virtual reality offers unique affordances that can benefit the scientific discovery process. However, virtual reality applications must maintain very high frame rates to provide immersion and prevent adverse events such as visual fatigue and motion sickness. Maintaining high frame rates can be challenging when visualizing scientific data that is large in scale. One successful technique for enabling interactive exploration of large-scale datasets is to create a large image collection from a structured sampling of camera positions, time steps, and visualization operators. This paper highlights our work to adapt this technique for virtual reality, and uses two authentic scientific datasets – a) a large-scale simulation of cancer cell transport and capture in a microfluidic device and b) a large-scale molecular dynamics simulation of graphene for creating extremely low friction interactions. We create a collection of omnidirectional stereoscopic images (three-dimensional surround-view panoramas), each of which captures all possible view angles from a given location. Therefore, virtual reality devices can always render local movements at full frame rates without loading a new image from the collection.

Keywords: Virtual reality · Image-based graphics · Large-scale visualization

1 Introduction

Sensors and simulations are producing data at ever-increasing rates, with tasks such as genome sequencing [17] and modeling galaxy formation [15] currently generating many petabytes of data. To help scientists make sense of these massive troves of data, new analysis techniques will be needed. Visualization has long been a useful tool for interpreting data. However, traditional visualization techniques often come up short when rendering large, complex datasets – either failing to achieve interactive frame rates or requiring a reduction in data size.

© The Author(s), under exclusive license to Springer Nature Switzerland AG 2022
G. Bebis et al. (Eds.): ISVC 2022, LNCS 13598, pp. 115–128, 2022.
https://doi.org/10.1007/978-3-031-20713-6_9

The Exascale Computing Project has identified a number of objectives for next-generation visualization software. Among them is research to develop "post-hoc approach[es] that support interactive exploration and understanding of data" [11]. One emerging technique that supports this model for post-hoc, yet interactive, analysis is the Cinema image-based visualization technique [1]. The Cinema approach involves rendering many views of a large-scale dataset to an image database. This database can then be interactively explored post-hoc to provide a similar experience to real-time visualization systems.

Utilizing emerging display technologies will also be vital in the scientific discovery process. Virtual reality (VR) has moved beyond purely experimental and gaming platforms and is poised to aid in tasks such as training and analysis to support data understanding and decision making [6]. VR combines a stereoscopic three-dimensional (S3D) display with head tracking to create an immersive experience that has been shown to enhance engagement and understanding in many situations [18,19]. S3D visualizations can help with tasks such as depth estimation and mental rotations of 3D objects [8] and head tracking offers a more natural interface for changing one's view and manipulating a visualization.

In this paper, we highlight our work on adapting the Cinema image-based approach for interactive VR immersion. Our workflow involves using production quality rendering software to create omnidirectional stereoscopic (ODS) images, which provides a 360° panoramic S3D view. This enables VR devices, such as head mounted displays (HMDs), to always render local view changes due to head rotation at full frame rates without needing to load a new image from the database. We demonstrate the power of this technique through two science drivers. The first is a large-scale multiphysics simulation of blood flowing through a microfluidic device to help capture and detect the presence of circulating tumor cells [20]. The second is a molecular dynamics simulation that shows how graphene can be used to substantially reduce friction between nanodiamond particles and a surface of diamondlike carbon [3]. Finally, we detail the development of a VR application that enables users to interactively view the ODS Cinema database and we present a performance evaluation of viewing large-scale data in VR.

2   Related Work

To situate our work in the context of prior efforts, we looked at research on image-based visualization and viewing large-scale scientific data in virtual reality.

2.1   Image-Based Visualization

Cinema [1] leverages layer and image-based rendering techniques. From a given perspective multiple renderings are performed, which can include an array of different visualization techniques and data quantities. These images can then be combined, layered, or replaced in different ways to explore the data from this given perspective. Further, all of these same renderings can be performed from a variety of views from around the dataset and for each time step of a simulation. This results in a database of images which can provide valuable insight into the data, while requiring orders of magnitude less storage space and I/O time than saving the raw simulation data.

While 2D Cinema images can show the perceived 3D model on the scene with less space and rendering resources, it can not provide information related to depth effectively due to the lack of depth cues. Whang [22] proposed to use varying relative size of front planes, shading, and motion parallax to improve the 3D immersive experience for 2D Cinema viewers. However, their work still stopped short of leveraging immersive display technologies.

Another image-based approach proposed by Yong et al. [5] uses panoramic images to provide an interactive virtual reality experience. Because the images give a 360° view of the environment from a single position, the user can look in any direction without the need to update the frame. Pre-rendering these frames eliminates the need for special purpose hardware capable of rendering them in real time. This also enables the scene to be arbitrarily complex. Rendering the scene from numerous positions enables the user to explore the environment from various perspectives. Our work takes this idea a step further by enabling a truly dynamic experience whereby visualization parameters can be interactively updated in addition to camera position.

2.2 Virtual Reality for Large-Scale Data Sets

There has long been interest in using virtual reality for investigating large-scale datasets produced by high-performance computing (HPC) simulations. Faigle et al. [7] highlight some of the requirements when merging the HPC and VR spaces. At the forefront is the need for the update rate of the HPC computing engine to not be tied to the update rate of the VR environment. Virtual reality visualizations must be allowed to render at high frame rates and therefore cannot be tied to bottlenecks in the computation or processing of simulation data.

Lütjens et al. developed a VR application for large-scale terrain data [13]. Their approach relied on level-of-detail (LOD) model reduction, tiling, and level streaming to maintain high frame rates. LOD enabled features of the terrain close to the user to be rendered in full detail while those far away could use fewer triangles. Tiling splits the entire terrain model into separate smaller pieces, and level streaming is a technique that only renders tiles with a specific distance from the user. These techniques result in only needing to render a modest amount of geometry from any given view point. While these techniques are well suited for large-scale terrain data, other datasets may not cover such a large physical area and therefore have a much larger percentage of the data close to the user.

Another technique that attempted to enable high frame rate virtual reality for large-scale data was proposed by Ge et al. [9]. Their technique involved only rendering points (rather than triangular meshes) from large-scale models. They created a decoupled server-client system, whereby the server would determine which points would actually be visible to the user. This limited number of points were then streamed to the client responsible for visualizing the data. The client could rapidly re-render the current set of points as the user's head position changed. At slower intervals, the server could recompute the visible set of points based on larger movements within a scene. Thus a user's view may temporarily have holes that later fill themselves in as the client receives updates from the server. This decoupling of tasks allows the VR client applications to always render a reasonable amount of geometry and thus maintain high frame rates. Similarly, our approach aims to decouple updates to the scene from view updates initiated by VR user head movement in order to maintain high frame rates.

3 Science Drivers

For our work on interactive image-based VR exploration, we visualized data from two authentic large-scale scientific simulations.

3.1 Cancer Cell Transport

Detecting circulating tumor cells (CTCs) at earlier stages is crucial for patient diagnostics and treatment. Microfluidic devices can help capture and detect the presence of CTCs [20]. To inform design of such microfluidic devices, a large-scale multiphysics model of blood flow was constructed that consists of CTCs, red blood cells (RBCs), and blood plasma. RBCs and CTCs were simulated using the Large-scale Atomic/Molecular Massively Parallel Simulator (LAMMPS) [21] coupled with fluid flow that was solved using the Parallel Lattice Boltzmann Solver (Palabos) [12]. The simulation was created based on a representative unit from a device layout with a domain size of $260 \times 25 \times 500\,\mu m$, as shown in Fig. 1. The fluid data is spatial-temporal volumetric data with fluid pressure scalars and velocity vectors. The cell data is spatial-temporal surface data embedded in 3D space. The fluid stress tensor, derived from velocity, was calculated during post-processing and used to calculate the shear force applied to cell surfaces.

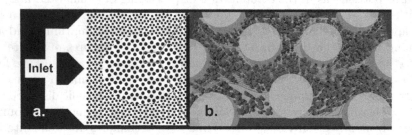

Fig. 1. (a) Microfluidic device with zoomed-in circular inset. The red box shows a representative unit for computational modeling. (b) Visualization of the simulation with RBCs (red), CTCs (green), streamlines (blue), and device microposts (beige). (Color figure online)

The simulation was performed on the Gaea high-performance computing cluster at Northern Illinois University. It took 34,560 core-hours to run 2.14 million time steps. After the first 400,000 time steps (used to reach quasi-equilibrium), RBC and CTC data was saved 1 out of every 10,000 time steps and fluid data was saved 1 out of every 25,000. With these output frequencies, cell and fluid outputs were not aligned and cell positions changed too much between successive time steps for viewing an animated visualization across time. Therefore a linear interpolation was used to generate intermediate data between raw time steps. The result was a total of 689 time steps that were saved, with each time step needing 74 MB for RBC data, 8 MB for CTC data, and 947 MB for the fluid data, thus consuming 709 GB of storage space for the entire simulation.

3.2 Graphene Superlubricity

Friction is the primary cause of mechanical energy dissipation in moving assemblies. Therefore, a large-scale molecular dynamics simulation was leveraged to gain insight on compounds that are capable of minimizing friction in a number of applications [3]. LAMMPS was used with the reactive force field (ReaxFF) module to simulate between 1.2 million and 10 million atoms, which provided insight on how graphene can wrap around nanodiamonds to form nanoscrolls with reduced contact area. This phenomenon creates superlubricity, but only in dry envrionments. The large-scale simulations (which took into account position, velocity, element type, molecular structure, and interatomic potentials for each individual atom) elucidated how the presence of a water layer inhibited scroll formation, and therefore caused higher friction.

Computations were performed on the Mira supercomputer at the Argonne Leadership Computing Facility. Each simulation used 16,000 nodes and took 2–4 million core-hours to run 50–100 million time steps. This work used data from one run that simulated a dry environment in which the graphene exhibited the nanoscrolling behavior. There were a total of 1,020 saved time steps, with raw atomic position and bond connectivity data only consuming 32.3 GB, but polygonal geometric data for atoms and bonds needing 4.8 TB storage space.

4   Cinema ODS Image Database

Often times, data from large-scale simulations are too big or complex to render at the high frame rates necessary for virtual reality applications. For example, there are approximately 3.3 million triangles and 87.7 million triangles in the models for each time step in the cancer cell transport and graphene superlubricity simulations respectively. While such scenes can be rendered in real-time, there are some drawbacks when doing so for VR. First, only more simple rendering techniques can be employed. Second, while able to be rendered at decent frame rates on a machine with a powerful GPU, they still may not be high enough for VR. Additionally, standalone VR devices are not powerful enough to render massive amounts of geometry – the Oculus Quest 2, for example, can only render approximately 1 million triangles while maintaining full frame rates [16].

Due to these limitations, and the fact that many HPC simulations output even larger and more complex models, we investigated leveraging non real-time rendering paired with image-based visualization for creating an interactive experience. To accomplish this, we adapted the Cinema image-based approach. Rather than using traditional planar rendering however, images are rendered in ODS format, thus providing S3D depth cues and a full 360° view of the data from a single image (see Fig. 2). When viewed in a VR application, this allows users to modify their view direction without loading a new image from the collection. Therefore updates to the visualization are decoupled from updates to a user's view, enabling VR devices to always maintain full refresh rates.

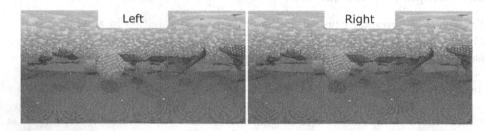

Fig. 2. Omnidirectional stereo rendering of a single time step from the graphene superlubricity simulation. Left and right portions are views for the left and right eye respectively, with each capturing a full 360° view of the scene.

The resulting Cinema ODS database will contain numerous images of a dataset representing different views, time steps, and visualization operators. Since the Cinema specification also supports additional files to be associated with each entry in the database, we also decided to support ODS videos. These videos can encapsulate all time steps – one video per combination of camera position/visualization operator. The purpose of the videos is to enable users to animate the visualization for a particular chosen set of visualization operators more efficiently than consecutively loading each image in a time series.

One caveat with using ODS images and videos is that they need to be rendered at fairly high resolutions. This is because only a fraction of the image is visible to a VR user when looking in any given direction. A recent survey of existing 360° images and videos concluded that the minimum resolution should be 3840×1920 pixels (per eye) in order to provide an immersive experience [23].

4.1   Rendering

Since a Cinema ODS database is created a priori, this also provides an opportunity to create higher quality visualizations using non real-time techniques. Therefore, the ODS images for both the cancer cell transport and graphene superlubricity databases were rendered using Blender 3.0 [4], a high-quality rendering software for 3D modeling and animation. Blender was chosen over other professional rendering software for two primary reasons – it is open-source and therefore easy to install on HPC systems, and it has a Python scripting interface making it easy to render many images in batch mode without user interaction.

ODS images for both databases used *pole merging* – a technique that reduces the interocular distance near the poles of the projection sphere. This technique has been shown to reduce visual discomfort associated with ODS binocular misalignment artifacts without negating the benefits stereo depth cues [14].

Custom materials were created and more advanced rendering techniques were utilized in order to create detailed visualizations. Between the two datasets, features such as bump/displacement mapping, transparency, reflections, global illumination, and shadows were used (see Fig. 3). Many of those techniques are often too complex to leverage when performing real-time rendering but can enhance the realism of a visualization and better enable data to be interpreted. Render style can also easily be made one of the visualization parameters of a Cinema ODS database if preference is unclear, thus enabling users to toggle between basic and high-quality renderings.

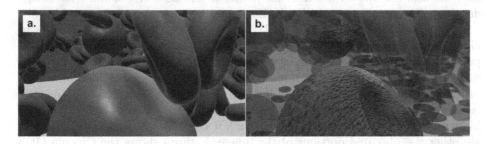

Fig. 3. Comparison of basic vs. high-quality materials and rendering. (a) Basic materials (smooth plastic-like look) and rendering (no transparency or shadows, local illumination). (b) High-quality materials (bump/displacement mapping to provide realistic texture) and rendering (transparency and shadows, global illumination).

The cancer cell transport image database contains 16,536 images – 689 time steps each with 24 permutations of visualization operators (three camera positions, with/without streamlines, cells colored solid vs. by magnitude of shear force, and RBCs rendered opaque vs. semi-transparent). The graphene superlubricity image database contains 4,080 images – 1020 time steps each with 4 permutations of visualization operators (two camera positions and with/without molecule bonds). Each ODS image was rendered at a resolution of 3840 × 3840 pixels encoded in JPEG format with a quality setting of 92/100. The resulting images for all time steps of each set of visualization parameters were then combined into WEBM videos using VP9 encoding and a playback speed of 24 frames per second with average bitrates between 31.4 Mbps and 38.7 Mbps.

Two HPC resources were used for rendering the cancer cell transport and graphene superlubricity databases – the Pittsburgh Supercomputing Center's

Bridges-2 and the Argonne Leadership Computing Facility's ThetaGPU. Rendering processes were distributed amongst many nodes/GPUs, whereby each process was responsible for rendering a fraction of the images in the entire database. For larger datasets that cannot fit in the memory of a single GPU/node, it would be possible to generate the image database by performing distributed rendering – splitting data needed for each single image amongst many processes.

5   Interactive Cinema ODS Viewer

We developed an interactive VR viewing application for Cinema databases that contain ODS images. The viewer application currently supports Cinema's *Spec D* specification, where each combination of available visual parameters corresponds to a pre-rendered image in the database. The application was developed using Babylon.js [2] with WebXR support. This choice was made since WebXR supports a wide variety of VR devices and the application is accessible via a web browser – no download or installation required. Once navigating to the web site, the user can specify a URL that points to the desired Cinema ODS image database. The database can either be hosted by a remote server or loaded locally.

A 3D graphical user interface (GUI) is dynamically generated based on visualization parameters present in the Cinema ODS database. The application supports three types of GUI elements – sliders, checkboxes, and radio buttons. Sliders are used for numeric parameters with regular intervals. Checkboxes are used for boolean parameters. Radio buttons are used for categorical parameters. Additionally, a 'play' button is created if video files are present. The GUI can be hidden, re-shown, or re-positioned using a VR controller, thus allowing users to see otherwise obscured portions of the image. Figure 4 shows the Cinema ODS viewer application and GUI for the graphene superlubricity dataset.

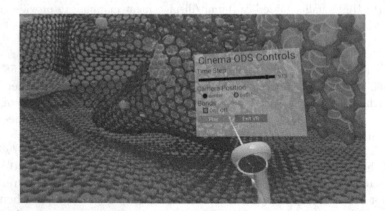

Fig. 4. Interactive virtual reality view of the Cinema ODS viewer application. The dynamically generated GUI on the middle-right part of the figure enables users to interactively modify visualization parameters present in the database.

Once a dataset is loaded in the Cinema ODS viewer, the GUI is created and the first image is loaded and used as a texture for a photo dome (large sphere that surrounds the camera). Subsequent updates to the GUI will trigger the viewer application to find the corresponding image in the database and update the photo dome's texture. Two photo domes are used, with only one visible at any given time, to double buffer image swaps. This prevents flickering between the time the new image is selected (thus unloading the prior image) and the time the new image is fully decoded and uploaded as a texture.

Pressing the 'play' button will trigger streaming of the appropriate ODS video (starting at the frame that corresponds to the currently viewed time step). Subsequent frames in the video will continuously be used to update the photo dome's texture. Pressing 'pause', having the video run to completion, or modifying any other GUI element will switch back to using images for the photo dome. The Cinema ODS viewing application is accessible at https://argonne-lcf.github.io/cinema-ods/. Source code can also be downloaded and run locally.

6   Evaluation

To evaluate the image-based VR workflow, we measured the performance of interactive exploration for large-scale datasets. First, we evaluated latency when updating the Cinema ODS visualization. To do so, we tested the viewer application under three different scenarios – remotely hosted image database accessed via 50 Mbps WiFi, remotely hosted image database accessed via 1 Gbps Ethernet, and locally hosted image database. A Windows laptop with an AMD Ryzen 9 4900 HS processor and 16 GB of RAM was used for all three scenarios.

We also evaluated the frame rate of the VR application to compare the rendering performance of image-based VR with traditional 3D rendering. The geometric models for both science datasets were converted to glTF format, a compressed format specifically designed for 3D geometric meshes [10]. Frame rates were measured using the Oculus Quest 2 as a standalone device and tethered to a Windows desktop with an NVIDIA RTX 3060 Ti GPU.

6.1   Visualization Latency

We wanted to measure the average latency in the WebXR viewer application. For this, we timed the delay between when a user selected a new option from the GUI and when the corresponding image from the database was displayed on the photo dome. The overall latency is comprised of three components – 1) time to select proper image in the database based on change to the GUI, 2) time to download the image from the hosting server to the VR application, and 3) time to decode the JPEG image and apply it as a texture on the photo dome.

Latency was measured under three conditions – remotely hosted image database accessed via 50 Mbps WiFi, remotely hosted image database accessed via 1 Gbps Ethernet, and locally hosted image database. A total of 48 images from each of the Cinema ODS databases were loaded under each test condition (representing all combinations of visualization options at a sample of time steps). Average latency results are summarized in Table 1.

Table 1. Average image update latency.

	50 Mbps WiFi	1 Gbps ethernet	Local
Select	1.1 ms	1.0 ms	1.0 ms
Download	485.8 ms	33.0 ms	13.7 ms
Decode/Texture	95.7 ms	95.4 ms	96.5 ms
Total	**582.6 ms**	**129.4 ms**	**111.2 ms**

On average, the Cinema ODS viewer application could achieve a visualization update rate of 1.7 images per second when using a 50 Mbps WiFi connection, 7.7 images per second when using a 1 Gbps Ethernet connection, and 9.0 images per second when hosting the database locally. While the image update rate is limited, the application can still update as a user looks around a given ODS image at the full refresh rate supported by the VR device.

On the 50 Mbps WiFi, image download time was the main source of latency. However, when using either 1 Gbps Ethernet or locally hosted image database, latency was dominated by decoding the JPEG and uploading it as a texture. Therefore, even though using a locally hosted the image database resulted in 2.41× faster downloads, the overall latency was only 1.16× less. This means that entire image databases can reside on remote servers without major degradation to image update rates as long as a sufficient network connection is used.

The Cinema ODS viewer application supports ODS videos that encode all time steps for each set of visualization parameters. Under all three network conditions, videos were able to smoothly play at the full 24 frames per second that they were encoded with. This was expected since the bandwidth of even the slowest network connection evaluated exceeded the average bitrate of the videos.

6.2 VR Frame Rate

In addition to update latency, we also wanted to compare the frame rate of viewing ODS images to the actual 3D geometry in virtual reality. Two separate VR applications were used – one that loaded a single image from the Cinema ODS database and one that loaded a single time steps' worth of 3D geometry rendered with basic materials and lighting. We ran the applications for 15 s while a user looked around the scene and measured how many frames the VR application could render. Both applications were tested using two separate hardware configurations – a standalone Oculus Quest 2, and a Windows desktop with an NVIDIA RTX 3060 Ti GPU tethered to the Oculus Quest 2 via link cable. Both science datasets were tested under each condition, with the cancer cell transport models containing approximately 3.3 million triangles and the graphene superlubricity models containing approximately 87.7 million triangles. Results for the average number of frames per second (fps) that could be achieved in each situation are summarized in Table 2.

Table 2. Average frames per second in a virtual reality application.

	Cancer cell transport		Graphene superlubricity	
	Cinema ODS	3D Models	Cinema ODS	3D Models
Standalone device (Quest 2)	89.8 fps	38.5 fps	89.8 fps	N/A
Tethered device (RTX 3060 Ti)	89.8 fps	89.8 fps	89.8 fps	43.5 fps

The first thing to note about the frame rates is that the Cinema ODS virtual reality application was always able to maintain full refresh rates (89.8 fps on the device'90 Hz display) regardless of the complexity of the underlying data or the power of the VR hardware. Rendering the 3D models, on the other hand, depended significantly on both the data's complexity and the VR hardware. When viewing the less complex geometry from the cancer cell transport simulation, a VR device tethered to the RTX 3060 Ti GPU could actually render the scene at full frame rates. However, the lower powered standalone device was only able to achieve 42.8% of its full frame rate. When viewing the more complex geometry from the graphene superlubricity simulation, even the tethered VR device struggled – achieving only 48.3% of its full frame rate. The standalone device wasn't even able to render the more complex scene at all, likely due to insufficient memory to store all the geometric data for the models.

As frame rates fail to match the refresh rate of the VR display, and especially as they dip below 60 fps, user experience begins to degrade. Low frame rates can cause adverse events, such as visual fatigue and sickness. Therefore, it is a critical component of our image-based VR technique that full frame rates can always be achieved. This makes our Cinema ODS approach well suited for interacting with large-scale datasets in virtual reality.

6.3 Qualitative Feedback

This work focused on developing the technology for enabling interactive image-based VR, and therefore a formal user evaluation was out of scope. However, we did have both a science researcher (blood flow expert) and members of the development team (i.e. not domain experts) use the system. According to the blood flow expert, the immersive VR application showed several important features that were not immediately apparent when viewing the data in ParaView. First, the egocentric view with head tracking enabled him to conveniently compare the spatially varying information at the interior of the simulation space. This was a task that had been difficult to achieve using standard planar projections where the camera is positioned outside the data domain.

Another benefit of investigating the data in VR was the ability to provide a first-person view along a stream path, moving along with the surrounding cells. Particularly insightful was the ability to see the effect of collisions with neighbors on cell trajectories. The traditional planar view of the data in ParaView was great at capturing the overall flow behavior. However, analyzing the relative motion and inter-cell collisions between cells was more informative in the VR application due to the stereo depth cues, egocentric view, and natural interaction for controlling the view direction.

For those who weren't domain experts, the immersive VR application provided an intuitive visualization without knowing the underlying scientific mechanics. Non-experts also noted that the interactivity provided by our Cinema ODS technique resulted in a more engaging application that better enabled data investigation as compared to simply watching a cinematic VR video.

7   Conclusion

This paper described an image-based technique for interactively viewing large-scale datasets in virtual reality. By rendering a database of omnidirectional stereoscopic images and videos, updates to the visualization became decoupled from updates to a user's view. This decoupling is critical for maintaining the high refresh rates necessary for VR applications.

We developed an image-based VR application that supports Cinema databases where images are rendered in ODS format. We tested the performance of both image update latency and viewing frame rate. For image update latency, our results showed a modest update rate (1.7–9.0 images per second). However, since this image update rate is decoupled from view updates based on a user's head movements, the VR application can always maintain full refresh rates. Therefore an approximately 100–600 ms delay between modifying a visualization parameter and seeing the update seems quite reasonable. For viewing frame rates, we compared image-based VR to standard rendering of 3D geometry. For our two large-scale datasets, the image-based VR was always able to maintain a frame rate equivalent to the display's refresh rate (90 Hz), whereas frame rate varied greatly (often well below interactive rates) depending on data complexity and graphics hardware when rendering 3D geometry in VR.

In the future, we would like to integrate Cinema ODS database creation in situ. I/O is a bottleneck for many HPC simulations. It would be advantageous to render data as its being simulated. This would result in more accurate visualizations as well as greatly reduce the output data size since rendered image data is often significantly smaller than raw simulation data. Additionally, we would like to add support for depth-augmented stereo panoramas and visualization layers. While traditional ODS images provide S3D depth cues and a full 360° view, they do not allow for head movement (side-to-side or up-and-down). Encoding depth information into ODS images would enable a small amount of head motion parallax that would create a more immersive experience. Adding layer support would update our viewer application from using Cinema's more basic *Spec D* specification to the more advanced *CIS* specification and potentially reduce the number of images needed in a database. Finally, we plan to conduct a formal study to evaluate the benefits of interactively viewing large-scale scientific datasets in an immersive image-based visualization application.

Acknowledgements. This research was supported in part by the Argonne Leadership Computing Facility, which is a U.S. Department of Energy Office of Science User Facility operated under contract DE-AC02-06CH11357. This work also used the Extreme Science and Engineering Discovery Environment (XSEDE) Bridges-2 at the Pittsburgh Supercomputing Center through allocation CIS210066, which is supported by National Science Foundation grant number ACI-1548562. We would also like to acknowledge the Center for Research Computing and Data at Northern Illinois University, where computations were performed on their Gaea high-performance computing cluster. Finally, we would like to thank Michael Hood and Subramanian Sankaranarayanan for their contributions towards generating the data from the science driver simulations.

References

1. Ahrens, J., Jourdain, S., O'Leary, P., Patchett, J., Rogers, D.H., Petersen, M.: An image-based approach to extreme scale in situ visualization and analysis. In: SC 2014: Proceedings of the International Conference for High Performance Computing, Networking, Storage and Analysis, pp. 424–434 (2014). https://doi.org/10.1109/SC.2014.40
2. Babylon.js. https://www.babylonjs.com/. Accessed 01 Mar 2022
3. Berman, D., Deshmukh, S.A., Sankaranarayanan, S.K.R.S., Erdemir, A., Sumant, A.V.: Macroscale superlubricity enabled by graphene nanoscroll formation. Science **348**(6239), 1118–1122 (2015). https://doi.org/10.1126/science.1262024
4. Blender online community: blender - a 3D modelling and rendering package. https://www.blender.org. Accessed 01 Mar 2022
5. Cai, Y., Heng, P., Wu, E., Liu, X., Li, H., Sun, Q.: An image-based virtual reality prototype system. J. Comput. Sci. Technol. **13**(5), 475–480 (1998). https://doi.org/10.1007/BF02948507. Sep
6. Dwyer, T., et al.: Immersive analytics: an introduction. In: Immersive Analytics. LNCS, vol. 11190, pp. 1–23. Springer, Cham (2018). https://doi.org/10.1007/978-3-030-01388-2_1
7. Faigle, C., Fox, G., Furmanski, W., Niemiec, J., Simoni, D.: Integrating virtual environments with high performance computing. In: Proceedings of IEEE Virtual Reality Annual International Symposium, pp. 62–68 (1993). https://doi.org/10.1109/VRAIS.1993.380797
8. Gaggioli, A., Breining, R.: Perception and cognition in immersive virtual reality. In: Emerging Communication: Studies on New Technologies and Practices in Communication. IOS Press (2001)
9. Ge, J., et al.: Point-based VR visualization for large-scale mesh datasets by real-time remote computation. In: Proceedings of the 2006 ACM International Conference on Virtual Reality Continuum and Its Applications, pp. 43–50. VRCIA 2006 (2006). https://doi.org/10.1145/1128923.1128931
10. glTF™. https://www.khronos.org/gltf/. Accessed 10 May 2022

11. Heroux, M.A., et al.: ECP software technology capability assessment report-public. Technical report, US Department of Energy's Exascale Computing Initiative (2020)
12. Latt, J., et al.: Palabos: parallel lattice Boltzmann solver. Comput. Math. Appl. **81**, 334–350 (2021). https://doi.org/10.1016/j.camwa.2020.03.022
13. Lütjens, M., Kersten, T.P., Dorschel, B., Tschirschwitz, F.: Virtual reality in cartography: immersive 3D visualization of the arctic Clyde inlet (Canada) using digital elevation models and bathymetric data. Multimodal Technol. Interact. **3**(1), 9 (2019). https://doi.org/10.3390/mti3010009
14. Marrinan, T., Papka, M.E.: Real-time omnidirectional stereo rendering: generating 360° surround-view panoramic images for comfortable immersive viewing. IEEE Trans. Vis. Comput. Graph. **27**(5), 2587–2596 (2021). https://doi.org/10.1109/TVCG.2021.3067780
15. Nelson, D., et al.: The IllustrisTNG simulations: public data release. Comput. Astrophy. Cosmo. **6**(1), 2 (2019). https://doi.org/10.1186/s40668-019-0028-x. May
16. Oculus for developers: performance and optimization. https://developer.oculus.com/documentation/unity/unity-perf. Accessed 16 Feb 2022
17. Schatz, M.C., Langmead, B.: The DNA data deluge: fast, efficient genome sequencing machines are spewing out more data than geneticists can analyze. IEEE Spectr. **50**(7), 26–33 (2013). https://doi.org/10.1109/MSPEC.2013.6545119
18. Schuchardt, P., Bowman, D.A.: The benefits of immersion for spatial understanding of complex underground cave systems. In: Proceedings of the 2007 ACM Symposium on Virtual Reality Software and Technology, pp. 121–124. VRST 2007 (2007). https://doi.org/10.1145/1315184.1315205
19. Sowndararajan, A., Wang, R., Bowman, D.A.: Quantifying the benefits of immersion for procedural training. In: Proceedings of the 2008 Workshop on Immersive Projection Technologies/Emerging Display Technologies. IPT/EDT 2008 (2008). https://doi.org/10.1145/1394669.1394672
20. Tan, J., Ding, Z., Hood, M., Li, W.: Simulation of circulating tumor cell transport and adhesion in cell suspensions in microfluidic devices. Biomicrofluidics **13**(6), 064105 (2019). https://doi.org/10.1063/1.5129787
21. Thompson, A.P., et al.: LAMMPS - a flexible simulation tool for particle-based materials modeling at the atomic, meso, and continuum scales. Comput. Phys. Commun. **271**, 108171 (2022). https://doi.org/10.1016/j.cpc.2021.108171
22. Whang, J.: Improving the perception of depth of image-based objects in a virtual environment. Master's thesis, Virginia Polytechnic Institute and State University (2020)
23. Xu, M., Li, C., Zhang, S., Callet, P.L.: State-of-the-art in 360° video/image processing: perception, assessment and compression. IEEE J. Sel. Top. Sign. Process. **14**(1), 5–26 (2020). https://doi.org/10.1109/JSTSP.2020.2966864

A Quantitative Analysis of Labeling Issues in the CelebA Dataset

Bryson Lingenfelter, Sara R. Davis$^{(\boxtimes)}$, and Emily M. Hand

University of Nevada, Reno, USA
sarad@nevada.unr.edu

Abstract. Facial attribute prediction is a facial analysis task that describes images using natural language features. While many works have attempted to optimize prediction accuracy on CelebA, the largest and most widely used facial attribute dataset, few works have analyzed the accuracy of the dataset's attribute labels. In this paper, we seek to do just that. Despite the popularity of CelebA, we find through quantitative analysis that there are widespread inconsistencies and inaccuracies in its attribute labeling. We estimate that at least one third of all images have one or more incorrect labels, and reliable predictions are impossible for several attributes due to inconsistent labeling. Our results demonstrate that classifiers struggle with many CelebA attributes not because they are difficult to predict, but because they are poorly labeled. This indicates that the CelebA dataset is flawed as a facial analysis tool and may not be suitable as a generic evaluation benchmark for imbalanced classification.

1 Introduction

CelebA is a widely used face dataset which contains $202,599$ images of $10,177$ people labeled with 40 binary facial attributes such as *big nose*, *bushy eyebrows*, *gray hair*, and *smiling*. The dataset was derived from the CelebFaces dataset, with attribute annotations provided by a "professional labeling company" [12]. CelebA attribute labels have proven useful for a variety of tasks including face recognition [21], semantic segmentation [9], detection and landmarking [16], and face editing [6]. Data is provided as both the original, in-the-wild images, and in a cropped and aligned format.

Despite the popularity of the dataset, we find there are a multitude of widespread, unaddressed attribute labeling issues. While the subjectivity of many attributes in the dataset makes complete analysis challenging, the majority of labels we are able to analyze have a large number of errors or inconsistencies. We use several techniques to evaluate label quality. We first create a list of contradicting attributes and find that 6.78% of images are labeled with attributes which directly contradict one another. We then relabel a random sample of 800 images for all non-subjective attributes and find that some attributes have false positive rates as high as 25%, while others have false negative rates as high as 22%. To evaluate subjective attributes, we use age estimation and semantic

G. Bebis et al. (Eds.): ISVC 2022, LNCS 13598, pp. 129–141, 2022.
https://doi.org/10.1007/978-3-031-20713-6_10

segmentation to provide estimates of age and feature size, and compare these estimates with the binary attributes in CelebA. We find that such attributes are highly inconsistent with these more fine-grained measures, preventing even near-state-of-the-art classifiers from achieving reasonable performance. Finally, we show that some attributes are correlated in ways that cannot be explained by dataset imbalance, indicating incorrect labeling or gender and racial bias. In total, we determine that at least 10 of the 40 attributes in CelebA have major issues such as frequent contradictions, incorrect labels, or significant inconsistency, and that most others suffer from sufficiently poor agreement to call into question their relevance as identity-specific features for downstream face processing tasks.

The remainder of this paper is organized as follows: in Sect. 2, we discuss related work. In Sect. 3, we estimate the number of labels which are categorically incorrect. Most CelebA labels are subjective and cannot be directly described as "correct" or "incorrect," so in Sect. 4 we analyze the consistency and agreement of subjective labels. Finally, we conclude in Sect. 5.

2   Related Work

Many previous works have used the CelebA dataset to evaluate attribute prediction and imbalanced classification methods [3,8,9,22]. Although the facial attributes were originally intended for improving face verification, CelebA has become popular as a generic benchmark for imbalanced classification [3,7,22]. However, few works have provided analysis of labeling issues. Hand et. al. [5] argue that the poor performance of state-of-the-art classifiers on many attributes is caused by ambiguous labeling, and provide examples of poor labels for the attributes *oval face, attractive, high cheekbones*, and *arched eyebrows*. They also show that many images labeled with *lipstick* are incorrectly labeled. However, they do not perform any dataset-wide analysis to properly assess the scope of these issues. Prior work has shown that there exist prevalent errors in common image benchmarks, and that these errors can impair comparison between methods [13]. However, these works generally only analyze datasets such as CIFAR and MNIST, for which each sample has a single label and error can be represented as confusion between a set of classes [14,23]. No comparable analysis exists for CelebA, which is difficult to definitely estimate label error for because each image can be labelled with any number of attributes, most of which are subjective. Other work on label errors largely focuses on accounting for them during training, rather than identifying and describing label error in a test set [19].

There has also been some work discussing the bias caused by subjective labeling and dataset imbalance. Prabhu et. al. [15] show that increasing the contribution of labels such as *attractive* and *wearing lipstick* to a generative model causes images to look like blond, white women. Wang et. al. [20] show that the imbalance present in CelebA results in classifiers amplifying bias. Other works have shown that bias amplification is an issue in large scale datasets exhibiting imbalance [24]. However, to our knowledge no other work has performed

Table 1. Contradicting attribute labels. % is the percentage of images in the full dataset with the label in the left column and a contradicting label from the middle column.

Label	Contradictions	%
No beard	5 o'Clock shadow, goatee, mustache	4.0%
5 o'clock shadow	goatee, mustache, no beard	47.9%
Straight hair	Wavy Hair	2.7%
Bald	Bangs, receding hairline, straight hair, wavy hair	33.3%

quantitative analysis of labeling issues in CelebA. We show that many CelebA labels, in addition to being subjective and imbalanced as shown in prior work, are frequently inconsistent or even completely incorrect.

3   Incorrect Labels

We first focus on labels which can be directly shown to be incorrect. For subjective labels, we do this by identifying contradicting labels. For non-subjective labels, we manually relabel random samples to determine the frequency of incorrect labels. Note that the random sampling is meant to demonstrate that there are data discrepancies, and to extrapolate the results to the entire dataset. We argue that the size of the dataset and the random selection provide a relatively accurate value of mislabeling, though it should not be considered the final ground truth: that can only be identified by relabeling the entire dataset, which is not a reasonable expectation for the scope of this paper.

3.1   Contradicting and Conflicting Labels

To determine the prevalence of incorrect labels for subjective attributes, we first count the number of labels which are contradicting (in direct opposition to one another). For example, it is not possible to have both *straight hair* and *wavy hair*. To determine how many labels in CelebA directly contradict another label, we define a list of all contradicting attributes. This is shown in Table 1. *No beard* contradicts with all facial hair labels other than *sideburns*. Depending on definition, *sideburns* may also contradict with *no beard*, but we find that this only applies to 128 images (0.06% of the dataset) so we do not include it. Similarly, *5 o'clock shadow* contradicts with other facial hair, *straight hair* contradicts with *wavy hair*, and *bald* contradicts with all hair labels. We find that 6.78% of images have at least one contradicting label based on this list, and that *bald* and *5 o'clock shadow* contradict with another label in one third or more images labeled with these attributes.

We also find that there are many labels, which, while not necessarily contradicting, conflict with one another. For example, a subject with light brown hair might be labeled both *brown hair* and *blond hair*. 2.33% of images labeled with

Fig. 1. The first four images in CelebA labeled as *double chin* but not *chubby*. None of these images contain a double chin.

a hair color are labeled with multiple hair colors, most commonly either both *brown hair* and *black hair* or *brown hair* and *blond hair* due to the unclear separation between classes. We also find that 38.1% of images labeled with *double chin* are not labeled with *chubby*. While *double chin* does not necessitate *chubby*, this is frequently indicative of bad labeling, as shown in Fig. 1. Similarly, while hair color labels don't contradict with *bald* because they may refer to facial hair, we find that this is very rarely the case. If we add these conflicts to our list of contradictions, we find that 9.84% of the dataset contains at least one pair of contradicting labels, and the contradiction frequency for bald rises by 9.0% to 42.3%.

3.2   Mislabeling

The absolute number of incorrect labels cannot be determined without relabeling the entire dataset, so we instead estimate labeling error by manually verifying a random sample. For each attribute for which labels can be clearly identified as correct or incorrect, we construct one randomly sampled subset of 400 images containing only positive instances, then another containing only negative instances. We then manually verify the correctness of the labels. To avoid sampling bias, a random seed of 0 is used for all attribute samples. We find that there are very few entirely non-subjective labels in CelebA; of the 40 total attributes, only 7 can be clearly defined. Error counts for these attributes along with their corresponding estimates of the mean and standard error for our sample count are shown in Table 2.

Note that images are only marked as incorrect in cases of clear error. *Eyeglasses* and the *wearing_** attributes are marked as false negatives if the clothing item is clearly in the image when labeled negatively, and as false positives if the clothing item is clearly not image when labeled positively. *Mouth slightly open* is marked as correct or incorrect according to the definition "visible space between lips." Although "slightly" implies there exists some upper bound to how open the mouth is, the dataset is consistently labeled with the assumption that any degree of open indicates "slightly open." Any alternative definition would drastically increase the number of false positives. *Wearing hat* also has a small amount of ambiguity. For our analysis we assume that hoods and bandanas count as hats. Without this assumption, the number of false positives rise to 26 and false negatives drop to 5. While using a binary label for gender assigned according to the opinion of a labeler is in itself questionable, for the purpose of this analysis we maintain CelebA's classification and only mark a *Male* label as definitively

Fig. 2. Examples of false positives (left to right): *eyeglasses, wearing earrings, wearing hat,* and *wearing necktie.*

"wrong" when the pictured person has consistently identified as the opposite of the gender with which they were labeled.

Examples of incorrectly labeled images are shown in Fig. 2. In addition to incorrect labels, we find that in 86 images (21.5%) correctly labeled as *wearing necklace*, the necklace is entirely cropped out in the aligned version. In many more images, the necklace is visible but too small or similar to clothing to be noticeable. This makes accurately predicting *wearing necklace* near-impossible for the aligned version of the dataset.

To estimate the total number of images in CelebA which have at least one error, we assume that attribute error rates are independent (i.e., one attribute being wrong does not make another attribute more likely to be wrong), and therefore that the likelihood of any error can be computed as $P(err) = P(err_{a_1}) \cdot P(err_{a_2}) \cdot ...$, where $P(err_{a_i}$ is the probability of attribute a_i being incorrectly labelled. Because details regarding label collection are not public, it is difficult to determine the extent to which this assumption holds. Because attributes are imbalanced, probabilities must be decomposed into

$$P(err_{a_i}) = P(err_{a_i}|a_i = 1) \cdot P(a_1 = 1) + P(err_{a_i}|a_i = 0) \cdot P(a_1 = 0)$$

Table 2. Number of false positives (FP) and false negatives (FN) for non-subjective attributes out of a sample of 400. Best Acc. Represents the accuracy of a theoretically perfect classifier based on our error estimates. PS-MCNN-LC [1], to our knowledge, provides the best reported results for CelebA.

Label	FP	FN	Best Acc.	PS-MCNN-LC
Eyeglasses	2 (0.5 ± 0.35%)	0 (0.0 ± 0.0%)	99.8%	99.8%
Mouth slightly open	5 (1.3 ± 0.56%)	86 (21.5 ± 2.05%)	89.0%	96.0%
Male	5 (1.3 ± 0.56%)	2 (0.5 ± 0.35%)	99.1%	98.8%
Wearing hat	14 (3.5 ± 0.92%)	9 (2.3 ± 0.74%)	97.1%	99.4%
Wearing earrings	53 (13.3 ± 1.70%)	44 (11.0 ± 0.82%)	87.9%	92.7%
Wearing necklace	102 (25.5 ± 2.18%)	39 (9.8 ± 1.48%)	82.4%	89.0%
Wearing necktie	56 (14.0 ± 1.73%)	3 (0.8 ± 0.43%)	92.6%	98.5%

We then use attribute correlation, as well as the error rate estimates in Table 2 to estimate the marginal distribution of error. From this we estimate that 34.3% of images in CelebA have at least one incorrect label among these seven. Note that almost all attributes are predominately negative (77% of all labels are negative), so the contribution of false negatives is far greater than the contribution of false positives. Combining this with the contradictions listed in Table 1, we estimate that 38.7% of images in CelebA have at least one incorrect label – because we can exactly compute contradictions for each image, we use Monte-Carlo sampling with exact contradiction labels combined with estimated mislabeling rates to obtain the best possible estimate.

Importantly, incorrect labels cannot be treated as random noise. Of the 102 images incorrectly labeled with *wearing necklace*, 100 are of women. Of the 56 images incorrectly labeled with *wearing necktie*, all are of men, most of whom are wearing a collared shirt and coat as shown in Fig. 2. Indeed, as shown in Table 2, we find that a the current state-of-the-art model is able to learn the error and perform better than a theoretically perfect classifier which accounts for incorrect labeling. We therefore suggest that these labeling issues were likely caused by labelers misunderstanding a set of reference images, resulting in systemic mislabeling. Details about CelebA data collection are not provided, so we are unable to determine the specific cause of these issues. These errors are far more problematic than random noise because classifiers are able to learn the noise. For example, a classifier trained on CelebA will likely that someone wearing a collared shirt is wearing a necktie even if they are not, because the training data is frequently mislabeled accordingly.

4   Inconsistent Labels

While incorrect labels are an issue for many attributes, most attributes are subjective and therefore cannot be directly relabeled or shown to contradict with other attributes. We instead show that many subjective attributes fail to capture quantitative information about the feature they describe or are strongly correlated with other, unrelated attributes.

4.1   Consistency

To evaluate label quality in subjective attributes, we take advantage of other facial analysis tasks that can be used to estimate quantitative information about subjective CelebA attributes. Semantic segmentation can be used to estimate the size of different facial regions, and age estimation can be used to estimate youth. We therefore compare all attributes which subjectively label the size of facial features (*big lips*, *big nose*, and *narrow eyes*) as well as *young*, which subjectively labels the age of the face, with these classifiers. We find that the subjective labels are highly inconsistent with respect to these quantitative metrics, preventing even near-state-of-the-art classifiers from achieving acceptable performance.

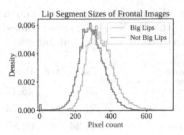

Fig. 3. Histogram of combined lip segment size for images labeled with *big lips* and images not labeled with *big lips*.

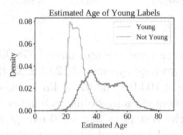

Fig. 4. Histogram of estimated ages for images labeled with *young* and images not labeled with *young*.

For age estimation, we use DEX [17] to estimate the age of all images in CelebA. For semantic segmentation, we use the DeepLabv3+ architecture [2] trained on the CelebA-Mask-HQ dataset, which annotates 18 facial regions for the 30,000 image CelebA-HQ dataset [10]. We predict part masks for all images in CelebA. We do note that using the DeepLabV3+ architecture as ground truth could be seen as problematic, since there is no guarantee that the algorithm will output the ground truth every time. *However*, DeepLabV3+ and other similar algorithms and architectures are capable of a higher level of consistency than human labeling as shown throughout this paper. For that reason, we believe that they are a reasonable baseline comparison. Because segment size is affected by pose, we restrict our analysis to frontal images to ensure consistent evaluation of part size. We use the HopeNet pose estimation network [18] to estimate head poses for all images in CelebA and discard all images with a pitch or roll not within $\pm10°$ or a yaw not within $-20°$ and $5°$. Because CelebA images are generally frontal, this leaves 84,970 out of 202,599 images for analysis.

To evaluate the consistency of size-based attributes we count the number of pixels contained in the segment associated with each attribute. We find that the attribute labels provided by CelebA do a poor job of discriminating these features. Images labeled with *big lips* have an average lip size of 343.1 ± 75.4 pixels, and images not labeled with *big lips* have an average lip size of 293.5 ± 73.2 pixels. This is shown in Fig. 3. We obtain similar results for *big nose* and *narrow eyes*: images labeled with *big nose* have an average nose size of 560.97 ± 69.81,

Table 3. F1 scores for linear classifiers using estimated quantitative metrics to predict subjective labels compared with a ResNet-18 classifier trained on CelebA. All attributes other than *young* are evaluated using only frontal images.

Attribute	Estimated	ResNet-18
Narrow eyes	38.31	45.47
Big lips	52.47	46.73
Big nose	46.34	64.89
Young	90.05	92.91
Mouth slightly open	93.93	95.70
Eyeglasses	95.03	98.10

with all other images having an average nose size of 518.96 ± 68.42. Images labeled with *narrow eyes* have an average eye size of 72.61 ± 33.42, with all other images having an average eye size of 104.01 ± 33.07. A linear classifier trained to predict these attributes using segment sizes (assuming a balanced distribution) is unable to reach an F1-score on the test data above 50 except for when predicting *big lips*, for which it achieves an F1-score of 52. This indicates the actual size of the features has little bearing on whether labelers described them as "big."

As shown in Fig. 4, we find that the *young* attribute is far more consistent, but still cannot be predicted completely reliably. The substantial overlap in estimated age between positive and negative instances demonstrates that even with reasonably consistent labeling, subjective binary attributes are highly flawed for representing non-binary features. A model with higher accuracy for *young* than a competitor may simply do a better job of capturing labeling bias than actually estimating age.

To demonstrate that the poor performance of these classifiers is not a result of bad segmentation and age estimation, we provide comparison to a ResNet-18 classifier trained to predict all 40 attributes. These results are shown in Table 3. Our classifier is pretrained on ImageNet and achieves an average test accuracy of 91.71%, which is reasonably close to the current state-of-the-art result of 92.98% [1]. Note that we compare to a generic ResNet model rather than current state-of-the-art because, to our knowledge, no work reporting better test performance has provided per-attribute F1 scores for CelebA [11]. Accuracy, the common metric, is poor for comparing performance on highly imbalanced attributes.

The ResNet classifier does not perform substantially better than using segment size or age estimation, and even performs slightly worse for *big lips*. To demonstrate that non-subjective attributes can be accurately estimated using quantitative classifiers, we also estimate *mouth slightly open* and *eyeglasses* using the mouth and glasses segments. While *mouth slightly open* is not entirely consistently labeled (as discussed in Sect. 3.2) and glasses propped on foreheads cause issues for our segment-size based classifier, we are still able to achieve satisfactory performance. We therefore suggest that these subjective, size-based labels are too inconsistent for any classifier to achieve reasonable performance.

4.2 Agreement

There are many other highly subjective labels we are unable to quantitatively estimate, many of which are just as inconsistent as the ones we can directly analyze. To demonstrate this, we measure attribute agreement across different images of the same person following the approach taken by [11]. Our analysis follows the observation that most facial attributes should not vary between different images of one person. While attributes such as *glasses, wavy hair*, and *no beard* may vary over time depending on the subject's current clothing and haircut, attributes such as *oval face, big nose*, and *narrow eyes* should be identically labeled for different images of the same person.

Label agreement is measured using Fleiss' κ [4], defined as $\frac{\bar{P}-P_e}{1-P_e}$, where P_e is the probability of two reviewers agreeing on a label by chance given its distribution, and $\bar{P}$ is the rate at which reviewers actually do agree in practice. The measure is most commonly used to determine agreement on a single sample between different reviewers. By treating labels for different images of the same person as different labels for the same sample, the metric can be directly used for CelebA. As shown in Table 4, the subjective attributes we are able to analyze using segment sizes actually have higher levels of agreement than the ones we are not able to analyze. Attributes which should remain consistent across images of the same person such as *oval face, narrow eyes*, and *point nose* have a κ measure below 0.5.

These results indicate that CelebA may not be an appropriate dataset for learning descriptions inherent to a single person. The poor label agreement suggests that labels are heavily affected by factors other than the person in the image. These may include pose, lighting, and image quality, but could also simply arise from the subjective opinions of different labelers. Because there is no way of knowing why an image was labeled in a particular way, any network trained to predict CelebA attributes will only be able to make accurate predictions by learning these biases, making attribute detection highly susceptible to manipulation in practice.

We note that, although CelebA is frequently used as a benchmark for a method's ability to predict on unbalanced data, label agreement as measured by Fleiss' κ is just as indicative of model performance than data balance. Despite the existence of many attributes such as *wearing hat* and *wearing glasses* which shouldn't necessarily agree across images of a subject, an attribute's κ is even more correlated (albeit by a very slight margin) with the F1 score of a generic ResNet-18 model than the percentage of samples in the majority class (0.358 > 0.352).

4.3 Correlated Labels

Counting contradictions, relabeling, and evaluating consistency with a quantitative classifier still leaves many attributes unanalyzed. While we are unable to directly evaluate the quality of these attributes, there are some correlations

Table 4. Average Fleiss κ agreement for the 40 attributes in CelebA. $\kappa < 0$ indicates agreement is worse than would be expected by random chance, $\kappa = 1$ indicates perfect agreement.

Rank	Attribute	κ	Rank	Attribute	κ
40	Blurry	−0.0181	39	Pale skin	0.1562
38	Mouth slightly open	0.2141	37	Narrow eyes	0.2378
36	Wearing hat	0.2489	35	Smiling	0.2551
34	Wearing necktie	0.2712	33	Double chin	0.2910
32	Wearing necklace	0.3113	31	High cheekbones	0.3178
30	Rosy cheeks	0.3282	29	Bags Under eyes	0.3388
28	Receding hairline	0.3405	27	Straight hair	0.3441
26	Brown hair	0.3719	25	Oval face	0.3881
24	Wearing earrings	0.3893	23	Chubby	0.3924
22	Eyeglasses	0.4150	21	Gray hair	0.4233
20	Wavy hair	0.4272	19	Bangs	0.4313
18	Pointy nose	0.4546	17	Black hair	0.4717
16	Sideburns	0.4759	15	Bushy eyebrows	0.4893
14	Mustache	0.4945	13	Bald	0.4981
12	Goatee	0.5062	11	5 o Clock shadow	0.5131
10	Arched eyebrows	0.5131	9	attractive	0.5140
8	Big nose	0.5585	7	Blond hair	0.5727
6	Heavy makeup	0.6302	5	No beard	0.6450
4	Big lips	0.7279	3	Wearing lipstick	0.7322
2	Young	0.8360	1	Male	0.9789

between subjective attributes which indicate poor labeling. As discussed by previous work, on average attributes have a gender skew of 80.0% [20]. For example, 27.9% of images labeled with *male* are labeled with *attractive*, whereas 67.9% of images not labeled with *male* are labeled with *attractive*. It is difficult to tell to what extent this is a result of bias in labeling rather than bias in data selection, but there are some cases were correlation is clearly indicative of bad labeling. The clearest example is *high cheekbones*, which has a correlation of 0.68 with *smiling*. 85.6% of images labeled *high cheekbones* are also labeled *smiling*, which is otherwise only applied to 48.2% of all images. This is likely because cheekbones appear higher while smiling, particularly when the smile is wide. Therefore, it is highly unlikely that *high cheekbones* provides an accurate label of cheekbone height irrespective of expression. Additionally, some gender correlations are too strong to be explained by data selection. We find that women are 3.1 times more likely to be labeled with *pointy nose*, whereas men are 2.9 times more likely to be labeled with *big nose*. This is despite the fact that the probability of a random male nose being larger than a random female nose in terms of segment size is just 54.3%, indicating gender bias substantially influences labeling.

Gender bias is also not the only bias encoded by subjective attributes. While the correlation between *big lips* and *big nose* in the validation set is fairly weak (0.054), our ResNet classifier described in Sect. 4.1 exaggerates this correlation to 0.091 due to related biases. Analysis of the 200 images which achieve the highest activations for these attributes show that they are heavily biased towards black men. 99% of people in the top activations for *big lips* are black, and 94% are male. 78% of people in the top activations for *big nose* are black, and 97% are male. None of the people in the images with the 200 lowest activations for either attribute are black.

5 Conclusion

While the subjectivity of CelebA labels makes their quality difficult to evaluate, we find that most labels we are able to quantitatively evaluate are poorly or inconsistently used. In particular, 10% or more instances of *5 o'clock shadow*, *bald*, *wearing earrings*, *wearing necklace*, and *wearing necktie* are used incorrectly or contradict another label. *Mouth slightly open* is labeled consistently enough to predict reliably, but the predictor does not match the label definition. Furthermore, subjective labels such as *big nose*, *big lips*, *narrow eyes*, and *young* are inconsistent with a quantitative classifier measuring the same feature. Attributes can also be shown to be poorly labeled through correlations. *High cheekbones* almost entirely overlaps with *smiling* and *pointy nose* is strongly negatively correlated with *male*. Other attributes clearly encode bias which is amplified by a classifier trained to predict those attributes. *Big lips* and *big nose*, while doing a poor job of estimating quantitative measures of lip and nose sizes, both encode racial bias which is learned by a classifier. In total, we find that there are 5 attributes which are clearly labeled incorrectly or contradict with another attribute more than 10% of the time, and another 5 attributes which are highly inconsistent or can be shown to be highly problematic through correlation with another attribute. There are many other attributes we are unable to evaluate, but are likely also poorly labeled. For example, a surprisingly high number (34.8%) of images labeled *male* are also labeled *bags under eyes*, and our ResNet classifier is unable to achieve an F1 greater than 50 for *oval face*. As a result of these issues, researchers should be cautious about making performance claims in regards to CelebA facial attribute classifiers. Future work should considering separating the most subjective attributes or even removing them from consideration entirely. It would also be beneficial to begin constructing another large scale face dataset that is more labelled in a more controlled manner than CelebA.

Acknowledgment. This material is based upon work supported by the National Science Foundation under Grant No. 1909707. Standard disclaimers apply.

References

1. Cao, J., Li, Y., Zhang, Z.: Partially shared multi-task convolutional neural network with local constraint for face attribute learning. In: Proceedings of the IEEE Conference on Computer Vision and Pattern Recognition, pp. 4290–4299 (2018)
2. Chen, L.C., Zhu, Y., Papandreou, G., Schroff, F., Adam, H.: Encoder-decoder with atrous separable convolution for semantic image segmentation. In: Proceedings of the European conference on computer vision (ECCV), pp. 801–818 (2018)
3. Dong, Q., Gong, S., Zhu, X.: Class rectification hard mining for imbalanced deep learning. In: Proceedings of the IEEE International Conference on Computer Vision, pp. 1851–1860 (2017)
4. Fleiss, J.L.: Measuring nominal scale agreement among many raters. Psychol. Bull. **76**(5), 378 (1971)
5. Hand, E., Castillo, C., Chellappa, R.: Doing the best we can with what we have: multi-label balancing with selective learning for attribute prediction. In: Proceedings of the AAAI Conference on Artificial Intelligence, vol. 32 (2018)
6. He, Z., Zuo, W., Kan, M., Shan, S., Chen, X.: AttGAN: facial attribute editing by only changing what you want. IEEE Trans. Image Process. **28**(11), 5464–5478 (2019)
7. Huang, C., Li, Y., Loy, C.C., Tang, X.: Learning deep representation for imbalanced classification. In: IEEE Conference on Computer Vision and Pattern Recognition (CVPR) (2016)
8. Huang, C., Li, Y., Loy, C.C., Tang, X.: Deep imbalanced learning for face recognition and attribute prediction. IEEE Trans. Pattern Anal. Mach. Intell. **42**(11), 2781–2794 (2019)
9. Kalayeh, M.M., Shah, M.: On symbiosis of attribute prediction and semantic segmentation. IEEE Trans. Pattern Anal. Mach. Intell. **45**, 1620–1635 (2019)
10. Lee, C.H., Liu, Z., Wu, L., Luo, P.: MaskGAN: towards diverse and interactive facial image manipulation. In: IEEE Conference on Computer Vision and Pattern Recognition (CVPR) (2020)
11. Lingenfelter, B., Hand, E.M.: Improving evaluation of facial attribute prediction models. In: 2021 16th IEEE International Conference on Automatic Face and Gesture Recognition (FG 2021), pp. 1–7 (2021). https://doi.org/10.1109/FG52635.2021.9667077
12. Liu, Z., Luo, P., Wang, X., Tang, X.: Deep learning face attributes in the wild. In: Proceedings of International Conference on Computer Vision (ICCV) (2015)
13. Northcutt, C.G., Athalye, A., Mueller, J.: Pervasive label errors in test sets destabilize machine learning benchmarks. In: Proceedings of the 35th Conference on Neural Information Processing Systems Track on Datasets and Benchmarks (2021)
14. Northcutt, C.G., Jiang, L., Chuang, I.L.: Confident learning: estimating uncertainty in dataset labels. J. Artif. Intell. Res. (JAIR) **70**, 1373–1411 (2021)
15. Prabhu, V.U., Yap, D.A., Wang, A., Whaley, J.: Covering up bias in celeba-like datasets with markov blankets: a post-hoc cure for attribute prior avoidance. arXiv preprint arXiv:1907.12917 (2019)
16. Ranjan, R., Sankaranarayanan, S., Castillo, C.D., Chellappa, R.: An all-in-one convolutional neural network for face analysis. In: 2017 12th IEEE International Conference on Automatic Face & Gesture Recognition (FG 2017), pp. 17–24. IEEE (2017)
17. Rothe, R., Timofte, R., Van Gool, L.: Deep expectation of real and apparent age from a single image without facial landmarks. Int. J. Comput. Vis. **126**(2), 144–157 (2018)

18. Ruiz, N., Chong, E., Rehg, J.M.: Fine-grained head pose estimation without keypoints. In: The IEEE Conference on Computer Vision and Pattern Recognition (CVPR) Workshops (2018)
19. Van Rooyen, B., Menon, A., Williamson, R.C.: Learning with symmetric label noise: The importance of being unhinged. In: Advances in Neural Information Processing Systems, vol. 28 (2015)
20. Wang, Z., et al.: Towards fairness in visual recognition: effective strategies for bias mitigation. In: Proceedings of the IEEE/CVF Conference on Computer Vision and Pattern Recognition, pp. 8919–8928 (2020)
21. Wang, Z., He, K., Fu, Y., Feng, R., Jiang, Y.G., Xue, X.: Multi-task deep neural network for joint face recognition and facial attribute prediction. In: Proceedings of the 2017 ACM on International Conference on Multimedia Retrieval, pp. 365–374 (2017)
22. Yang, J., et al.: Hierarchical feature embedding for attribute recognition. In: Proceedings of the IEEE/CVF Conference on Computer Vision and Pattern Recognition, pp. 13055–13064 (2020)
23. Yao, Y., Liu, T., Han, B., Gong, M., Deng, J., Niu, G., Sugiyama, M.: Dual t: Reducing estimation error for transition matrix in label-noise learning. In: Advances in Neural Information Processing Systems, vol. 33, pp. 7260–7271 (2020)
24. Zhao, J., Wang, T., Yatskar, M., Ordonez, V., Chang, K.W.: Men also like shopping: reducing gender bias amplification using corpus-level constraints. In: Proceedings of the 2017 Conference on Empirical Methods in Natural Language Processing (2017)

Object Detection and Recognition

Recognition of Aquatic Invasive Species Larvae Using Autoencoder-Based Feature Averaging

Shaif Chowdhury[✉] and Greg Hamerly[✉]

Baylor University, Waco, TX 76798, USA
shaif_chowdhury1@baylor.edu, greg_hamerly@baylor.edu

Abstract. The spread of invasive aquatic species disrupts ecological balance, damages natural resources, and adversely affects agricultural activity. There is a need for automated systems that can detect and classify invasive and non-invasive aquatic species using underwater videos without human supervision. In this paper, we intend to classify the larvae of invasive species like Zebra and Quagga mussels. These organisms are native to eastern Europe, but are invasive in United States waterways. It's important to identify invasive species at the larval stage when they are mobile in the water and before they have established a presence, to avoid infestations. Video-based underwater species classification has several challenges due to variation of illumination, angle of view and background noise. In the case of invasive larvae, there is added difficulty due to the microscopic size and small differences between aquatic species larvae. Additionally, there are challenges of data imbalance since invasive species are typically less abundant than native species. In video-based surveillance methods, each organism may have multiple video frames offering different views that show different angles, conditions, etc. Since, there are multiple images per organism, we propose using image set based classification which can accurately classify invasive and non-invasive organisms based on sets of images. Image set classification can often have higher accuracy even if single image classification accuracy is lower. Our system classifies image sets with a feature averaging pipeline that begins with an autoencoder to extract features from the images. These features are then averaged for each set corresponding to a single organism. The final prediction is made by a classifier trained on the image set features. Our experiments show that feature averaging provides a significant improvement over other models of image classification, achieving more than 97% F1 score to predict invasive organisms on our video imaging data for a quagga mussel survey.

Keywords: Invasive species · Quagga mussels · Classification · Image set · Autoencoder · Feature averaging

© The Author(s), under exclusive license to Springer Nature Switzerland AG 2022
G. Bebis et al. (Eds.): ISVC 2022, LNCS 13598, pp. 145–161, 2022.
https://doi.org/10.1007/978-3-031-20713-6_11

1   Introduction

Zebra mussels (*Dreissena polymorpha*) and Quagga mussels (*Dreissena bugensis*) are not native to North American waters and probably arrived as freshwater stowaways in commercial vessels from Europe in the 1980s [30]. Zebra mussels spread rapidly, cause ecological disruption, and clog water pipes and other machinery [8,30]. Due to economical and environmental damage it is important to detect and prevent the spread of these invasive species. Adult zebra mussels are easy to identify but they can spread quickly by laying millions of eggs per season. By the time these invasive species have established themselves in a waterway, eradicating or mitigating their presence becomes very difficult and costly. Thus it is important to detect and monitor zebra mussels at the larval (aka veliger) stage [22]. Detection of veligers is usually done by collecting water samples and using microscopy with cross-polarized light for identification [22], or using DNA-based methods [9]. Microscopy is expensive, time-consuming, and requires expert manual analysis. DNA-based methods are time-consuming, expensive, and are able to detect veliger presence but not *prevalence*. It's important to have an automated process that can monitor both veliger presence and prevalence [12].

Recently, there has been a lot of research in classifying fish and other underwater species [3,39]. But, there can be some unique challenges in classifying veligers of invasive species. First, fish and other adult underwater species have large and recognizable patterns, while veligers are difficult to distinguish from other organisms even for human experts. Secondly, there are a lot of other native planktonic organisms present in the water samples. Moreover, veligers can be rare depending on the season, which creates a data imbalance problem both at the training and testing stage [22]. Additionally, images collected from water samples might vary in illumination, background noise, and viewpoint orientation. Therefore, any solution for detecting invasive veligers must take the aforementioned challenges into account.

Fig. 1. 1. Adult zebra mussels that are easily recognizable. But our problem is about detecting zebra mussels at larval (veliger) stage, so the spread of invasive species can be stopped. 2. Some images of veligers from our dataset. The first row contains images of invasive veligers, and the second row contains images of other non-invasive organisms.

Our dataset comes from a video capture of a water sample. First, organisms in the video are tracked and then cropped images are extracted for each organism. This has been done by proprietary software developed by a private company, and is based on a Kalman filter. For each tracked organism, we group together extracted images and aim to classify the set as either invasive or non-invasive. That means our prediction model is based on image set classification, i.e. classification based on multiple images of same object [25]. Experts provided ground truth by inspecting the tracked objects in the video and the extracted images.

Image set based classification is often used in face detection with multiple instances of the same person recorded from surveillance videos. These datasets generally contain images of faces captured under different poses, expressions, or illumination [24,36]. An image set-based approach can perform better than single image classification, given that they take advantage of the multiple instances available [36,41]. The general solution to this problem entails reducing the dimension of the images, followed by aggregation of features of images in the same set. The second step is to use a similarity or distance measure with a nearest neighbour classifier [35]. This is both computationally expensive and unreliable for images with fine-grained differences.

Our dataset has two primary classes: invasive and non-invasive. Each organism has a varying number of images, depending on how long the organism was in the video frame. Our solution uses a feature extraction model followed by a final classifier. For feature extraction we have considered both hand-crafted and deep learning based methods. Hand-crafted features generally use a filter to encode some characteristics of an image like edges, color, shape, etc. Some popular hand-crafted feature descriptors are SIFT, HOG, HSV, color histogram, PCA, etc. [27]. More recently, methods based on deep learning can learn complex image features more accurately [11]. So we used a convolutional autoencoder to extract features from individual images [28,37].

In the last decade, convolutional neural networks based methods have been able to achieve significant improvement in many machine learning tasks, especially image classification. In particular, non-linear activation functions, batch normalization, pooling etc. have improved network performance [5]. In our case, we use a convolution autoencoder to map images to lower-dimensional features. Autoencoders use an encoder to create latent representation from an image and then a decoder is used to reconstruct the original image [21]. The loss is calculated based on the difference between original and reconstructed image and is optimized over the training period. Since the latent representation is created over multiple layers, it presents an opportunity to use different activation functions and create features that are appropriate for the problem.

Another challenge in our invasive species dataset is that the images are taken in different angles and illuminations as shown in Figs. 1 and 2, with groups of invasive and non-invasive images of the same organism placed side by side. The variations come from the organisms moving in three dimensions as they pass through the video frame. Thus we need a machine learning pipeline that is invariant to different conditions [2]. One technique is to train different models for different purposes and then use an ensemble for the final prediction. This is of course more expensive to train and might also introduce bias towards certain types of data variations. For example, the ensemble model might overfit on images of low illumination and do poorly against images of high illumination. Another technique is to augment the dataset, which aims to create data variations resulting in a more balanced dataset [38]. This approach can involve changing brightness of some images with low illumination and using them to balance the dataset [18]. Several papers propose using morphological transformations or generative adversarial networks to create augmented data samples [42]. These ideas are relevant to our problem, especially since we also have data imbalance in favor of non-invasive species. But generative adversarial networks with classification models are difficult to train, risk overfitting, and are computationally expensive.

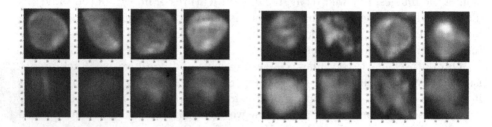

Fig. 2. These are groups of four images placed in same row taken from the same organism. As shown, the images have a lot of variation in terms of viewpoint and illumination, making it difficult to accurately classify individual organism.

In this paper we present a feature averaging process to create a representation from an image set which makes classification robust to varying illumination and object orientation and also reduces generalization error [24]. The key idea is that using the average of features from multiple images reduces the effect of illumination or viewpoint changes, compared to the use of a single image [23]. Some researchers have used linear subspace methods to represent mean or basis image from image sets [35]. But we have decided to use element-wise average of autoencoder features, which provides a more flexible and robust representation of the image set, while capturing the fine details at the same time.

Our classification pipeline is based on two neural networks. At first we extract features from each image of an organism using the encoding portion of a convolutional autoencoder network. Then we average these features across images of the same organism to create a single feature vector for the organism. Finally, we use a neural network classifier to predict if the organism is invasive or non-invasive. Our main contribution here is to present a classification approach that takes advantage of multiple instances, and can accurately and reliably classify invasive and non-invasive larvae despite the presence of variation in illumination and viewpoint. Our experiments also show the robustness of the autoencoder-based feature averaging process compared to other classification models. The balanced accuracy of this method is 97% on the test data, which is a significant improvement from other previous models which were convolutional neural networks similar to VGGNet [40]. In the results section, we provide more detailed results including F1-score, recall, and balanced accuracy. We also compare our results with other methods of classifying underwater images or image sets like CNN, PCA+CNN, SVM, etc.

In the next section we provide a literature survey on the problem of aquatic invasive species detection and responses, image set classification, and neural network models for feature extraction. In the methodology section we discuss details of our classification pipeline, network structure, loss functions, and the dataset. In the results section we describe the evaluation metrics and the experimental results and analysis.

2 Related Work

The problem of aquatic invasive species (AIS) is not new, but approaches for detection and identification of invasive mussels are costly and can be ineffective at preventing infestation due to the time required. Common approaches for detecting invasive mussels include microscopy or environmental DNA (eDNA). Here we review some approaches for detection of invasive species as well as some plans to stop further spread.

2.1 Aquatic Invasive Species

Most of the early techniques for detection of zebra mussels in larval stage are based on microscope photography. Conn et al. [7] provide a framework to detect and differentiate between larval and post-larval stages of zebra mussel (Dreissena polymorpha) and the Dark False mussel (Mytilopsis leucophaeata). This photographic guide aims to help personnel involved with the monitoring of these organisms. The other notable work in this area is from Johnson et al. [22], which uses cross-polarizing filters for microscopy retrofitted to detect the presence of zebra mussel veligers much faster with improved accuracy. This technique is useful for rapid detection as well as counting of veligers in a water sample.

A recent study by Gingera et al. [16] is based on water samples from Lake Winnipeg during early May and late October. This is an eDNA-based technique to identify the presence of zebra and quagga mussels. The results of the study show that zebra mussels were detected in 0–33.3% of all water samples per site studied during the early season and 42.9–100% during the late season. Finally, Feist et al. [14] provides a detailed review of eDNA-based approaches to detect and combat the spread of zebra and quagga mussels along with discussion on all the important discoveries and novel revelations made along the way.

Other than detection, there is a lot of research on how to trace and combat the presence of zebra and quagga mussels. The Massachusetts Department of Conservation and Recreation [13] has a rapid response plan to combat spread of zebra mussels, which involves collection of water samples, early detection of invasive species, marking of GPS position for infested locations followed by risk assessment and necessary response.

2.2   Local Responses to Aquatic Invasive Species

Now we look at some of the different states across western United States and ways they monitor and control aquatic invasive species. In the state of Texas many freshwater fisheries and other aquatic resources are managed by the Texas Parks and Wildlife Department (TPWD). Experts from TPWD and their partner organizations monitor Texas water bodies for the spread of zebra and quagga mussels at least twice per year. There are different amounts of infestation in different lakes. For example, Lake Worth in Tarrant County, Lake Brownwood, Inks Lake, and Medina Lake in the Colorado and San Antonio River basins have been designated as *infested* which indicates a sustained significant presence of zebra mussels in those lakes. On the other hand, International Amistad Reservoir in the Rio Grande basin had the first detection of quagga mussels in a Texas reservoir in February 2022.

In California quagga mussels have spread in Southern California reservoirs fed by the Colorado River. The state of California has added legislation requiring all reservoir owners and managers to assess the possibility of zebra and quagga mussels spread [31]. The Arizona Game and Fish Department (AZGFD) urges pet stores and aquarium owners to check for zebra mussels infestations [1].

Overall, the spread of invasive species is estimated to have an economic impact of $219 billion in the United States. It impacts different types of water infrastructure along with fishing, boating, and hunting. Worldwide it is estimated to have an economic impact of more than $4 trillion. This makes automated early detection and monitoring of invasive mussels crucial to reducing environmental and economic damage [43].

2.3   Classification with Image Sets

Our dataset contains multiple images of the same organism taken from video sample with different pose and illumination. Because of that, we chose an approach based on image set classification. Over the years there has been a lot of interest in image set-based classification [15,25,47], especially in the area of face recognition [19], handwritten digit recognition [20], shape recognition [10] and object recognition from different viewpoints [25]. The general procedure for image set classification is: (1) images of the same class are grouped together, (2) a model is learned to represent the set, and (3) for classifying test data a similarity measurement is used to match the set with a particular class. So, the key problem of image set classification is to capture the intrinsic properties of the set and use those for classification.

Most image set classification approaches can be categorized into two different types: parametric and non-parametric models [47]. Parametric models assume that each population follows a certain distribution, determined by a fixed set of parameters. In this method each image set is modelled using a distribution function and a similarity measure is used make the final classification.

Non-parametric methods do not require a pre-determined number of parameters in the model, but allow the data to determine the complexity of the model. These methods create a representation for each image set often based on statistical features and then a distance measure is used for the prediction. These methods represent image sets in different ways [47], such as linear subspaces [25, 46], affine subspaces [4], and nonlinear manifolds [15, 45].

Linear subspace methods place images in a low dimensional linear subspace and use subspace distance as a measure of similarity. Yamaguchi et al. [46] represented face images from different directions to create a subspace with the image sequence and use mutual subspace method as a distance measure. Kim et al. [25] developed a discriminative model, which maximizes the canonical correlations within sets in the same class.

The nonlinear manifold method represents images from the same set as a nonlinear manifold. Wang et al. propose a manifold learning approach [45], representing each manifold as a collection of linear models. Image sets from the test data are mapped to the manifold and matched against manifolds from the training set. The final classification is made by calculating the manifold-manifold distance (MMD).

Our method uses a convolutional autoencoder to represent image sets. Autoencoders, which are often deep networks, are used extensively with images to learn compressed representations and mappings for dimensionality reduction. A simpler and widely-used data dimensionality reduction technique is principal component analysis (PCA). PCA represents the data based on the orthogonal directions of maximum variance. PCA can give a poor representation for images with large number of features and low variance concentration [26]. The nonlinearity of neural networks on the other hand allows autoencoders to compress much more complex data while retaining information about the internal structure [21, 26].

2.4   Underwater Image Classification

A lot of underwater image classification problems have similar challenges of variation in brightness, image quality and viewpoint orientations. Raitoharju et al. [32] proposed a data enrichment algorithm to improve neural network-based classification of aquatic macroinvertebrates. They created new images by rotations and mirroring of older images, which increases the dataset size, leading to better classification accuracy. Schoening et al. [34] propose an image patch based feature representation for the problem of seafloor classification. The paper from Chuang et al. [6] compared supervised and unsupervised feature extraction methods for fish species recognition. Their experiments show that an unsupervised approach gives more accurate predictions of fish species. For many underwater species recognition problems the choice of feature extraction and representation method is crucial. In the next section, we discuss the use of autoencoders for feature extraction from images.

2.5   Autoencoders

Autoencoders were initially proposed by Hinton et al. [21] and are frequently used for learning feature representations. Since then it has been used and studied for image representation, compression, and dimensionality reduction in wide range of data types. Liu et al. [28] proposed autoencoder features to predict well failures using an SVM for final classification. The paper also compared the use of hand-crafted features with autoencoder features for classification. Most neural networks are trained to predict a target value or label Y given an input X, and a loss function is used to measure the difference between true and predicted labels. Autoencoders instead use a combination of layers as an encoder to create a low dimensional representation and then use more layers as a decoder to reconstruct the input. The loss function is calculated using the difference between the input and reconstructed output data. The gradients are propagated through the decoder and encoder networks. There are multiple variants of autoencoders that are applicable in wide range of problems. Vincent et al. [44] proposed denoising autoencoders which tries to reconstruct an image from a noised input image, thereby making the model robust to noise. Goroshin et al. [17] proposed an autoencoder architecture that limits the model's ability to reconstruct inputs which are not near the data manifold. The paper also shows that using different activation functions in the intermediate layers of autoencoder can be used to learn different features with interesting properties. Rifai et al. [33] adds a penalty term to the loss function which makes the model better at capturing the local directions of the data.

3   Methodology

Our prediction algorithm uses two steps: feature set generation and classification. The training process involves two different models: an autoencoder trained to generate features from images, and a classifier trained to discriminate between invasive and non-invasive organisms. Figure 3 shows the steps involved for feature averaging.

3.1   Solution Description

Consider image set S, which contains different images of the same organism. S has n images x_1 through x_n, each of size (a, b). Our goal is to create a vector r of size $z \ll a \cdot b$, which is a single representation of S. An autoencoder is used for feature extraction. Image x_i in the set has a corresponding feature vector f_i of size z, so there will be n feature vectors for n images in the set. Now these features are combined to create an average representation r of size z, where $r = \left(\sum_{i=1}^{n} f_i \right) / n$. The addition is done element-wise to create a final feature which is of the same size as the features from individual images. The autoencoder starts with an input size of $(a, b, 3)$ and the final layer of the encoder has an output size of z. Now, we should look at the details of the neural network architecture used for feature extraction.

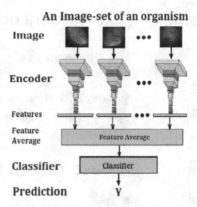

An Image-set of an organism

Image

Encoder

Features

Feature Average

Classifier

Prediction

Fig. 3. Diagram of the feature averaging pipeline. The images in the set are from the same organism. Image features are extracted from all images using the encoder and the average feature is used for final classification.

3.2 Convolutional Autoencoder

Let us assume we have images of size $(a, b, 3)$ given as input to the autoencoder. The autoencoder network $\Phi = \{\phi_e, \phi_d\}$ is formed of an encoder ϕ_e that creates a latent vector of size l_z and the decoder ϕ_d reconstructs the input image with the same size. The network architecture is based on the VGG model [40], which allows us to compare the performance with a VGG based CNN model. The VGG based model generally uses convolution filters of size 3×3, pooling layers of stride size 2×2, and dense layers with decreasing output size. The final layer of the encoder is fully connected from the encoder to the decoder. The encoder output size is z, which is the size of the latent vector features l_z. The decoder reconstructs the image with a series of dense layers, convolution layers, and up-sampling layers. Where the encoder uses a pooling layer, the decoder uses an up-sampling layer. We have used ReLU as activation in convolution layers and TanH in the final dense layer. The loss function is mean square error between the input image and the reconstructed image. The parameters are learned using the Adam optimizer. When using an autoencoder for feature extraction, we use the output of the last encoder layer.

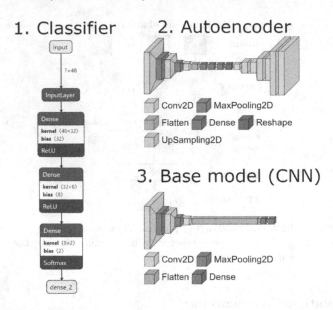

Fig. 4. (1) The classifier starts with features of size 48 and provides an output of size 2, which is used to make the prediction. ? × 48 stand for the batch-size variable along with the input feature size. (2) The autoencoder, with the input size of $(40, 40, 3)$. The output of the encoder is 48 features, which are used for feature averaging. (3) The CNN based model used for comparison.

3.3 Classification Model

Once the autoencoder has been trained, it can be used to extract features from every image. These features are averaged within a set to give us a feature and label pair for each organism. Now, we have a neural network based classifier that is trained to predict the label from the features. The input features reduced by two dense layers with ReLU activation function. If the input to the classifier network has z features, we train the three layers of the classifier network to reduce from size z to the output size. The final layer has the output size of 2 with a softmax activation function, using categorical cross-entropy loss. We train the network with the Adam optimizer, and use a dropout layer for regularization. Figure 4 presents a diagram of the classification model, autoencoder model, and CNN-based base model. Figure 6 shows images of organisms reconstructed by autoencoder, and Fig. 7 shows some images that were misclassified by the base CNN model.

3.4 Activation Functions

For the autoencoder we use two types of activation functions. For the convolution layers we use ReLU activation, which is defined as $\text{ReLU}(x) = \max(0, x)$. This function eliminates negative values and eliminates the vanishing gradient problem observed with other activation function [29]. For the encoder's output layer we use hyperbolic tangent $\text{TanH}(x) = (e^x - e^{-x})/(e^x + e^{-x})$. The output of $\text{TanH}(x)$ is in the range $[-1, 1]$. This limits the range of the autoencoder's output (latent) features, which regularizes against extreme feature values [29].

We used softmax activation at the final layer of classification. Softmax converts a real-valued vector into a discrete probability distribution [29]; the outputs are in the range $[0, 1]$, with their sum being 1. For softmax activation the output $f(x)$, given input x of size k is computed as $f(x)_i = \exp(x_i)/(\sum_{j=1}^{k} \exp(x_j))$.

3.5 Loss Functions

The loss function for the autoencoder network is mean-squared error: $\text{MSE}(Y, \hat{Y}) = \frac{1}{n} \sum_{i=1}^{n} (Y_i - \hat{Y}_i)^2$, where Y is the true label, $\hat{Y}$ is the predicted label, and n is the number of pixels. MSE in this case is the average of pixel-wise squared error between the input and generated images.

The classifier portion of the network uses categorical cross-entropy as the loss function. We use categorical encoding to encode the target label to numerical features with values between values of 0 to 1. Cross-entropy loss is computed from the sum of the negative logarithm of predictions made by the Neural Network. For our case with n samples and $C = 2$ categories,if ground truth is given by Y and prediction by $\hat{Y}$, where $Y, \hat{Y} \in [0, 1]$, the cross-entropy loss is $\text{CE}(Y, \hat{Y}) = -\sum_{i=1}^{n} \sum_{c=1}^{C} Y_{ic} \cdot \log(\hat{Y}_{ic}) = -\sum_{i=1}^{n} (Y_{i1} \cdot \log(\hat{Y}_{i1}) + Y_{i2} \cdot \log(\hat{Y}_{i2}))$.

3.6 Base Model

For comparison we use a CNN-based model to classify individual images (as opposed to classifying a set of images per organism). This "base model" has two convolution layers of size 3×3 with a max pooling layer after each one, one convolution layer of size 5×5, and fully-connected dense layers. The final layer has softmax activation with categorical cross-entropy loss. We use the Xavier initializer and the Adam optimizer for training. We train for 20 epochs with a batch size of 32 and learning rate .001.

3.7 Dataset

Our dataset contains a total of $4,374$ organisms with a total of $112,788$ images. There are 674 invasive organisms (quagga mussels) with $19,101$ images and $3,700$ non-invasive organisms with $93,687$ images. On average each organism has 25.78 images. The average image size is 22.56×19.46 pixels. We resize each image to a fixed size of $40 \times 40 \times 3$ and use that as an input to the autoencoder. We trained multiple autoencoder models with latent feature size of 48, 16 and 64. We trained a classifier for each latent representation. Table 1 gives more details on the number of parameters for each model.

Table 1. These are details about the neural network models used. The first row presents an autoencoder with an output vector of 64 features. The following two rows give details of the encoder and decoder which are used to construct that autoencoder. Next, we have the details of autoencoders with latent vectors of 48 and 16 features. This is followed by the classifiers and the base neural network model.

Model type	# Parameters	# Convolution layers	# Dense layers
Autoencoder (64 features)	38, 297	7	3
Encoder (64 features)	28, 089	3	2
Decoder (64 features)	10, 208	4	1
Autoencoder (48 features)	34, 281	7	3
Encoder (48 features)	26, 073	3	2
Decoder (48 features)	8, 208	4	1
Autoencoder (16 features)	26, 249	7	3
Encoder (16 features)	22, 041	3	2
Decoder (16 features)	4, 208	4	1
Classifier(64 features)	2, 362	0	3
Classifier(48 features)	1, 850	0	3
Classifier(16 features)	276	0	3
Base model (CNN)	204, 512	3	3

4   Results

4.1   Evaluation Metric

Our dataset has class imbalance, and the cost of a false negative (missing an invasive larvae) is potentially high. Therefore, accuracy alone is not sufficient to evaluate model performance. Thus we look at the following performance metrics:

Recall: Recall measures the percentage of the true invasive examples that are correctly predicted by the model. Recall is not affected by imbalance because it is only dependent on the invasive group. Recall $= TP/(TP + FN)$.

F1 Score: F1 score combines precision (which is $TP/(TP + FP)$) and recall using the harmonic mean. With equal weight for both, F1 $=$ $2 \cdot \text{precision} \cdot \text{recall}/(\text{precision} + \text{recall}) = 2TP/(2TP + FP + FN)$.

Balanced Accuracy: Balanced Accuracy (BAC) is the average of the individual accuracy of each class. BAC $= (1/2) \cdot (TP/(TP + FN) + TN/(FP + TN))$.

4.2   Quantitative Analysis

We split the dataset into train and test data for both the autoencoder and classifier. We use 80% for training and validation and 20% for testing. The dataset is shuffled before each training iteration to validate the results. The shuffle is applied over organisms, so that the images from same organism are not in both training and test data. We train the autoencoder for 20 epochs and the classifier for 200 epochs. We use the Xavier initializer and the Adam optimizer with a learning rate of .001. Figure 5 shows the training accuracy and loss against the number of training epochs. Then we show the comparative performance of our model against other popular machine learning methods.

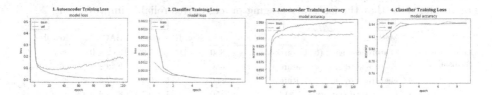

Fig. 5. 1. Autoencoder training loss against number of epochs. 2. Similarly, Classifier training loss vs epochs. 3. Autoencoder training accuracy. 4. Classifier training accuracy.

4.3 Comparative Analysis

We shuffle the dataset for both the autoencoder and classifier, perform 10 iterations of training and use the average score to compare the result. We also compare the results with other machine learning methods like a convolutional neural network, PCA + neural network, SVM classifier, and PCA + KNN. The results are in Table 2. For the base neural network we report the accuracy on individual images and also on organisms (image sets) based on majority vote. The autoencoder-based feature average achieves highest accuracy with 48 features.

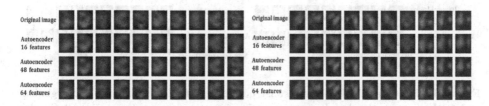

Fig. 6. Images of invasive and non-invasive species reconstructed by the autoencoders. Notice that larger autoencoder features create better reconstructions which also improves the accuracy of the final classification.

Fig. 7. These are some of the images incorrectly classified by the Base Neural Network (VGG). A lot of these images have low brightness or have different viewpoints that causes incorrect prediction.

Table 2. Experimental results on three evaluation metrics: F1, BAC, and Recall. The results at the top are based on classification of image set of each organism (each prediction is for one organism). The results at the bottom are based on individual images of all organisms in the test set (each prediction is for an individual image). We have also reported the accuracy with under-sampling method, where we have used a subset of the non-invasive images to balance the two classes. For PCA we report accuracy on individual images and similar feature averaging for organisms-wise results. The results show that the feature averaging process gives reliable improvement.

Type	#	Method	Test size	F1 score	BAC	Recall
Classify each organism	1	Feature averaging (64 features)	850	$97.1 \pm 0.9\%$	$98.2 \pm 0.7\%$	$96.3 \pm 0.5\%$
	2	Feature averaging (48 features)	850	$97.1 \pm 0.3\%$	$98.2 \pm 0.3\%$	$96.3 \pm 0.4\%$
	3	Feature averaging (16 features)	850	$90.5 \pm 0.3\%$	$95.2 \pm 1.2\%$	$88.8 \pm 1.5\%$
	4	Base neural network (CNN)	850	$88.1 \pm 0.7\%$	$89.4 \pm 0.3\%$	$82.5 \pm 0.6\%$
	5	PCA (feature average) + Neural network	850	$86.7 \pm 0.6\%$	$92.5 \pm 0.7\%$	$85.5 \pm 0.4\%$
Classify each image	6	Base neural network (CNN)	20,196	$80.2 \pm 1.2\%$	$89.3 \pm 1.6\%$	$80.1 \pm 1.4\%$
	7	Base neural network (under-sampling)	20,196	$82.2 \pm 1.1\%$	$87.5 \pm 1.5\%$	$82.7 \pm 1.1\%$
	8	PCA + Neural network	20,196	$66.8 \pm 1.1\%$	$82.9 \pm 1.3\%$	$54.9 \pm 0.9\%$
	9	SVM	20,196	$74.6 \pm 0.6\%$	$83.0 \pm 0.3\%$	$79.3 \pm 0.8\%$
	10	PCA+ 3-nearest neighbour	20,196	$64.2 \pm 10.0\%$	$78.7 \pm 5.0\%$	$68.1 \pm 9.0\%$

For single images, a convolutional neural network has F1 score of 80%. Compared with single image classification, image set-based classification performs better in many cases [36,41]. Our results show that autoencoder-based feature averaging improves the accuracy significantly over single image classification and has consistent performance comparable to state-of-the-art image set classification techniques. Moreover, it shows that feature fusion applied over an image set before classification has an advantage over voting after classification (Fig. 8).

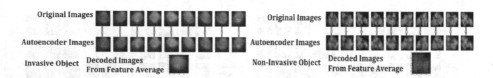

Fig. 8. 1. These are the invasive reconstruction created from images of an organism and at the bottom the decoder reconstruction from average representation. 2. Similar average representation of a Non-invasive organism

5   Conclusion

The spread of aquatic invasive species is a large, critical problem with global impact. We presented a framework to detect invasive mussel larvae from water sample videos. Our approach uses image sets and feature averaging to create representative features for each organism, which is then used for classification. We use two different neural networks: a convolutional autoencoder to create the features, and a classifier. Our experiments show that this method is robust and an improvement over other techniques.

Our goal is to create end-to-end prediction model. We want to incorporate additional relevant information such as organism movement, image/object size, weather, season, water conditions, etc. We would also like to extend this work to other invasive species including green crabs, Asian carp, hydrilla, and northern snakehead.

Acknowledgments. Funding for this project is provided by Texas Parks and Wildlife Department (TPWD). We would like to acknowledge the significant help from Ryan McManamay, Micah Bowman, Jordan Jatko, and Mark Lueders from Baylor's Department of Environmental Science.

References

1. Arizona Game and Fish: Invasive zebra mussels found in "moss ball" aquarium product. azgfd.com/invasive-zebra-mussels-found-in-moss-ball-aquarium-product-sold-at-aquarium-and-pet-supply-stores/
2. Benton, G., Finzi, M., Izmailov, P., Wilson, A.G.: Learning invariances in neural networks (2020). https://doi.org/10.48550/ARXIV.2010.11882
3. Bochinski, E., Bacha, G., Eiselein, V., Walles, T.J., Nejstgaard, J.C., Sikora, T.: Deep active learning for in situ plankton classification. In: International Conference on Pattern Recognition, pp. 5–15 (2018)
4. Cevikalp, H., Triggs, B.: Face recognition based on image sets. In: CVPR Proceedings, pp. 2567–2573 (2010)
5. Chai, J., Zeng, H., Li, A., Ngai, E.W.: Deep learning in computer vision: a critical review of emerging techniques and application scenarios. Mach. Learn. Appl. **6**, 100134 (2021)
6. Chuang, M.C., Hwang, J.N., Williams, K.: Supervised and unsupervised feature extraction methods for underwater fish species recognition. In: ICPR Workshop on Computer Vision for Analysis of Underwater Imagery, pp. 33–40 (2014)
7. Conn, D., Lutz, R., Hu, Y.P., Kennedy, V.: Guide to the Identification of Larval and Postlarval Stages of Zebra Mussels, Dreissena spp. and the Dark False Mussel, Mytilopsis leucophaeata. NEW YORK SEA GRANT, STONY BROOK, NY (USA), January 1993
8. Connelly, N.A., O'Neill, C.R., Knuth, B.A., Brown, T.L.: Economic impacts of zebra mussels on drinking water treatment and electric power generation facilities. Environ. Manag. **40**(1), 105–112 (2007)
9. Cowart, D.A., Breedveld, K.G., Ellis, M.J., Hull, J.M., Larson, E.R.: Environmental DNA (eDNA) applications for the conservation of imperiled crayfish (decapoda: Astacidea) through monitoring of invasive species barriers and relocated populations. J. Crustac. Biol. **38**(3), 257–266 (2018)
10. Daliri, M.R., Torre, V.: Robust symbolic representation for shape recognition and retrieval. Pattern Recogn. **41**(5), 1782–1798 (2008)
11. Deng, Y., Loy, C.C., Tang, X.: Image aesthetic assessment: an experimental survey. IEEE Sig. Process. Mag. **34**, 80–106 (2017)
12. Durán, C., Lanao, M., Anadón, A., Touyá, V.: Management strategies for the zebra mussel invasion in the Ebro river basin. Aquat. Invasions **5**(3), 309–16 (2010)

13. ENSR International: Rapid response plan for the zebra mussel (dreissena polymorpha) in Massachusetts (2005). https://www.mass.gov/doc/zebra-mussel-3/download

14. Feist, S.M., Lance, R.F.: Advanced molecular-based surveillance of quagga and zebra mussels: a review of environmental DNA/RNA (eDNA/eRNA) studies and considerations for future directions. NeoBiota **66**, 117 (2021)

15. Fitzgibbon, A.W., Zisserman, A.: Joint manifold distance: a new approach to appearance based clustering. In: CVPR Proceedings, vol. 1, p. I (2003)

16. Gingera, T.D., Bajno, R., Docker, M.F., Reist, J.D.: Environmental DNA as a detection tool for zebra mussels dreissena polymorpha (Pallas, 1771) at the forefront of an invasion event in Lake Winnipeg, Manitoba. Canada. Manag. Biol. Invasions **8**(3), 287 (2017)

17. Goroshin, R., LeCun, Y.: Saturating auto-encoders (2013). https://doi.org/10.48550/ARXIV.1301.3577

18. Gutierrez, P., Cordier, A., Caldeira, T., Sautory, T.: Data augmentation and pretrained networks for extremely low data regimes unsupervised visual inspection. In: Optical Metrology (2021)

19. Hadid, A., Pietikainen, M.: From still image to video-based face recognition: an experimental analysis. In: Sixth IEEE International Conference on Automatic Face and Gesture Recognition, pp. 813–818 (2004)

20. Hinton, G.E., Dayan, P., Revow, M.: Modeling the manifolds of images of handwritten digits. IEEE Trans. Neural Netw. **8**(1), 65–74 (1997)

21. Hinton, G.E., Salakhutdinov, R.R.: Reducing the dimensionality of data with neural networks. Science **313**(5786), 504–507 (2006)

22. Johnson, L.E.: Enhanced early detection and enumeration of zebra mussel (dreissena spp.) veligers using cross-polarized light microscopy. Hydrobiologia **312**(2), 139–146 (1995)

23. Khashman, A.: Face recognition using neural networks and pattern averaging. In: ISNN Proceedings (2006)

24. Khashman, A.: Intelligent face recognition: local versus global pattern averaging. In: Australian Conference on Artificial Intelligence (2006)

25. Kim, T.K., Kittler, J., Cipolla, R.: Discriminative learning and recognition of image set classes using canonical correlations. IEEE Trans. Pattern Anal. Mach. Intell. **29**(6), 1005–1018 (2007)

26. Kovenko, V., Bogach, I.: A comprehensive study of autoencoders applications related to images. In: Proceeding of the International Conference on Information Technology and Interactions (IT&I-2020), pp. 43–54 (2020)

27. Lin, W., Hasenstab, K., Moura Cunha, G., Schwartzman, A.: Comparison of handcrafted features and convolutional neural networks for liver MR image adequacy assessment. Sci. Rep. **10**(1), 1–11 (2020)

28. Liu, J., Jaiswal, A., Yao, K.T., Raghavendra, C.S.: Autoencoder-derived features as inputs to classification algorithms for predicting well failures. In: SPE Western Regional Meeting (2015)

29. Nwankpa, C., Ijomah, W., Gachagan, A., Marshall, S.: Activation functions: comparison of trends in practice and research for deep learning (2018). https://doi.org/10.48550/ARXIV.1811.03378

30. O'Neill, Jr., C.R., Dextrase, A.: The introduction and spread of the zebra mussel in North America. In: Proceedings of The Fourth International Zebra Mussel Conference, March 1994

31. Pacific Gas and Electric: Prevent the spread of quagga and zebra mussels. pge.com/en_US/about-pge/environment/what-we-are-doing/quagga-and-zebra-mussel-prevention-program/quagga-and-zebra-mussel-prevention-program.page
32. Raitoharju, J., et al.: Data enrichment in fine-grained classification of aquatic macroinvertebrates. In: 2nd Workshop on Computer Vision for Analysis of Underwater Imagery, pp. 43–48 (2016)
33. Rifai, S., Vincent, P., Muller, X., Glorot, X., Bengio, Y.: Contractive auto-encoders: explicit invariance during feature extraction. In: ICML (2011)
34. Schoening, T., Kuhn, T., Nattkemper, T.W.: Seabed classification using a bag-of-prototypes feature representation. In: ICPR Workshop on Computer Vision for Analysis of Underwater Imagery, pp. 17–24 (2014)
35. Shafait, F., et al.: Fish identification from videos captured in uncontrolled underwater environments. ICES J. Mar. Sci. **73**(10), 2737–2746 (2016)
36. Shah, S.A., Nadeem, U., Bennamoun, M., Sohel, F., Togneri, R.: Efficient image set classification using linear regression based image reconstruction. In: CVPR Workshop Proceedings, pp. 99–108 (2017)
37. Shoeibi, A., et al.: A comprehensive comparison of handcrafted features and convolutional autoencoders for epileptic seizures detection in EEG signals. Expert Syst. Appl. **163**, 113788 (2021)
38. Shorten, C., Khoshgoftaar, T.M.: A survey on image data augmentation for deep learning. J. Big Data **6**, 1–48 (2019)
39. Siddiqui, S.A., et al.: Automatic fish species classification in underwater videos: exploiting pre-trained deep neural network models to compensate for limited labelled data. ICES J. Marine Sci. **75**(1), 374–389 (07 2017)
40. Simonyan, K., Zisserman, A.: Very deep convolutional networks for large-scale image recognition (2014). https://doi.org/10.48550/ARXIV.1409.1556
41. Sun, H., Zhen, X., Zheng, Y., Yang, G., Yin, Y., Li, S.: Learning deep match kernels for image-set classification. In: CVPR Proceedings, pp. 3307–3316 (2017)
42. Taylor, L., Nitschke, G.S.: Improving deep learning with generic data augmentation. IEEE Symposium Series on Computational Intelligence, pp. 1542–1547 (2018)
43. Texas Parks and Wildlife Department: TPWD aquatic invasive species management FY 2020–2021. tpwd.texas.gov/landwater/water/aquatic-invasives/media/Statewide
44. Vincent, P., Larochelle, H., Bengio, Y., Manzagol, P.A.: Extracting and composing robust features with denoising autoencoders. In: ICML Proceedings, pp. 1096–1103 (2008)
45. Wang, R., Shan, S., Chen, X., Gao, W.: Manifold-manifold distance with application to face recognition based on image set. In: CVPR Proceedings, pp. 1–8 (2008)
46. Yamaguchi, O., Fukui, K., Maeda, K.I.: Face recognition using temporal image sequence. In: Proceedings of the Third IEEE International Conference on Automatic Face and Gesture Recognition, pp. 318–323 (1998)
47. Zhao, Z.Q., Xu, S.T., Liu, D., Tian, W.D., Jiang, Z.D.: A review of image set classification. Neurocomputing **335**, 251–260 (2019)

Subspace Analysis for Multi-temporal Disaster Mapping Using Satellite Imagery

Azubuike M. Okorie and Sokratis Makrogiannis(✉)

Division of Physics, Engineering, Mathematics and Computer Science,
Delaware State University, Dover, DE, USA
smakrogiannis@desu.edu
http://miviclab.org/

Abstract. We propose an automated disaster mapping technique using pre- and post-disaster satellite imagery. We first find the geometric transformation for automatic image registration by matching regions represented by shape and intensity descriptors. We produce piece-wise constant approximations of the two images using the delineated regions. We perform linear subspace learning in the joint regional space and project the samples onto the orthogonal to tangent subspace to produce a change map and identify the outliers using statistical tests. We tested our method on multiple disaster datasets that is, four wildfire events and two flooding events. We validated our results by measuring the overlap score (DSC), and classification accuracy of our disaster map and ground-truth data. We performed comparisons to representative change detection techniques, namely Gabor Two-Level Clustering (G-TLC), and spectral index-based detection methods. Performance metrics indicated that the proposed Subspace Learning-based Disaster Mapping (SLDM) method produced more accurate change maps than the compared methods for multiple types of disaster events. Visual interpretation of the proposed SLDM method confirms its capacity for creating change maps for disaster mapping.

1 Introduction

In the wake of a disaster, timely intervention or response is paramount to reduce fatalities, infrastructural damage, risk of environmental hazards, health risks and other consequences. Natural disaster events include wildfires, floods, landslides, earthquakes, and tsunamis. A first step leading to timely intervention of the response team is to identify the areas that have been impacted by the disaster. This process is often termed *disaster-mapping*. In the past few decades, the increase in the number of remote sensing satellite data and the coordination of the International Charter Space and Major Disasters has made it possible for the acquisition and usage of multi-source images, including very high resolution (VHR) optical images and thermal images, for image-based disaster mapping techniques [25].

One of the objectives of disaster mapping using remote sensing images is to produce a change map that correctly delineates the area(s) that have been

G. Bebis et al. (Eds.): ISVC 2022, LNCS 13598, pp. 162–173, 2022.
https://doi.org/10.1007/978-3-031-20713-6_12

affected by disaster. At the early stages of disaster mapping research, accurate change maps were produced manually by visual analysis [16,25]. Nevertheless, manual techniques are labor-intensive, inefficient and subject to the proficiency of experts. Recently, researchers have invested resources to develop automated disaster mapping techniques and improve the efficiency of such techniques. Contributions to the field of disaster mapping range from classical image analysis tools to machine learning techniques [9,25]. Moreover, in the current era of artificial intelligence, the field of disaster mapping has received significant contributions from deep learning techniques. Reviews of image processing techniques for disaster mapping/assessment are available in [9,25] and [6]. Although some image-based disaster mapping techniques may be developed based on pre- or post-disaster data only [4], other works propose multi-temporal change detection techniques, that utilize pre- and post-disaster images for disaster mapping [11,12,23].

Multi-temporal change detection techniques for disaster mapping are developed on the assumption that changes caused by a disaster are easily detected by evaluating the difference between pre- and post-disaster images. Utilizing information from pre-disaster data for disaster mapping offers additional information that would assist to accurately map the area(s) that were impacted. Thus, basic image processing techniques, such as image subtraction, have been used for disaster mapping [9]. Notwithstanding, one major disadvantage of using basic image processing techniques for disaster-mapping purposes is that they may falsely detect differences caused by brightness [9]. Other image processing techniques for monitoring disaster events compute differences between spectral indices, such as the normalized-differenced vegetation index (NDVI) [17,22], normalized-differenced water index (NDWI) [14,27], and normalized burn ratio (NBR) [19]. The use of spectral indices may be limited to multi-spectral data, or restricted to certain disaster events. Other multi-temporal disaster mapping techniques that have been proposed include principal component analysis (PCA) based methods [24], feature extraction-based classification methods like the two level clustering technique for change detection using Gabor features (G-TLC) [11], a method that uses wavelet features and Kohonen clustering [10], and PCA k-means (PCAKM) clustering [2]. Additional unsupervised feature-based clustering techniques for change detection in satellite imagery have been proposed in [7,8]. Despite the good reported performances of clustering and feature-based clustering techniques proposed in the literature above, these methods may face limitations to map disasters accurately, especially when applied to high- or very-high-resolution images, due to high computational complexity [26].

Recently, deep learning techniques have produced state-of-the-art performances in the fields of image processing and analysis. Deep learning techniques have also been developed for multi-temporal disaster mapping. Sublime et al. [23], proposed a deep learning technique for automatic disaster mapping using joint-autoencoders and decoders. The method produced relatively high accuracy for the particular application to Tohoku tsunami, especially for detection of flooded areas. Nevertheless, it presented some limitations including moderate performance accuracy for classification of destroyed buildings. The authors in [28] utilized autoencoder models to detect changes in very high resolution images (VHR). In their method, feature learning is defined implicitly and enabled to learn complex features from VHR images, unlike other methods that make assumptions of predefined linear transformations. The authors in [1] proposed a convolutional U-Net architecture for multi-temporal disaster mapping using four-spectral bands. Each pair is composed of high resolution (0.6 m) pre- and post-disaster WorldView images. This method uses supervised-learning, and requires substantial amounts of labeled data for training, which are usually not available for remote sensing and especially in our studies.

Although deep learning techniques for multi-temporal disaster mapping have proven to produce good results, they present their own challenges. The unavailability of labeled data by experts is a major domain challenge in remote sensing. This limitation implies that in some methods of the literature, the networks may need to be trained on the test image, which means that parts of the test image need to be labeled to train the net. Also, deep learning techniques require high-performance hardware for training due to high computational complexity. Despite the good characteristics of existing methods, and deep learning techniques, there is an unmet need for change detection algorithms that can perform well for multiple disaster events with low requirements for manual labeling. In this paper, we propose a subspace learning-based disaster mapping (SLDM) technique that identifies and characterizes changes between pre- and post-disaster images. We employ principles of subspace learning [15,20] in the joint space generated by multiple time points to estimate the disaster map. This method is motivated by the assumption that unaffected regions are expected to lie on a principal subspace, or close to it. Conversely, the affected regions are expected to lie further away from the principal subspace. Our experiments on multiple datasets support the validity of this approach, and provide a framework that is adaptable to different types of disaster events.

2   Subspace Learning-Based Disaster Mapping

The main stages of the proposed method are (i) region delineation, (ii) region mapping and matching, and (iii) disaster mapping by subspace learning, as shown in Fig. 1. We detail the region delineation and disaster mapping stages next.

2.1   Region Delineation

First, let L denote the locations of areas that have been hit by a natural disaster. Our task is to identify the affected areas in L, automatically, using remotely sensed satellite images L_b and L_a acquired before and after the natural disaster, respectively. L_b and L_a are also referred to as pre-disaster and post-disaster images, respectively. Our goal is to obtain an image map, showing the regions(s) that have been affected by disaster.

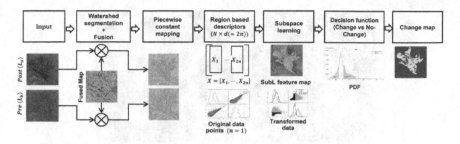

Fig. 1. Flowchart of the proposed subspace learning-based disaster mapping algorithm.

In this stage, we delineate the regions of the two images that serve as the basic image elements of automated co-registration and disaster mapping. To generate these regions, or superpixels, we employ watershed segmentation based on Parzen kernel density edge estimation [13] and morphological reconstruction.

First, we apply a median filter to the input image L_x, to reduce the effect of noise on edge estimation. Secondly, we estimate edge maps using Parzen kernel density estimation. Next, we apply the regional $h-$minima transform to reduce the local minima of the edge map that do not correspond to meaningful regions. We specify the height of minima to be filtered by the parameter h_{min}. The sensitivity of edge maps depends on the following parameters: Parzen kernel length$-pkl$, Parzen bandwidth$-pbw$, and h_{min}.

Finally, we perform watershed segmentation on the $h_{min}-$transformed edge map. Watershed segmentation produces a closed region map R_x that we use in the next stages.

2.2 Segmentation Fusion

We introduce a *multivalued fusion* method to fuse the input and reference region maps. The goal is to obtain a common set of regions for both time points that accommodates subspace learning.

We propose to perform multivalued region fusion by combining the signed distance maps of input and reference superpixels followed by morphological reconstruction to remove small/noisy regions. In particular, given the super-pixel binary map $B = \{p \in \Omega | L(p) = 1\}$, the distance transform computes a map DM such that at each pixel p, $X(p)$ is the smallest distance from p to B^c, i.e.,

$$DM(p) = \min\{dist(p,q)|q \in B^c\} = \min\{dist(p,q)|L(q) = 0\},$$

where $dist(.,.)$ is a pair-wise distance function, in our case, the Euclidean distance. The signed distance map is therefore given as

$$J_x = -DM(B_x^c) \setminus (DM(B_x) \cup (B_x + 0.5)), \tag{1}$$

with $x = a, b$. The fused signed distance map becomes

$$J = 0.5(J_a \cup J_b). \tag{2}$$

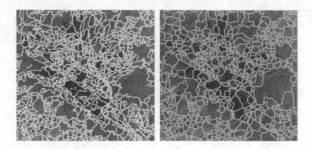

Fig. 2. Example of segmentation fusion. Post-disaster regions (yellow), pre-disaster regions (cyan) and fused regions (green). (Color figure online)

We then apply h-minima transform on J to remove local minima of the fused distance map, followed by watershed segmentation to produce the fused regions. We map the fused regions onto all registered bands in both time points. We show an example of segmentation fusion in Fig. 2.

2.3 Subspace Learning for Disaster Mapping

Here we use subspace learning techniques to compute tangent distances [3, 5, 15, 20, 21] that will be used for identifying the damaged regions. Motivated from manifold learning principles, our premise is that the pre- and post-disaster regions not affected by the disaster will lie close to a principal subspace formed by regional multi-band descriptors obtained from the fused superpixels. Conversely, the damaged regions will lie further away from the principal subspace. We approximate the principal subspace by a tangent space. We will identify the level of damage caused by a disaster using distances from the tangent space, which are known as tangent distances.

Let S : {*descriptors of regions of no damage*} be the region descriptors that are concentrated close to a manifold that is generated by the unknown relationships of the multi-temporal no-disaster region descriptors in the two time points.

We approximate the manifold by a linear principal space S_p with respect to a query region r_q using the tangent distance given by

$$td(r_q, S_p) = \min_{r \in S_p} \|r_q, r\|_2. \tag{3}$$

Following this formulation, the region descriptors corresponding to the disaster areas, will lie further away from S_p relative to the no-disaster region descriptors.

We compute the pre- and post-disaster piecewise constant approximation maps L_a^R and L_b^R from the input images L_a and L_b using the labeled map R produced by segmentation fusion or the reference segmentation in the case of SLDM. The objective is to reduce the statistical variability of the samples without losing the changes we intend to detect.

Let X_{a_i} and X_{b_i}, for $i = 1, \ldots, n$, be the vectorized forms of $L_{a_i}^R$ and $L_{b_i}^R$, respectively, where n is the number of spectral bands. We form a $N \times 2n$ matrix $X = [X_{a_1}, X_{b_1}, \ldots, X_{a_n}, X_{b_n}]$. We scale the data matrix X by calculating the z-score of each column. Let $\mathbf{Z}$ denote the z-scaled matrix.

Next, we apply PCA to the matrix $\mathbf{Z}$ to obtain the eigenvalues $\lambda_k, k = 1, \ldots, 2n$ be the eigenvalues of the covariance matrix Σ arranged in descending order of magnitude, with corresponding eigenvectors $\mathbf{w}_k, k = 1, \ldots, 2n$. We project $\mathbf{Z}$ to the space spanned by $\{\mathbf{w}_1, \mathbf{w}_2, \ldots, \mathbf{w}_{2n}\}$ as follows

$$W = [W_1, W_2, \ldots, W_{2n}] = \mathbf{Z} \cdot [\mathbf{w_1}, \mathbf{w_2}, \ldots, \mathbf{w_{2n}}]^{\mathbf{T}}. \tag{4}$$

We define the principal subspace S_p as the hyperplane spanned by the first p components, $W_1, \ldots, W_p$.

We assume that the unaffected regions will be approximated with vectors X that lie close to the principal subspace S_p, whereas the regions changed by the disaster will lie further from this space. We propose to use these distances to define the change map L_d^R, that is, $L_d^R := d(X, S_p)$. By definition, this vector distance is given by projection onto the orthogonal subspace, which yields

$$L_d^R := d(W, S_p) = \|W - \mathbf{Z} \cdot (\mathbf{w}_1 + \mathbf{w}_2 + \ldots + \mathbf{w}_p)^T\|_2 \tag{5}$$

$$= \|W_o\|_2 = \|\mathbf{Z} \cdot (\mathbf{w_{p+1}} + \ldots + \mathbf{w_{2n}})^{\mathbf{T}}\|_2, \tag{6}$$

where $\| \cdot \|_2$ denotes the ℓ_2 norm, and W_0 denotes the orthogonal subspace.

3   Determining the Changed and Unchanged Regions

Given the set of points $X \subset \mathbb{R}^{N \times d}$ in the orthogonal space produced by subspace learning, we estimate the probability density using kernel density estimation. The sample set $x_1, \ldots, x_n \in \mathbb{R}^d$, with $n \leq N$, consists of the feature map with priors $p(x_k), \ k = 1, \ldots, n$.

We anticipate that the peak and the minimum of the probability density curve would correspond to the no-change and noisy regions, respectively. The data points satisfying $\tau_n < p(\mathbf{x}) < \tau_d$ correspond to regions $R_i, i = 1, 2$ that are candidates for changes caused by the disaster, where τ_d and τ_n are the detection and noise margins respectively.

These regions divide the orthogonal space into two semi-spaces. We estimate the total probability on each region R_i bounded by the tangent space and reject the candidate points that lie in the region of lower probability. We determine the regional probabilities by the areas under the estimated pdf and choose the maximizing region as the detection region R_d:

$$R_d = \arg \max_i P\{\mathbf{x} \in R_i\}. \tag{7}$$

Figure 3 shows an example of the estimated density, the detection region in green color and the rejected region in gray.

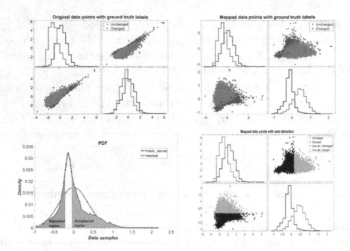

Fig. 3. Scatterplots of original data points, mapped data points, decision density function, and the subspace data points identified as changes caused by disaster (in green color). (Color figure online)

4   Experiments, Results and Discussion

4.1   Experimental Setup

We evaluate the effectiveness of the proposed method by testing it on datasets of two floods in Oroville, CA, USA *(O-FL)* and Brazil *(B-FL)*, and four wildfires in Pisa, Italy *(PI-FI)*, Fort McMurray, Canada *(FM-FI)*, San Bernardino, CA, USA *(SB-FI)* and Yosemite national park, CA, USA *(Y-FI)*. According to the information on ESA earth-watching, the six disaster events were severe, and caused hundreds of residents to vacate their homes, significant infrastructural damage, waste of resources, and loss of lives.

We obtained pre- and post-disaster images from the United States Geological Survey (USGS) glovis archive. The technical characteristics of the images are provided in Table 1. We utilized the near-infra-red (NIR) bands from both times in all our experiments. We generated the ground-truth of the cropped region of interest in each case manually by visual interpretation/analysis using the information provided on the ESA's earth watching - environmental hazards website. The pre- and post-disaster images and the ground-truth change map of the above datasets are displayed in Fig. 4.

To reduce the effect of atmospheric conditions, we performed cloud, cloud-shadow, and no-data removal on both pre-disaster and post-disaster images at the preprocessing stage using a mask generated by FMask [29], and registration information.

Table 1. Technical details of the datasets

Data	Satellite	Acquisition dates		ROI size	Resolution
		Pre-disaster	Post-disaster		
O-FL	Sentinel-2	12-Dec-2016	30-Jan-2017	1500 × 1500	10 m
B-FL	Landsat 8 OLI	18-May-2014	5-Jul-2014	3001 × 3000	30 m
PI-FI	Landsat 8 OLI	24-Oct-2017	25-Sep-2018	731 × 818	30 m
FM-FI	Landsat 8 OLI	1-Oct-2015	12-May-2016	2200 × 2200	30 m
SB-FI	Landsat 8 OLI	17-Jul-2016	18-Aug-2016	1800 × 2200	30 m
Y-FI	Landsat 8 OLI	5-Jun-2013	9-Sep-2013	3000 × 3000	30 m

4.2   Results and Discussion

Our method performs complete registration [18] and disaster mapping given multi-temporal images. Disaster mapping requires accurate registration of the pre- and post-disaster images in a common space. Therefore it is important to evaluate the performance of the registration stage.

Our first experiments included an evaluation of registration accuracy. The root mean square error measures of our method against ground truth transformations are: B-FL (0.100), PI-FI (0.318), FM-FI (0.327), SB-FI (0.026) and Y-FI (0.576). We note that the RMSE values are smaller than 1 pixel, indicating high accuracy that meets the requirements of multi-temporal disaster mapping. We note here that the multi-temporal images in the Oroville fire dataset were already co-registered, so no registration was applied to them.

We also evaluated the accuracy of the proposed subspace learning-based disaster mapping technique against manually generated ground truth data. We compared the performance of our SLDM techniques to image differencing, spectral index differencing, namely normalized-differenced spectral indices (d-NDVI), and disaster specific indices - normalized burn ratio (d-NBR) and normalized differenced water index (d-NDWI), and the Gabor Two-level Clustering (G-TLC) [11]. Furthermore, SLDM-SF symbolizes SLDM with segmentation fusion, in contrast to SLDM that symbolizes our method without using fusion. We made this distinction to evaluate the effect of segmentation fusion on performance. The results produced by the proposed SLDM techniques and the compared methods are shown in Fig. 4. Table 2 contains a summary of delineation and classification accuracy rates of all disaster mapping methods under consideration.

With respect to average DSC, Table 2 shows that SLDM and SLDM-SF outperformed other compared methods on wildfires, while SLDM is the second best on floods. We observe that at least one version of the SLDM technique produced greater DSC than G-TLC on all datasets except for the Oroville flood, and Pisa fires. All versions of SLDM produced at least 0.006 higher DSCs on SB-FI, and 0.064 higher on FM-FI. SLDM produced > 0.9 DSC on SB-FI, outperforming the non-SLDM techniques. SLDM-SF was the top performing method on Y-FI, with an improvement of at least 0.034 in DSC versus the non-SLDM techniques.

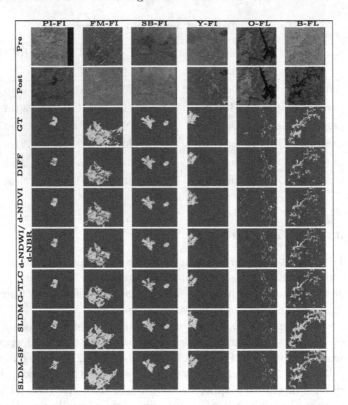

Fig. 4. Comparison between our SLDM techniques with other methods. (left to right) Oroville flood (O-Fl), Brazil flood (B-FL), Pisa fires (PI-FI), Fort McMurray fires (FM-FI), San-Bernardino fires (SB-FI), and Yosemite fires (Y-FI). (top to bottom) Pre-disaster image, post-disaster image, ground-truth, image difference (DIFF), differenced spectral indices (d-NDVI, d-NBWI, and d-NBR), G-TLC, SLDM, and SLDM-SF disaster maps. The difference image for G-TLC was calculated using log ratio.

In Fig. 4 we observe that the detection maps by SLDM techniques on B-FL, FM-FI, SB-FI, and Y-FI are more accurate than non-SLDM techniques. G-TLC and DNDVI show better performance on O-FL, and PI-FI.

Both SLDM techniques produced better average DSC than image differencing-based (DIFF) techniques on the flood data, and produced better DSC on all data except O-FL. Similarly, both SLDM techniques produced better average DSC on all data than spectral index-based detection except on floods, where D-NDWI is the best performing method. The detection rates of SLDM techniques are more accurate than d-NDVI on O-FL, B-FL, FM-FI, SB-FI and Y-FI. SLDM produced lower rates than D-NDVI and D-NBR on PI-FI. D-NBR also produced greater DSC than SLDM only on Y-FI. D-NDWI also outperformed SLDM techniques on O-FL data, which is likely caused by the limited resolution of O-FL images that could favor pixel-level analysis.

In comparison with a state-of-the-art technique, G-TLC, we observe in Table 2 and Fig. 4 that both SLDM techniques produced more accurate detection in terms of DSC than G-TLC on B-FL, FM-FI, and SB-FI. On O-FL, G-TLC yielded better performance than all SLDM techniques. On Y-FI, SLDM-SF performed better than G-TLC in terms of DSC.

We also hypothesized that segmentation fusion would improve the detection and classification performance of the proposed framework. Comparison of average accuracy rates supports this hypothesis on wildfires, but not on floods.

We note here that straightforward application of the compared methods produced only moderate detection rates. Therefore, to establish equal standards for evaluation and comparison, in the reported results we applied the pre- and post-processing steps that we proposed in our methods, including filtering, and removal of small regions based on the cumulative distribution function, on all the compared methods.

Table 2. Classification performance comparisons on flood and wild-fire datasets.

		Compared methods					
Wildfires	Metric	DIFF	D-NDVI	D-NBR	G-TLC	SLDM	SLDM-SF
PI-FI	ACC	0.991	**0.993**	0.992	**0.994**	0.992	0.991
	DSC	0.764	**0.838**	0.801	**0.850**	0.793	0.770
FM-FI	ACC	0.896	0.902	0.903	0.902	**0.921**	**0.909**
	DSC	0.680	0.709	0.703	0.711	**0.789**	**0.775**
SB-FI	ACC	0.990	0.989	**0.991**	0.988	**0.991**	0.988
	DSC	0.889	0.872	0.894	0.860	**0.904**	**0.900**
Y-FI	ACC	**0.989**	0.970	0.977	**0.978**	0.970	0.979
	DSC	0.719	0.701	0.744	**0.744**	0.731	**0.781**
Mean	ACC	*0.967*	*0.966*	*0.966*	*0.965*	*0.969*	*0.969*
	DSC	*0.763*	*0.780*	*0.786*	*0.791*	*0.804*	*0.806*
Floods	Metric	DIFF	D-NDVI	D-NDWI	G-TLC	SLDM	SLDM-SF
O-FL	ACC	**0.989**	0.984	**0.989**	**0.989**	0.987	0.986
	DSC	**0.719**	0.604	0.718	**0.721**	0.634	0.604
B-FL	ACC	0.923	0.943	**0.946**	0.927	0.926	0.926
	DSC	0.544	0.639	0.670	0.575	**0.716**	0.692
Mean	ACC	*0.956*	*0.963*	*0.967*	*0.958*	*0.957*	*0.956*
	DSC	*0.631*	*0.621*	*0.694*	*0.648*	*0.675*	*0.648*

5   Conclusion

In this work, we proposed a subspace learning-based disaster mapping technique that delineates, maps, and identifies region entities to perform disaster mapping from pre- and post-disaster imagery. We formulated disaster mapping as a subspace learning problem and proposed a tangent distance measure to express the degree of damage.

The validation results indicate that the proposed method is capable of producing accurate maps for timely response to disaster events. Furthermore, the concept of subspace learning is extensible to multiple dimensions and to other techniques for finding mappings, such as manifold learning.

Acknowledgments. This research was supported by the National Institute of General Medical Sciences of the National Institutes of Health (NIH) (award #SC3GM113754) and by the Army Research Office under grant #W911NF2010095.

References

1. Bai, Y., Mas, E., Koshimura, S.: Towards operational satellite-based damage-mapping using u-net convolutional network: a case study of 2011 Tohoku earthquake-tsunami. Remote Sens. **10**(10), 1626 (2018). https://doi.org/10.3390/rs10101626
2. Celik, T.: Unsupervised change detection in satellite images using principal component analysis and k-means clustering. IEEE Geosci. Remote Sens. Lett. **6**, 772–776 (2009). https://doi.org/10.1109/LGRS.2009.2025059
3. Chang, J.M., Kirby, M.: Face recognition under varying viewing conditions with subspace distance. In: Proceedings of International Conference on Artificial Intelligence and Pattern Recognition (AIPR-09), Orlando, FL, pp. 16–23 (2009)
4. Dell'Acqua, F., Gamba, P., Polli, D.: Mapping earthquake damage in VHR radar images of human settlements: preliminary results on the 6th April 2009, Italy case, pp. 1347–1350. IEEE (2010). https://doi.org/10.1109/IGARSS.2010.5653973
5. Fitzgibbon, A.W., Zisserman, A.: Joint manifold distance: a new approach to appearance based clustering. In: 2003 IEEE Computer Society Conference on Computer Vision and Pattern Recognition. Proceedings, vol. 1, p. I. IEEE (2003)
6. Gillespie, T.W., Chu, J., Frankenberg, E., Thomas, D.: Assessment and prediction of natural hazards from satellite imagery. Prog. Phys. Geogr. **31**(5), 459–470 (2007)
7. Gong, M., Su, L., Jia, M., Chen, W.: Fuzzy clustering with a modified MRF energy function for change detection in synthetic aperture radar images. IEEE Trans. Fuzzy Syst. **22**, 98–109 (2014). https://doi.org/10.1109/TFUZZ.2013.2249072
8. Gupta, N., Ari, S., Panigrahi, N.: Change detection in landsat images using unsupervised learning and RBF-based clustering. IEEE Trans. Emerg. Top. Comput. Intell. 1–14 (2019). https://doi.org/10.1109/TETCI.2019.2932087
9. Joyce, K.E., Belliss, S.E., Samsonov, S.V., McNeill, S.J., Glassey, P.J.: A review of the status of satellite remote sensing and image processing techniques for mapping natural hazards and disasters. Prog. Phys. Geogr. **33**(2), 183–207 (2009)
10. Khandelwal, P., Singh, K.K., Singh, B., Mehrotra, A.: Unsupervised change detection of multispectral images using wavelet fusion and Kohonen clustering network. Int. J. Eng. Technol. **5**(2), 1401–1406 (2013)
11. Li, H., Celik, T., Longbotham, N., Emery, W.J.: Gabor feature based unsupervised change detection of multitemporal SAR images based on two-level clustering. IEEE Geosci. Remote Sens. Lett. **12**(12), 2458–2462 (2015). https://doi.org/10.1109/LGRS.2015.2484220
12. Ma, Y., Chen, F., Liu, J., He, Y., Duan, J., Li, X.: An automatic procedure for early disaster change mapping based on optical remote sensing. Remote Sens. **8**(4), 272 (2016)

13. Makrogiannis, S., Vanhamel, I., Fotopoulos, S., Sahli, H., Cornelis, J.P.: Watershed-based multiscale segmentation method for color images using automated scale selection. J. Electron. Imaging **14**(3), 033007 (2005)
14. Memon, A.A., Muhammad, S., Rahman, S., Haq, M.: Flood monitoring and damage assessment using water indices: a case study of Pakistan flood-2012. Egypt. J. Remote Sens. Space Sci. **18**(1), 99–106 (2015)
15. Moghaddam, B.: Principal manifolds and probabilistic subspaces for visual recognition. IEEE Trans. Pattern Anal. Mach. Intell. **24**(6), 780–788 (2002)
16. Mori, N., Takahashi, T., Yasuda, T., Yanagisawa, H.: Survey of 2011 Tohoku earthquake tsunami inundation and run-up. Geophys. Res. Lett. **38**(7) (2011)
17. Navarro, G., Caballero, I., Silva, G., Parra, P.C., Vázquez, Á., Caldeira, R.: Evaluation of forest fire on madeira island using sentinel-2a MSI imagery. Int. J. Appl. Earth Obs. Geoinf. **58**, 97–106 (2017)
18. Okorie, A., Makrogiannis, S.: Region-based image registration for remote sensing imagery. Comput. Vis. Image Underst. **189**, 102825 (2019)
19. Quintano, C., Fernández-Manso, A., Fernández-Manso, O.: Combination of landsat and sentinel-2 MSI data for initial assessing of burn severity. Int. J. Appl. Earth Obs. Geoinf. **64**, 221–225 (2018)
20. Rifai, S., Dauphin, Y.N., Vincent, P., Bengio, Y., Muller, X.: The manifold tangent classifier. In: Advances in Neural Information Processing Systems, vol. 24 (2011)
21. Simard, P.Y., LeCun, Y.A., Denker, J.S., Victorri, B.: Transformation invariance in pattern recognition—tangent distance and tangent propagation. In: Orr, G.B., Müller, K.-R. (eds.) Neural Networks: Tricks of the Trade. LNCS, vol. 1524, pp. 239–274. Springer, Heidelberg (1998). https://doi.org/10.1007/3-540-49430-8_13
22. Soltani, K., Ebtehaj, I., Amiri, A., Azari, A., Gharabaghi, B., Bonakdari, H.: Mapping the spatial and temporal variability of flood susceptibility using remotely sensed normalized difference vegetation index and the forecasted changes in the future. Sci. Total Environ. **770**, 145288 (2021)
23. Sublime, J., Kalinicheva, E.: Automatic post-disaster damage mapping using deep-learning techniques for change detection: case study of the Tohoku tsunami. Remote Sens. **11**(9), 1123 (2019)
24. Torres, R., Mouginis-Mark, P., Self, S., Garbeil, H., Kallianpur, K., Quiambao, R.: Monitoring the evolution of the pasig-potrero alluvial fan, pinatubo volcano, using a decade of remote sensing data. J. Volcanol. Geoth. Res. **138**(3–4), 371–392 (2004)
25. Voigt, S., Kemper, T., Riedlinger, T., Kiefl, R., Scholte, K., Mehl, H.: Satellite image analysis for disaster and crisis-management support. IEEE Trans. Geosci. Remote Sens. **45**, 1520–1528 (2007). https://doi.org/10.1109/TGRS.2007.895830
26. Wang, S., et al.: Fast parameter-free multi-view subspace clustering with consensus anchor guidance. IEEE Trans. Image Process. **31**, 556–568 (2021)
27. Wang, Z., Liu, J., Li, J., Zhang, D.D.: Multi-spectral water index (MUWI): a native 10-m multi-spectral water index for accurate water mapping on sentinel-2. Remote Sens. **10**(10), 1643 (2018)
28. Xu, Y., Xiang, S., Huo, C., Pan, C.: Change detection based on auto-encoder model for VHR images. In: MIPPR 2013: Pattern Recognition and Computer Vision, vol. 8919, p. 891902. International Society for Optics and Photonics (2013). https://doi.org/10.1117/12.2031104
29. Zhu, Z., Wang, S., Woodcock, C.E.: Improvement and expansion of the FMASK algorithm: cloud, cloud shadow, and snow detection for landsats 4-7, 8, and sentinel 2 images. Remote Sens. Environ. **159**, 269–277 (2015)

Open-Set Plankton Recognition Using Similarity Learning

Ola Badreldeen Bdawy Mohamed[1], Tuomas Eerola[1](✉) (iD), Kaisa Kraft[2](iD),
Lasse Lensu[1](iD), and Heikki Kälviäinen[1](iD)

[1] Computer Vision and Pattern Recognition Laboratory,
School of Engineering Science, Lappeenranta-Lahti University of Technology LUT,
Lappeenranta, Finland
`tuomas.eerola@lut.fi`
[2] Finnish Environment Institute, Marine Research Centre, Helsinki, Finland

Abstract. Automatic plankton recognition provides new possibilities to
study plankton populations and various environmental aspects related
to them. Most of the existing recognition methods focus on individual
datasets with a known set of classes limiting their wider applicability.
Automated plankton imaging instruments capture images of unknown
particles and the class (plankton species) composition varies between
geographical regions and ecosystems. This calls for an open-set recognition method that is able to reject images from unknown classes and can
be easily generalized to new classes. In this paper, we show that a flexible
model capable of high classification accuracy can be obtained by utilizing similarity learning and a gallery set of known plankton species. The
model is shown to generalize well for new plankton classes added in the
gallery set without retraining the model. This provides a good basis for
the wider utilization of plankton recognition methods in aquatic research.

Keywords: Plankton recognition · Open-set classification · Metric
learning

1 Introduction

Phytoplankton are microscopic organisms that grow at a rapid rate. Combined
with their ability to produce organic compounds from inorganic material, phytoplankton are considered the foundation of the marine food web by supporting
all other living organisms in the ocean. As a by-product of the photosynthetic
operation, phytoplankton are one of the main producers of oxygen on the Earth.
Because of the critical roles it plays both as a sustainer of marine ecosystems and
as a regulator of a global climate change, monitoring phytoplankton populations
over time and space is essential.

Recent technological advancements have resulted in the emergence of automated and semi-automated plankton imaging instruments with continuously
improving image resolution and output rates. This has opened novel possibilities

© The Author(s), under exclusive license to Springer Nature Switzerland AG 2022
G. Bebis et al. (Eds.): ISVC 2022, LNCS 13598, pp. 174–183, 2022.
https://doi.org/10.1007/978-3-031-20713-6_13

to study plankton communities. However, to fully utilize the large image volumes in plankton research automatic methods are needed to analyze the image data. The main image analysis task to be solved is plankton recognition, i.e., classifying the images based on the species they contain.

Convolutional neural networks (CNNs) have shown to reach close-to-human level accuracy in various image recognition tasks and plankton recognition is not an exception [9,12]. However, they are known to struggle in open-set settings where the class composition of training data differs from the data for which the trained model is applied. Typical CNN-based classification models tend to classify the images from a new class to one of the known classes often with a high confidence, and to include new classes to the models, they need to be retrained. These are major problems for plankton recognition as the plankton species vary between different regions and seasons. Retraining a separate model for each dataset is not feasible. Therefore, there is a need for a recognition model that 1) is able to predict when the image contains a previously unknown plankton species and 2) can be generalized to new classes without retraining the whole model.

In this paper, we address these challenges by proposing a novel open-set plankton recognition method utilizing metric learning. The idea is to learn such image embeddings that the plankton images from the same species are close to each other and the images from the different species are far from each other in the feature space (see Fig. 1). The recognition method consists of a gallery set of known species and a learnt similarity metric allowing to compare query images to the gallery images. Similarity in this context corresponds to likelihood that the images belong to the same class. This further allows to define a threshold value for similarity enabling open-set classification: if no similar images are found in the gallery set, the query image is predicted to belong to an unknown class. Furthermore, new classes can be added by simply including them into gallery set as the model does not necessarily need to learn class-specific image features.

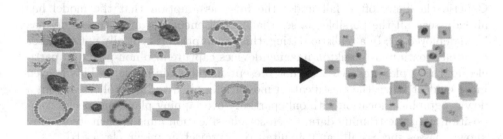

Fig. 1. Similarity metric learning for plankton images.

We propose to train the similarity metric using the angular margin loss (Arc-Face) [5] combined with Generalised mean pooling (GeM) [20] allowing to aggregate of the deep activations to rotation and translation invariant representations.

ArcFace uses a similarity learning mechanism that allows distance metric learning to be solved in the classification task by introducing the Angular Margin Loss. This allows straightforward training of the model and only adds negligible computational complexity. In the experimental part of the work, we show that the proposed method obtains high plankton image classification accuracy and outperforms the previously proposed model utilizing OpenMax [1] layer in open-set classification. We further show that the method generalizes well to new classes added to the gallery set without retraining. This makes it straightforward to apply the model to new datasets with only partly overlapping plankton species composition.

2   Related Work

2.1   Plankton Recognition

In hope of mitigating the laborious task of manually classifying the plankton images, various automatic approaches have been proposed. Modern imaging devices often utilize flow cytometry and are able to produce separate images of individual particles rendering the plankton recognition task as an image classification problem. Traditional plankton recognition methods utilize hand-crafted image features such as shape and texture (see e.g. [2]). Recently, CNNs have replaced hand-crafted features and have shown recognition performance which is comparable to human experts [9,13]. Such recognition models have already been implemented into operational phytoplankton recognition systems [11]. A typical approach utilizes common CNN architectures (e.g., ResNet), pre-trained models, and transfer learning [12,18]. However, also custom architectures have been proposed to address the fine-grained nature of the classification problem [3,4].

2.2   Open-Set Classification

Generic classifiers often fall under the false assumption that the model has already seen all the possible classes that it will encounter after the model has been deployed [7]. In a realistic setting, this assumption is typically not true. For example, continuous plankton imaging devices capture also non-plankton particles and rare plankton particles not present in the training data. This is even more evident when the classification model is applied to data collected from a new geographical location with only partially overlapping plankton species composition with the training data. Open-set classification aims to identify already known classes successfully and simultaneously reject unknown classes [7].

Bendale et al. [1] proposed the OpenMax which is an additional layer that allows deep neural networks to perform open-set recognition. The method utilizes meta-recognition to analyze activation scores and identify when the recognition model is likely to fail. Based on the distribution of the activation vector values, the OpenMax layer calculates the probability of an image being from an unknown class.

In the case of plankton recognition the open-set problem is often formulated as an anomaly detection problem where the model is trained to both correctly classify the known classes and to filter abnormal classes by training the model to produce high and low entropy distributions for the normal classes and abnormal classes respectively. Yuchun et al. [19] proposed a loss function which contains three loss terms to detect the anomalies and to maintain the classification accuracy for the images belonging to the normal classes by incorporating the expected cross-entropy loss, the expected Kullback-Leibler (KL) divergence, and the Anchor loss. The model was tested on classes of plankton images containing also bubbles or random suspending particles.

Walker et al. [22] utilized a large background set of images which do not belong to the target classes (classes to be recognized) and hard negative mining to find images that are more likely to cause false negatives. The training set was then complemented with these challenging images to improve the classifiers ability to recognize when the images are from novel classes. While promising results were obtained on open-set plankton recognition the method requires that a labeled background set is available which limits the usability of the method.

2.3 Classification by Metric Learning

The aim of deep metric learning is to obtain image embedding vectors that model the similarity between images. It is commonly utilized in person [23] and animal re-identification [15], as well as, content based image retrieval [6], but has been also successfully applied to more traditional image recognition problems such as vehicle attribute recognition [16]. The main benefit of metric learning is that training with the full set of target classes is not needed which makes metric learning more suitable for open-set recognition than traditional classification models.

The most common approaches for deep metric learning include triplet-based learning strategies and classification-based metric learning. The first approach learns the metric by sampling image triplets with and anchor, positive, and negative examples [10]. The loss function is defined in such a way that the distance (similarity) from the embeddings of the anchors to the positive samples are minimized, and the distance from the anchors to the negative samples are maximized. The second approach approximates the classes using learnt proxies [14] or class centers [5] that provide the global information needed to learn the metric. This makes it possible to formulate the loss function based on the softmax loss and allows to avoid the challenging triplet mining step.

Recently, metric learning has been utilized also in plankton classification. Teigen et al. [21] studied the viability of few-shot learners in correctly classifying plankton images. A Siamese network was trained using the triplet loss and used to determine the class of a query image. Two scenarios were tested: the multiclass classification and the novel class detection. A model trained to distinguish between five classes of plankton using five reference images from each class was able to achieve a reasonable accuracy. In the novel class detection, however, the model was able to filter out only 57 images out of 500 unknowns. Furthermore, the used triplet loss approach suffers from the high cost of the triplets mining and exponentially increasing computations as the number of classes increases.

3   Proposed Method

The proposed method for plankton recognition is based on similarity metric and a gallery set of known classes. To obtain the similarity metric, a CNN model is trained using the Angular Margin loss (ArcFace) [5]. Given an image as input, the trained CNN model outputs an embedding vector and a similarity of two images is quantified by computing the cosine distance between the image embeddings as

$$d_{cos}(\boldsymbol{v_1}, \boldsymbol{v_2}) = \frac{\boldsymbol{v_1} \cdot \boldsymbol{v_2}}{||\boldsymbol{v_1}|| \; ||\boldsymbol{v_2}||}, \tag{1}$$

where $\boldsymbol{v_1}$ and $\boldsymbol{v_2}$ are the embedding vectors. The embedding vector will be discussed further below.

To perform the plankton recognition for a query image, the embedding vector is first computed using the trained model. Then the distances to the embedding vectors of gallery set images are computed and the label is given based on the most similar image. See Fig. 2 for the overview of the method. It should be noted that since the image embeddings for gallery set can be computed and stored beforehand the query image recognition can be done efficiently by computing the cosine similarities between the vectors (simple dot product if the vectors are L^2 normalised). If the similarity between the query image and the most similar gallery set image exceeds the predetermined threshold the query image is labelled as unknown providing the basis for the open-set recognition. The metric learning approach increases inter-class separability while decreasing intra-class variation making the recognition less sensitive to selected threshold values when compared to a traditional classification approach with class probability thresholding. The threshold values can be tuned by minimizing the amount of misclassifications in the validation set.

Since the method learns to quantify the similarity (likelyhood that the images originate from the same class) instead of representations for individual classes,

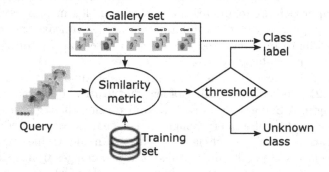

Fig. 2. The proposed method.

the set of plankton species for which the method is applied can differ from the set of classes in the training set. Therefore, to utilize the trained model on a new dataset with different set of classes due to, for example, different geographical region or ecosystem, one must only select and label a new gallery set. The gallery set requires considerably less labeled images per class than model training. Technically, even just one gallery image per class is enough to apply the method if intra-class variation is very small. However, a very small amount of gallery images may lead to a subpar recognition performance.

The method can be used with any backbone architecture, but ResNet-18 [8] has been found to produce a high classification accuracy on plankton image data with low computation cost [11]. We further propose to use Generalised mean pooling (GeM) [20] to aggregate the deep activations and to construct a representation that is invariant to both rotation and translation of the plankton. The embedding vector v aggregated through GeM can be written as

$$ v = [v_1 \ldots v_k \ldots v_C]^\top , \quad v_k = \left(\frac{1}{|\mathcal{X}_k|} \sum_{x \in \mathcal{X}_k} x^{p_k} \right)^{\frac{1}{p_k}} , \quad k \in \{1 \ldots C\}, \quad (2) $$

where $\mathcal{X}_k$ is a set of elements of the feature map k and C is the number of channels. The greater the power parameter p_k, the more the network values strong features. One of the major benefits of GeM is that p_k is also learnable so it can be optimized during the learning process.

3.1   Angular Margin Loss

ArcFace [5] utilizes the Angular Margin Loss to learn a distance metric for the classification task. The idea behind the method is to consider the weights of the last fully-connected layer as class centers. Normalization is used to distribute embeddings on a hypersphere with predefined radius which makes it possible to utilize geodesic distance. The loss is formulated as:

$$ L = -\frac{1}{N} \sum_{i=1}^{N} \log \frac{e^{s(\cos(\theta_{y_i} + m))}}{e^{s(\cos(\theta_{y_i} + m))} + \sum_{j=1, j \neq y_i}^{n} e^{s \cos \theta_j}}, \quad (3) $$

where s is the feature scale (hypersphere radius), θ_{y_i} is an angle between embedding and the class center (vector of weights) of the correct class y_i, θ_j is an angle between weight vector for class j and the predicted embedding vector, N and n are the batch size and number of classes, respectively. m is a predefined additive margin that is used to increase inter-class separability while decreasing intra-class variation. The most notable benefits of the ArcFace method include the lack of need for triplet mining and a better class separability.

4   Experiments

4.1   Data

The data was collected from the Baltic Sea using an Imaging FlowCytobot (IFCB) [17] that capture grayscale images of individual phytoplankton (see

Fig. 3). The SYKE-plankton_IFCB_2022 dataset consists of 63 074 images representing 50 different classes of phytoplankton manually labeled by an expert. Due to the varying rarity of plankton species, the dataset is highly imbalanced and the number of images per class varies from 19 to 12 280 images. For detailed description of the data, see [11]. The dataset has been made publicly available[1].

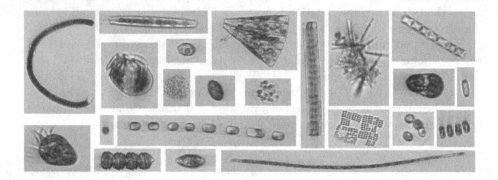

Fig. 3. Example images from the dataset.

To prepare the data for the training phase, several preprocessing steps were done. The images were resized to have a standard dimension [224,224]. Resizing was done using bicubic interpolation and the aspect ratio was maintained by padding with the background color. The dataset was split into the training, validation and test subsets with a ratio 6:2:2. To address the large class imbalance, undersampling was utilized for large classes and data augmentation with random affine transformations for small classes in order to create a balanced training set with 2 000 images per class.

4.2   Description of Experiments

To evaluate the open-set classification accuracy 10 classes were selected as unknowns and excluded from the training set. The remaining 40 classes were used for training. The gallery set was constructed by randomly selecting 100 images per class from the training set. The experiment was repeated 5 times in such a way that each class was selected as unknown once.

ResNet-18 was used as the backbone architecture for all experiments. The network was trained from scratch using Adam optimizer. A fixed learning rate of 1e-5 was used to train 200 epoch with a batch size of 64. The main two hyperparameters related to ArcFace are the hypersphere radius s and the additive angular margin penalty m. s and m were set to 2.39 and 0.95, respectively. The threshold values for open-set classification were defined for each class separately based on the validation set. The thresholds were found based on the distance between the query image and all the images in the gallery set. For OpenMax a pretrained ResNet-18 was used as a backbone.

---

[1] http://doi.org/10.23728/b2share.abf913e5a6ad47e6baa273ae0ed6617a.

4.3   Results

Table 1 shows the comparison between the proposed metric learning based method and the OpenMax method. The classification of the knowns presents the results in traditional closed-set setting with the same 40 classes included in both the training and test sets. The classification accuracy with the proposed method varied between 92.5% and 95.4%. These are comparable accuracies with baseline CNN classifiers obtained with the similar datasets (96% accuracy with 32 classes of phytoplankton [3] and 97% accuracy with 50 classes [11]). The classification of the knowns with the threshold shows the results when the test set contains only images from the known classes, but the threshold is applied to filter out predicted unknowns. As it can be seen, the accuracy decreases only little, which indicates that the known classes are only rarely classified as unknowns. The classification of the unknowns shows how many percentage of images from the previously unseen classes were correctly classified as the unknowns and the open-set classification shows results with 41 classes (40 known classes + unknowns). As it can be seen, the proposed method outperforms OpenMax in both recognition accuracy and ability to reject images from previously unseen classes.

Table 1. Mean classification accuracies and standard deviations over all 5 subexperiments.

	Classification of knowns	Classification of knowns+threshold	Classification of unknowns	Open-set recognition
OpenMax [1]	93.85 ± 0.84%	91.96 ± 0.68%	41.80 ± 8.10%	90.65 ± 0.39%
Proposed	94.60 ± 1.05%	93.27 ± 0.95%	65.20 ± 6.43%	92.33 ± 0.90%

One benefit of the proposed similarity learning approach is that by including images to the gallery set it allows to generalize the method to new classes without retraining the model itself. To study the method's ability to generalize, example images from the 10 unknown classes were included into the gallery set. Two experiments were carried out: 1) the gallery set and the query set contained images from all 50 classes (40 classes used to train the similarity model and 10 unknown classes), and 2) the gallery set and the query set contained images only from the 10 classes that were not included in the training. The results are shown in Table 2. While a drop in accuracy can be observed due to considerably more challenging tasks and a mismatch between training and test set distributions, a reasonably high accuracy was obtained.

Table 2. Capability to generalize to previously unseen classes.

	Top-1	Top-2	Top-3	Top-4	Top-5
50 classes (10 new)	$84.48 \pm 1.90\%$	$91.96 \pm 0.99\%$	$94.69 \pm 0.70\%$	$95.88 \pm 0.41\%$	$96.57 \pm 0.38\%$
10 classes (all new)	$74.07 \pm 7.08\%$	$90.21 \pm 3.29\%$	$95.68 \pm 2.03\%$	$97.78 \pm 1.60\%$	$98.91 \pm 0.70\%$

5   Conclusions

In this paper, a similarity learning approach to tackle the open-set plankton recognition problem was proposed. The method consists of a similarity metric learned using angular margin loss and a gallery set of known plankton species. The feature embeddings produced by the similarity learning model allow to compute the similarities between images and to find the most similar image (species) in the gallery set of known plankton species. Moreover, by setting similarity thresholds, the method is able to recognize when the query image contains a plankton species not present in the gallery set, enabling open-set recognition. The proposed method was shown to accurately recognize plankton species and it outperformed OpenMax in the open-set recognition task. Furthermore, we showed that the proposed method can adapt to new classes added to the gallery set without retraining the similarity learning model. This is a promising step towards a general-purpose plankton recognition method applicable to different datasets with varying class compositions, promoting the wider utilization of automatic plankton recognition for aquatic research.

Acknowledgements. The research was carried out in the FASTVISION and FASTVISION-plus projects funded by the Academy of Finland (Decision numbers 321980, 321991, 339612, and 339355).

References

1. Bendale, A., Boult, T.: Towards open set deep networks. In: Conference on Computer Vision and Pattern Recognition, pp. 1563–1572 (2016)
2. Bueno, G., et al.: Automated diatom classification (part A): handcrafted feature approaches. Appl. Sci. **7**(8), 753 (2017)
3. Bureš, J., Eerola, T., Lensu, L., Kälviäinen, H., Zemčík, P.: Plankton recognition in images with varying size. In: International Conference on Pattern Recognition Workshops, pp. 110–120 (2021)
4. Dai, J., Wang, R., Zheng, H., Ji, G., Qiao, X.: ZooplanktoNet: deep convolutional network for zooplankton classification. In: OCEANS Conference, pp. 1–6 (2016)
5. Deng, J., Guo, J., Xue, N., Zafeiriou, S.: ArcFace: additive angular margin loss for deep face recognition. In: Conference on Computer Vision and Pattern Recognition, pp. 4690–4699 (2019)
6. Dubey, S.R.: A decade survey of content based image retrieval using deep learning. IEEE Trans. Circuits Syst. Video Technol. **32**(5), 2687–2704 (2021)

7. Geng, C., Huang, S.J., Chen, S.: Recent advances in open set recognition: a survey. IEEE Trans. Pattern Anal. Mach. Intell. **43**(10), 3614–3631 (2020)
8. He, K., Zhang, X., Ren, S., Sun, J.: Deep residual learning for image recognition. In: Proceedings of the IEEE Conference on Computer Vision and Pattern Recognition, pp. 770–778 (2016)
9. Henrichs, D.W., Anglès, S., Gaonkar, C.C., Campbell, L.: Application of a convolutional neural network to improve automated early warning of harmful algal blooms. Environ. Sci. Pollut. Res. **28**(22), 28544–28555 (2021)
10. Hoffer, E., Ailon, N.: Deep metric learning using triplet network. In: International Workshop on Similarity-Based Pattern Recognition, pp. 84–92 (2015)
11. Kraft, K., et al.: Towards operational phytoplankton recognition with automated high-throughput imaging, near real-time data processing, and convolutional neural networks. Front. Marine Sci. **9** (2022)
12. Lumini, A., Nanni, L.: Deep learning and transfer learning features for plankton classification. Econ. Inform. **51**, 33–43 (2019)
13. Mitra, R., et al.: Automated species-level identification of planktic foraminifera using convolutional neural networks, with comparison to human performance. Mar. Micropaleontol. **147**, 16–24 (2019)
14. Movshovitz-Attias, Y., Toshev, A., Leung, T.K., Ioffe, S., Singh, S.: No fuss distance metric learning using proxies. In: International Conference on Computer Vision, pp. 360–368 (2017)
15. Nepovinnykh, E., Eerola, T., Kalviainen, H.: Siamese network based pelage pattern matching for ringed seal re-identification. In: Winter Conference on Applications of Computer Vision Workshops, pp. 25–34 (2020)
16. Ni, X., Huttunen, H.: Vehicle attribute recognition by appearance: computer vision methods for vehicle type, make and model classification. J. Sig. Process. Syst. **93**(4), 357–368 (2021)
17. Olson, R., Sosik, H.: A submersible imaging-in-flow instrument to analyze nano- and microplankton: imaging flowcytobot. Limnol. Oceanogr. Methods **5**(6), 195–203 (2007)
18. Orenstein, E., Beijbom, O.: Transfer learning and deep feature extraction for planktonic image data sets. In: Winter Conference on Applications of Computer Vision, pp. 1082–1088 (2017)
19. Pu, Y., Feng, Z., Wang, Z., Yang, Z., Li, J.: Anomaly detection for in situ marine plankton images. In: International Conference on Computer Vision, pp. 3661–3671 (2021)
20. Radenović, F., Tolias, G., Chum, O.: Fine-tuning CNN image retrieval with no human annotation. IEEE Trans. Pattern Anal. Mach. Intell. **41**(7), 1655–1668 (2018)
21. Teigen, A.L., Saad, A., Stahl, A.: Leveraging similarity metrics to in-situ discover planktonic interspecies variations or mutations. In: Global Oceans 2020: Singapore-US Gulf Coast, pp. 1–8 (2020)
22. Walker, J., Orenstein, E.: Improving rare-class recognition of marine plankton with hard negative mining. In: International Conference on Computer Vision, pp. 3672–3682 (2021)
23. Ye, M., Shen, J., Lin, G., Xiang, T., Shao, L., Hoi, S.C.: Deep learning for person re-identification: a survey and outlook. IEEE Trans. Pattern Anal. Mach. Intell. **44**(6), 2872–2893 (2021)

Sensor Fusion Operators for Multimodal 2D Object Detection

Morteza Mousa Pasandi, Tianran Liu, Yahya Massoud[(✉)],
and Robert Laganière

University of Ottawa, Ottawa, ON, Canada
ymass049@uottawa.ca

Abstract. Autonomous driving requires effective capabilities to detect road objects in different environmental conditions. One promising solution to improve perception is to leverage multi-sensor fusion. This approach aims to combine various sensor streams in order to best integrate the information coming from the different sensors. Fusion operators are used to combine features from different modalities inside convolutional neural network architectures. In this study, we provide a framework for evaluating early fusion operators using different 2D object detection architectures. This comparative study includes element-wise addition and multiplication, feature concatenation, multi-modal factorized bilinear pooling, and bilaterally-guided fusion. We report quantitative results of the performance as well as an analysis of computational costs of these operators on different architectures.

Keywords: Convolutional neural networks · Sensor fusion · Fusion operators · Object detection · Autonomous driving

1 Introduction

Nowadays, intelligent vehicles include several sensors of different types in order to produce robust perception systems. In that context, multi-modal sensor fusion represents a way to enhance the accuracy and reliability of perception algorithms and methods. Deep convolutional networks are particularly well adapted for sensor fusion as the network architecture can be designed to accommodate multiple branches coming from different sensor streams that eventually merge or fuse together to produce a single output.

Different strategies can be used to implement sensor fusion in a neural network. Early fusion aims at combining the input modalities before performing the feature extraction step. Late fusion is usually done at the very end of the network by fusing the high-level feature maps before making a final classification or detection decision. Mid-level fusion is performed on intermediate deep representations and applies further processing of the fused feature maps in order to come up with a final decision. However, no matter which strategy is used to implement a sensor fusion architecture, one has to make a decision on how fusion will be performed at the junction point where the branches from the different modalities merge.

The choice of an appropriate fusion mechanism is therefore a critical factor toward building a robust sensor fusion architecture. The fusion mechanism will enable proper interaction between the different modalities and their corresponding feature maps. Several fusion operators have been proposed in the recent literature. Some are based on simple element-wise arithmetic operators such as summation and multiplication, or on order statistics such as median or min/max operations. Although computationally efficient, these element-wise approaches generally do not provide good perceptual robustness as they are unable to capture all interactions between the different modalities and their associated feature maps. In order to design more advanced fusion operators, we need to capture the intrinsic interrelation between features. This idea seems to constitute an interesting alternative to simple fusion operators. But before adding computational complexity to a network, one must assess the efficacy of such complex fusion operators.

[1] presented an idea of employing learnable fusion mechanisms for the task of 3D object detection, and proposed extending such contribution to other tasks while exploring other variations of fusion modules. The objective of this paper is to experimentally compare the performance of different fusion operators in the context of multi-modal road user detection using deep neural networks. To do so, we selected an object detection architecture and use LiDAR and camera fusion as an illustrative application of sensor fusion. The performance of this architecture is then tested for different choices of fusion mechanisms. Our objective is to demonstrate the impact of a fusion operator on the precision of a detection network.

Section 2 presents some recent works in sensor fusion. Section 3 describes the detection network used in this experimental study. Section 4 introduces the different fusion operators. Section 5 present the experimental results. Section 6 is a conclusion.

2   Related Work

MV3D [2] presents a sensor fusion framework that leverages both camera and LiDAR sensors. The proposed architecture uses cylindrical frontal view projection of the LiDAR sensor to further enhance the performance of its frontal view branch. Each of the modalities is fed into a feature extraction network, then a 3D region-proposal generation step is applied. After that, region proposals are fed into a deep-fusion mechanism to enable interaction between all three modalities. Finally, the output of the deep-fusion mechanism is fed to classification and regression branches. It is worth noting that the deep-fusion mechanism comprises of a branching version of the element-wise mean fusion.

FrustumPointNets [3] uses RGB-D data for the tasks of object detection and localization. The framework applies a robust 2D detector to the RGB image to extract accurate 2D region-proposals, then aims to extract and segments 3D frustums from each region proposal by using the depth information. PointFusion [4] is a two-stage framework that uses inputs from both camera and LiDAR. PointFusion applies a SOTA 2D detector on the image, then fuses the extracted feature maps with the corresponding 3D points extracted from the raw LIDAR point cloud to mitigate any loss of information, not having to encode the whole raw point cloud.

AVOD [5] incorporates a two-stage architecture to operate on both camera and LiDAR sensors, while the intermediate fusion mechanism is an element-wise mean operation, followed by a series of fully-connected layers for each modality. ContFuse [6] is an end-to-end framework that uses the idea of continuous convolution to project frontal view feature maps extracted from a frontal view stream into BEV, then fuses these projected feature maps with original BEV feature maps extracted from a BEV feature extractor. The fusion mechanism is a simple element-wise summation. [1] proposes a two-stream multi-modal multi-view sensor fusion architecture that operates on LiDAR BEV representation, LiDAR frontal view features (height, depth, and intensity), and RGB images. Early learnable fusion for the frontal view stream is employed to boost performance. Moreover, learnable mid-level fusion is applied with multi-task learning to bypass the limited nature of fixed fusion operations (e.g. addition or multiplication). MMF [7] employed a strategy of using two sensors (LiDAR and camera) to learn four tasks and showed that a target task (3D object detection) can benefit from multi-task learning. MMF framework aimed at using RGB image as well as projection-based representations for LiDAR point clouds to simultaneously perform the following tasks: 2D and 3D object detection, online mapping, and depth completion.

3   Camera-LiDAR 2D Object Detector

The objective of this paper is to study the impact of various fusion operators on the performance of a sensor fusion framework. Therefore, we chose a multi-sensor fusion architecture that uses both LiDAR and camera inputs to perform 2D road object detection. We performed our experiments without introducing changes to the original network. Instead, we evaluated the performance by replacing the fusion operator that combines both input modalities. In Fig. 1, we show the architecture of the sensor fusion network. The objective behind our model selection is to combine both good performance and low complexity.

The camera stream processes a colored input image to detect 2D objects. The downside of using camera only is the impact of, among others, adverse lighting and weather conditions, noise, reflections, and limited depth cues. These challenging situations will negatively affect the performance of an image-based object detector. The LiDAR stream aims at complementing the visual information with 3D information provided in the form of 3D point clouds. In order to have compatible representations from both modalities, we opted for a frontal view representation of the LiDAR data by projecting intensity, depth, and height maps on the camera view.

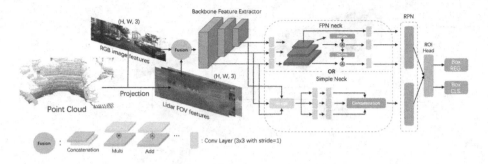

Fig. 1. Overall architecture of our sensor fusion framework. This network is used to assess and analyze the effectiveness of different fusion operators in a 2D detection task.

Both camera and LiDAR frontal views are then combined using a fusion operator forming the sensor fusion head of this early fusion network. The outcome of the fusion operation is then fed into the 2D object detection to perform inference. The architecture of the 2D detection network is inspired by popular detection frameworks such as Faster-RCNN [8] and Cascade-RCNN [9].

We use ResNet-30 [10] and Swin Transformer Tiny [11] as our feature extraction backbone networks. ResNet-30 has an initial layer containing 32 filters and a 7×7 kernel size, followed by three stages containing $\{4, 4, 6\}$ basic blocks and $\{32, 64, 128\}$ filters, respectively. Swin Transformer Tiny has a window size of 7 with four stages containing $\{96, 192, 384, 768\}$ embedding sizes, respectively. To further process the output of the backbone network, we employ one of two types of necks, namely Simple neck or a Feature Pyramid Network (FPN) neck [12]. Simple neck has three stages, each stage containing 96 Filters, resulting in 288 output channels after concatenation of all stages.

Lastly, Faster-RCNN [8] and Cascade-RCNN [9] are used as detection heads. Faster-RCNN employs a region proposal network (RPN) and a region-of-interest (ROI) detection head for generating object proposals. It extracts a fixed-length feature vector from each region proposal, based on which it assigns a classification score and a predicted bounding box. The outcome of both the RPN and the feature maps extracted from the neck are then fed into the ROI detection head to infer 2D objects. Cascade-RCNN is based on a sequential arrangement of three identical ROI heads, each feeding the next cascaded Faster RCNN detector. Figure 2 illustrates how both early- and mid-level fusion are applied in the proposed framework. Early fusion applies the fusion operation on the inputs, then feeds the fused inputs to the backbone network, while mid-level fusion feeds inputs to two parallel backbone networks first, then applies the fusion operation on the two output feature maps.

4   Sensor Fusion Operators

Fusion operators can be classified into two categories: (1) fixed and (2) learnable operators. The first category includes basic and computationally efficient

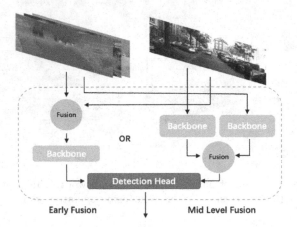

Fig. 2. Left: early fusion fuse inputs then feeds the outcome to the backbone network. Right: mid-level fusion feeds inputs to two backbone networks first, then fuses the output feature maps.

fusion methods such as element-wise summation, mean, max, or the concatenation operation. However, these methods are generally not robust enough to adequately capture the interactions between related features of different modalities. At the price of higher computational cost and training complexity, more sophisticated fusion schemes have been introduced. [13] proposed bilinear-pooling as a robust fusion mechanism. Despite the expressiveness of bilinear pooling, its use is impractical from a computational perspective. The authors present more efficient way to implement factorized versions of the robust bilinear-pooling fusion mechanism in deep learning architectures leading to multi-modal factorized bilinear pooling (MFB). MFB has been used in [14] for detecting activity in videos. MFB's implementation was further studied and optimized in [1] in order to be adapted for the task of 3D object detection. As a mid-level fusion mechanism, [1] showed a significant performance increase compared to element-wise fusion operators. Bilateral Guided Aggregation (BGA) is another fusion mechanism that has been applied in [15] to preserve Semantic features in semantic segmentation tasks. BGA aims at fusing multi-modal features with a cross-modal attention mechanism embedded into a neural sub-network. BGA has also been used in [16] to merge frontal view features with bird's eye view features in a camera-lidar fusion network. In our work, we employ and analyze both multi-modal factorized bilinear pooling (MFB) and bilateral guided fusion (BGF) as potential learnable fusion mechanisms. Both fusion mechanisms are illustrated in Fig. 3.

Multi-modal Factorized Bilinear Pooling. First, both colored image ($\mathcal{I}_{rgb}$) and LiDAR features ($\mathcal{I}_{lidar}$) are projected into a high-dimensional space using a convolutional layer that expands the number of channels from 3 to 6. The aforementioned step produces two expanded feature maps ($\mathcal{F}_a$) and ($\mathcal{F}_b$) as described

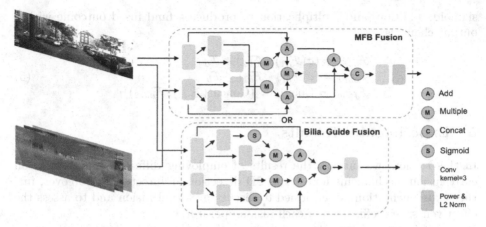

Fig. 3. The structure of two learnable fusion mechanisms: multi-modal factorized bilinear pooling (MFB) and bilateral guided fusion (BGF).

in Eq. 1. Then, each feature map is fed into two convolutional layers while preserving the size of the channel dimension (6 filters), producing four new feature maps: $\{\mathcal{F}_{a1}, \mathcal{F}_{a2}, \mathcal{F}_{b1}, \mathcal{F}_{b2}\}$. All four feature maps are then mixed together based on Eqs. 2 and 3. Then, two operations (addition and multiplication) are applied in parallel to $\mathcal{F}_{out1}$ and $\mathcal{F}_{out2}$. The multiplication outcome is then fed into a convolutional layer with 6 filters. Finally, the outcome of both convolution and addition operations is concatenated and fed into a final convolutional layer which reduces the channel dimension from 12 to 3 channels, followed by power and L_2 normalization. The final process is described in Eq. 4.

$$\begin{aligned}\mathcal{F}_a &= \mathrm{Conv}_{3 \to 6}(\mathcal{I}_{rgb}) \\ \mathcal{F}_b &= \mathrm{Conv}_{3 \to 6}(\mathcal{I}_{lidar})\end{aligned} \qquad (1)$$

$$\mathcal{F}_{out1} = \mathcal{F}_{b1} * \mathcal{F}_{a2} + \mathcal{F}_a \qquad (2)$$

$$\mathcal{F}_{out2} = \mathcal{F}_{b2} * \mathcal{F}_{a1} + \mathcal{F}_b \qquad (3)$$

$$\begin{aligned}\mathcal{F}_{mul} &= \mathcal{F}_{out1} * \mathcal{F}_{out2} \\ \mathcal{F}_{add} &= \mathcal{F}_{out1} + \mathcal{F}_{out2} \\ \mathcal{F}_{pre} &= \mathrm{Concat}(\mathrm{Conv}_{6 \to 6}(\mathcal{F}_{mul}), \mathcal{F}_{add}) \\ \mathcal{F}_{final} &= \mathrm{Norm}(\mathrm{Conv}_{12 \to 3}(\mathcal{F}_{pre}))\end{aligned} \qquad (4)$$

Bilateral Guided Fusion. Similar to steps 1 and 2 in MFB, both input modalities are first projected into a high-dimensional space using convolutions (Eq. 1), then fed into convolutions to produce four feature maps: $\{\mathcal{F}_{a1}, \mathcal{F}_{a2}, \mathcal{F}_{b1}, \mathcal{F}_{b2}\}$. Finally, all four feature maps are mixed based on Eq. 5 with a combination of sigmoid, addition, and multiplication to produce a final fused outcome with 3 output channels.

$$\mathcal{F}_{out1} = (\sigma(\mathcal{F}_{a1}) * \mathcal{F}_{a2}) + \mathcal{F}_a$$
$$\mathcal{F}_{out2} = (\sigma(\mathcal{F}_{b1}) * \mathcal{F}_{b2}) + \mathcal{F}_b \qquad (5)$$
$$\mathcal{F}_{final} = \text{Conv}_{12 \to 3}(\text{Concat}(\mathcal{F}_{out1}, \mathcal{F}_{out2}))$$

5   Experimental Results

In this section, we present the results of employing different operators in an early fusion mechanisms for various 2D detection architectures. Moreover, further experimentation is performed to discuss mid-level fusion and to assess the effectiveness and efficiency of each fusion operator.

5.1   Experimental Setting

To assess the effectiveness of early sensor fusion mechanisms, we train and evaluate four different models on the KITTI 2D object detection benchmark [17]. We rely on KITTI's validation set to showcase our experimental results and ablation study by following the same split suggested in [18]. Faster-RCNN variants are trained using stochastic gradient descent, while Cascade-RCNN with Swin Transformer is trained using the AdamW [19] optimizer. All architectures are trained on the 2D detection task for "Car" and "Pedestrian" classes. Models are trained for 30 epochs, while applying horizontal flipping as a data augmentation strategy. Detection accuracy is reported for three different categories: easy, moderate, and hard. We use average-precision (AP%) to report the detection accuracy for each class in all three difficulty levels.

5.2   Evaluation of Early Sensor Fusion

In Table 1, we compare and contrast the results of five early fusion operators and their impact on the performance of four 2D object detectors. The baseline detection accuracy for each architecture is called "No Fusion", where the detector operates on the colored image only without LiDAR information, hence, no early fusion mechanism is being applied. Other fusion operators are: (1) element-wise addition "Add", (2) feature concatenation "Concat", (3) element-wise multiplication "Multi", (4) bilaterally-guided fusion "BGF", and (5) multi-modal factorized bilinear pooling "MFB".

For the first set of experiments which use the R30 Simple Neck Faster-RCNN detector, MFB consistently outperforms all other early fusion operators in all difficulty levels for both classes of interest. Compared to the second-best fusion operator, MFB scores an increase of (+4.37%) and (+3.76%) in the moderate category for both car and pedestrian classes, respectively. In the second set of experiments, we use the R30 FPN Faster-RCNN detector. Feature concatenation yields better results for the pedestrian class, while BGF performs better for the

Table 1. Comaparing 2D detection accuracy of different early stage fusion operators on Faster-RCNN and Swin Transformer

Model components	Fusion operation	Car ($AP_{70}\%$)			Pedestrian ($AP_{50}\%$)		
		Easy	Moderate	Hard	Easy	Moderate	Hard
R30 Simple Neck Faster-RCNN	No fusion	78.04	56.03	47.25	29.04	24.55	20.93
	Add	77.45	59.18	48.34	30.73	23.25	19.52
	Concat	83.48	65.74	56.05	36.63	27.60	23.97
	Multi	77.09	56.39	47.51	28.98	22.18	18.71
	BGF	84.82	66.73	58.44	34.09	28.36	24.76
	MFB	**85.52**	**71.1**	**59.2**	**37.2**	**32.12**	**29.98**
R30 FPN Faster-RCNN	No fusion	89.92	81.26	72.56	63.18	53.12	46.18
	Add	92.57	81.88	71.7	54.27	45.32	38.28
	Concat	93.48	84.21	74.42	**65.59**	**55.41**	**47.94**
	Multi	87.39	70.25	62.6	58.18	48.91	42.2
	BGF	**93.79**	**84.89**	**76.15**	64.57	54.99	47.45
	MFB	92.93	82.37	72.23	64.12	53.15	47.11
R30 FPN Cascade-RCNN	No fusion	92.49	84.38	73.75	62.33	52.89	44.9
	Add	93.82	85.42	75.33	63.62	52.61	44.31
	Concat	94.49	87.5	77.74	70.21	58.98	50.41
	Multi	90.9	77.23	67.53	64.85	54.44	46.38
	BGF	**94.9**	**88.4**	**78.38**	**71.25**	**61.11**	**52.48**
	MFB	93.21	85.34	76.93	66.88	56.13	48.53
Swin FPN CascadeRCNN	No fusion	93.85	81.66	71.56	58.98	50.02	43.12
	Add	90.35	77.76	67.78	59.50	50.70	43.29
	Concat	94.87	86.36	77.76	**71.3**	**60.83**	**52.05**
	Multi	91.49	76.05	66.00	60.73	50.62	43.50
	BGF	95.38	85.81	77.68	67.66	56.78	47.9
	MFB	**96.57**	**88.12**	**78.13**	67.20	58.10	50.11

car class. That being said, both feature concatenation and BGF are on par. If we compare their performance based on the moderate difficulty, we find that BGF is superior to concatenation by (+0.68%) for the car class, but inferior to concatenation by (−0.42%) for the pedestrian class. When incorporated with R30-FPN Cascade-RCNN, BGF outperforms other fusion methods for both car and pedestrian classes in all difficulty levels.

Finally, we evaluate the Swin FPN Cascade-RCNN detector and observe MFB fusion outperforming other early fusion methods in the car class. As for the pedestrian class, it follows a similar pattern to R30-FPN Faster-RCNN, where feature concatenation outperforms all other fusion methods.

Based on the aforementioned results, we conclude the superiority of the learnable fusion mechanisms, both MFB and BGF, over other less-sophisticated fusion operators when detecting the car class. Using feature concatenation as the fusion operator yields overall good results, and even superior to learnable fusion in two cases only for the pedestrian class.

5.3   Evaluation of Mid-Level Sensor Fusion

In order to assess the importance of mid-level fusion, we train two ResNet30 in parallel, then fuse the extracted features from each network. Table 2 shows and contrasts the results between early- and mid-level fusion on the same model architecture, an R30 FPN Faster-RCNN 2D object detector. Sophisticated learnable fusion mechanisms prove ineffective in the case of mid-level fusion for both car and pedestrian class, while more simple element-wise addition or feature concatenation are scoring higher detection accuracy. Moreover, mid-level fusion with element-wise addition is superior to early fusion in the case of pedestrian detection, scoring an increase of (+2.25%), (+3.97%), and (+3.46%) in easy, moderate, and hard categories, respectively.

Table 2. Difference between early fusion and mid-level fusion. The reported results compare two different backbone feature extractors.

Model components	Fusion operation	Car ($AP_{70}\%$)			Pedestrian ($AP_{50}\%$)		
		Easy	Moderate	Hard	Easy	Moderate	Hard
R30 FPN Faster-RCNN Early Fusion	No Fusion	89.92	81.26	72.56	63.18	53.12	46.18
	Add	92.57	81.88	71.7	54.27	45.32	38.28
	Concat	93.48	84.21	74.42	**65.59**	**55.41**	**47.94**
	Multi	87.39	70.25	62.6	58.18	48.91	42.2
	BGF	**93.79**	**84.89**	**76.15**	64.57	54.99	47.45
	MFB	92.93	82.37	72.23	64.12	53.15	47.11
R30 FPN Faster-RCNN Mid-level Fusion	No Fusion	90.44	79.97	70.12	53.4	46.13	39.33
	Add	93.14	**83.80**	**73.88**	**67.84**	**59.38**	**51.40**
	Concat	**93.97**	83.77	73.65	67.12	58.18	50.53
	Multi	93.70	82.87	72.64	63.64	54.25	46.46
	BGF	93.41	82.50	72.44	60.75	51.91	44.72
	MFB	93.75	82.87	72.08	59.8	50.54	43.00

5.4   Complexity Analysis

Computation Overhead. In Table 3, we compare the computational complexity of five different object detectors without applying any fusion mechanisms. In terms of the number of learnable parameters, R30-FPN Faster-RCNN has the least capacity with 18.4M parameters, compared to Swin Tiny FPN Cascade-RCNN which has 72.5M parameters. R30 Simple Neck Faster-RCNN

Table 3. Comparison of the complexity of each model and their required floating point operations per second (FLOPS)

Model	Computation metrics	
	Parameters (Million)	FLOPS (Giga)
R30 Simple Neck Faster-RCNN	18.88	**79.44**
R30 FPN Faster-RCNN	**18.4**	191.71
2 Stream R30 FPN Faster-RCNN	20.87	217.78
R30 FPN Cascade-RCNN	46.2	219.51
Swin Tiny FPN Cascade-RCNN	72.5	336.13

has 79.44 GFLOPS, which is four times more efficient compared to Swin Tiny FPN Cascade-RCNN which has 336.13 giga-FLOPS.

An interesting aspect that should be emphasized is the relation between the number of parameters and GFLOPS for different fusion mechanisms. In Fig. 4, we compare concatenation to two learnable fusion mechanisms (MFB and BGF) by applying them on three different architectures: (1) R30 Simple Neck Faster-RCNN, (2) R30 FPN Faster-RCNN, and (3) Swin FPN Cascade-RCNN.

Normally, concatenation by itself does not add up more learnable parameters to the architecture, except for Swin FPN Cascade-RCNN. In contrast, both MFB and BGF add more learnable parameters to the model. That being said, the impact of concatenation on increasing GFLOPS is comparable, and in some cases even higher than both MFB and BGF.

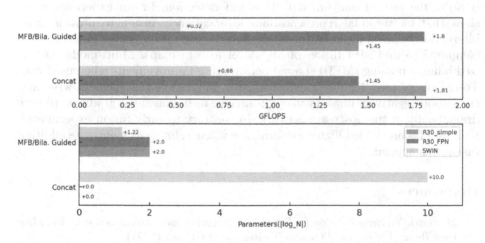

Fig. 4. Showing the relation between number of parameters (log-scaled) and the amount of GFLOPS when using different fusion operators. Even though learnable fusion mechanisms add up more learnable parameters to the architecture, their GFLOPS is still on par, and in some cases more efficient compared to feature concatenation.

Kernel Size of MFB. As denoted in [1], MFB was used with a kernel of size (1×1). In this work, we aimed to assess this design choice by comparing the usage of kernel size (1×1) and (3×3). We perform such experiments on R30 FPN Faster-RCNN architecture. In Table 4, we observe that (3×3) usually yields superior detection accuracy for both car and pedestrian classes, with only one exception in the moderate case for the pedestrian class.

Table 4. Comparing different kernel size options in MFB Fusion module. K_1: 1×1 kernel size, K_3: 3×3 kernel size. *Mid-level* flag denotes whether the setting was used in mid- or early-fusion. All four experiments were performed on Resnet 30 FPN Faster-RCNN architecture.

Exp	K_1	K_3	Mid-level	Car $AP_{70\%}$			Pedestrian $AP_{50\%}$		
				Easy	Moderate	Hard	Easy	Moderate	Hard
(a)	√		√	92.93	82.01	71.42	58.8	50.43	42.11
(b)		√	√	**93.75**	**82.87**	72.08	59.8	50.54	43.00
(c)	√			92.71	81.48	71.82	63.66	**54.12**	46.28
(d)		√		92.93	82.37	**72.23**	**64.12**	53.15	**47.11**

6   Conclusion

In this work, we provide a comprehensive analysis of both effectiveness and efficiency of various fusion operators when employed in different architectures to perform the task of multi-modal 2D object detection. In our experiments, we show that multi-modal representations leverage early fusion to provide more interaction between input features. Moreover, early fusion proves more effective compared to mid-level fusion of high-level feature maps. Multi-modal factorized bilinear pooling (MFB) showed performance improvements when used with Transformer-based 2D object detector. Also, we observe that element-wise multiplication negatively impacts the performance as it causes the gradients to vary dramatically in the upstream network. In contrary to early fusion experiments, mid-level fusion yielded higher performance when a simple element-wise addition fusion was applied.

References

1. Massoud, Y.: Sensor fusion for 3D object detection for autonomous vehicles. Master's thesis, Université d'Ottawa/University of Ottawa (2021)
2. Chen, X., Ma, H., Wan, J., Li, B., Xia, T.: Multi-view 3D object detection network for autonomous driving. In: Proceedings of the IEEE Conference on Computer Vision and Pattern Recognition, pp. 1907–1915 (2017)
3. Qi, C.R., Liu, W., Wu, C., Su, H., Guibas, L.J.: Frustum pointnets for 3D object detection from RGB-D data. In Proceedings of the IEEE Conference on Computer Vision and Pattern Recognition, pp. 918–927 (2018)

4. Xu, D., Anguelov, D., Jain, A.: Pointfusion: deep sensor fusion for 3D bounding box estimation. In: Proceedings of the IEEE Conference on Computer Vision and Pattern Recognition, pp. 244–253 (2018)
5. Ku, J., Mozifian, M., Lee, J., Harakeh, A., Waslander, S.L.: Joint 3D proposal generation and object detection from view aggregation. In: 2018 IEEE/RSJ International Conference on Intelligent Robots and Systems (IROS), pp. 1–8. IEEE (2018)
6. Liang, M., Yang, B., Wang, S., Urtasun, R.: Deep continuous fusion for multi-sensor 3D object detection. In: Ferrari, V., Hebert, M., Sminchisescu, C., Weiss, Y. (eds.) ECCV 2018. LNCS, vol. 11220, pp. 663–678. Springer, Cham (2018). https://doi.org/10.1007/978-3-030-01270-0_39
7. Liang, M., Yang, B., Chen, Y., Hu, R., Urtasun, R.: Multi-task multi-sensor fusion for 3D object detection. In: Proceedings of the IEEE/CVF Conference on Computer Vision and Pattern Recognition, pp. 7345–7353 (2019)
8. Chen, X., Gupta, A.: An implementation of faster RCNN with study for region sampling. arXiv preprint arXiv:1702.02138 (2017)
9. Cai, Z., Vasconcelos, N.: Cascade R-CNN: delving into high quality object detection. In: Proceedings of the IEEE Conference on Computer Vision and Pattern Recognition, pp. 6154–6162 (2018)
10. He, K., Zhang, X., Ren, S., Sun, J.: Deep residual learning for image recognition. In: Proceedings of the IEEE Conference on Computer Vision and Pattern Recognition, pp. 770–778 (2016)
11. Liu, Z., et al.: Swin transformer: hierarchical vision transformer using shifted windows. In: Proceedings of the IEEE/CVF International Conference on Computer Vision, pp. 10012–10022 (2021)
12. Lin, T.-Y., Dollár, P., Girshick, R., He, K., Hariharan, B., Belongie, S.: Feature pyramid networks for object detection. In: Proceedings of the IEEE Conference on Computer Vision and Pattern Recognition, pp. 2117–2125 (2017)
13. Yu, Z., Yu, J., Fan, J., Tao, D.: Multi-modal factorized bilinear pooling with co-attention learning for visual question answering. In: ICCV, pp. 1839–1848 (2017)
14. Rahman, Md.A., Laganière, R.: Mid-level fusion for end-to-end temporal activity detection in untrimmed video. In: BMVC (2020)
15. Changqian, Yu., Gao, C., Wang, J., Gang, Yu., Shen, C., Sang, N.: Bisenet v2: bilateral network with guided aggregation for real-time semantic segmentation. Int. J. Comput. Vision 129(11), 3051–3068 (2021)
16. Deng, J., Zhou, W., Zhang, Y., Li, H.: From multi-view to hollow-3D: hallucinated hollow-3D R-CNN for 3D object detection. IEEE Trans. Circuits Syst. Video Technol. 31(12), 4722–4734 (2021)
17. Geiger, A., Lenz, P., Urtasun, R.: Are we ready for autonomous driving? The KITTI vision benchmark suite. In: Conference on Computer Vision and Pattern Recognition (CVPR) (2012)
18. Chen, X., Kundu, K., Zhu, Y., Ma, H., Fidler, S., Urtasun, R.: 3D object proposals using stereo imagery for accurate object class detection. IEEE Trans. Pattern Anal. Mach. Intell. 40(5), 1259–1272 (2017)
19. Loshchilov, I., Hutter, F.: Decoupled weight decay regularization. arXiv preprint arXiv:1711.05101 (2017)

Learning When to Say *"I Don't Know"*

Nicholas Kashani Motlagh[1]([envelope])[iD], Jim Davis[1], Tim Anderson[2],
and Jeremy Gwinnup[2]

[1] Department of Computer Science and Engineering, Ohio State University,
Columbus, USA
{kashanimotlagh.1,davis.1719}@osu.edu
[2] Air Force Research Laboratory, Wright-Patterson AFB, Dayton, USA
{timothy.anderson.20,jeremy.gwinnup.1}@us.af.mil

Abstract. We propose a new Reject Option Classification technique to identify and remove regions of uncertainty in the decision space for a given neural classifier and dataset. Such existing formulations employ a learned rejection (remove)/selection (keep) function and require either a known cost for rejecting examples or strong constraints on the accuracy or coverage of the *selected* examples. We consider an alternative formulation by instead analyzing the complementary *reject* region and employing a validation set to learn per-class softmax thresholds. The goal is to maximize the accuracy of the selected examples subject to a natural randomness allowance on the *rejected* examples (rejecting more incorrect than correct predictions). We provide results showing the benefits of the proposed method over naïvely thresholding calibrated/uncalibrated softmax scores with 2-D points, imagery, and text classification datasets using state-of-the-art pretrained models. Source code is available at https://github.com/osu-cvl/learning-idk.

Keywords: Reject Option Classification · Confusion · Uncertainty

1 Introduction

Neural classifiers have shown impressive performance in diverse applications ranging from spam identification to medical diagnosis to autonomous driving. However, the typical argmax softmax decision function forces these networks to sometimes yield unreliable predictions. For example, the 10-class feature space shown in Fig. 1a displays many regions of class overlap/confusion. It can be desirable to abstain from accepting predictions within highly confusing regions. These low-confidence decisions could be discarded or potentially given to a more complex model (or human analyst) to resolve. Our task is to identify these confusing regions by learning an auxiliary rejection/selection function on predictions. We show the results of using a particular rejection function (described later) in Fig. 1b and 1c, where plots are generated for the *selected* and *rejected* examples. Clearly, these plots show much stronger classifiable selected examples while further supporting the confusability of the rejected examples.

G. Bebis et al. (Eds.): ISVC 2022, LNCS 13598, pp. 196–210, 2022.
https://doi.org/10.1007/978-3-031-20713-6_15

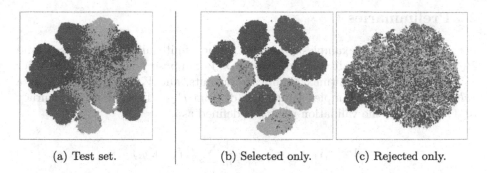

(a) Test set.   (b) Selected only.   (c) Rejected only.

Fig. 1. t-SNE plots of logits from a weakly-trained ResNet20 [16] model on CINIC10 [7] using a) all, b) selected only, and c) rejected only.

One simple solution to detect under-confident predictions is to threshold the softmax value of the argmax decision. However, naïvely thresholding at 0.5 (the boundary of being more confidently correct) or some other ad hoc threshold may not be ideal or optimal. Reject Option Classification methods [5,11–14,21,22] aim to address this problem by endowing a classifier with a *learned* rejection threshold to reject (remove) or select (keep) predictions, enabling the model to "know what it doesn't know."

There are three main types of approaches to learning a rejection function. First, the cost-based approach [5] minimizes an objective that uses a *user-defined* cost for making a rejection. However, applications without a known rejection cost can not leverage this approach. The next type of approach is the bounded-improvement model [21], which maximizes coverage (percentage of examples selected) under the constraint that the *select accuracy* (accuracy of selected examples) is lower-bounded by a user-defined amount. For example, a classifier may be required to have a select accuracy of $\geq 95\%$ while trying to maximize the number of selected predictions (coverage). Lastly, the bounded-coverage model [12] maximizes the select accuracy under the constraint that the *coverage* is lower-bounded by a user-defined amount. For example, it may be necessary to accept $\geq 90\%$ of examples while maximizing the select accuracy.

These previous works focus on user-defined constraints of accuracy and coverage for the selected examples. Here, we present a new Reject Option Classification approach that instead focuses on a natural randomness property desired of *reject* regions. This randomness property is not directly applicable to the complementary select regions and holds across any neural classifier and dataset pairing. Our contributions are summarized as follows:

1. Fast post-processing method applicable to any pretrained classifier/dataset.
2. No user-defined costs/constraints for rejection, select accuracy, or coverage.
3. Additional approach that reduces computation for large datasets.

2 Preliminaries

Let $\mathcal{X}$ be the space of examples, $\mathcal{Y} = \{1, ..., c\}$ be a finite label set of c classes, and $P_{\mathcal{X}\mathcal{Y}}$ be the joint data distribution over $\mathcal{X} \times \mathcal{Y}$. Suppose f is a *trained* classifier $f : \mathcal{X} \to [0, 1]^c$ with softmax/confidence outputs, and $V_m = \{(x_i, y_i)\}_{i=1}^m$ is a *validation* set of m examples sampled i.i.d. from $P_{\mathcal{X}\mathcal{Y}}$. The empirical accuracy (0–1) of f w.r.t. the validation set V_m is defined as

$$Acc(f|V_m) \quad = \quad 1 - \frac{1}{m} \sum_{i=1}^m \ell(f(x_i), y_i) \tag{1}$$

where $\ell(f(x_i), y_i) = \mathbb{1}[\text{argmax}(f(x_i)) \neq y_i]$ is the 0/1 loss using the indicator function on the argmax decision rule.

A Reject Option Classifier $H_{(f, g_\tau)}$ is defined by a tuple (f, g_τ) where f is the previously defined trained classifier and $g_\tau : [0, 1]^c \to \{0, 1\}$ is a rejection function (1:reject, 0:select) with a per-class threshold vector $\tau \in [0, 1]^c$. We can write the rejection function for a given example (x_i, y_i) as

$$g_\tau(f(x_i)) = \mathbb{1}[\max(f(x_i)) \leq \tau_{\text{argmax}(f(x_i))}]$$

Hence, $H_{(f, g_\tau)}$ is

$$H_{(f, g_\tau)}(x_i) = \begin{cases} \text{reject}, & g_\tau(f(x_i)) = 1 \\ f(x_i), & g_\tau(f(x_i)) = 0 \end{cases}$$

The performance of a Reject Option Classifier can be evaluated using *coverage* (ϕ) and/or *select accuracy* on the validation set V_m. The *coverage* is the proportion of the examples *selected* by g_τ, using

$$\phi(H_{(f, g_\tau)}|V_m) \quad = \quad \frac{1}{m} \sum_{i=1}^m (1 - g_\tau(f(x_i))) \tag{2}$$

The empirical select accuracy w.r.t. the labeled validation set V_m (when the coverage is greater than 0) is

$$SelAcc(H_{(f, g_\tau)}|V_m) \quad = \quad 1 - \frac{\sum_{i=1}^m \ell(f(x_i), y_i) \cdot (1 - g_\tau(f(x_i)))}{\sum_{i=1}^m (1 - g_\tau(f(x_i)))} \tag{3}$$

A trade-off exists between the coverage and select accuracy of a Reject Option Classifier since the only way to *increase* select accuracy is by rejecting more misclassified examples (*decreasing* coverage). Hence, Reject Option Classification problems are typically formulated by either constraining coverage or select accuracy and maximizing the other, as described in the next section.

3   Related Work

As previously mentioned, prior approaches to Reject Option Classification employ strong user-defined constraints. In the case where a cost of rejection is available, [5] provides an optimal strategy when the data distribution $P_{\mathcal{X}\mathcal{Y}}$ is known. In [22], a model is proposed for binary classification with additional user-defined classification costs using Receiver Operating Characteristic (ROC) analysis. For cases where the cost of rejection is not defined or available, two other constraint-based strategies have been proposed: bounded-improvement and bounded-rejection models.

In [21], the *bounded-improvement* model is proposed, where the objective is to maximize the coverage ϕ such that the select accuracy has a lower bound of a^*, as given by

$$\max \phi(H_{(f,g)}|V_m) \quad s.t. \quad SelAcc(H_{(f,g)}|V_m) \geq a^* \tag{4}$$

They use ROC analysis to determine optimal decision thresholds in the case of two classes. Furthermore, they assume a classifier can provide output scores (*e.g.*, softmax) proportional to posterior probabilities. In [11], an algorithm is proposed to learn the optimal rejection function when perfect select accuracy is possible for a classifier. The later work of [13] explores the bounded-improvement model in the context of deep neural networks. They propose an algorithm to learn an optimal threshold that statistically guarantees (under a user-defined confidence level) that the *theoretical* select accuracy is greater than a specified target accuracy a^*.

Alternatively, the *bounded-coverage* model has the objective of maximizing the select accuracy such that the coverage has a lower bound of c^*, as given by

$$\max SelAcc(H_{(f,g)}|V_m) \quad s.t. \quad \phi(H_{(f,g)}|V_m) \geq c^* \tag{5}$$

In [12], the bounded-coverage model is formalized, and a method is provided to obtain uncertainty scores from any black-box classifier. In [14], a joint training scheme is proposed to simultaneously learn a neural classifier and rejection function that provides the highest accuracy for the desired coverage c^*.

Our proposed method focuses on the *rejected* region rather than the *selected* region. We do not require user-defined costs for rejection nor lower bounds for select accuracy or coverage. Instead, we learn per-class rejection thresholds subject to a natural randomness property desirable of any reject region. Our formulation employs an *upper bound* of randomness (or confusion) expected/desired for a rejection region at a proposed significance level. As multiple viable rejection regions could exist, we maximize in tandem the select accuracy.

4   Proposed Method

Consider a *strong* neural classifier (*e.g.*, 99% accuracy) and an overall rejection threshold chosen to reject all but the single highest scoring prediction. Though the threshold yields 100% select accuracy (with 1 example), the coverage of the model is far too small (again, just 1 example) for any practical application. Furthermore, the classification accuracy in the remaining reject region would be very high (undesired). Next, consider a *weak* classifier having a large confusion region and a reject threshold set to 0 (reject none, select all). Though the threshold yields 100% coverage of the examples, the model's select accuracy (of all examples) could be too low to be worth using.

We argue that an *ideal* reject threshold (or set of per-class thresholds) should aim to produce a reject region that has <u>at most</u> random-chance classification accuracy. We certainly do *not* want to reject significantly more *correct* than *incorrect* predictions. As multiple viable rejection region sizes may exist, each adhering to at most random-chance classification behavior, the reject region corresponding to the highest accuracy in the complementary accept region should be chosen. Such an approach offers a naturally constrained analysis of reject regions that can be used to filter out indecision areas of *any* neural network and dataset pairing. However, a method must be provided to test a reject region for adherence to the upper-bound randomness requirement. We base our method on a Binomial distribution.

Consider a series of flips of a fair coin with $P(\text{heads}) = P(\text{tails}) = 0.5$ (random chance). Let Z be the number of observed heads after 100 tosses. The expected value of Z is 50, but in reality, the number of heads can deviate from this ideal. The Binomial distribution with $p = 0.5$ can be used to calculate the probability of seeing $Z = k$ heads in n trials. The corresponding Binomial CDF can be used to assess the probability of seeing *at most* k heads

$$P(Z \leq k) = BinomCDF(k; n, p) = \sum_{i=0}^{k} \binom{n}{i} p^i (1-p)^{n-i} \qquad (6)$$

We now shift focus from coin flips to the successes/failures of a classifier. Let $R_\tau = \{(x, y) \in V_m \mid H_{(f, g_\tau)}(x) = \text{reject}\}$ be the set of rejected examples from V_m using threshold τ, where $|R_\tau| = n$. As previously mentioned, we desire a reject region with accuracy $\leq 50\% + \xi$, for some small ξ. Note that ξ largely depends on the size of R_τ (smaller n may allow larger ξ in Binomial probability).

We employ the Binomial CDF model in Eq. 6 (with $p = 0.5$) along with the *actual* number of classification successes k^* of validation examples (having ground truth) in R_τ to assess adherence to the desired upper bound random state of R_τ. If $BinomCDF(k^*; n, 0.5) = 1 - \delta$, this means the probability of getting a *higher* number of correct classifications in the reject region, assuming random behavior, is δ. For example, if $\delta = .05$, there is only a 5% chance of observing $>k^*$ correct classifications assuming random chance behavior. Thus, for a given significance level δ, a proposed reject region has too many correct classifications if $BinomCDF(k^*; n, 0.5) > 1 - \delta$, and therefore must not be accepted. Only when $BinomCDF(k^*; n, 0.5) \leq 1 - \delta$ is the region viable. As multiple sizes of a reject region could be deemed viable, we seek to maximize the select accuracy to ensure the highest performing select region from the corresponding set of viable reject regions. To learn the desired per-class rejection thresholds τ, our overall objective, B-CDF$_\delta$, for k^* observed successes in the examined reject region is

$$\max SelAcc(H_{(f,g_\tau)}|V_m) \quad s.t. \quad BinomCDF(k^*; n, 0.5) \leq 1 - \delta \qquad (7)$$

As we are thresholding the softmax scores of the classifier, an important aspect to consider is network calibration, which aims to better align softmax values to true probabilities. Prior Reject Option Classification methods [5, 11–14, 21, 22] did not employ calibration. However, we believe it is an important component to model classification uncertainty properly. Previous work has provided various methods to calibrate networks, including temperature scaling [15]. When learning global or per-class thresholds, global temperature scaling is unnecessary (as it is a monotonic operation on the argmax softmax values). Therefore, as promoted in [24], we use *per-class* temperature scaling to better model class-conditional uncertainty before learning per-class rejection thresholds.

The algorithm for our approach is relatively direct and fast to run. We first compute a list of possible rejection thresholds per-class given a validation set. For each class c, we identify examples predicted as class c. Then, we choose potential thresholds from those examples' calibrated softmax scores. Since we are maximizing select accuracy across viable reject regions, we need only employ thresholds corresponding to the *incorrect* predictions. Next, for a given threshold and class, we extract the corresponding reject region and evaluate the Binomial constraint at a significance level δ. The algorithm chooses the threshold resulting in the highest select accuracy with acceptable reject regions. If multiple thresholds admit the same select accuracy, we choose the smallest threshold (producing the highest coverage). Experiments will demonstrate performance trade-offs across various significance levels δ.

5 Experiments

As previous Reject Option Classification methods require strong user/application-defined constraints on select accuracy or coverage, we can not directly compare the bounded-improvement and bounded-coverage models to our method. We instead compare a baseline model (Base) that never rejects any predictions (threshold of 0). Additionally, we compare a naïve method that thresholds the softmax values at 0.5. Here, we employ with and without calibration variations, Naïve-Cal and Naïve-NoCal, respectively. For our proposed Binomial-CDF method (B-CDF$_\delta$), we present results across different significance values $\delta \in \{0.05, 0.1, 0.5, 0.75, 0.95\}$. We use per-class temperature scaling calibration [24] for B-CDF$_\delta$ and the Naïve-Cal approaches.

We evaluate on different modalities: synthetic 2-D point-sets, benchmark image classification datasets, and common text classification datasets. We report and compare various accuracy (ideal, select, reject) and coverage metrics.

We additionally examine the generalization capability of thresholds from validation data to test data. Lastly, we provide an alternative formulation using associated confidence intervals to avoid the computational complexity of the Binomial CDF for very large datasets with vast reject regions.

5.1   Synthetic Data

To initially test our approach, we designed 8 multi-class 2-D point datasets with varying amounts of class overlap. We split these datasets into two subsets characterized by class overlap: equal-density and unequal-density. We sampled train-validation-test partitions having 1K-1K-4K examples per-class. We used a test set 4X larger than the training set to better measure the true performance of the learned thresholds.

For each dataset, we trained a simple neural network consisting of a single hidden layer of 10 nodes followed by a ReLU activation and an output layer consisting of the number of classes (2–4). We trained the network for 50 epochs using a half period cosine learning rate scheduler (with an initial learning rate of 0.1 and no restarts) and an SGD optimizer with 0.9 momentum. We selected the model from the epoch with the highest validation accuracy. We repeated this process ten times (producing 10 models) using different random seed initializations to provide meaningful statistics on the results [8].

5.1.1   Equal Density Overlap

For the first 4 datasets, each class is *uniformly* sampled from a defined rectangular region and positioned such that varying amounts of overlap occur. The top of Table 1 shows the resulting test datasets. Here, the *ideal* reject regions are shown in black and are due to *theoretically* equivalent class densities. To compare results from different reject thresholds, we computed the accuracy of the rejection function (1-reject, 0-select) w.r.t. the ideal reject region, defined as the *Ideal Decision Accuracy* (IDA).

We see the IDA scores of the different approaches in Table 1. We report the mean IDA score and the standard deviation over the ten trained models for each method and dataset. We also computed one-sided T-tests at the 0.05 significance level [8] against the highest mean IDA, and we bold all approaches whose mean is not significantly less than the top-scoring mean IDA.

The first two datasets (Synthetic 1 and Synthetic 2) are binary datasets that demonstrate weaknesses in the Naïve approaches. We see that the Naïve methods match Base in IDA as they rejected no examples. In two-class datasets, the smallest maximum-softmax score is 0.5. Hence, rejecting examples with the trivial 0.5 threshold is unlikely as both softmax values must be exactly 0.5. On the other hand, some B-CDF$_\delta$ approaches did reject confusing examples, with the B-CDF$_{.05/.10}$ variants yielding the highest IDA for Synthetic 1 and 2. In Synthetic 3, the B-CDF$_{.05/.10}$ variants produced the best results. Synthetic 4 again demonstrates the capability of B-CDF$_\delta$ to better model the ideal reject region, where all δ values gave statistically similar results above the other methods.

5.1.2   Unequal Density Overlap

Table 2 shows similarly configured datasets as Table 1 except that we used isotropic Gaussian distributions rather than uniform squares to sample the datasets. We also varied the density ratio of examples sampled per-class to evaluate regions of varying confusion. Here, the theoretical reject region is an infinitely

Table 1. The mean/std ideal decision accuracy (IDA) of different approaches on four **equal** density synthetic datasets (R:B:G:Y) over 10 runs.

	Synthetic 1	Synthetic 2	Synthetic 3	Synthetic 4
Density Ratio	1:1:0:0	1:1:0:0	1:1:1:0	1:1:1:1
Method	IDA↑	IDA↑	IDA↑	IDA↑
Base	74.4	0.0	64.5	56.3
Naïve-NoCal	74.4±0.0	0.0±0.0	70.4±0.9	61.0±0.3
Naïve-Cal	74.4±0.0	0.0±0.0	71.6±1.3	64.5±1.2
B-CDF$_{.05}$	**76.7**±1.0	**90.5**±29.7	**88.4**±2.4	**93.0**±1.3
B-CDF$_{.10}$	**76.3**±0.9	70.8±44.9	**88.1**±2.2	**93.2**±1.4
B-CDF$_{.50}$	75.1±1.6	4.4±6.0	85.4±3.6	**93.7**±1.7
B-CDF$_{.75}$	74.6±0.1	3.0±6.3	80.5±4.5	**93.7**±1.8
B-CDF$_{.95}$	74.4±0.0	0.0±0.0	71.3±4.4	**93.1**±2.0

thin line along the maximum posterior decision boundaries. However, this line could be a region *in practice* due to the sampling of the datasets. Therefore, instead of employing IDA, we report and compare the select accuracy, reject accuracy, and coverage of the approaches.

We see in the 2-class datasets Synthetic 5 and 6 that the Base and Naïve methods have full coverage. However, the proposed algorithm identified viable reject regions in the sampled data. In Synthetic 5, the B-CDF$_{.05}$ variant improved the select accuracy by +2.8% over the Base and Naïve methods, with a 54.3% reject accuracy. In Synthetic 6, the B-CDF$_{.05}$ method scored a reject accuracy of 61.5%, slightly larger than expected. Since thresholds are learned and ensured on validation data, this overage could occur on test data when using a strong model with a small reject region and different sampling of the data. Later in Sect. 5.4, we will show a more detailed generalization experiment from validation to test data on real datasets. In Synthetic 7 and 8, we see that most B-CDF$_\delta$ approaches rejected more examples than Base and Naïve methods with reject accuracy near 50%. The B-CDF$_{.05}$ variant improved the select accuracy over Base (+7% and +11.6%, respectively), while maintaining a viable reject accuracy of 52.2%.

5.2   Image Datasets

We next evaluated the approaches on the benchmark image classification datasets CIFAR10 [17], CIFAR100 [17], FGVC-Aircraft [20], and ImageNet [9] using pretrained state-of-the-art CNN and transformer models. These datasets

Table 2. The mean select accuracy (SA), reject accuracy (RA), and coverage (ϕ) of different approaches on four Gaussian **unequal** density synthetic datasets (R:B:G:Y) over 10 runs.

	Synthetic 5			Synthetic 6			Synthetic 7			Synthetic 8		
Density Ratio	2:1:0:0			2:1:0:0			4:2:1:0			6:5:4:3		
Method	SA↑	RA↓	ϕ↑	SA↑	RA↓	ϕ↑	SA↑	RA↓	ϕ↑	SA↑	RA↓	ϕ↑
Base	88.4	–	100	66.6	–	100	82.9	–	100	71.4	–	100
Naïve-NoCal	88.4	–	100	66.6	–	100	84.2	42.7	96.3	75.6	42.3	87.3
Naïve-Cal	88.4	–	100	66.6	–	100	84.8	42.3	94.9	75.8	41.6	87.1
B-CDF$_{.05}$	91.2	54.3	92.6	66.7	61.5	95.5	89.9	52.2	80.7	83.0	52.2	62.4
B-CDF$_{.10}$	90.5	52.8	94.5	66.7	61.9	95.9	89.5	51.2	82.2	82.6	51.6	63.9
B-CDF$_{.50}$	88.9	44.6	98.8	66.7	53.8	98.4	87.0	46.7	89.2	81.0	49.7	69.3
B-CDF$_{.75}$	88.6	38.7	99.6	66.6	–	100	85.6	44.1	92.9	80.1	48.6	72.4
B-CDF$_{.95}$	88.4	–	100.0	66.6	–	100	84.1	39.3	96.8	78.9	46.4	77.0

contain various numbers of classes ranging from 10 to 1K. Since all reject approaches are post-processing methods, only the logits/softmax values of a trained model and the truth targets are needed. For CIFAR10, CIFAR100, and FGVC-Aircraft, we used pretrained state-of-the-art NAT CNNs [18]. For ImageNet, we used the pretrained BEiT large transformer [2]. None of the aforementioned datasets have a fixed train-validation-test partitioning of the data. Therefore, we report scores on the validation set for ImageNet and the test set for CIFAR10, CIFAR100, and FGVC-Aircraft. Table 3 shows the results of the various approaches.

Note that when comparing results from two different thresholds, if one yields higher select accuracy and lower reject accuracy (regardless of the coverage change), it is a definite improvement. If one has higher select accuracy and *higher* reject accuracy, as long as the reject accuracy is within the acceptability level of the Binomial, then this is still considered an improvement.

CIFAR10. The Base approach scored 98.4% select accuracy indicating that the model is already strong. Both Naïve approaches rejected a few examples, with Naïve-Cal scoring slightly higher select accuracy and lower reject accuracy than Naïve-NoCal. The highest select accuracy of 99.3% was given by B-CDF$_{.05}$ with a coverage of 98.0% and a reject accuracy of 58.7%. Though seemingly high, the B-CDF$_\delta$ approach statistically permits higher reject accuracy for smaller reject regions (consider the possible number of heads appearing on a small number of fair coin tosses). Comparing B-CDF$_\delta$ to Naïve-Cal, the B-CDF$_{.50}$ variant had a

Table 3. The select accuracy (SA), reject accuracy (RA), and coverage (ϕ) of different approaches on four benchmark vision datasets.

Method	CIFAR10			CIFAR100			FGVC Aircraft			ImageNet		
	SA↑	RA↓	ϕ↑	SA↑	RA↓	ϕ↑	SA↑	RA↓	ϕ↑	SA↑	RA↓	ϕ↑
Base	98.4	–	100	88.3	–	100	90.1	–	100	88.4	–	100
Naïve-NoCal	98.5	57.1	99.9	89.3	24.5	98.5	96.3	58.4	83.5	91.7	45.1	92.8
Naïve-Cal	98.6	48.8	99.6	91.8	40.1	93.4	93.2	33.3	94.8	90.6	38.5	95.7
B-CDF$_{.05}$	99.3	58.7	97.9	97.8	55.9	77.3	98.3	45.4	84.4	97.4	52.7	79.7
B-CDF$_{.10}$	99.2	55.6	98.3	97.3	53.1	79.7	98.0	42.8	85.7	96.9	49.5	81.9
B-CDF$_{.50}$	98.9	42.5	99.2	94.8	42.3	87.7	96.2	28.6	91.0	94.6	36.8	89.1
B-CDF$_{.75}$	98.5	20.0	99.9	92.3	32.6	93.4	93.9	21.6	94.7	92.1	27.7	94.1
B-CDF$_{.95}$	98.4	–	100	89.3	21.3	98.6	91.1	14.9	98.6	89.7	22.5	98.0

lower reject accuracy (42.5%) and higher select accuracy (98.9%), demonstrating better performance.

CIFAR100. The Base approach scored 88.3% select accuracy. The Naïve-Cal method rejected about 5% more examples than Naïve-NoCal, yielding a higher select accuracy (91.8%) and a lower reject accuracy (40.1%). The B-CDF$_{.75}$ variant matched the coverage of Naïve-Cal while increasing select accuracy (+0.5%) and decreasing reject accuracy (−7.5%). These improvements indicate that the B-CDF$_\delta$ approach can better model confusion over the Naïve methods.

FGVC-Aircraft. The Base approach scored 90.1% select accuracy. The Naïve-Cal method outperformed Naïve-NoCal in coverage (94.8%, 83.5%, respectively) and reject accuracy (33.3% and 58.4%, respectively) but scored lower select accuracy (93.2% and 96.3%, respectively). Compared to Naïve-Cal, the B-CDF$_{.50/.75}$ variants scored much lower reject accuracy (−4.7% and −11.7%, respectively) and similar coverage (−3.8% and −0.1%, respectively) with increased select accuracy (+3.0% and +0.7%, respectively), indicating better performance.

ImageNet. The Base approach scored 88.4% select accuracy. The Naïve-NoCal and Naïve-Cal approaches achieved a higher select accuracy (91.7% and 90.6%, respectively) with reasonable reject accuracy (45.1% and 38.5%, respectively) and fairly high coverage (92.8% and 95.7%, respectively). Comparing the Naïve-Cal approach to B-CDF$_\delta$, the B-CDF$_{.50/.75}$ variants performed better in select accuracy (+4.0% and +1.5%, respectively) and reject accuracy (−1.7% and −10.8%, respectively). Nearly all B-CDF$_\delta$ approaches scored higher select accuracy and reasonable reject accuracy (as desired). We found that per-class thresholds varied widely on this dataset (and others with many classes).

5.3 Text Datasets

We next evaluated the approaches on the IMDB sentiment analysis [19] and AG News [23] text classification datasets. These datasets contain fewer classes than

Table 4. The select accuracy (SA), reject accuracy (RA), and coverage (ϕ) of different approaches on text datasets.

	IMDB			AG News		
Method	SA↑	RA↓	ϕ↑	SA↑	RA↓	ϕ↑
Base	94.7	–	100	94.7	–	100
Naïve-NoCal	94.7	–	100	94.8	30.0	99.9
Naïve-Cal	94.7	–	100	94.9	33.3	99.8
B-CDF$_{.05}$	96.3	53.4	96.3	96.7	55.8	95.1
B-CDF$_{.10}$	96.2	52.7	96.5	96.7	54.8	95.3
B-CDF$_{.50}$	95.6	49.8	97.9	95.6	46.0	98.2
B-CDF$_{.75}$	95.5	48.0	98.3	95.4	39.8	98.8
B-CDF$_{.95}$	94.7	18.2	99.9	94.7	–	100

the image datasets (2 and 4, respectively). We utilized near state-of-the-art off-the-shelf pretrained BERT transformers [10] for the evaluations. Both datasets do not include a validation set, hence we report results on the test data. Table 4 shows the results for text classification using the IMDB and AG News datasets.

IMDB. The Base approach was fairly strong and scored a select accuracy of 94.7%. Like in the 2-class synthetic datasets, the Naïve approaches failed to reject any examples. However, the B-CDF$_\delta$ method rejected some examples with B-CDF$_{.05}$ giving a reasonable reject accuracy (53.4%) and greater select accuracy (+1.6%). Other B-CDF$_\delta$ variants yielded higher select accuracy with reject accuracy near 50%, except B-CDF$_{.95}$ which selected nearly all examples with 18.2% reject accuracy and coverage of 99.9%.

AG News. The Base method scored a select accuracy of 94.7%. The Naïve-NoCal and Naïve-Cal approaches rejected only a few examples, improving select accuracy by +0.1% and +0.2%, respectively. The B-CDF$_\delta$ approach rejected more examples than Naïve-Cal, with B-CDF$_{.05}$ scoring the highest select accuracy (96.7%) with acceptable reject accuracy (55.8%). Moreover, all other B-CDF$_\delta$ variants (except B-CDF$_{.95}$) scored higher select accuracy than both Naïve methods, with a reasonable reject accuracy.

5.4   Generalization from Validation to Test Data

We now present results on how the learned reject thresholds generalize from a validation set to a test set. We employed CINIC10 [7] (imagery) and Tweet Eval Emoji [3] (text) as both contain a proper train-validation-test partitioning. We utilized a weakly-trained ResNet20 CNN [16] for CINIC10 and an off-the-shelf pretrained BERT transformer [10] for Tweet Eval Emoji. Table 5 shows the results of rejection thresholds learned from validation and applied to test data.

CINIC10 contains 90K training, 90K validation, and 90K testing examples. Given that the validation set here is large (equal to the test set), we expect

Table 5. The generalization of select accuracy (SA), reject accuracy (RA), and coverage (ϕ) of thresholds learned on validation and applied to test data for CINIC10 and Tweet Eval Emoji.

Method	CINIC10						Tweet Eval Emoji					
	Val			Test			Val			Test		
	SA↑	RA↓	ϕ↑	SA↑	RA↓	ϕ↑	SA↑	RA↓	ϕ↑	SA↑	RA↓	ϕ↑
Base	81.8	–	100	81.5	–	100	32.6	–	100	47.9	–	100
Naïve-NoCal	83.5	31.4	96.9	83.1	29.7	96.9	58.5	22.5	28.0	74.7	24.7	46.5
Naïve-Cal	87.7	40.2	87.7	87.5	39.3	87.4	69.3	24.0	19.1	79.4	28.5	38.2
B-CDF$_{.05}$	93.4	51.6	72.5	93.2	51.0	72.2	92.9	30.3	3.6	93.7	35.3	21.7
B-CDF$_{.10}$	93.2	51.2	73.0	93.0	50.6	72.8	90.7	30.1	4.1	92.4	35.0	22.5
B-CDF$_{.50}$	92.6	49.9	74.8	92.4	49.3	74.6	82.8	29.2	6.4	89.1	33.8	25.6
B-CDF$_{.75}$	92.1	49.2	76.1	92.0	48.4	75.8	79.7	28.4	8.2	86.6	33.1	27.7
B-CDF$_{.95}$	91.5	48.1	77.7	91.4	47.3	77.4	71.3	27.4	11.9	82.0	32.8	30.7

thresholds to behave similarly across validation and test. We see that select accuracy, reject accuracy, and coverage all transfer well to the test set (nearly a one-to-one match). The earlier Figs. 1b and 1c depict t-SNE embeddings computed using the select and reject sets given by B-CDF$_{.05}$.

Tweet Eval Emoji contains 45K training, 5K validation, and 50K testing examples with 21 classes. For this dataset, the validation set is 10X *smaller* than the test set. Although, we observe that all metrics here tend to be higher (desired) on the test set across all approaches, which shows that the proposed algorithm compensates in the proper direction. However, in Table 2 the reject accuracy of the B-CDF$_\delta$ approach on Synthetic 6 was larger than expected due to the smaller validation set. We additionally examined a larger validation set on Synthetic 6 and saw expected generalization performance.

5.5   Alternative Confidence Interval Formulations

Given the computational complexity of evaluating the Binomial CDF on very large reject regions, we provide alternative confidence interval methods with a similar goal but lower computational complexity. The objective remains the same as B-CDF$_\delta$, but the randomness evaluation uses a one-sided confidence interval to determine whether the lower bound on *true* accuracy given the *observed* accuracy is reasonable (less than or equal to 50%). We present results using the Clopper-Pearson interval [6], the Wilson interval with and without continuity correction (Wilson-CC and Wilson-NoCC, respectively) [4], and the Agresti Coull interval [1]. Closed-form equations exist for Wilson-CC, Wilson-NoCC, and Agresti Coull. Table 6 shows the results using these confidence intervals.

On these datasets, the Clopper-Pearson and Wilson-CC approaches arrive at the same solutions as the original B-CDF$_{.05}$ approach. However, Wilson-NoCC

Table 6. The select accuracy (SA), reject accuracy (RA), and coverage (ϕ) of alternative confidence interval approaches on four benchmark vision datasets.

Method	CIFAR10			CIFAR100			FGVC Aircraft			ImageNet		
	SA ↑	RA ↓	ϕ↑	SA ↑	RA ↓	ϕ↑	SA ↑	RA ↓	ϕ↑	SA ↑	RA ↓	ϕ↑
Base	98.4	–	100	88.3	–	100	90.1	–	100	88.4	–	100
Naïve-NoCal	98.5	57.1	99.9	89.3	24.5	98.5	96.3	58.4	83.5	91.7	45.1	92.8
Naïve-Cal	98.6	48.8	99.6	91.8	40.1	93.4	93.2	33.3	94.8	90.6	38.5	95.7
B-CDF$_{.05}$	99.3	58.7	97.9	97.8	55.9	77.3	98.3	45.4	84.4	97.4	52.7	79.7
Clopper-Pearson	99.3	58.7	97.9	97.8	55.9	77.3	98.3	45.4	84.4	97.4	52.7	79.7
Wilson-CC	99.3	58.7	97.9	97.8	55.9	77.3	98.3	45.4	84.4	97.4	52.7	79.7
Wilson-NoCC	99.3	59.8	97.7	98.2	57.8	75.6	98.7	49.1	82.5	97.7	54.9	78.1
Agresti-Coull	99.3	59.8	97.7	98.2	57.8	75.6	98.8	49.7	82.3	97.8	55.0	78.0

and Agresti-Coull typically score higher select accuracy at the cost of higher reject accuracy and lower coverage. The Agresti-Coull method scored the highest select accuracy, highest reject accuracy, and lowest coverage for all experiments. We showed results based on $\delta=.05$, but for all significance levels examined in this paper, we found that Clopper-Pearson and Wilson-CC approaches matched B-CDF$_\delta$. These results demonstrate that Clopper-Pearson and Wilson-CC could be interchanged with B-CDF$_\delta$ to reduce computational complexity, if desired.

5.6   Discussion

We evaluated multiple approaches on equal-density synthetic datasets and showed that the B-CDF$_\delta$ method provides the highest accuracy to the ideal decision function. On unequal-density synthetic data, real-world imagery, and text datasets, our approach performed the best at specific δ values, yielding the highest select accuracy while keeping a reasonable and statistically viable reject accuracy (near 50%). Furthermore, given a user preference for select accuracy or coverage in a specific application, the user could examine different δ values to best suit the task. Higher values of δ provide increased coverage, while lower values of δ provide increased select accuracy. Overall, we found that lower values of δ seem preferable across multiple datasets and could be used as a default. We have also shown that thresholds learned on large validation sets transfer well to test sets. Lastly, we presented an alternative formulation using related confidence intervals and showed that they could provide similar performance at reduced computational complexity. Therefore, when given very large datasets with extensive reject regions, it is recommended to use alternative formulations.

6   Conclusion

Given the growing adoption of neural networks in various applied tasks, the need for confident predictions is becoming increasingly important. We proposed a Binomial-CDF approach to automatically detect and filter out regions of confusion for any neural classifier and dataset pairing. This post-processing technique leverages a validation set to learn per-class rejection thresholds that can identify and reject regions in the decision space based on random-chance classification. This approach is applicable when strong constraints on select accuracy or coverage are unavailable. We demonstrated that the approach provides a favorable scoring of select and reject accuracy on 2-D points, imagery, and text datasets. In future work, we plan to develop a joint-training objective to learn the rejection function during the training of the neural network.

Acknowledgements. This research was supported by the U.S. Air Force Research Laboratory under Contract #GRT00054740 (Release #AFRL-2022-3339).

References

1. Agresti, A., Coull, B.A.: Approximate is better than "exact" for interval estimation of binomial proportions. Am. Stat. **52**(2) (1998)
2. Bao, H., Dong, L., Piao, S., Wei, F.: BEiT: BERT pre-training of image transformers. In: ICLR (2022)
3. Barbieri, F., Camacho-Collados, J., Neves, L., Espinosa-Anke, L.: TweetEval: unified benchmark and comparative evaluation for tweet classification. In: EMNLP (2020)
4. Brown, L.D., Cai, T.T., DasGupta, A.: Interval estimation for a binomial proportion. Stat. Sci. **16**(2) (2001)
5. Chow, C.K.: On optimum recognition error and reject tradeoff. IEEE Trans. Inf. Theory **16**(1), 41–46 (1970)
6. Clopper, C.J., Pearson, E.S.: The use of confidence or fiducial limits illustrated in the case of the binomial. Biometrika **26**(4) (1934)
7. Darlow, L.N., Crowley, E.J., Antoniou, A., Storkey, A.J.: CINIC-10 is not imagenet or CIFAR-10. arXiv preprint arxiv:1810.03505 (2018)
8. Davis, J., Frank, L.: Revisiting Batch Normalization. In: ECCV (2022)
9. Deng, J., Dong, W., Socher, R., Li, L.J., Li, K., Fei-Fei, L.: ImageNet: a large-scale hierarchical image database. In: CVPR (2009)
10. Devlin, J., Chang, M.W., Lee, K., Toutanova, K.: BERT: pre-training of deep bidirectional transformers for language understanding. In: Human Language Technologies (2019)
11. El-Yaniv, R., Wiener, Y.: On the foundations of noise-free selective classification. J. Mach. Learn. Res. **11** (2010)
12. Franc, V., Prusa, D., Voracek, V.: Optimal Strategies for Reject Option Classifiers. arXiv preprint arxiv:2101.12523 (2021)
13. Geifman, Y., El-Yaniv, R.: Selective classification for deep neural networks. In: NIPS (2017)
14. Geifman, Y., El-Yaniv, R.: SelectiveNet: a deep neural network with an integrated reject option. In: ICML (2019)
15. Guo, C., Pleiss, G., Sun, Y., Weinberger, K.Q.: On calibration of modern neural networks. In: ICML (2017)
16. He, K., Zhang, X., Ren, S., Sun, J.: Deep residual learning for image recognition. In: CVPR (2016)

17. Krizhevsky, A., Hinton, G., et al.: Learning multiple layers of features from tiny images (2009)
18. Lu, Z., Sreekumar, G., Goodman, E., Banzhaf, W., Deb, K., Boddeti, V.: Neural Architecture Transfer. IEEE Trans. Pattern Anal. Mach. Intell. **43**(09) (2021)
19. Maas, A.L., Daly, R.E., Pham, P.T., Huang, D., Ng, A.Y., Potts, C.: Learning word vectors for sentiment analysis. In: Human Language Technologies (2011)
20. Maji, S., Chicago, T., Rahtu, E., Kannala, J., Blaschkó, M., Vedaldi, A.: Fine-Grained Visual Classification of Aircraft. arXiv preprint arxiv:1306.5151 (2013)
21. Pietraszek, T.: Optimizing abstaining classifiers using ROC analysis. In: ICML (2005)
22. Tortorella, F.: An optimal reject rule for binary classifiers. In: Advances in Pattern Recognition (2000)
23. Zhang, X., Zhao, J., LeCun, Y.: Character-level convolutional networks for text classification. In: NIPS (2015)
24. Zhao, Y., Chen, J., Oymak, S.: On the Role of Dataset Quality and Heterogeneity in Model Confidence. arXiv preprint arxiv:2002.09831 (2020)

Multi-class Detection and Tracking of Intracorporeal Suturing Instruments in an FLS Laparoscopic Box Trainer Using Scaled-YOLOv4

Mohsen Mohaidat[1(✉)], Janos L. Grantner[1], Saad A. Shebrain[2],
and Ikhlas Abdel-Qader[1]

[1] Electrical and Computer Engineering, Western Michigan University, Kalamazoo, MI, USA
{mohsen.mohaidat,janos.grantner,abdelqader}@wmich.edu
[2] School of Medicine, Western Michigan University, Kalamazoo, MI, USA
saad.shebrain@med.wmich.edu

Abstract. Intracorporeal suturing is one of the most critical skills in the Fundamentals of Laparoscopic Surgery (FLS) training. Assessment of skills acquisition requires a significant amount of the supervisory surgeons' time, and it can be a very subjective decision. This study uses an object detection algorithm, Scaled-YOLOv4, in conjunction with a centroid tracking algorithm to evaluate the surgeon's skills during advanced intracorporeal suturing. We proposed a system capable of locating and tracking surgical instruments as well as providing an evaluation of the performance of the surgeons. Since the accuracy of the detection is crucial to our proposed tracking system, we evaluated the detection performance using the mean average precision and inference time metrics. An average precision of 85.50% was achieved for the detection of the needle, and 100% was achieved for the work field area.

Keywords: Laparoscopic surgery training · Object detection · Suturing video data · Needle tracking

1 Introduction

Minimally invasive surgery (MIS) is one of the enhanced methods used in surgical treatments, and it has received enormous attention in recent years while considering the patients' surgical experiences and the skills of surgeons executing these procedures. MIS's goal is to achieve improved surgical performance through smaller, fewer incisions and with executing higher precision and efficacy surgical procedures [1]. In addition, to increase liability and improve patient safety in healthcare delivery, all MIS surgery procedures must be trained for and professionally assessed [2].

Before performing laparoscopic surgery, surgeons must gain a wide range of skills, such as suturing, injection, anastomosis, needle insertion and others [3, 4]. To achieve this goal, training programs for laparoscopic surgery have been introduced and integrated

G. Bebis et al. (Eds.): ISVC 2022, LNCS 13598, pp. 211–221, 2022.
https://doi.org/10.1007/978-3-031-20713-6_16

into hospital curricula. To develop surgical skills for more complicated tasks, facilitate resident training and enhance surgical competency, several surgery simulators have been developed [5].

A commonly used program for acquiring laparoscopic suturing skills is the Fundamentals of Laparoscopic Surgery (FLS) [6]. In spite of the fact that FLS provides a good platform for acquiring the basic skills required, it does not adequately capture the full complexity of the laparoscopic skills needed for the operating room [7]. Therefore, to enhance the skills of laparoscopic surgeons, various training methods have been proposed which not only increase the skill level of surgeons but also evaluate their performance. The performance assessment provides feedback on the level of the surgeon's expertise and is commonly based on tracking the surgeon's performance during a task operation [8]. In order to achieve this important goal when suturing intracorporeal, it is necessary to monitor and assess the performance of residents by tracking the movements of the tips of the surgical tools in complex environments, such as suturing in tight spaces [9].

By using the FLS laparoscopic box trainer, in this study we propose a robust, multi-class detection and tracking system for complex intracorporeal suturing tasks. For the Intracorporeal Suturing task in a FLS Box Trainer, this system should be able to locate and identify all instruments. As an additional contribution, a measurement algorithm is proposed not only for the general evaluation of the FLS metrics (i.e., time and error), but also for detecting whether or not the trainee is operating in the designated field of work. Upon failure to meet that criterion, a notification will appear on the monitor to alert the trainee to the problem. In this study, a deep learning approach based on Scaled-YOLOv4 has been proposed, which has been trained on our custom intracorporeal suturing dataset to detect and track all the instruments in a real-time manner.

This paper is organized as follows. In Sect. 2, we provide an overview of related work regarding the detection of FLS instruments by using Convolutional Neural Networks (CNN). Section 3 describes the methodologies proposed for the training algorithms and a novel method for evaluating advanced suturing. Section 4 presents the experimental setup. The results are discussed in Sect. 5. Lastly, conclusions and plans for future research are given in Sect. 6.

2 Related Works

In recent years, deep learning technologies have gained more attention in various applications [10]. In some complex applications, humans could be completely removed, and Deep Neural Network models and unsupervised learning methods would take their place [11].

Oquendo et al. [11] proposed a motion-tracking system and algorithms using a magnetic sensing system that automatically evaluates the trainees' performance in two trials of intracorporeal suturing in a custom pediatric laparoscopic box trainer. During a pediatric laparoscopic suturing task, 32 surgical residents were evaluated using a validated and novel machine learning algorithm. To determine the most appropriate algorithm in terms of speed and accuracy, Soviany et al. [12] examined two types of state-of-the-art methods: Two-Stage object detectors (Faster R-CNNs) and Single-Stage Object

Detectors (MobileNet-SSDs, SSD300s). According to the researchers, the performance differences between a two-stage detector and a single-stage detector were insignificant when applied to simple images. Our dataset for intracorporeal suturing contains only simple images, so we used a single-stage detector for our analysis.

Peng et al. [13] proposed a method for autonomous recognition of multiple surgical instruments' tips based on the arrow object bounding box (OBB)-YOLO network prediction, which recognizes the localization of an instrument. Koskinen et al. [14] trained and evaluated YOLOv5-l on a dataset of 4900 to 5900 frames, with approximately 20 surgical settings and 17 micro-instruments, for knot tying and interrupted suturing tasks, to perform tool detection.

Schwaner et al. [15] presented an application of the Learning from Demonstration method to implement a fully autonomous bi-manual surgical suturing task, including steps such as needle pick up, insertion, re-grasping, and extraction, and hand-over with a custom surgical robot system. Pryor et al. [16] investigated localization and autonomous robotic control of needles in the context of a magneto-suturing system using neural network-based segmentation and classification techniques in a closed-loop feedback control system.

The development of deep learning architectures for detecting surgical tools in the laparoscopic video has also been the subject of several medical research studies [17–19]. Sugimori et al. [20] used YOLOv2 to detect tips of surgical instruments in images extracted from nine video recordings of carotid endarterectomies. A study conducted by Cho et al. [17] aimed to detect the tooltips of instruments using two open source detectors, RetinaNet and YOLOv2, and then localized them by using colored points. Alkhamaiseh et al. [18] compared the performance of two deep learning algorithms, YOLOv5 and scaled YOLOv4, in a pattern cutting exercise, for the purpose of detecting the movement of the tip of the scissors. A laparoscopic box trainer tool tip tracking task was implemented using Fast-RCNN by Fathabadi et al. [19]. According to [21], a scaled YOLOv4 has demonstrated faster and more accurate object detection in comparison to other single-stage detectors.

3 Methodology

The proposed method employs an open-source deep learning algorithm for detecting and tracking intracorporeal suturing laparoscopic instruments in a FLS box trainer by using multi-class detection and tracking methods. The simplicity of this algorithm allows the recognition process to be executed more quickly and yet deliver satisfying results when compared to other algorithms. The workflow of the proposed work is given in Fig. 1. Our custom dataset was used to pre-train the model, which used the Scaled-YOLOv4 architecture [22] from Torchvision's models repository. Thus, to train the model, we expanded and augmented our previous laparoscopic box trainer dataset [21] by incorporating extracted frames from various laparoscopic intracorporeal suturing training videos using Roboflow augmentation tools [23].

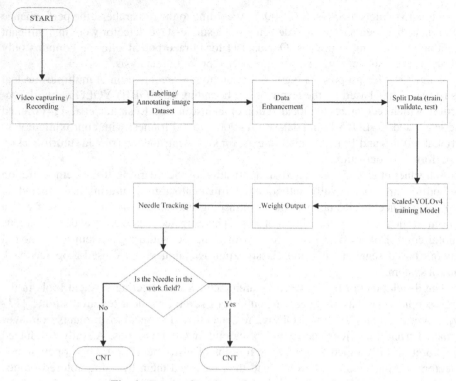

Fig. 1. Process flowchart of the proposed method

3.1 Scaled-YOLOv4 Architecture

An image is divided into N x N grids in accordance with the logic of the YOLO algorithm. The Mish-Function serves as an activation function in the YOLO algorithm. The leaky ReLU functions are used instead of the mish function in the tiny-YOLO series to reduce the computational cost. YOLOv4 Scaled-Stage is based on a Cross-Stage Partial Network (CSP) developed by Wang C et al. [22] for scaling large and small networks. As the backbone of its architecture, YOLOv4-CSP uses a slightly modified version of CSPDarkNet53, whereas YOLOv4 uses the CSP approach [22].

3.2 Measurement Algorithm

To track the needle and find out whether it is inside the field of work, i.e., the region of interest (ROI) or it is out of it, a measurement algorithm based on the Euclidean Distance Transformation [24] has been developed. For passing this test, variable Distance between the center of the needle and the center of the field of work is continuously measured, and it is compared with the bounding box coordinates of the ROI. If the needle is out of the ROI, a notification will be displayed on the monitor screen. In Eq. 1, during each frame, Distance represents the distance between two points, and variable Pix represents the set of pixel points that contain all the pixels of the extracted object.

$$D[A][B] = min\{Distance[(A_x, A_y), (B_x, B_y)], (A, B) \in pix\}$$
$$Distance[(A_x, A_y), (B_x, B_y)] = \sqrt{(B_x - A_x)^2 + (B_y - A_y)^2}$$
(1)

As suturing occurs in tight spaces during an actual operation, surgeon trainees should execute the suturing test in a very tight space, too [9]. In this study, we have referred to the red sponge carrier as the working area, which we have classified as an object called ROI. Considering that the location of the working field area cannot be guaranteed and may vary, we have trained our model to detect this area.

4 Experimental Setup

The Intelligent Box-Trainer System (IBTS) [22] facilitates a variety of FLS training exercises, including tooltip tracking, intracorporeal suturing, pattern cutting, and peg transfer. In this work, intracorporeal suturing was carried out to detect all the objects used in the task and track the needle driver and notify the trainee whether it is inside or outside of the ROI. These scenarios are illustrated in Figs. 2 and 3.

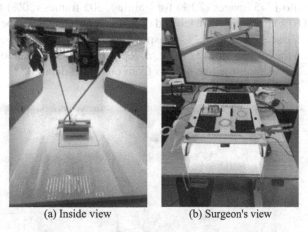

(a) Inside view   (b) Surgeon's view

Fig. 2. The IBTS for intracorporal suturing task

Fig. 3. Execution of the intracorporal suturing task in the intelligent fuzzy controllers laboratory

4.1 Dataset

To train the model for detecting intracorporeal suturing instruments and field of work (ROI), 2500 images were randomly chosen from 12 different intracorporeal suturing video recordings (i.e., 18500 frames). All images have been resized to 640 by 640 pixels to work with the Scaled-YOLOv4 darknet framework. Thereafter, this dataset was subdivided into 1745 images (70%) for training, 505 frames (20%) for validation, and 250 frames (10%) for testing. We labeled the dataset by using the LabelImg tool [25] for five classes: "Tissue", "Needle", "L-Grasper,", "Grasper" and "ROI" and saved it as a.txt file, based on the Scaled-YOLO format. A representation of the annotated image is shown in Fig. 4. It illustrates the five objects from our IBTS dataset.

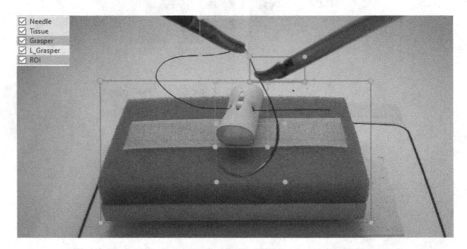

Fig. 4. Labeling of objects inside the IBTS using the LabelImg tool

Table 1 shows the number of objects and the processes of splitting classes. During the distribution phase, we ensured that a wide variety of frames were used for each class.

Table 1. Class splitting distribution

	Objects per class				
Split process	Needle	Grasper	L-Grasper	Tissue	ROI
Training	1063	1112	1165	1634	1740
Validation	329	310	304	453	497
Testing	191	188	178	228	238

4.2 Software Implementation

A Momentum optimizer with a learning rate of 0.04 was used for the region proposal and classification network. We fed our network with images of 640×640 pixels and performed 10,000 iterations with 64 batches. The final output was a bounding box for each detected object as a class label (Needle, Grasper (i.e., Needle Driver), left Grasper (L-Grasper), Tissue, and ROI with its confidence score. In this study, our intelligent laparoscopic box trainer software has been developed using Python, and the feasibility of this work has been evaluated on a Windows PC along with a P100-PCIe GPU.

5 Results

In Sect. 2, we described that how our proposed model was trained and constructed. In Fig. 5, the training loss and validation loss for each iteration are shown for 10,000

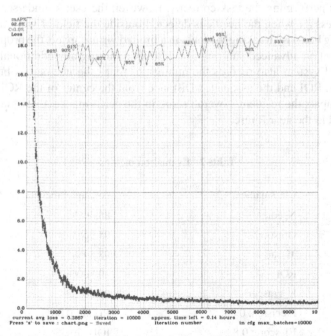

Fig. 5. Training Loss and the mAP for the scaled-YOLOv4 by darknet

iterations. The output with the highest precision (i.e., the best weight file) was chosen to be used in our research. mAP@0.5 provides a measure of the mean average precision at the 50% intersection-over-union threshold, which evaluates if a model generalizes well on a never-before-seen dataset. The blue curve represents the learning error for the training dataset (specifically, the Complete Intersections-Over-Union (CIoU) loss for the Scaled-YOLOv4) [21]. During the training process, our model generated output training files every 1000 iterations, as well as files with the highest mAP. Figure 5 illustrates that the highest mAP occurs at 6800 iterations when the mAP reaches 95%. To the track needle position, the best output file was chosen, out of all generated, since it has the highest mAP.

The measures precision, recall, F1-score, and mAP have been used as the criteria to evaluate the performance of the Scaled-YOLOv4 algorithm. The F1 score, the model's test accuracy, is the harmonic mean of precision and recall. The highest possible value of the F1-score is 0.88, which indicates a perfect precision, 0.88, and recall, 0.88. In addition, mAP, 0.95 is calculated by taking the mean of average precision (AP) of all the classes, as shown in Table 2. Furthermore, precision and recall were computed using the Intersection over Union (IOU) threshold. The IOU was calculated as the ratio between the overlap area and the union area of the ground truth and the prediction labels. Then, the average precision was calculated from the precision-recall curve.

The detection and tracking results are presented in Fig. 6, which illustrates that all objects have been detected where a threshold degree of accuracy was determined to be at least 70%, so the class bounding box with a higher IOU will only be presented. All objects have been detected ideally with 100% accuracy. When the needle is within the ROI bounding box, the system does not display warnings or distance measurements, as the trainee is performing the task correctly. However, the user's guide screen displays a warning message when the needle is detected outside the field of work area (i.e., the ROI bounding box). By tracking the tools in a limited virtual space, the proposed system can implement an advanced suturing test without requiring any additional equipment. The proposed system also records the number of times the needle has been detected outside of the ROI and the associated Distance from the center of the ROI, which will negatively impact the resident's overall score in the performance assessment system to be developed in the near future.

Table 2. Evaluation metrics

Class Id	Class name	Average Precision (AP)
0	Needle	85.50%
1	Grasper	95.96%
2	Tissue	98.89%
3	ROI	100.00%
4	L_grasper	92.86%
	Precision: 0.88	Recall: 0.88
	F1-score: 0.88	IOU: 70.38

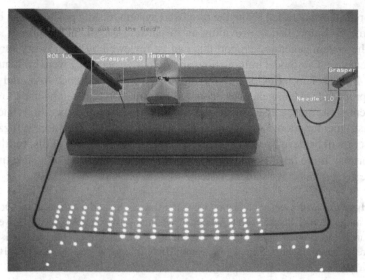

Fig. 6. Detection and tracking result shown in sample frame of the intracorporeal suturing task video

6 Discussion

The accuracy of the centroid tracking algorithm is entirely dependent on the quality of the detection. Due to this and on the grounds of the results of a previous study [22] that showed the Scaled-YOLOv4 had delivered decent detection quality for the same dataset, Scaled-YOLOv4 has been used in this study. The loss function that has been used is based on the YOLOv4 loss function [22], which is a combination of classification loss, localization loss, and confidence loss. As illustrated in Fig. 5, we can guarantee that we will choose the low loss with the high mAP after the training process.

In advanced laparoscopic intracorporeal suturing, it is imperative to emphasize the importance of both the needle and the ROI since the purpose of advanced suturing is to keep tools in a very tight space, and the needle is the moving object that is required to be within the ROI-designated field of work area. According to our results, the detection precision mAP for the needle is 85.5%, and for the ROI it is 100%. Because the ROI is fully detectable, there is no loss of detection in all video frames. As a result, we conclude that detecting the needle was challenging at some points during the suturing operation. It is possible for the needle to either be hidden behind other objects or positioned parallel to the camera's field of view, in which case the needle will look like the thread. These cases, however, would not present a problem since we focus on tracking the needle outside of the ROI, where detection is more accessible due to a smaller number of objects present.

7 Conclusion and Future Work

In this paper, we propose using a centroid tracking method to track the needle position in the FLS box trainer to evaluate the trainees' performance while they carry out advanced intracorporeal suturing tasks. Using the proposed system, needle positions can be determined frame by frame, hence, providing an impartial assessment of surgery skills. In addition, the system generates a report that can be reviewed by supervisory surgeons at their convenience. Our model training time and detection accuracy were evaluated using the scaled-YOLOv4 in terms of mean average precision, inference loss, and training loss. The proposed system generates adequate information that can be used to develop an intelligent performance assessment system soon. Based on the operation time, errors, surgical instrument motion, and distance quality in the field of work area, a fuzzy logic-based system will be developed to assess the laparoscopic suturing skills. Furthermore, after performing more testing and evaluation, our proposed system may also qualify as a real-time performance assessment system.

Acknowledgment. With great appreciation we thank the faculty and residents of the Department of Surgery at the Homer Stryker M.D. School of Medicine, Western Michigan University, for their assistance and support during the development of our database. Our Dataset is publicly available, free of charge, at https://drive.google.com/drive/folders/1F97CvN3GnLj-rqg1tk2rHu8x 0J740DpC.

References

1. Zhu, J., et al.: Intelligent soft surgical robots for next-generation minimally invasive surgery. Adv. Intell. Syst. **3**, 2100011 (2021)
2. Kohn, L.T., Corrigan, J.M., Donaldson, M.S.: To Err is Human: Building a Safer Health System. Report of the Institute of Medicine (2000)
3. Chellali, A., et al.: Achieving interface and environment fidelity in the virtual basic laparoscopic surgical trainer. Int. J. Hum. Comput. Stud. **96**, 22–37 (2016)
4. Oh, D., et al.: Surgical techniques for totally laparoscopic caudate lobectomy. J. Laparoendosc. Adv. Surg. Tech. **26**, 689–692 (2016)
5. Lahanas, V., Georgiou, E., Loukas, C.: Surgical simulation training systems: box trainers, virtual reality and augmented reality simulators. Int. J. Adv. Robot. Autom. **1**, 1–9 (2016)
6. McKendy, K.M., et al.: Establishing meaningful benchmarks: the development of a formative feedback tool for advanced laparoscopic suturing. Surg. Endosc. **31**(12), 5057–5065 (2017). https://doi.org/10.1007/s00464-017-5569-y
7. Leijte, E., Arts, E., Witteman, B., Jakimowicz, J., De Blaauw, I., Botden, S.: Construct, content and face validity of the eoSim laparoscopic simulator on advanced suturing tasks. Surg. Endosc. **33**(11), 3635–3643 (2019). https://doi.org/10.1007/s00464-018-06652-3
8. Yamazaki, Y., et al.: Automated surgical instrument detection from laparoscopic gastrectomy video images using an open source convolutional neural network platform. J. Am. Coll. Surg. **230**, 725-732.e1 (2020). https://doi.org/10.1016/j.jamcollsurg.2020.01.037
9. Bilgic, E., Alyafi, M., Hada, T., Landry, T., Fried, G.M., Vassiliou, M.C.: Simulation platforms to assess laparoscopic suturing skills: a scoping review. Surg. Endosc. **33**(9), 2742–2762 (2019). https://doi.org/10.1007/s00464-019-06821-y
10. Lundervold, A.S., Lundervold, A.: An overview of deep learning in medical imaging focusing on MRI https://doi.org/10.1016/j.zemedi.2018.11.002
11. Oquendo, Y.A., Riddle, E.W., Hiller, D., Blinman, T.A., Kuchenbecker, K.J.: Automatically rating trainee skill at a pediatric laparoscopic suturing task. Surg. Endosc. **32**(4), 1840–1857 (2017). https://doi.org/10.1007/s00464-017-5873-6

12. Soviany, P., Ionescu, R.T.: Optimizing the trade-off between single-stage and two-stage deep object detectors using image difficulty prediction. In: Proceedings - 2018 20th International Symposium on Symbolic and Numeric Algorithms for Scientific Computing, SYNASC 2018, pp. 209–214. Institute of Electrical and Electronics Engineers Inc. (2018). https://doi.org/10.1109/SYNASC.2018.00041
13. Peng, J., Chen, Q., Kang, L., Jie, H., Han, Y.: Autonomous recognition of multiple surgical instruments tips based on arrow OBB-YOLO network. IEEE Trans. Instrum. Meas. **71**, 1–13 (2022)
14. Koskinen, J., Torkamani-Azar, M., Hussein, A., Huotarinen, A., Bednarik, R.: Automated tool detection with deep learning for monitoring kinematics and eye-hand coordination in microsurgery. Comput. Biol. Med. **141**, 105121 (2022)
15. Schwaner, K.L., Iturrate, I., Andersen, J.K.H., Jensen, P.T., Savarimuthu, T.R.: Autonomous bi-manual surgical suturing based on skills learned from demonstration. In: 2021 IEEE/RSJ International Conference on Intelligent Robots and Systems (IROS), pp. 4017–4024. IEEE (2021)
16. Pryor, W., et al.: Localization and control of magnetic suture needles in cluttered surgical site with blood and tissue. In: 2021 IEEE/RSJ International Conference on Intelligent Robots and Systems (IROS), pp. 524–531. IEEE (2021)
17. Cho, S.M., Kim, Y.G., Jeong, J., Kim, I., Lee, H.J., Kim, N.: Automatic tip detection of surgical instruments in biportal endoscopic spine surgery. Comput. Biol. Med. **133**, 104384 (2021). https://doi.org/10.1016/j.compbiomed.2021.104384
18. Alkhamaiseh, K.N., Grantner, J.L., Shebrain, S., Abdel–Oader, I.: Towards automated performance assessment for laparoscopic box trainer using cross-stage partial network. In: 2021 Digital Image Computing: Techniques and Applications (DICTA), pp. 1–7 (2021). https://doi.org/10.1109/DICTA52665.2021.9647393
19. Fathabadi, F.R., Grantner, J.L., Shebrain, S.A., Abdel-Qader, I.: Multi-class detection of laparoscopic instruments for the intelligent box-trainer system using faster R-CNN architecture. In: Proceedings of the SAMI 2021 - IEEE 19th World Symposium Applied Machine Intelligence Informatics, pp. 149–154 (2021). https://doi.org/10.1109/SAMI50585.2021.9378617
20. Sugimori, H., Sugiyama, T., Nakayama, N., Yamashita, A., Ogasawara, K.: Development of a deep learning-based algorithm to detect the distal end of a surgical instrument. Appl. Sci. **10**, 4245 (2020)
21. Mohaidat, M., Grantner, J.L., Shebrain, S.A., Abdel-Qader, I.: Instrument detection for the intracorporeal suturing task in the laparoscopic box trainer using single-stage object detectors. In: 2022 IEEE International Conference on Electro Information Technology (eIT), pp. 455–460 (2022). https://doi.org/10.1109/eIT53891.2022.9813888
22. Wang, C.-Y., Bochkovskiy, A., Liao, H.-Y.M.: Scaled-yolov4: scaling cross stage partial network. In: Proceedings of the IEEE/CVF Conference on Computer Vision and Pattern Recognition, pp. 13029–13038 (2021)
23. Roboflow: Image Augmentation – Roboflow. https://docs.roboflow.com/image-transformations/image-augmentation. Accessed 15 Jul 2022
24. He, K., Zhang, X., Ren, S., Sun, J.: Deep residual learning for image recognition. In: Proceedings of the IEEE Conference on Computer Vision and Pattern Recognition, pp. 770–778 (2016)
25. Tzutalin, D.: LabelImg is a graphical image annotation tool and label object bounding boxes in images. https://github.com/tzutalin/labelImg. Accessed 15 Jul 2022

Deep Learning II

A New Approach to Visual Classification Using Concatenated Deep Learning for Multimode Fusion of EEG and Image Data

Alankrit Mishra and Garima Bajwa[(✉)]

Department of Computer Science, Lakehead University, Thunder Bay, Canada
{amishra1,garima.bajwa}@lakeheadu.ca

Abstract. In this work, we explore various approaches for automated visual classification of multimodal inputs such as EEG and Image data for the same item, focusing on finding an optimal solution. Our new technique examines the fusion of EEG and Image data using a concatenation of deep learning models for classification, where the EEG feature space is encoded with 8-bit-grayscale images. This concatenated-based model achieves a 95% accuracy for the 39 class EEG-ImageNet dataset, setting a new benchmark and surpassing all prior work. Furthermore, we show that it is computationally effective in multimodal classification when human subjects are presented with visual stimuli of objects in three-dimensional real-world space rather than images of the same. These findings will improve machine visual perception and bring it closer to human-learned vision.

Keywords: EEG · Images · Multimodal visual classification · Deep learning · Machine vision

1 Introduction

In classification problems, searching for similar patterns is the first thought in mind. The human brain learns to classify things on the go in a semi-supervised approach. It is fascinating to observe that one-half of the human brain searches for similar patterns, while the other labels are based on intuition. In contrast, machines employ binary logic to discover patterns in a supervised environment [25]. They lack the intuition that the human mind possesses. The same applies in the case of visual classification [17], but a distinctive micro-pattern can sometimes make a classification task difficult for humans, whereas machines outperform in finding that pattern. As a result, given that humans and machines perceive visual cues in different ways, our aim is to find the best approach to combine human cognition with machine perception for improved visual classification.

Integration with evoked potentials (human visual perception) through the brain-computer interface (BCI) will enable a new form of automated annotation

G. Bebis et al. (Eds.): ISVC 2022, LNCS 13598, pp. 225–236, 2022.
https://doi.org/10.1007/978-3-031-20713-6_17

of brain-based images [14] compared to the current state where much manual effort is required to annotate or label a visual stimulus. Also, joint representational learning will especially contribute to imaging systems (e.g. diagnosis, surveillance, object tracking), as the AI vision system will learn directly and integrate with human observative decisions. It can provide vital suggestions, such as a new region of interest that was not perceived by the human eye due to [6], and it can later learn to filter out non-interesting regions using temporal and spatial joint learning.

2   Related Work

The visual classification task with EEG signal data was initially performed by Kaneshiro et al. [12] in 2015, who proposed a linear discriminant analysis framework based on representational similarity to classify 12 different object categories and obtained an accuracy of 28.87% in their proposed data set, known as the object category-EEG data set. Zhang et al. [31] also proposed a unique approach to visual classification with an EEG dataset using an 8-bit heatmap scaling to convert raw EEG signals into images. A pre-trained MobileNet was used to extract deep features from these images and obtained a classification performance of 95.33% with an SVM classifier. Marini et al. [19] found that EEG signals demonstrated stronger and more sustained event-related desynchronization (ERD) in the [8–13] Hz frequency band for real objects compared to their images, possibly due to 3-D stereoscopic differences, in addition to a late persistent parietal amplitude modulation consistent with an old-new' memory advantage for actual objects over images.

Ilievski et al. [11] and Guillaumin et al. [7] showed robust performance for visual classification using multimodal learning with text and image as cross-modal input. Similarly, Owens et al. [21] and Arandjelovic et al. [2] performed visual classification using shared visual and auditory space modalities.

Spampinato et al. [28] introduced multimodal visual classification using EEG and image data. Their methodology showed outstanding results until later, when it was revealed that the EEG data were not correctly filtered, adding bias to the data. This revelation voided the results of this approach and all other derived works that have used unfiltered data. Palazzo et al. [23] corrected the dataset used by [28] and later published the filtered EEG-ImageNet dataset which we have used in this study.

3   Datasets

Visual classification with multimodal image and EEG data learning has been an emerging study since 2017 [28]. As a result, there are only a limited number of publicly available databases, so collecting additional data was not a priority of our research. This research focused on two existing multimodal datasets for visual classification tests shown in Table 1.

3.1 EEG-ImageNet

The EEG-ImageNet dataset was published by Spampinato et al. [28] and later updated [23] due to filtering issues and signal bias caused by EEG drift. We used the recently updated dataset, commonly known as EEG-ImageNet. It was created by recording EEG signals from six subjects using a 128-channel actiCAP electrode system. The recordings included each subject viewing 2000 images (50 images per class with 40 classes from a subset of ImageNet [4] dataset). The signals were recorded for 500 ms for each trial at a sampling rate of 1000 Hz Hz. The total number of trials was 12,000 for 40 classes; however, due to low-quality samples and some missing trials in the dataset, we used 11,682 trials for 39 classes, approximately 50 images for each class. All data from class "*mushrooms*" (labeled 33 in the dataset) were excluded, and some classes did not have all 50 images with the corresponding EEG recordings tagged. We followed the processing by Pallazzo et al. [23] and used the variant [5–95] Hz of the data set for this study, as it performed comparatively better than [14–70] Hz for the classification of EEG data [20,22,23].

Table 1. Parameters of the two publicly available datasets.

Datasets	Trials	Stimulus	Classes	Subjects	Stimuli	Stimuli per class	Rec. per stimulus	Sampling rate
EEG-ImageNet [23]	11,682	Image	39	6	1947	50*	440ms	1000 Hz
Marini et al. [18]	4,224	Image	2	22	96	48	800ms/1600ms	512 Hz
		Real	2	22	96	48	800ms/1600ms	512 Hz

*There are approximately 50 images for each class.

3.2 Visual Stimuli EEG Dataset: Real-World 3D Objects and Corresponding 2D Image Stimuli

Marini et al. [18] introduced an EEG dataset with two distinct but similar visual stimuli. It consisted of 24 subjects viewing 3D real-world kitchen and garage objects, and their corresponding images while recording EEG signals. Each subject's data had 192 trials, 96 of which were real-world objects, and the other 96 were exact-size photographs of the same items. A 128-electrode setup was used to record the signal data at 512 Hz sampling rate. The entire length of each raw signal was 2800 ms (−800 to 2000 ms), of which 800 ms (0 to 800 ms) was the actual response of subjects observing the stimulus, and the next 800 ms (800 to 1600 ms) were with their eyes closed before switching to the subsequent trial.

The unwanted artifacts of the original data were removed. However, the raw EEG signals were not processed for ERP analysis. We used various processing techniques, including normalizing the data using a z-score and then baseline correcting the signal in the prestimulus period (−200 to 0 ms) to give zero-centered values with a unitary standard deviation. We used data from 22 participants, since two of them (two and seven) had fragmentary data. For optimization, we clipped the signal data (0 to 800 ms) for deep learning models and (0 to 1600 ms) for conventional machine classifiers.

4   Data Encoding and Processing

We use various data extraction and encoding techniques to optimize the feature space and process the data for optimal model configuration and performance.

4.1   Classical Feature Extraction for EEG Data

The EEG visual stimuli datasets usually have more categorical information in the alpha, beta, and gamma frequency bands of the signal, as observed by previous studies [5,28,30]. We performed a periodogram spectral analysis to use the relative band power average of all signals as a feature in each trial. This analysis is best suited for low-frequency resolution in small-length signal datasets [1]. These feature sets are then fed to machine learning classifiers with various mixed PCA pipelines and feature selection encoding (Sect. 5.1).

4.2   Classical Feature Extraction for Image Data

Histogram of Oriented Gradients, or HOG, a classic feature descriptor applied as a feature extractor for various computer vision applications, computes the features from histograms using both the image gradient's magnitude and angle [3]. We used the HOG filter on the image data to produce a one-dimensional feature vector fed into the classifiers to assess the baseline accuracy.

4.3   Principal Component Analysis (PCA) Encoding

PCA is a statistical encoder for converting high- to low-dimensional data by picking the main components that capture the most relevant information about the data set. We employed PCA encoders to compress the feature dimension of both images and EEG data to evaluate the differences in classification results by utilizing only the main components with 99% variance.

4.4   Grayscale-Image Encoding for EEG Data

We used the grayscale-image encoder from our previous work [20], which was designed as a feature extractor to convert the 128-channel EEG signal values to an 8-bit grayscale heatmap image. This encoding method was modified from the Zhang et al. [31] technique used in EEG classification.

The data was processed using two strategies with the grayscale-image encoder. In the first method, each EEG trial's grayscale image was cloned three times ($512 \times 440 \times 3$) to match the input shape of the CNN-based models. Hence, the input shape for EEG-ImageNet was ($11682 \times 512 \times 440 \times 3$), and the Marini et al. dataset was ($4224 \times 512 \times 440 \times 3$). In the second method, we stacked the EEG signals of all subjects corresponding to the same stimulus trial as represented in Fig. 1. Thus, unlike the first method of replicating the same image three times, the images of every subject will be considered as a channel. This

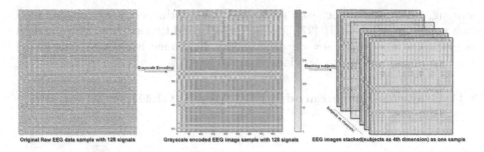

Fig. 1. Representation of the input sample of grayscale-image encoded EEG data with each subject as a dimension for every visual stimulus.

processing approach turned out to be more efficient than the first one, as it uses data from different subjects as separate dimensions. The shape of the input data for EEG-ImageNet was $(1947 \times 512 \times 440 \times 6)$, and the Marini et al. dataset was $(192 \times 512 \times 440 \times 22)$, given six subjects and 22 subjects in the respective datasets.

5   Methods and Model Implementation

5.1   Conventional Machine Learning Classifiers

We used Decision Tree, Random Forest, K-Nearest Neighbor, Support Vector Machine (SVM), Multilayer Perceptron, and Logistic Regression as traditional machine learning classifiers in our evaluation. These model configurations were default setups from the sklearn library [24]. For our experiments, we modified the SVM kernel to RBF. The baseline classification accuracy using one-dimensional feature vectors collected in Sects. 4.1 and 4.2 was determined using these classifiers.

5.2   LSTM-Based EEG Model (LEM) [20]

The LSTM-based EEG Model (introduced in our previous work [20]) has an input layer with the same shape as each sample of raw EEG data. It was first linked to 50 stacked bidirectional LSTMs [9], then to two stacks of common LSTMs (128 and 50), and finally to a dense layer of 128 neurons. To train the model with a softmax classifier, we employed the adam optimizer. Each input EEG data sample has the shape (ts, ch), where "ts" represents the number of time points, and "ch" represents the number of channels in each trial.

5.3   CNN-Based Image Model (CIM) [20]

The model architecture included an input layer representing the shape of the image data to be supplied, a functional model layer that fits CNN-based pretrained models, a 128-neuron dense layer and a softmax classification layer. For training, we applied a stochastic gradient descent optimizer. Pre-trained models such as ResNet [8], VGG16 [27], MobileNet [10], and EfficientNet [29] were used as functional models for several experiments mentioned in Sect. 6. This model was first introduced in our previous work [20].

5.4 Grayscale-Image Encoded EEG Model (GEM)

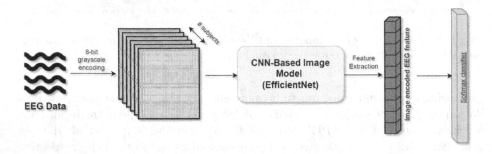

Fig. 2. A representation of the Grayscale-Image Encoded EEG Model (GEM) (modified from our previous work [20])

The GEM architecture consists of a pipeline framework based on our previous study [20] in which the raw EEG data signal data are first converted to an image feature set using the Grayscale-Image encoder mentioned in Sect. 4.4. Then it was fed to a CIM (EfficientNet), a functional model layer for classification. Efficient-Net was used as it was shown to have the best performance for grayscale-image encoded EEG data [31]. Figure 2 illustrates the GEM model design.

5.5 Concatenation-Based Models [20]

A concatenation-based technique often combines the data obtained from two or more machine learning models and then labels those features. To predict the different classes in our datasets, we integrate the penultimate levels of the models, i.e., fully connected layers, immediately before the classification layer, a softmax layer. Concatenated models are popular multimodal deep learning models due to their fast convergence and generalization since different modalities do not lose any feature value during joint learning, which aids in the final classification. We used two designs, concatenated LEM [20] or GEM model (EEG data as input) with CIM model (image stimuli as input) to perform multimodal joint learning visual classification experiments, as shown in Figs. 3a and 3b.

6   Experiments and Results

We investigated the performance of Marini et al. [18] dataset and compared it with the EEG ImageNet [23] dataset using various combinations of encodings mentioned in Sect. 4 and classification models mentioned in Sect. 5.

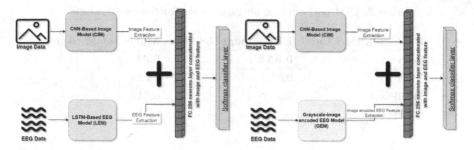

(a) LEM concatenated with CIM [20]   (b) GEM concatenated with CIM

Fig. 3. Multimodal deep learning visual classification using concatenation design (based on our previous approach [20])

6.1 Baseline Visual Classification for EEG and Image Data

In our initial experiments, we obtained a baseline visual classification performance using EEG data and the corresponding image stimulus data to find the degree of distinct visual information present in the classical features of the data.

Table 2a shows the baseline performance of the best data processing, encoding (Sect. 4) and classifier implementation (Sect. 5.1) on the image data for the EEG-ImageNet and Marini et al. datasets. We observed a slight drop in accuracy when the feature space was reduced using PCA. To evaluate the baseline accuracy of the EEG data, we used the first 1600 ms of the EEG sequence for the Marini et al. dataset and 440 ms for EEG-ImageNet. The raw EEG signal was processed to extract the average band power of the alpha and beta bands (Sect. 4.1). Table 2b shows the best baseline performance obtained for each dataset.

Table 2. Baseline visual classification for EEG and Image data

(a) Image stimuli

Image Dataset	# of classes	Accuracy	Best Classifier Setup
Marini et al.	2	0.67	HOG - Gaussian Naïve Bayes
Marini et al.	2	0.65	HOG+PCA - Logistic Regression
EEG-ImageNet	39	0.05	HOG - SVM
EEG-ImageNet	39	0.04	HOG+PCA - Gaussian Naïve Bayes

(b) EEG data

EEG Dataset	# of classes	Accuracy	Best Classifier
EEG-ImageNet	39	0.15	Multilayer perceptron
Marini et al.	2	0.53	Logistic Regression

6.2 Classification Using Deep Learning Models

To compare the results with previous baseline performances, we continue our efforts to evaluate the depth of classification using various state-of-the-art deep learning classifier models.

Table 3. CIM performance on Image data for the two datasets

DL Classifier Model	EEG-ImageNet Acc	Marini et al. Acc
ResNet	**0.85**	**0.81**
VGG 16	0.63	0.72
MobileNet	0.33	0.63
AlexNet	0.2	0.54

To classify images, we used different CNN-based image models (Sect. 5.3). The image stimulus of each trial was first resized ($224 \times 224 \times 3$) to be fed to the CIM models. Table 3 shows the classification results for both datasets, with the ResNet model having the best performance. For the LEM classifier, the EEG data were used as is from the dataset. However, for the GEM classifier, we applied grayscale-image encoded EEG data (Sect. 4.4). The visual classification using the EEG data is shown in Table 4. Marini et al. and the EEG ImageNet datasets obtained better visual classifications when the EEG signals were grayscale encoded. Furthermore, GEM performed better when each subject's data were stacked as a distinct channel dimension.

Table 4. Comparison of our visual classification on EEG data with SOTA models

Marini et al. dataset		
EEG data Encoding	**Classifier models**	**Marini et al. [18] Acc**
Raw EEG data	LSTM based Model (LEM)	0.5
Grayscale image encoded EEG data	EfficientNet + SVM (rbf)	0.52
Grayscale image encoded EEG data with all 22 subjects as channel	**EfficientNet + SVM (rbf)**	**0.73**
EEG-ImageNet (results as shown in our previous work [20])		
EEG data Encoding	**Classifier models**	**EEG-ImageNet -Acc**
Raw EEG data	Stacked LSTMs [28]	0.22
Raw EEG data	SyncNet [16]	0.27
Raw EEG data	EEGNet [15]	0.32
Raw EEG data	EEG-ChannelNet [23]	0.36
Raw EEG data	GRUGate Transformer [30]	0.46
Raw EEG data	LSTM based Model (LEM) [20]	0.26
Grayscale image encoded EEG data	EfficientNet + SVM (rbf) [20]	0.64
Grayscale image encoded EEG data with all 6 subjects as channel	**EfficientNet + SVM (rbf) [20]**	**0.70**

6.3   Hemispherical Brain Region Classification Comparison

In this experiment, our objective was to estimate the categorization potency of the EEG signal data based on the left and right hemispherical regions of the brain with various traditional and deep learning classifiers (Sects. 6.1 and 6.2). We selected a group of 12 electrodes around the left (C3) and right (C4) motor cortex electrodes as the hemispherical regions. Table 5 lists the top results for traditional and deep learning classifiers in both datasets. Classification was marginally improved in the left motor cortex region compared to the right for the Marini et al. dataset. However, it is interesting to note that the right hemispherical region provided better visual classification accuracy for the EEG-ImageNet dataset.

Table 5. Visual classification based on the hemispherical regions of the brain

Exp.	Implementation approach	Classifier Model Used	Dataset	Acc (Left-hem)	Acc (Right-hem)
1	Alpha and beta band average as features	Decision Tree	Marini et al.	0.51	0.51
2	Alpha and beta band average as features	Gaussian Naïve Bayes	Marini et al.	**0.53**	0.5
3	Grayscale image-encoded EEG data Model (GEM)	EfficientNet	Marini et al.	**0.52**	0.51
4	Alpha and beta band average as features	Random Forest	EEG-ImageNet	0.05	0.05
5	Alpha and beta band average as features	Multilayer Perceptron	EEG-ImageNet	0.06	**0.07**
6	Grayscale image-encoded EEG data Model (GEM)	EfficientNet	EEG-ImageNet	0.13	**0.28**

6.4 Visual Classification Using Multimodal Deep Learning

The previous experiments were carried out to separately evaluate the visual classification performance of EEG and Image stimuli data. The isolation of these different input modes in various classifiers gave us a baseline understanding of the accuracy. In this section, we test our joint learning experiments using concatenation-based models (Sect. 5.5).

Table 6 illustrates the performance comparison of our models with the state-of-the-art multimodal visual classification approaches (Image and EEG data as inputs). Additionally, the LEM model concatenated with the CIM model was compared with the GEM model concatenated with the CIM using the EEG-ImageNet dataset. The results indicated that our GEM-based concatenation model outperformed the other architectures and reached 95% accuracy for the EEG-ImageNet. Using this result, we further used this model approach to evaluate the performance of joint learning on the Marini et al. dataset. We similarly obtained a performance improvement for this dataset (78%) compared to using a single EEG only modality (73%, Table 4).

Table 6. Multimodal deep learning visual classification using Image+EGG data as cross modal input.

Exp.	Implementation approach	Model Used	Dataset	Accuracy
1	Regression-based Model [28]	LEM feature regressed with CIM	EEG-ImageNet	0.03
2	Siamese network [23]	Joint learning with 1D CNN and ResNet	EEG-ImageNet	0.91
3	Vertical Stacking [20]	ResNet pretained and LEM (end to end)	EEG-ImageNet	0.70
4	LEM - based Concatenation Model [20]	LEM concatenated with CIM	EEG-ImageNet	0.82
5	GEM - based Concatenation Model	GEM concatenated with CIM	EEG-ImageNet	**0.95**
6	GEM - based Concatenation Model	GEM concatenated with CIM	Marini et al.(image stimuli)	0.72
7	GEM - based Concatenation Model	GEM concatenated with CIM	Marini et al. (real object stimuli)	0.78

6.5 Visual Classification for Real Object Versus Image as Stimuli

As discussed in Sect. 1, the Marini et al. dataset had two different types of EEG recording trials for each visual stimulus data; one when the subject observed the real-world object and the other with planar images of the same object. We applied best-performing deep learning approaches of visual classification to investigate whether machine learning classification improves in the above-mentioned differences in visual stimuli. We found a marginal improvement in classification performance with real object stimuli using the traditional machine learning app-roach. However, the GEM-based concatenation classifier provided a 6% increase in accuracy when the visual stimuli were real objects compared to planar images, as shown in Table 7.

Table 7. Visual classification using real objects versus planar images stimuli

Exp.	Implementation approach	Model Used	Marini et al. dataset	Acc (Image stimuli)	Acc (Object stimuli)
1	Baseline classification Model	ML classifiers	EEG	0.48	0.5
2	LSTM-based EEG Model (LEM)	Stacked (BiLSTM + LSTMs) and 128 FC	EEG	0.51	0.51
3	Grayscale image-encoded EEG data Model (GEM)	EfficientNet	EEG	0.49	0.52
4	GEM - based Concatenation Model	GEM concatenated with CIM	Image + EEG	0.72	0.78

7   Discussion

The datasets used in this work are resourceful but challenging. With 39 classes (a significantly high number in EEG studies), the EEG ImageNet dataset is one of the benchmark datasets for the overall EEG classification problem. However, even though the Marini et al. dataset has two classes, it is worth noting that there are 192 visual stimulus trials, of which 96 are for real-world object stimuli and the remaining 96 are for image stimuli. This makes it harder to classify using deep learning models, as they require a large number of samples to train from scratch. We chose these two datasets to evaluate the optimal performance of our proposed visual classification models.

The baseline classification experiments provided the seed results to compare the stretch of improvement that we achieved while designing more complex clas-sifier architectures. While experimenting with many deep learning architectures for visual classification, we found that the grayscale-image encoded EEG Model (GEM) was best suited for visual classification of challenging datasets such as EEG-ImageNet [23] and Marini et al. [19]. It performed better as we accommo-dated the two-dimensional feature information from all 128 channels in a single image by stretching rather than compressing each channel's feature space.

We got mixed results for the experiments based on the hemisphere mentioned in Table 5. The strong ERP in the hemispherical region of the motor cortex is contralateral to the dominant hand (right-handed subjects in the dataset by Marini et al.). However, this information was not available in the EEG-ImageNet dataset.

We also compared different multimodal deep learning approaches on our datasets. Unlike other modalities, such as text and audio tagged with images, it is harder for machines to classify patterns from EEG signals because they are more volatile and noisy [23]. The concatenation-based approach with the grayscale encoding of EEG data allowed us to accommodate all data (such as electrodes and the entire set of features for all modalities), unlike other approaches where you have to select the best electrodes [26] to reduce complexity or the need to select partial information for each modality [13,23,28]. The GEM-based concate-nation model also helped to discover that machine perception can be enhanced with real-world objects as stimuli instead of images.

8   Conclusion

To conclude this study, we evaluated different approaches to improve visual classification using a multimodal fusion of brainwave (EEG) and image features using EEG-ImageNet and Marini et al. datasets with two key takeaways. First, we designed a state-of-the-art approach to visual classification, the Grayscale-Image encoded EEG model (GEM), which provides a new benchmark performance accuracy of 95% in multimodal deep learning classification. Second, we found that automated visual classification can be improved for multimodal inputs when the stimulus for EEG recording is a real-world object rather than an image.

References

1. Akin, M., Kiymik, M.K.: Application of periodogram and AR spectral analysis to EEG signals. J. Med. Syst. **24**(4), 247–256 (2000)
2. Arandjelovic, R., Zisserman, A.: Look, listen and learn. In: Proceedings of the IEEE International Conference on Computer Vision, pp. 609–617 (2017)
3. Dalal, N., Triggs, B.: Histograms of oriented gradients for human detection. In: 2005 IEEE Computer Society Conference on Computer Vision and Pattern Recognition (CVPR'05), vol. 1, pp. 886–893. IEEE (2005)
4. Deng, J., Dong, W., Socher, R., Li, L.J., Li, K., Fei-Fei, L.: ImageNet: a large-scale hierarchical image database. In: 2009 IEEE Conference on Computer Vision and Pattern Recognition, pp. 248–255. IEEE (2009)
5. Fares, A., Zhong, S., Jiang, J.: Region level bi-directional deep learning framework for EEG-based image classification. In: 2018 IEEE International Conference on Bioinformatics and Biomedicine (BIBM), pp. 368–373. IEEE (2018)
6. Funke, C.M., et al.: Five points to check when comparing visual perception in humans and machines. J. Vis. **21**(3), 16–16 (2021)
7. Guillaumin, M., Verbeek, J., Schmid, C.: Multimodal semi-supervised learning for image classification. In: 2010 IEEE Computer Society Conference on Computer Vision and Pattern Recognition, pp. 902–909. IEEE (2010)
8. He, K., Zhang, X., Ren, S., Sun, J.: Deep residual learning for image recognition. CoRR abs/1512.03385 (2015)
9. Hochreiter, S., Schmidhuber, J.: Long short-term memory. Neural Comput. **9**(8), 1735–1780 (1997)
10. Howard, A.G., et al.: MobileNets: efficient convolutional neural networks for mobile vision applications. CoRR abs/1704.04861 (2017)
11. Ilievski, I., Feng, J.: Multimodal learning and reasoning for visual question answering. In: Advances in Neural Information Processing Systems, vol. 30 (2017)
12. Kaneshiro, B., Guimaraes, P., et al.: A representational similarity analysis of the dynamics of object processing using single-trial EEG classification. PLoS ONE **10**(8), e0135697 (2015)
13. Kavasidis, I., Palazzo, S., Spampinato, C., Giordano, D., Shah, M.: Brain2Image: converting brain signals into images. In: Proceedings of the 25th ACM International Conference on Multimedia, pp. 1809–1817 (2017)
14. Koelstra, S., Mühl, C., Patras, I.: EEG analysis for implicit tagging of video data. In: 2009 3rd International Conference on Affective Computing and Intelligent Interaction and Workshops, pp. 1–6 (2009)

15. Lawhern, V.J., et al.: EEGNet: a compact convolutional neural network for EEG-based brain-computer interfaces. J. Neural Eng. **15**(5), 056013 (2018)
16. Li, Y., Dzirasa, K., Carin, L., Carlson, D.E., et al.: Targeting EEG/LFP synchrony with neural nets. In: Advances in Neural Information Processing Systems, vol. 30 (2017)
17. MacInnes, J., Santosa, S., Wright, W.: Visual classification: expert knowledge guides machine learning. IEEE Comput. Graph. Appl. **30**(1), 8–14 (2010)
18. Marini, F., Breeding, K.A., Snow, J.C.: Dataset of 24-subject EEG recordings during viewing of real-world objects and planar images of the same items. Data Brief **24**, 103857 (2019)
19. Marini, F., Breeding, K.A., Snow, J.C.: Distinct visuo-motor brain dynamics for real-world objects versus planar images. Neuroimage **195**, 232–242 (2019)
20. Mishra, A., Raj, N., Bajwa, G.: EEG-based image feature extraction for visual classification using deep learning. In: 2022 Third International Conference on Intelligent Data Science Technologies and Applications (IDSTA) In Press. IEEE (2022). https://intelligenttech.org/IDSTA2022/IDSTApackingList/26_DTL2022_RC_8931.pdf
21. Owens, A., Wu, J., McDermott, J.H., Freeman, W.T., Torralba, A.: Ambient sound provides supervision for visual learning. In: Leibe, B., Matas, J., Sebe, N., Welling, M. (eds.) ECCV 2016. LNCS, vol. 9905, pp. 801–816. Springer, Cham (2016). https://doi.org/10.1007/978-3-319-46448-0_48
22. Palazzo, S., Spampinato, C., et al.: Correct block-design experiments mitigate temporal correlation bias in EEG classification. arXiv preprint arXiv:2012.03849 (2020)
23. Palazzo, S., Spampinato, C., et al.: Decoding brain representations by multimodal learning of neural activity and visual features. IEEE Trans. Pattern Anal. Mach. Intell. **43**(11), 3833–3849 (2020)
24. Pedregosa, F., et al.: Scikit-Learn: machine learning in Python. J. Mach. Learn. Res. **12**, 2825–2830 (2011)
25. Phoha, S.: Machine perception and learning grand challenge: situational intelligence using cross-sensory fusion. Front. Robot. AI **1**, 7 (2014)
26. Raghu, S., Sriraam, N., Temel, Y., Rao, S.V., Kubben, P.L.: EEG based multi-class seizure type classification using convolutional neural network and transfer learning. Neural Netw. **124**, 202–212 (2020)
27. Simonyan, K., Zisserman, A.: Very deep convolutional networks for large-scale image recognition. arXiv preprint:1409.1556 (2014)
28. Spampinato, C., Palazzo, S., et al.: Deep learning human mind for automated visual classification. In: Proceedings of the IEEE Conference on Computer Vision and Pattern Recognition, pp. 6809–6817 (2017)
29. Tan, M., Le, Q.V.: EfficientNet: rethinking model scaling for convolutional neural networks. CoRR abs/1905.11946 (2019)
30. Tao, Y., et al.: Gated transformer for decoding human brain EEG signals. In: 2021 43rd Annual International Conference of the IEEE Engineering in Medicine & Biology Society (EMBC), pp. 125–130. IEEE (2021)
31. Zhang, H., Silva, F.H.S., Ohata, E.F., Medeiros, A.G., Rebouças Filho, P.P.: Bidimensional approach based on transfer learning for alcoholism pre-disposition classification via EEG signals. Front. Human Neurosci. **14** (2020)

Deep Learning-Based Classification of Plant Xylem Tissue from Light Micrographs

Sean Wu[1]([✉]), Reem Al Dabagh[1], Anna L. Jacobsen[2], Helen I. Holmlund[1], and Fabien Scalzo[1,3]

[1] Seaver College, Pepperdine University, Malibu, CA 90265, USA
sean.wu@pepperdine.edu
[2] California State University Bakersfield, Bakersfield, CA 93311, USA
[3] Department of Computer Science, University of California, Los Angeles (UCLA), Los Angeles, CA 90095, USA

Abstract. Anatomical studies of plant hydraulic traits have traditionally been conducted by manual measurements of light micrographs. An
automated process could expedite analysis and broaden the scope of
questions that can be asked, but such an approach would require the ability to accurately classify plant cells according to their type. Our research
evaluates a deep learning-based model which accepts a cropped cell image
input alongside a broader cropped image which incorporates contextual
information of that cell type's original cropped image, and learns to segregate these plant cells based off of the features of both inputs. Whilst a
single cropped image classification yielded adequate results with outputs
matching the ground-truth labels, we discovered that a second image
input significantly bolstered the model's learning and accuracy (98.1%),
indicating that local context provides important information needed to
accurately classify cells. Finally our results imply a future application of
our classifier to automatic cell-type detection in xylem tissue image cross
sections.

1 Introduction

Plants are important global producers of oxygen and they serve as an important
food source for many animals. This makes plants essential for the existence of
most life on Earth. Most plant life on land is limited to some extent by water
availability. While most plants have some basic adaptations to control water loss
(such as a waxy cuticle covering the leaves and the ability to regulate water loss
through stomata), some plants have adapted to thrive in dry regions such as the
desert and chaparral ecosystems of southern California [1,2]. During drought,
some of the most dehydration tolerant chaparral shrubs can survive internal
water pressures that are more negative than -10 MPa, absolute pressures that
are equivalent to approximately 100 times Earth's atmospheric pressure [3,4].

The ability of some plants to survive extreme dehydration is attributed
in part to anatomical characteristics of the plant vascular tissue system. The

G. Bebis et al. (Eds.): ISVC 2022, LNCS 13598, pp. 237–248, 2022.
https://doi.org/10.1007/978-3-031-20713-6_18

vascular tissue system is composed, in part, of xylem. Xylem tissue transports water from the roots to the leaves. The xylem tissue contains several cell types with distinct functions [5], that may be divided into three cellular classifications. 1) Tracheary elements are elongate tubes with a large diameter for the passive transport of water, which is pulled through the plant by evaporation from the leaves (i.e., transpiration). They have a thick secondary cell wall and are dead upon maturity, facilitating their function of long-distance transport. There are two types of tracheary elements that may be found within chaparral shrubs, vessel elements and tracheids. 2) Fibers are also elongate cells, but they function primarily as mechanical support for the stem or root by means of their thick cell walls with a narrow lumen. 3) Parenchyma cells are short cells that have thin primary cell walls and are typically alive at maturity. They function in short-distance transport and storage of water and starch (long-term sugar reserves). There are two types of parenchyma cells that may occur within the xylem, axial parenchyma and ray parenchyma. While all flowering plants have these three cell types present in the xylem, structural adaptations within each cell type can improve whole-plant dehydration tolerance. Additionally, different species may differ greatly in the proportions of these cell type classes within their xylem, with the amount of different cell type classes linked to differences in plant function [6,7].

Small changes in xylem cell characteristics can have a large impact on their function. For example, there is a tradeoff between hydraulic efficiency (which contributes to greater sugar production and growth) and resistance to freezing-induced gas bubble (embolism) formation in the vascular system (which can lead to whole-plant mortality), with large diameter tracheary elements being efficient but highly vulnerable to embolism [8–10]. In a similar way, tracheary element implosion resistance (measured as the cell wall thickness to breadth ratio, $(t/b)^2$) also corresponds to dehydration-induced embolism resistance [11,12]. Although not directly conducting water, the fibers provide mechanical support (estimated by parameters such as wall thickness and lumen diameter) that increases embolism resistance and the mechanical strength of the stem [2,12]. The proportion of the parenchyma within the xylem can indicate the plant's relative carbon stores, with implications for tradeoffs related to carbon starvation and drought tolerance [5,6,13].

Traditionally, all these measurements related to plant anatomy have been taken manually or semi-automatically from light micrographs of transverse stem sections. However, given the difficulty of scaling up time-intensive measurements to whole ecosystems or the globe, it is compelling to find faster ways to measure key xylem traits without compromising accuracy. There is a need for automated, scalable software tools that could automatically analyze large datasets efficiently. An accurate but automated way to measure anatomical traits could also allow us to take advantage of increasingly available large image datasets [14]. In short, a faster means of measuring key characteristics of xylem anatomy would greatly broaden the scope of questions that can be asked about plant structure and function. We tackle this problem in this paper by introducing a deep learning-based model for classification of plant cells.

2   Related Works

In recent years, cell type classification with machine learning has received significant attention particularly in the medical field. Researchers have made breakthrough findings in cancer cell type classifications [15] and cardiovascular research [16], for example, where different types of white blood cells were segregated through popular machine learning techniques such as Deep Learning, or a Random Forest algorithms [17].

Although some prior studies have used semi-automated approaches to classify plant cells [18], and there exists commercially available software such as Win-CELL (Regent Instruments, Inc.), there are relatively few previous applications of machine learning to plant hydraulic anatomy. Previous studies have applied machine learning algorithms to topics such as plant disease classification [19] and plant leaf classification [20]; however few studies have been conducted on machine learning at the cellular level. Those studies at this microscopic level have mainly been focused on the segmentation of plant tissues, then possibly classifying those segmented images [14, 21–24]. To our best knowledge, we are the first group to design a cascade-like machine learning model to classify tracheary elements (vessels), fibers, and parenchyma cells in plants, with discussions on the effects of inputting a contextualized image alongside the image to be classified.

3   Dataset and Problem Definition

Our dataset for this project consists of light micrographs of transverse stem and root sections of three chaparral shrub species native to the Santa Monica Mountains in southern California: *Ceanothus crassifolius* (CCR), *Ceanothus oliganthus* (CO), and *Frangula californica* (FCA). The samples were collected in 2007 at Cold Creek Canyon (34°05′36.0″N, 118°39′02.9″W). Samples were taken from three individuals of each species to account for genetic and phenotypic variation among individuals. Thin circular slices of the stems and roots (transverse sections or "cross-sections") were cut using a sledge microtome (Model 860 Sledge Microtome, American Optical Corp., Buffalo, NY, USA). The cross-sections were stained with I_2KI (to show starch) and mounted in glycerol on microscope slides. Images of the cross-sections were taken at 100× or 200× magnification using a light microscope with an attached digital camera (Olympus BH-2, Olympus Imaging Corp., Center Valley, PA; Spot Insight 2, v. 18.2 Color Mosaic, Diagnostic Instruments, Inc., Sterling Heights, MI). Multiple (non-overlapping) images were taken of each cross section, with each image showing at least 200 cells. Our final dataset included 26 CCR, 22 CO, and 37 FCA images. The goal for this research project is to classify three functionally distinct plant cell types found in the xylem tissue (vessel, fiber, and parenchyma). Our objective is to construct a machine learning model that learns the features of these plant cell types alongside its surrounding characteristics to classify them with high accuracy. Flowering plants have two types of conductive tracheary elements: vessels

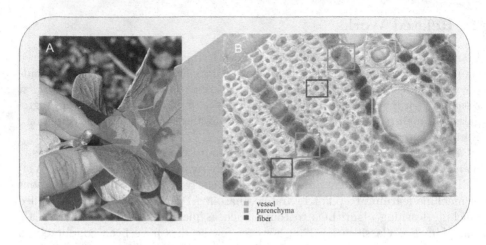

Fig. 1. (A) Chaparral shrub stem cut transversely as to prepare cross sections. (B) Micrograph of transverse cross section with labeled cell types. Boxes are placed as for cropping. Scale bar = 50 μm.

(typically larger diameter, composed of multiple cells) and tracheids (typically smaller diameter, composed of a single cell). However, it can be difficult to distinguish tracheids from other cell types in light micrographs, as large tracheids can appear similar to small vessels and small tracheids can appear similar to fibers. Thus, we did not attempt to identify tracheids in this study; we tried to avoid using images of tracheids. For labeled vessels, we selected large cells that were most likely vessels and not tracheids. However, it is possible that some tracheids were incorrectly labeled as vessels or fibers. Additionally, the roots of some shrubs contained gelatinous fibers, which are morphologically distinct from the more common sclerenchyma fibers. We categorized all fibers (gelatinous and sclerenchyma) as falling within the cell type class of "fibers" for this study. Finally, we did not distinguish between axial and ray parenchyma, but rather categorized them all within the cell type class of "parenchyma".

All of the original images were re-scaled to 1600×1200 for each image cross section regardless of the shrub species. We utilized a manual image cropping software called *makesense.ai* to crop the individual cells. We discarded all the extremely zoomed out images and chose the images with good resolution. Since vessels are the least abundant compared to fibers and parenchyma, we started with cropping the vessels and cropping approximately the same amount for fibers and parenchyma. The cells that are not fully shown in the image, i.e. are in the corner or blurry, were not cropped. This process is depicted in Fig. 1. This cropping process produced 790 unique images of vessels, fibers, and parenchyma cells.

When splitting our data into training and testing sets, our group decided to train a model on two shrub species and use the third species as an external validation. All models were run three times, with different species used as the test and training sets each time.

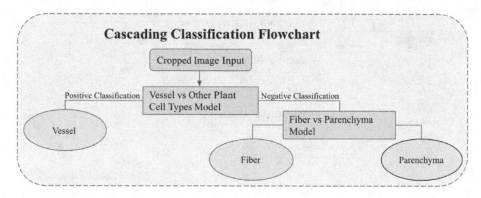

Fig. 2. Illustration of cascade-like framework to achieve a multi-class classification while avoiding its potential sub-class confusions. This is attained by splitting the classifier into two binary deep-learning classification models.

4   Methodology

Our research presents a cascade-like approach to classifying plant cell-types and consists of two separate models, each for their own classification task of varying complexity. Additionally to the cascade-like models, we then propose the effects of inputting two image inputs to the machine learning model- the first being a cropped image of either a vessel, fiber, or parenchyma, and the second being a broader image that displays some context around that cropped image.

4.1   Data Augmentation and Pre-processing

To mitigate the minute number of cropped training images that we obtained, some data augmentation was implemented to give our model more generalization. By using a PyTorch transform, each cropped cell type image was augmented in terms of a random rotation between 0 and 180° ten times.

Our data loading consists of a three step process of pre-processing the images. The first step is to resize each cropped image to $(224, 224)$ (width, height) pixels, as the pre-trained ResNet-18 was trained on this image size on ImageNet [25]. Following, we normalize the features in each of the data sets by calculating the mean and standard deviation for the data set as a whole and computing a z score standardization for each image, ultimately modifying each image to have roughly a mean of 0 and standard deviation of 1. Lastly, each pixel value in the RGB channels are transformed into a range spanning from 0–1 by a division of 255 through a PyTorch Tensor.

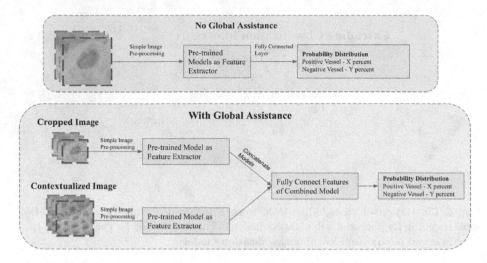

Fig. 3. Portrayal of our experiments of the advantages of an additional cropped image input to potentially enhance classification results.

4.2 Cascading-Like Model

Due to the fact that a multi-class cell type classification assignment may be harder for features to be classified, our group trained and optimized one model on categorizing vessels vs other cell types, and the other on classifying fibers vs parenchyma cells.

As depicted in Fig. 2, the intuition is to deliver a cropped cell image to two potential classification models. First, the cropped cell image will be sent to the a model that will classify it as a vessel or non-vessel. If the first model were to classify that cropped image was a vessel, then the classification task would be complete, however, in the case where the image is a non-vessel, then the second model will classify that cropped image as a fiber or parenchyma.

4.3 Global Contextualization Approach

While local patches can capture detailed information about the texture of a cell, it lacks the contextual information necessary to classify some cells. The reasoning behind this approach is due to the potential similarity of fiber and parenchyma cell class types when strictly cropped with little to no surrounding information, particularly for fibers and axial parenchyma. However, when including a secondary image with surrounding information, we hypothesize a preferable more concise model.

To achieve the contextualized photos, we took the image dimensions of each cropped plant cell image and re-cropped a new globalized image that is 140 pixels longer and taller than the original cropped image. As illustrated in Fig. 3, we decided to extract the features of the original cropped image and the globalized cropped image separately in a chosen feature extraction model, then concatenate the features in a wrapper class where those added features are fully connected into a probability distribution of two classes.

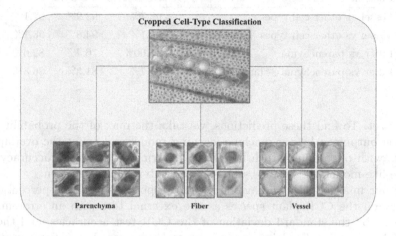

Fig. 4. Depiction of the cell-type classification we hope to achieve with deep learning.

5   Experiments and Results

To fulfill our research goal, we trained one pipeline that consists of two binary classification models that classifies one cropped plant cell type input, and a second pipeline consisting of two binary classification models, that classifies two image inputs as a plant cell type. For our baseline classification models, we appropriated three popular deep learning models: ResNet-18, VGG-16, and DeiT, as feature extractors by freezing the weights previously trained on ImageNet, and only training the fully connected layer [25–27].

For each model, our data was partitioned into three data sets. The training data, which was permuted to choose two of the three plant species for training and the third plant species as an external validation, was assigned an approximate [90, 10] train-validation split after augmenting. This was done by implementing a random number generator, where on the $1/10th$ probability scenario, that image alongside its augmented counterparts would be sent to the validation data, which was subsequently used for hyper-parameter tuning. Figure 4 illustrates our end goal for classifying these xylem cell-types. We chose an initial learning rate of 0.1 and decreased it by a magnitude of 10 every n steps depending on the sub-problem we were trying to solve.

5.1   Model Evaluation Metric

The accuracy of each of our models are evaluated based on the number of predictions the model gets correct on the external test set divided by the length of

Table 1. These are the scores for each baseline pre-trained convolutional neural networks with the bare cropped image inputs, and the cropped image input with contextual assistance.

Baseline models	ResNet-18	VGG-16	DeiT
Vessel vs other cell types	96.7%	93.9%	97.1%
Vessel vs other cell types + large patches	98.1%	94.8%	98.1%
Fiber vs parenchyma	91.00%	76.4%	82.6%
Fiber vs parenchyma + large patches	91.7%	81.3%	86.8%

the test set. To find these predictions, we take the max of the probability distribution outputted by our machine learning model and count the overlapping corrects with our ground truth labels. To determine the overall accuracy of a cascade-like model, the average score of both sub-models are taken.

For our final models, we have decided to report results by a percentage of accuracy on the CCR plant species as the external test with an error margin calculated by the standard deviation of the CCR test accuracies, and the CO and FCA accuracies. By doing so, we hope to have created classification models that will yield similar test results within the error margin on other unseen species.

5.2   Baseline Results

To determine which pre-trained feature extractor to use, we trained both models without data augmentation on the three chosen neural networks (ResNet-18, VGG-16, DeiT) to determine initial results. Our group decided that ResNet-18 was the most accurate and efficient feature extractor for our research goals, because without any augmentation, it is clear that ResNet-18 has the best performance for all sub-problems. Additionally, the information shown in Table 1 starts to strengthens our claim of contextualized images providing classification assistance, as marginal improvements are evident in the contextualized image models.

5.3   Results

Our hypothesis of adding a contextualized image to the machine learning model proved to be accurate. Table 2 shows that adding a global patch for vessel classification improved the vessel vs non-vessels by 5.7% correctly classifying 211/213 vessels, fiber vs parenchyma by 2.8%, and escalating the overall accuracy by 4.2%. As a justification for our cascade-like architecture, the total accuracy of a trained and optimized multi-class classification model with data augmentation and global patch input is also visualized to be evidently worse than both the non-global patch and with global patch cascade-like models.

Table 2. A comparison of the performance of ResNet-18 with augmented images and global patches vs ResNet-18 with just data augmentation. Large patches are shown to increase classification accuracy. A justification for our cascading-like model is supported when compared with the multi-class classification results. Abbreviation Notes: (Ves, Fib, Par, aug) = (Vessel, Fiber, Parenchyma, augmentation

Cascading model	Ves. vs other	Fib. vs par.	Overall accuracy
Large patches + data aug.	99.1 ± 1.2%	97.2 ± 4.3%	98.1 ± 2.6%
Data aug.	93.4%	94.4%	93.9%
Non-cascading model	Ves. vs other	Fib. vs par.	Overall accuracy
Large patches + data aug.	x	x	90.1%

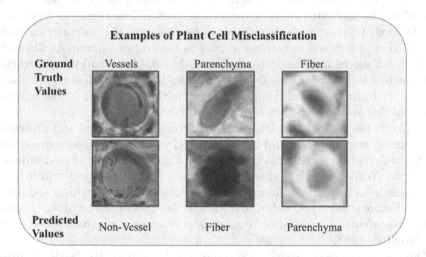

Fig. 5. Representation of the cropped plant cell images that were misclassified by our model

6 Discussion

In this study, we used a novel application of machine learning to classify plant cell types in xylem tissue. We discovered that applying two cascading models (vessels vs non-vessels and fibers vs parenchyma) achieved more accurate results than a single model to classify the three cell types. Vessels have a more distinctive shape compared to fibers and parenchyma, which likely explains why the accuracy score in the first model is higher than in the second model comparing fibers and parenchyma. We ran the cascading models three times and found some variation depending on which two species were used for training and which one species was used for testing the model. This likely reflects interspecific variation in cell characteristics and the cell types present (e.g., the lack of tracheids in FCA) and the challenge of fine-tuning a model that can be accurately applied to a broad selection of species.

Additionally, we discovered that incorporating the larger context ("patches") surrounding each plant cell improved the accuracy of our classification model. The appearance and size of plant cells is naturally variable within cell types (even within a single image), due to a variety of genetic, environmental, or developmental factors. Thus, the context can greatly increase the confidence in cell classification (e.g., vessels are larger than fibers). Also, some cell types can be classified based on the pattern that they form within the tissue. For example, parenchyma in xylem tissue form lines ("rays") through the fibers and vessels, as shown in Fig. 1. Future models may be able to incorporate contextual information with even greater success.

Another challenge to our current framework is that some cells would overlap with other cells in the cropped rectangular frame which may cause the machine to analyze the undesired overlapping cell as part of the region of interest for classification. When cropping parenchyma for instance, the parenchyma that is directly next to it would sometimes appear in the cropped frame. As illustrated in Fig. 5, our model misclassified some parenchyma, fibers, and vessels, whether it be due to a lack of image quality, or similarity in features. In our future work, we may try to implement a cropping technique that is similar to the magnetic lasso tool that would crop the cell at its exact borders.

While promising, our current framework could be expanded and diversified. For example, we could train and test this model using images from more species, more developmental stages, and grown under a greater variety of environmental conditions. While some cell characteristics are fairly conserved within a cell type, there is an incredible amount of morphological diversity within and among species. Future studies may determine whether our model can be broadly applied across ecosystems, growth forms (e.g., woody vs non-woody tissue), and organs (e.g., stem vs root).

Our cascading model framework could also be applied to classify a greater number of cell types. For this study, we adopted a simplified classification system for the three most abundant cell type classes (vessel, fiber, and parenchyma). However, future models may further distinguish cell types, such as between ray vs axial parenchyma, libriform vs gelatinous fibers, and vessels vs tracheids. A more detailed model would also likely benefit from the cascading model framework and contextual information.

7   Conclusion

Our study produced a novel approach to classifying plant cell types from light micrographs with high accuracy. Our model may provide a foundation for future models that are capable of detecting, classifying, and measuring plant cells from unprocessed light micrographs. Our framework might also be applied to other times of image datasets, such as micro-computed tomography. With the increasing availability of large image datasets, such a model would greatly broaden the utility of these resources for research teams that lack the manpower for manual analysis.

Acknowledgements. We would like to thank the Keck Foundation for their grant to Pepperdine University to support our Data Science program. We would also like to thank R. Brandon Pratt for help with shrub sample collection.

References

1. Rundel, P.W.: California chaparral and its global significance. In: Underwood, E.C., Safford, H.D., Molinari, N.A., Keeley, J.E. (eds.) Valuing Chaparral. SSEM, pp. 1–27. Springer, Cham (2018). https://doi.org/10.1007/978-3-319-68303-4_1
2. Jacobsen, A.L., Pratt, R.B., Ewers, F.W., Davis, S.D.: Cavitation resistance among 26 chaparral species of southern California. Ecol. Monogr. **77**(1), 99–115 (2007)
3. Davis, S.D., Ewers, F.W., Sperry, J.S., Portwood, K.A., Crocker, M.C., Adams, G.C.: Shoot dieback during prolonged drought in Ceanothus (Rhamnaceae) chaparral of California: a possible case of hydraulic failure. Am. J. Bot. **89**(5), 820–828 (2002)
4. Venturas, M.D., MacKinnon, E.D., Dario, H.L., Jacobsen, A.L., Pratt, R.B., Davis, S.D.: Chaparral shrub hydraulic traits, size, and life history types relate to species mortality during California's historic drought of 2014. PLoS ONE **11**(7), e0159145 (2016)
5. Pratt, R.B., Jacobsen, A.L.: Conflicting demands on angiosperm xylem: tradeoffs among storage, transport and biomechanics. Plant, Cell Environ. **40**(6), 897–913 (2017)
6. Pratt, R., Jacobsen, A., Ewers, F., Davis, S.: Relationships among xylem transport, biomechanics and storage in stems and roots of nine Rhamnaceae species of the California chaparral. New Phytol. **174**(4), 787–798 (2007)
7. Jacobsen, A.L., Agenbag, L., Esler, K.J., Pratt, R.B., Ewers, F.W., Davis, S.D.: Xylem density, biomechanics and anatomical traits correlate with water stress in 17 evergreen shrub species of the Mediterranean-type climate region of South Africa. J. Ecol. **95**(1), 171–183 (2007)
8. Davis, S.D., Sperry, J.S., Hacke, U.G.: The relationship between xylem conduit diameter and cavitation caused by freezing. Am. J. Bot. **86**(10), 1367–1372 (1999)
9. Hacke, U.G., Sperry, J.S.: Functional and ecological xylem anatomy. Perspect. Plant Ecol. Evol. Syst. **4**(2), 97–115 (2001)
10. Pittermann, J., Sperry, J.S.: Analysis of freeze-thaw embolism in conifers. The interaction between cavitation pressure and tracheid size. Plant Physiol. **140**(1), 374–382 (2006)
11. Hacke, U.G., Sperry, J.S., Pockman, W.T., Davis, S.D., McCulloh, K.A.: Trends in wood density and structure are linked to prevention of xylem implosion by negative pressure. Oecologia **126**(4), 457–461 (2001). https://doi.org/10.1007/s004420100628
12. Jacobsen, A.L., Ewers, F.W., Pratt, R.B., Paddock, W.A., III., Davis, S.D.: Do xylem fibers affect vessel cavitation resistance? Plant Physiol. **139**(1), 546–556 (2005)
13. Pratt, R.B., et al.: Starch storage capacity of sapwood is related to dehydration avoidance during drought. Am. J. Bot. **108**(1), 91–101 (2021)
14. Biswas, S., Barma, S.: A large-scale optical microscopy image dataset of potato tuber for deep learning based plant cell assessment. Sci. Data **7**(1), 1–11 (2020)
15. Nissim, N., Dudaie, M., Barnea, I., Shaked, N.T.: Real-time stain-free classification of cancer cells and blood cells using interferometric phase microscopy and machine learning. Cytometry A **99**(5), 511–523 (2021)

16. Ding, S., et al.: Predicting heart cell types by using transcriptome profiles and a machine learning method. Life **12**(2), 228 (2022)

17. Abdullah, E., Turan, M.K.: Classifying white blood cells using machine learning algorithms. Int. J. Eng. Res. Dev. **11**(1), 141–152 (2019)

18. Ziemińska, K., Westoby, M., Wright, I.J.: Broad anatomical variation within a narrow wood density range–a study of twig wood across 69 Australian angiosperms. PLoS ONE **10**(4), e0124892 (2015)

19. Ramesh, S., Hebbar, R., Niveditha, M., Pooja, R., Shashank, N., Vinod, P., et al.: Plant disease detection using machine learning. In: 2018 International Conference on Design Innovations for 3Cs Compute Communicate Control (ICDI3C), pp. 41–45. IEEE (2018)

20. Priya, C.A., Balasaravanan, T., Thanamani, A.S.: An efficient leaf recognition algorithm for plant classification using support vector machine. In: International Conference on Pattern Recognition, Informatics and Medical Engineering (PRIME-2012), pp. 428–432. IEEE (2012)

21. Wolny, A., et al.: Accurate and versatile 3D segmentation of plant tissues at cellular resolution. Elife **9**, e57613 (2020)

22. Vu, Q.D., et al.: Methods for segmentation and classification of digital microscopy tissue images. Front. Bioeng. Biotechnol. **7**, 53 (2019)

23. Garcia-Pedrero, A., et al.: Convolutional neural networks for segmenting xylem vessels in stained cross-sectional images. Neural Comput. Appl. **32**(24), 17927–17939 (2020). https://doi.org/10.1007/s00521-019-04546-6

24. Resente, G., et al.: Mask, train, repeat! Artificial intelligence for quantitative wood anatomy. Front. Plant Sci. **12**, 767400 (2021)

25. He, K., Zhang, X., Ren, S., Sun, J.: Deep residual learning for image recognition. In: Proceedings of the IEEE Conference on Computer Vision and Pattern Recognition, pp. 770–778 (2016)

26. Tammina, S.: Transfer learning using VGG-16 with deep convolutional neural network for classifying images. Int. J. Sci. Res. Publ. (IJSRP) **9**(10), 143–150 (2019)

27. Touvron, H., Cord, M., Douze, M., Massa, F., Sablayrolles, A., Jégou, H.: Training data-efficient image transformers & distillation through attention. In: International Conference on Machine Learning, PMLR, pp. 10347–10357 (2021)

VampNet: Unsupervised Vampirizing of Convolutional Networks

Trong-Lanh R. Nguyen[1,2]([✉]), Thierry Chateau[2], and Guillaume Magniez[1]

[1] Safran Electronics & Defence, Boulogne-Billancourt, France
t-lanh.nguyen@doctorant.uca.fr
[2] Clermont Auvergne Université, CNRS, Clermont Auvergne INP, Institut Pascal,
63000 Clermont-Ferrand, France

Abstract. Numerous applications need to concurrently solve multiple tasks. We present an unsupervised method enabling to create from two pre-trained neural networks A and B, a network B' approximating B while feeding on a part of A's layers. This "Vampire" Network allows to significantly reduce the combined weight of the two networks. We propose the following contributions: (1) we show that two networks of the same structure but trained on different tasks display quite strong linear properties between their layers; (2) an unsupervised algorithm replacing part of the vampire network's features by linear projections of features from the first network; (3) we show that the vampire network thereby created significantly reduces the number of additional parameters needed to accomplish the second task, and thus the computational load of the full system.

Keywords: Neural network · Compression · Multitask

1 Introduction

Deep Convolutional Neural Networks (DCNN) are widely used for different tasks such as detection, semantic segmentation or depth estimation. Since some applications like autonomous driving need to combine theses different outputs, Multi-task models seem to be a relevant solution. It consists in generating networks performing several related tasks at once on the same input, effectively sharing resources between tasks [2]. One major convenience of such methods is the inductive bias that arises during the training step, that allows one task to benefit from the training of others, both raising the convergence speed and the generalisation abilities of the trained network [2]. Another interesting property for embedded applications is the reduction of the model size due to some shared parts. However, most of the proposed approaches assume that all tasks must be trained jointly with available annotated data-sets. Moreover, adding a new task without modifying the performances of existing ones is also a important feature from an industrial point of view.

We propose VampNet: 1) Given two DCNN networks $\mathcal{N}_A$ (that we will call Master network) and $\mathcal{N}_B$, already trained on two different but related task A

G. Bebis et al. (Eds.): ISVC 2022, LNCS 13598, pp. 249–261, 2022.
https://doi.org/10.1007/978-3-031-20713-6_19

and B, we formulate a framework to build a new network $\mathcal{N}_{B'}$ that approximates $\mathcal{N}_B$ under the challenging hypothesis:

- no annotated learning base is available,
- the master network $\mathcal{N}_A$ must not be modified,
- the model size of the new network $\mathcal{N}_{B'}$ must be lower than $\mathcal{N}_B$

Since both networks estimate related tasks, they should be correlated. We study this assumption and show that a very simple linear relation can be applied to replace features in $\mathcal{N}_B$ by features from $\mathcal{N}_A$. The new generated network $\mathcal{N}_{B'}$ is then called VampNet (from Vampire): it saves some computation by using some simple linear projections of $\mathcal{N}_A$ features (so-called *vampirizing* thereafter) resulting in a strong reduction of the size of the two merged networks. Figure 1 presents an overview of VampNet.

When using a classical DCNN $\mathcal{N}_B$ (*i.e.*: without skip connections) replacing the full feature map of a layer has as consequence that the preceding layers of the network do not have to be computed anymore. This implies that the deeper a full layer is replaced, the lower the resulting global network size is. This is why we focus thereafter on vampirizing a layer (*i.e.*: the full feature map of the layer).

We demonstrate our method on several public data-sets for two related tasks: semantic segmentation and depth estimation. Moreover, we provide a thorough ablation study to analyse linear correlation between layers and the proposed model that select the vampirized layer.

The next section presents some relevant works linked to multitask learning, network merging and correlation based feature analysis. Section three describes the core of our model while section four shows and analyses the experiments provided in order to evaluate the VampNet framework.

In this paper, we use the following nomenclature for convolutional neural networks:

- a **feature** extracted by a convolutional layer is a single channel of its output volume. Each element of a channel is then a **sample** of the feature, as it is the result of a dot product with the convolution kernel for a different patch of the input volume.
- a **feature-map** is the set of features computed by a convolutional layer.

2   Related Work

In order to assess the proposed VampNet model with the wide literature, we consider three aspects: 1) correlation based feature analysis, 2) neural network merging and 3) multitask neural networks.

2.1   Correlation-Based Feature Map Analysis

Since the proposed method relies on the assumption that there are linear links between features of two correlated task networks, we first review relevant works dealing with linear analysis for neural networks.

[7] uses Canonical Cross Correlation (CCA) between feature maps to compare learned representations. By comparing in-training feature maps to their fully trained version, the authors are able to study the training dynamics of a network. They explore the application of CCA to model compression.

[13] notes that multiple trainings of the same network starting from different random initial states usually converge toward solutions with similar performances, and that learned feature maps of a same layer often correlate with each other across the solutions. The authors show that it is possible to find a one-to-one, then a few-to-one mapping between features of the same layer of two versions of the same network, using activations' correlation as distance metric.

2.2   Multitask Neural Networks

Multitask learning [2,14] encompasses learning methods aiming to accomplish multiple tasks at the same time. The main interest of this kind of approach is inductive bias: by learning two different but related tasks, more meaningful features are trained. Each task can thus benefit from features that would not have appeared with its sole training gradient.

Multitask neural network are the deep learning pendant of multitask learning. Two families stand out fairly distinctively [9]: approaches that have a "hard sharing" of weights, *i.e.* using a common body of computations, and approaches that have a "soft sharing" of weights, *i.e.* giving each task its own trainable weights but putting constraints between them.

2.3   Networks Merging

While in multitask learning specific networks are trained to estimate several tasks, networks merging considers two existing networks which are mixed to produce a lightweight one. [12] introduces a post-training merging and compression method based on the convolution kernels' weights' values. The approach consists in a separation of kernels into 1×1 convolutions, a K-means clustering of those new kernels, followed by a Huffman encoding of the found centroids. A codebook can then be used to get back the full kernels. The clustering step has the effect that retrieved kernels are not exactly equal to the original ones. The authors suggest to make up for the changes in performances by fine-tuning the model on the original training data.

[10] proposes a cascaded architecture to speed up classifiers' ability to discard negatives, replacing a monolithic network by a sequence of smaller classifiers called *stages*. Stages are of increasing abstraction level and size, the later ones only being computed if the earlier did not return a negative result. Because each subsequent stage must be of higher abstraction than the preceding one, building such an abstraction at each stage would induce a substantial amount of computing for examples that are not early rejected. To avoid that, the author gives each stage access to all the features extracted by the previous one, a stage only adding layers and/or channels to the preceding stage. All the stages are

trained at the same time under a composite loss. As the sharing is unidirectional, the later stages do influence the convergence of the earlier ones but not *vice versa*.

In this paper, we propose a model that starts from several assumptions: 1) we have two existing trained networks like in network merging, 2) no annotated data-set is available like in unsupervised learning and 3) the function of the master network should not be changed.

3   Method

This section describes the core of the proposed model, relying on that correlated tasks trained using two networks with the same structure generate correlated Feature Maps (FM) within the two networks. After defining how to compute linearities between FMs, we propose a simple way, using a convolutional operator, to replace a feature by a linear projection of one vampirized from another task network. Since replacing the full FM of a layer is very interesting to save both computation time and model size, we propose a layer selection relation to automatically choose where replacing a layer while keeping a good trade-off between performances and computation budget.

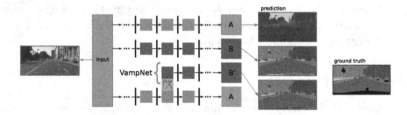

Fig. 1. Overview of the method: computations are spared by reusing results from a related network. In a first time, features of two networks $\mathcal{N}_A$ and $\mathcal{N}_B$ are compared with each other by linear regression. Features from $\mathcal{N}_A$ with the smallest residuals can then be used to predict features from $\mathcal{N}_B$ by linear projection, thus creating the network $\mathcal{N}'_B$, approximating $\mathcal{N}_B$. In this example, the displayed results are from fully replacing UNet layer 11.

3.1   Linearity Between Feature Maps

Given two networks: $\mathcal{N}_A$ and $\mathcal{N}_B$ with the same structure but trained on two different tasks (A and B), we are interested in replacing some features of $\mathcal{N}_B$ by linear projections of features of $\mathcal{N}_A$, without using any annotated data. This strategy, called VampNet ($\mathcal{N}_B$ acts like a vampire when it gets some already computed features of $\mathcal{N}_A$) is motivated by:

- The network $\mathcal{N}_A$ won't be modified: it can be mandatory in some industrial contexts (i.e. such network has already been certificated for task A).

- The resulting new $\mathcal{N}_B$ network will save computation time.
- We argue that if task A and B are correlated, The new $\mathcal{N}_B$ network will keep good performances.

Let $\mathbf{F}^{A,l}(\mathbf{X})$ be a 3D-tensor function returning the feature map associated to layer $l \in \{1,..,N_l\}$ of network $\mathcal{N}_A$ for the input tensor $\mathbf{X}$. Moreover, we define $f_{w,h,c}^{A,l}(\mathbf{X})$ a function returning the feature sample value for layer l, channel $c \in \{1,..,N_c^l\}$, and position $w \in \{1,..,N_w^l\}$, $h \in \{1,..,N_h^l\}$. $\mathbf{F}_c^{A,l}(\mathbf{X}) \doteq \mathbf{F}_{:,:,c}^{A,l}(\mathbf{X})$ is a function computing the 2D-slice feature matrix from channel c of tensor $\mathbf{F}^{A,l}(\mathbf{X})$ and $\mathbf{f}_c^{A,l}(\mathbf{X}) \doteq \text{vec}(\mathbf{F}_c^{A,l})(\mathbf{X})$ the vectorization of $\mathbf{F}_c^{A,l}(\mathbf{X})$. The linear relation between the feature computed by channel c of layer l of network $\mathcal{N}_A$ and the feature computed by the channel c' of the same layer of network $\mathcal{N}_B$ can be expressed by:

$$\mathbf{f}_c^{B,l}(\mathbf{X}) = \left[\mathbf{f}_{c'}^{A,l}(\mathbf{X}) \; 1 \right] \mathbf{w} \tag{1}$$

with $\mathbf{w}$ a parameter vector of size 2.

Given a set of input images $\mathcal{X} \doteq \{\mathbf{X}_1,...\mathbf{X}_{n_x}\}$, estimating $\mathbf{w}$ is given by the resolution of the following linear system:

$$
\begin{bmatrix}
\mathbf{f}_c^{B,l}(\mathbf{X}_1) \\
\vdots \\
\mathbf{f}_c^{B,l}(\mathbf{X}_i) \\
\vdots \\
\mathbf{f}_c^{B,l}(\mathbf{X}_{N_x})
\end{bmatrix}
=
\begin{bmatrix}
\mathbf{f}_{c'}^{A,l}(\mathbf{X}_1) & 1 \\
\vdots & \vdots \\
\mathbf{f}_{c'}^{A,l}(\mathbf{X}_i) & 1 \\
\vdots & \vdots \\
\mathbf{f}_{c'}^{A,l}(\mathbf{X}_{N_x}) & 1
\end{bmatrix}
\mathbf{w}
\tag{2}
$$

However, the number of equations of this linear system is huge ($N_x \times N_w^l \times N_h^l$) and solving it becomes too complex. We propose a sub-sampling strategy to reduce the number of equations using only a subset of all possible pixels of the features.

Let $s_w^l(i)$ and $s_h^l(i)$ be two sub-sampling functions providing width and height indexes of a feature of layer l for $i \in \{1,..,N_s^l\}$ and with $N_s^l << N_w^l \times N_h^l$. Sub-sampling vectors associated to the network $\mathcal{N}$ can be defined as:

$$\hat{\mathbf{f}}_c^{\cdot,l}(\mathbf{X}) \doteq \|_{i=1}^{N_s^l} \mathbf{F}_{s_w^l(i),s_h^l(i),c}^{\cdot,l}(\mathbf{X}) \tag{3}$$

with $\|$ the concatenation operator. The linear equation 2 can be approximated from a new one, changing full vectors to sub-sampled ones. Several sub-sampling strategies can be defined.

3.2 Ranking Linearity Between Features

When data are standardized (zero-mean and unit-std), the residue between the linear prediction and the set of target values is a simple way to estimate linearity. We define $\tilde{\mathbf{f}}_c^{\cdot,l}(\mathbf{X})$ returning the standardized sub-sampled vector by applying

$\tilde{\mathbf{f}}_c^{,l}(\mathbf{X}) = \frac{1}{\sigma_{\hat{\mathbf{f}}_c^{,l}}}.(\hat{\mathbf{f}}_c^{,l}(\mathbf{X}) - \overline{\hat{\mathbf{f}}_c^{,l}})$ with $\sigma_{\hat{\mathbf{f}}_c^{,l}}$ the standard deviation (std) and $\overline{\hat{\mathbf{f}}_c^{,l}}$ the mean of $\hat{\mathbf{f}}_c^{,l}(\mathbf{X})$ over $\mathbf{X}$, and compute the residue by:

$$r_{c,c'}^l = \frac{1}{N_x} \sum_{\mathbf{X}\in\{\mathcal{X}\}} \|\tilde{\mathbf{f}}_c^{B,l}(\mathbf{X}) - [\tilde{\mathbf{f}}_{c'}^{A,l}(\mathbf{X}), 1]\tilde{\mathbf{w}}\|_2 \tag{4}$$

The residue provides a natural way to predict if two features are correlated. We propose to compute a feature-wise residue matrix between the same layer of networks $\mathcal{N}_A$ and $\mathcal{N}_B$.

3.3 Vampirizing a Feature Using a Convolutional Operator

The simple model we propose to replace a feature is two-steps:

Selection of the closest feature in $\mathcal{N}_A$ given the feature $\mathbf{F}_c^{B,l}$ of channel c of layer l of network $\mathcal{N}_B$, we define the association function providing the closest feature's channel for the same layer of $\mathcal{N}_A$ by:

$$t_c^l(c) \doteq \underset{c'\in\{1,..,N_c^l\}}{\operatorname{argmin}} \ r_{c,c'}^l \tag{5}$$

Replace by Convolution. The vampire network $\mathcal{N}_B$ replaces one of its features by the selected one of $\mathcal{N}_A$ applying a linear projection. It can be done very simply using a biased convolutional 1×1 kernel. Given a linear relation estimated by $\mathbf{w} = [a, b]^T$ between $\mathbf{f}_c^{B,l}$ and $\mathbf{f}_{s_c^l(c)}^{A,l}$, the associated feature of network $\mathcal{N}_B$ can be replaced by:

$$F_c^{B,l} = F_{t_c^l(c)}^{A,l} * K \tag{6}$$

with K a kernel of size $1 \times 1 \times (N_c + 1)$ defined by:

$$K \doteq \left[\|_{i=1}^{N_c} a.\delta_i^{t_c^l(c)} \| b \right] \tag{7}$$

with δ the Kronecker function and $\|$ the concatenation operator. The bias b is provided by a virtual last channel with unit values.

3.4 Vampirizing a Layer

Replacing a layer is very important in order to save high computational cost. When VampNet replaces a full layer, it does not have to compute the layers before it anymore. Vampirizing a layer is achieved by replacing all of its features. The simple way to do that is by the strategy presented in the previous subsection (Fig. 2).

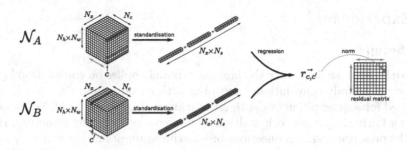

Fig. 2. Sampling method: in a given layer, for a feature pair c from $\mathcal{N}_A$ and c' from $\mathcal{N}_B$, we take a same random set of N_s pixels in the volumes extracted by both networks. N_h and N_w are the spacial dimensions, N_x is the data-set's size, and N_c is the number of features.

3.5   Automatic Selection of the Layer to Be Replaced

VampNet should produce a new model that approximates the original $\mathcal{N}_B$ net with a lower inference computation cost. Choosing the layer to be replaced is very important. The Deeper this layer is, the higher the computation gain will be. However, we expect that the correlation decreases along the layers. Since the new network must approximate an existing one for a given task, we propose to define a layer-to-vampirize selection function with two terms:

Computation Budget Loss. Let $C_l(\mathcal{N}_B)$ the computation cost of the new network when replacing layer l of network $\mathcal{N}_B$ and $C_0(\mathcal{N}_B)$ the cost of $\mathcal{N}_B$ without any replacement. We propose to define a loss function by:

$$\mathcal{L}_C(C_l(\mathcal{N}_B)) \doteq \frac{C_0(\mathcal{N}_B) - C_l(\mathcal{N}_B)}{C_0(\mathcal{N}_B)} \tag{8}$$

Accuracy Loss. The new network should provide good performances while using a large number of features coming from a network trained for another task. Like in knowledge distillation, we consider the output of $\mathcal{N}_B$ as annotations that should be estimated by $\mathcal{N}'_B$. We then propose to estimate the accuracy between the two networks according to the layer to be replaced with a typical metric for the targeted task: $\mathcal{L}_A$. In the semantic segmentation case, we choose to use the *mean Intersection over Union* metric (mIoU).

We propose a layer-to-vampirize selection function that combines both the accuracy and the computation budget terms:

$$\hat{l}_v = \operatorname*{argmin}_{l \in \{1,..,N_l\}} \lambda \mathcal{L}_C(C_l(\mathcal{N}_B)) + (1 - \lambda)\mathcal{L}_A(\mathcal{N}'^{l}_B) \tag{9}$$

4   Experiments

4.1   Setup

Networks and Tasks. Since the proposed model applies on convolution layers, we study it on fully convolutional networks with encoders and decoders like the ones used for segmentation or depth estimation tasks. We use the UNet network as it is a fairly simple network with such an encoding/decoding structure. However, the presence of skip-connections breaks the assumption that when replacing a layer, the previous ones don't have to be computed anymore. We will compare the impact of such connections into the network structure by comparing UNet with a degraded version of it without skip-connections that we will call Encode/Decoder-like (or ED-like). Figure 3 shows The evolution of VampNet model size related to the vampirized layer with (UNet) and without (ED-like) skip-connections. On the left figure, the model size (y-axis) is computed as a ratio related to the original network size. The middle and right figures illustrate the layers that do not need to be computed (within the overlay areas) if we choose to replace the layer 14 (red line in the left figure). In this case, the new model size would be about 1% of the original for both networks (that value can also be read in Table 1). When using skip connections, some layers before the replaced one still have to be computed while all preceding layers can be forgotten in the case of ED-like networks (no skip connections). In the case of UNet and similar architectures however, the first and last layers do not contain many parameters in comparison to the central ones which have a lot more channels, and computing them does not cost a lot, it is visible as the low variation rate on both sides of the left figure. The difference between the two networks' model sizes is drawn in green on the left figure.

We chose two tasks for experiments: 1) Depth estimation that consists in estimating a dense depth map from a monocular image [1,4] and 2) semantic segmentation that associates a semantic class to each pixel of an input image [6,8]. These two tasks are known to be quite related [15]. Depth estimation is selected as the task to be vampirized (A) and semantic segmentation as the task to be approximated (B). Evaluation of the performance of the semantic segmentation task is achieved using the classical Mean Intersection Over Union criteria (mIoU) on a testing data-set.

Data-Sets and Implementation Details. Different data-sets have been used to train the depth estimation network (called $\mathcal{N}_D$) and the semantic segmentation network (called $\mathcal{N}_S$). $\mathcal{N}_D$ was trained using ApolloScape [11] (sequences from road n° 3 for training and sequences from road n° 2 for validation) while $\mathcal{N}_S$ was trained using Cityscapes [3] (2975 images). Related to Semantic segmentation, we use the 19 default Cityscapes training classes.

The implementation we use was made in the PyTorch framework using a single GPU. For sub-sampling during the linear analysis, we chose a selection function that get a constant spatial coverage such as each sample covers $1/16^{th}$ of the features For example, for input images of resolution 256×256, the first

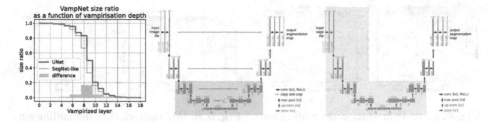

Fig. 3. Visualisation of saved computation: on the left, the evolution of the saved network volume; On the right the two studied architectures: UNet in the middle and ED-like on the right. The overlays are an example of what can be removed if we choose to vampirize layer 14, shown as a red line on the left graph. The x-axis units of the left graph correspond to blue arrows in the networks. (Color figure online)

layer's output is also 256×256 that is 65536 pixels, we sample 4096 of them. For the middle layers, the spatial resolution drops to 16×16 that is 256 pixels, and we sample 16 of them. This is one of the possible strategies that provides a computational solution. Moreover, the analysis is achieved on a set of 1000 images.

4.2 Linearity

Feature-Based Linearity. Since the main hypothesis of VampNet is that a task B feature can be replaced by a linear projection of a task A feature, we first study the loss of accuracy according to the number of replaced filters in a layer. Figure 4 shows such evolution for several layers (3, 7, 11 and 15) for both ED-like and UNet networks. We define the loss of accuracy as the mIoU degradation: a degradation of 0% means that the VampNet version of the segmentation network outputs the exact same segmentation maps as the original network. This figure shows that the more features are approximated, the more the network loses in accuracy, which is not surprising. However, it also appears that it does not increase according to the depth. It means that two networks with correlated tasks share linear information into deep layers: for example, replacing features in layer 11 yields better results than replacing features in layer 15 (for both tested networks). It is counter-intuitive because we expected that features grow in abstraction levels and should become more specific to the task [5].

Layer-Based Linearity. Since the best strategy to reduce the computation budget is to replace all the features of a layer, the next experiment evaluates the loss of accuracy (mIoU) according to the replaced layer (See Fig. 5). Like in the previous experiment, we observe that mIoU degradation does not increase monotonically according to the depth. The general shape of the curve outlines that layer-wise linearity seems to be better in the decoder (from layer 10).

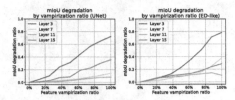
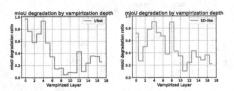

Fig. 4. mIoU degradation depending on feature replacement ratio at varying depths.

Fig. 5. mIoU degradation depending on vampirization depth for full feature map replacement.

4.3 Trade-Off Selection Between the Accuracy and Computational Budget

This section studies the couple accuracy, computation budget and the influence of the function that selects the layer to be replaced.

Table 1 present the couple mIoU degradation and size ratio related to the replaced layer for the two networks. It confirms that replacing encoding layers does not provide good performances for both accuracy and computational budget. Regarding UNet, mIoU degradation is below 10% for layers 9 to 11: the first decoding layers. The model size decreases along layers but we observe a high reduction between layers 9 and 11. This is directly linked to the network auto-encoder-like structure with many parameters near the embedded middle representation. The UNet variant without skip connection does not seem to follow the same variations and mostly presents a degradation of about 10% at layer 11.

Table 1. mIoU degradation and size ratio for a given vampirization layer

Layer		0	1	2	3	4	5	6	7	8
UNet	% degradation	96.94	76.38	58.02	72.18	93.73	57.30	34.25	14.31	15.46
	% size	99.99	99.86	99.74	99.22	98.96	96.87	95.82	87.47	83.30
ED-like	% degradation	71.97	26.87	50.27	78.27	90.77	72.70	67.40	37.75	90.04
	% size	99.99	99.86	99.60	99.08	98.03	95.95	91.77	83.42	66.72
Layer		9	10	11	12	13	14	15	16	17
UNet	% degradation	4.88	8.44	8.14	42.66	10.08	23.82	35.57	34.89	26.02
	% size	49.90	20.67	12.31	5.01	2.92	1.09	0.57	0.17	0.04
ED-like	% degradation	42.63	35.03	10.55	24.53	43.36	33.04	28.43	36.23	22.26
	% size	33.31	16.61	8.26	4.09	2.00	0.95	0.43	0.17	0.04

The layer to be replaced must be selected according to the desired trade-off between the accuracy and the computation budget. Adjusting this trade-off is achieved by a selection function that uses a hyper-parameter λ described in

Sect. 3.5. Figure 6 studies the evolution of the accuracy loss and model compression for $\lambda \in [0,1]$. For small values of λ, the mIoU degradation is low while the model size ration is about 50 for UNet and 8% for its variant without skip connection. As λ increases, the mIoU degradation also increases while the model size ratio decreases.

Figure 7 shows, according to selected layer to be replaced when $\lambda \in [0,1]$, a 2D parametric representation of the accuracy loss and model compression rate. Since we want to minimize both the degradation and model size, the best layer to be replaced is the one that provide an accuracy loss/size ratio, near the origin. This graph confirms that layers 11 is a good candidate for both networks. It will be selected for $\lambda = 0.5$.

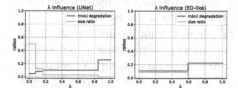
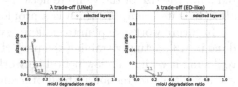

Fig. 6. Evolution of the size ratio and mIoU degradation when varying λ from 0 to 1.

Fig. 7. Pareto front of selected layers for $\lambda \in [0,1]$.

Figure 8 Shows some output examples from using VampNet on layer 11 of UNet for a semantic segmentation task with depth estimation as master network. The UNet original segmentation network has $28M$ parameters while it VampNet approximation reduces the model size to $3M$ (12.31% of the size, that is 87.69% compression). Differences mainly occur on class boundaries and for small objects.

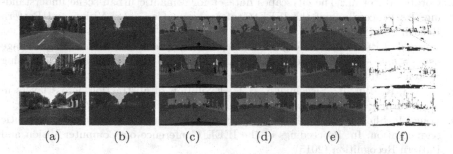

(a)   (b)   (c)   (d)   (e)   (f)

Fig. 8. Examples of results for a vampirization of layer 11 of the UNet network, with the input image (a), the output of $\mathcal{N}_A$ (b), the ground-truth of task B (c), the output of $\mathcal{N}_B$ (d), the output of $\mathcal{N}_B'$ (e), and the error mask between $\mathcal{N}_B$ and $\mathcal{N}_B'$ (f).

5   Conclusion

We introduced vampire networks, an approach to reduce the cumulative size of two networks performing related tasks by replacing features of one of them by a linear projection of the features of the other, while leaving that last one's performances untouched. We explained our method of selecting which features to replace by analyzing the linearity between them, and of computing the projection parameters, all of this in an unsupervised fashion. We showed that while replacing some features in a layer can somewhat reduce the needed resources, the true potential appears if we are able to replace a whole layer, in which case big portions of the vampire network can be discarded at once. We also showed how skip-connection can impede that alleviation. Our approach is oriented toward reducing the size of the vampire network; by approximating its features we over-all reduce its accuracy, which is a problem that we do not solve here.

In future works we plan to explore several ideas: taking inspiration of what is done in [13], actually training the projection instead of computing it, potentially replacing it with a shallow neural network could prove interesting. We could also use a multiple regression instead of a singular one to predict features. The goal of our approach being to add new tasks in a cascading manner, experiments with more than two tasks, meaning multiple source networks, should also be done. A last idea would be to see how well this method works with networks of different architectures.

References

1. Alhashim, I., Wonka, P.: High quality monocular depth estimation via transfer learning. ArXiv (2019)
2. Caruana, R.: Multitask learning. Mach. Learn. **28**, 41–75 (1997). https://doi.org/10.1023/A:1007379606734
3. Cordts, M., et al.: The cityscapes dataset for semantic urban scene understanding. In: Proceedings of the IEEE Conference on Computer Vision and Pattern Recognition (2016)
4. Eigen, D., Puhrsch, C., Fergus, R.: Depth map prediction from a single image using a multi-scale deep network. In: Advances in Neural Information Processing Systems (2014)
5. Kozma, R., Ilin, R., Siegelmann, H.T.: Evolution of abstraction across layers in deep learning neural networks. Procedia Comput. Sci. **144**, 203–213 (2018)
6. Long, J., Shelhamer, E., Darrell, T.: Fully convolutional networks for semantic segmentation. In: Proceedings of the IEEE Conference on Computer Vision and Pattern Recognition (2015)
7. Raghu, M., et al.: SVCCA: singular vector canonical correlation analysis for deep learning dynamics and interpretability. In: NIPS 2017: Proceedings of the 31st International Conference on Neural Information Processing Systems (2017)
8. Ronneberger, O., Fischer, P., Brox, T.: U-Net: convolutional networks for biomedical image segmentation. In: Navab, N., Hornegger, J., Wells, W.M., Frangi, A.F. (eds.) MICCAI 2015. LNCS, vol. 9351, pp. 234–241. Springer, Cham (2015). https://doi.org/10.1007/978-3-319-24574-4_28

9. Ruder, S.: An overview of multi-task learning in deep neural networks. ArXiv (2017)
10. Martin, S., et al.: OnionNet: sharing features in cascaded deep classifiers. In: Proceedings of the British Machine Vision Conference (BMVC) (2016)
11. Huang, X., et al.: The ApolloScape open dataset for autonomous driving and its application. IEEE Trans. Pattern Anal. Mach. Intell. **42**(10), 2702–2719 (2019)
12. Chou, Y.-M., et al.: Unifying and merging well-trained deep neural networks for inference stage. In: IJCAI: Proceedings of the Twenty-Seventh International Joint Conference on Artificial Intelligence (2018)
13. Li, Y., et al.: Convergent learning: do different neural networks learn the same representations? In: ICLR (2016)
14. Zhang, Y., et al.: An overview of multi-task learning. Natl. Sci. Rev. **5**(1), 30–43 (2018)
15. Zamir, A.R., et al.: Taskonomy: disentangling task transfer learning. In: CVPR: The IEEE Conference on Computer Vision and Pattern Recognition (2018)

RSI-Grad-CAM: Visual Explanations from Deep Networks via Riemann-Stieltjes Integrated Gradient-Based Localization

Mirtha Lucas[1]([envelope]) [iD], Miguel Lerma[2] [iD], Jacob Furst[1] [iD], and Daniela Raicu[1] [iD]

[1] DePaul University, Chicago, IL 60604, USA
mlucas3@depaul.edu, {jfurst,draicu}@cdm.depaul.edu
[2] Northwestern University, Evanston, IL 60208, USA
mlerma@math.northwestern.edu

Abstract. Neural networks are becoming increasingly better at tasks that involve classifying and recognizing images. At the same time techniques intended to explain the network output have been proposed. Here we examine three such techniques: Gradient-based Class Activation Mapping (Grad-CAM), Integrated Gradients (IG), and Integrated Grad-CAM, and introduce a new technique, that we call Riemann-Stieltjes Integrated Grad-CAM (RSI-Grad-CAM) that overcomes some of the shortcomings of those and similar techniques. Like Grad-CAM, our method can be applied to any layer of the network, and like Integrated Gradients it is not affected by the problem of vanishing gradients. For efficiency, gradient integration is performed numerically at the layer level using a Riemann-Stieltjes sum approximation. Compared to Grad-CAM, heatmaps produced by our algorithm are better focused in the areas of interest, and their numerical computation is more stable.

1 Introduction

The visualization of features captured by convolutional neural networks (CNN) helps explain how they make their predictions. This is a field of rapid development in which many techniques have been proposed, tested, and validated. Methods to provide explanations for the predictions of a CNN can be grouped into three main categories: primary attribution methods, layer attribution methods and neuron attribution methods [5].

Primary attribution methods evaluate the contribution of each input to the output of a model. This approach is model-agnostic, meaning that primary attribution methods work the same regardless of the internal structure of the network or machine learning system used. Some examples are Integrated Gradients (IG) [13] and Local Interpretable Model-Agnostic Explanations (LIME) [7].

Layer attribution methods evaluate the contribution of each neuron in a given layer to the output of the model. These methods are useful to determine the location of medium and high level features such as the spacial location of

© The Author(s), under exclusive license to Springer Nature Switzerland AG 2022
G. Bebis et al. (Eds.): ISVC 2022, LNCS 13598, pp. 262–274, 2022.
https://doi.org/10.1007/978-3-031-20713-6_20

the various elements that compose an image. Some examples are Gradient-based Class Activation Mapping (Grad-CAM) [10] and Grad-CAM++ [2].

Neuron attribution methods evaluate the contribution of each input feature to the activation of given hidden neurons. Both primary and layer attribution methods can be converted into neuron attribution methods by replacing the network output with any neuron activation. They may be useful when we are interested in determining how the activation of a given neuron, rather than the network output, depends on the input of the network. It is also possible to combine the effect of the input on a given neuron and the effect of the neuron on the network output, as in the Neuron Conductance method described in [4].

In our study we look at three gradient based methods: Gradient Guided Class Activation Map (Grad-CAM, a layer attribution method) [10], Integrated Gradients (a primary attribution method) [13], and Integrated Grad-CAM (layer attribution method) [9]. We examine their advantages and limitations, and propose a modification of Grad-CAM in which gradients are replaced with integration of gradients computed at any layer rather than the input layer. This allows our method to simultaneously overcome the limitations of grad-CAM, and Integrated Gradients, namely vulnerability to the vanishing gradients problem, and be applicable to arbitrary hidden networks.

2 Previous Work

Here we look at three gradient-based techniques: Grad-CAM, Integrated Gradients, and Integrated Grad-CAM.

Grad-CAM. Introduced in [10], this method uses the gradients of any target concept flowing into a convolutional layer to produce a heatmap, also called saliency map or localization map,[1] intended to highlight the regions of the image that contribute to predicting the concept.

Grad-CAM works as follows. First we must pick a convolutional layer A, consisting of a number of feature maps, also called channels, $A^1, A^2, \ldots, A^N$ (where N is the number of feature maps in the picked layer), all of them with the same dimensions. When the network is fed with an input image, the channels/feature maps of the hidden layers are expected to capture progressively higher features of the image (beginning with edge detection, shapes, textures, geometric shapes, and ultimately whole categories such as "dog" and "cat"). We will use the term "channels" when referring to the third dimension of a layer, and "feature maps" if we want to stress their feature capturing role.

Let A^k be the k-th feature map of the chosen layer, and let A_{ij}^k be the activation of the unit in the position (i, j) of the k-th feature map. Then, the localization map, or "heatmap," is obtained by combining the feature maps of

---

[1] We will be using the terms *heatmap*, *saliency map*, and *localization map* interchangeably.

the layer using weights w_k^c that capture the contribution of the k-th feature map to the output y^c of the network corresponding to class c.

In order to compute the weights, we pick a class c and determine how much the network output y^c depends of each unit of the k-th feature map, as measured by the gradient $\partial y^c / \partial A_{ij}^k$, which can be computed by using the backpropagation algorithm. The gradients are then averaged thorough the feature map to yield a weight w_k^c, as indicated in Eq. (1). Here Z is the size (number of units) of the feature map.

$$w_k^c = \overbrace{\frac{1}{Z} \sum_i \sum_j}^{\text{global average pooling}} \underbrace{\frac{\partial y^c}{\partial A_{ij}^k}}_{\text{gradients via backprop}} \tag{1}$$

The next step consists of combining the feature maps A^k with the weights computed above, as shown in Eq. (2). Note that the combination is also followed by a Rectified Linear Unit function $\text{ReLU}(x) = \max(x, 0)$, because we are interested only in the features that have a positive influence on the class of interest. The result $L_{\text{Grad-CAM}}^c$ is called *class-discriminative localization map* by the authors. It can be interpreted as a coarse heatmap of the same size as the chosen convolutional feature map.

$$L_{\text{Grad-CAM}}^c = \text{ReLU} \underbrace{\left(\sum_k w_k^c A^k \right)}_{\text{linear combination}} \tag{2}$$

After the heatmap has been produced, it is min-max normalized and upsampled via bilinear interpolation to the size of the original image, and overlapped with it to highlight the areas of the input image that contribute to the network output corresponding to the chosen class (see Fig. 1).

Fig. 1. Original image (left). Grad-CAM locating a dog (center) and a cat (right).

The method is very general, and can be applied to any (differentiable) network outputs.

In spite of its success, Grad-CAM is vulnerable to the *vanishing gradients problem* that happens when some or all the gradients get zero or near zero, $(\partial y^c / \partial A_{ij}^k \approx 0)$. This happens e.g. when the network output is near saturation, i.e., when the value of the output is very close to its maximum (say 100% score assigned to a class). In this instance, any increase in the value is very small (almost zero). The gradients can vanish at hidden layers too.

Integrated Gradients. Introduced in [13], Integrated Gradients avoids the vanishing gradients problem by using the result of integrating gradients along a set of network inputs obtained by interpolating between a *baseline* input (e.g. a black image) and the actual desired input. A deep network can be interpreted as a multivariate function $F : \mathbb{R}^d \rightarrow [0, 1]$ from its d inputs to the prediction $F(x)$ of the network for a given input $x \in \mathbb{R}^d$. The goal is to determine which pixels in the image contribute to the prediction of the network. To accomplish that, instead of using a single image, the method uses a sequence of interpolated images between a baseline x' and the given image x:

$$\gamma(\alpha) = x' + \alpha(x - x') \qquad 0 \leq \alpha \leq 1 \qquad (3)$$

Each interpolated image is a combination of $\gamma(0) = x'$ (baseline) and $\gamma(1) = x$ (given image). Then, the gradient of the network output with respect to each input pixel x_i is integrated as shown in Eq. (4).

$$\texttt{IntegratedGrads}_i(x) :: = (x_i - x'_i) \times \int_{\alpha=0}^{1} \frac{\partial F(x' + \alpha \times (x - x'))}{\partial x_i} \, d\alpha \qquad (4)$$

A problem with the Integrated Gradients method is that it is designed for working with the network inputs and may miss features captured at hidden (intermediate) layers.

Integrated Grad-CAM. Introduced in [9], Integrated Grad-CAM produces heatmaps by integrating Grad-CAM saliency maps produces by a set of interpolated images between a baseline x' and a final image x.

$$M^c = \int_{\alpha=0}^{1} \text{ReLU} \left(\sum_k \sum_{i,j} \frac{\partial y^c(\alpha)}{\partial A_{ij}^k} \Delta_k(\alpha) \right) d\alpha \qquad (5)$$

where $\Delta_k(\alpha) = A^k(\alpha) - A^k(0)$. Here $\partial y^c(\alpha)/\partial A_{ij}^k$ represents the partial derivative of the network output y^c with respect to A_{ij}^k when the input $\gamma(\alpha) = x' + \alpha(x - x')$ is fed to the network, and $A_{ij}^k(\alpha)$ is the value of the activation in location (i, j) of the k-th feature map of the chosen layer. The explanation map can be computed numerically using a Riemann sum for the integral:

$$M^c \approx \sum_{\ell=1}^{m} \text{ReLU} \left(\frac{1}{m} \sum_k \sum_{i,j} \frac{\partial y^c(\alpha_\ell)}{\partial A_{ij}^k} \Delta_k(\alpha_\ell) \right) \qquad (6)$$

where m is the number of interpolation steps, and $\alpha_\ell = \ell/m$. Finally, M^c is upsampled to the dimensions of the input image via bilinear interpolation.

3   Methodology

In this section we will introduce a novel attribution method combining ideas from Grad-CAM and Integrated Gradients, but essentially different from the approach used in Integrated Grad-CAM. In the next section we will provide metrics showing how our method overperforms Grad-CAM and Integrated Grad-CAM.

Like the Integrated Gradients attribution method, our algorithm feeds the network with a set of inputs obtained by interpolation between a baseline and a final input. Then, it computes a weight for each feature map to be used like in Grad-CAM, except that instead of gradients it uses the integral of those gradients to compute the weight assigned to each feature map.

The computation of the integrated gradients is formally equivalent to the numerical computation of a Riemann-Stieltjes Integral [6]. We start with a brief explanation of the concepts and mathematical techniques behind our method.

3.1   Motivation and Theoretical Background

Our technique aims to replace the gradients of the activations A_{ij}^k used by Grad-CAM with their integral as the network is fed by a sequence of interpolated images (recall that k indexes the feature maps within a given layer, and (i, j) is the location of each of the units of the feature map). The main motivation is that we are not interested in how much the output network y^c for a given class c changes for an infinitesimal change of the activations A_{ij}^k, but how much it changes along the whole interval of values taken by each activation A_{ij}^k as the image fed to the network goes from baseline to final image. The idea behind this technique is inspired by the *gradient theorem for line integrals* [15, p. 374]: a line integral through a gradient field ∇F of a scalar vector field $F : \mathbb{R}^n \to \mathbb{R}$ along a given curve $\gamma : [0, 1] \to \mathbb{R}^n$ equals the difference between the values of the scalar field at the endpoints $\mathbf{p} = \gamma(0)$ and $\mathbf{q} = \gamma(1)$ of the curve:

$$F(\mathbf{q}) - F(\mathbf{p}) = \int_\gamma \nabla F(\mathbf{x}) \cdot d\mathbf{r} = \int_\gamma \sum_{i=1}^n \frac{\partial F}{\partial x_i} dx_i = \sum_{i=1}^n \int_\gamma \frac{\partial F}{\partial x_i} dx_i \qquad (7)$$

Each term $\int_\gamma \frac{\partial F}{\partial x_i} dx_i$ of the final sum is the contribution of the i-th variable x_i to the total change of F. In our method the function will be the output of the network for a given class y^c, and the variables of integration will be the activations A_{ij}^k. The gradients are $\partial y^c / \partial A_{ij}^k$, and the term corresponding to the contribution of unit (i, j) in feature map k will be $\int_\gamma \frac{\partial y^c}{\partial A_{ij}^k} dA_{ij}^k$.

Note that the A_{ij}^k are not independent variables, but (potentially complicated) functions of the network inputs. An integral in which the variable of integration is replaced with a function is called a Riemann-Stieltjes integral [6]. In general, the integral of a function f with respect to another function g is expressed like this:

$$\int_a^b f(x) \, dg(x) \qquad (8)$$

where $g(x)$ is called the *integrator*. In our problem the activations A_{ij}^k will play the role of integrators. This kind of integral can be numerically approximated with a modification of a Riemann sum as follows:

$$\int_a^b f(x)\,dg(x) \approx \sum_{\ell=1}^m f(x_\ell)[g(x_\ell) - g(x_{\ell-1})] \tag{9}$$

where $x_\ell = a + \frac{\ell}{m}(b - a)$.

3.2   Riemann-Stieltjes Integration of Gradients

In our method we use a Riemann-Stieltjes integral like Eq. (8) with $f = \partial y^c / \partial A_{ij}^k$ as integrand, and $g = A_{ij}^k$ in the role of integrator, so the weight assigned to feature map k of the chosen layer for a given class c will be:

$$w_k^c = \frac{1}{Z} \sum_{i,j} \int_{\alpha=0}^{\alpha=1} \frac{\partial y^c(\alpha)}{\partial A_{ij}^k} \, dA_{ij}^k(\alpha) \tag{10}$$

where α is the interpolating parameter varying between 0 and 1.

The approximate value of the integral in Eq. (10) is given by the following *Riemann-Stieltjes sum*, as in Eq. (9):

$$\int_{\alpha=0}^{\alpha=1} \frac{\partial y^c(\alpha)}{\partial A_{ij}^k} \, dA_{ij}^k(\alpha) \approx \sum_{\ell=1}^m \left\{ \frac{\partial y^c(\alpha_\ell)}{\partial A_{ij}^k} \times \Delta A_{ij}^k(\alpha_\ell)) \right\} \tag{11}$$

where $\alpha_\ell = \ell/m$ and $\Delta A_{ij}^k(\alpha_\ell) = A_{ij}^k(\alpha_\ell) - A_{ij}^k(\alpha_{\ell-1})$. Hence, the following is a numerical approximation of the w_k^c:

$$w_k^c = \frac{1}{Z} \sum_{i,j} \left(\sum_{\ell=1}^m \left\{ \frac{\partial y^c(\alpha_\ell)}{\partial A_{ij}^k} \times \Delta A_{ij}^k(\alpha_\ell) \right\} \right) \tag{12}$$

3.3   Metrics

We will compare the performance of Grad-CAM, Integrated Grad-CAM and our RSI-Grad-CAM using two quantitative evaluation approaches, with and without ground truth.

Quantitative Evaluations Without Ground Truth. Following [2] we use quantitative evaluations that do not require ground truth. This metric measures how much the prediction of the network changes when the original image is replaced by the parts of the image highlighted by the heatmap produced by the attribution method being tested. Given an image I and a heatmap L^c generated for this image for class c, we find an *explanation map* $E^c = L^c \odot I$, where $\odot$ represents the Hadamard (element-wise) product of L^c and I. Figure 2 shows an example of image, heatmap, and resulting explanation map.

Fig. 2. Original image, heatmap, and explanation map.

Feeding the network with an image I we obtain an output Y^c = predicted probability of class c. If we feed the network with the explanation map E^c we will obtain an output O^c. For a good attribution method we expect O^c to be close to the predicted probability Y^c. Based on this idea, the following metrics are defined:

$$\text{Percentage Average Drop} = \frac{100}{N} \sum_{i=1}^{N} \frac{\max(0, Y_i^{c_i} - O_i^{c_i})}{Y_i^{c_i}} \tag{13}$$

$$\text{Increase in Confidence} = \frac{1}{N} \sum_{i=1}^{N} \mathbb{1}(Y_i^{c_i} < O_i^{c_i}) \tag{14}$$

where $\mathbb{1}$ is the indicator function with value 1 if the argument is true, and 0 if it is false, i is an index running through the image dataset, and c_i is the class predicted by the network when fed with the ith image.

Intuitively, the "drop" is the proportion of decrease of the network output when replacing the original image with the explanation map, and the Percentage Average Drop is the average of the drop through the image dataset multiplied by 100 (lower is better). The Increase in Confidence is the proportion of images for which the explanation map produces a network output larger than the network output produced by the original image (higher is better).

Quantitative Evaluations with Ground Truth. With an image dataset containing ground-truth bounding boxes, we can use metrics indicating in what extent the heatmaps overlapped the bounding boxes. Here we use the *Pixel Energy*, defined as $\frac{\sum L_{(i,j)\in bbox}^c}{\sum L_{(i,j)\in bbox}^c + \sum L_{(i,j)\notin bbox}^c}$, i.e., the sum of pixel intensities in the part of the heatmap inside the bounding box divided by the total sum of intensities of the heatmap for the entire image (see energy-based pointing game in Sect. 4.3 of [14]). When comparing two heatmaps generated by the same input image, higher pixel energy is better. Range goes from 0 to 1.

4   Implementation and Testing

4.1   Implementation

We call our algorithm RSI-Grad-CAM (for "Riemann-Stieltjes Integrated Gradient Class Activation Map"). The computation of the weights w_k^c and the final linear combination of feature maps $\sum_k w_k^c A^k$ are straightforward. The application of a ReLU at the end allows to select only the units that contribute positively to the score of the selected class.

In our implementation, when computing the weights, we also selected only units in which activations, integrated gradients, and activation total increments $(A_{ij}^k(m) - A_{ij}^k(0))$ are all positive. This allows the algorithm to ignore extraneous elements that do not contribute to the chosen class score. For instance, if an image contains a 'dog' and a 'cat', and we are interested in locating only the dog, the area of the image containing the cat is expected to produce negative integrated gradients, negative activations, and negative activation total increments in the feature maps more strongly linked to the 'dog' output. As a consequence, we expect that ignoring those units will produce heatmaps that are sharper and better focused in locating the elements of the image related to the output of the chosen class.

After a heatmap has been produced at the layer level, it is min-max normalized and upsampled to the original size and overlaid to highlight the elements of the input image that most contribute to the output corresponding to the desired class. Following [13] we pick a black image as baseline, since it naturally represents absence of image for natural elements.

Figure 3 shows heatmaps generated by our RSI-Grad-CAM method and two other methods. The heatmaps generated by our method do a better job at locating the object (at the last convolutional layer of the network) and its parts (at a layer before the last one).

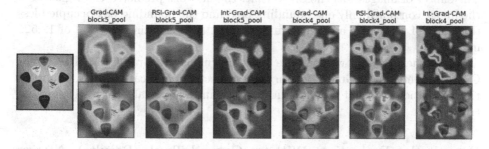

Fig. 3. Heatmaps generated by Grad-CAM, our RSi-Grad-CAM, and Integrated Grad-CAM at the last (block5_pool) and next to the last block (block4_pool)) of a VGG19 network when fed with the image shown at the left (a set of guitar picks).

4.2   Quantitative Evaluations

The examples shown in the previous section are illustrative. Here we use the quantitative metrics introduced in Sect. 3.3 to evaluate our attribution technique. For that purpose, we use a common image classification network working on a fairly large dataset with a variety of images of objects and natural elements, as detailed below.

Dataset and Model. We used the VGG-19 network pretrained on ImageNet [11], with input shape 224 × 224 × 3, and performed experiments on a subset of the validation dataset used for the ImageNet Large Scale Visual Recognition Challenge 2012 (ILSVRC2012) [8]. The ILSVRC2012 dataset is a subset of ImageNet with 50,000 images from 1,000 categories, annotated with labels and rectangular bounding boxes obtained using the Amazon Mechanical Turk [12]. Figure 4 shows two randomly selected images with their bounding boxes.

 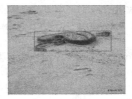

Fig. 4. Two images from the ILSVRC2012 dataset. Left: image of Alp mountains with two bounding boxes. Right: image of a sea snake, with one bounding box.

In all the tests we picked a convolutional block and computed heatmaps generated by each of the attribution methods at the maxpooling layer of the block. The subset of images was chosen so that: the network predicted the right class, the image contained only one bounding box, and the bounding box occupied less that 50% of the image area. The final dataset used contained a total of 12,525 images.

In the next section we compare the performance of Grad-CAM, RSI-Grad-CAM and Integrated Grad-CAM in three aspects: numerical stability, quantitative evaluations without ground truth, and quantitative evaluations with ground truth.

Quantitative Evaluations Without Ground Truth (Results). Now we look at the results of applying Average Drop and Increment in Confidence, introduced in Sect. 3.3.

In order to determine if these metrics depend on the predicted probability, the graphics shown in Fig. 5 and 6 were obtained by sorting the images by predicted probability, and computing averages across a fix length rolling window. In our experiments the window had a width of 1000 samples, so each point in the

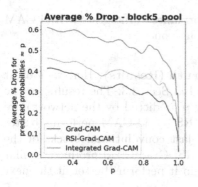

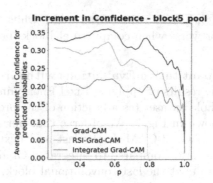

Fig. 5. Average % drop and Increment in Confidence at the last convolutional block.

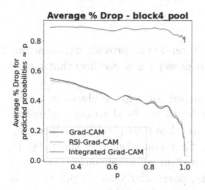

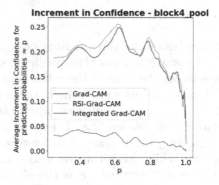

Fig. 6. Average % drop and Increment in Confidence at the next to the last convolutional block.

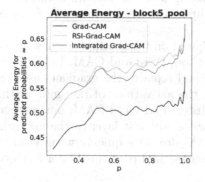

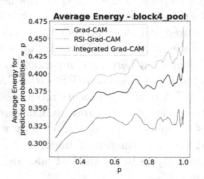

Fig. 7. Average energy at the last and next to the last convolutional blocks

graph represents the average metric obtained for 1000 consecutive samples (the p coordinate in the graph is also the average probability of the 1000 elements contained in the sliding window). We found that the performance of Grad-CAM was the best at the last convolutional block, but our method RSI-Grad-CAM did slightly better than Grad-CAM, while the performance of Integrated Grad-CAM got worse when computed at blocks below the last one.

Quantitative Evaluations with Ground Truth (Results). Here we look at the results of applying Pixel Energy introduced in Sect. 3.3. The results for the whole dataset (as a function of the probability p predicted by the network) are shown in Fig. 7. We observe that our method RSI-Grad-CAM performs better than Grad-CAM at the last and next to the last convolutional blocks of the network. Compared to Integrated Grad-CAM, RSI-Grad-CAM produces similar results at the last convolutional block, but again it performs better at the next to the last block.

5   Conclusions

We have examined three attribution techniques intended to provide explanations about how CNNs make their predictions, and proposed a new method that better implements the goals of those techniques.

Grad-CAM uses gradients of the network output for a given class computed at an arbitrary convolutional layer. Those gradients are used to determine the relative contribution of each feature map in that layer to produce a heatmap highlighting the regions of the network input that contribute to the network output. While this technique works relatively well in many situations, its performance suffers when any of the network layers, particularly its output layer, is near saturation level. Integrated Gradients overcomes the problem caused by the network output saturation by integrating the gradients of the network outputs with respect to the inputs of the network along a set of outputs obtained by interpolation from a baseline to the desired input. However, it may miss features captured at hidden layers of the network.

Integrated Grad-CAM offers a solution based on integrating saliency maps. We include it here for comparison to our method, RSI-Grad-CAM. Unlike Integrated Grad-CAM, our RSI-Grad-CAM method replaces the gradients used by Grad-CAM with gradients integrated using the activations of the units of the internal layer as integrators. Compared to Integrated Grad-CAM, our method has comparable performances only when used at the last layer of the network, but the performance of Integrated Grad-CAM degrades quickly when used at hidden layers below the last one, and then our method performs better at those layers.

Compared to Grad-CAM we observe that the results of applying our RSI-Grad-CAM method yields better results when applied to images in which the network outputs are near saturation and has a better numerical stability. Furthermore, it is better suited to detect small details within the region of interest when used at layers right below the last one—such small details are expected to be captured at hidden layers below the last one, and we find empirically that our method works better on those layers.

6   Future Work

Any method based on line integrals depends on the integration path used. In our algorithm we feed the network using a set of images linearly interpolated between a baseline and the desired input. A possible area of research would be to explore alternate integration paths.

Alternatively, there is a degree of arbitrariness in the choice of the baseline (a blank image in our case). Ideally the baseline should be an input that produces equal outputs for all classes. However it is unlikely that only one output has such property, so additional conditions on the baseline may need to be imposed depending on heuristic arguments (such as darker baselines being preferred to bright ones as indicative of "no features present") and practical considerations such as final performance.

Although our experiments provide enough evidence in support of the good performance of RSI-Grad-CAM compared to the other attribution methods examined here, there is still room to try our method on additional network models and datasets from other domains such as, e.g., medical imaging. The sanity checks for saliency methods described in [1] are also a line of research worth exploring.

Another line of work would be to replace Grad-CAM with our RSI-Grad-CAM algorithm in existing works, such as the method proposed in [3] for use in embedding networks.

References

1. Adebayo, J., Gilmer, J., Muelly, M., Goodfellow, I.J., Hardt, M., Kim, B.: Sanity checks for saliency maps. CoRR abs/1810.03292 (2018). https://arxiv.org/abs/1810.03292
2. Chattopadhyay, A., Sarkar, A., Howlader, P., Balasubramanian, V.N.: Grad-CAM++: generalized gradient-based visual explanations for deep convolutional networks. In: 2018 IEEE Winter Conference on Applications of Computer Vision (WACV) (2018). https://doi.org/10.1109/wacv.2018.00097
3. Chen, L., Chen, J., Hajimirsadeghi, H., Mori, G.: Adapting Grad-CAM for embedding networks (2020). https://arxiv.org/abs/2001.06538
4. Dhamdhere, K., Sundararajan, M., Yan, Q.: How important is a neuron? (2018). https://arxiv.org/abs/1805.12233
5. Kokhlikyan, N., et al.: Captum: a unified and generic model interpretability library for PyTorch (2020). https://arxiv.org/abs/2009.07896
6. Protter, M.H., Morrey, C.B.: The Riemann—Stieltjes integral and functions of bounded variation. In: A First Course in Real Analysis. Undergraduate Texts in Mathematics. Springer, NY (1991). https://doi.org/10.1007/978-1-4419-8744-0_12
7. Ribeiro, M.T., Singh, S., Guestrin, C.: Why should I trust you?: explaining the predictions of any classifier. In: Proceedings of the 2016 Conference of the North American Chapter of the Association for Computational Linguistics: Demonstrations (2016). https://doi.org/10.18653/v1/N16-3020
8. Russakovsky, O., et al.: ImageNet large scale visual recognition challenge. Int. J. Comput. Vis. **115**(3), 211–252 (2015). https://doi.org/10.1007/s11263-015-0816-y

9. Sattarzadeh, S., Sudhakar, M., Plataniotis, K.N., Jang, J., Jeong, Y., Kim, H.: Integrated grad-CAM: sensitivity-aware visual explanation of deep convolutional networks via integrated gradient-based scoring (2021). https://arxiv.org/abs/2102.07805

10. Selvaraju, R.R., Cogswell, M., Das, A., Vedantam, R., Parikh, D., Batra, D.: Grad-CAM: visual explanations from deep networks via gradient-based localization. Int. J. Comput. Vis. **128**(2), 336–359 (2019). https://doi.org/10.1007/s11263-019-01228-7

11. Simonyan, K., Zisserman, A.: Very deep convolutional networks for large-scale image recognition. In: Bengio, Y., LeCun, Y. (eds.) ICLR (2015). https://dblp.uni-trier.de/db/conf/iclr/iclr2015.html#SimonyanZ14a

12. Sorokin, A., Forsyth, D.A.: Utility data annotation with amazon mechanical turk. In: 2008 IEEE Computer Society Conference on Computer Vision and Pattern Recognition Workshops, pp. 1–8 (2008)

13. Sundararajan, M., Taly, A., Yan, Q.: Axiomatic attribution for deep networks. In: Precup, D., Teh, Y.W. (eds.) Proceedings of the 34th International Conference on Machine Learning. Proceedings of Machine Learning Research, vol. 70, pp. 3319–3328. PMLR (2017). https://proceedings.mlr.press/v70/sundararajan17a.html

14. Wang, H., et al.: Score-CAM: score-weighted visual explanations for convolutional neural networks. In: Proceedings of the IEEE/CVF Conference on Computer Vision and Pattern Recognition Workshops, pp. 24–25 (2020)

15. Williamson, R., Trotter, H.: Multivariable Mathematics, 4th edn. Pearson Education Inc. (2004)

Deep Labeling of fMRI Brain Networks Using Cloud Based Processing

Sejal Ghate[1], Alberto Santamaria-Pang[2], Ivan Tarapov[2], Haris Sair[3],
and Craig Jones[3,4(✉)]

[1] Department of Biomedical Engineering, JHU, Baltimore, MD, USA
sghate1@jhu.edu
[2] Health AI, Microsoft, Redmond, WA, USA
{alberto.santamariapang,ivan.tarapov}@microsoft.com
[3] Department of Radiology and Radiological Science, JHU, Baltimore, MD, USA
hsair1@jhmi.edu, craigj@jhu.edu
[4] Department of Computer Science, JHU, Baltimore, MD, USA

Abstract. Resting state fMRI is an imaging modality which reveals brain activity localization through signal changes, in what is known as Resting State Networks (RSNs). This technique is gaining popularity in neurosurgical pre-planning to visualize the functional regions and assess regional activity. Labeling of rs-fMRI networks require subject-matter expertise and is time consuming, creating a need for an automated classification algorithm. While the impact of AI in medical diagnosis has shown great progress; deploying and maintaining these in a clinical setting is an unmet need. We propose an end-to-end reproducible pipeline which incorporates image processing of rs-fMRI in a cloud-based workflow while using deep learning to automate the classification of RSNs. We have architected a reproducible Azure Machine Learning cloud-based medical imaging concept pipeline for fMRI analysis integrating the popular FMRIB Software Library (FSL) toolkit. To demonstrate a clinical application using a large dataset, we compare three neural network architectures for classification of deeper RSNs derived from processed rs-fMRI. The three algorithms are: an MLP, a 2D projection-based CNN, and a fully 3D CNN classification networks. Each of the networks was trained on the rs-fMRI back-projected independent components giving > 98% accuracy for each classification method.

Keywords: Resting state fMRI · Independent component analysis · Neural network classification · AzureML

1 Introduction

Functional magnetic resonance imaging (fMRI) is a technique to understand time-varying, spatially related signal changes in the brain. Since its introduction, fMRI has revolutionized our understanding of neuroscience and human cognition [1]. fMRI relies on Blood Oxygen Level Dependent (BOLD) signal change that is modulated by oxygen uptake in functionally active regions of the brain [2]. Resting state fMRI (rs-fMRI) is a method to measure intrinsic signal fluctuations without a specific task-based

© The Author(s), under exclusive license to Springer Nature Switzerland AG 2022
G. Bebis et al. (Eds.): ISVC 2022, LNCS 13598, pp. 275–283, 2022.
https://doi.org/10.1007/978-3-031-20713-6_21

paradigm and is gaining popularity for brain activity localization in neurosurgical pre-planning such as for the eloquent cortex in the brain [3]. The benefits of using rs-fMRI are that highly correlated brain networks/components at rest can be reproduced across multiple subjects for appropriate assessment of functional brain regions. Moreover, rs-fMRI eliminates the need for active patient participation and other task-related logistical/demographic considerations such as cognitively challenged patients for language mapping.

Independent Component Analysis (ICA) [4] is a mathematical algorithm to separate 3D + time rs-fMRI data into 3D spatial maps of statistically independent components (ICs) having strong 1D temporal coherence. ICA is advantageous in that it is a blind-source separation technique that does not require a-priori information for clustering of temporal signals. Group-ICA is a popular method for performing ICA across a cohort to identify Resting State Networks (RSNs) common to the group as opposed to subject-level ICA which separates actual neuronal signals from noise for a single subject. Labeling of these spatial-temporal RSNs can be time consuming and subjective requiring expertise, thus creating the need for an objective and accurate algorithm for automated classification.

Over the past few years, deep learning has been gaining popularity to classify relevant RSNs from rs-fMRI ICA results. Kam et. Al. Proposed a novel spatial-temporal deep-learning framework to identify noise components from true RSNs, using a 3D CNN for spatial ICA maps and 1D CNN on ICA time series [5]. Other studies such as Vergun et. Al., Zhao et al. used deep learning for RSN classification of a smaller number of ICs (~5–10) [6, 7]. Deep learning based rs-fMRI classification was also used for disease classification in Alzheimer's disease and schizophrenia [8, 9]. Our work is similar to Joliot et al.'s in investigating neural network for classifying ICA signals for a greater number of RSNs (>40) [10]. Though, in their work, subject specific contributions from group-ICA results were not used as part of their deep learning training data. In our study, we use the group-ICA results back-projected to individual subjects to highlight variability of the same RSN across different subjects, while also classifying a higher number of RSNs (58) displaying deep networks.

Our goal was to architect a reproducible Azure Machine Learning [11] cloud-based medical imaging concept pipeline for fMRI analysis integrating the popular toolkit FMRIB Software Library (FSL) [12] and to use it for a reproducible end-to-end image processing and deep-learning rs-fMRI classification framework. Figure 1 shows a schematic of our concept pipeline. This workflow incorporates both group-ICA processing and classification of RSNs on a single platform without the hassle of individual software processing and expert labeling. To the best of our knowledge, this is the first study that performed classification on over 50 RSNs and that will enable the inclusion of a hierarchy in the labeled networks. We plan to make of public access our pipeline architecture code and methods for further reproducibility.

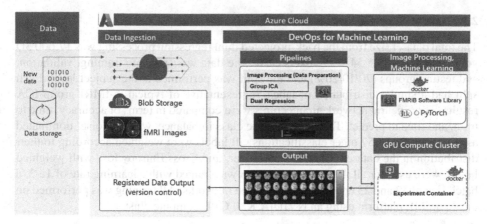

Fig. 1. Schematic of the concept imaging pipeline.

2 Methods

2.1 Data

To demonstrate feasibility and reproducibility, we used the 1000 Functional Connectomes Project publicly available dataset for our experiments. The 176 subjects (106M/70F) from the Beijing-Zhang cohort were selected (mean age of 21.2 ± 1.9) all data acquired on a 3T scanner, and the fMRI data had a TR $= 2$ s, more details on the projects website [17].

2.2 fMRI Resting State Analysis

The rs-fMRI analysis was composed of three main steps: (1) standard pre-processing pipeline to resample image volumes to a standard reference coordinate system; (2) performing group ICA to estimate group level components; and (3) dual regression analysis to estimate group components at the subject level.

Step 1: The pre-processing pipeline consisted of several steps implemented using FSL [13] including motion correction (MCFLIRT with standard parameters), spatial smoothing (FWHM $= 7$mm), temporal filter (default high pass filter), and registration (resampling to MNI standard space using FLIRT).

Step 2: Group ICA of rs-fMRI was performed using FSL MELODIC. The MELODIC model order was set to 100 ICs and was selected based on highest variability amongst respective ICs. ICA output maps were reviewed and labeled as RSNs based on anatomic location by a neuroradiologist with 12 years of fMRI expertise. There were 58 unique labels identified for classification. Two classes, 'Noise' and 'Unknown' were used for ICs that did not display true RSNs.

Step 3: We used the dual regression (back-projection) algorithm implemented in FSL to estimate group components per subject. This was implemented in two stages. Stage 1, regress the group ICA spatial maps (from Step 2) into each subject's 4D dataset to resulting in a set of time courses; and Stage 2, regress the time courses into the same 4D dataset to get a subject-specific set of spatial maps [14]. All the processing components were executed using Azure Machine Learning Cloud-based analytics.

2.3 Neural Network Methods

The total dataset size from the back-projected dual regression processing was 17,600 3D volumes of size 45 * 54 * 45 voxels each. The data was split into training, validation, and testing groups (70/10/20%) and the split was performed at the subject level. Each split had a similar distribution of labels representative of typical rs-fMRI group-ICA results. Three neural network architectures were compared in terms of accuracy, time to train, and time to predict. To account for the class imbalance, where 'Noise' dominated as compared to the 57 other classifications, all labels were weighted according to their distribution in the dataset. The SGD optimizer, and Cross Entropy loss with weighted labels, were used for all three networks. Data was trained with a learning rate of 1e-3, a batch size of 32 and 25 epochs across all three networks. All training was performed on the AzureML platform using an NVIDIA K80 GPU compute cluster.

MLP: We chose to first incorporate a multi-layer perceptron (MLP), as opposed to CNNs, to understand the voxel-voxel interactions through the fully connected layers. Three fully connected hidden layers were used of 200 neurons each, with ReLU activation and a dropout of 66% after the second layer. No down sampling or data augmentation was performed on the dataset before training.

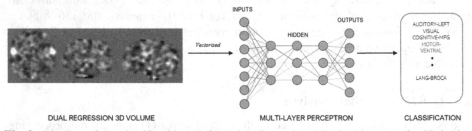

Fig. 2. Pipeline of the classifications: (left) Axial, Coronal and Sagittal images of a 3D back-projected rs-fMRI dataset is flattened and input to the (middle) Multi-Layer Perceptron consisting of 3 hidden layers of 200 neurons each, and finally (right) classifying a specific RSN label.

2.5D Neural Network: The novel 2D data representation was constructed from the back-projected 3D volumes transformed into 3-channel 2D slices by projecting the sum of the voxel information across each of the axial, sagittal and coronal planes and setting them in the red, green and blue channel, respectively. Each of the projected image intensities were scaled to an RGB intensity range (0–255). This transformation thus retained all the information yet drastically reduced input volume size. A 2D ResNet (resnet-50 in PyTorch) with pretrained weights was trained on these images using the same hyper-parameters as the previous model (Fig. 3).

3D Neural Network: A pretrained 3D ResNet architecture (r3d_18 in PyTorch) from the Torchvision video models was trained on the 3D fMRI cluster volumes. No additional data augmentation was performed on the datasets prior to training.

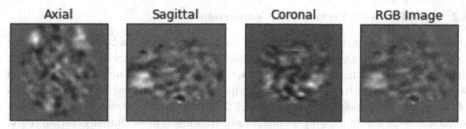

Fig. 3. The input of the 2.5D network is a constructed RGB image based on (left) an axial projection of the back-projection of the fMRI IC (red channel), (middle-left) sagittal projection (green channel), (middle-right) coronal projection (blue), and (right) the 2.5D resulting RGB image.

3 Results

3.1 fMRI Resting State Analysis

We architected a reproducible Azure Machine Learning [11] cloud-based medical imaging concept pipeline for fMRI analysis integrating the popular toolkit FMRIB Software Library (FSL). The core components of the concept pipeline are: 1) data ingestion component using a Blob Storage Container [15]; 2) Docker container with Ubuntu 18.04, FSL v6.0 [12] and Miniconda [16]; 3) a Python script to run FSL; and 4) configurable compute cluster. The pipeline is capable to orchestrate end-to-end steps or individual steps based on the configuration. We integrate modularity by building docker containers for required processing steps, one to run FSL-based image analytics and another Docker container built around the PyTorch image libraries. To enable full reproducibility, the pipeline automatically tracks datasets, code version control and Anaconda environments (and code dependencies). Similarly, the analysis pipeline has full traceability of input parameters for downstream analysis. All the algorithms packaged in docker containers and executed from the Azure Machine Learning Cloud. Figure 2 below shows an example of an image registration output using FLIRT (pre-processing step) when executed in the pipeline. The image in gray is the rs-fMRI volume (spatial component), red contours correspond to the reference image. Once individual dual regression volumes were estimated, they were used to train a classifier to semantically predict the resting state components (Fig. 4).

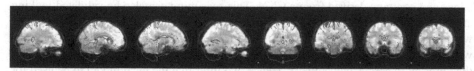

Fig. 4. Example of a representative registration of a subject (grayscale) and the reference image (red contours). (Color figure online)

3.2 Neural Network Performance Comparison

Our results indicate that all three neural networks could be used as an accurate classifier to classify the RSNs, showcasing greater than 98% testing accuracy in all models. Since the hyperparameters used were the same across all models, and no data augmentation was performed on the training dataset, a comparison was conducted based on accuracies obtained and time taken to train the model for optimization purposes. Table 1 below summarizes the training, testing accuracies and duration of model training and inference.

Table 1. Summary of the training and testing rs-fMRI classification accuracy and total training time taken.

Model	Training accuracy	Testing accuracy	Training duration	Inference duration
MLP	99.8%	100%	5 min	1.9 s
2.5D	99.4%	99%	33 min	23 s
3D	98.1%	98%	12 h 23min	904 s

As shown in Table 1 above, the MLP neural network reached a 100% testing classification accuracy, while the 2.5D and 3D models reached 99% and 98% testing classification accuracies.

Another important factor is the time to train each network considering future planned work with larger datasets. Training and inference were fastest for the MLP (5 min and ~2 s, respectively), while the longest training and inference time was taken by the 3D CNN model training (over 12 h for training and 15 min for inference).

4 Discussion

The purpose of training our dataset on three different models was to understand which model would be most efficient for deployment and resulted in accurate classifications. Though all models gave excellent accuracies, the MLP had a 100% accuracy on the test data and the shortest inference time. Though CNN architectures are more commonly used for image classification problems, we believe that the MLP was able to extract voxel-to-voxel interaction at a lower level as opposed to high-level features such as edges and contours derived from a CNN. This reasoning can also be validated looking at the back projected rs-fMRI images which do not display any strong edges or contours when qualitatively and visually assessing the image. Additionally, since only 200 neurons were used in the hidden layers, the number of parameters would be considerably fewer than present in a 3D-CNN network. Hence, we infer that the ideal model to be used for further studies would be the MLP given the fast inference time for deployment purposes and similar accuracy to the convolutional architectures.

Another factor that may have led to such high accuracies is the distinct variability amongst different networks and the deep labeling performed in the dataset. Labels were annotated in such a way that each label comprised of a functional name (e.g., 'Language',

'Motor', or 'Visual') along with the anatomical region of the functional network (e.g., 'Ventral', 'Dorsal', 'Superior', etc.). Table 2 displays examples of the labels used in the classification. The purpose of this sequence adopted during the labeling is the emergence of certain hierarchies between sub-networks that can also be easily distinguished while classification. The labels displayed show lowest-level specific brain networks.

Table 2. Example labels of rs-fMRI networks.

DMN-PCC-MID	EXECUTIVE-POSTERIOR-LEFT
ATTENTION-DORSAL-IPS-MID	MOTOR-VENTRAL
VISUAL-LINGUAL-ANTERIOR	SENSORY-DORSAL-HAND-RIGHT
DMN-CINGULATE-MID	SALIENCE-INSULA-POSTERIOR
COGNITIVE-MFG	LANG-BROCA

Since the current study incorporates back-projected data from a group-ICA processing conducted for a model order of 100 independent components, the RSNs produced account for ICs that may display a deeper classification of RSNs compared to a group-ICA study with model order 20. As an extension of the current study, we aim to perform group-ICA on the cloud-based FSL pipeline for different predefined independent component model orders, to generate greater variability in the dataset which may include higher level, bigger RSNs as well as deeper, more specific RSNs. Additionally, the current dataset only includes one demographic of data acquired from Beijing. With the FSL image processing pipeline in the cloud, we plan to conduct an experiment on all subjects across every cohort present in the 1000 Functional Connectomes dataset, creating a dataset that is representative across different demographics.

The inclusion of RSNs with different levels of hierarchies and comprehensive labeling enables the extension of this study not just for multi-class classifications but also for multi-label classification providing information across taxonomies of functional networks and their respective anatomical regions. This would be particularly beneficial to identify two ambiguous RSNs that may overlap with each other as a result of coherence during ICA separation. The results from the deep learning classifications can be used to further create a hierarchical classification model.

In realistic scenarios, end-to-end cloud-based systems must be capable of not only training and deploying AI models but to pre-process large amounts of data using computational tools that were not originally designed to be operated in the cloud. This scenario poses the challenge of how to architect robust cloud systems so that they benefit from new capabilities from cloud computing while they can efficiently integrate standardized medical imaging libraries (such as FSL) to provide an end-to-end cloud-based pipeline. We plan to make our pipeline core components publicly available and further optimize the integration of FSL and enable parallel processing to minimize the processing time.

5 Conclusions

We have demonstrated interoperability of well-established image processing libraries with state-of-the art cloud-based architectures for a large dynamic imaging modality like fMRI. We have efficiently processed rs-fMRI image data by integrating image processing libraries such as FSL for a large cohort in a scalable cloud-based environment. This step is critical when needed to apply and optimize machine learning algorithms at large scale in realistic scenarios. We have compared the performance of three neural network architectures to perform classification of deeper RSNs representing over 50 functional regions, with the MLP providing fastest inference times with a testing accuracy of 100%. This study provides a foundation for an end-to-end rs-fMRI processing and classification pipeline which can be extended to more robust multi-label/hierarchical classifications in the future.

References

1. Glover, G.H.: Overview of functional magnetic resonance imaging. Neurosurgery Clinics **22**(2), 133–139 (2011)
2. Lin, A.L., Way, H.M.: Functional magnetic resonance imaging. Pathobiology of Human Disease: A Dynamic Encyclopedia of Disease Mechanisms, 4005–4018 (2014)
3. Nandakumar, N., et al.: Automated eloquent cortex localization in brain tumor patients using multi-task graph neural networks. Med. Image Anal. **74**, 102203 (2021)
4. Griffanti, L., et al.: Hand classification of fMRI ICA noise components. Neuroimage **154**, 188–205 (2017)
5. Kam, T.-E.: A deep learning framework for noise component detection from resting-state functional MRI. In: Shen, D., Liu, T., Peters, T.M., Staib, L.H., Essert, C., Zhou, S., Yap, P.-T., Khan, A. (eds.) MICCAI 2019. LNCS, vol. 11766, pp. 754–762. Springer, Cham (2019). https://doi.org/10.1007/978-3-030-32248-9_84
6. Vergun, S., et al.: Classification and extraction of resting state networks using healthy and epilepsy fMRI data. Front. Neurosci. **10**, 440 (2016)
7. Zhao, Y., et al.: Automatic recognition of fMRI-derived functional networks using 3-D convolutional neural networks. IEEE Trans. Biomed. Eng. **65**(9), 1975–1984 (2017)
8. Duc, N.T., Ryu, S., Qureshi, M.N.I., Choi, M., Lee, K.H., Lee, B.: 3D-deep learning based automatic diagnosis of Alzheimer's disease with joint MMSE prediction using resting-state fMRI. Neuroinformatics **18**(1), 71–86 (2020)
9. Qureshi, M.N.I., Oh, J., Lee, B.: 3D-CNN based discrimination of schizophrenia using resting-state fMRI. Artif. Intell. Med. **98**, 10–17 (2019)
10. Nozais, V., et al.: Deep learning-based classification of resting-state fMRI independent-component analysis. Neuroinformatics **19**(4), 619–637 (2021)
11. lgayhardt: What are machine learning pipelines? - Azure Machine Learning. https://docs.microsoft.com/en-us/azure/machine-learning/concept-ml-pipelines. Accessed 09 Jul 2022
12. Woolrich, M.W., et al.: Bayesian analysis of neuroim-aging data in FSL. Neuroimage **45**, S173–S186 (2009)
13. Woolrich, M.W., Behrens, T.E.J., Beckmann, C.F., Jenkinson, M., Smith, S.M.: Multilevel linear modelling for FMRI group analysis using Bayesian inference. Neuroimage **21**(4), 1732–1747 (2004)
14. Nickerson, L., Smith, S.M., Öngür, D., Beckmann, C.F.: Using dual regression to investigate network shape and amplitude in functional connectivity analyses. Front Neurosci. **11**, 115 (2017). https://doi.org/10.3389/fnins.2017.00115

15. tamram: Introduction to Blob (object) storage - Azure Storage. https://docs.microsoft.com/enus/azure/storage/blobs/storage-blobs-introduction. Accessed 09 Jul 2022
16. Miniconda — Conda documentation. https://docs.conda.io/en/latest/miniconda.html. Accessed 09 Jul 2022
17. http://fcon_1000.projects.nitrc.org/fcpClassic/FcpTable.html

Semantic Segmentation Using Neural Ordinary Differential Equations

Seyedalireza Khoshsirat[✉] and Chandra Kambhamettu

VIMS Lab, University of Delaware, Newark, DE 19716, USA
{alireza,chandrak}@udel.edu

Abstract. The idea of neural Ordinary Differential Equations (ODE) is to approximate the derivative of a function (data model) instead of the function itself. In residual networks, instead of having a discrete sequence of hidden layers, the derivative of the continuous dynamics of hidden state can be parameterized by an ODE. It has been shown that this type of neural network is able to produce the same results as an equivalent residual network for image classification. In this paper, we design a novel neural ODE for the semantic segmentation task. We start by a baseline network that consists of residual modules, then we use the modules to build our neural ODE network. We show that our neural ODE is able to achieve the state-of-the-art results using 57% less memory for training, 42% less memory for testing, and 68% less number of parameters. We evaluate our model on the Cityscapes, CamVid, LIP, and PASCAL-Context datasets.

Keywords: Semantic segmentation · Neural ODE · Deep learning

1 Introduction

Neural Ordinary Differential Equations. In machine learning, we try to iteratively find a function that best describes the data. There are two basic approaches to finding this function. The first approach is to directly approximate the function by an analytical or numerical method. An ordinary linear regression falls into this category. The second approach is to approximate the derivative of the function. This results in an Ordinary Differential Equation (ODE) which by solving, we get the approximation of the function. We can parameterize the derivative of the function as a neural network.

Now, consider a residual network [15] where all the hidden states have the same dimension. Such networks generate an output by doing a sequence of transformations to a hidden state [6]:

$$\mathbf{h}_{t+1} = \mathbf{h}_t + f(\mathbf{h}_t, \theta_t) \tag{1}$$

By adding infinite number of layers, we get the continuous dynamics of hidden units using an ODE defined by a neural network [6]:

$$\frac{d\mathbf{h}(t)}{dt} = f(\mathbf{h}(t), t, \theta) \tag{2}$$

© The Author(s), under exclusive license to Springer Nature Switzerland AG 2022
G. Bebis et al. (Eds.): ISVC 2022, LNCS 13598, pp. 284–295, 2022.
https://doi.org/10.1007/978-3-031-20713-6_22

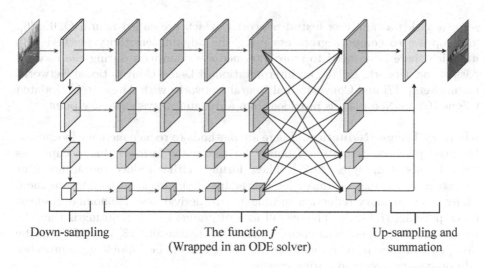

Down-sampling   The function f Up-sampling and
                    (Wrapped in an ODE solver)   summation

Fig. 1. The overall structure of the proposed method. The down-sampling uses convolutions with *stride* = 2. For the up-sampling, we use bilinear interpolation to avoid the checkerboard artifact [31].

where $f(\mathbf{h}(t), t, \theta)$ is a neural network layer parameterized by θ at layer t. By solving the integral:

$$\mathbf{h}(t) = \mathbf{h}(t_0) + \int_{t_0}^{T} f(\mathbf{h}(t), t, \theta)\, dt, \tag{3}$$

we can get the output value of a hidden layer at some depth T.

Semantic Segmentation. Semantic segmentation refers to the process of assigning each pixel in an image to a class label. Current state-of-the-art neural networks for semantic segmentation require a considerable amount of memory for training (especially with high-resolution images). Based on the fact that neural ODEs use less memory [6], in this paper we propose a novel neural ODE design for the semantic segmentation task. We evaluate our model on the Cityscapes [8], CamVid [2], LIP [12], and PASCAL-Context [28] datasets and show that it is able to produce the state-of-the-art results using 57% less memory for training, 42% less memory for testing, and 68% less number of parameters.

2   Related Work

Neural ODEs. Recently, several works have analyzed the relationship between dynamical systems and deep neural networks. In [40], the authors propose the idea of using continuous dynamical systems as a tool for machine learning. In [25], it has been shown that many effective networks, such as ResNet [15], PolyNet [43], FractalNet [19], and RevNet [11], can be interpreted as different numerical discretizations of differential equations. When the discretization step approaches zero, it yields a family of neural networks, which are called neural ODEs [6]. [6] proposes to compute gradients using the adjoint sensitivity method [33], in which there is no need to store intermediate quantities during the forward pass of the network. In [46], an interpretation of Dense Convolutional Networks (DenseNets) [17] and Convolutional Neural Networks with Alternately Updated Clique (CliqueNets) [41] is provided from a dynamical systems view point.

Memory Usage Reduction. There are methods to reduce memory footprints. Reduced precision formats are binary floating-point formats that occupy less than 32 bits (four bytes) [9,27]. These formats either reduce the accuracy or add some processing overhead for converting high precision to low precision. Many other memory reduction techniques are derivatives of binomial gradient check-pointing [7,14,35]. The overall idea of gradient checkpointing is that the results of cheap operations such as batch normalization [18] or ReLU can be dropped and then recomputed later. All the gradient check-pointing approaches add processing overhead during training.

Semantic Segmentation. Current state-of-the-art methods for semantic segmentation are based on convolutional neural networks. These networks have different architectures. Encoder-decoder or hourglass networks are used in many computer vision tasks like object detection [22], human pose estimation [29], image-based localization [26], and semantic segmentation [1,23,30]. Generally, they are made of an encoder and decoder parts such that, the encoder gradually reduces the feature maps resolution and captures high-level semantic information, and the decoder gradually recovers the low-level details. Because these networks lose the image details during the encoder path, they are not able to achieve the highest results without using skip connections. Spatial pyramid pooling models perform spatial pyramid pooling [13,20] at different grid scales or apply several parallel atrous convolution [4] with different rates. These models include the two well-known PSPNet [44] and DeepLab [5]. High-resolution representation networks [10,16,39,45] try to maintain a high-resolution hidden state from input to output. By doing low-resolution convolutions in parallel streams, high-level features are gained while low-level details are not lost. Since these networks require a lot of memory, they first down-sample the input image to a lower resolution before the main body. Some approaches [3,4] do post-processing, such as conditional random fields, on the network's output to improve the segmentation details, especially around the object boundaries. These approaches add some processing overhead to training and testing.

Semantic Segmentation Using Neural ODEs. There are only a few methods for semantic segmentation that have partially incorporated neural ODEs in the network design. In [32], a U-Net is modified to use neural ODEs. In this design, the repeated residual blocks in each branch are replaced by a neural ODE that wraps around only one convolutional block. Although U-Net is a well-known network, more recent networks can achieve higher results than U-Net. In this paper, we design our network based on the HRNetV2 [39] which can achieve the state-of-the-art accuracy on the Cityscapes [8], CamVid [2], and LIP

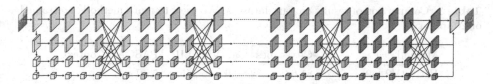

Fig. 2. The baseline network is created by repeating the last module from HRNetV2 [39] which has four branches with different feature-map resolutions. We use skip connections at the module level (not drawn). So, each module is treated as a residual block. Each small block in a module consists of one set of batch normalization [18], ReLU, and convolutional layers. This network is not a neural ODE and is trained similarly to HRNetV2.

[12] datasets. Similar to [32], another modified U-Net is introduced in [21]. This time, instead of replacing a branch with a neural ODE block, a neural ODE block is added at the end of each branch. In [38], a novel approach that combines neural ODEs and the Level Set method is proposed. This approach parameterizes the derivative of the contour as a neural ODE that implicitly learns a forcing function describing the evolution of the contour. This approach is limited to the segmentation of images with one target class.

3   Method

We introduce a baseline network that is trained without the use of neural ODEs. Then we introduce a neural ODE equivalent to the baseline network. Our goal is to compare the results step by step, from a state-of-the-art network to the baseline network, then to the neural ODE network.

3.1   Baseline Network

At the time of writing, one of the state-of-the-art methods in semantic segmentation is HRNetV2 [39]. We try to adopt this network architecture and turn it into a residual form such that each module is like a residual block. To this aim, we repeat the last module in series, multiple times and treat each one of them as a residual unit (as depicted in Fig. 2). This way, the network consists of multiple residual modules, each module has four branches with different feature-map resolutions, and each branch has multiple residual blocks. In our experiments in this paper, we repeat the main module six times to keep the number of parameters close to HRNetV2. We use this baseline network to gradually evaluate the design of our neural ODE network.

3.2   SegNode

Since the baseline network has an overall residual form, we can turn it into a neural ODE. In this form, a single or multiple modules act as the function f in

Table 1. Comparison of results on four datasets. We use † to mark methods pretrained on Mapillary.

Method	Cityscapes	CamVid	LIP	PASCAL-Context
HRNetV2 [39]	81.6	80.9	55.9	54.0
HRNetV2+OCR [42]	83.0	81.7	56.6	56.2
HRNetV2+OCR† [42]	84.2	–	–	–
U-Node [32]	78.1	77.3	51.3	49.7
NODEs-UNet [21]	79.5	78.8	52.9	50.9
Baseline network	81.7	81.0	55.9	53.9
SegNode	81.8	81.1	55.8	54.1
SegNode+OCR	83.1	**82.0**	**56.7**	**56.2**
SegNode+OCR†	**84.5**	–	–	–

Eq. 1. This module (or modules) is wrapped in an ODE solver. Since the main module has four convolutional streams with different resolutions and number of channels, we use convolutional layers to create the input feature-maps with the corresponding resolution and number of channels. The resulting four tensors are fed to the ODE solver. The output of the ODE solver has the same format as its input. By using four convolutional layers, the number of channels of the output feature maps is changed to the number of classes. Then, the feature maps are re-scaled to the higher resolution using bilinear interpolation and added together to produce the final output (as shown in Fig. 1). Bilinear interpolation is used to avoid the checkerboard artifact [31]. We call our network SegNode for short.

4   Experiments

We evaluate our approach on four datasets: Cityscapes [8], CamVid [2], LIP [12], and PASCAL-Context [28]. Additionally, since the existing neural ODE methods for semantic segmentation have not been evaluated on these datasets, we train and test the two U-Net based methods [21,32] on these datasets and report their accuracy.

4.1   Setup

We pretrain our baseline and SegNode networks on ImageNet [37] and use the pre-trained networks in all our experiments. We use the mean Intersection over Union (mIoU) metric to compare all the methods.

For the baseline network, we use AdamW optimizer [24] with a weight decay of 0.05 and batch size of 16. We apply the "polynomial" learning rate policy with a poly exponent of 0.9 and an initial learning rate of 0.0001.

For SegNode, we use the Runge-Kutta ODE solver provided by [6]. Also, we use the adjoint sensitivity method [33] which is available in the same implementation. We use the SGD optimizer with a base learning rate of 0.1, a momentum

Table 2. A comparison of a few important empirical computational measures on an NVIDIA Tesla V100 32 GB for CamVid [2] dataset. The training time per epoch is calculated using the maximum batch size possible. Our method requires the least amount of memory, but the longest computation time for training and testing.

Method	Maximum batch size for 32 GB	Memory usage for batch size 24 (GB)	Memory usage for testing one image (GB)	Training time per Epoch (Seconds)	Testing time per image (Milliseconds)	Number of parameters (Millions)
U-Net [34]	36	21.8	0.8	**10**	4	31.0
PSPNet [44]	24	31.2	0.8	18	5	23.7
Deeplab v3 [5]	24	31.3	1.0	24	16	58.6
HRNetV2 [39]	24	31.1	1.2	18	48	65.8
Baseline network	24	31.9	1.2	19	49	70.9
SegNode	**62**	**13.4**	**0.7**	34	117	**20.9**

of 0.9, and no weight decay. The polynomial learning rate decay function is used with a poly exponent of 0.9.

For both the baseline network and SegNode, similar to HRNetV2 [39], we use a stem for the input image, which consists of two stride-2 3×3 convolutions to decrease the resolution to 1/4, and is connected to the main body. The main body outputs the feature maps with the same resolution (1/4), which are then made larger as the original resolution using bilinear interpolation. Each stream in the main body has 48, 96, 192, and 384 channels respectively from the highest resolution to the lowest. We use two modules in the main body to achieve the highest accuracy.

4.2 Cityscapes

The Cityscapes dataset [8] contains 5k high quality pixel-level finely annotated street images. The finely annotated images are divided into 2,975/500/1,525 images for training, validation, and testing. Also, the dataset contains additional 20k coarsely annotated images. There are 30 classes, and 19 classes among them are used for evaluation. We train on the training, validation, and coarse sets to get the highest accuracy on the test set.

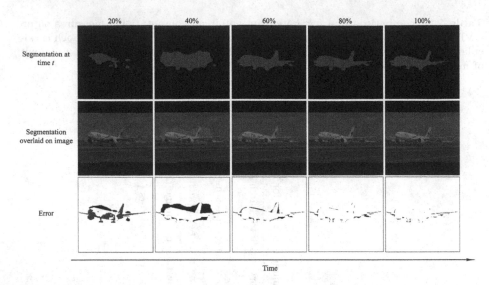

Fig. 3. Segmentation results from trajectories at different times. This image shows how the gradual transformations correct the segmentation over time.

4.3 CamVid

Compared to Cityscapes [8], CamVid [2] is a much smaller dataset focusing on semantic segmentation for driving scenarios. The original version is composed of 701 annotated images in 32 classes with size 960×720 from five video sequences. However, most literature only focuses on the protocol proposed in [1] which splits the dataset into 367 training, 101 validation, and 233 test images in 11 classes. We follow this protocol for training on CamVid.

4.4 LIP

The LIP dataset [12] contains 50,462 human images with detailed annotations. The dataset is divided into 30,462 training, 10,000 validation, and 10,000 test images. The model evaluation is done on 20 categories (including the background label). We follow the common testing protocol [36,39] and resize the images to 473×473.

4.5 PASCAL-Context

The PASCAL-Context dataset [28] adds annotations for more than 400 additional categories to the PASCAL VOC 2010 dataset. It contains 4,998 training and 5,105 validation images, subsets of PASCAL VOC 2010 dataset. The dataset annotations cover 100% of pixels while the previous annotations covered around 29%. We follow [39,42] and evaluate our method on 59 sub-categories.

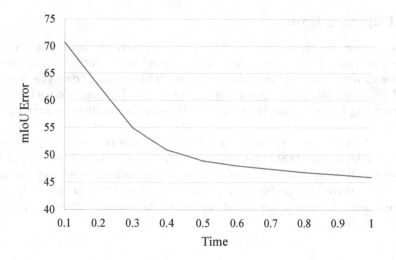

Fig. 4. The average mean IoU error of the trajectories during solving time, calculated on the PASCAL-Context validation set.

4.6   Results

Table 1 compares the results of our proposed method to different variants of HRNetV2 and existing neural ODE methods. On average our method performs better than HRNetV2 and its variants by a small margin.

We tried and improved the existing neural ODE methods in our implementation by increasing the number of parameters and tuning hyper-parameters. Still, our proposed design can achieve higher accuracy by a large margin. The main reason is that we started our design from a better-performing network architecture and modified it step-by-step towards the final design.

4.7   Empirical Computational Cost

In this section, we provide an empirical comparison between our approach and a few well-known networks. We use an NVIDIA Tesla V100 32GB with the same network hyper-parameters as used before. All the experiments are implemented in Python using PyTorch. The results are calculated on CamVid [2] dataset with an image size of 480×360.

Table 2 compares a few important empirical computational measures. Our method requires the least amount of memory, but the longest computation time for training and testing by a large margin. In particular, compared to HRNetV2 [39], while our method has 68% less number of parameters, it requires 57% less memory for training and 42% less memory for testing. On the other side, HRNetV2 requires 47% less training time and 59% less testing time.

4.8   Trajectory Error

In this section, we show how the ODE solver gradually improves its output during test time. Figure 3 visualizes the segmentation output of the network trajectories over time for one sample image. This figure shows the steps that the ODE solver takes during solving the network. To generate each step, the corresponding hyper-parameter of the ODE solver is modified to partially solve its input.

Figure 4 shows the average mean IoU error of the trajectories over time for all the samples in the PASCAL-Context validation set. One of the biggest issues with neural ODEs is that they require more computational resources during test time. To alleviate this problem, it is possible to sacrifice accuracy for speed. As an example, by sacrificing 3% of accuracy, the required computational time decreases by 50%.

5   Conclusion

Based on a current state-of-the-art network, we proposed a novel neural ODE design for semantic segmentation. The new idea of neural ODEs helped us to reduce the memory requirement with the cost of more processing time. While using a notably less amount of memory, our method (SegNode) was able to achieve state-of-the-art results. The proposed method can be used for all the computer vision tasks that can make use of dense 2D predictions such as human pose estimation and object detection tasks.

References

1. Badrinarayanan, V., Kendall, A., Cipolla, R.: SegNet: a deep convolutional encoder-decoder architecture for image segmentation. IEEE Trans. Pattern Anal. Mach. Intell. **39**(12), 2481–2495 (2017)
2. Brostow, G.J., Fauqueur, J., Cipolla, R.: Semantic object classes in video: a high-definition ground truth database. Pattern Recognit. Lett. **30**(2), 88–97 (2009)
3. Chandra, S., Kokkinos, I.: Fast, exact and multi-scale inference for semantic image segmentation with deep Gaussian CRFs. In: Leibe, B., Matas, J., Sebe, N., Welling, M. (eds.) ECCV 2016. LNCS, vol. 9911, pp. 402–418. Springer, Cham (2016). https://doi.org/10.1007/978-3-319-46478-7_25
4. Chen, L.C., Papandreou, G., Kokkinos, I., Murphy, K., Yuille, A.L.: DeepLab: Semantic image segmentation with deep convolutional nets, atrous convolution, and fully connected CRFs. IEEE Trans. Pattern Anal. Mach. Intell. **40**(4), 834–848 (2017)
5. Chen, L.C., Papandreou, G., Schroff, F., Adam, H.: Rethinking atrous convolution for semantic image segmentation. arXiv preprint arXiv:1706.05587 (2017)
6. Chen, T.Q., Rubanova, Y., Bettencourt, J., Duvenaud, D.K.: Neural ordinary differential equations. In: Advances in Neural Information Processing Systems, pp. 6571–6583 (2018)
7. Chen, T., Xu, B., Zhang, C., Guestrin, C.: Training deep nets with sublinear memory cost. arXiv preprint arXiv:1604.06174 (2016)

8. Cordts, M., et al.: The cityscapes dataset for semantic urban scene understanding. In: Proceedings of the IEEE Conference on Computer Vision and Pattern Recognition, pp. 3213–3223 (2016)
9. Courbariaux, M., David, J.P., Bengio, Y.: Low precision storage for deep learning. arXiv preprint arXiv:1412.7024 (2014)
10. Fourure, D., Emonet, R., Fromont, E., Muselet, D., Tremeau, A., Wolf, C.: Residual conv-deconv grid network for semantic segmentation. arXiv preprint arXiv:1707.07958 (2017)
11. Gomez, A.N., Ren, M., Urtasun, R., Grosse, R.B.: The reversible residual network: backpropagation without storing activations. In: Advances in Neural Information Processing Systems, pp. 2214–2224 (2017)
12. Gong, K., Liang, X., Zhang, D., Shen, X., Lin, L.: Look into person: self-supervised structure-sensitive learning and a new benchmark for human parsing. In: Proceedings of the IEEE Conference on Computer Vision and Pattern Recognition, pp. 932–940 (2017)
13. Grauman, K., Darrell, T.: The pyramid match kernel: discriminative classification with sets of image features. In: Tenth IEEE International Conference on Computer Vision (ICCV 2005) Volume 1, vol. 2, pp. 1458–1465. IEEE (2005)
14. Griewank, A., Walther, A.: Algorithm 799: revolve: an implementation of check-pointing for the reverse or adjoint mode of computational differentiation. ACM Trans. Math. Softw. $26(1)$, 19–45 (2000)
15. He, K., Zhang, X., Ren, S., Sun, J.: Identity mappings in deep residual networks. In: Leibe, B., Matas, J., Sebe, N., Welling, M. (eds.) ECCV 2016. LNCS, vol. 9908, pp. 630–645. Springer, Cham (2016). https://doi.org/10.1007/978-3-319-46493-0_38
16. Huang, G., Chen, D., Li, T., Wu, F., van der Maaten, L., Weinberger, K.Q.: Multi-scale dense networks for resource efficient image classification. arXiv preprint arXiv:1703.09844 (2017)
17. Huang, G., Liu, Z., Van Der Maaten, L., Weinberger, K.Q.: Densely connected convolutional networks. In: Proceedings of the IEEE Conference on Computer Vision and Pattern Recognition, pp. 4700–4708 (2017)
18. Ioffe, S., Szegedy, C.: Batch normalization: accelerating deep network training by reducing internal covariate shift. arXiv preprint arXiv:1502.03167 (2015)
19. Larsson, G., Maire, M., Shakhnarovich, G.: FractalNet: ultra-deep neural networks without residuals. arXiv preprint arXiv:1605.07648 (2016)
20. Lazebnik, S., Schmid, C., Ponce, J.: Beyond bags of features: spatial pyramid matching for recognizing natural scene categories. In: 2006 IEEE Computer Society Conference on Computer Vision and Pattern Recognition (CVPR 2006), vol. 2, pp. 2169–2178. IEEE (2006)
21. Li, D., et al.: Robust blood cell image segmentation method based on neural ordinary differential equations. Comput. Math. Methods Med. **2021** (2021)
22. Lin, T.Y., Dollár, P., Girshick, R., He, K., Hariharan, B., Belongie, S.: Feature pyramid networks for object detection. In: Proceedings of the IEEE Conference on Computer Vision and Pattern Recognition, pp. 2117–2125 (2017)
23. Long, J., Shelhamer, E., Darrell, T.: Fully convolutional networks for semantic segmentation. In: Proceedings of the IEEE Conference on Computer Vision and Pattern Recognition, pp. 3431–3440 (2015)
24. Loshchilov, I., Hutter, F.: Decoupled weight decay regularization. arXiv preprint arXiv:1711.05101 (2017)
25. Lu, Y., Zhong, A., Li, Q., Dong, B.: Beyond finite layer neural networks: bridging deep architectures and numerical differential equations. arXiv preprint arXiv:1710.10121 (2017)

26. Melekhov, I., Ylioinas, J., Kannala, J., Rahtu, E.: Image-based localization using hourglass networks. In: Proceedings of the IEEE International Conference on Computer Vision, pp. 879–886 (2017)
27. Micikevicius, P., et al.: Mixed precision training. arXiv preprint arXiv:1710.03740 (2017)
28. Mottaghi, R., et al.: The role of context for object detection and semantic segmentation in the wild. In: Proceedings of the IEEE Conference on Computer Vision and Pattern Recognition, pp. 891–898 (2014)
29. Newell, A., Yang, K., Deng, J.: Stacked hourglass networks for human pose estimation. In: Leibe, B., Matas, J., Sebe, N., Welling, M. (eds.) ECCV 2016. LNCS, vol. 9912, pp. 483–499. Springer, Cham (2016). https://doi.org/10.1007/978-3-319-46484-8_29
30. Noh, H., Hong, S., Han, B.: Learning deconvolution network for semantic segmentation. In: Proceedings of the IEEE International Conference on Computer Vision, pp. 1520–1528 (2015)
31. Odena, A., Dumoulin, V., Olah, C.: Deconvolution and checkerboard artifacts. Distill 1(10), e3 (2016)
32. Pinckaers, H., Litjens, G.: Neural ordinary differential equations for semantic segmentation of individual colon glands. arXiv preprint arXiv:1910.10470 (2019)
33. Pontryagin, L.S.: Mathematical Theory of Optimal Processes. Routledge (2018)
34. Ronneberger, O., Fischer, P., Brox, T.: U-Net: convolutional networks for biomedical image segmentation. In: Navab, N., Hornegger, J., Wells, W.M., Frangi, A.F. (eds.) MICCAI 2015. LNCS, vol. 9351, pp. 234–241. Springer, Cham (2015). https://doi.org/10.1007/978-3-319-24574-4_28
35. Rota Bulò, S., Porzi, L., Kontschieder, P.: In-place activated batchnorm for memory-optimized training of DNNs. In: Proceedings of the IEEE Conference on Computer Vision and Pattern Recognition, pp. 5639–5647 (2018)
36. Ruan, T., Liu, T., Huang, Z., Wei, Y., Wei, S., Zhao, Y.: Devil in the details: towards accurate single and multiple human parsing. In: Proceedings of the AAAI Conference on Artificial Intelligence, vol. 33, pp. 4814–4821 (2019)
37. Russakovsky, O., et al.: ImageNet large scale visual recognition challenge. Int. J. Comput. Vision 115(3), 211–252 (2015)
38. Valle, R., Reda, F., Shoeybi, M., Legresley, P., Tao, A., Catanzaro, B.: Neural odes for image segmentation with level sets. arXiv preprint arXiv:1912.11683 (2019)
39. Wang, J., et al.: Deep high-resolution representation learning for visual recognition. arXiv preprint arXiv:1908.07919 (2019)
40. Weinan, E.: A proposal on machine learning via dynamical systems. Commun. Math. Stat. 5(1), 1–11 (2017)
41. Yang, Y., Zhong, Z., Shen, T., Lin, Z.: Convolutional neural networks with alternately updated clique. In: Proceedings of the IEEE Conference on Computer Vision and Pattern Recognition, pp. 2413–2422 (2018)
42. Yuan, Y., Chen, X., Wang, J.: Object-contextual representations for semantic segmentation. In: Vedaldi, A., Bischof, H., Brox, T., Frahm, J.-M. (eds.) ECCV 2020. LNCS, vol. 12351, pp. 173–190. Springer, Cham (2020). https://doi.org/10.1007/978-3-030-58539-6_11
43. Zhang, X., Li, Z., Change Loy, C., Lin, D.: PolyNet: a pursuit of structural diversity in very deep networks. In: Proceedings of the IEEE Conference on Computer Vision and Pattern Recognition, pp. 718–726 (2017)
44. Zhao, H., Shi, J., Qi, X., Wang, X., Jia, J.: Pyramid scene parsing network. In: Proceedings of the IEEE Conference on Computer Vision and Pattern Recognition, pp. 2881–2890 (2017)

45. Zhou, Y., Hu, X., Zhang, B.: Interlinked convolutional neural networks for face parsing. In: Hu, X., Xia, Y., Zhang, Y., Zhao, D. (eds.) ISNN 2015. LNCS, vol. 9377, pp. 222–231. Springer, Cham (2015). https://doi.org/10.1007/978-3-319-25393-0_25

46. Zhu, M., Chang, B., Fu, C.: Convolutional neural networks combined with Runge–Kutta methods. Neural Comput. Applic. (2022). https://doi.org/10.1007/s00521-022-07785-2

Video Analysis and Event Recognition

Graphing the Future: Activity and Next Active Object Prediction Using Graph-Based Activity Representations

Victoria Manousaki[1,2](✉) , Konstantinos Papoutsakis[2] ,

and Antonis Argyros[1,2](✉)

[1] Computer Science Department, University of Crete, Heraklion, Greece
[2] Institute of Computer Science, Foundation for Research and Technology - Hellas (FORTH),
Heraklion, Greece
{vmanous,papoutsa,argyros}@ics.forth.gr

Abstract. We present a novel approach for the visual prediction of human-object interactions in videos. Rather than forecasting the human and object motion or the future hand-object contact points, we aim at predicting (a) the class of the ongoing human-object interaction and (b) the class(es) of the next active object(s) (NAOs), i.e., the object(s) that will be involved in the interaction in the near future as well as the time the interaction will occur. Graph matching relies on the efficient Graph Edit distance (GED) method. The experimental evaluation of the proposed approach was conducted using two well-established video datasets that contain human-object interactions, namely the MSR Daily Activities and the CAD120. High prediction accuracy was obtained for both action prediction and NAO forecasting.

Keywords: Activity prediction · Next active object prediction · BP-GED

1 Introduction

Prediction provides smart agents the ability to take a look into the future in order to proactively foresee possible outcomes or adverse, high-risk events. This enables them to plan timely responses for early intervention or corrective actions [15,16,26]. Such a competence is rather important when it comes to the observation of the environment or scenes in a wide variety of applications such as assistive robots in domestic or industrial environments [30] or pedestrian/obstacle trajectory prediction for autonomous vehicles [36] and more. Our study focuses on prediction of the semantics of a partially observed activity, before its completion, and of the next active objects that will be involved in order to complete the ongoing activity. Specifically, the proposed approach aspires to model the spatio-temporal relationships between the human and the visible scene objects in order to predict the classes of a varying number of the next active objects that will be handled by the human in order to complete the ongoing activity. Current methods lack the ability to predict more than one next active object [7,9,11].

G. Bebis et al. (Eds.): ISVC 2022, LNCS 13598, pp. 299–312, 2022.
https://doi.org/10.1007/978-3-031-20713-6_23

To the best of our knowledge, this is the first approach that is able to jointly predict the semantics of the ongoing activity and multiple next active objects. Moreover, one aspect that can be of great importance to such prediction systems is the ability to forecast the time in which NAOs will be involved in the current scenario. Our method is the first to predict NAOs along with the time that they will be involved in the activity.

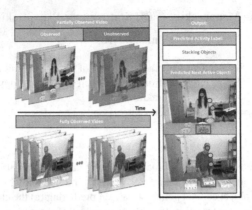

Fig. 1. By matching a partially executed and observed activity, to a prototype, fully observed one, we are able to infer correspondences of similar objects and human joints between the two videos. This, in turn, enables to perform activity and next-active-object prediction in the partially observed activity. The example in this figure refers to the "stacking objects" activity, which is performed with a different number and types of objects in the partially and the fully observed activities.

In this paper, we propose to jointly forecast the activity and the objects that will participate in the execution of the activity till its completion. Instead of predicting the interaction hotspots [19,20,25] of a NAO, we propose a holistic understanding of the activity regarding the human and objects present in the scene. Our approach is based upon calculating the dissimilarity of graphs representing the entities that constitute the activity [29]. Specifically, the human body joints of the acting person and the scene objects are represented as nodes of a graph and the semantic and motion relations between the nodes are represented as edges. The dissimilarity of graphs is calculated using the graph edit distance (GED) [1].

We showcase our approach on video datasets of human-object interactions of varying complexity. The well-known MSR-Daily Activities dataset [37] includes activities where none or one object is handled by a single subject. We further evaluate the performance of the proposed method using the CAD-120 dataset [18] that contains long and complex activities. Instances of the activities are performed by different subjects using different types and a varying number of objects. As an example, different executions of the "stacking objects" activity are performed using 4 boxes and 5 plates, respectively (see Fig. 1). The main contributions can be summarized as follows:

- We propose Graphing The Future (GTF), a method that can jointly predict the activity label and the next-active-objects by calculating the dissimilarity of videos with the use of GED as well as the time instance at which these objects will be used in the ongoing activity.
- Our work is the first to address the prediction of multiple NAOs in human-object interaction scenarios.
- GTF models the pairwise correspondences of objects and human joints between two comparing videos based on their semantic similarity as well as their (intra-video) spatio-temporal relationships in each video. Therefore, predictions are in principle possible even when a particular interaction with an object of a specific class has never been observed before.

2 Related Work

Activity Prediction: Action prediction aims to forecast the label of an action based on limited/partial observations. The majority of the proposed methods that tackle this problem consider (first person) egocentric videos [2,33,35,41,43], mainly due to the availability of large amounts of relevant video data and annotations [6,13,31]. In [12], Video Transformers are proposed to accurately anticipate future actions. Without supervision the method learns to focus on the image areas where the hands and objects appear, while attends the most relevant frames for the prediction of the next action. Rodin et al. [34] tackles the problem of anticipation in untrimmed videos in an attempt to generalize and deal with unconstrained conditions in real world scenarios. An advantage of the work proposed by Furnari et al. [10,11] is the ability to make predictions not only in first-person but also in third-person videos. Their work focuses on making predictions using multiple modalities such as RGB frames, optical flow and object-based features. Their architecture uses one LSTM for encoding the past time steps while the second LSTM makes predictions about the future. Manousaki et al. [22,23] focused their work on predicting action sequences by using temporal alignment algorithms. They aligned complete and partially observed actions using the Segregational Soft Dynamic Time Warping (SSDTW) algorithm by fusing the human and object motion. Wu et al. [39] opted to solve the problem of activity prediction by exploring spatio-temporal relations between humans and objects. They used a graph-based neural network to encode the spatial relations between video entities at different time-scales.

Next-Active-Object Prediction: Having correctly predicted the activity label, recent studies focus their attention on predicting the next-active-object. Dessalene et al. [7] define an active object as the object presently *in contact with a hand* while next-active-object is the object which *will next come into contact with that hand*. We argue that an object can be the next-active-object without having the need to come in contact with the hand. For example, imagine a scenario in which a hand pushes an object, which comes in contact with another object which is pushed, too. The hand never comes in contact

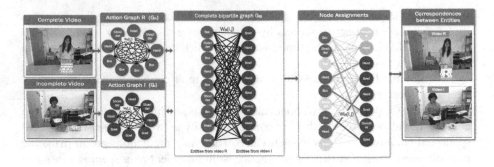

Fig. 2. Graph matching of a complete video (reference) and an incomplete/partially observed (test) video. First, the fully connected graphs of each video are created based on the video entities. On the basis of these graphs, a bipartite graph between the action graphs is constructed. By calculating the GED, we are able to correspond nodes between the two original action graphs.

with the second object. However, the second object is definitely part of the interaction. So, we define next-active-object as the object that is the next to be involved in the progress of an action.

In the course of an activity many actions can take place. These actions can be performed with or without the use of objects. Some consecutive actions may use the same object. In case there is no change of the active object between actions, the object used in consequent actions is not considered as next-active-object only because the action has changed. Our work differs from other approaches towards the prediction of objects. Other approaches [12,43] perform prediction of the object of the next segment/action, which in some cases can be the current active object of the ongoing segment. Liu et al. [20] predict future hand trajectories and object interaction hotspots, while in [42] hand-object contact prediction (contact or no-contact) is modelled using hand and object tracks throughout the video. This task if different from our target task of next-active-object prediction.

The first approach to tackle the problem of next-active-object prediction was Furnari et al. [9]. A sliding window was utilized in conjunction with an object detector in order to model each tracked trajectory and classify it as passive or active using random forests. The paper argues that the next-active-object can be distinguished from its frames immediately before it turns active. One very interesting characteristic of the method they propose is its ability to generalise to unseen object classes. However, their experiments show a loss of accuracy when dealing with unseen object classes thus proposing to train the method with the object classes that will be present in the test set for better results.

The work of Dessalene et al. [7] employs graphs to predict the partially observed action and produce Contact Anticipation Maps which provide pixel-wise information of the anticipated time-to-contact involving one hand, either the left or the right. Also, they perform next-active-object segmentation by localizing candidate next active objects. These localizations are evaluated with the calculation of the Intersection over Union (IoU) value of the bounding boxes produced from the Faster-RCNN model. This work predicts the hand-object time-to-contact in egocentric videos but this does imply that this can be the next-active-object or that this object will be used immediately. Also, this is trained on annotated object classes of the dataset which implies that it cannot generalize to unseen object classes.

3   The Proposed Method - GTF

We introduce the GTF method that jointly tackles the tasks of activity prediction and of next active object(s) prediction in videos using graph-based representation of an activity and graph matching technique based on the Graph Edit Distance measure to compare pairs of videos. The *activity prediction* task can be defined as the problem of inferring the label of an ongoing activity before its actual completion. Let an activity, noted as A, that starts at time t_s and ends at time t_e, thus has a duration $d = t_e - t_s$. Its observation time is defined in proportions of 10% of d. The goal is to predict the correct class as early as possible which implies access to fewer observations. We also note the task of *next-active-object prediction* as the problem of the inference of the semantic label of an object that will be used in the progress of an activity. Multiple objects may be used in the progress of a given activity A. Related works [7,11] predict the next-active-object in the segment preceding it's use, i.e., an amount of time (measured in seconds) before the start of the action that involves the object of interest.

Our approach relies on a graph-based representation of an activity that is captured in video. The entities in a video regard the tracked human skeletal joints and the observable/visible objects. Each video entity is represented as a node of an undirected graph, which also models both semantic information (object label) and its motion (2D or 3D trajectory). Each graph edge connecting two nodes represents the semantic similarity and the spatio-temporal relationships of the interconnected video entities, as described in Sect. 3. Our goal is to devise a novel approach that is able to identify human joints and/or objects in two different videos, one fully and one partially observed video, that exhibit similar behaviors and interactions with other entities using bipartite graph-matching. As shown in Fig. 2 a fully and a partially observed video are represented as two action graphs whose nodes represent the detected and tracked objects and human joints.

Video Representation: Given a video of duration T frames, it can be seen, at an object-level, as a complete and undirected graph, noted as $G = (V, E)$. In the course of a video, entities such as human body joints and foreground objects are localized and tracked using 2D or 3D human body pose estimation and tracking as well as object detection methods, respectively. Each graph node is noted as $v \in V$ and graph edges are noted as $e_{ij} = (v_i, v_j) \in E$ between nodes $v_i, v_j \in V$, where $i \neq j$. The relations between the nodes describe their dissimilarity in the form of edge weights. The dissimilarity is described based on the semantic dissimilarity s_i and the motion dissimilarity m_i. The edge weight between two connected nodes is defined as the weighted sum of the semantic and motion dissimilarity as follows:

$$w_{ij} = (1 - \lambda) * m_{ij} + \lambda * s_{ij}. \tag{1}$$

The parameter $lamda \in [0,1]$ is user-defined and controls the contribution of the semantic and motion information. On the extremity of $lamda = 0$, only motion information is considered while when $lamda = 1$, only semantic information is used. In the experimental section of this paper, we present an investigation of the effect of this parameter on the performance of the proposed method.

Semantic Dissimilarity: The weights s_{ij} represent the semantic dissimilarity between the labels of the nodes v_i and v_j. The node labels are retrieved based on ground truth annotations or object recognition methods. The semantic similarity of nodes v_i and v_j with recognized labels l_i and l_j is described as $S(l_i, l_j)$ and is estimated using the WordNet [8] lexical database and the Natural Language Toolkit [21] to compute the path-based Wu-Palmer scaled metric [40]. The similarity is in the range $(0, 1]$ with 1 identifying identical words so semantic weight is:

$$s_{ij} = 1 - S(l_i, l_j). \tag{2}$$

Motion Dissimilarity: Each node in the graph is described by a feature vector which can encode information such as the 2D/3D human joint location, the 2D/3D location of the object centroid or any other feature such as appearance, optical flow, etc. The extracted motion features for each dataset are described in Sect. 4.2. The acquired 2D/3D skeletal-based pose features or the 2D/3D object-based pose features are described by a trajectory $t(v_i)$ encoding the movement of the video entity during the activity. A pair of trajectories $t(v_i)$ and $t(v_j)$ can be aligned temporally using the Segregational Soft Dynamic Time Warping (SSDTW) [22] algorithm. The alignment cost of the trajectories $t(v_i)$ and $t(v_j)$ describes the motion dissimilarity of the graph nodes v_i and v_j and is divided by the summation of the length of the trajectory of the incomplete sequence $t(v_i)$ and the length of the trajectory of the reference sequence $t(v_j)$ that matched with $t(v_i)$ as proposed by the authors [22]. Thus, the weight m_{ij} of an edge connecting the graph nodes v_i and v_j is:

$$m_{i,j} = \frac{SSDTW(t(v_i), t(v_j))}{(len(t(v_i)) + len(t(v_j)))}. \tag{3}$$

Graph Operations: Having represented one partially observed and one complete video as graphs, we estimate their dissimilarity by using Graph Edit Distance (GED) [1]. GED is calculated by considering the edit operations (insertions, deletions and substitutions of nodes and/or edges) that are needed in order to transform one graph into another with minimum cost. Our GTF approach is inspired by the approach of Papoutsakis et al. [29] which uses the GED in order to solve the problem of co-segmentation in triplets of videos. Different from [29] we propose to assess the GED between a pair of videos in order to perform activity prediction. Comparably to [29] our approach is based on semantic and motion similarity of the entities but instead of using the EVACO cosegmentation method [28] to compute the alignment cost of the co-segmented sub-sequences we employ the SSDTW algorithm [22] to align the trajectories between pairs of nodes. The SSDTW algorithm has been shown to have better performance in aligning incomplete/ partially observed sequences for the task of action prediction.

We create a graph for each video G_I ((I)ncomplete video) and G_R ((R)eference video) and assess their graph distance. W_I and W_R are the dissimilarity matrices of action graphs G_I and G_R with size $N_I \times N_I$ and $N_R \times N_R$, respectively, where N_I and N_R are the number of vertices of each graph. As seen in Fig. 2 the next step is to create the bipartite graph G_{IR} of the action graphs G_I and G_R. The edge weights W_H connecting the nodes of graph G_I to nodes of graph G_R are calculated using Eq. (1). In order to calculate the GED on the bipartite graph we need to employ the Bipartite Graph Edit Distance (BP-GED) which solves an assignment problem on the complete bipartite graph using the Kuhn-Munkres algorithm [24]. The weights of the complete bipartite graph G_{IR} are: $W_{IR} = \begin{bmatrix} 0_{N_I,N_I} & W_H \\ W_H{}^T & 0_{N_R,N_R} \end{bmatrix}$ where $0_{x,y}$ stands for an $x \times y$ matrix of zeros. The solution of this assignment problem requires the definition of the graph edit operations and their associated costs.

Node Operations: Consist of node insertions, deletions and substitutions. The cost of inserting and deleting a node v is:

$$nd_{in}(empty\_node \to v_i) = \tau_v, \quad nd_{del}(v_i \to empty\_node) = \tau_v \quad (4)$$

while the cost of substitution of node v with node u is:

$$nd_{sb}(v_i \to u_j) = [\frac{1}{2\tau_v} + \exp(-a_v * W_H(i,j) + \sigma_v)]^{-1}. \quad (5)$$

The parameters of the cost operations for the nodes where set experimentally to $\tau_v = 0.4$, $\alpha_v = 0.1$ and $\sigma_v = 0.0$.

Edge Operations: also consist of insertions, deletions and substitutions. The costs of inserting and deleting an edge from node n of graph G_I to node u of graph G_R is:

$$e_{in}(e_{ij}^{G_I} \to e_{mn}^{G_R}) = \tau_e, \quad e_{del}(e_{ij}^{G_I} \to e_{mn}^{G_R}) = \tau_e. \quad (6)$$

Finally, the cost of edge substitution is defined as:

$$e_{sb}(e_{ij}^{G_I} \to e_{mn}^{G_R}) = \left[\frac{1}{2\tau_e} + exp(-\alpha_e \cdot (W_I(i,j) + W_R(m,n))/2 + \sigma_e)\right]^{-1}. \quad (7)$$

The parameters of the cost operations for the edges where set experimentally to $\tau_e = 0.3$, $\alpha_e = 0.1$ and $\sigma_e = 100$.

Action Distance: The dissimilarity between a pair of graphs (G_I, G_R) is computed by the BP-GED which calculates the exact GED [1]. With GED the minimum edit operations are calculated for transforming graph G_I to graph G_R. The dissimilarity, denoted as BP-GED(G_I, G_R), in the work of [29] is normalized by the total number

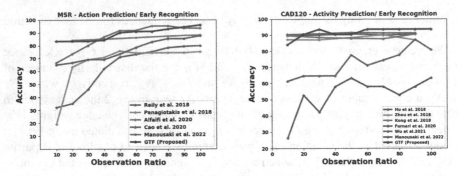

Fig. 3. Activity prediction results for the (left) MSR Daily Activities and (right) CAD-120 datasets for different observation ratios.

of objects. This normalization is effective when looking for commonalities between videos but is ineffective for activity prediction. In our work we need to be flexible in the number of objects that can be used during an activity while discarding irrelevant objects. In order to achieve this, we found that the best option is to normalize by the number of pairs of matched objects (MO). This helps us to assess our method on the objects that are important for the prediction and discard objects that may be present but with no use in the activity performed. Thus, the dissimilarity $D(G_I, G_R)$ of graphs G_I, G_R is defined as:

$$D(G_I, G_R) = BP\text{-}GED(G_I, G_R)/MO. \tag{8}$$

4   Experiments

4.1   Datasets

MSR Daily Activity 3D Dataset [37]: The activities contained in this dataset involve human-object interactions in trimmed video executions. The dataset contains 16 activity classes the executions of which are performed by male and female subjects, the first time by standing up and the second by laying down. The dataset contains the 3D locations of the human body joints. The evaluation split of the related works [22, 23, 32] is used for a fair comparative evaluation.

CAD-120 Dataset [18]: Contains complex activities that represent human-object interactions performed by different subjects. The activities are performed using 10 different objects and are observed from varying viewpoints. Each of the 10 activities contains interactions with multiple object classes in different environments. The dataset provides annotations regarding the activity and sub-activity labels, object labels, affordance labels and temporal segmentation of activities. The split of the related work [39] is used for a fair comparative evaluation.

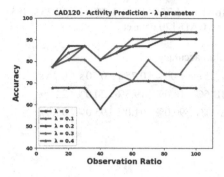 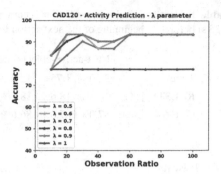

Fig. 4. Exploration of the user-defined λ parameter on the CAD-120 dataset. The values of the λ parameter are in the range $[0, 1]$. Some curves may be partially visible due to occlusions. Plots are separated in two figures to aid readability.

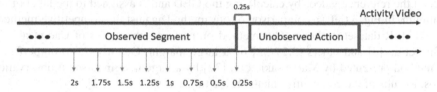

Fig. 5. Observing the activity and making object predictions for $[2\,s, 1.75\,s, 1.5\,s, 1.25\,s, 1\,s, 0.75\,s, 0.5\,s, 0.25\,s]$ before the beginning of the next action as in [11].

4.2 Feature Extraction

The employed datasets are recorded from a third-person viewpoint, therefore they provide information for the whole or upper body of the acting subjects. We decided to align with the existing work of [22] and consider only the upper body human joints for both datasets. For the MSR Daily Activity 3D Dataset the features used are the 3D joint angles and 3D skeletal joint positions [22]. Object classes and 2D object positions are obtained from YoloV4 [4]. For the CAD-120 Dataset the 3D location of the joints of the upper body are used. As for the objects, the ground truth labels are used along with their 3D centroid locations [22,23].

4.3 Evaluation Metrics

Activity Prediction: Activities are observed in a range from 10% to 100% of their total duration with steps equal to 10%. At every step, the accuracy of the predicted activity label is evaluated compared to the ground truth.

Next-Active-Object Prediction: At variable time steps before the start of the next segment (see Fig. 5) where the next-active-object will be used, we estimate the accuracy of the predicted object label compared to the ground truth label. Also, we calculate the time at which the next-active-object will be used in the activity. For the aforementioned time steps the prediction error is calculated as the difference of the predicted time of use and the ground truth time, divided by the length of the video.

Table 1. Next-active-object prediction accuracy for [2 s, 1.75 s, 1.5 s, 1.25 s, 1 s, 0.75 s, 0.5 s, 0.25 s] before the beginning of the next action for the CAD-120 dataset.

	Next-active-object prediction accuracy							
Time	2.00 s	1.75 s	1.50 s	1.25 s	1.00 s	0.75 s	0.50 s	0.25 s
RULSTM [11]	18.6%	18.6%	18.0%	18.6%	18.6%	19.3%	20.0%	22.0%
GTF (proposed)	87.0%	87.0%	86.6%	89.1%	90.0%	91.0%	95.0%	97.0%

4.4 Results

Activity Prediction/Early Recognition: Activity label prediction is performed by considering observation ratios in chunks of 10% until the end of the video. The label prediction at 100% can be regarded as activity recognition. The test video is compared with all the reference videos by calculating the GED and is assigned to the label of the minimum. In Fig. 3 (left) a comparison of our method against the competitive methods for the MSR dataset is shown. Our method outperforms the works of Cao et al. [5], Alfaifi et al. [3] and others [3,27,32] by a large margin. Our work also outperforms the method presented by Manousaki et al. [22] by a large margin at small observation ratios. Results of the competitive methods are taken as shown in [22].

CAD-120 is a challenging dataset due to the number of objects and their interchangeability in different executions of activities. In this dataset, our method outperforms the works of Manousaki et al. [22], Furnari et al. [11] and other competitive methods [14,17,44] by a large margin. It also outperforms the approach of Wu et al. [39] that holds the state-of-art performance, for all observation ratios greater than 20% (see Fig. 3, right). The results of the [14,17,44] and [39] methods are taken from the work of Wu et al. [39] while for our previous work (Manousaki et al. [22]) we trained and tested using the activities (instead of actions) with the parameters mentioned in that paper.

The Impact of Parameter λ: Edge weights are determined based on the proportion of the semantic and motion information they convey. This proportion is quantified by the user-defined parameter λ (see Eq. (1)). In Fig. 4 we present results that explore the impact of λ on the performance of our approach on the CAD-120 dataset. When $\lambda = 0$ (only motion features) and $\lambda = 1$ (only semantic features) the results are alike in terms of having the lowest ability to make accurate predictions. Their combination carries a lot more information and gives the best results. Some values are not visible in the plots because for different values of the λ parameter, accuracy values remain the same. After experimental evaluation the best value across datasets is $\lambda = 0.8$.

Next-Active-Object Prediction: Our method is designed to accommodate videos captured from a third-person viewpoint as we need to have a view of the human joints and the surrounding objects. The most related work to ours is the work of Dessalene et al. [7] which is currently limited only to egocentric videos. This does not allow for a comparison with that approach. We compare our method to the recent work of Furnari et al. [11]. This work performs on both egocentric and third-view datasets and is the

Table 2. Time prediction error is the offset of the predicted time of the next-active-object use to the ground truth time of use compared to video length. Predictions are made from 0.25 s to 2 s prior to the start of the next action.

CAD120	Next-active-object time prediction error							
Time	2.00 s	1.75 s	1.50 s	1.25 s	1.00 s	0.75 s	0.50 s	0.25 s
GTF (Proposed)	0.471	0.463	0.46	0.457	0.443	0.405	0.36	0.325

Table 3. Accuracy for predicting multiple next-active-objects for different observation ratios.

CAD120	Multiple next-active-objects prediction accuracy								
Observation ratio	10%	20%	30%	40%	50%	60%	70%	80%	90%
GTF (proposed)	41.7%	43.2%	45.6%	45.6%	47.1%	47.1%	48.6%	50%	55.9%

method that [7] compares with. Their performance is comparable for the task of next-active-object prediction. However, instead of following their experimental scheme and evaluating only the accuracy of the prediction of the next-active-object, we also evaluate the accuracy of the prediction in relation to the time prior to the start of the action where the next-active-object will be used. Predictions are made in the range [2 s, 1.75 s, 1.5 s, 1.25 s, 1 s, 0.75 s, 0.5 s, 0.25 s] before the beginning of the action (see Fig. 5). As seen in Table 1 our method can correctly predict more objects as we move closer in time while [11] can predict less accurately the objects and is not affected by the time horizon. By comparing the graph of the partially observed video with those of the reference videos, the pair of graphs that have the smaller graph edit distance and object correspondences between the graphs are estimated (test and reference videos may have different number of objects). The work of Furnari et al. [11] is tested using the CAD120 dataset and the publicly available implementation. We extracted the 1024-dimensional features by using TSN [38] and calculated object features using the ground truth annotations. Their code accommodates the extraction of predictions at different seconds before the beginning of the action as described above.

Next-Active-Object Time Prediction: Another aspect of great importance is the ability to forecast the time at which the object will be used in the activity. With the use of the GTF method we are able to compare the partially observed video with the reference videos from the training. After finding the pair of graphs that have the smaller graph edit distance, we acquire the information about object correspondences. This ability to infer the object correspondences between the two videos allows us to have the same number of objects between the videos in order to perform video alignment with the use of SSDTW. The alignment provides the ability to find the point of the reference video that corresponds to the current point in time in the test video (matching point). This projection of time from the reference video to the test one, permits the forecasting of the time at which the next-active-objects will be engaged in the interaction. The prediction error is calculated as the offset of the predicted time of use from the ground truth time of use of the next-active-object compared to the duration of the video. The error is calculated upon the correct predictions of the next-active-object. In Table 2 we observe that this error is low, which means that we are able to accurately predict the time at which the next-active-object will be used in the activity.

Multiple Next-Active-Objects Prediction: Our method is capable of predicting not just one, but multiple next-active-objects. These predictions can be performed at different observation ratios from to 10% to 90% (an observation ratio equal to 100% means that the whole video is observed, so next object prediction is not defined). The accuracy for each observation ratio for the predicted next-active-objects is presented at Table 3. The prediction is made through the correspondence of the objects between the reference and test graphs. By knowing the order in which the objects in the reference video are used, we can infer the order in which the objects of the test video will be used. After finding the matching point (see the previous section) we can infer the order of the matched objects from that point till the end. Prediction of multiple next-active-objects is challenging due to long time horizons involved and the related increased uncertainty.

5   Conclusions

We introduced GTF, a method that is based on matching complete and partially observed videos which are represented as graphs, with the use of Bipartite Graph matching. Human joints and objects were represented as nodes whereas their semantic and motion similarity was captured by the edges. We showed that through this formulation and process, we are able to perform activity and next-active-object prediction providing state-of-art results. Moreover, we proposed to solve the problem of predicting the time at which the next-active-object will be used as well as the prediction of multiple next-active-objects. Future research will be focused on compiling and experimenting with larger and more complex datasets of human-object interactions in which users will be handling a broader variety of objects in several ways.

Acknowledgements. This research was co-financed by Greece and the European Union (European Social Fund-ESF) through the Operational Programme "Human Resources Development, Education and Lifelong Learning" in the context of the Act "Enhancing Human Resources Research Potential by undertaking a Doctoral Research" Sub-action 2: IKY Scholarship Programme for PhD candidates in the Greek Universities. The research work was also supported by the Hellenic Foundation for Research and Innovation (HFRI) under the HFRI PhD Fellowship grant (Fellowship Number: 1592) and by HFRI under the "1st Call for HFRI Research Projects to support Faculty members and Researchers and the procurement of high-cost research equipment", project I.C.Humans, number 91.

References

1. Abu-Aisheh, Z., Raveaux, R., Ramel, J.Y., Martineau, P.: An exact graph edit distance algorithm for solving pattern recognition problems. In: ICPRAM (2015)
2. Abu Farha, Y., Ke, Q., Schiele, B., Gall, J.: Long-term anticipation of activities with cycle consistency. In: Akata, Z., Geiger, A., Sattler, T. (eds.) DAGM GCPR 2020. LNCS, vol. 12544, pp. 159–173. Springer, Cham (2021). https://doi.org/10.1007/978-3-030-71278-5_12

3. Alfaifi, R., Artoli, A.M.: Human action prediction with 3D-CNN. SN Comput. Sci. **1**(5), 1–15 (2020). https://doi.org/10.1007/s42979-020-00293-x

4. Bochkovskiy, A., Wang, C.Y., Liao, H.Y.M.: YOLOv4: optimal speed and accuracy of object detection. arXiv preprint arXiv:2004.10934 (2020)

5. Cao, K., Ji, J., Cao, Z., Chang, C.Y., Niebles, J.C.: Few-shot video classification via temporal alignment. In: CVPR, pp. 10618–10627 (2020)

6. Damen, D., et al.: Rescaling egocentric vision: collection, pipeline and challenges for EPIC-KITCHENS-100. Int. J. Comput. Vis. **130**(1), 33–55 (2021). https://doi.org/10.1007/s11263-021-01531-2

7. Dessalene, E., Devaraj, C., Maynord, M., Fermuller, C., Aloimonos, Y.: Forecasting action through contact representations from first person video. In: IEEE PAMI (2021)

8. Fellbaum, C.: WordNet and WordNets (2005)

9. Furnari, A., Battiato, S., Grauman, K., Farinella, G.M.: Next-active-object prediction from egocentric videos. J. Vis. Commun. Image Represent. **49**, 401–411 (2017)

10. Furnari, A., Farinella, G.M.: What would you expect? Anticipating egocentric actions with rolling-unrolling LSTMs and modality attention. In: IEEE ICCV, pp. 6252–6261 (2019)

11. Furnari, A., Farinella, G.M.: Rolling-unrolling LSTMs for action anticipation from first-person video. IEEE Trans. Pattern Anal. Mach. Intell. **43**(11), 4021–4036 (2020)

12. Girdhar, R., Grauman, K.: Anticipative video transformer. In: IEEE ICCV, pp. 13505–13515 (2021)

13. Grauman, K., et al.: Ego4D: around the world in 3,000 hours of egocentric video. In: IEEE CVPR, pp. 18995–19012 (2022)

14. Hu, J.F., Zheng, W.S., Ma, L., Wang, G., Lai, J., Zhang, J.: Early action prediction by soft regression. IEEE Trans. Pattern Anal. Mach. Intell. **41**(11), 2568–2583 (2018)

15. Hu, X., Dai, J., Li, M., Peng, C., Li, Y., Du, S.: Online human action detection and anticipation in videos: a survey. Neurocomputing **491**, 395–413 (2022)

16. Kong, Yu., Fu, Y.: Human action recognition and prediction: a survey. Int. J. Comput. Vis. **130**, 1366–1401 (2022). https://doi.org/10.1007/s11263-022-01594-9

17. Kong, Y., Gao, S., Sun, B., Fu, Y.: Action prediction from videos via memorizing hard-to-predict samples. In: Proceedings of the AAAI Conference on Artificial Intelligence, vol. 32, No. 1 (2018)

18. Koppula, H., Gupta, R., Saxena, A.: Learning human activities and object affordances from RGB-D videos. Int. J. Robot. Res. **32**(8), 951–970 (2013)

19. Liu, M., Tang, S., Li, Y., Rehg, J.M.: Forecasting human-object interaction: joint prediction of motor attention and actions in first person video. In: ECCV (2020)

20. Liu, S., Tripathi, S., Majumdar, S., Wang, X.: Joint hand motion and interaction hotspots prediction from egocentric videos. In: IEEE CVPR, pp. 3282–3292 (2022)

21. Loper, E., Bird, S.: NLTK: the natural language toolkit. arXiv preprint arXiv:cs/0205028 (2002)

22. Manousaki, V., Argyros, A.A.: Segregational soft dynamic time warping and its application to action prediction. In: VISIGRAPP (5: VISAPP), pp. 226–235 (2022)

23. Manousaki, V., Papoutsakis, K., Argyros, A.: Action prediction during human-object interaction based on DTW and early fusion of human and object representations. In: Vincze, M., Patten, T., Christensen, H.I., Nalpantidis, L., Liu, M. (eds.) ICVS 2021. LNCS, vol. 12899, pp. 169–179. Springer, Cham (2021). https://doi.org/10.1007/978-3-030-87156-7_14

24. Munkres, J.: Algorithms for the assignment and transportation problems. J. Soc. Ind. Appl. Math. **5**(1), 32–38 (1957)

25. Nagarajan, T., Feichtenhofer, C., Grauman, K.: Grounded human-object interaction hotspots from video. In: IEEE ICCV, pp. 8688–8697 (2019)

26. Oprea, S., et al.: A review on deep learning techniques for video prediction. IEEE PAMI (2020)

27. Panagiotakis, C., Papoutsakis, K., Argyros, A.: A graph-based approach for detecting common actions in motion capture data and videos. Pattern Recognit. **79**, 1–11 (2018)
28. Papoutsakis, K., Panagiotakis, C., Argyros, A.A.: Temporal action co-segmentation in 3D motion capture data and videos. In: IEEE CVPR, pp. 6827–6836 (2017)
29. Papoutsakis, K.E., Argyros, A.A.: Unsupervised and explainable assessment of video similarity. In: BMVC, p. 151 (2019)
30. Petković, T., Petrović, L., Marković, I., Petrović, I.: Human action prediction in collaborative environments based on shared-weight LSTMs with feature dimensionality reduction. Appl. Soft Comput. **126**, 109245 (2022)
31. Ragusa, F., Furnari, A., Livatino, S., Farinella, G.M.: The MECCANO dataset: understanding human-object interactions from egocentric videos in an industrial-like domain. In: IEEE WACV, pp. 1569–1578 (2021)
32. Reily, B., Han, F., Parker, L.E., Zhang, H.: Skeleton-based bio-inspired human activity prediction for real-time human–robot interaction. Auton. Robot. **42**(6), 1281–1298 (2017). https://doi.org/10.1007/s10514-017-9692-3
33. Rodin, I., Furnari, A., Mavroeidis, D., Farinella, G.M.: Predicting the future from first person (egocentric) vision: a survey. Comput. Vis. Image Underst. **211**, 103252 (2021)
34. Rodin, I., Furnari, A., Mavroeidis, D., Farinella, G.M.: Untrimmed action anticipation. In: Sclaroff, S., Distante, C., Leo, M., Farinella, G.M., Tombari, F. (eds) Image Analysis and Processing (ICIAP 2022). ICIAP 2022. LNCS, vol. 13233, pp. 337–348. Springer, Cham (2022). https://doi.org/10.1007/978-3-031-06433-3_29
35. Sener, F., Singhania, D., Yao, A.: Temporal aggregate representations for long-range video understanding. In: Vedaldi, A., Bischof, H., Brox, T., Frahm, J.-M. (eds.) ECCV 2020. LNCS, vol. 12361, pp. 154–171. Springer, Cham (2020). https://doi.org/10.1007/978-3-030-58517-4_10
36. Wang, C., Wang, Y., Xu, M., Crandall, D.J.: Stepwise goal-driven networks for trajectory prediction. IEEE Robot. Autom. Lett. **7**(2), 2716–2723 (2022)
37. Wang, J., Liu, Z., Wu, Y., Yuan, J.: Mining actionlet ensemble for action recognition with depth cameras. In: IEEE CVPR, pp. 1290–1297 (2012)
38. Wang, L., et al.: Temporal segment networks: towards good practices for deep action recognition. In: Leibe, B., Matas, J., Sebe, N., Welling, M. (eds.) ECCV 2016. LNCS, vol. 9912, pp. 20–36. Springer, Cham (2016). https://doi.org/10.1007/978-3-319-46484-8_2
39. Wu, X., Wang, R., Hou, J., Lin, H., Luo, J.: Spatial–temporal relation reasoning for action prediction in videos. Int. J. Comput. Vis. **129**(5), 1484–1505 (2021). https://doi.org/10.1007/s11263-020-01409-9
40. Wu, Z., Palmer, M.: Verb semantics and lexical selection. arXiv preprint arXiv:cmp-lg/9406033 (1994)
41. Xu, X., Li, Y.L., Lu, C.: Learning to anticipate future with dynamic context removal. In: IEEE CVPR, pp. 12734–12744 (2022)
42. Yagi, T., Hasan, M.T., Sato, Y.: Hand-object contact prediction via motion-based pseudo-labeling and guided progressive label correction. arXiv preprint arXiv:2110.10174 (2021)
43. Zatsarynna, O., Abu Farha, Y., Gall, J.: Multi-modal temporal convolutional network for anticipating actions in egocentric videos. In: IEEE CVPR, pp. 2249–2258 (2021)
44. Zhou, B., Andonian, A., Oliva, A., Torralba, A.: Temporal relational reasoning in videos. In: ECCV, pp. 803–818 (2018)

Detecting Fall Actions of Videos by Using Weakly-Supervised Learning and Unsupervised Clustering Learning

Jiaxin Zhou[ID] and Takashi Komuro[✉][ID]

Saitama University, Saitama 338-8570, Japan
shuu.j.681@ms.saitama-u.ac.jp, komuro@mail.saitama-u.ac.jp

Abstract. A framework has been proposed for detecting fall actions from videos to solve the problem of imbalance between fall action data and Activity of Daily Life (ADL) data. In the framework, a 3D-convolutional variational auto-encoder (VAE) was used to reconstruct ADL videos, and reconstruction errors were used to recognize fall actions. In this paper, we propose an improved method using unsupervised clustering learning to cluster fall actions. The 3D-convolutional VAE extracts representations from videos, and additionally proposed fully-connected VAE to gather those representations into two clusters, where representations of fall actions are distinguished from distribution of ADL data. The experimental results showed that our method achieved a promising level of accuracy and better generalization ability compared to methods using supervised learning with well-labeled data. We further show visualization results of latent variables during unsupervised clustering, which showed the representations were clustered into two distinct clusters.

Keywords: Fall detection · Auto-encoder · Weakly-supervised learning · Unsupervised clustering learning

1 Introduction

Population aging is a widespread problem across the world and is very severe in highly developed countries. Since solitary elderly people are more likely to fall indoors and cannot obtain assistance in time, demands for stable fall-detecting systems are increasing. However, it is challenging to detect whether a person falls by using computer vision due to complicated real-life situations.

Until the age of deep learning, hand-crafted features were extracted from images and were used to detect fall actions. However, they are not sufficient to discriminate against fall actions due to complicated human behaviors, viewpoints of cameras, and other factors. Recently, deep learning methods using supervised neural networks have been proposed to detect fall actions. In those methods [10,23], neural networks were used to classify input data as fall actions or normal actions by training with manually labeled data. If supervised neural networks

G. Bebis et al. (Eds.): ISVC 2022, LNCS 13598, pp. 313–324, 2022.
https://doi.org/10.1007/978-3-031-20713-6_24

are trained with enough, balanced, and well-labeled data, they perform well. However, there is a problem in the field of fall detection that well-labeled data is not abundant, since it is labor-consuming to label each frame of hours of videos with tags of falling, sitting, drinking water, and other actions in daily life. There is another problem that quantities of Activity of Daily Life (ADL) data and fall action data are imbalanced. In most videos, fall actions do not happen or happen only within several seconds, and the rest is about activities of daily life. Those problems can adversely affect the performance of supervised neural networks.

Therefore, some researchers proposed utilizing the idea of anomaly detection [15] for fall detection, since there is sometimes an imbalance between regular events and anomalous events like ADL data and fall action data. Some methods using unsupervised neural networks [7, 26] were proposed to overcome the imbalance between anomalous data and regular data. In these methods, auto-encoders (AE) which are a kind of unsupervised neural network and do not depend on well-labeled data were used to detect abnormal events. First, AE-based networks learn the distribution of regular videos by compressing and reconstructing regular videos. When training is finished, an abnormal sample is input to the networks and still is reconstructed to be normal, which makes reconstruction errors large, and the sample is classified as an anomaly. Those methods belong to weakly supervised learning, which uses data with imprecise labels since training data has imprecise labels, namely training data only contains regular videos.

A framework [27] has been proposed for fall detection has been proposed where a Variational Auto-encoder (VAE) [14] with 3D-convolutional residual blocks [12] learns to reconstruct ADL videos, and reconstruction errors are used to recognize fall actions. In this paper, the contributions of our work are as follows:

i) We propose an improved method using unsupervised clustering learning to cluster fall actions. The 3D-convolutional VAE extracts representations from videos, and we further propose a fully-connected VAE to gather those representations into two distinct clusters, where representations of fall actions are distinguished from distribution of ADL data.

ii) The experimental results show that the proposed method obtain better accuracies and generalization ability than methods using supervised learning with well-labeled data.

iii) We verify that a combination of weakly supervised learning and unsupervised cluster learning can be used to ease the lack of well-labeled data, and abundant ADL data can be taken good use of to overcome the adverse effect of imbalanced data.

2   Related Work

2.1   Fall Detection

Until the age of deep learning, handcrafted features were used to detect fall actions, such as fitting an ellipse to a body [16, 21]. In these methods, whether a fall action happens or not is detected depending on variations of the short and long axis, the area, etc. of the fitted ellipse in videos. For example, if a vertical and thin ellipse becomes horizontal, it may indicate that a fall action happened. Such hand-crafted features are not sufficient to discriminate against fall actions.

In some studies, handcrafted features were used as inputs to neural networks for fall detection. For example, skeleton information is extracted by using Microsoft Kinect, treated as biomechanical features, and then used as inputs to a recurrent neural network with long short-term memory units [25]. Since visual information is lost when extracting skeleton information, and the performance may become unstable, it would be more appropriate to directly use pixel-level information to train neural networks. Due to complicated human behaviors, viewpoints of cameras, and other factors, it is more reasonable to automatically extract features by using deep neural networks.

Recently, supervised learning methods using deep neural networks have been proposed to detect fall actions [1,10,23]. In these methods, a neural network is trained with manually labeled data to classify input data as a fall action or a normal action. Well-labeled data usually is precious since it is tiresome to label tags on a large amount of data, and lacking well-labeled data will lead to the overfitting of supervised neural networks. Moreover, the amount of fall action data and the amount of ADL data are imbalanced. Therefore, a large amount of ADL data is abandoned to keep the balance and allow supervised neural networks to work normally, which further aggravates the lack of well-labeled data.

2.2 Weakly Supervised Learning

Since there is an imbalance between fall action data and ADL data like anomalous videos and regular videos, the idea of anomaly detection [15] was proposed to detect fall actions. Anomaly detection is a kind of weakly supervised learning method since training data with imprecise labels is used. In the case of fall detection, all training data is from ADL videos.

A spatiotemporal auto-encoder [7,26] was proposed to detect abnormal events. In these methods, AE-based networks were used to model regular video data, and the networks learn how to reconstruct regular videos. When training is finished, if an abnormal sample is an input, the networks still try to reconstruct it to be a regular video, which makes reconstruction errors large, and the sample is classified as an anomaly. The higher the reconstruction error is, the more possibly an abnormal event happens. An AE-based network was also proposed for fall detection, and experiments were conducted using a fall dataset consisting of thermal and depth images [22]. A 3D-convolutional VAE network for detecting fall actions using RGB videos was proposed [27]. In this method, the network learned a data distribution of ADL videos that follows a normal distribution, which made representations of ADL videos compact in a latent space. Since representations learned by a VAE are more compact than those learned by an AE, they are more discriminative for fall action recognition. Additionally, a region extraction technique was proposed to make the network focus on learning human actions from RGB videos.

2.3   Unsupervised Clustering Learning

Using handcrafted thresholds of reconstruction errors cannot detect fall actions well in various situations, but metrics such as clustering learned for different situations can overcome that weakness.

Some classical clustering methods such as k-means [19] and Gaussian Mixture Models [5] tend to suffer from the curse of dimensionality [3] when high-dimensional data such as videos are input. Various clustering methods such as spectral clustering [17], density-based clustering [9], etc., were proposed to take good use of more flexible distance metrics to process high-dimensional data. However, they lead to other problems such as memory and time-consuming.

With the development of deep learning, some methods assembled both representation learning and clustering learning. Deep Embedding Clustering (DEC) was proposed [24] in which an auto-encoder compresses the dimensionality of input data, and minimized the KL divergence between predictions and auxiliary target distribution. DEC achieved progressive performance on clustering tasks. Variational Deep Embedding (VaDE) [13] and Gaussian Mixture VAE (GMVAE) [8] were proposed respectively where there was an assumption that low-dimensional latent space of compressed input data follows a mixture of gaussian distribution. Besides, we refer to [20] for a comprehensive literature study of clustering with deep learning.

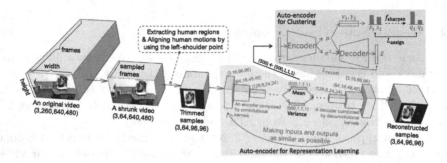

Fig. 1. Overview of our framework for fall detection. A 3D-convolutional VAE [27] extracts representations from videos (as shown with a background of light orange), and a fully-connected VAE gathers those representations into two distinct clusters (as shown with a background of light blue). (Color figure online)

3   Method

An overview of our framework for fall detection is shown in Fig. 1. There are mainly two parts to the framework. A 3D-convolutional VAE [27] learns representations of ADL data by reconstructing ADL videos since videos include lots of redundant information and should be reduced to lower dimensionality. Additionally, a fully-connected VAE is needed to further cluster all representations of ADL data and fall action data into two distinct clusters since a discriminative boundary between representations of ADL data and fall action data is still not clear enough for classification.

Handcrafted thresholds of reconstruction errors are usually used to distinguish fall actions since videos of fall actions are reconstructed worse than ADL videos by VAEs according to previous research [7,22,26,27]. However, it is more reasonable to directly cluster representations in the high-dimensional latent space using a deep neural network. Therefore, we propose to use additional fully-connected VAE (FCVAE) that learns cluster centers of distributions of ADL data and fall action data as shown in the part with a light blue background in Fig. 1.

Representations $\{x_1, x_2, ..., x_i, ...\}$, $x_i \in \mathbb{R}^D$, where D denotes dimensionality, are extracted by the trained encoder of 3D-convolutional VAE from both ADL data and fall action data and are taken as a set. Then, the FCVAE learns to distinguish between ADL data and fall action data by simultaneously learning two cluster centers denoted by γ_1, $\gamma_2 \in \mathbb{R}^D$ and reconstructing input data.

In the branch of clustering learning, cluster centers are firstly initialized by using k-means, and similarity s_{ij} between representation embeddings $\{\mu_1, \mu_2, ..., \mu_i, ...\}$, $\mu_i \in \mathbb{R}^D$ and cluster centers in the high-dimensional latent space is calculated using Student's t-distribution following [18,24]:

$$s_{ij} = \frac{(1 + \|\mu_i - \gamma_j\|^2)^{-1}}{\sum_{j'}(1 + \|\mu_i - \gamma_{j'}\|^2)^{-1}},$$

where $i = 1, 2, ..., N$, $j = 1, 2$. Those values of similarities are normalized between 0 and 1 using

$$s_{ij} \leftarrow \frac{s_{ij}}{\sum_{j'} s_{ij'}}$$

and compose a distribution (s_{i1}, s_{i2}) which represents label assignment possibility. We additionally apply a sharpening function to obtain pseudo ground truth [4,11]

$$q_{ij} = f_{\text{sharpen}}(s_{ij}) = \frac{s_{ij}^2}{\sum_{j'} s_{ij'}^2}$$

which can reduce the entropy of assignment distribution, namely encouraging the network to make an assignment as certain as possible. We use a KL divergence loss between predicted assignment distribution (s_{i1}, s_{i2}) and the pseudo ground truth (q_{i1}, q_{i2}) to gradually reduce the entropy as follows:

$$L_{\text{assign}} = \sum_{i=1}^{N} \sum_{j=1}^{2} s_{ij} \log \frac{s_{ij}}{q_{ij}}.$$

Clustering learning and reconstruction learning are conducted simultaneously. Reconstruction learning of x_i is needed since it implicitly makes middle representation embeddings be assigned based on input data. We use an MSE loss during the reconstruction learning as follows:

$$L_{\text{recon}} = \sum_{i=1}^{N} \|x_i - \hat{x}_i\|^2.$$

Finally, the optimization objective is $L = \alpha L_{\text{assign}} + \beta L_{\text{recon}}$. The larger α is, the more obvious the clustering effect is. It is reasonable if α is much bigger than β. We set $\alpha = 0.8$ and $\beta = 0.2$ in this study.

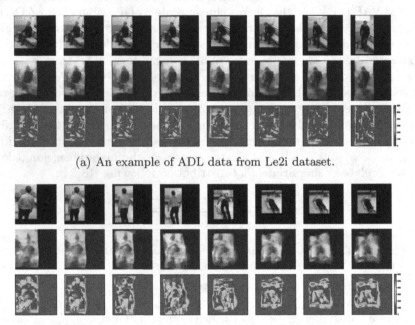

(a) An example of ADL data from Le2i dataset.

(b) An example of fall action data from Le2i dataset.

Fig. 2. Examples including input images (top), reconstructed images (middle), and heatmaps of reconstruction errors (bottom). (For better showing, 16 frames are resampled to 8 frames.)

4   Experiment

We conducted experiments using a PC having a 4.2 GHz i7-7700K CPU, 16 GB RAM, and a GTX 1070 GPU. As shown in Table 1, we compared networks with supervised learning, networks with weakly supervised learning only, and networks with weakly supervised learning and unsupervised clustering, which use the same architecture with different numbers of layers, for training and evaluating on different datasets and cropped images [27].

Table 1. Experimental results of different networks by using evaluation of reconstruction error thresholds.

Method	Learning fashion	Training set (#Fall/#ADL)	Evaluation set (#Fall/#ADL)	TPR (%)	TNR (%)	ACC (%)	F1 (%)	MCC
ResVAE-18 (proposed)	Weakly supervised learning Unsupervised clustering learning	HQFD (0/12266) HQFD (0/12266)	HQFD (282/300) Le2i (130/200)	90 97.5	87.9 96	88.9 96.6	88.7 **95.5**	**0.778** **0.928**
ResVAE-18 [27]	Weakly supervised learning	HQFD (0/12266) HQFD (0/12266)	HQFD (282/300) Le2i (130/200)	94 92.3	83.7 84	88.7 87.3	**88.9** 85.1	**0.778** 0.748
ResVAE-34 [27]	Weakly supervised learning	HQFD (0/12266) HQFD (0/12266)	HQFD (282/300) Le2i (130/200)	80.5 92.3	83.3 84.5	82 87.6	81.2 85.4	0.639 0.753
ResNet-18	Supervised learning	HQFD (225/9812) HQFD (225/240) HQFD (282/12266) HQFD (282/300)	HQFD (57/2454) HQFD (57/60) Le2i (130/200) Le2i (130/200)	5.3 75.4 0.8 93.8	100 96.7 100 79.5	97.8 86.3 60.9 85.2	10 84.3 1.5 83.3	0.227 0.741 0.68 0.717
ResNet-34	Supervised learning	HQFD (225/9812) HQFD (225/240) HQFD (282/12266) HQFD (282/300)	HQFD (57/2454) HQFD (57/60) Le2i (130/200) Le2i (130/200)	17.5 47.5 2.3 70.8	100 98.3 100 79.5	98.1 73.5 61.5 76.1	29.9 63.5 4.5 70	0.415 0.535 0.119 0.501

TPR denotes the true positive rate, which is a measure of how many falling samples were classified correctly. TNR denotes the true negative rate, which is a measure of how many ADL samples are classified correctly. ACC denotes average accuracy. F1 denotes the F1-score, which is the harmonic average of the precision and recall. MCC denotes the Matthews correlation, coefficient which is a balanced measure of the quality of binary classifications. The closer an MCC value is to a positive one, the better the prediction is.

4.1 Dataset

We used the High Quality Simulated Fall Dataset (HQFD) [2] and the Le2i Fall Dataset (Le2i) [6].

ADL videos have a resolution of 640 × 480, multiple frames and RGB channels. They are separated into several segments, and each segment included 16 frames which were uniformly sampled from 64 frames. The region of human motion was extracted from an entire image by using the AlphaPose estimator and was resized to 96 by 96 pixels. Regarding fall action data for evaluation, we manually trimmed each video to exactly include one fall action at first and then applied the same preprocessing operations as those on the ADL data. The data structure was in the form of (3, 16, 96, 96), which denotes 3 channels (RGB), 16 frames, a height of 96, and a width of 96. As training sets for weakly supervised learning, all samples were ADL data. As evaluation sets for weakly supervised learning, besides all fall samples, there was also a moderate amount of ADL samples. Some examples of ADL data and fall action data are shown in Fig. 2.

HQFD. The HQFD dataset contains 275 fall videos and 85 ADL videos which range from 50 s to 35.5 min in duration. They were captured by RGB cameras from 5 different viewpoints. After preprocessing, there were 12266 ADL samples and 282 fall samples. An evaluation set for weakly supervised learning consisted of 282 fall samples and 300 ADL samples.

Le2i. The Le2i dataset contains 192 fall videos and 57 ADL videos which were captured by a single RGB camera and range from 10 s to 45 s in duration. After preprocessing, there were 834 ADL samples and 130 fall samples. Some videos after preprocessing with too few frames were abandoned. An evaluation set for weakly supervised learning consisted of 130 fall samples and 200 ADL samples.

4.2   Implementation

The encoder and decoder of the 3D-convolutional VAE (ResVAE) respectively consisted of 8 residual blocks named ResVAE-18 or 16 residual blocks named ResVAE-34 [27]. Each residual block comprised two batch normalization layers, two activation layers, and two convolution layers (or transposed convolution layers). The networks were optimized using an Adam optimizer with a learning rate of 0.0001. The batch size was 32 in ResVAE-18 and 24 in ResVAE-34.

The encoder of the FCVAE consisted of two full-connected layers with ReLU activation layers and another two full-connected layers with following dimensions: Input data (dim $= 512$) $\rightarrow$ FC(dim $= 2048$) $\rightarrow$ FC(dim $= 2048$) $\rightarrow$ FC-μ(dim $= 512$) & FC-σ^2(dim $= 512$). The decoder consisted of two full-connected layers with ReLU activation layers and another full-connected layer with following dimensions: $z = \mu + \sigma \times \epsilon \sim N(0, I)$ (dim $= 512$) $\rightarrow$ FC(dim $= 2048$) $\rightarrow$ FC(dim $= 2048$) $\rightarrow$ FC(dim $= 512$). Cluster centers were also regarded as parameters and were jointly optimized with the FCVAE using an Adam optimizer with a learning rate of 0.0001 and a batch size of 64.

For the training of ResVAEs, networks were trained for 500 epochs. For the training of FCVAEs, networks were trained for 100 epochs. For training of standard ResNets, training was stopped if the value of the loss function was consecutively less than 0.00001 for ten epochs.

For evaluation using a threshold of reconstruction errors, the mean and variance of reconstructed errors of ADL samples in the evaluation dataset are calculated, and reconstruction errors of all samples are normalized using the mean and variance of training samples. The threshold was determined so that 85% of the ADL samples are always classified as normal samples. An unknown sample is classified as falling if its normalized reconstructed error is larger than a threshold.

For evaluation using unsupervised clustering learning, we used unsupervised classification accuracy:

$$\text{ACC} = \max_{m} \frac{1}{n} \sum_{i=1}^{n} 1\{l_i = m(c_i)\},$$

where l_i denotes the ground-truth label, c_i denotes the cluster assignment, and m denotes possible bijection functions between clusters and labels. Since there are only two classes, fall action data, and ADL data, there are two bijection functions.

4.3   Results and Analysis for Learning of ResVAE

Reconstructed data learned by the ResVAE and difference heatmaps between input data and reconstructed data were shown in Fig. 2. In heatmap images of ADL data shown in Fig. 2(a), it was seen that pixels of the subject and block edges are reconstructed well since motion changes smoothly, and blobs of reconstruction errors were rare. However, in heatmap images of Fig. 2(b), at the falling moment, many blobs of large reconstruction errors were produced, since the pose of falling was a rare case in the training data, and ResVAE cannot reconstruct it well.

As shown in Table 1, in the experiments using imbalanced data, supervised ResNets performed badly, which showed that imbalanced data was fatal for supervised learning. To maintain the balance, a lot of ADL data must be abandoned. The accuracy of supervised learning methods with balanced data sharply increased compared with those with imbalanced data. Since abandoning ADL data was unnecessary for weakly supervised learning methods, ResVAEs had better performance than standard ResNets.

For training and evaluation on different datasets with different persons and situations, the performance of ResVAEs was still better than that of standard ResNets. The ResVAEs showed good generalization ability since the proposed method adopts a kind of weakly supervised learning architecture.

Besides, the result of ResVAE-34 was worse than that of ResVAE-18 when training and evaluating on the same dataset. A possible reason was that ResVAE-34 may need more training for obtaining stable and better performance. Another possible reason was that overfitting happens in ResVAE-34 due to deeper layers.

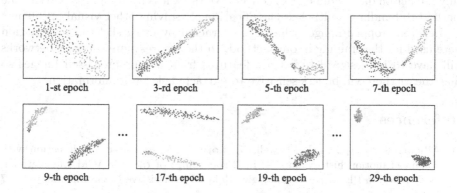

Fig. 3. Visualization results of representation embeddings in the 500-dimensional latent space during clustering learning period.

4.4   Results and Analysis for Learning of FCVAE

Visualization results of representation embeddings learned by FCVAE during clustering learning are shown in Fig. 3. At the beginning (e.g. the first epoch), the boundary of ADL data and fall action data was unclear, and a part of the sample points was mixed up. With training going on, similar representations were continuously gathered, and discrepant representations were continuously made distant. Finally, sample points formed two clear clusters, and classification results were obtained by using a metric of unsupervised classification accuracy.

As shown in Table 1, the proposed network with additional clustering learning that was trained on the HQFD dataset and evaluated on the Le2i dataset obtained a large improvement in the aspect of generalization ability. It was shown that measurements learned by deep neural networks were superior to handcrafted thresholds of reconstruction errors.

5   Conclusion

We proposed a fully-connected VAE (FCVAE) with a combination of weakly supervised learning and unsupervised clustering learning to detect fall actions. The experimental results showed that the proposed method achieved a competitive level of accuracy and better generalization ability compared with supervised learning with well-labeled data. Our method overcame the imbalance between ADL data and fall action data, and obtain good generalization ability when the network is evaluated on different datasets.

6   Future Work

The proposed method can be used in tasks of binary classification. However, not only fall action data is difficult to collect. We think it is meaningful to extend the method to handling multi-class classification for solving other visual problems.

Besides, cropped images which are extracted by using skeleton information were used for the training in our method. In the future, more complex networks will have to be designed to extract features from non-preprocessed images so that the method will be less sensitive to extracted skeleton information.

References

1. Albawendi, S., Appiah, K., Powell, H., Lotfi, A.: Video based fall detection with enhanced motion history images. In: Proceedings of the 9th ACM International Conference on PErvasive Technologies Related to Assistive Environments, pp. 1–7 (2016)
2. Baldewijns, G., Debard, G., Mertes, G., Vanrumste, B., Croonenborghs, T.: Bridging the gap between real-life data and simulated data by providing a highly realistic fall dataset for evaluating camera-based fall detection algorithms. Healthc. Technol. Lett. **3**(1), 6–11 (2016)
3. Bellman, R.E.: Adaptive Control Processes: A Guided Tour. Princeton University Press, Princeton (2015)
4. Berthelot, D., Carlini, N., Goodfellow, I., Papernot, N., Oliver, A., Raffel, C.A.: MixMatch: a holistic approach to semi-supervised learning. In: Advances in Neural Information Processing Systems, vol. 32. Curran Associates, Inc. (2019)

5. Bishop, C.M.: Pattern Recognition and Machine Learning. Springer, Heidelberg (2006)
6. Charfi, I., Miteran, J., Dubois, J., Atri, M., Tourki, R.: Optimized spatio-temporal descriptors for real-time fall detection: comparison of support vector machine and adaboost-based classification. J. Electron. Imaging **22**(4), 041106 (2013)
7. Chong, Y.S., Tay, Y.H.: Abnormal event detection in videos using spatiotemporal autoencoder. In: Cong, F., Leung, A., Wei, Q. (eds.) ISNN 2017. LNCS, vol. 10262, pp. 189–196. Springer, Cham (2017). https://doi.org/10.1007/978-3-319-59081-3_23
8. Dilokthanakul, N., et al.: Deep unsupervised clustering with gaussian mixture variational autoencoders. CoRR (2016)
9. Ester, M., Kriegel, H.P., Sander, J., Xu, X., et al.: A density-based algorithm for discovering clusters in large spatial databases with noise. In: KDD, vol. 96, pp. 226–231 (1996)
10. Fan, Y., Levine, M.D., Wen, G., Qiu, S.: A deep neural network for real-time detection of falling humans in naturally occurring scenes. Neurocomputing **260**, 43–58 (2017)
11. Grandvalet, Y., Bengio, Y.: Semi-supervised learning by entropy minimization. In: Saul, L., Weiss, Y., Bottou, L. (eds.) Advances in Neural Information Processing Systems, vol. 17. MIT Press (2005)
12. Hara, K., Kataoka, H., Satoh, Y.: Learning spatio-temporal features with 3D residual networks for action recognition. In: Proceedings of the IEEE International Conference on Computer Vision Workshops, pp. 3154–3160 (2017)
13. Jiang, Z., Zheng, Y., Tan, H., Tang, B., Zhou, H.: Variational deep embedding: An unsupervised and generative approach to clustering. arXiv preprint arXiv:1611.05148 (2016)
14. Kingma, D.P., Welling, M.: Auto-encoding variational bayes. arXiv preprint arXiv:1312.6114 (2013)
15. Kiran, B.R., Thomas, D.M., Parakkal, R.: An overview of deep learning based methods for unsupervised and semi-supervised anomaly detection in videos. J. Imaging **4**(2), 36 (2018)
16. Lin, C.Y., Wang, S.M., Hong, J.W., Kang, L.W., Huang, C.L.: Vision-based fall detection through shape features. In: Proceedings of the IEEE Second International Conference on Multimedia Big Data (BigMM), pp. 237–240. IEEE (2016)
17. Luxburg, U.V.: A tutorial on spectral clustering (2007)
18. Van der Maaten, L., Hinton, G.: Visualizing data using t-SNE. J. Mach. Learn. Res. **9**(11) (2008)
19. MacQueen, J., et al.: Some methods for classification and analysis of multivariate observations. In: Proceedings of the Fifth Berkeley Symposium on Mathematical Statistics and Probability, Oakland, CA, USA, vol. 1, pp. 281–297 (1967)
20. Min, E., Guo, X., Liu, Q., Zhang, G., Cui, J., Long, J.: A survey of clustering with deep learning: From the perspective of network architecture. IEEE Access **6**, 39501–39514 (2018)
21. Nguyen, V.A., Le, T.H., Nguyen, T.T.: Single camera based fall detection using motion and human shape features. In: Proceedings of the Seventh Symposium on Information and Communication Technology, pp. 339–344 (2016)
22. Nogas, J., Khan, S.S., Mihailidis, A.: Deepfall: non-invasive fall detection with deep spatio-temporal convolutional autoencoders. J. Healthc. Inform. Res. **4**(1), 50–70 (2020)
23. Nunez-Marcos, A., Azkune, G., Arganda-Carreras, I.: Vision-based fall detection with convolutional neural networks. Wirel. Commun. Mob. Comput. **2017** (2017)

24. Xie, J., Girshick, R., Farhadi, A.: Unsupervised deep embedding for clustering analysis. In: International Conference on Machine Learning, pp. 478–487. PMLR (2016)
25. Xu, T., Zhou, Y.: Elders' fall detection based on biomechanical features using depth camera. Int. J. Wavelets Multiresolut. Inf. Process. **16**(02), 1840005 (2018)
26. Zhao, Y., Deng, B., Shen, C., Liu, Y., Lu, H., Hua, X.S.: Spatio-temporal autoencoder for video anomaly detection. In: Proceedings of the 25th ACM International Conference on Multimedia, pp. 1933–1941 (2017)
27. Zhou, J., Komuro, T.: Recognizing fall actions from videos using reconstruction error of variational autoencoder. In: 2019 IEEE International Conference on Image Processing (ICIP), pp. 3372–3376 (2019)

Multi-property Tensor-Based Learning for Abnormal Event Detection

Nikolaos Bakalos[1]([✉]) [iD], Nikolaos Doulamis[1], Anastasios Doulamis[1], and Konstantinos Makantasis[2]

[1] National Technical University of Athens, 15773 Athens, Greece
bakalosnik@mail.ntua.gr
[2] Institute of Digital Games, University of Malta, Msida 2080, MSD, Malta

Abstract. In this paper, we propose a novel abnormal event detection scheme for video surveillance systems using an unsupervised learning process. Our contribution includes intra and inter property feature encoding to reduce information redundancy within (intra) and across (inter) image features. Intra property encoding is carried out using convolutional auto-encoders. Inter-property encoding is performed using an unsupervised tensor-based learning mode to handle the dimensionality issue arising in cases when different properties are inter-related together. Comprehensive experiments are performed on two benchmarks: Avenue, and ShanghaiTech.

Keywords: Abnormal event · Convolutional auto-encoders · Tensor learning

1 Introduction

Abnormal event detection in video surveillance, a process to detect specific frames containing an anomaly, has been drawn a great attention in image processing research mainly due to its advantages in many applications [1–4]. Examples include surveillance in industrial environments [2] or critical infrastructures [3] for safety/security and quality assurance, traffic flow management [4] and intelligent monitoring of public places [5].

Some works address abnormal event detection as a multi-class classification problem under a supervised paradigm [2, 3]. The main, however, limitation of such approaches is that abnormal events sporadically occur in real-world videos. Additionally, what is an abnormal event is vague and tough to model. This means that the distribution of normal versus abnormal events is severely imbalanced which result in low classification performance. One solution to address this issue is to use semi-supervised learning [6, 7]. However, again the problem of data imbalance among normal and abnormal cases cannot be handled. For this reason, the abnormal event detection problem is modeled as *outlier detector*. In particular, the model learns the normality from data samples and then it identifies the abnormal events as the ones which deviate from the normal learnt cases [8–10].

In this context, unsupervised learning has been applied to handle abnormal event detection [11–13]. The methods partition the normal space into coherent clusters in

© The Author(s), under exclusive license to Springer Nature Switzerland AG 2022
G. Bebis et al. (Eds.): ISVC 2022, LNCS 13598, pp. 325–335, 2022.
https://doi.org/10.1007/978-3-031-20713-6_25

contrast to the outlier-detector models that they use a common global model for the whole normal space. Then, the abnormality is detected as those events which cannot be represented by the normal space. Usually, k-means clustering algorithm is utilized (as in [11]) combined with SVM learning.

In this paper, we handle the abnormal event detection problem as an unsupervised learning paradigm. However, the limitations of the current approaches in this field, such as the work of [11], are: i) the number of clusters, that a normal space is partitioned to, is a priori given and ii) the model assumes no interrelations for events across different clusters, conditions that are not valid for real-life cases. To address these difficulties, in this paper, we introduce a framework for intra and inter property (feature) encoding to take into account property interrelations. In addition, a tensor-based unsupervised learning scheme is incorporated to handle the dimensionality issue arising in cases when different properties are inter-related together.

1.1 Related Work

We concentrate on works handling abnormal event detection either as an outlier detection or using deep/unsupervised learning schemes. Regarding outlier detection, the works of [8, 10, 14] learn dictionary of sub-events, through a training process, and then those events that do not lie in the partitioned sub-space are marked as abnormal ones.

Regarding deep learning, the work of [13] employs convolutional auto-encoders (ConvAE) to learn temporal regularity in videos, while auto-encoders are exploited in [15] to learn feature and reconstruct the input images. Then, one-class Support Vector Machines (SVMs) are used for detecting the abnormal events. The work of [16] introduces a hybrid scheme which aggregates ConvAE with Long Short-Term Memory (LSTM) encoder-decoder. Recently, deep generative models have been applied [17–20]. These models are trained to produce normal events while the abnormal ones are given as the difference between the original frames and the generated ones.

Recently, unsupervised learning models are utilized for abnormal event detection. In [21], the anomalies in videos are scored independently of temporal ordering and without any training by simply discriminating between abnormal frames and the normal ones. Other approaches exploit on-line incremental coding [22], deep cascading neural networks [12], and unmasking (a technique previously used for authorship verification in text documents) [23]. Recently, the works of [11, 31, 32] incorporate autoencoders and supervised learning for abnormal event detection. Other approaches employ tracking algorithms to extract salient motion information which is then classified either as normal or abnormal [24, 25]. However, tracking fails in complex visual scenes of multiple humans' presence.

1.2 Our Contribution

Our approach uses a two-fold scheme towards unsupervised abnormal event detection; the *Intra and Inter-Property Encoding*. In this way, we eliminate the correlated information within and across image property features of video frames. Intra property encoding is implemented through auto-encoders as in [11], while a novel tensor-based unsupervised learning model is utilized as far as inter-property encoding is concerned. The current approaches, such as the work of [11], adopts a simple concatenation mechanism for fusing the intra-property compressed latent features. However, such an approach inherently implies that each property representation is independent from each other, an assumption which it is not valid. For example, the gradient property is highly correlated with the appearance as well as the saliency property. To address this difficulty, in this paper, we introduce an alternative approach for fusing the intra-property compressed latent features together using a tensor-based unsupervised learning model. Tensor-based learning i) addresses the assumption that the partitions of the normal event space are a priori known and ii) reduces the dimensionality of space removing the inter-relationships across different properties. Tensor learning compacts the normal space partitioning, increasing the performance and generalization of the abnormal event detection.

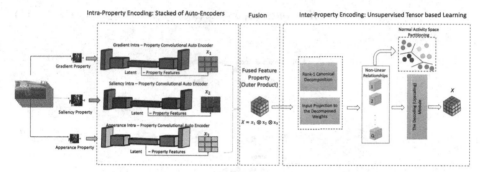

Fig. 1. The proposed twofold architecture for abnormal event detection.

2 Intra/Inter Property Encoding

Figure 1 presents the proposed methodology consisting of two main parts; *the intra and inter property encoding.*

2.1 Intra-property Encoding

The first part of the proposed methodology includes a set of convolutional auto-encoders each associated for an image property. The purpose of these auto-encoders is to reduce the redundant information of a property extracting key property components in a hidden (latent) way. In this paper, three image properties are considered; the appearance, the gradient and the saliency.

The first two property features are in a similar line with previous works such as [11], while saliency property is extracted to make our abnormal event detector more generic to different event types. The Appearance Property consists of the actual frame capturing. The Motion Property captures the movement of objects by taking as input the gradient of the frame. Specifically, batches of 10 frames (current frame plus the previous 9) are used to compute the gradient vector of each frame. Finally, the Saliency Property reflects how likely a window of the frame covers an object of any category. This property creates a saliency map with the same size as the frame that covers all objects in an image in a category independent manner.

2.2 Inter-property Encoding

To generate a reliable partition of the feature space, we need to appropriately combine all into a stacked representation so as to extract inter-property relations. The current approaches such as the work of [11] adopt a simple concatenation mechanism, which implies that each property is independent, an assumption that is not valid in a visual analysis. In this paper, we fuse the intra-property features through the outer product of them. In particular, let us denote as x_i, $i = 1,\ldots,$ N the N compressed (encoded) version of an image property (N $= 3$ in our case). Then, the fused feature is

$$X = outer(x_1, x_2, \ldots, x_N) \tag{1}$$

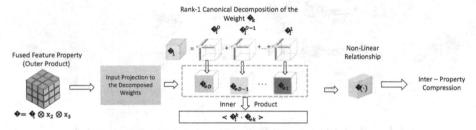

Fig. 2. The tensor-based learning algorithm adopted in the unsupervised tensor-based network

In Eq. (1) function $outer(\cdot)$ implements the outer product operator of the tensors x_i and it produces all possible correlations of the compressed property features, since we are not a priori aware which correlations of the property space should be taken into account. However, this generates quite large tensors of high redundant information, confusing the direct application of an unsupervised clustering (e.g., k-means) for normal space partitioning. To overcome this difficulty, we introduce a novel tensor-based unsupervised learning, with the main purpose of partitioning the normal space based on the fused tensor information X.

3 Tensor-Based Unsupervised Learning for Inter-property Encoding

The inter-property encoding part is also an autoencoder but we now involve non-linear neuron operations instead of convolutions through a tensor-based scheme (see Fig. 2).

3.1 Unsupervised Tensor-Based Learning

Let us assume that we form a neural network-based auto-encoder, in which its inputs/outputs coincide with tensors X. Each neuron implements a non-linear relationship $g(\cdot)$, relied on the sigmoid function. We also assume that we have Q neurons at the hidden layer. The input X is weighted through parameters w_i and the inner product $< w_i, X >$ is given as input to $g(\cdot)$. The response of the i-th hidden neuron is

$$u_i = g(< w_i, X >) \tag{2}$$

weights w_i are tensors since the input X is a hyper-cube.

In Eq. (2), tensor u_i is a transformed version of X at the i-th hidden neuron. The decoder part receives as input the compressed signal u_i and transforms it to an output signal which should be as close as possible to X. In the decoder, tensor u_i are first weighted by parameters v and then are inputted to neurons to generate an estimate $\widehat{X}$ of X.

$$\widehat{X} = < y, g(< v, u_i >) > \tag{3}$$

In Eq. (3), y denotes the parameters that weigh the outputs of the decoder to produce estimates of X. Since the network weights are huge due to the outer product, a tensor-based unsupervised learning is proposed for reducing significantly its parameters and consequently the number of data samples.

3.2 The Rank-1 Canonical Decomposition of Network Parameters

Let us assume that the weights w_i are rank-1 canonically decomposed into the weights $w_i^1, w_i^2, \ldots, w_i^D$, where w_i^D refers to the D-th rank-1 canonical decomposition of the weight w_i [26]. Therefore, we have that

$$w_i = w_i^D \otimes \cdots \otimes w_i^1 \tag{4}$$

In Eq. (4), the $\otimes$ refers to the Kronecker product of the tensors $w_i^1, w_i^2, \ldots, w_i^D$. Using tensor algebra, the inner product of $< w_i \cdot X >$ can be written as

$$< w_i, X > = < w_i^D \otimes \cdots \otimes w_i^1, X > =$$

$$= < w_i^l, X_{\neq l} > \tag{5}$$

where $X_{\neq l}$ is a transformed version of the input signal X independent from the l-th rank-1 canonical decomposition w_i^l. More specifically, the $X_{\neq l}$ is given as

$$X_{\neq l} = X(w_i^D \odot \ldots w_i^{l+1} \odot w_i^{l-1} \cdots \odot w_i^1) \tag{6}$$

In Eq. (6) the $\odot$ denotes the Khatri-Rao product in tensor algebra. Using Eq. (5) and (6) one can re-write the encoding part of Eq. (2) as

$$u_i = g(< w_i, X >) = g(< w_i^l, X_{\neq l} >) \tag{7}$$

In a similar way, we can re-write the decoding part of the network using rank-1 canonical decomposition.

3.3 The Learning Algorithm

Using Eq. (7) we are able to train the network with a significant reduction in the number of its parameters. We initially fix all the weights $w_i^1, w_i^2, \ldots, w_i^D$ apart from the l-th. This way, the transformed version $X_{\neq l}$ is computer from Eq. (6). Then, using the backpropagation algorithm, we update only the weight w_i^l to minimize the error so that network output resembles as much as possible the respective inputs. Therefore, network parameters are solved in an iterative way with respect to one of the D canonical decomposed weight vectors, assuming the remaining fixed [27].

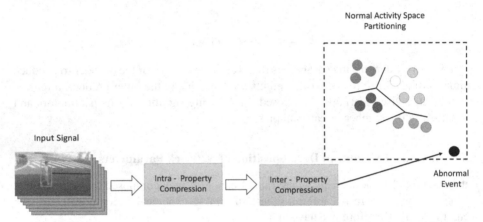

Fig. 3. Our approach for Abnormal Event Detection as outliers of normal space partitioning by the unsupervised tensor learning algoirthm

3.4 Unsupervised Abnormal Event Detection

The output of the encoding part of the unsupervised tensor-based learning module is used to partition the normal activity space into sub-groups. This is depicted in Fig. 3. Therefore, a way for detecting an abnormal event detection compared with a normal activity is to compare the event with respect to its distance to the normal activity space. In case that the reconstructed error with respect to the normal activity subgroups (representing by the tensors u_i) is high the event is considered not normal and therefore abnormal.

4   Experimental Evaluation

The proposed method was tested using two popular benchmarking datasets, namely the Avenue [10] and Shanghai Tech [28]. The Avenue dataset includes 16 training videos and a total of 15,328 frames as well as 21 test videos or 15,324 test frames. For each frame ground truth locations of anomalies are provided. The Shanghai Tech dataset consists of 330 training and 107 testing videos. It contains of about 130 abnormal events.

The proposed method was implemented in Python. The autoencoders that implement the feature extraction (Appearance, Gradient and Saliency) were implemented in Tensorflow and Keras, while the tensor based autoencoder was implemented in PyTorch using the Tensorly library. The hyperparameter optimization of the learning algorithms was determined using the Hyperband optimization method of [29], which employs a principled early-stopping strategy to allocate resources, allowing it to evaluate orders-of-magnitude more configurations than black-box procedures like Bayesian optimization methods [30].

Table 1. Abnormal event detection based on frame level AUC.

Method	Avenue dataset	Shanghai tech dataset	XD-Violence
Lu et al. [10]	80.9	-	-
Hasan et al. [13]	70.2	60.9	-
Del Giorno et al.	78.3	-	-
Smeureanu et al. [31]	84.6	-	-
Ionescu et al. [23]	80.6	-	-
Luo et al. [28]	81.7	68.0	-
Liu et al. [18]	85.1	72.8	-
Liu et al. [32]	84.4	-	-
Sultani et al. [33]	-	76.5	75.68
Wu et al. [34]	-	-	75.41
Tian et al. [35]	-	**97.21**	**77.81**
Ionescu et al. [11]	**90.4**	84.9	-
Our method	86.9	79.8	77.31

The Area Under Curve (AUC) metric was employed in assessing the performance of the proposed method and the compared ones. The AUC is computed with regard to ground-truth annotations at the frame-level and it is a common metric for many abnormal event detection methods. The performance comparison of our method with other implementations is presented in Table 1. As we can see in the table above our outperforms most techniques. [35] reaches a very high AUC score in the ShangaiTech dataset, however, this method does not perform as well across other datasets. [11] performs better in both Avenue and ShangaiTech datasets. However, [11] uses an initial human detection step for preprocessing. This allows only for the detection of abnormalities relevant to specific objects, such as humans, that can be identified by the object detection method, while also introducing a computational overhead as a result of the frame preprocessing. Instead, our approach can be generalized to any type of object classes, such as falling debris, natural disaster detection et which can be seen as abnormal events.

Figure 4 indicates the limitation of [11] in using k-means for normal event space partitioning. It is clear that the number of clusters selected is highly related with the application scenario used. In this figure, we have implemented the approach of [11] without the use of the initial object detection algorithm for different numbers of clusters. This is the reason of why the results are not the same as Table 1, which they have been optimized for a particular dataset. As is observed, the maximum accuracy is achieved for different numbers of clusters between different datasets.

This drawback is also illustrated by the introduction of noise in the input video stream. The multi-property processing and the frame wide analysis of our method results in robustness towards noise introduced to the stream. Such noise can be the result of poor visibility conditions. We have compared our method with a method that resembles the one presented in [11]. It is worth mentioning here that the comparison was done not with the actual model of [11], but rather with an implementation of the method from the paper authors. Figure 5 presents this comparison with our method and [11] in this aspect. The figure illustrates the variance of AUC scores as the input signal's SNR drops. The noise introduced is simple Gaussian noise.

The response of our system to various abnormalities in a test video can be viewed in Fig. 6. In the figure we have averaged the reconstruction errors in batches of 10 frames, for presentation purposes. The frames above are representative of the state captured in the bounding boxes in the graph. The annotation of abnormalities comes from the ground truth dataset.

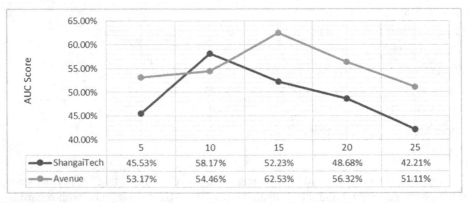

	5	10	15	20	25
ShangaiTech	45.53%	58.17%	52.23%	48.68%	42.21%
Avenue	53.17%	54.46%	62.53%	56.32%	51.11%

Fig. 4. Performance difference between different number of k in the Shangai and Avenue Dataset.

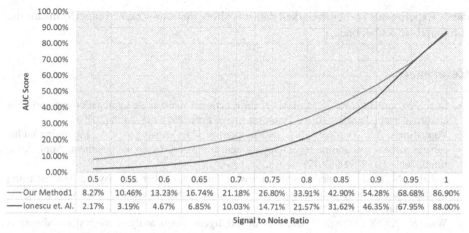

	0.5	0.55	0.6	0.65	0.7	0.75	0.8	0.85	0.9	0.95	1
Our Method1	8.27%	10.46%	13.23%	16.74%	21.18%	26.80%	33.91%	42.90%	54.28%	68.68%	86.90%
Ionescu et. Al.	2.17%	3.19%	4.67%	6.85%	10.03%	14.71%	21.57%	31.62%	46.35%	67.95%	88.00%

Signal to Noise Ratio

Fig. 5. Performance difference between different levels of noise in the video stream, Avenue Dataset.

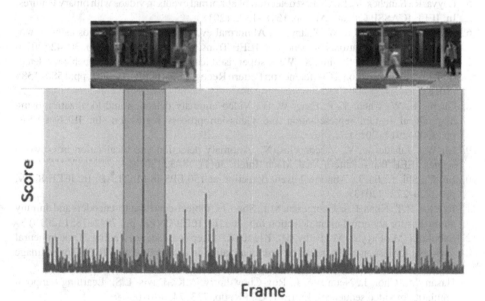

Frame

Fig. 6. Captured abnormalities and system response (Avenue Dataset). Axis x presents the frame batch while axis y represents the average reconstruction error. Above the detected abnormalities the annotated ground-truth data is presented

5 Conclusions

In this paper we introduce a novel method for abnormal event detection in video systems based on an intra/inter property feature information redundancy reduction. Intra property redundancy reduction is carried out using auto-encoders while the inter property one through tensor-based learning to take into account all potential interrelations of them. Experiments on benchmarked datasets show that our scheme outperforms all the compared works but one.

References

1. Lee, S., Kim, H.G., Ro, Y.M.: BMAN: bidirectional multi-scale aggregation networks for abnormal event detection. IEEE Trans. on Image Proc. **29**, 2395–2408 (2020)
2. Voulodimos, A.S., Doulamis, N.D., Kosmopoulos, D.I., Varvarigou, T.A.: Improving multi-camera activity recognition by employing neural network based readjustment. Appl. Artif. Intell. **26**(1–2), 97–118 (2012)
3. Bakalos, N., et al.: Protecting water infrastructure from cyber and physical threats: using multimodal data fusion and adaptive deep learning to monitor critical systems. IEEE Signal Process. Mag. **36**(2), 36–48 (2019)
4. Wan, S., Xu, X., Wang, T., Gu, Z.: An intelligent video analysis method for abnormal event detection in intelligent transportation systems. IEEE Trans. Intell. Transp. Syst. (to be Published)
5. Leyva, R., Sanchez, V., Li, C.: Fast detection of abnormal events in videos with binary features. In: IEEE ICASSP Calgary AB, pp. 1318–1322 (2018)
6. Yan, S., Smith, J.S., Lu, W., Zhang, B.: Abnormal event detection from videos using a two-stream recurrent variational autoencoder. IEEE Trans. Cogn. Dev. Syst. **12**(1), 30–42 (2020)
7. Sun, X., Zhu, S., Wu, S., Jing, X.: Weak supervised learning based abnormal behavior detection. In: 24th International Conference on Pattern Recognition (ICPR), Beijing, pp. 1580–1585 (2018)
8. Cheng, K.-W., Chen, Y.-T., Fang, W.-H.: Video anomaly detection and localization using hierarchical feature representation and Gaussian process regression. In: IEEE CVPR, pp. 2909–2917 (2015)
9. Li, W., Mahadevan, V., Vasconcelos, N.: Anomaly detection and localization in crowded scenes. IEEE Trans. Pattern Anal. Mach. Intell. **36**(1), 18–32 (2014)
10. Lu, C., Shi, J., Jia, J.: Abnormal event detection at 150 FPS in MATLAB. In: IEEE ICCV, pp. 2720–2727 (2013)
11. Ionescu, R.T., Khan, F.S.. Georgescu, M.I., Shao, L.: Object-centric auto-encoders and dummy anomalies for abnormal event detection in video. In: IEEE CVPR, pp. 7842–7851 (2019)
12. Sabokrou, M., Fayyaz, M., Fathy, M., Klette, R.: Deep- cascade: cascading 3D deep neural networks for fast anomaly detection and localization in crowded scenes. IEEE Trans. Image Process. **26**(4), 1992–2004 (2017)
13. Hasan, M., Choi, J., Neumann, J., Roy-Chowdhury, A.K., Davis, L.S.: Learning temporal regularity in video sequences. In: IEEE CVPR, pp. 733–742 (2016_
14. Ren, H., Liu, W., Olsen, S.I., Escalera, S., Moeslund, T.B.: Unsupervised behavior-specific dictionary learning for abnormal event detection. In: Proceedings of the BMVC, pp. 28.1–28.13 (2015)
15. Xu, D., Ricci, E., Yan, Y., Song, J., Sebe, N.: Learning deep representations of appearance and motion for anomalous event detection. In: BMVC (2015)
16. Wang, L., Zhou, F., Li, Z., Zuo, W., Tan, H.: Abnormal event detection in videos using hybrid spatio-temporal autoencoder. In: 25th IEEE International Conference on Image Processing (ICIP), Athens, 2018, pp. 2276–2280 (2018)
17. Ravanbakhsh, M., Nabi, M., Sangineto, E., Marcenaro, L., Regazzoni, C., Sebe, N.: Abnormal event detection in videos using generative adversarial nets. In: IEEE ICIP, pp. 1577–1581 (2017)

18. Liu, W., Luo, W., Lian, D., Gao, S.: Future frame prediction for anomaly detection—A new baseline. In: IEEE CVPR, pp. 6536–6545 (2018)
19. Lee, S., Kim, H.G., Ro, Y.M.: STAN: spatio-temporal adversarial networks for abnormal event detection. In: IEEE ICASSP, pp. 1323–1327 (2018)
20. Sun, C., Jia, Y., Song, H., Wu, Y.: Adversarial 3D convolutional auto-encoder for abnormal event detection in videos. IEEE Transactions on Multimedia, (to be Published)
21. Del Giorno, A., Bagnell, J., Hebert, M.: A discriminative framework for anomaly detection in large videos. In: Proceedings of ECCV, pp. 334–349 (2016)
22. Dutta, J.K., Banerjee, B.: Online detection of abnormal events using incremental coding length. In: Proceedings of AAAI, pp. 3755–3761 (2015)
23. Ionescu, R.T., Smeureanu, S., Alexe, B., Popescu, M.: Un-masking the abnormal events in video. In: IEEE ICCV, pp. 2895–2903 (2017)
24. Mo, X., Monga, V., Bala, R., Fan, Z.: Adaptive sparse representations for video anomaly detection. IEEE Trans. Circuits Syst. Video Technol. **24**(4), 631–645 (2014)
25. Jiang, F., Wu, Y., Katsaggelos, A.K.: A dynamic hierarchical clustering method for trajectory-based unusual video event detection. IEEE Trans. Image Process. **18**(4), 907–913 (2009)
26. Makantasis, K., Doulamis, A.D., Doulamis, N.D., Nikitakis, A.: Tensor-based classification models for hyperspectral data analysis. IEEE Trans. Geosci. Remote Sens. **56**(12), 6884–6898 (2018)
27. Makantasis, K., Doulamis, A., Doulamis, N., Nikitakis, A., Voulodimos, A.: Tensor-based nonlinear classifier for high-order data analysis. In: IEEE International Conference on Acoustics, Speech and Signal Processing (ICASSP), Calgary, AB, 2018, pp. 2221–2225 (2018)
28. W. Luo, W. Liu, and S. Gao. "A Revisit of Sparse Coding Based Anomaly Detection in Stacked RNN Framework. In: Proceedings of ICCV, pp. 341–349 (2017)
29. Li, L., Jamieson, K., DeSalvo, G., Rostamizadeh, A., Talwalkar, A.: Hyperband: a novel bandit-based approach to hyperparameter optimization. J. Mach. Learn. Res. **18**(1), 6765–6816 (2016)
30. Kaselimi, M., et al.: Bayesian-optimized bidirectional LSTM regression model for non-intrusive load monitoring. In: ICASSP 2019–2019 IEEE International Conference on Acoustics, Speech and Signal Processing (ICASSP). IEEE (2019)
31. Smeureanu, S., Ionescu, R.T., Popescu, M., Alexe, B.: Deep appearance features for abnormal behavior detection in video. In: Battiato, S., Gallo, G., Schettini, R., Stanco, F. (eds.) ICIAP 2017. LNCS, vol. 10485, pp. 779–789. Springer, Cham (2017). https://doi.org/10.1007/978-3-319-68548-9_70
32. Liu, Y., Li, C.-L., Poczos, B.: Classifier two-sample test for video anomaly detections. In: Proceedings of BMVC (2018)
33. Sultani, W., Chen, C., Shah, M.: Real-world anomaly detection in surveillance videos. In: Proceedings of CVPR, pp. 6479–6488 (2018)
34. Wu, P., et al.: Not only look, but also listen: learning multimodal violence detection under weak supervision. In: Vedaldi, A., Bischof, H., Brox, T., Frahm, J.-M. (eds.) ECCV 2020. LNCS, vol. 12375, pp. 322–339. Springer, Cham (2020). https://doi.org/10.1007/978-3-030-58577-8_20
35. Tian, Y., Pang, G., Chen, Y., Singh, R., Verjans, J.W., Carneiro, G.: Weakly-supervised Video Anomaly Detection with Robust Temporal Feature Magnitude Learning (2021). arXiv:2101.10030

Depth-Based vs. Color-Based Pose Estimation in Human Action Recognition

Filip Malawski[✉][iD] and Bartosz Jankowski

Institute of Computer Science, AGH University of Science and Technology,
Krakow, Poland
{fmal,bjankows}@agh.edu.pl

Abstract. Recent advances in deep learning resulted in the emergence of accurate models for human pose estimation in color videos. Distance between automatically estimated and manually annotated joint positions is commonly used for the evaluation of such methods. However, from a practical point of view, pose estimation is not a goal by itself. Therefore, in this work, we study how useful are state-of-the-art deep learning pose estimation approaches in a practical scenario of human action recognition. We compare different variants of pose estimation models with the baseline provided by the Kinect skeleton tracking, which, until recently, was the most widely used solution in such applications. We present a comprehensive framework for pose-based action recognition evaluation, which consists of both classical machine learning approaches, including feature extraction, selection, and classification steps, as well as more recent end-to-end methods. Extensive evaluation on four publicly available datasets shows, that by using state-of-the-art neural network models for pose tracking, color-based action recognition matches, or even outperforms, that of the depth-based one.

Keywords: Pose estimation · Human action recognition · Depth modality · Color modality · Kinect

1 Introduction

Automatic human action recognition (HAR) is a widely researched topic in the field of computer vision, due to multiple possible applications in domains such as human-robot and human-computer interaction [14], sports analysis [9] or physical rehabilitation [12]. Early attempts at tracking human motion and recognizing actions from color videos included methods such as background subtraction, estimation of changes between frames (e.g. optical flow), or gradient-based person detection (e.g. histogram of oriented gradients) [20]. Once consumer-level, affordable depth sensors were released on the market, the interest of the scientific community shifted towards depth-based human motion tracking. The Microsoft Kinect sensor became very popular, due to its built-in pose (skeleton) estimation algorithm, which provided 3D positions of 20 joints, in real-time, and with

© The Author(s), under exclusive license to Springer Nature Switzerland AG 2022
G. Bebis et al. (Eds.): ISVC 2022, LNCS 13598, pp. 336–346, 2022.
https://doi.org/10.1007/978-3-031-20713-6_26

reasonable accuracy and robustness. A wide range of methods was proposed for action recognition based on either skeleton estimation alone, or a multimodal combination of the skeleton, color, and depth data [5]. Recently, with extensive development of deep learning, multiple neural network architectures were proposed to accurately estimate pose from color videos, with no need for depth data, making effective HAR possible even with mid-level mobile devices [19].

Pose estimation algorithms are commonly evaluated by comparing joint position estimation to manually prepared ground truth annotations. However, in any practical application, knowing joint positions is only a middle step and not a final goal by itself. Therefore, in this work, we evaluate pose estimation algorithms by their usefulness in the context of one of their main applications, namely action recognition. Instead of focusing on pixel-level metrics, we consider accuracy in distinguishing actions based on provided joint estimations. We compare, in terms of HAR, state-of-the-art pose estimation neural networks using Kinect skeleton tracking as a baseline, given that this was the most widely used consumer-level motion tracking solution, prior to the emergence of deep learning color-based approaches.

In particular we want to answer three research questions regarding HAR applications: 1) Is color-based pose estimation as accurate as depth-based? 2) How much more effective is 3D tracking compared to 2D tracking? 3) How does neural network complexity correspond to the accuracy and efficiency of HAR?

To ensure a fair comparison between pose estimation methods we present a holistic framework for action recognition based on joint positions. Our framework includes both classical machine learning methods, such as feature extraction and selection followed by the classification, as well as end-to-end approaches, such as convolutional or recurrent neural networks. We conduct extensive experiments, comparing HAR accuracy between Kinect skeleton tracking and several variants of two state-of-the-art deep learning pose estimation methods. We perform the evaluation on four publicly available HAR datasets, using multiple machine learning approaches to action classification. We consider employing 3D or 2D only joint positions in order to study the importance of 3D tracking. Finally, we analyze the results in terms of accuracy and efficiency.

2   Related Work

2.1   Pose Estimation

One of the first neural network architectures for pose estimation was Deep-Pose [17], which performed a regression of joint location using a 7-layer convolutional neural network. Moreover, a cascade of pose regressors was proposed by the authors in order to fully capture both the context and the details. PoseNet [11] adapted 22-layer GoogLeNet [16], with six inception modules, for the pose regression task. Authors of [8] proposed DensePose - a model for estimating a 3D surface-based representation of the human body. More recent BlazePose [3] employs an encoder-decoder heat map-based network followed by a regression encoder network, to estimate 33 joint positions in 3D. This model is currently part of the MediaPipe framework.[1] MoveNet is yet another recent solution, employing feature pyramid networks [13] and CenterNet [23], with focus on fast processing.

2.2 Action Recognition

Due to the popularity of the Kinect sensor, many skeleton-based solutions have been proposed for action recognition. EignJoints action descriptor employs differences between joint positions together with principal component analysis [22]. Histograms of oriented joints are used for view-invariant action recognition in [21]. Authors of [1] propose a rate-invariant analysis of skeletal shape trajectories. In [18] joints, edges and surfaces are used as input for a recurrent neural network for learning action representations. Convolutional neural networks are also used to create an efficient representation of skeleton sequences [10].

3 Methods

In this work, we decided to employ and compare against the Kinect baseline two state-of-the-art pose estimators, namely BlazePose and MoveNet. We present a holistic framework for the evaluation of pose estimation algorithms in HAR scenario, to provide a comprehensive comparison.

3.1 Data Loading and Preprocessing

Our pipeline starts with loading and preprocessing the data, followed by optional feature extraction and optional feature selection, and finished with different classification methods, see Fig. 1. Since each of the datasets employed in the experiments (see Sect. 4.1) has a different file structure and naming convention, the data loading layer includes separate modules for loading each dataset. It is followed by pose estimation layer, responsible for computing and caching results from different pose estimators. This is an easily extensible solution, which provides a unified data and metadata format for subsequent stages.

The preprocessing layer allows applying any number of data transformation operations. In this work, we apply three preprocessing steps. The first is to select relevant joints. Estimation of face parts (e.g. eyes or mouth position) is provided by pose estimators, but those would introduce more noise than useful information when used in action recognition, therefore they are filtered out in this stage. Also, at this point, we can decide to use 2D or 3D positions, as well as select joints specifically for the given dataset (e.g. one of the employed datasets considers only lower body parts). The second preprocessing step is to interpolate the estimated joint position sequence to a common length. This is necessary, as most classifiers require fixed-length input. Also, this aids in making the action recognition process robust to different motion speeds. The last step is to take

---

[1] https://google.github.io/mediapipe/solutions/pose.html.

the first derivative of the data (in the time dimension) - we consider velocities instead of positions, in order to make the classification robust to different body structures and different positions of persons in the video frames.

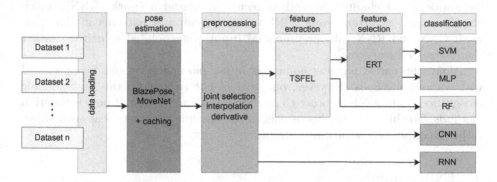

Fig. 1. Architecture of the action recognition framework

3.2   Feature Extraction and Classification

Feature extraction is a crucial step in classical machine learning approaches. While many handcrafted features have been proposed in the literature, those are prone to be scenario-specific. Therefore, for our comparison, we decided to employ an automated approach, in which a large number of features is computed and then filtered with the feature selection process. Time Series Feature Extraction Library (TSFEL) [2] computes 60 different features in statistical, temporal and spectral domains, including wavelet-based features. Two of them (MFCC and LPCC) are audio-specific and therefore those are not used in our experiments. All other features are computed per channel, where a channel is a single component of coordinates of a single joint. E.g. in the case of Kinect pose estimation, there are 20 joints tracked in 3D, which results in 60 channels. Some of the features result in a sequence of values rather than a single value, therefore the final feature vector is large. Depending on the pose estimator, selected joints, and used dimensions (2D/3D) the number of extracted features ranges from 10K to 57K. Such representation carries a substantial redundancy of information, which needs to be reduced before feeding the features to a classifier. Therefore, we employ feature extraction on the basis of extremely randomized trees (ERT) [7]. ERT is an ensemble classifier, that computes feature importance at each step when growing the classification tree. Using min-max normalized importance we select a minimal subset of features for which total importance is at least 0.5. This operation greatly reduces the final feature vector size, which ranges approx. from 200 to 1.7K, while preserving relevant information.

The final step of our pipeline is classification. To make our comparison more comprehensive we consider both classical machine learning classifiers, as well as end-to-end approaches. Full feature extraction and selection are applied when using support vector machines (SVM) and multilayer perceptron (MLP) classifiers. Random forest (RF) classifier employs full feature vector, as it performs feature importance estimation internally, similar to ERT. We consider two end-to-end approaches - 1D convolutional neural network (CNN) which learns 1D convolutions per channel, as well as recurrent neural network (RNN), which employs gated recurrent units (GRU) to find temporal patterns in the data. Both CNN and RNN take preprocessed input (interpolated velocities) rather than extracted features.

Along the entire pipeline numerous hyper-parameters could be optimized with various methods. However, our goal is not to achieve the best possible recognition accuracy, but rather to provide a fair comparison of pose estimation methods. To this end, we choose reasonable baseline parameters at each stage, rather than perform wide optimization.

4 Experiments

4.1 Datasets

In our experiments, we employ four publicly available datasets. Our main requirement for selecting the datasets was that they would include synchronized Kinect and RGB data, with a fully visible single person (multi-pose estimation is not considered in this work). While several action recognition datasets are publicly available, only a small number contains both Kinect and RGB data, and some of those are no longer available or otherwise not usable in our scenario (e.g. one of the considered datasets had only videos with inpainted joint positions). Our final selection includes datasets as described further in this Section. See also Table 1 for more details. All datasets have videos in resolution 640 × 480.

UTD-MHAD [4]. University of Texas at Dallas Multimodal Human Action Dataset contains 27 actions, mostly performed with one or two hands, with a small subset of leg and full body actions. The person is located in the center of the frame, with a mostly clear background.

FFD [15]. Fencing Footwork Dataset contains 6 full-body actions from the fencing training domain. Due to the specifics of the actions only lower-body parts are considered and only in 2D (actions are recorded in side-view). Also, 4 out of 6 actions are different variations of the same exercise, with similar trajectories, but different dynamics. Learning to distinguish between those variations is the main goal of this dataset. The action is performed in the center of the frame, with a mostly clear background.

KARD [6]. Kinect Activity Recognition Dataset contains 18 actions similar to those in the UTD-MHAD dataset - most performed with hands, some including leg or body movement. The person is located in the center of the image, with clear background.

Table 1. Datasets summary (A - number of actions, P - number of persons, R - number of repetitions of action per person)

Name	A	P	R	Actions
UTD-MHAD	27	8	4	Right arm swipe to the left, Right arm swipe to the right, Right hand wave, Two hand front clap, Right arm throw, Cross arms in the chest, Basketball shoot, Right hand draw x, Right hand draw circle (clockwise), Right hand draw circle (counter clockwise), Draw triangle, Bowling (right hand), Front boxing, Baseball swing from right, Tennis right hand forehand swing, Arm curl (two arms), Tennis serve, Two hand push, Right hand knock on door, Right hand catch an object, Right hand pick up and throw, Jogging in place, Walking in place, Sit to stand, Stand to sit, Forward lunge (left foot forward), Squat (two arms stretch out)
FFD	6	10	11	Step forward, Step backward, Rapid lunge, Incremental speed lunge, Lunge with waiting, Jumping-sliding lunge
KARD	18	10	3	Horizontal arm wave, High arm wave, Two hand wave, Catch Cap, High throw, Draw X, Draw Tick, Toss Paper, Forward Kick, Side Kick, Take Umbrella, Bend, Hand Clap, Walk, Phone Call, Drink, Sit down, Stand up
UT-Kinect	10	10	2	Walk, Sit down, Stand up, Pick up, Carry, Throw, Push, Pull, Wave hands, Clap hands

UT-Kinect [21]. University of Texas Kinect-Action3D Dataset contains 10 actions including full body and hand motion. The person is located in different parts of the image and moves around in some actions. Also, the background is cluttered, which may constitute a challenge for color-based pose estimation.

4.2 Evaluation Protocol

As stated in Sect. 3 we decided to compare the Kinect with two state-of-the-art pose estimators, namely BlazePose, which has a total of six variants, and MoveNet, which has two variants. BlazePose has three basic variants - Lite, Heavy and Full - each with better accuracy than the previous, but at the cost of longer computation time. Those can run either in static mode, in which each frame is processed separately, or non-static mode, in which information from the previous frame is used for tracking in order to decrease the computation time. BlazePose estimates 33 joint positions in 3D. MoveNet has two variations, Lightning - the faster, but a less accurate one, and Thunder - slower, but more accurate. It estimates only 17 joints in 2D. Our reference, the Kinect, estimates 20 joints in 3D. See Table 2 for more details.

All datasets were evaluated using leave-one-person-out cross-validation, thus each experiment run included n folds (n equal to the number of subjects in the dataset), and in each fold, one subject was used for validation and all other were used for training. Scores presented in this Section are accuracy metric averaged over all folds.

As described in Sect. 3.2 no systematic hyper-parameter search was performed, as this was not the goal of this study. Instead, reasonable set of hyper-parameters was manually selected, based on our previous experience. SVM classifier has regularization parameter $C = 1$ and employs radial basis function (RBF) kernel, with $\gamma = 1/(n * v)$, where $n =$ number of features and $v =$ variance of the training samples. MLP has two hidden layers with sizes 64 and 32. RF creates 100 trees with no depth limit, using Gini impurity to measure the split quality. CNN has two blocks, each containing two 1D convolutional layers followed by 1D max-pooling layer. The first block has layers with 32 filters, and the second one with 64 filters. The two blocks are followed by a dense layer with a size of 64. RNN has a single GRU layer with 32 filters followed by a dense layer with a size of 64.

4.3   Results

The comparison of pose estimators in terms of tracked joints and processing time is presented in Table 2. Times were measured on a PC with Intel Core i5 2.5 GHz processor. The Kinect pose estimation is performed on the Kinect device, therefore time per frame does not apply, however, pose data is provided with 30 frames per second.

Results for each dataset are presented in: Table 3 (UTD-MHAD), Table 4 (FFD), Table 5 (KARD) and Table 6 (UTKinect). Pose estimator versions are abbreviated as follows: MedaPipe: (L) Lite, (LS) Lite static, (H) Heavy, (HS) Heavy static, (F) Full, (FS) Full static; MoveNet (L) Lightning, (T) Thunder. The *feat.* column denotes the number of selected features, which is relevant only for SVM and MLP classifiers. Best results per dimensionality (2D/3D) are indicated with boldface.

4.4   Discussion

In experiments with the UTD-MHAD dataset best action recognition accuracy (0.92) for both the 2D and the 3D scenarios was obtained with the Full BlazePose estimator and SVM classifier (equally with the MLP for the 3D case), little over the Kinect baseline (0.89 for 2D and 0.91 for 3D). Lighter BlazePose models performed almost as well as the Full, still outperforming the Kinect in the 2D case. Moreover, 2D estimation was sufficient, as 3D tracking provided little to no improvement in most cases. MoveNet pose estimations proved to be significantly less efficient for action recognition (best accuracy 0.81).

Regarding the FFD dataset only 2D tracking was considered, as actions are recorded from side-view and depth estimation is irrelevant. Kinect pose estimation with SVM classifier outperformed all other approaches, obtaining accuracy

Table 2. Pose estimators - tracked joints and processing time

Pose estimator	Variant	Time per frame (ms)	Frames per sec.	Num. of joints	Joints
Kinect		n/a	30	20	Head, Spine, Shoulder center, Shoulders, Elbows, Wrists, Hands, Hip center, Hips, Knees, Ankles, Feet
BlazePose	Lite	43	23	33	Nose, Eyes, Ears, Mouth, Shoulders, Elbows, Wrists, Pinky fingers, Index fingers, Thumbs, Hips, Knees, Ankles, Heels, Feet index fingers
	Lite Static	94	10.5		
	Heavy	65	15.5		
	Heavy St	112	9		
	Full	229	4.5		
	Full Static	280	3.5		
MoveNet	Lightning	45	22	17	Nose, Eyes, Ears, Shoulders, Elbows, Wrists, Hips, Knees, Ankles
	Thunder	135	7.5		

Table 3. UTD-MHAD dataset action recognition accuracy

Pose estimator	2D						3D					
	Feat.	SVM	MLP	RF	CNN	RNN	Feat.	SVM	MLP	RF	CNN	RNN
Kinect	1147	0.89	0.89	0.86	0.84	0.81	1097	0.91	0.91	0.89	0.87	0.84
BlazePose L	1053	0.91	0.89	0.88	0.86	0.76	1205	0.91	0.89	0.89	0.81	0.50
BlazePose Ls	1136	0.91	0.87	0.88	0.83	0.68	1320	0.90	0.89	0.88	0.75	0.27
BlazePose H	999	0.90	0.90	0.89	0.87	0.79	1094	0.90	0.90	0.88	0.80	0.48
BlazePose Hs	1069	0.91	0.88	0.87	0.88	0.71	1223	0.90	0.91	0.88	0.75	0.36
BlazePose F	963	0.90	0.90	0.89	0.85	0.79	1045	0.90	0.91	0.91	0.82	0.42
BlazePose Fs	1002	**0.92**	0.90	0.89	0.85	0.73	1122	**0.92**	**0.92**	0.89	0.79	0.16
MoveNet L	1719	0.68	0.67	0.67	0.56	0.21	–	–	–	–	–	–
MoveNet T	1350	0.76	0.81	0.81	0.78	0.54	–	–	–	–	–	–

Table 4. FFD dataset action recognition accuracy

Pose estimator	2D					
	Feat.	SVM	MLP	RF	CNN	RNN
Kinect	287	**0.84**	0.81	0.78	0.77	0.72
BlazePose L	380	0.78	0.75	0.75	0.71	0.56
BlazePose Ls	384	0.79	0.77	0.75	0.72	0.56
BlazePose H	342	0.79	0.78	0.77	0.71	0.65
BlazePose Hs	349	0.80	0.79	0.76	0.70	0.62
BlazePose F	319	0.80	0.80	0.76	0.73	0.62
BlazePose Fs	317	0.79	0.78	0.75	0.71	0.62
MoveNet L	619	0.71	0.68	0.70	0.59	0.41
MoveNet T	509	0.75	0.72	0.71	0.61	0.44

Table 5. KARD dataset action recognition accuracy

Pose estimator	2D						3D					
	Feat.	SVM	MLP	RF	CNN	RNN	Feat.	SVM	MLP	RF	CNN	RNN
Kinect	524	0.97	**0.98**	0.96	0.92	0.72	518	0.98	0.98	0.97	0.95	0.76
BlazePose L	539	0.97	**0.98**	0.97	0.92	0.84	555	0.97	0.98	0.96	0.91	0.62
BlazePose Ls	617	0.97	0.96	0.96	0.95	0.79	651	0.97	0.96	0.96	0.86	0.49
BlazePose H	515	0.96	0.97	0.96	0.92	0.86	538	0.97	0.97	0.96	0.90	0.61
BlazePose Hs	567	0.97	0.97	0.96	0.92	0.84	600	0.98	0.97	0.96	0.87	0.47
BlazePose F	529	0.97	**0.98**	0.96	0.94	0.86	521	0.98	**0.99**	0.96	0.89	0.53
BlazePose Fs	581	0.97	0.97	0.96	0.94	0.83	585	0.98	0.98	0.96	0.89	0.36
MoveNet L	817	0.87	0.88	0.87	0.78	0.47	–	–	–	–	–	–
MoveNet T	665	0.91	0.94	0.93	0.88	0.73	–	–	–	–	–	–

Table 6. UTKinect dataset action recognition accuracy

Pose estimator	2D						3D					
	Feat.	SVM	MLP	RF	CNN	RNN	Feat.	SVM	MLP	RF	CNN	RNN
Kinect	415	**0.90**	0.89	0.83	0.74	0.78	385	0.89	0.90	0.87	0.77	0.85
BlazePose L	495	0.78	0.81	0.74	0.65	0.63	511	0.78	0.82	0.81	0.53	0.36
BlazePose Ls	545	0.78	0.81	0.77	0.65	0.64	556	0.77	0.85	0.80	0.43	0.23
BlazePose H	438	0.75	0.79	0.77	0.71	0.63	454	0.82	0.88	0.82	0.60	0.28
BlazePose Hs	528	0.76	0.83	0.78	0.65	0.58	535	0.78	0.87	0.85	0.50	0.33
BlazePose F	458	0.79	0.83	0.76	0.71	0.65	469	0.83	0.88	0.83	0.59	0.29
BlazePose Fs	489	0.80	0.86	0.81	0.69	0.67	499	0.85	**0.92**	0.83	0.54	0.35
MoveNet L	621	0.68	0.74	0.69	0.39	0.24	–	–	–	–	–	–
MoveNet T	556	0.78	0.82	0.73	0.43	0.44	–	–	–	–	–	–

0.84, while best BlazePose result was 0.80. Since this dataset focuses on distinguishing similar actions on the basis of dynamics rather than trajectories, a possible explanation is that the Kinect skeleton tracking is more stable. Again, MoveNet was less efficient (best accuracy 0.75), however with a smaller gap than the one observed in the UTD-MHAD results.

KARD dataset experimental results indicate that BlazePose and Kinect pose estimations are equally well suited for recognizing actions, both obtaining close to perfect results with MLP classifier (Kinect 0.98 for 2D and 3D, BlazePose 0.98 and 0.99 accordingly). MoveNet falls behind with the best accuracy of 0.94 obtained with the Thunder variant.

UTKinect dataset proved to be more difficult for the color-based pose estimators, probably due to the cluttered background and more movement present in the videos. Results obtained with BlazePose and MoveNet pose estimations are generally worse than those obtained on the basis of Kinect, however, the highest accuracy (0.92) was actually achieved with the BlazePose Full static variant. The best accuracy of the Kinect-based approach is 0.90, while that of MoveNet-based is only 0.82.

Considering all experiments, color-based pose estimation performed very well. BlazePose pose estimation obtained the highest accuracy in 3 out of 4 datasets. We can observe, that factors that are challenging for color-based approaches are motion dynamics and cluttered background. There is little difference in action recognition accuracy based on 2D and 3D joint positions, even though the 3 datasets that employed 3D positions contained together over 50 actions. We can expect that for some actions depth estimation will be relevant, however, those will probably be rare in most practical scenarios. Also, we can observe that lighter variants of the BlazePose estimator in most scenarios perform almost as well as the full one, even though their processing is much faster. In all experiments, end-to-end approaches were inferior to the classical machine learning methods. This is most likely due to the low sizes of the datasets, as well as the relatively simple architectures of the employed CNN and RNN. In terms of processing times, BlazePose Lite and MoveNet Lightning both achieve close to real-time performance, with 22–23 frames per second (target would be 30, as this is the frame rate in most consumer-level cameras). It is worth noting, that further processing of the joint positions is very fast, due to the low amount of data (up to 33 joints in 2D or 3D), therefore there is almost no additional computational overhead introduced by the action recognition itself.

5 Conclusions

In this work, we presented a study of color-based pose estimation in action recognition. Our holistic framework provided a comprehensive evaluation of different pose estimators and their variants, using the Kinect as a baseline. To conclude answers to the research questions stated in Sect. 1: 1) state-of-the-art color-based pose estimation performs equally well as depth-based one (and sometimes even better) in the HAR context, 2) 2D tracking is as effective as 3D tracking for most actions, 3) lighter variants of the BlazePose estimator are much faster, yet almost as effective as the Full one. However, MoveNet proved to be less useful for HAR, even with the more accurate Thunder variant.

Acknowledgements. The research presented in this paper was supported by the National Centre for Research and Development (NCBiR) under Grant No. LIDER/37/0198/L-12/20/NCBR/2021.

References

1. Amor, B.B., Su, J., Srivastava, A.: Action recognition using rate-invariant analysis of skeletal shape trajectories. IEEE Trans. Pattern Anal. Mach. Intell. **38**(1), 1–13 (2015)
2. Barandas, M., et al.: TSFEL: time series feature extraction library. SoftwareX **11**, 100456 (2020)
3. Bazarevsky, V., Grishchenko, I., Raveendran, K., Zhu, T., Zhang, F., Grundmann, M.: BlazePose: on-device real-time body pose tracking. arXiv preprint arXiv:2006.10204 (2020)
4. Chen, C., Jafari, R., Kehtarnavaz, N.: UTD-MHAD: a multimodal dataset for human action recognition utilizing a depth camera and a wearable inertial sensor. In: 2015 IEEE International Conference on Image Processing (ICIP), pp. 168–172. IEEE (2015)

5. Chen, C., Jafari, R., Kehtarnavaz, N.: A survey of depth and inertial sensor fusion for human action recognition. Multimed. Tools Appl. **76**(3), 4405–4425 (2017)
6. Gaglio, S., Re, G.L., Morana, M.: Human activity recognition process using 3-D posture data. IEEE Trans. Human-Mach. Syst. **45**(5), 586–597 (2014)
7. Geurts, P., Ernst, D., Wehenkel, L.: Extremely randomized trees. Mach. Learn. **63**(1), 3–42 (2006)
8. Güler, R.A., Neverova, N., Kokkinos, I.: DensePose: dense human pose estimation in the wild. In: Proceedings of the IEEE Conference on Computer Vision and Pattern Recognition, pp. 7297–7306 (2018)
9. Host, K., Ivašić-Kos, M.: An overview of human action recognition in sports based on computer vision. Heliyon, e09633 (2022)
10. Ke, Q., Bennamoun, M., An, S., Sohel, F., Boussaid, F.: A new representation of skeleton sequences for 3D action recognition. In: Proceedings of the IEEE Conference on Computer Vision and Pattern Recognition, pp. 3288–3297 (2017)
11. Kendall, A., Grimes, M., Cipolla, R.: PoseNet: a convolutional network for real-time 6-DoF camera relocalization. In: Proceedings of the IEEE International Conference on Computer Vision, pp. 2938–2946 (2015)
12. Liao, Y., Vakanski, A., Xian, M.: A deep learning framework for assessing physical rehabilitation exercises. IEEE Trans. Neural Syst. Rehabil. Eng. **28**(2), 468–477 (2020)
13. Lin, T.Y., Dollár, P., Girshick, R., He, K., Hariharan, B., Belongie, S.: Feature pyramid networks for object detection. In: Proceedings of the IEEE Conference on Computer Vision and Pattern Recognition, pp. 2117–2125 (2017)
14. Lou, M., Li, J., Wang, G., He, G.: AR-C3D: action recognition accelerator for human-computer interaction on FPGA. In: 2019 IEEE International Symposium on Circuits and Systems (ISCAS), pp. 1–4. IEEE (2019)
15. Malawski, F., Kwolek, B.: Recognition of action dynamics in fencing using multimodal cues. Image Vis. Comp. **75**, 1–10 (2018)
16. Szegedy, C., et al.: Going deeper with convolutions. In: Proceedings of the IEEE Conference on Computer Vision and Pattern Recognition, pp. 1–9 (2015)
17. Toshev, A., Szegedy, C.: DeepPose: human pose estimation via deep neural networks. In: Proceedings of the IEEE Conference on Computer Vision and Pattern Recognition, pp. 1653–1660 (2014)
18. Wang, H., Wang, L.: Beyond joints: learning representations from primitive geometries for skeleton-based action recognition and detection. IEEE Trans. Image Proc. **27**(9), 4382–4394 (2018)
19. Wang, J., et al.: Deep 3D human pose estimation: a review. Comput. Vis. Image Underst. **210**, 103225 (2021)
20. Weinland, D., Ronfard, R., Boyer, E.: A survey of vision-based methods for action representation, segmentation and recognition. Comput. Vis. Image Underst. **115**(2), 224–241 (2011)
21. Xia, L., Chen, C., Aggarwal, J.: View invariant human action recognition using histograms of 3D joints. In: 2012 IEEE Computer Society Conference on Computer Vision and Pattern Recognition Workshops(CVPRW), pp. 20–27. IEEE (2012)
22. Yang, X., Tian, Y.: Effective 3D action recognition using EigenJoints. J. Vis. Commun. Image R **25**(1), 2–11 (2014)
23. Zhou, X., Wang, D., Krähenbühl, P.: Objects as points. arXiv preprint arXiv:1904.07850 (2019)

Cross-Domain Learning in Deep HAR Models via Natural Language Processing on Action Labels

Konstantinos Bacharidis[1,2]([⊠])[iD] and Antonis Argyros[1,2][iD]

[1] Computer Science Department, University of Crete, Heraklion, Greece
{kbacharidis,argyros}@csd.uoc.gr
[2] Foundation for Research and Technology - Hellas, Heraklion, Greece
{kbach,argyros}@ics.forth.gr

Abstract. Nowadays, deep learning approaches lead the state-of-the-art scores in human activity recognition (HAR). However, the supervised nature of these approaches still relies heavily on the size and the quality of the available training datasets. The complexity of activities of existing HAR video datasets ranges from simple coarse actions, such as sitting, to complex activities, consisting of multiple actions with subtle variations in appearance and execution. For the latter, the available datasets rarely contain adequate data samples. In this paper, we propose an approach to exploit the action-related information in action label sentences to combine HAR datasets that share a sufficient amount of actions with high linguistic similarity in their labels. We evaluate the effect of inter- and intra-dataset label linguistic similarity rate in the process of a cross-dataset knowledge distillation. In addition, we propose a deep neural network design that enables joint learning and leverages, for each dataset, the additional training data from the other dataset, for actions with high linguistic similarity. Finally, in a series of quantitative and qualitative experiments, we show that our approach improves the performance for both datasets, compared to a single dataset learning scheme.

Keywords: Human action recognition · Natural language processing · Deep learning · Video understanding

1 Introduction

In recent years deep learning has become the dominant learning direction in several research fields, including computer vision. Human activity recognition (HAR) is one of its challenging sub-fields, with a wide range of applications from Human-Robot Collaboration (HRC) and assistive technologies for daily living, to surveillance and entertainment. Deep learning models have dominated the field due to their high representational power, long-range temporal modelling capacity, as well as their end-to-end training capabilities. The majority of these models rely on a supervised learning process, with the most powerful ones requiring large-scale datasets with diverse video content and action/activity sets, especially for layer-related hard optimization cases, such as 3D convolutional

G. Bebis et al. (Eds.): ISVC 2022, LNCS 13598, pp. 347–361, 2022.
https://doi.org/10.1007/978-3-031-20713-6_27

filter-based ones. However, the number of publicly available large-scale HAR datasets is rather small. The most common workaround to improve performance and generalization on small-scale datasets is to exploit a model that has been trained on large-scale image or video recognition datasets, such as ImageNet [9] or Kinetics [4], as a generic feature extractor and only train a shallow temporal model on the target dataset [14], or fine-tune the entire spatio-temporal model [11,26], a concept known as *transfer learning*.

Another direction is to consider action category commonalities between dataset pairs, and apply a joint learning scheme (*multi-task learning*) for the two action domains [21], leveraging of additional data for the class set that lies in the shared label space, referred as *supervised Domain Adaptation (DA)* [30]. The evaluation of the contribution of this learning tactic is carried out in carefully selected dataset pairs that fulfill the criteria of having a sufficient number of common action classes and similar motion and appearance characteristics, in order to constrain the distribution gap due to the *domain shift*. In the existing literature, there exists only a limited number of such dataset pairs, which are defined via manual evaluation of the aforementioned attributes [5,7]. Under this premise, the development of a generalized framework for automatically evaluating the potential compatibility of two or more datasets, is an interesting but still unaddressed research direction. Our work is an attempt to tackle this problem, with a flexible and interpretive domain adaptation-oriented dataset association process based on label linguistic similarities for the considered datasets.

2   Related Work

Cross-Domain Learning in Action Recognition: aims at reducing the distribution gap between the feature spaces of the considered domains through joint modelling. To achieve this, existing works have incorporated feature distribution similarity measures, such as the Kullback-Leibler (KL) divergence, and the Maximum Mean Discrepancy (MMD), along with the task of image [2,17], video classification [5,31]. Expanding on the task of action recognition, a set of deep learning works, instead of only relying on distribution similarity error metrics, attempt to reduce the domain gap at feature level, by introducing domain alignment layers that consider batch-level statistics and cross-domain batch contamination strategies [3,21] in their designs of a cross-dataset HAR learning deep model, which operates on the concatenated label set of the datasets.

Dataset Association: has been considered in numerous works, as a means to increase the generalization of models, expand the supported label space, and handle imbalanced datasets [22,27]. In the contexts of video cross-domain learning and DA, existing works have combined dataset pairs with a range of approaches. These approaches include simple strategies, such as formulating a new dataset comprised of the union of the label sets [21] or re-annotating the labels of the second dataset following the annotation protocol of the first [15]. Delving into the task of DA, a set of works considers only common actions between datasets

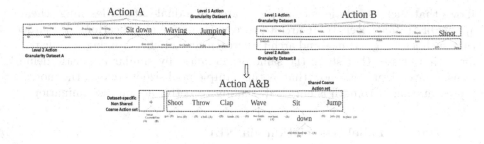

Fig. 1. Hierarchical action label decomposition in coarse, fine action levels via verb-POS analysis. Datasets: *MHAD (A), J-HMDB (B)*

to define the basis in which the shared latent subspace is defined [12,25]. This set of common action classes can be further expanded by grouping semantically similar action labels, considering notions such as word semantic similarity and lexical hierarchy. These linguistic associations are usually exploited indirectly via the inherent linguistic knowledge of the annotators, either in the form of direct relabelling of the source dataset to the target [5], or, to provide annotations regarding linguistic and semantic relations between the two label sets [28]. The advantage of the second approach is that these intermediate annotations allow to further analyze the characteristics of the datasets, to compute the general relevance score between the datasets, as well as to generation of a range of dataset label fusions, by considering stronger or weaker label associations.

Different from these works, our work does not utilize annotators for the derivation of the linguistic similarity between the labels, but instead exploits the word semantic similarities and relations from large lexical databases, such as WordNet [19], to define and control the strength of the label associations. In addition, by exploiting dataset relevance statistics, in a similar basis with the work of Yoshikawa et al [28], we are able to evaluate the resulting association. Finally, we investigate the impact of the cross-dataset linguistic similarity rate requirements and single dataset inter-class linguistic label sentence correlation rate on the potential performance gain in a HAR deep model design that exploits the joint label space in a multi-task learning scheme. The core design direction for this model follows the principles of HAR-oriented DA models, and can be related with the work of Bousmalis et al. [2], in that we also follow a combined dataset-wise (private) and shared subspace learning scheme. In addition, compared to [2] despite mitigating the problem of cross-domain knowledge transfer to the task of action recognition, our model design aims to learn discrete representations for both datasets and their respective action sets (*multi-task learning*).

3   Proposed Method

The proposed method provides a framework for the relation of video HAR datasets based on the linguistic similarities of their label sentences. Our work shows that such associations can be exploited in a dual-dataset learning scheme applicable to any deep HAR architecture with minor modifications. We argue that such learning schemes and architectures access a richer training sample pool for action classes that share the same or semantically similar linguistic definitions. Our experiments show that as this sample pool size increases, the model's representational strength is enriched, leading to better action discrimination.

3.1   Dataset Label Association via NLP

The proposed method pipeline operates as follows. First, we present the NLP tools utilized in the computation of label linguistic similarity, and, a label decomposition process that provides an interpretive and precise definition of the linguistic association between action labels. This process transforms the label set of each dataset into two action granularity-based label sets, (a) a *coarse-grained* action set, consisting of simple verb-based labels that denote the common action motif between a set of associated actions (for the actions *get the cup* and *get the bottle*, coarse label is the verb *get*), and, (b) a *fine-grained* action set, with the initial labels enriched with coarse-grained membership information. Subsequently, we present a process to define association rules between a dataset pair and highlight key elements and assumptions of this dataset relation process.

Dataset-Wise Label Association and Hierarchical Decomposition: In our recent work [1] we presented an NLP-assisted label sentence analysis approach to define a two-level action tree hierarchy from a given set of action labels, either focusing on a specific part-of-speech (POS) or by exploring the semantic relations between the entire label (via word-ordering & semantic content similarities) relying on the work of Yuhua Li et al. [16]. In this work, we also follow a verb-POS action label direction to group semantically similar labels based on verb commonalities, or high verb semantic content similarity.

For the latter case, we evaluate the semantic relation between the verbs of the label sentences based on two metrics. The first metric expresses the semantic relation as defined within the WordNet [19] semantic knowledge base. We define the verb semantic similarity rate between a label pair by thresholding the normalized (to $[0, 1]$) length of the shortest path between the word (verb) nodes relatively to the common word-ancestor node, as defined in WordNet, following the direction of Redmon and Farhadi [22]. The second metric follows a more simplified direction and directly compares the word embeddings of the two words (verbs), generated via the Word2Vec [18] embedding model, using the cosine similarity metric. We found that combining these metrics best expresses the relation between the label sentences in terms of verb semantic content similarity.

Given the detected label associations we can define a two-level action hierarchy based on the verb semantic similarities between the action classes. The first action tree level, consists of a set of coarse action classes, defined by the *shared* verbs,[1] indicating the presence of a common coarse motion pattern between the related actions. The second level contains the fine-grained action classes, belonging to the dataset's original set, enriched with info regarding the *coarse* class to which each fine-grained label has been clustered. We should mention that a more complex hierarchy could surface more informative clues,[2] however more complex semantic relation trees are scheduled to be explored in the future.

Inter-dataset Label Association: In a similar fashion, to associate a dataset pair, we utilize NLP to identify action labels that are common or exhibit high semantic similarity, focusing only on the verb POS sets (coarse classes), and fuse the two action trees into a shared, two-level action tree hierarchy. The first level now contains a set of coarse action classes that correspond to the verb-POS elements that are shared between the class sets of the dataset pair, indicating a similar coarse action primitive, as well as the remaining unique coarse classes of both datasets. The second level consists of the fine-grained classes for which a coarser action class was defined. Figure 1 shows a simplified illustration.

In more detail, for a pair of datasets A, B, with isolated verb label sets noted as T_A and T_B, we define the shared coarse action label set C, with the verbs-POS of the labels k, l in A, B, whose verbs are the same, $T_A \cap T_B$, or, (a) the relative path length in WordTree between $verb_k \in T_A, verb_l \in T_B \leq 0.5$, and (b) the cosine similarity between $verb_k \in T_A, verb_l \in T_B \geq 0.9$. The gains for each dataset from this formulation depend on the portion of action labels for each dataset that are shared. A simple, intuitive criterion to define the dataset label set fusion compatibility, is to set thresholds on the minimum portion of labels of each dataset that needs to be included in the shared, coarse label set. Based on this, we can define the label set compatibility for the dataset pair as follows:

Criterion for Assessing the Dataset Label Set Compatibility: $|C \cap T_A| \geq t_1|T_A|$ *and* $|C \cap T_B| \geq t_2|T_B|$ *conditioned that* $\frac{t_1+t_2}{2} \geq t_3$, *with* $t_1, t_2, t_3 \in (0, 1]$.

The parameters t_1, t_2, t_3 determine the required degree of similarity between the two datasets in order to consider the content of their action sets as correlated. Thresholds t_1, t_2, express the portion of the dataset's class set that is encapsulated in the generated *coarse* action class set C. The degree of the overall dataset pair similarity rate is expressed with t_3. The higher the t_3 value, the larger becomes the requirement for the datasets to exhibit higher label semantic associations. With that in mind, we can define levels for the dataset association power (*low, partial, high*) by setting dataset-appropriate values for t_3. For this purpose in our experiments we evaluated the aspect of inter-dataset compatibility by defining the dataset association levels, (a) $t_3 < 0.3$ - *low*, (b) $0.3 < t_3 < 0.6$ - *partial*, and, (c) $0.6 < t_3 < 0.9$ - *high*, with $t_3 = 1$ signifying full association.

---

[1] For associated labels with different verbs, with high semantic similarity, the verb of 1st label is used as a coarse label.

[2] For example, we could add a level that defines associations based on nouns, referring to the presence of common objects in different actions.

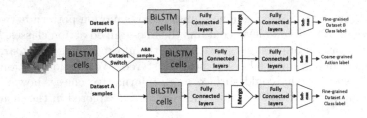

Fig. 2. Baseline BiLSTM DNN for dual-dataset learning. Batch consists of both dataset samples. Each sample contains also a scalar $\in [0, 1]$, indicating dataset membership.

The Importance of Intra-dataset Label Similarity: The information gain from the fusion of two datasets will be higher as the amount of associated classes increases. A factor that affects the gain is the dataset-wise intra-class label similarity. Ideally, a high label relation threshold (high cosine similarity, short-length paths between words in WordTree) guarantees that only labels with close semantic contents are associated, and exploit the coarser representation knowledge that is acquired from this learning scheme. However, it is interesting to examine the effect of subtle linguistic relations between labels that have been included in the shared set, and the ones that were not. To express this in *set theory*, for the two datasets A and B, and their shared action set C, we define the relative complement of B in A as $A_D : (T_A - T_B)$, and the one of A in B as $B_D : (T_B - T_A)$. Our goal is to assess the performance of the dataset association learning scheme based on the degree of the lexical similarity between the labels in A_D and the ones in C, and, in similar fashion, for B_D and C. In a similar factor assessment direction to the one described for the dataset fusing compatibility, in our experiments we examine the effect of the linguistic similarity rate between the intersection C, and non-intersection, A_D (or B_D) sets, under the same three association levels (*no, partial, high*). In addition, since it is difficult to find different dataset pairs that satisfy these conditions, we design a simple algorithm which, given the requested association condition, splits the MPII Cooking Activities [23], into two subsets whose label sets satisfy the requirements. Details in the next section.

3.2   Dual-Dataset Learning Deep Architecture

We now present design directions, applicable to the majority of HAR DNNs, that allow the utilization of the dataset association scheme in a dual-dataset learning format, improving the model's performance on one or both datasets.

The simplest HAR DNN design that allows the support of a dual-dataset learning functionality is to merge the datasets into a new expanded action set, $A \cup B$, and classify an input sequence to the unified action label set. In this work we propose a DNN structure, that mimics the hierarchical action decomposition and dataset relation scheme that we defined earlier. It is a triple-branch DNN design (Fig. 2), consisting of two distinct sub-nets assigned to model each dataset and an additional sub-net that handles the spatio-temporal modelling of the shared coarser actions. Moreover, skip connections introduce the learned coarse-grained representation as complementary information in the fine-grained sub-nets, guiding them to learn representations towards finer action details.

Regarding the objective function, the network learns a shared representation of two different distributions, thus, we need to evaluate the learned representation for the shared coarse action labels. For this we follow the guidelines of cross-domain learning approaches and use the Maximum Mean Discrepancy (MMD) loss [10] to compute the marginal distribution between the domain distributions. The loss function to be minimized is defined as:

$$L = L_{task} + L_{MMD}(Gen, Fine_A) + L_{MMD}(Gen, Fine_B), \tag{1}$$

where L_{task} refers to the classification problem between the coarse and fine action classes, and L_{MMD} refers to the MMD domain distribution distance loss. In detail, the classification loss is defined as the cross-entropy loss for the two action granularities (coarse, fine):

$$L_{task} = - \sum_{k=0}^{K} T_k^{gen} log\left(Y_k^{gen}\right) - \sum_{i=0}^{1} \sum_{j=0}^{J} w_{i,j} T_{i,j}^{fine} log\left(Y_{i,j}^{fine}\right), \tag{2}$$

with (a) the w_i vector denoting the dependencies between the fine-grained action classes of the dataset i (details in [1]), T^{gen} denoting the ground-truth labels for the joint coarse-grained action set, (c) T_i^{fine} being the ground-truth fine-grained labels for dataset i, and, (d) (Y^{gen}, Y_i^{fine}) being the estimated action classes for the coarse- and the fine-grained action sets for dataset i.

The L_{MMD} loss, is actually the summation of two MMD losses, between the learned shared distribution and each dataset-specific learned distribution. Intuitively, regarding the two design directions, the first is simpler to define and learns a mapping from both input domains to the distinct concatenated output label set. However, HAR model of this design can be harder to train. The reason can be thought as a potential combination of, a) model capacity inadequacy due to the fine-grained label space significant expansion, and, b) label cases with similar characteristics combined with data scarcity, resulting in weaker representations for each class that easily lead to mis-classifications.

3.3   Factors that Affect Learning

The performance of cross-domain and dataset fusion learning such as the one we propose, is affected by a number of factors. The most important one that affects the efficiency of learning in HAR datasets is the differentiation in the dataset characteristics, such as whether the actions are performed in a constrained or unconstrained environment, under a fixed or with multiple viewing angles, the presence of moving objects in the background etc. In HAR cross-domain learning and domain-adaptation setups, the examined datasets share similar action characteristics and are defined under more controlled conditions, such as environments with static scenes with minimal background motions and noise. This allows for the impact on the representation difference to be smaller since the appearance feature manifold is more constrained. To further restraint the effect of such elements, in our experiments we limit the processing area in the actor's region, removing any background information that may induce a negative affect.

A consequence of the aforementioned domain-related differences between the datasets is the distance between the learned representational sub-space in the feature manifold to which the action set of each dataset is mapped to. Ideally, when working with an action set consisting of the union of the label sets, for the cases of actions that are shared, or associated via linguistic similarities, we expect the learned representations to be mapped closely in feature space. However, in the appearance domain (RGB), variations in the background or in the actor/object characteristics can expand the feature representation subspace of each action and increase the representation gap between actions with similar coarse motion motifs (take a bottle and grab a glass). To constrain the representation gap for such cases we can work with high-level representation spaces, such as optical flow (OF) or pose-based feature representations. In our experiments we also follow this direction by utilizing OF data of, (a) *the entire scene*, (b) *human body part regions*.

4   Experimental Setup

We evaluate the benefits and constraints of the proposed learning and DNN design scheme on three known HAR datasets of ranging action complexity. The first dataset pair consists of the Berkeley's MHAD [20] (11-classes) and J-HMDB [13] (21-classes) datasets. The specific dataset pair shares a number of six coarser classes. The coarser action set for this dataset pair consists of (a) the common coarser classes for both datasets, (b) the remainder of the coarser action classes for the dataset A (MHAD), and, (c) the remainder of the coarser action classes for the dataset B (J-HMDB). A simplified illustration is shown in Fig. 1.

The third dataset that has been explored is Max Planck's Cooking dataset (MPII Cooking Activities [23]), which is used to better understand the significance and impact of the similarity rate on the proposed learning scheme. Specifically, it's action label size and complexity as well as the high inter-class similarity (appearance&motion characteristics) between its action label set makes it ideal to serve as the experimental basis for evaluating the inter- and intra-dataset cases, presented in Sect. 3.1. To adjust MPII Cooking to this format, we designed a simple algorithmic process that splits the dataset into two subsets that satisfy the specifications of different scenarios of inter- and intra-dataset label linguistic similarity. Details are presented in the next subsection.

For the reported scores, for MPII and J-HMDB, we report the accuracy score on split-1, whereas for MHAD, we follow the provided train/test scheme. Regarding input sources, we focus on the OF domain, and consider two feature design strategies, (a) OF estimates on the actor's region, and, (b) OF estimates on distinct body-parts of the actor. OF data were generated with TV-L1 [29].

4.1   Inter- and Intra-dataset Evaluation

To evaluate the notions in Sect. 3.1, instead of searching for dataset pairs that satisfy the inter- and intra-dataset similarity cases, we manually construct them. For this, we designed a simple algorithmic pipeline that splits MPII Cooking Activities into two subsets $MPII_A$, $MPII_B$, that satisfy a specified configuration for inter- and intra-dataset label linguistic similarity.

To decouple the inter- and intra-dataset similarity factors and assess their impact, the algorithmic process[3] contains two functionality sets:

Inter-dataset: generate random splits of the dataset class set into two subsets, under the condition that the similarity rate between class sets of the two subsets satisfies the required threshold, t_3. To evaluate the satisfaction of the requested inter-dataset similarity, we estimate the inter-dataset similarity score. For this, we identify the verb-POS of the labels that have been assigned to each subset and compare them using the metrics presented in Sect. 3.1. The achieved score is evaluated based on t_3. If the threshold is not satisfied the process is repeated.

Intra-dataset: To evaluate intra-dataset similarity for each of the possible similarity rate scenarios, the initial step of the dataset splitting algorithm is to define an intersecting class set $MPII_C$, and then proceed to gradually add the non-intersecting classes to each subset, checking after each insertion the satisfaction of the conditions of each case. This format allows for all generated splits for each condition to share the same common coarse action set, in order to exclude the impact of this factor from the assessment.

The examined association scenarios for the non-intersecting subsets of $MPII_A$, $MPII_B$, noted as $MPII_{A_D}$, $MPII_{B_D}$, with the intersection $MPII_C$, are:

(1) $MPII_{A_D}$, $MPII_{B_D}$ with a relative large portion of labels with high similarity with the ones in $MPII_C$,

(2) $MPII_{A_D}$, $MPII_{B_D}$ with a relative small portion of labels with high similarity with the ones in $MPII_C$,

(3) $MPII_{A_D}$ with a large portion of labels with high similarity with the ones in $MPII_C$, and, $MPII_{B_D}$ a low,

(4) $MPII_{B_D}$ with a large portion of labels with high similarity with the ones in $MPII_C$, and, $MPII_{A_D}$ a low.

In detail, the process begins with the construction of the label self-similarity matrix (LSM), by computing the pairwise cosine similarity of their respective word-embeddings. Based on the LSM scores, we select the N most similar label pairs, and use them as the basis for the intersection label set, $MPII_C$, assigning from each pair, $label_i$ in subset $MPII_A$, and, $label_j$ in $MPII_B$. The rest of the labels, $MPII - MPII_C$ serve as the label pool to construct $MPII_{A_D}$, $MPII_{B_D}$.

---

[3] The process utilizes the label set, and, the respective word embeddings.

Table 1. Performance difference between a single dataset (NM), and, a dual dataset (M) DNN designs. Inputs are OF frame sequences. For MPII, splits are A-31 classes, B-33 classes, with intersection similarity rate of 0.38, leading to 11 coarse classes.

Architecture	Datasets Acc.%, Input: OF			
Design	$MHAD/JHMDB$		$MPII_A/MPII_B$	
NM-lstm	60.18	38.75	28.17	29.65
M-lstm	**63.59**	**41.87**	**36.45**	**29.74**
NM-I3D [4]	86.37	49.89	47.05	48.33
M-I3D	**90.67**	49.58	46.62	**49.83**

This process involves first clustering these labels, using k-means, based on the linguistic similarity of their verb-POS with the verb-POS of the labels in $MPII_C$, which allows the detection of the labels with the most impact on the intra-dataset similarity scores, $\mathbf{Sim}(MPII_{A_D}, MPII_C)$, $\mathbf{Sim}(MPII_{B_D}, MPII_C)$. For each label in each cluster, we use LSM to find each most similar label in the same cluster, and, in $MPII_C$. We assign each of the two labels to the subset, whose label in $MPII_C$ exhibits the highest similarity with it. After all non-intersecting labels have been assigned to one of the subsets, we compute the intra-dataset similarity scores to evaluate their satisfaction. If the requested thresholds are unsatisfied, we randomly select one label from the clusters with the highest dissimilarity and assign the label to the opposite subset, and, recompute the similarity rates. The process repeats until the goal constraints are satisfied.

4.2   Feature Extraction

For optical flow (OF), 16-OF frame sequences were used for the I3D network. Contrary, for the case of the Bi-LSTM based architecture, the OF frames were fed to VGG-16 [24]. We then extracted 2D feature maps from the last 2D layer, resulting in a frame-wise feature tensor of 7-by-7-by-512 for the sequence. For the second input modality, we follow the work of Chéron et al [6], to generate frame-wise CNN-based features for the actor's right hand, left hand, upper body, full body and full image regions, utilizing the positions of body joints. This results in frame-wise 5×4096 feature maps. The final descriptor formulation stage of PCNN [6] involves a feature map aggregation scheme, that defines a *spatial descriptor* for each part by computing minimum and maximum values for this part following a *max* and *min* pooling scheme, leading to a 1×512 feature vector for each part per frame, and finally concatenating the resulting body part *spatial descriptors*. In this work we consider motion attributes by using OF as input.

4.3   Temporal Modelling Architectures

For the evaluation of the proposed DNN directions, we compared baseline single-dataset architectures to their modified proposed dual-dataset versions.

Table 2. Action recognition performance for the MHAD, JHMDB and MPII datasets between a single dataset (NM), and, a dual dataset (M) DNN designs, d refers to the usage of the MMD loss besides cross-entropy. Input source pose OF features [6].

| Architecture | Datasets Acc.%, Input: Body-part OF | | | |
Design	$MHAD/JHMDB$		$MPII_A/MPII_B$	
NM-lstm	75.18	42.28	32.48	38.33
M-lstm	70.89	47.43	30.39	31.54
M-lstm$_d$	**80.31**	**55.29**	**36.02**	**39.14**

Table 3. Inter-dataset similarity threshold and accuracy. Random split of MPII Cooking under a inter-dataset similarity requirement t_3. At each scenario we generate a new splitting of MPII into $MPII_A$ and $MPII_B$ datasets, C contains $MPII_A \cap MPII_B$.

| Threshold | MPII Acc.%, Input: Body-Part OF | | |
Value	Subsets (A/B)	C	Acc. %
NM-lstm	37/27	–	**25.50**/30.00
$t_3 < 0.3$, M-lstm$_d$	37/27 (0.2)	14	20.62/**30.87**
NM-lstm	31/33	–	32.48/38.33
$t_3 \in (0.3, 0.6)$, M-lstm$_d$	31/33 (0.38)	11	**36.02/39.14**
NM-lstm	53/11	–	21.04/48.98
$t_3 > 0.6$, M-lstm$_d$	53/11 (0.72)	10	**23.84/55.37**

Baseline BiLSTM DNN and Modification: we design a two-layer BiLSTM net with three Fully-Connected (FC) top layers, with activation functions, Leaky ReLU x2 and soft-max for classification. Inputs are frame-wise deep embeddings. To support dual-dataset learning, the modifications involve the use of a BiLSTM layer as a shared temporal modelling layer between the datasets, followed by decoupling into three sub-nets tasked with representation learning for datasets A, B, and, *set C of coarse classes*. In detail, the coarse-level sub-net consists of a BiLSTM layer followed by a two-level FC layer set, with Leaky ReLU and soft-max. This sub-net generates probability distribution estimates for coarse-grained classes. Contrary, the fine-grained sub-nets consist of a BiLSTM layer followed by a three-FC layer set, with the first two using Leaky ReLU and dropout, and the last a soft-max. The second FC layer input is the concatenation of the feature maps of the first FC layers of the coarse and the dataset-specific sub-net.

I3D [4] and Modification: We maintain the original design up until the last receptive field up-sampling layer-block, using the pre-trained weights on ImageNet [8] and Kinetics [4], and fine-tune the last layers on the new datasets. The design modifications to support the dual-dataset learning scheme, follow the same coarse- and fine-grained sub-network structural principles as previous with the difference of replacing BiLSTM with Conv3D layers.

Table 4. Dataset-wise intra-class linguistic similarity impact. Random split of MPII Cooking with $t_{Ssim} = 0,34$. A, B refer to $MPII_A, MPII_B$, C to $MPII_A \cap MPII_B$.

Threshold	MPII Acc.%, Input: Body-part OF	
Value	# classes of (A/B/C)	Acc.
A/B	7/57	37.30/21.01%
Intra-Case 1	7 (0.32)/ 57 (0.31)/ 4	**44.69/23.15**%
A/B	31/33	21.39/23.72%
Intra-Case 2	31(0.54)/ 33 (0.33)/ 4	**25.83/30.51**%
A/B	29/35	23.63/25.24%
Intra-Case 3	29(0.52)/ 35(0.38)/ 4	**30.09/29.32**%
A/B	10/54	43.38/20.12%
Intra-Case 4	10 (0.33)/ 54 (0.46)/ 4	**55.18/24.89**%

5   Experimental Results

The first set of experiments, shown in Tables 1 and 2, illustrate the contribution of a dual-dataset learning strategy, relying on the label-centered linguistic fusion and action decomposition methodology. We can observe that for both modalities and architecture variations there is a clear benefit, with improvements in accuracy reaching up to 9%. An additional observation is that the BiLSTM-based DNN appears to benefit the most, with improvements being observed in both datasets and modalities. Contrary, the proposed design scheme in an I3D-based model, appears to assist recognition on the small-sized subsets, following the observed learning trend reported in existing dual-dataset learning works [21]. It is noted that in this experimental setup, MHAD has 9 training samples/class (a single view was used), compared to J-HMDB that has around 3–4 times more samples/class. For MPII Cooking, for the specific split, $MPII_B$ has on average 44 samples/class, as opposed to the 47 of $MPII_A$. We aim to publicly release the MPII splits created for intra-dataset evaluation.

MMD Loss Contribution: Table 2 presents the contribution of the distribution adaptation part of the objective function. We observe that for the body part OF modality the inclusion of this term is crucial for the success of the proposed method, improving recognition accuracy on both datasets.

Inter-dataset Label Similarity Rate: In Table 3 we present our findings on the role of the inter-dataset label similarity rate on the proposed learning strategy effectiveness. The results on 3 split versions of the MPII Cooking that satisfy each case (*low, partial, high* relation), show that for the proposed method to be beneficial, the pair has to show partial to high label set linguistic association.

Intra-dataset Label Similarity Rate: In Table 4 we present our findings on the role of the intra-dataset label similarity rate. The obtained results for the 4 identified scenarios (see Sect. 4.1), indicate that the presence of subtle linguistic similarities between the labels in the intersecting and non-intersecting subsets of a dataset, appear to affect the contribution of the proposed dataset fusion and joint learning scheme. This can be observed from the fact that the inclusion of new labels (in the smaller dataset A), that have high similarity with the labels in the intersecting subset, leads to a decrease in the recognition accuracy.

6   Conclusions and Discussion

We proposed an approach to fuse HAR datasets pairs by exploiting NLP to identify linguistic similarities on the label sets. To exploit such associations, we designed a DNN to allow joint dataset learning, leveraging the dataset association knowledge under a multi-task learning scheme. We evaluated parameters that control its effectiveness like the intra-dataset label similarity. Our method positively affects the performance of HAR DNNs, however its effectiveness requires careful consideration of dataset characteristics and label linguistic similarity.

An aspect of the method open for discussion is the context information locality in Word2Vec's embeddings and the fact that WordTree represents general notions of word semantics. As such, they do not encode semantic relations between a word and other parts-of-speech that co-exist in a sentence. Word2Vec relies on local statistics, incorporates the local context information of the neighboring words to the target word, defined within the corpus. This can lead to semantic context ambiguities, with words associated to different semantic interpretations. In simpler action datasets, this is not an issue as the label sentence length and semantic context is constrained and simplified. However, for fine-grained datasets larger sentences and multiple verbs/nouns are encountered. Thus, a global word context relationship will lead to more informative embeddings. Non-local embedding methods or DNNs with text sequential ordering and long-range dependency modelling mechanisms will be ideal for label similarity evaluation in such datasets. We aim to explore such methods to enrich the semantic context our method considers.

Acknowledgments. This research work was supported by the Hellenic Foundation for Research and Innovation (HFRI) under the "1st Call for H.F.R.I Research Projects to support Faculty members and Researchers and the procurement of high-cost research equipment", project I.C. Humans, number 91. The authors also gratefully acknowledge the support of NVIDIA Corporation with the donation of a GPU.

References

1. Bacharidis, K., Argyros, A.: Improving deep learning approaches for human activity recognition based on natural language processing of action labels. In: 2020 International Joint Conference on Neural Networks (IJCNN), pp. 1–8 (2020)
2. Bousmalis, K., Trigeorgis, G., Silberman, N., Krishnan, D., Erhan, D.: Domain separation networks. In: Lee, D., Sugiyama, M., Luxburg, U., Guyon, I., Garnett, R. (eds.) Advances in Neural Information Processing Systems, vol. 29 (2016)
3. Carlucci, F.M., Porzi, L., Caputo, B., Ricci, E., Bulo, S.R.: Autodial: automatic domain alignment layers. In: 2017 IEEE International Conference on Computer Vision (ICCV), pp. 5077–5085. IEEE (2017)
4. Carreira, J., Zisserman, A.: Quo vadis, action recognition? A new model and the kinetics dataset. In: CVPR, pp. 6299–6308. IEEE (2017)
5. Chen, M.H., Kira, Z., AlRegib, G., Yoo, J., Chen, R., Zheng, J.: Temporal attentive alignment for large-scale video domain adaptation. In: Proceedings of the IEEE/CVF International Conference on Computer Vision, pp. 6321–6330 (2019)
6. Chéron, G., Laptev, I., Schmid, C.: P-CNN: pose-based CNN features for action recognition. In: ICCV, pp. 3218–3226. IEEE (2015)
7. Csurka, G.: Domain adaptation for visual applications: a comprehensive survey. arXiv preprint arXiv:1702.05374 (2017)
8. Deng, J., Dong, W., Socher, R., Li, L.J., Li, K., Fei-Fei, L.: ImageNet: a large-scale hierarchical image database. In: CVPR. IEEE (2009)
9. Deng, J., Dong, W., Socher, R., Li, L.J., Li, K., Fei-Fei, L.: ImageNet: a large-scale hierarchical image database. In: 2009 IEEE Conference on Computer Vision and Pattern Recognition, pp. 248–255. IEEE (2009)
10. Gretton, A., Borgwardt, K.M., Rasch, M.J., Schölkopf, B., Smola, A.: A kernel two-sample test. J. Mach. Learn. Res. **13**(25), 723–773 (2012)
11. Hara, K., Kataoka, H., Satoh, Y.: Learning spatio-temporal features with 3D residual networks for action recognition. In: Proceedings of the IEEE International Conference on Computer Vision Workshops, pp. 3154–3160 (2017)
12. Jamal, A., Namboodiri, V.P., Deodhare, D., Venkatesh, K.: Deep domain adaptation in action space. In: BMVC, vol. 2, p. 5 (2018)
13. Jhuang, H., Gall, J., Zuffi, S., Schmid, C., Black, M.J.: Towards understanding action recognition. In: ICCV, pp. 3192–3199. IEEE (2013)
14. Karpathy, A., Toderici, G., Shetty, S., Leung, T., Sukthankar, R., Fei-Fei, L.: Large-scale video classification with convolutional neural networks. In: Proceedings of the IEEE conference on Computer Vision and Pattern Recognition (2014)
15. Li, A., Thotakuri, M., Ross, D.A., Carreira, J., Vostrikov, A., Zisserman, A.: The AVA-kinetics localized human actions video dataset. arXiv preprint arXiv:2005.00214 (2020)
16. Li, Y., McLean, D., Bandar, Z.A., Crockett, K., et al.: Sentence similarity based on semantic nets and corpus statistics. IEEE Trans. Knowl. Data Eng. **8**, 1138–1150 (2006)
17. Long, M., Wang, J., Ding, G., Sun, J., Yu, P.S.: Transfer feature learning with joint distribution adaptation. In: 2013 IEEE International Conference on Computer Vision, pp. 2200–2207 (2013). https://doi.org/10.1109/ICCV.2013.274
18. Mikolov, T., Chen, K., Corrado, G., Dean, J.: Efficient estimation of word representations in vector space. arXiv preprint arXiv:1301.3781 (2013)
19. Miller, G.A.: WordNet: a lexical database for English. Commun. ACM **38**(11), 39–41 (1995). https://doi.org/10.1145/219717.219748

20. Ofli, F., Chaudhry, R., Kurillo, G., Vidal, R., Bajcsy, R.: Berkeley MHAD: a comprehensive multimodal human action database. In: IEEE WACV. IEEE (2013)
21. Perrett, T., Damen, D.: DDLSTM: dual-domain LSTM for cross-dataset action recognition. In: Proceedings of the IEEE/CVF Conference on Computer Vision and Pattern Recognition, pp. 7852–7861 (2019)
22. Redmon, J., Farhadi, A.: YOLO9000: better, faster, stronger. In: Proceedings of the IEEE Conference on Computer Vision and Pattern Recognition, pp. 7263–7271 (2017)
23. Rohrbach, M., Amin, S., Andriluka, M., Schiele, B.: A database for fine grained activity detection of cooking activities. In: CVPR, pp. 1194–1201. IEEE (2012)
24. Simonyan, K., Zisserman, A.: Very deep convolutional networks for large-scale image recognition. arXiv preprint arXiv:1409.1556 (2014)
25. Sultani, W., Saleemi, I.: Human action recognition across datasets by foreground-weighted histogram decomposition. In: Proceedings of the IEEE Conference on Computer Vision and Pattern Recognition, pp. 764–771 (2014)
26. Tran, D., Wang, H., Torresani, L., Ray, J., LeCun, Y., Paluri, M.: A closer look at spatiotemporal convolutions for action recognition. In: Proceedings of the IEEE Conference on Computer Vision and Pattern Recognition, pp. 6450–6459 (2018)
27. Yao, Y., Wang, Y., Guo, Y., Lin, J., Qin, H., Yan, J.: Cross-dataset training for class increasing object detection. arXiv preprint arXiv:2001.04621 (2020)
28. Yoshikawa, Y., Shigeto, Y., Takeuchi, A.: MetaVD: a meta video dataset for enhancing human action recognition datasets. Comput. Vis. Image Underst. **212**, 103276 (2021)
29. Zach, C., Pock, T., Bischof, H.: A duality based approach for realtime TV-L^1 optical flow. In: Hamprecht, F.A., Schnörr, C., Jähne, B. (eds.) DAGM 2007. LNCS, vol. 4713, pp. 214–223. Springer, Heidelberg (2007). https://doi.org/10.1007/978-3-540-74936-3_22
30. Zhang, J., Li, W., Ogunbona, P., Xu, D.: Recent advances in transfer learning for cross-dataset visual recognition: a problem-oriented perspective. ACM Comput. Surv. (CSUR) **52**(1), 1–38 (2019)
31. Zhang, X.Y., Shi, H., Li, C., Zheng, K., Zhu, X., Duan, L.: Learning transferable self-attentive representations for action recognition in untrimmed videos with weak supervision. In: AAAI, vol. 33, pp. 9227–9234 (2019)

Computer Graphics

Visualizing Data Flows in Computer Graphics Programs for Code Comprehension and Debugging

Ying Zhu[✉]

Georgia State University, Atlanta, USA
yzhu@gsu.edu

Abstract. OpenGL is the most widely used API and programming language in college-level computer graphics courses. However, OpenGL programs are difficult to comprehend and debug because they involve programming for both CPU and GPU and the data transfer between them. Modern OpenGL is a complex data flow machine with multiple programmable stages, and it is difficult to trace the partially hidden data flows in the source code written in C++, OpenGL, and OpenGL Shading Language. We have developed a web-based data visualization tool to analyze OpenGL source code and generate interactive data flow diagrams from the source code. The diagrams can help novice programmers build clear mental images of complex data flows. The source code viewer and the data flow diagram are synchronized so that a user can select an OpenGL API call, and the corresponding component in the data flow diagram is highlighted, and vice versa. A programmer can visually step through the data flows and detect specific bugs that are otherwise difficult to find. The main contribution of this paper is an interactive learning tool for computer graphics education.

Keywords: Software visualization · Debugging · Code comprehension · Computer graphics · Computer science education

1 Introduction

Real-time 3D graphics programming is essential to virtual reality, augmented reality, CAD, scientific visualization, game development, and visual simulations. Computer graphics applications can be developed with high-level tools such as game engines (e.g., Unity and Unreal) or low-level programming languages and APIs such as OpenGL [36], Direct3D [26], Vulkan [37], and Metal [3]. Among them, shader-based OpenGL is the most commonly taught programming language in college-level computer graphics courses [6].

College students generally consider OpenGL programming difficult to learn. There are several reasons for this. First, a real-time computer graphics program is a parallel program that runs on both CPU and GPU. Therefore, an OpenGL programmer needs to write code for two different processors and handle the data

© The Author(s), under exclusive license to Springer Nature Switzerland AG 2022
G. Bebis et al. (Eds.): ISVC 2022, LNCS 13598, pp. 365–376, 2022.
https://doi.org/10.1007/978-3-031-20713-6_28

transfer between them. Second, OpenGL is a low-level language that requires programmers to implement many low-level details such as data transfer from CPU to GPU, 3D transformations, lighting, texture mapping, etc.

Third, OpenGL is a complex data flow machine with multiple programmable stages [2], but data flows in an OpenGL program are not always explicitly expressed in the source code. Many data flows are created by multiple OpenGL API calls that are difficult to understand. Data connections are often based on implicit connections between API calls. In addition, there can be multiple ways to transfer the same type of data from CPU to GPU. Some parts of the data flows are hidden and can only be understood by a deep understanding of the 3D graphics pipeline and the OpenGL language. A subtle error in data flow construction can cause the program to malfunction without warning messages. 3D graphics debugging tools are also not very helpful in detecting data flow errors. An experienced 3D graphics programmer may be able to mentally connect these low-level details to create a mental picture of data flows, but novice computer graphics programmers often have difficulty making such connections. As a result, students find OpenGL programs difficult to understand and debug, particularly data flows between a CPU and a GPU.

There is a lack of tools to support OpenGL learning. Most computer graphics courses were taught using traditional methods, such as textbooks, PowerPoint slides, websites, and PDF documents. Innovative learning tools are needed to address some of the difficulties discussed above. This is the primary motivation for this project.

To help students better understand and debug 3D graphics programs, we have developed a web-based, interactive visualization tool for creating data flow diagrams in OpenGL programs through static code analysis. The diagrams provide a clear view of both the explicit and hidden data flows, helping students construct a mental model of the program's data flows. The source code viewer and the interactive data flow diagram are synchronized so that a student can select an OpenGL API call, and the corresponding component in the data flow diagram will be highlighted, and vice versa. The data flow diagrams serve as an instructional scaffolding technique to help students understand the sophisticated source code. Using these diagrams, a programmer can visually step through the data flows and detect certain bugs that are otherwise difficult to find.

2   Related Work

2.1   OpenGL in Computer Science Education

There are many programming languages or libraries for 3D graphics programming. OpenGL [36] is a cross-platform programming language and API specification for computer graphics. WebGL [38] is a variation of OpenGL for web-based applications. In this paper, we use the term OpenGL to cover both OpenGL and WebGL. Vulkan [37] is the successor of OpenGL as the cross-platform industry standard but is much more complicated to learn and code. Direct3D [26] is the 3D graphics library developed by Microsoft for Windows and Xbox platforms.

Metal [3] is a 3D graphics library developed by Apple for Mac computers, iPads, and iPhones.

We collected and analyzed 30 publicly accessible online syllabi of undergraduate computer graphics courses taught in North American universities within the last six years (2017–2022). The course titles are Computer Graphics, Introduction to Computer Graphics, Interactive Computer Graphics, and Fundamentals of Computer Graphics.

The survey showed that shader-based OpenGL is the most widely taught programming language (GLSL) and library (OpenGL API) in college-level computer graphics courses. They were taught in 19 of the 30 courses we surveyed. The other courses used C, Java, or Python but did not use any graphics programming libraries. Vulkan was briefly introduced in one course. Direct3D and Metal were not taught in any of the courses we surveyed. This finding is consistent with an earlier survey by Balreira, et al. [6]. Based on this survey, we decided to focus on analyzing and visualizing OpenGL programs.

2.2 Program Comprehension and Debugging

Previous studies have shown that there is very little correspondence between the ability to write a program and the ability to read one, and therefore both need to be taught [35]. An essential skill for code comprehension is code tracing, which is also important for debugging [25]. Debugging and code tracing are among the most challenging issues for students learning programming [25,35].

Previous studies have also shown that creating proper mental models is important for program comprehension [8] and debugging [30]. A study by Fix et al. [16] showed that experts had more sophisticated mental models than novices and could use them more effectively to debug programs. One of the most influential theories for program comprehension is the two-phase theory by Pennington [31]. Based on this theory, programmers go through two phases to understand a program. Programmers first develop a mental model about the program's control flow and then a mental model about the program's data flow. Visualization can help novice programmers build such models. For example, the study by Navarro-Prieto and Canas [28] showed that visual data flow programming could help build mental models for data flow.

2.3 Benefits of Program Visualization for Code Comprehension and Debugging

Based on the software visualization taxonomy by Price, et al. [34], the proposed visualization belongs to the category of program visualization and the sub-category of data flow visualization (B.1.2 in [34]).

Many previous studies have shown that software visualization can help program comprehension and debugging [4,5,12,14,15,17,18,20,22–24,29,39]. For example, Nguyen, et al. [29] showed that a Callflow diagram can help improve the comprehension of parallel programs. Jacobs, et al. [19] and Pilskalns, et al. [32] used reverse engineered UML diagrams to help debugging.

Although there are many visual data flow programming languages, there are relatively few program visualization tools for data flow analysis and very few for computer graphics programs. We studied many surveys of software visualization [7,10,11,13,21,22] and found only a small number of software visualizations that explicitly visualize data flows. For example, Message Passing net (MP net) is a formal model for visualizing the message communication within MPI applications [40]. Butler, et al. [9] developed a taxonomy to help users manually create a data flow diagram in binary software for vulnerability analysis. Mysore, et al. [27] developed a Data Flow Tomography tool to visualize the interactions between complex and interwoven components of a software system. Our work is different from previous work because our focus is on computer graphics programs.

2.4   Program Visualization for Computer Graphics

There is very little previous work on visualizing computer graphics programs. In our previous work [33], we developed a program visualization tool that could automatically generate data flow diagrams from OpenGL API logs. This visualization tool could help detect certain bugs but might not be helpful for program comprehension. First of all, the program must be executable, which is not always possible. When a bug is found in a diagram, it may not be easy to trace back to a particular line of code when there are many similar function calls.

The key difference in our work is that we try to automatically generate data flow diagrams through static code analysis, not OpenGL API call logs. In our case, the program does not need to be executable. So the visualization can be used throughout the development process. Since the diagram is synchronized with the source code, if a bug is detected in the diagram, it can be quickly traced back to the source code.

3   OpenGL Overview

3.1   Program Structure

An OpenGL program consists of a host program and a number of shader programs. The host program is typically written in C or C++, uses OpenGL API and other libraries, and runs on the CPU. Shaders are written in OpenGL Shading Language and run on GPU. The most commonly used shaders are vertex shader(s) and fragment shader(s).

The host program loads 3D geometry data and passes them to shader programs as vertex attributes. It also passes uniform variables (e.g., transformation matrices and lighting parameters) and texture images to shader programs.

A vertex program receives vertex attributes and performs model, view, and projection transformations. It then passes the data to a fragment shader that calculates lighting, texture mappings, and perhaps other tasks. The data is then passed to graphics hardware for the final processing and display.

3.2   Data Flows in OpenGL

There are three types of data flows in OpenGL programs.

- **Vertex attribute connections:** Connect a vertex array in a host program to a vertex attribute variable in a shader program.
- **Uniform variable connections:** Connect a variable in a host program to a uniform variable in a shader program.
- **Texture sampler connections:** Connect a texture object in a host program to a sampler variable in a shader program.

In a typical OpenGL program, data needs to be transferred from a host program (running on the CPU) to a shader program (running on the GPU). For example, vertex positions in a host program need to be connected to the vertex position variable in a shader program. If the connection is broken, the vertex positions will not be transferred to the shader, and the object is not displayed. If the vertex positions are connected to the wrong shader variable, the object may be displayed incorrectly. Therefore, identifying a broken or misdirected data connection is an important part of the debugging process. However, it is not always easy to identify a broken or misdirected data connection by reading source code, especially for long programs. Drawing a data flow diagram makes it easier.

3.3   Explicit and Implicit Links

A data flow diagram contains nodes and links. Each node is a variable in either a host program or a shader program. The link between two variables is established by certain OpenGL API calls involving either or both variables. There are two types of links: explicit links and implicit links. An explicit link is created by one OpenGL API that contains both variables. For example, vPos = glGetAttribLocation(shaderProgram, "vPos"); establishes an explicit link between host program variable vPos and shader variable vPos because both variables appear in the same OpenGL API call.

An implicit link is established by two or more OpenGL API calls that each contains one variable. Implicit links are more difficult to identify because the two OpenGL API calls may be in different parts of the program, and it requires a deeper understanding of how OpenGL works. For example, the two API calls below establish a link between variable vPos and VBO vertexArrayBufferID. These two variables are in two different API calls.

```
glBindBuffer(GL_ARRAY_BUFFER, vertexArrayBufferID);
...
glVertexAttribPointer(vPos, numComponentsPerVertex,
    GL_FLOAT, GL_FALSE, 0, BUFFER_OFFSET(0));
```

4   Creating Data Flow Diagrams (DFDs)

Our data flow diagram consists of three symbols: data store (rectangle), process (rounded rectangle), and data connection (arrow). A data store must be connected to a process and cannot be connected directly to another data store. Here a data store is a 3D graphics data structure, such as a vertex buffer object, a vertex attribute, a uniform variable, or a texture sampler. A process is a function, usually an OpenGL API.

In this work, we only visualize data transfer from CPU to GPU, not the data transfer between shaders on GPU. Data transfer between shaders is not programmable and is entirely hidden from programmers.

Three types of data are transferred from CPU to GPU: vertex attributes, uniform variables, and textures. Accordingly, there are three types of data flow diagrams. In the following sections, we will discuss the rules for creating each type of data flow diagram (DFD).

4.1 Vertex Attribute DFD

Each vertex has multiple attributes, such as position, normal vectors, and texture coordinates. These attributes are stored as arrays in the main memory and need to be transferred to the GPU memory. Specifically, each vertex attribute in the OpenGL host program needs to be connected to an "in" (input) variable in a vertex shader via a sequence of OpenGL API calls. First, a Vertex Buffer Object (VBO) is generated by calling `glGenBuffers()`. Each VBO must be bound with a buffer using `glBindBuffer()`. The array that stores a vertex attribute (e.g., position) is copied to a VBO by calling `glBufferData()`. The buffer (or sub-buffer) bound with the VBO is then connected with an "in" variable in a vertex shader by calling `glEnableVertexAttribArray()` and `glVertexAttribPointer()`. The "in" variable is in the GPU memory.

If the code is correct, there should be an unbroken path between a vertex attribute array and its corresponding input variable in a vertex shader. An error can be visually detected if the path is broken or the path connects a vertex attribute to the wrong input variable in a shader. Therefore, the DFD can help programmers detect errors in data flows.

4.2 Uniform Variable DFD

Uniform variables contain the data used by shader programs to calculate transformations, lighting, camera projection, texture mapping, etc. Uniform variables are usually specified on a per-object (not per-vertex) basis. Each uniform variable in the OpenGL host program needs to be connected to a uniform variable in a shader program via OpenGL API calls.

If the code is correct, there should be an unbroken path between each uniform variable in the host program and its corresponding uniform variable in a shader program.

4.3 Texture Sampler DFD

A texture object stores texture images and their related parameters. The texture object is connected to a sampler variable in a shader program via multiple OpenGL API calls. First, a texture object is bound to a texture unit via `glActiveTexture()` and `glBindTexture()`. A sampler variable in a shader program is connected with a sampler variable in the host program via `glGetUniformLocation()`. The texture unit index is connected with the sampler variable in the host program via `glUniform*()`.

Figure 1 shows how a texture data flow can be constructed by analyzing specific parameters in specific OpenGL API calls.

If the code is correct, there should be an unbroken path between the texture object and its corresponding sampler variable in a shader program.

4.4   Interactive Visualization

We have developed an interactive web interface to help students connect the OpenGL source code with data flow diagrams (Fig. 2). We build our program using JavaScript and HTML based on the open-source project diagrams.net [1]. The web interface has a source code window and a DFD window. Users copy and paste their source code into the source code window. Our program will automatically detect data flow connections based on the rules discussed above and create a data flow diagram. If a user selects a line of code in the source code window, the corresponding component in the DFD will be highlighted. If a user clicks on a component in a DFD, the corresponding line of code will be highlighted in the source code window. Such synchronized views will help students better understand how data flows are implemented in OpenGL programs. It helps students detect bugs in DFD and quickly trace the problem back to the source code.

4.5   When to Draw a Data Flow Diagram?

The following guidelines may help students decide which type of data flow diagram they need to draw.

- If an object is not displayed or not displayed correctly, draw a vertex attribute connection diagram for the vertex position array.
- If the transformation is incorrect, draw a uniform variable diagram for transformation parameters, such as transformation matrices.
- If the lighting is incorrect, draw a uniform variable connection diagram for the lighting parameters and a vertex attribute connection diagram for the normal array.
- If the texture mapping is incorrect, draw a texture connection diagram and a vertex attribute connection diagram for the vertex

5   A Debugging Case Study

The example below shows how to use DFD to detect a subtle error that is otherwise difficult to find. Due to space limitations, we only show the OpenGL API calls, not the complete program.

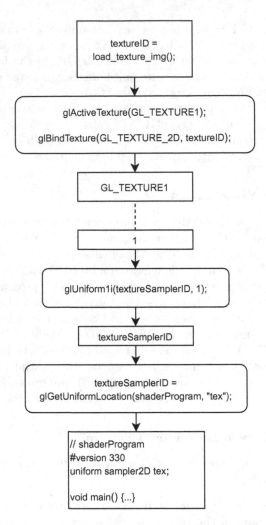

Fig. 1. This figure shows how to construct texture data flows by identifying parameters in specific OpenGL API calls. The parameters that indicate data connections are marked in red. The dashed line indicates an implicit connection by matching numbers (1 and GLTEXTURE1). (Color figure online)

```
...
glActiveTexture(GL_TEXTURE1);
glBindTexture(GL_TEXTURE_2D, textureObjID);
...
textureSamplerID =
    glGetUniformLocation(shader, "tex");
...
glUniform1i(textureSamplerID, 2);
```

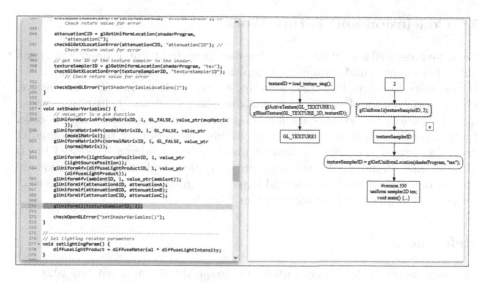

Fig. 2. This screenshot shows the UI of our program. A box in the data flow diagram (*glUniform1i()*) is selected, and the corresponding line of code is highlighted in the source code window. This DFD also shows a broken data flow, indicating an error in the code. There is no link between *GL_TEXTURE1* and the texture unit number *2* because the text unit numbers do not match.

In this case, the texture object is bound with texture unit 1 (`glActiveText ure(GL_TEXTURE1)`), but the textureSamplerID is connected with texture unit 2 (`glUniform1i(textureSamplerID, 2)`). The text unit numbers do not match. Therefore, the texture image is not transferred properly to the shader program on GPU. This error is often difficult to detect by running or reading the code because there is no error message, these two lines of code are buried in a long program, and the connection between these two lines is not obvious. However, in the automatically generated data flow diagram (Fig. 2), it is clear that texture data flow is broken.

6 Discussion

Due to the complexity of coding, it is not always possible to automatically detect data connections by analyzing the parameters of OpenGL API calls. We plan to add features that allow users to manually select and group OpenGL API calls to help the program analyze the code and generate DFDs.

There are different ways of transferring data from CPU to GPU. Due to space limitations, we did not discuss vertex element arrays, vertex array buffer (VAO), or uniform buffer object (UBO). However, the approach discussed above can also be applied to VAO and UBO.

7 Conclusion and Future Work

We have presented a method to visualize data flows in OpenGL programs. It can help programmers understand the complex data flow between CPU and GPU. It also helps to detect bugs that are otherwise difficult to find. The interactive, synchronized views of source code and data flow diagrams help programmers quickly connect the visual data flow diagrams with the abstract source code. Since OpenGL is still the most widely taught programming tool in computer graphics courses, our tool can benefit many college students interested in 3D graphics programming. We are improving our static code analysis functions to handle more sophisticated code and expand program visualization to general-purpose GPU programming tools such as CUDA.

References

1. diagrams.net (2022). https://github.com/jgraph/drawio. Accessed July 2022
2. Angel, E., Shreiner, D.: Interactive Computer Graphics: A Top-Down Approach with Shader-Based OpenGL, 6 edn. Pearson (2011)
3. Apple: Metal (2022). https://developer.apple.com/documentation/metal. Accessed July 2022
4. Asenov, D., Hilliges, O., Müller, P.: The effect of richer visualizations on code comprehension. In: Proceedings of the Conference on Human Factors in Computing Systems, pp. 5040–5045. ACM (2016)
5. Bacher, I., Namee, B.M., Kelleher, J.D.: On using tree visualisation techniques to support source code comprehension. In: Proceedings of the 2016 IEEE Working Conference on Software Visualization (VISSOFT), pp. 91–95. IEEE (2016)
6. Balreira, D.G., Walter, M., Fellner, D.W.: A survey of the contents in introductory computer graphics courses. Comput. Graph. **77**, 88–96 (2018)
7. Bedu, L., Tinh, O., Petrillo, F.: A tertiary systematic literature review on software visualization. In: Proceedings of the 7th IEEE Working Conference on Software Visualization (VISSOFT), pp. 33–44. IEEE (2019)
8. Blackwell, A.F., Petre, M., Church, L.: Fifty years of the psychology of programming. Int. J. Hum Comput Stud. **131**, 52–63 (2019)
9. Butler, K., et al.: Creating a user-centric data flow visualization: a case study. In: Yamamoto, S., Mori, H. (eds.) HCII 2019. LNCS, vol. 11569, pp. 174–193. Springer, Cham (2019). https://doi.org/10.1007/978-3-030-22660-2_12
10. Caserta, P., Zendra, O.: Visualization of the static aspects of software: a survey. IEEE Trans. Vis. Comput. Graph. **17**, 913–933 (2011)
11. Chotisarn, N., et al.: A systematic literature review of modern software visualization. J. Vis. **23**, 539–558 (2020). https://doi.org/10.1007/s12650-020-00647-w
12. Cornelissen, B., Zaidman, A., Deursen, A.V.: A controlled experiment for program comprehension through trace visualization. IEEE Trans. Softw. Eng. **37**, 341–355 (2011)
13. Cornelissen, B., Zaidman, A., Deursen, A.V., Moonen, L., Koschke, R.: A systematic survey of program comprehension through dynamic analysis. IEEE Trans. Softw. Eng. **35**, 684–702 (2009)

14. Dias, M., Orellana, D., Vidal, S., Merino, L., Bergel, A.: Evaluating a visual approach for understanding JavaScript source code. In: Proceedings of the IEEE/ACM International Conference on Program Comprehension, vol. 20, pp. 128–138. IEEE (2020)

15. Duru, H.A., Çakır, M.P., İşler, V.: How does software visualization contribute to software comprehension? A grounded theory approach. Int. J. Hum.-Comput. Interact. **29**(11), 743–763 (2013)

16. Fix, V., Wiedenbeck, S., Scholtz, J.: Mental representations of programs by novices and experts. In: Proceedings of the INTERACT 1993 and CHI 1993 Conference on Human Factors in Computing Systems, pp. 74–79. ACM (1993)

17. Ghaleb, T.A., Alturki, M.A., Aljasser, K.: Program comprehension through reverse-engineered sequence diagrams: a systematic review. J. Softw. Evol. Process **30**, e1965 (2018)

18. Hendrix, D., Cross, J.H., Maghsoodloo, S.: The effectiveness of control structure diagrams in source code comprehension activities. IEEE Trans. Softw. Eng. **28**, 463–477 (2002)

19. Jacobs, T., Musial, B.: Interactive visual debugging with UML. In: Proceedings of the 2003 ACM Symposium on Software Visualization, pp. 115–122. ACM (2003)

20. Klerkx, J., Verbert, K., Duval, E.: Enhancing learning with visualization techniques. In: Spector, J.M., Merrill, M.D., Elen, J., Bishop, M.J. (eds.) Handbook of Research on Educational Communications and Technology, pp. 791–807. Springer, New York (2014). https://doi.org/10.1007/978-1-4614-3185-5_64

21. Koschke, R.: Software visualization in software maintenance, reverse engineering, and re-engineering: a research survey. J. Softw. Maint. Evol. **15**, 87–109 (2003)

22. Lemieux, F., Salois, M.: Visualization techniques for program comprehension - a literature review. In: Fujita, H., Mejri, M. (eds.) New Trends in Software Methodologies, Tools and Techniques, pp. 22–47. IOS Press (2006)

23. Lommerse, G., Nossin, F., Voinea, L., Telea, A.: The visual code navigator: an interactive toolset for source code investigation. In: Proceedings of the IEEE Symposium on Information Visualization (InfoVis), pp. 24–31. IEEE (2005)

24. Ma, L., Ferguson, J., Roper, M., Wood, M.: Investigating and improving the models of programming concepts held by novice programmers. Comput. Sci. Educ. **21**, 57–80 (2011)

25. Medeiros, R.P., Ramalho, G.L., Falcao, T.P.: A systematic literature review on teaching and learning introductory programming in higher education. IEEE Trans. Educ. **62**, 77–90 (2019)

26. Microsoft: Direct3D (2022). https://docs.microsoft.com/en-us/windows/win32/directx. Accessed July 2022

27. Mysore, S., Mazloom, B., Agrawal, B., Sherwood, T.: Understanding and visualizing full systems with data flow tomography. SIGOPS Oper. Syst. Rev. **42**, 211–221 (2008)

28. Navarro-Prieto, R., Cañas, J.J.: Are visual programming languages better? The role of imagery in program comprehension. Int. J. Hum Comput Stud. **54**, 799–829 (2001)

29. Nguyen, H.T., et al.: Visualizing hierarchical performance profiles of parallel codes using CallFlow. IEEE Trans. Vis. Comput. Graph. **27**, 2455–2468 (2021)

30. Pancake, C.M., Utter, S.: Models for visualization in parallel debuggers. In: Proceedings of the 1989 ACM/IEEE Conference on Supercomputing, pp. 627–636 (1989)

31. Pennington, N.: Comprehension strategies in programming. In: Empirical Studies of Programmers: Second Workshop, pp. 100–113. Ablex Publishing Corp. (1987)

32. Pilskalns, O., Wallace, S., Ilas, F.: Runtime debugging using reverse-engineered UML. In: Engels, G., Opdyke, B., Schmidt, D.C., Weil, F. (eds.) MODELS 2007. LNCS, vol. 4735, pp. 605–619. Springer, Heidelberg (2007). https://doi.org/10.1007/978-3-540-75209-7_41

33. Podila, S., Zhu, Y.: A visualization tool for 3D graphics program comprehension and debugging. In: Proceedings of the IEEE Working Conference on Software Visualization (VISSOFT), pp. 111–115 (2016)

34. Price, B.A., Baecker, R.M., Small, I.S.: A principled taxonomy of software visualization. J. Vis. Lang. Comput. **4**, 211–266 (1993)

35. Robins, A., Rountree, J., Rountree, N.: Learning and teaching programming: a review and discussion. Comput. Sci. Educ. **13**, 137–172 (2003)

36. The Khronos Group: OpenGL (2022). https://www.khronos.org/opengl/. Accessed July 2022

37. The Khronos Group: Vulkan (2022). https://www.vulkan.org/. Accessed July 2022

38. The Khronos Group: WebGL (2022). https://www.khronos.org/webgl/. Accessed July 2022

39. Umphress, D.A., Hendrix, T.D., Cross, J.H., Maghsoodloo, S.: Software visualizations for improving and measuring the comprehensibility of source code. Sci. Comput. Program. **60**, 121–133 (2006)

40. Šurkovský, M.: MP net as abstract model of communication for message-passing applications. In: Proceedings of the 16th ACM International Conference on Computing Frontiers, pp. 263–267. ACM (2019)

A Practical Algorithm for Degree-k Voronoi Domains of Three-Dimensional Periodic Point Sets

Philip Smith[(✉)] and Vitaliy Kurlin[(✉)]

Computer Science department, University of Liverpool, Liverpool L69 3BX, UK
{Philip.Smith3,vitaliy.kurlin}@liverpool.ac.uk
http://kurlin.org

Abstract. Degree-k Voronoi domains of a periodic point set are concentric regions around a fixed centre consisting of all points in Euclidean space that have the centre as their k-th nearest neighbour. Periodic point sets generalise the concept of a lattice by allowing multiple points to appear within a unit cell of the lattice. Thus, periodic point sets model all solid crystalline materials (periodic crystals), and degree-k Voronoi domains of periodic point sets can be used to characterise the relative positions of atoms in a crystal from a fixed centre. The paper describes the first algorithm to compute all degree-k Voronoi domains up to any degree $k \geq 1$ for any two or three-dimensional periodic point set.

Keywords: Degree-k Voronoi Domains · Periodic point sets · Crystals

1 Introduction: Motivations and Key Contributions

A *discrete set* $C \subset \mathbb{R}^n$ consists of (possibly, infinitely many) points whose pairwise distances have a positive lower bound. The *Voronoi domain* $Z_1(C; p)$ or Wigner-Seitz cell or Brillouin zone of a point $p \in C$ consits of all ambient points in $\mathbb{R}^n$ that are (non-strictly) closer to p than to all other points of C. Figure 1 shows Voronoi domains in yellow when C is a lattice and p is the origin.

For any $k \geq 1$, the *degree-k Voronoi domain* $Z_k(C; p)$ consists of all points in $\mathbb{R}^n$ that have p as its k-th nearest neighbour in C, thus covering relative positions of distant points beyond the closest neighbours, see Fig. 1. Our key example of C is a periodic point set that generalises the concept of a lattice by allowing multiple points to lie within a unit cell of the lattice. Such periodic point sets geometrically model any solid crystalline material (briefly, a *crystal*) whose atoms are represented by points, possibly with added chemical types.

Key physical properties of a crystal depend on atomic interactions beyond immediate neighbours within larger degree-k Voronoi domains. These domains were called k-th Brillouin zones in [13] for lattices and later helped compute density functions [12, Theorem 6.1], which distinguish all periodic point sets in general position up to isometry in $\mathbb{R}^3$. Section 7 in [12] described how density functions detected a previously missing crystal in the Cambridge Structural

© The Author(s), under exclusive license to Springer Nature Switzerland AG 2022
G. Bebis et al. (Eds.): ISVC 2022, LNCS 13598, pp. 377–391, 2022.
https://doi.org/10.1007/978-3-031-20713-6_29

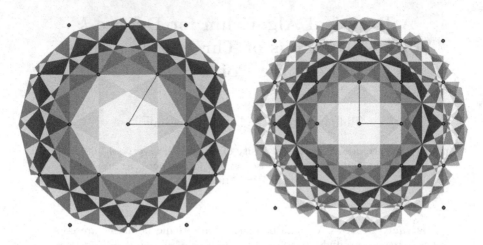

Fig. 1. The degree-k Voronoi domain is the union of polygons of the same colour, and has the origin as its k-th nearest neighbour among all lattice points. **Left**: the hexagonal lattice, degrees $1 \leq k \leq 12$. **Right**: the square lattice, degrees $1 \leq k \leq 20$. (Color figure online)

Database. This paper complements [12] by describing structural results and a practical algorithm for degree-k Voronoi domains for three-dimensional periodic point sets.

The first algorithm to compute Voronoi domains for periodic point sets appeared in [9], but did not consider degree-k Voronoi domains for $k \geq 2$. The algorithm for dual periodic Delaunay triangulations or mosaics was recently improved in [23]. Previously, degree-k Voronoi domains were studied and computed only for lattices whose motif is a single point [13].

In the more restrictive case of lattices, the Teaching and Learning Package of Cambridge University [25] visualises the degree-k Voronoi domains only for:

- the square and hexagonal lattices up to $k = 10$ and $k = 6$ respectively;
- the cubic, body centred cubic and face centred cubic lattices up to $k = 5$.

Again restricted to lattices, Andrew et al. [1] described an algorithm which approximates the domains simply by assigning each point of a fixed square/cubical grid at a given resolution to the appropriate degree-k Voronoi domain.

Degree-k Voronoi domains relate to the more widely known order-k Voronoi domains, which have been studied for a long time. Only recently degree-k Voronoi domains have begun to be properly investigated [10, 11].

One could extend algorithms that compute order-k Voronoi domains to construct the desired degree-k Voronoi domains. Though there are many algorithms that for order-k Voronoi domains in dimension 2 [8], to the best of the authors' knowledge, there is no publicly available algorithm for order-k Voronoi domains in dimension 3, which has motivated us to propose the algorithm in this paper.

We substantially improve on the past work in two ways: by generalising to any periodic point set, and by computing exactly the polytopes that comprise each domain, which can be used for visualisations and precise computations.

- Theorem 6 will describe the structure of the degree-k Voronoi domain $Z_k(C; p)$ from Definition 4 for any point p in a periodic point set $C \subset \mathbb{R}^n$.
- The total volume of the degree-k Voronoi domains $Z_k(C; p)$ over all points p in a motif M of a periodic set $C \subset \mathbb{R}^n$ is *independent of k*, see Theorem 7.
- The algorithm in Sect. 4 computes any degree-k Voronoi domain $Z_k(C; p)$ of a periodic point set in polynomial time in the motif size of C, see Theorem 17. The actual runtime takes only milliseconds on a modest laptop, see Sect. 5.

Section 2 defines necessary concepts. Section 3 states Theorems 6 and 7. Section 4 describes the practical algorithm for computing degree-k Voronoi domains of periodic point sets in dimensions two and three. Section 5 contains experimental analysis whose polynomial complexity is justified in Theorem 17.

2   Background Definitions from Computational Geometry

Any point $p \in \mathbb{R}^n$ can be represented by the vector $\boldsymbol{p}$ from the origin $0 \in \mathbb{R}^n$ to p. The symbol $\boldsymbol{p}$ also denotes all equal vectors with the same length and direction. We use only the Euclidean distance $|\boldsymbol{p} - \boldsymbol{q}|$ between points $p, q \in \mathbb{R}^n$. The *perpendicular bisector* between p and q is an $\mathbb{R}^{n-1}$-dimensional subspace composed of all points that are equidistant from p and q, and has the property that $\boldsymbol{p} - \boldsymbol{q}$ is perpendicular to this subspace. For a standard orthonormal basis $\boldsymbol{e}_1, \ldots, \boldsymbol{e}_n$ of $\mathbb{R}^n$, the lattice $\mathbb{Z}^n \subset \mathbb{R}^n$ consists of all points with integer coordinates.

Definition 1 (*lattice Λ, periodic point set C*). For n linearly independent vectors $\boldsymbol{v}_1, \ldots, \boldsymbol{v}_n$ in $\mathbb{R}^n$, the set of integer combinations $\Lambda = \{\sum_{i=1}^n c_i \boldsymbol{v}_i \,|\, c_i \in \mathbb{Z}\}$ is called a *lattice*. The *unit cell* spanned by this basis is the parallelepiped $U = \{\sum_{i=1}^n t_i \boldsymbol{v}_i \,|\, t_i \in [0, 1)\}$. The lattice generated by this basis or unit cell is denoted by $\Lambda(U)$. A *motif* $M \subset U$ is a finite subset of U, and the *periodic point set* C for M and Λ is the *Minkowski* sum $M + \Lambda = \{p + \boldsymbol{v} \,|\, p \in M, v \in \Lambda\}$, see Fig. 2(right) for the doubled square cell $2U$ with $k = 2$. ∎

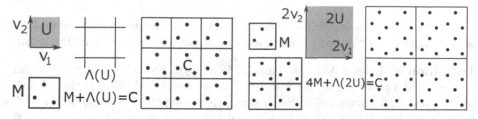

Fig. 2. Left: the green lattice Λ is generated by the orthonormal basis $\boldsymbol{v}_1, \boldsymbol{v}_2$. The blue motif M consists of three points in the square unit cell U. The periodic set $C = \Lambda + M$ is the Minkowski sum of the lattice and the finite motif M of points. **Right**: if a unit cell $U \subset \mathbb{R}^n$ has m motif points, then the 2-extended unit cell has $2^n m$ motif points. (Color figure online)

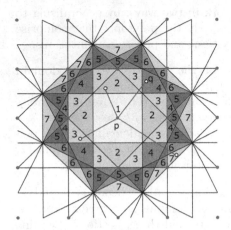

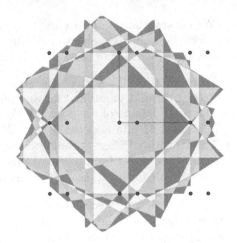

Fig. 3. Four red line segments $[p, q]$ go from the centre p to points q in polygons with indices $k = \text{ind}(q)$ from Definition 5 and intersect $k - 1$ bisectors. (Color figure online)

Fig. 4. Degree-k Voronoi domains of a periodic set (not a lattice) with a 2-point motif.

The periodic point set C can be thought of as the union of translates of M by all vectors of Λ, and hence is invariant under translations by all vectors of Λ. If a periodic point set C is invariant *only* under translations by vectors $v \in \Lambda$, then the lattice Λ and its unit cell U are called *primitive* for C.

One can consider any lattice Λ as a periodic point set on the lattice 2Λ with a motif of 2^n points inside the 2-extended unit cell more formally as follows.

Definition 2 (*k*-extended unit cell kU). Let a unit cell $U \subset \mathbb{R}^n$ have a basis $v_1, \ldots, v_n \in \mathbb{R}^n$ and a finite motif $M \subset U$ of m points. For any integer $k > 1$, the *k-extended unit cell* kU has motif $M + \sum_{i=1}^{n} c_i v_i$ of $k^n m$ points obtained from M by k^n translations along the vectors $\sum_{i=1}^{n} c_i v_i$ with $c_i \in \{0, \ldots, k-1\}$. ∎

Degree-k Voronoi domains of periodic point sets are introduced in Definition 4 as the relative complement between sequential index-k Voronoi domains below.

Definition 3 (Index-k Voronoi domains $V_k(C; p)$). For a finite or periodic set $C \subset \mathbb{R}^n$ and a point $p \in C$, the *index-k Voronoi domain* $V_k(C; p)$ is the (closure of the) set of all points $q \in \mathbb{R}^n$ such that p is among the k nearest points of C to q. In particular, $V_1(C; p)$ is the classical Voronoi domain $V(C; p)$. ∎

The index-k Voronoi domain $V_k(C; p) \subset \mathbb{R}^n$ is defined as a closed set above to cover all cases where p has equal distances to several neighbours, so a k-th neighbour of p may not be unique. Unlike order-k Voronoi domains which tile

$\mathbb{R}^n$ [15], index-k Voronoi domains form a nested sequence. Any $V_k(C;p)$ is *star-convex*, which means it contains all line segments connecting $\partial V_k(C;p)$ to p. Indeed, if $p \in C$ is among the k nearest to $q \in \partial V_k(C;p)$, then any intermediate point in the line segment $[p,q]$ has p among its k nearest neighbours of C.

An order-k Voronoi domain [14] is defined for a k-point subset $Q \subset A \subset \mathbb{R}^n$ and consists of all points for whom the points in Q are the closest k points in A.

Definition 4 (Degree-k Voronoi domains $Z_k(C;p)$). For any periodic point set $C \subset \mathbb{R}^n$ and $p \in C$, the *degree-k Voronoi domain* is the difference between successive closed index-k Voronoi domains: $Z_k(C;p) = V_k(C;p) - V_{k-1}(C;p)$ for $k \geq 1$, $V_0(C;p) = \emptyset$, which differs from order-k Voronoi domains in [14]. ∎

Figure 4 shows degree-k Voronoi domains for a point in the periodic point set C that has a 2-point motif. For a point $p \in C \subset \mathbb{R}^n$, any $q \in \mathbb{R}^n$ belongs to exactly one degree-k Voronoi domain $Z_k(C;p)$ for some $k \geq 1$, hence $\cup_{k=1}^{+\infty} Z_k(C;p)$ covers $\mathbb{R}^n$ without overlaps. Unlike index-k Voronoi domains which are closed, $Z_k(C;p)$ are neither open nor closed for $k > 1$. The closure of the domain $Z_k(C;p)$ includes all points q for whom p is a non-unique k-th nearest neighbour within C.

3   The Geometric Structure of Degree-k Voronoi Domains

The main results of this section are Theorem 6 describing the structure of degree-k Voronoi domains and Theorem 7 saying that the total volume of the degree-k Voronoi domains for all motif points is independent of k for a fixed set. So all coloured regions in Fig. 3 have the same area, which might seem surprising.

Definition 5 (Zone index $\text{ind}(q;C;p)$). For a periodic set $C \subset \mathbb{R}^n$ and $p \in C$, let $b(C;p)$ be the set of perpendicular bisectors between p and all other points of C. For any $q \in \mathbb{R}^n$, consider the half-open line segment $[p,q)$ joining p to q, but not including q, see Fig. 3. Let i be the number of bisectors from $b(C;p)$ that intersect $[p,q)$. The *zone index* of q relative to $b(C;p)$ is $\text{ind}(q;C;p) = i+1$. ∎

For any point q in the closed Voronoi domain $V_1(C;p)$, the half-open segment $[p,q)$ belongs to the interior of $V_1(C;p)$, and hence doesn't intersect any bisectors from $b(C;p)$. Consider other polytopes obtained from $\mathbb{R}^n$ by cutting out all bisectoral hyperplanes between p and other points $q \in C$. The zone indices of these polytopes can be computed in gradual increments as we travel radially outwards from p and count intersecting bisectors, see Fig. 3.

The following structural description of a degree-k Voronoi domain $Z_k(C;p)$ justifies its spherical shape consisting of polytopes of the same degree k.

Theorem 6 (Structure of Voronoi domains). For any point p in a periodic point set $C \subset \mathbb{R}^n$, the closure of the degree-k Voronoi domain $Z_k(C;p)$ is a union of convex polytopes whose interior points have zone index k. Moreover, the closure of the degree-k Voronoi domain is spherical in the sense that its image under the radial projection $Z_k(C;p) \to S^{n-1}$ covers the whole unit sphere $S^{n-1} \subset \mathbb{R}^n$. ∎

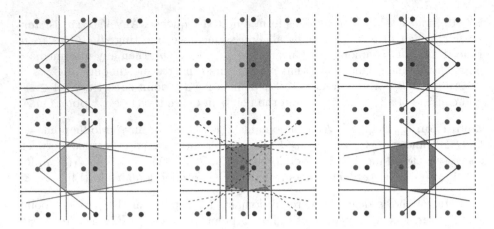

Fig. 5. Top left: the Voronoi domain of the red point is bounded by red and black bisectors. **Top middle:** both Voronoi domains of the red and blue points form the Voronoi domain $V(\varLambda; 0)$ of the lattice $\varLambda$ of C. **Top right:** the Voronoi domain of the blue point is bounded by blue and black bisectors. **Bottom left:** the degree-2 Voronoi domain of the red point in C. **Bottom middle:** both degree-2 Voronoi domains form $V(\varLambda; 0)$ after applying translations of the polygons that form the degree-2 Voronoi domains. **Bottom right:** the degree-2 Voronoi domain of the blue point. (Color figure online)

Proof. First we prove that any point $q \in \mathbb{R}^n$ that has the central point p as its exact k-th nearest neighbour in C should have zone index $\mathrm{ind}(q; C; p) = k$, see Definition 5. Let us slide a point s along the half-open line segment $[p, q)$ starting from the central point p as in Fig. 3. While s is in the interior of $V_1(C; p)$, our point s has p as exactly its 1st nearest neighbour in C and $\mathrm{ind}(s; C; p) = 1$.

When we slide the point s further along the half-closed line segment $[p, q)$, the zone index $\mathrm{ind}(s; C; p)$ jumps up only when we intersect a bisector separating p from another point of C. If we intersect $i \geq 1$ bisectors, then $\mathrm{ind}(s; C; p)$ jumps by i. As the final point $s = q$ has p as its exact k-th nearest neighbour in C, s will intersect $k - 1$ bisectors as it travels along $[p, q)$, and so the zone index becomes k. Then $Z_k(C; p)$ is a finite union of convex polytopes (obtained from $\mathbb{R}^n$ by cutting out bisectors) that includes all index k points. The boundary of any such polytope includes points of index at most $k - 1$ ('internal' faces closer to p) and points of index k ('external' faces further away from p).

So the closure of $Z_k(C; p)$ is the union of all convex polytopes whose internal points have zone index k. Then any straight ray R emanating from p either contains points of index k, hence intersects the interior of $Z_k(C; p)$, or R passes through an intersection point a of several bisectors. In the latter case, when a point s moves along R via the intersection a, the index of s can change from $k' < k$ to $k'' > k$. Then any small neighbourhood of a contains points of all intermediate indices from k' to k'' (including k). So the closure of $Z_k(C; p)$ contains a and its image under the radial projection covers the sphere S^{n-1}. $\square$

Figure 5 illustrates the key idea for the periodic point set $C \subset \mathbb{R}^2$, which has the primitive square unit cell $[-1,1] \times [-1,1]$ containing the red point at $(-0.25, 0)$ and the blue point at $(0.25, 0)$. The bottom row in Fig. 5 shows how the polygons of the degree-2 Voronoi domain can be rearranged to form the classical degree-1 Voronoi domain in the first row, see the proof of Theorem 7 below.

Theorem 7 (volumes of a degree-k Voronoi domain, extending [13, Section 2.2]). For a periodic point set $C = \Lambda + M$, the sum of the volumes of the degree-k Voronoi domains $Z_k(C; p)$ over all motif points $p \in M$ is independent of k. ∎

Definition 8 (open subdomains) $V^{(k)}(C; 0)$. A lattice Λ of a periodic set $C = \Lambda + M$ is *primitive* if C is not a Minkowski sum $\Lambda' + M'$ whose motif M' has a smaller number of points than M. Then the *subdomain* $V^{(k)}(C; 0)$ in the interior of the Voronoi domain $V(\Lambda; 0)$ consists of all points that have a unique k-th nearest neighbour in the set C. So this subdomain $V^{(k)}(C; 0)$ is obtained from the classical Voronoi domain $V(\Lambda; 0)$ around the origin 0 by removing the measure 0 subset of points that have several k-th nearest neighbours in C. ∎

Definition 9 (subzone Z_k°). Let Λ be a primitive lattice of a periodic set C. The open *subzone* $Z_k^\circ(C; p)$ in the interior of the degree-k Voronoi domain $Z_k(C; p)$ consists of all points that have a unique closest node in Λ. ∎

Since $V^{(k)}(C; 0)$ is in the interior of $V(\Lambda; 0)$, the origin 0 is a unique closest point of Λ to every point of $V^{(k)}(C; 0)$. Since $Z_k^\circ(C; p)$ is in the interior of $Z_k(C; p)$, every point of $Z_k^\circ(C; p)$ has a unique k-th nearest neighbour in C.

Definition 10 (half-open Voronoi domain $\tilde{V}(\Lambda; 0)$). For a lattice $\Lambda \subset \mathbb{R}^n$, the closed Voronoi domains $V(\Lambda; q)$ of the lattice points $q \in \Lambda$ tile $\mathbb{R}^n$, overlapping only at their boundaries. We define a *half-open Voronoi domain* $\tilde{V}(\Lambda; 0) \subset V(\Lambda; 0)$ to be such that all translational copies tile $\mathbb{R}^n$ without overlaps. ∎

A half-open Voronoi domain $\tilde{V}(\Lambda; 0)$ differs from $V(\Lambda; 0)$ only by a measure 0 subset and can be obtained by removing boundary points of $V(\Lambda; 0)$ until there remains exactly one representative of each class of boundary points that are related via lattice translations. Definition 11 adapts the piecewise shifts f_i from the case of lattices in [13, p. 754] to any periodic point set $C \subset \mathbb{R}^n$.

Definition 11 (piecewise shift f_k). For any periodic set $C \subset \mathbb{R}^n$ with lattice Λ, any point $p \in V^{(k)}(C; 0)$ has a unique k-th nearest neighbour $p_k \in C$. Since all translates of $\tilde{V}(\Lambda; 0)$ cover $\mathbb{R}^n$ without overlaps, p_k is contained in a translate $\tilde{V}(\Lambda; 0) + q_k$ for a unique lattice node $q_k \in \Lambda$. Then we set $f_k(p) = p - q_k$. ∎

Lemma 12. The map $f_k : V^{(k)}(C; 0) \to \bigcup\limits_{p \in C \cap \tilde{V}(\Lambda;0)} Z_k^\circ(C; p)$ is a bijection. ∎

Proof. We first show that the image of f_k is in $\bigcup_{p \in C \cap \tilde{V}(\Lambda;0)} Z_k^\circ(C;p)$. Any $p \in V^{(k)}(C;0)$ has a unique k-th nearest neighbour $p_k \in C$, which is covered by a unique translate $\tilde{V}(\Lambda;0) + q_k$ for some $q_k \in \Lambda$. Shifting these neighbouring relations by $-q_k$, we conclude that $f_k(p) = p - q_k$ has the unique k-th neighbour $p' = p_k - q_k \in C$, which is covered by $\tilde{V}(\Lambda;0)$. Then $f_k(p) = p - q_k \in Z_k^\circ(C;p') \subset \bigcup_{p \in C \cap \tilde{V}(\Lambda;0)} Z_k^\circ(C;p)$. To prove that f_k is injective, let $p, p' \in V^{(k)}(C;0)$ have unique k-th neighbours $p_k, p_k' \in C$, which are covered by unique translates of $\tilde{V}(\Lambda;0)$ along $q_k, q_k' \in \Lambda$, respectively. If $q_k = q_k'$, then $f_k(p) - f_k(p') = p - p'$, so that $p \neq p'$ implies $f_k(p) \neq f_k(p')$. Otherwise, if $q_k \neq q_k'$, then $f_k(p) \neq f_k(p')$ since they lie in the interiors of two different translates of $\tilde{V}(\Lambda;0)$. To prove that f_k is surjective, any point q in the target set belongs to a $Z_k^\circ(C;p_k)$ for $p_k \in C \cap \tilde{V}(\Lambda;0)$. Then q has p_k as its unique k-th neighbour in C and a unique closest lattice node $q_k \in \Lambda$ such that $V(\Lambda,0) + q_k$ covers q. Subtracting q_k, we conclude that $p = q - q_k$ has $p_k - q_k$ as its unique k-th neighbour in C and 0 as its unique closest lattice node in Λ. So $p \in V^{(k)}(C;0)$ and $f_k(p) = q$.   □

Proof of Theorem 7. By Lemma 12 the shifts f_k from Definition 11 translate different pieces of the Voronoi domain $V(\Lambda;0)$ to the union of degree-k Voronoi domains over all motif points (modulo measure 0), so the volumes are equal.   □

4   Computing Degree-k Voronoi Domains of a Periodic Set

Let the dimension $n = 2$ or 3. The **algorithm input** consists of:

- a unit cell U given by a basis $v_1, \ldots, v_n$ with rational coordinates in practice;
- a finite motif $M \subset U$ of points given by their coefficients in the basis of U;
- a degree $k \geq 1$ and a point $p \in M$ that will be the centre of the degree-k Voronoi domains $Z_k(C;p)$ of the periodic point set $C = \Lambda + M \subset \mathbb{R}^n$.

Up to rigid motions, we can assume that the point $p \in M$ is at the origin.

The output is the degree-k Voronoi domains $Z_i(C;0)$, $i = 1, \ldots, k$. Each domain is a union of polygons ($n = 2$) or polytopes ($n = 3$) defined by:

- vertices: arbitrarily ordered points in $\mathbb{R}^n$;
- edges: unordered pairs of vertices indexed above;
- 2-dimensional faces: cyclically ordered lists of edges indexed above for $n = 3$.

We introduce the algorithm for $n = 2$ in the plane $\mathbb{R}^2$ for simplicity, while the natural extension to $\mathbb{R}^3$ will be described in an extended version.

Stage 1: Cell Reduction. A given basis of a unit cell U is reduced to a Minkowski basis [22], see Lemma 15. A basis reduction is needed due to Lemma 13 below.

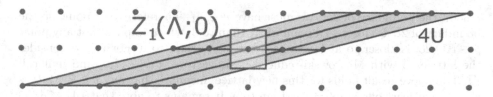

Fig. 6. If a unit cell U is not reduced, the extension by any fixed factor k may not cover even the degree-1 Voronoi domain $Z_1(\Lambda; 0)$, see Lemma 13.

Lemma 13 (insufficiency of cell extensions). For any $k > 1$, any lattice $\Lambda \subset \mathbb{R}^n$ has a unit cell U whose k-extension doesn't cover the domain $V(\Lambda; 0)$. ∎

Proof. The example in Fig. 6 can be generalised for any lattice $\Lambda \subset \mathbb{R}^n$ as follows. One can choose a basis $v_1, \ldots, v_n$ of Λ in such a way that the nearest neighbour of the origin $0 \in \mathbb{R}^n$ is the vertex v_2 of the unit cell spanned by this basis. If we add the multiple $(k+1)v_1$ to v_2, then the vertex v_2 of the initial unit cell U will not be covered by the k-extended cell U_k based on $v_1, v_2 + (k+1)v_1, \ldots, v_n$, see Fig. 6. Indeed, to reach the vertex v_2, we need $k+1$ subtractions from $v_2 + (k+1)v_1$. Hence at least the $(k+1)$-extension of the cell U_k is needed. □

The degree-1 Voronoi domain is covered by the 2-extension of a Minkowski-reduced cell for $n = 2, 3$ as proved in [16, Appendix A.1]. For degrees $k > 1$, we need the stronger Lemma 14 covering any degree-k Voronoi domain.

Lemma 14. Let $n = 2$ or 3. For any unit cell U with a Minkowski-reduced basis, the unit cell $2kU \subset \mathbb{R}^n$ (symmetrically extended around $0 \in \mathbb{R}^n$) covers the degree-k Voronoi domain $Z_k(C; 0) \subset \mathbb{R}^n$ for any periodic set $C = \Lambda + M$. ∎

Lemma 14 states that $Z_k(C; 0)$ is covered by $2kU$ (if U is Minkowski-reduced). Since the boundary of $Z_k(C; 0)$ is defined by bisectors between 0 and other points in C, we need to consider points that lie in the $4k$-extended unit cell.

Lemma 15 (*Minkowski-reduced* basis, Lemma 2.2.1 in [22]). A basis $v_1, \ldots, v_n$ of a lattice $\Lambda \subset \mathbb{R}^n$ is *Minkowski-reduced* if and only if for any $i = 1, \ldots, n$ and integers $c_1, \ldots, c_n \in \mathbb{Z}$ such that $c_i, \ldots, c_n$ have no common integer factor $c > 1$, the inequality $|\sum_{i=j}^{n} c_j v_j| \geq |v_j|$ holds. ∎

Lemma 16 (sufficiency of Minkowski-reduced cell extensions). For a unit cell U of a lattice $\Lambda \subset \mathbb{R}^n$, $n \leq 3$, with a Minkowski-reduced basis $v_1, \ldots, v_n$, let Λ_i, $i \geq 1$, be the set of all points of Λ on the boundary of the $2i$-extended unit cell $2iU$ whose centre of symmetry is the origin 0. Then any point $p \in \mathbb{R}^n \backslash 2iU$ is closer to at least one point of Λ_i than to $0 \in \mathbb{R}^n$. ∎

Proof. Set $i = 1$. By Appendix A.1 in [16], the Voronoi cell $V(\Lambda; 0)$ is strictly within $2U$. Any point p on the boundary of $2U$ belongs to the Voronoi domain $V(\Lambda; v)$ of a lattice point $v \in \Lambda \backslash 0$. $2U + v$ must strictly contain $V(\Lambda; v)$, and as

p is on the boundary of $2U$, we must have $v \in \Lambda_1$. Therefore, any point on the boundary of $2U$ is closer to a point of Λ_1 than to 0, which implies that any point $p \in \mathbb{R}^n \backslash 2U$ is closer to at least one point of Λ_1 than to 0. For $i \geq 1$, consider the lattice $i\Lambda$ with Minkowski-reduced basis vectors $i\boldsymbol{v}_1, \ldots, i\boldsymbol{v}_n$ and unit cell iU. The above result holds for this new lattice, meaning that any $p \in \mathbb{R}^n \backslash 2iU$ is closer to at least one point of $i\Lambda_1$ than to 0. It remains to note that $i\Lambda_1 \subset \Lambda_i$. $\square$

Proof of Lemma 14. It suffices to prove that $V_k(\Lambda; 0) \subset 2kU$ only for a lattice Λ, i.e. for a periodic set with a single point in a motif M. Indeed, adding any extra points to M can only make the Voronoi domain $V_k(\Lambda + M; 0)$ smaller than $V_k(\Lambda; 0)$. Let U be the unit cell with a Minkowski-reduced basis $\boldsymbol{v}_1, \ldots, \boldsymbol{v}_n$. Take any point $p \in \mathbb{R}^n - 2kU$. Applying Lemma 16 for $i = 1, \ldots, k$, we conclude that p has k neighbours in $\cup_{i=1}^k \Lambda_i$ that are closer to p than 0. Hence p can not have 0 among its k nearest neighbours in Λ. Then p is outside the k-th Voronoi domain $V_k(\Lambda; 0)$. So $p \in \mathbb{R}^n - V_k(\Lambda; 0)$, $\mathbb{R}^n - 2kU \subset \mathbb{R}^n - V_k(\Lambda; 0)$, $V_k(\Lambda; 0) \subset 2kU$. $\square$

Stage 2: Sorting Points from the Extended Motif. If the original motif $M \subset \mathbb{R}^n$ had m points including the origin $0 \in \mathbb{R}^n$, the $4k$-extended motif M_k has $(4k)^n m$ points for any dimension n. All these points are inserted into a balanced binary tree whose keys for comparison are distances to the origin.

Stage 3: A Loop over Motif Points. The loop processes all motif points from the $2k$-extended cell (except 0) in increasing order of their distance to $0 \in \mathbb{R}^n$.

For any point $p \neq 0$ in the extended motif M_k, the vector $0.5\boldsymbol{p}$ represents the mid-point of the line segment $[0, p] \subset \mathbb{R}^2$. The bisector line $L(p) \subset \mathbb{R}^2$ between 0 and p has the parametric equation $0.5\boldsymbol{p} + t\boldsymbol{p}_\perp$, where $t \in \mathbb{R}$ and the unit vector $\boldsymbol{p}_\perp$ is orthogonal to $\boldsymbol{p}$ and anti-clockwisely oriented relative to $0 \in \mathbb{R}^2$.

In the loop of Stage 3, for each point $p \in M_k \backslash \{0\}$, the bisector $L(p)$ is intersected with all previous bisectors. The resulting intersection points can be ordered according to the direction of $L(p)$. We keep these intersection points in a balanced binary tree $T(p)$ whose key for comparison is the parameter t in the equation of $L(p)$. So a tree $T(q)$ of ordered intersections of $L(q)$ will be maintained for every point q in the extended motif M_k. This tree is implemented using the multimap structure in C++ for fast searching and insertions. Every oriented edge $e \subset L(q)$ between successive intersection points has an ordered pair of polygons attached to this edge. This pair is kept as extra information in the tree $T(q)$, for example assigned to the initial vertex a of e in Fig. 7.

To avoid unbounded regions, we restrict all polygons to a large square S containing the extended motif M_k. Every polygon Q in the current splitting of S by previous bisectors has the index $\text{ind}(Q)$ defined similarly to Definition 5 as the number of intersections of all previous bisectors with a line segment $[0, q)$ for any internal point $q \in Q$, see Fig. 3. After finding a new intersection point a of the bisector $L(p)$ with a previous bisector $L(q)$, we follow the steps below.

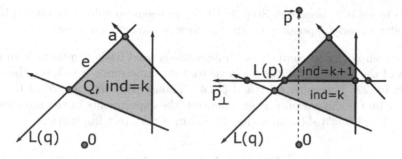

Fig. 7. Left: the blue convex polygon Q after cutting out all bisectors and before inserting the bisector of a more distant point p of the set C. **Right:** the new bisector $L(p)$ meets the previous four bisectors, creates four intersection points, then splits Q. (Color figure online)

Step 3a: insert the intersection point a into the binary trees $T(p), T(q)$ according to its positions relative to other intersections of $L(p)$, $L(q)$, respectively.

Step 3b: the appearance of the new intersection point a in the previous bisector $T(q)$ subdivides an edge $e \subset L(q)$ and we mark the two polygons that are attached to the edge e and should be later split by $L(p)$.

Step 3c: splitting the polygons marked in Step 3b. After finding all intersections of $L(p)$ with previous bisectors, we split each marked polygon Q into two smaller polygons and update their zone indices: the polygon closer to 0 keeps its current index, while we increment by 1 the index of the more distant polygon.

Theorem 17 says that degree-k Voronoi domains can be computed in polynomial time in the number m of motif points. The polynomial dependence on m and k seems inevitable, because in general position $m(4k)^n$ bisectors between a fixed centre p and its neighbours in a k-extended motif can intersect each other.

Theorem 17 (Algorithm complexity). Let the dimension be $n \leq 3$, and let a periodic point set $C \subset \mathbb{R}^n$ have a motif of m points in a Minkowski-reduced basis. Then the complexity to compute the first k degree-i Voronoi domains, $Z_i(C; p)$, $i = 1, \ldots, k$, is $O(m^n(4k)^{n^2}(n\log(4k) + \log m))$ for any point $p \in C$. ∎

Proof. Starting from a reduced basis in Stage 1, the $4k$-extended motif M_k consists of $m(4k)^n$ points. Sorting these points according to their distance from the origin at Stage 2 takes $O(m(4k)^n(n\log(4k) + \log m))$ time. Stage 3 loops over $m(4k)^n$ points and computes all n-fold intersections of $m(4k)^n$ bisectors, which explains the extra n-th power in the factor $m^n(4k)^{n^2}$. Inserting intersection points into binary trees and marking polyhedra at Stage 3 requires only a logarithmic time in the number of intersection points between $O(m^{n-1}(4k)^{n(n-1)})$ 1-dimensional lines (intersections of $n-1 \geq 2$ bisectors in any dimension $n \geq 3$)

and up to $m(4k)^n$ bisectors. Step 3c similarly needs to split only $O(m^n(4k)^{n^2})$ polyhedra linearly depending on the number of intersection points.   □

The complexity to compute a Minkowski-reduced basis is quadratic in logarithms of the lengths of initial basis vectors for dimensions $n \leq 3$, see the exact bounds in [22, Theorems 4.2.1 and 5.0.4]. Though the dependence of the time estimate on the dimension n is exponential, the experiments in the next section for $n = 2$ and $n = 3$ show that the algorithm is very fast in practice.

5   Experiments on Degree-k Voronoi Domains for $n = 2, 3$

The complexity bound from Theorem 17 has been experimentally illustrated as follows. In $\mathbb{R}^2$ we chose 6 different lattices: the square, hexagonal and rectangular lattices, plus 3 more generic ones, as shown in Fig. 8. Given one of these lattices and a fixed number $m \in [1, 50]$, we randomly generated m motif points to get a periodic point set. Repeating the random generation of motif points 100 times for each of the 6 lattices, we get 600 periodic point sets in total for each $m \in [1, 50]$, see Fig. 9 for two periodic point sets with $m = 2$. In Figs. 10, 11, 12 and 13, each cross represents the mean result, such as runtime in milliseconds, over the 600 periodic point sets of every value of the number m of motif points considered. All experiments were performed on a MacBook Pro with 2.3 GHz, 8 GB RAM.

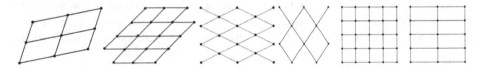

Fig. 8. The 2D lattices in the experiments in Sect. 5. **1st:** a (black) generic lattice with basis $(1.25, 0.25)$, $(0.25, 0.75)$. **2nd:** a (blue) hexagonal lattice with basis $(1, 0)$, $(0.5, \sqrt{3}/2)$. **3rd:** an (orange) rhombic lattice with basis $(1, 0.5)$, $(1, -0.5)$. **4th:** a (purple) rhombic lattice with basis $(1, 1.5)$, $(1, -1.5)$. **5th:** a (red) square lattice with standard basis $(1, 0)$, $(0, 1)$. **6th:** a (green) rectangular lattice with basis $(2, 0)$, $(0, 1)$. (Color figure online)

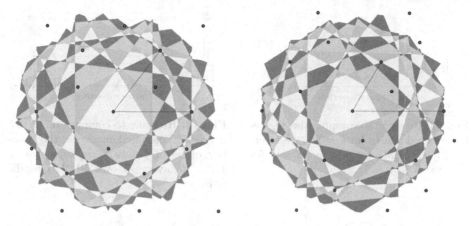

Fig. 9. The first 12 degree-k Voronoi domains of $0 \in \mathbb{R}^2$ for: **Left:** A periodic point set with basis $(1, 0.5)$, $(1, -0.5)$; **Right:** A periodic point set with basis $(1.25, 0.25)$, $(0.25, 0.75)$. In each image, the basis vectors are shown by thin black lines.

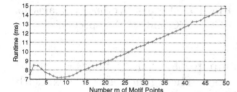

Fig. 10. Runtime for 8 degree-k Voronoi domains for $m = 1, \ldots, 50$ motif points, averaged over 600 2D periodic sets.

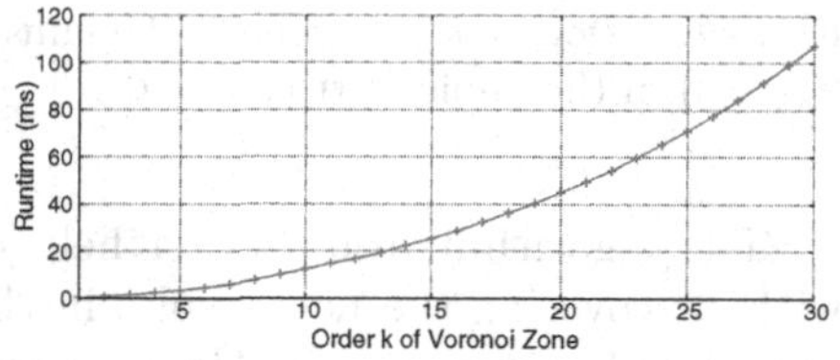

Fig. 11. Runtime for degree-k Voronoi domains for $k = 1, \ldots, 30$, averaged over 600 2D periodic sets for $m = 1, \ldots, 5$.

Figure 10 indicates that starting from about $m = 10$, the runtime increases almost linearly with respect to the number m of motif points as expected by Theorem 17. Figure 11 indicates that the runtime for $n = 2$ follows a slow quadratic increase with respect to the degree k of Voronoi domains, see Theorem 17 (Fig. 14).

The 3D experiments were for periodic sets with m motif points randomly generated for the cubic lattice. Figure 15 shows degree-5 Voronoi domains for the FCC (face-centred cubic) and BCC (body-centred cubic) lattices, and HCP (hexagonal close packing). Figures 12 and 13 illustrate the time in Theorem 17 for $n = 3$.

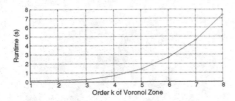

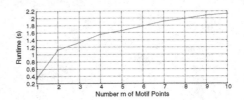

Fig. 12. Runtime to compute the degree-k Voronoi domains for $k = 1, \ldots, 8$, averaged over 10 3D periodic point sets for each value of $m = 1, \ldots, 5$.

Fig. 13. Runtime to compute the first 5 degree-k Voronoi domains as the number of motif points takes values $m = 1, \ldots, 10$, averaged over 10 3D periodic point sets.

Fig. 14. Degree-k Voronoi domains $Z_k(\Lambda; 0)$ in the cubic lattice, $k = 4, 5, 6$.

Fig. 15. Degree-5 Voronoi domains for FCC, BCC and HCP respectively.

The algorithm from Sect. 4 helped compute the density functions in [12] without covering the new results in this paper. These functions were explicitly described for any periodic 1D sequence in [5]. The C++ code for the algorithm in Sect. 4 is available by request. This research opened the wider area of Geometric Data Science studying point sets up to isometry. Persistent homology turned out to be a weaker isometry invariant than previously anticipated [24], but complete isometry invariants with continuous and computable metrics were recently constructed in [17]. Isometry invariants and continuous metrics of periodic sets were initiated in [2,21], see the recent progress in [3,4,6,7,18–20,26–30].

References

1. Andrew, R.C., Salagaram, T., Chetty, N.: Visualising higher order Brillouin zones with applications. Eur. J. Phys. **38**(3), 035501 (2017)
2. Anosova, O., Kurlin, V.: Introduction to periodic geometry and topology. arXiv:2103.02749 (2021)
3. Anosova, O., Kurlin, V.: An isometry classification of periodic point sets. In: Lindblad, J., Malmberg, F., Sladoje, N. (eds.) DGMM 2021. LNCS, vol. 12708, pp. 229–241. Springer, Cham (2021). https://doi.org/10.1007/978-3-030-76657-3_16
4. Anosova, O., Kurlin, V.: Algorithms for continuous metrics on periodic crystals. arXiv:2205.15298 (2022)
5. Anosova, O., Kurlin, V.: Density functions of periodic sequences. In: Discrete Geometry and Mathematical Morphology (2022)
6. Bright, M., Cooper, A., Kurlin, V.: Welcome to a continuous world of 3-dimensional lattices. arxiv:2109.11538 (2021)

7. Bright, M.J., Cooper, A.I., Kurlin, V.A.: Geographic-style maps for 2-dimensional lattices. Acta Crystallographica Sect. A **79**(1), (2023)
8. Chan, T.M.: Random sampling, halfspace range reporting, and construction of k-levels in three dimensions. SIAM J. Comput. **30**(2), 561–575 (2000)
9. Dolbilin, N., Huson, D.: Periodic Delone tilings. Per. Math. Hung. **34**, 57–64 (1997). https://doi.org/10.1023/A:1004272423695
10. Edelsbrunner, H., Garber, A., Ghafari, M., Heiss, T., Saghafian, M.: On angles in higher order brillouin tessellations and related tilings in the plane. arxiv:2204.01076
11. Edelsbrunner, H., Garber, A., Ghafari, M., Heiss, T., Saghafian, M., Wintraecken, M.: Brillouin zones of integer lattices and their perturbations. arxiv:2204.01077
12. Edelsbrunner, H., Heiss, T., Kurlin, V., Smith, P., Wintraecken, M.: The density fingerprint of a periodic point set. In: Symposium on Computational Geometry, pp. 32:1–32:16 (2021)
13. Edelsbrunner, H., Iglesias-Ham, M.: On the optimality of the FCC lattice for soft sphere packing. SIAM J. Discrete Math. **32**(1), 750–782 (2018)
14. Edelsbrunner, H., Osang, G.: A simple algorithm for higher-order Delaunay mosaics and alpha shapes. Algorithmica, 1–19 (2022). Springer
15. Edelsbrunner, H., Seidel, R.: Voronoi diagrams and arrangements. Discrete Comput. Geom. **1**(1), 25–44 (1986). https://doi.org/10.1007/BF02187681
16. Hart, G., Jorgensen, J., Morgan, W., Forcade, R.: A robust algorithm for k-point grid generation and symmetry reduction. J. Phys. Commun. **3**(6), 065009 (2019)
17. Kurlin, V.: Complete invariants for finite clouds of unlabeled points. arxiv:2207.08502
18. Kurlin, V.: A complete isometry classification of 3D lattices. arxiv:2201.10543
19. Kurlin, V.: Exactly computable and continuous metrics on isometry classes of finite and 1-periodic sequences. arXiv:2205.04388 (2022)
20. Kurlin, V.A.: Mathematics of 2-dimensional lattices. Found. Comput. Math. (to appear)
21. Mosca, M., Kurlin, V.: Voronoi-based similarity distances between arbitrary crystal lattices. Cryst. Res. Technol. **55**(5), 1900197 (2020)
22. Nguyen, P.Q., Stehlé, D.: Low-dimensional lattice basis reduction revisited. ACM Trans. Algorithms **5**(4) (2009). https://doi.org/10.1145/1597036.1597050
23. Osang, G., Rouxel-Labbé, M., Teillaud, M.: Generalizing CGAL periodic Delaunay triangulations. In: European Symposium on Algorithms, pp. 75:1–75:17 (2020)
24. Smith, P., Kurlin, V.: Families of point sets with identical 1D persistence. arxiv:2202.00577 (2022)
25. TLP. https://www.doitpoms.ac.uk/tlplib/brillouin_zones/index.php
26. Torda, M., Goulermas, J.Y., Kurlin, V., Day, G.M.: Densest plane group packings of regular polygons, Phys. Rev. E **106**(5), 054603 (2022). APS
27. Vriza, A., et al.: Molecular set transformer: attending to the co-crystals in the Cambridge structural database. Digital Discovery (2022)
28. Widdowson, D., Kurlin, V.: Resolving the data ambiguity for periodic crystals. In: Advances in Neural Information Processing Systems (NeurIPS), vol. 35 (2022)
29. Widdowson, D., Mosca, M., Pulido, A., Cooper, A., Kurlin, V.: Average minimum distances of periodic sets. MATCH Commun. Math. Comput. Chem. **87**, 529–559 (2022)
30. Zhu, Q., et al.: Analogy powered by prediction and structural invariants. J. Am. Chem. Soc. **144**, 9893–9901 (2022)

End-to-End Deep Neural Network for Illumination Consistency and Global Illumination

Huang Jingtao and Takashi Komuro[✉]

Saitama University, Saitama 338-8570, Japan
komuro@mail.saitama-u.ac.jp

Abstract. In this study, we propose a real-time method for realizing illumination consistency and global illumination in augmented reality (AR). The proposed method uses pix2pix, which is a generative adversarial network (GAN) for image-to-image translation. The network takes an image with k channels as the input, and attempts to generate reflections and shadows of a virtual object corresponding to the illumination condition. We also propose an approach for improving the applicability of the method by combining RGB information with geometric information (normal and depth) as the network input. For evaluating the proposed method, we created a synthetic dataset by using Unreal Engine 4, which can render computer graphics (CG) images with global illumination. The results of an experiment indicated that although generated images were not completely the same as the ground truth, the proposed method reproduced natural-looking reflections and shadows of a virtual object.

Keywords: Augmented reality · Illumination consistency · Global illumination · Generative adversarial network

1 Introduction

Rendering virtual objects seamlessly onto real-world scenes is a very important goal of augmented reality (AR). This difficult task requires the objects to be lit consistently with the surfaces in their vicinity and that the interplay of light between the objects and their surroundings to be properly simulated. Specifically, the objects should cast shadows and reflect light as real objects would do. This visual coherence of illumination between the real world and virtual objects is called illumination consistency. In order to add more realistic lighting to AR scenes, it is necessary to take into account not only the light that comes directly from light sources (direct illumination) but also the light that is reflected on other surfaces (indirect illumination). Environmental objects affect the rendering of reflections and shadows of virtual objects. A group of algorithms used for calculating indirect illumination between environment and virtual objects is called global illumination.

G. Bebis et al. (Eds.): ISVC 2022, LNCS 13598, pp. 392–403, 2022.
https://doi.org/10.1007/978-3-031-20713-6_30

Most of existing solutions for achieving illumination consistency and global illumination in AR involve two steps: illumination estimation and virtual object rendering. In the first step, a panoramic high dynamic range (HDR) map needs to be generated in order to obtain the illumination information of a scene. In the second step, reflections and shadows of virtual objects are rendered according to the illumination information. The HDR environment map can be generated by placing light probes in the real environment, such as a spherical mirror or a 360-degree camera [1–3]. As an another approach, Kán et al. rotated a mobile device about 360° to scan the surrounding environment for reconstructing an HDR environment map [4]. In recent years, with the progress of research on deep learning, convolutional neural network (CNN) solutions for estimating HDR illumination information from a low dynamic range (LDR) image with a limited field of view have been proposed [5,6]. However, with these two-step solutions, it is difficult to render a virtual object in real-time because it takes time to dynamically construct the environment map and compute the global illumination.

Recently, end-to-end solutions, in which an input is received from one end and an output is produced at the other end and all intermediate processing is implemented by deep learning, have been used to implicitly estimate the illumination information of a scene. Thomas et al. [7] proposed a method for generating a global illumination scene from a direct illumination scene using pix2pix [8], which is an image transformation network based on the Generative Adversarial Network (GAN). Wang et al. [9] used pix2pixHD [10] for directly generating diffuse reflections and shadows of virtual objects. However, existing end-to-end solutions have been applied only to simple scenes, in which the intensity of light sources was constant, and the positions of light sources and environment objects were fixed. In addition, these studies only used a dataset with one virtual object to train a neural network.

In this study, we try to extend existing end-to-end solutions to be applicable to more complex scenes, in which the light sources and environment objects are not fixed. We use an end-to-end network to generate the reflections and shadows of a virtual object from RGB and geometric information of a scene, in order to achieve illumination consistency and global illumination.

2   Proposed Method

2.1   Generating Reflections and Shadows of Virtual Objects

We use pix2pix [8], which is a GAN-based image-to-image translation network, in order to realize illumination consistency and global illumination in AR.

As shown in Fig. 1, the pix2pix network consists of a generator and a discriminator. The generator network is an auto-encoder, which takes an image with k channels as the input, and that attempts to generate the reflections and shadows of a virtual object corresponding to the illumination information.

The discriminator is a deep convolutional neural network, taking either the ground truth output or the generated output from the generator, and classifies them into real or fake, where "real" means that the input is an image that is

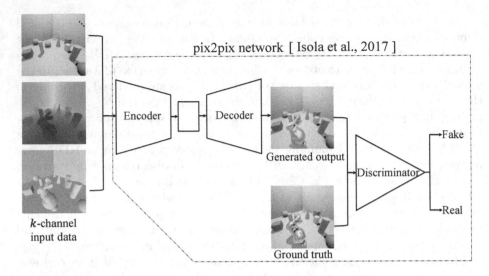

Fig. 1. Overview of the proposed method. k-channel data consisting of RGB and geometry information is input to pix2pix [8] network.

rendered by a global illumination algorithm. Thus, the generator and discriminator play a min-max adversarial game where the generator tries its best to fool the discriminator into thinking that the generated output is from the real distribution and the discriminator tries to learn from the real and generated images to classify them. This game will continue until the discriminator is unable to distinguish between real and generated images.

The loss function defines how the error between the network outputs $G(x)$ and the ground truth y is computed during training. For the network, the min-max adversarial game refers to the minimization of the generator loss and the maximization of the discriminator's loss:

$$\mathcal{L}_p = \min_G \max_D \mathcal{L}_{GAN}(G, D) + \lambda \mathcal{L}_{L1}(G) \tag{1}$$

where the discriminator seeks to maximize the average of the log probability of real images (ground truth) and the log of the inverse probability for fake images (generated outputs). The generator seeks to minimize the log of the inverse probability predicted by the discriminator for fake images:

$$\mathcal{L}_{GAN}(G, D) = E_{(x,y)}[\log D(x, y)] \\ + E_x[\log(1 - D(x, G(x)))] \tag{2}$$

while L_1 loss is used to reduct the artifact of generated outputs:

$$\mathcal{L}_{L1}(G) = E_{(x,y)}[|y - G(x)|] \tag{3}$$

2.2   Combination of RGB and Geometric Data

We combine RGB and geometric data (normal and depth) as the input to the network in order to improve the applicability of our method. Since normals provide information of surface orientations, and depths provide structural information of a scene, the network could robustly generate reflections and shadows of a virtual object in a complex scene.

9-Channel Data Concatenating RGB, Depth, and Normal Data. As the first solution, we concatenate the 3-channel RGB data of the background scene, the 3-channel depth data of the entire scene containing both the background and the virtual object, which is created by duplicating a single-channel depth data, and the 3-channel normal data of the entire scene into an image with 9 channels as shown in Fig. 2.

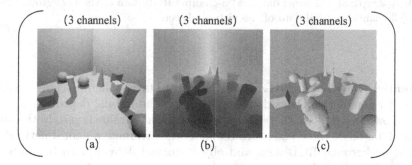

Fig. 2. A sample of 9-channel data: (a) 3-channel RGB data of the background scene, (b) 3-channel depth data of the entire scene, and (c) 3-channel normal data of the entire scene.

In the background scene, there are several objects which are lit by light sources and cast shadows in various directions. The directions and intensities of shadows are highly correlated with the positions and intensities of light sources. Thus, the shadow information provided by the RGB data is needed to estimate illumination information. Since structure information of objects determines the shape of shadows, we use the scene depth data to provide structure information of both background and virtual objects. The surface orientations are related to the luminance of reflected light, and we used the scene normal data to provide information of surface orientations, which would help better rendering of reflections.

6-Channel Data Concatenating RGB and Normal Data. Since the geometry of background scene is difficult to obtain without using a depth sensor, we propose an optional solution for combining RGB and geometric information. In this solution, we concatenate the 3-channel RGB data of the background scene

and the 3-channel normal data of the virtual object into an image with 6 channels
as shown in Fig. 3.

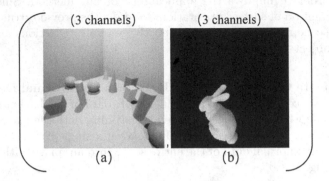

Fig. 3. A sample of 6-channel data: (a) 3-channel RGB data of the background scene,
and (b) 3-channel normal data of the virtual object.

3-Channel Data Fusing RGB and Normal Data. There is another simpli-
fication for combination that does not require an additional depth sensor.

As shown in Fig. 3(b), there are many pixels whose value is zero in the object
normal data. Since these pixels are redundant for training a neural network, we
fuse the background RGB data and object normal data into an image with 3
channels as shown in Fig. 4.

Fig. 4. A sample of 3-channel data.

3   Experiment

3.1   Creating a Dataset

We created a synthetic dataset by using Unreal Engine 4 [11], which can render CG images with global illumination, to evaluate the proposed method.

For generating image sets, we built virtual scenes, each of which consisted of three elements: a background scene, a virtual object, and a camera as shown in Fig. 5. In the background scene, we put 20 objects that have simple geometric structures and two different point light sources: a brighter one and a darker one, in a cube room. The positions of background objects and light sources were randomly determined for each scene. Then, the virtual object with a complex geometric structure was placed in the middle of the room with the fixed position and orientation. We used 14 kinds of virtual objects with the 3D models downloaded from the Stanford 3D Scanning Repository. Finally, We placed a camera on a hemisphere that was centered on the virtual object with randomly changing the (θ, φ) of the spherical coordinate system (r, θ, φ).

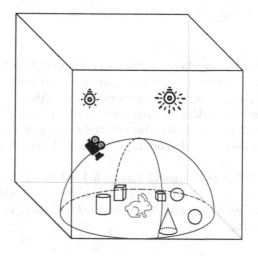

Fig. 5. Overview of the virtual scene.

We used two kinds of metallic materials for virtual objects: nickel and steel. The nickle material has blurred surfaces while the steel material reflects the surrounding scene clearly as shown in Fig. 6. These materials were rendered using the parameters shown in Table 1.

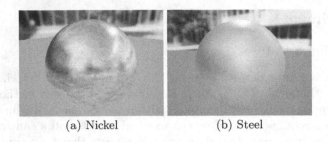

(a) Nickel   (b) Steel

Fig. 6. The materials used in the experiment.

Table 1. The parameters of the materials used in the experiment.

Parameter	Material	
	Nickel	Steel
BaseColor	(0.95, 0.95, 0.95)	(0.5, 0.5, 0.5)
Metallic	1	1
Specular	0	0
Roughness	0.4	0.2

In order to create the synthetic dataset of k-channel input data as shown in Fig. 7, two types of CG images were rendered first: (a) background RGB data and (b) scene RGB data (used as the ground truth). After rendering the scene RGB data, (c) scene depth data and (d) scene normal data were extracted from the g-buffer of Unreal Engine 4. We also created (e) object mask to generate (f) object normal data and (g) 3-channel input data. All images were created with 256×256 pixels.

We rendered 1,000 sets of images for each kind of virtual object and each material. Since there were 14 kinds of virtual objects, a total of 14,000 image sets were created for each material. We used 10,000 of them for training and the rest of them for testing.

3.2   Training the Network

We trained the network with a batch size of 1 for 200 epochs, using the Adam optimization algorithm with a fixed learning rate of 0.0002. We conducted training using a PC having a 2.9 GHz i7-10700 CPU, 32 GB RAM, and an NVIDIA GeForce RTX 2070 Super GPU. The training took approximately three days for each types of input data.

3.3   Qualitative Results

Figure 8 shows the results of generated images for the nickel material. The nickel material has higher roughness and there is little reflection of the surrounding

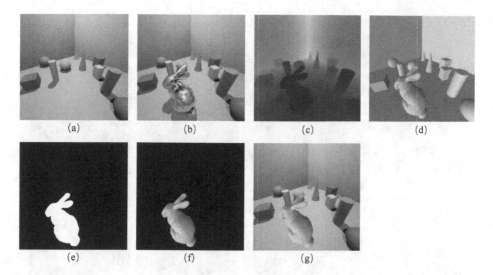

Fig. 7. A sample of the image sets in our synthetic dataset: (a) background RGB data, (b) scene RGB data, (c) scene depth data, (d) scene normal data, (e) object mask, (f) object normal data, and (g) generated 3-channel input data.

scene. As shown in Fig. 8(a), our method successfully reproduced the base color and the specular reflection of nickel material. In Fig. 8(b), although the reproduced reflection is not similar to that of the ground truth, our method reproduced natural-looking reflection. By comparing the results of three different inputs, we found that 6-channel input data produced the smoothest metal surfaces and 3-channel and 9-channel input data tend to produce more noises and undesired artifacts. In Fig. 8(c) and (d), the results show that the network learned from the background objects to generate shadows of a virtual object. Although the shape of the shadows is incorrect, the color and direction match the shadows of the background objects.

Figure 9 shows the results of generated images for the steel material. The results demonstrate that the network generated colorful reflections of the surrounding scene on the surface of virtual objects. Although our input data was provided in a limited view, the network learned to generate indirect reflections from the walls.

In most cases, although generated images were not completely the same as the ground truth, the proposed method reproduced natural-looking reflections and shadows of a virtual object, which is probably thanks to the use of a GAN-based network.

In some cases, however, our method failed to correctly reproduce the shadows of a virtual object as shown in Fig. 10. The reason may be that the structure of the virtual object is too complex, which causes the exact shape of the shadows to be difficult to predict.

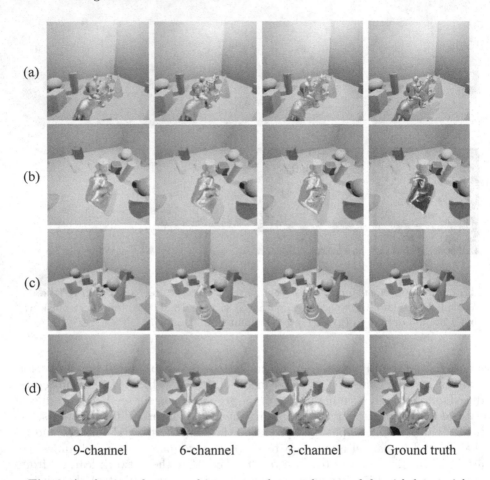

(a)

(b)

(c)

(d)

| 9-channel | 6-channel | 3-channel | Ground truth |

Fig. 8. A selection of generated images on the test dataset of the nickel material.

3.4   Quantitative Results

The peak signal-to-noise ratio (PSNR) and the structural similarity index measure (SSIM) for each type of input data were calculated by using 4,000 pairs of generated results and ground truth, in order to quantitatively evaluate the performance of our method. The result for each material is shown in Table 2. We found that the performance of 6-channel input data showed the highest SSIM and PSNR values though the differences among the types of input data are small.

We also measured the computational speed of image generation on the PC which was used for training the network. The results are shown in Table 3, and they prove that our method can generate images with illumination consistency and global illumination in real-time.

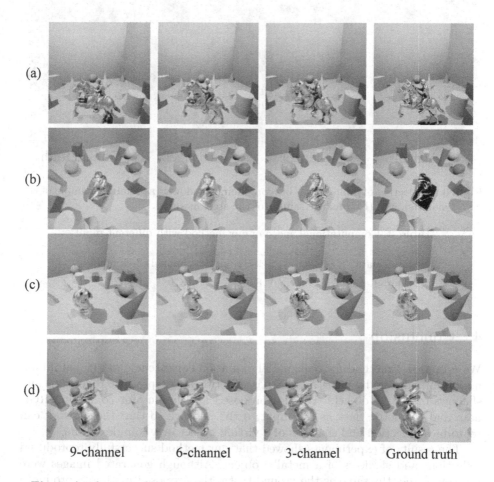

Fig. 9. A selection of generated images on the test dataset of the steel material.

Table 2. PSNR and SSIM values for each material.

Material	Metric	9-channel	6-channel	3-channel
Nickel	PSNR	24.9450	25.1183	24.7196
	SSIM	0.9068	0.9124	0.9060
Steel	PSNR	26.6663	26.6974	26.8725
	SSIM	0.9143	0.9147	0.9146

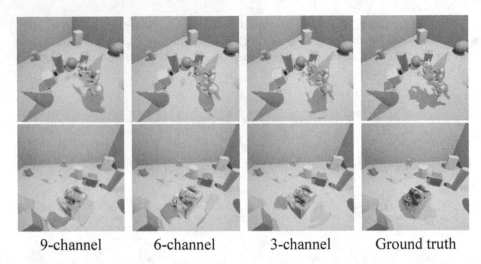

| 9-channel | 6-channel | 3-channel | Ground truth |

Fig. 10. A selection of failure cases of reproducing shadows: (a) a failure sample of the nickel material, and (b) a failure sample of the steel material.

Table 3. Computational speed of our method with different input.

Input data	9-channel	6-channel	3-channel
Computational speed (ms)	8.4229	8.1379	8.3075

4   Conclusion

We proposed a method for realizing illumination consistency and global illumination in real time by using a GAN-based network to reproduce reflections and shadows of virtual objects. We also proposed a technique for combining RGB data and geometric data as the input to the network so that the network can reproduce reflection and shadows of a virtual object in a complex scene.

The results of experiments showed that our method successfully reproduced reflections and shadows of a metallic object. Although generated images were not completely the same as the ground truth, the proposed method reproduced natural-looking reflections and shadows thanks to the use of a GAN-based network.

The neural network was trained with a synthetic dataset in our experiment. In the future, a real world dataset will have to be created so that we can verify whether the proposed method is applicable to a real scene.

References

1. Debevec, P.: Image-based lighting. In: Proceedings of the ACM Special Interest Group on Graphics and Interactive Techniques 2006 Courses, p. 4-es (2006)
2. Pessoa, S.A., et al.: Illumination techniques for photorealistic rendering in augmented reality. In: Proceedings of the Symposium on Virtual and Augmented Reality 2008, pp. 223–232 (2008)
3. Tuceryan, M.: AR360: dynamic illumination for augmented reality with real-time interaction. In: Proceedings of the IEEE International Conference on Information and Computer Technologies 2019, pp. 170–174 (2019)
4. Kán, P., Unterguggenberger, J., Kaufmann, H.: High-quality consistent illumination in mobile augmented reality by radiance convolution on the GPU. In: Bebis, G., et al. (eds.) ISVC 2015. LNCS, vol. 9474, pp. 574–585. Springer, Cham (2015). https://doi.org/10.1007/978-3-319-27857-5_52
5. Gardner, M.-A., et al.: Learning to predict indoor illumination from a single image. ACM Trans. Graph. **36**(6), Article no. 176 (2017)
6. Hold-Geoffroy, Y., Sunkavalli, K., Hadap, S., Gambaretto, E., Lalonde, J.-F.: Deep outdoor illumination estimation. In: Proceedings of the IEEE Conference on Computer Vision and Pattern Recognition 2017, pp. 7312–7321 (2017)
7. Thomas, M.M., Forbes, A.G.: Deep illumination: approximating dynamic global illumination with generative adversarial network. arXiv preprint arXiv:1710.09834 (2017)
8. Isola, P., Zhu, J.-Y., Zhou, T., Efros, A.A.: Image-to-image translation with conditional adversarial networks. In: Proceedings of the IEEE Conference on Computer Vision and Pattern Recognition 2017, pp. 1125–1134 (2017)
9. Wang, X., Wang, K., Lian, S.: Deep consistent illumination in augmented reality. In: Adjunct Proceedings of the IEEE International Symposium on Mixed and Augmented Reality 2019, pp. 189–194 (2019)
10. Wang, T.-C., Liu, M.-Y., Zhu, J.-Y., Tao, A., Kautz, J., Catanzaro, B.: High-resolution image synthesis and semantic manipulation with conditional GANs. In: Proceedings of the IEEE Conference on Computer Vision and Pattern Recognition 2018, pp. 8798–8807 (2018)
11. https://www.unrealengine.com

Pruning-Based Topology Refinement of 3D Mesh Using a 2D Alpha Mask

Gaétan Landreau[1,2](✉) and Mohamed Tamaazousti[2](✉)

[1] Meero, 75002 Paris, France
gaetan.landreau@meero.com
[2] Université Paris-Saclay, CEA-LIST, 91120 Palaiseau, France
mohamed.tamaazousti@cea.fr

Abstract. Image-based 3D reconstruction has increasingly stunning results over the past few years with the latest improvements in computer vision and graphics. Geometry and topology are two fundamental concepts when dealing with 3D mesh structures. But the latest often remains a side issue in the 3D mesh-based reconstruction literature. Indeed, performing per-vertex elementary displacements over a 3D sphere mesh only impacts its geometry and leaves the topological structure unchanged and fixed. Whereas few attempts propose to update the geometry and the topology, all need to lean on costly 3D ground-truth to determine the faces/edges to prune. We present in this work a method that aims to refine the topology of any 3D mesh through a face-pruning strategy that extensively relies upon 2D alpha masks and camera pose information. Our solution leverages a differentiable renderer that renders each face as a 2D soft map. Its pixel intensity reflects the probability of being covered during the rendering process by such a face. Based on the 2D soft-masks available, our method is thus able to quickly highlight all the incorrectly rendered faces for a given viewpoint. Because our module is agnostic to the network that produces the 3D mesh, it can be easily plugged into any self-supervised image-based (either synthetic or natural) 3D reconstruction pipeline to get complex meshes with a non-spherical topology.

Keywords: Topology · 3D deep-learning · Computer graphics

1 Introduction

The image-based 3D reconstruction task aims at building a 3D representation of a given object/scene depicted in a set of images. From a very early age, humans learn to apprehend their surrounding 3-dimensional environment and thus have high cognitive abilities for mentally representing the whole 3D scene structure from a single image. Doing so for any vision algorithm is way more challenging since computers do not have such sensitive prior knowledge. Inferring 3D information from a lower dimensional 2D space is thus an arduous task in visual computing. Whereas literature has tackled image-based 3D reconstruction for

G. Bebis et al. (Eds.): ISVC 2022, LNCS 13598, pp. 404–415, 2022.
https://doi.org/10.1007/978-3-031-20713-6_31

decades in computer vision and graphics with robust and renowned techniques such as Structure-from-Motion [14], the latest learning-based approaches address the problem through the new prism of deep neural networks [4,9,21].

The single-image-based 3D reconstruction issue even brings the challenge one step above as input information is solely constrained to a single image. From a general perspective, the latest contributions in single-image 3D reconstruction chose to work with mesh structures rather than 3D point clouds or voxels since they offer a well-balanced trade-off between computational requirements and tiny 3D details retrieval. Meshes also embed a notion of connectivity between vertices, contrary to the point cloud representation where such valuable property is inherently missing.

The rendering operation somehow fills the gap between the 3D world and the 2D image plane by mimicking the optical image formation process. Whereas the procedure is well-known in graphics for decades, it has only been brought into computer vision learning-based approaches for a few years. Indeed, the rasterization stage involved in any rendering process is intrinsically non-differentiable (since it requires a face selection step), making its integration in any deep architecture intractable from a backward loss computational perspective. The latest progress has led a few years ago to single-image 3D reconstruction methods where 3D ground truth labels are no longer needed: supervisory signal directly comes from a differentiable renderer at the 2-dimensional image level.

There are two main ways to update the topology of any mesh during 3D object reconstruction: by either pruning some edges/ faces or, on the other hand, by adopting the opposite strategy and thus adding edges or vertices at the correct location to generate new faces onto the mesh surface. Single-image 3D reconstruction methods that require 3D supervision already apply these techniques in their training pipeline [16,18,22]. However, most of the current state-of-the-art methods in self-supervised single-image 3D reconstruction -where 3D labels are thus no more needed- perform mesh reconstruction with a roughly similar approach. An Encoder-Decoder network iteratively learns to predict an elementary per-vertex displacement on a 3D template sphere to faithfully reconstruct, as better as possible, the mesh associated with the input images. Such a strategy only affects the geometry of the mesh and thus does not get consideration for its topology. Indeed, vertice position impacts edges length and dihedral face angles but leaves the overall topology unchanged: two faces sharing an edge at the beginning of the training still do so at the end. These topological considerations, yet fundamental when embracing 3D mesh structures, are often bypassed in the current self-supervised single image-based 3D reconstruction literature. We thus claim that the latest advances in differentiable rendering [12,20] are informative enough to address this fundamental concept.

Our work thus brings topological considerations to the self-supervised image-based 3D reconstruction issue. From a general perspective, our method leverages the differentiable renderer from [20] to catch up through an efficient and fast procedure the most likely mesh's faces to prune without accounting for costly 3D supervision, as done in [16,18,22]. As far as we are informed, no attempts in the current literature exist in this direction. Our work is thus in line with self-supervised image-based 3D reconstruction methods, while our topological refinement method is agnostic to the mesh reconstruction network used.

We summarise our contribution through:

- A fast and efficient strategy to prune faces on a 3D mesh by only leveraging 2D alpha masks and camera pose.
- An agnostic topological refinement module to the 3D mesh reconstruction network.

2   Related Works

Differentiable Renderer. Since our work aims to be integrated within a deep architecture as an add-on module to perform complex 3D mesh reconstruction, we naturally focus on existing state-of-the-art differentiable renderers. Even though they perform much better than their differentiable counterparts, they can not be plugged into learning-based networks: there will be a network layer where back-propagation can no longer take place. OpenDR [15] paved the way in 2014 regarding differentiable rendering. However, the such topic has only gained significant interest over the past few years in deep learning-based computer vision tasks. Compelling progress was reached in 2017 by Hiroharu Kato *et al.* with an approximated gradient-based strategy called NMR [10]. But SoftRasterizer [12] designed the first differentiable framework without gradient approximation through a probability-distance-based formulation whereas Chen *et al.* designed their differentiable renderer with foreground-background pixel consideration in their DIB-R [1] method. In addition to those renderers that are thus primarily designed to work with mesh, other types of renderers [8,17] also emerged a few years ago to address the rendering of implicit 3D shape surfaces.

Single Image-Based 3D Reconstruction. Initiating works [2,5,27] related to learning-based single image 3D reconstruction extensively leveraged on 3D datasets [23,25] to let the generative network apprehends the 3D structure it must learn. These methods lack the physical image formation process during training since there is no need to consider it as soon as 3D labels are accessible. In this way, existing 3D loss functions are sufficient to predict feasible 3D mesh structures from a 3D sphere template. While tremendous works have leveraged over 3D labels, the current trend in single image-based 3D reconstruction instead tries to advantage differentiable renderers and thus limit the need for expensive 3D supervision. It led in the last few years to a new path of work called self-supervised image-based 3D reconstruction [7,9,11,19] where 3D ground truth meshes are no more needed. Differentiable rendering allows to render the predicted 3D mesh onto a 2D image plane and gets a meaningful 2D supervision signal to train a mesh reconstruction network in an end-to-end way.

Topology. Implicit-based methods spontaneously handle complex topology since any 3D object parameterises in a continuous 3-dimensional vector field where the notion of connectivity is absent. Generated surfaces do not suffer from resolution limitations as soon as the 3D space is continuously defined. Works relying on such formulation produce outstanding results but often require extensive use of 3D supervision [21], even though the latest research achieved reconstructing 3D implicit surfaces without 3D labels [13,17].

The topological issue on explicit-based formulation are already addressed when it comes to supervise the mesh generation with 3D labels. Pix2Mesh [24] leverages the capacity of Graph Neural Networks and their graph unpooling operation to add new vertices on the initial template mesh during training. With the same will to add a new vertex/face, GEOMetrics [22] considers an explicit adaptive face splitting strategy to locally increase face density and thus ensure that the generated mesh will have enough detail around the most complex regions. The face splitting decision relies on local curvature consideration with a fixed threshold. These two methods adopt a progressive mesh growing strategy and thus start from a low-resolution template mesh to end up with a 3D mesh which is complex only in the most challenging regions to reconstruct.

On the other hand, Junyi Pan *et al.* [18] paved the way to prune irrelevant faces onto 3D mesh surface. They introduced a face-pruning method through a 3D point cloud-based error-estimation network. While [18] used a fixed scalar threshold to determine whether or not to prune a face, Total3D [16] proposes a refined version of such a method by performing edge pruning with an adaptive thresholding strategy set on 3D local considerations.

To the best of our knowledge, such topological issue on 3D mesh structures is currently not addressed in the state of the art methods that extensively rely on 2D cues for training. Generated meshes are thus always isomorphic to a 3D sphere.

3   Method

We introduce our method and the associated framework in this section. We draft a complete overview of our methodology before digging into the implementation details of the module we designed.

Regarding the notation, we denote by $I \in \mathbb{R}^{H \times W \times 4}$ the source RGBα image, where α therefore refers to the (ground-truth) alpha mask. We aim to refine the topology of a mesh $\mathbf{M} = (V, F)$ where V and F respectively stand for the set of vertices and faces. We assume such mesh was obtained from a genus-0 template shape by any single-image 3D mesh reconstruction network (fed with either the RGB image or its alpha mask counterpart). Finally, the camera pose θ is parametrized by an azimuth and an elevation angle, leaving the distance between the object and the camera fixed.

3.1   General Overview

As we extensively rely on the 2D information from α (even though the 3D corresponding camera pose θ is needed) to perform topological refinement over the mesh surface, we must lean on a renderer to get back onto 2D considerations.

We consider the differentiable one from PyTorch3D [20] since it allows the generation of meaningful per-face rendered maps that one can aggregate to produce the final rendered mask. The core idea of our work is to identify the faces that were re-projected the worst onto the 2D image plane during the rasterization procedure through the prior information from α. Figure 1 depicts the general overview of our face-pruning method.

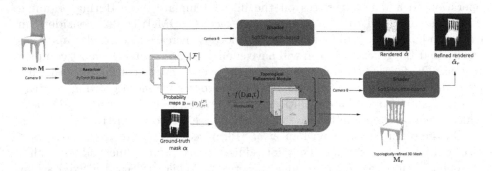

Fig. 1. Architecture overview of our method. *Based on a 3D mesh* **M** *and a camera pose* θ, *our module leverages PyTorch3D rasterizer to detect and prune onto the mesh surface by only getting consideration for the ground-truth alpha mask* α.

Detecting those faces is driven through the computation of an Intersection over Union (IoU) score between each per-face rendered map with ground-truth α. Those faces can then be removed from the 3D mesh surface or directly discarded in the shader stage of the renderer. Inspired by the thresholding strategy introduced in TMN [18], we get consideration for t, an adaptative threshold based on the IoU score distribution γ/Γ and quantile Q_τ, $\tau \in [0, 1]$.

$$t = Q_\tau(\gamma/\Gamma) \tag{1}$$

In a similar fashion line to what TMN [18] did for the thresholding strategy in their pipeline architecture, the setting of τ influences the number of pruned faces: the lower τ is, the lower the number of faces detected as wrongly projected will be.

3.2 Implementation Details

We implement our topological refinement strategy onto the renderer from the PyTorch3D [20] library. The renderer's modularity offered by [20] is worth mentioning since the entire rendering procedure can be adjusted as desired. We paid attention to the rasterization stage for its connivance with the one from Soft-Rasterizer [12].

One of the core differences between those two frameworks in the silhouette rasterization process concerns the number of faces involved: while PyTorch3D only considers for each pixel location p_i the top-K closest faces from the camera center, SoftRasterizer equally considers all the faces of $\mathbf{M}$. We denote by $\mathbf{P} \in \mathbb{R}^{K \times (H \times W)}$ the intermediate probability map produced by [20] which is highly related to the one originally introduced in [12]. Considering any 2D pixel location $p_i = (x_i; y_i) \in \{0, ..H-1\} \times \in \{0, ..W-1\}$ and the kth closest face f_k^i, the distance based probability tensor $\mathbf{P}$ is expressed through:

$$\mathbf{P}[k, p_i] = \left(1 + e^{-d(f_k^i, p_i)/\sigma}\right)^{-1} \tag{2}$$

where $d(f_k^i, p_i)$ stands for the Euclidean distance between p_i and f_k^i, while σ is a hyperparameter to control the sharpness of the rendered silhouette image. Both d and σ are defined in SoftRasterizer [12].

It is worth emphasizing the indexing notation of $\mathbf{P}$. Indeed, face indexes f_k^i and $f_{k'}^{i'}$, $\{i, k\} \neq \{i', k'\}$ might refer to the same physical face on $\mathbf{M}$ because a rendered one is likely to cover an area larger than a single pixel. One could already build up an aggregation function to render a final predicted alpha mask from $\mathbf{P}$ but the computational cost would not be optimal.

We thus introduced $\mathcal{F}$ as the set of unique faces from $\mathbf{P}$ involved in the rendering of $\mathbf{M}$. The larger K is, the more likely the cardinality of $\mathcal{F}$ will get close to the total number of faces in the original mesh $|F|$.

We denote by $\mathbf{D} = \{D_j\}_{j=1}^{|\mathcal{F}|} \in \mathbb{R}^{|\mathcal{F}| \times (H \times W)}$ the probability map tensor, as defined in [12], that accounts (contrary to $\mathbf{P}$) on all the unique faces (indexed f_j) involved in the rendering process. Following Eq. 2 formulation, we have for any pixel location p_i:

$$D_j[p_i] = \left(1 + e^{-d(f_j, p_i)/\sigma}\right)^{-1} \tag{3}$$

Our module status on pruning the face f_j considering the degree of overlap between the ground truth $\boldsymbol{\alpha}$ and the corresponding probability map D_j. Since each face $f_j \in \mathcal{F}$ contributes to the final rendered, an Intersection over Union (IoU) term is computed per face:

$$\begin{cases} \gamma_j = \sum_{p_i \in \alpha} \min\left(D_j[p_i], \boldsymbol{\alpha}[p_i]\right) \\ \Gamma_j = \sum_{p_i \in \alpha} \max\left(D_j[p_i], \boldsymbol{\alpha}[p_i]\right) \end{cases} \tag{4}$$

The ratio γ_j/Γ_j gives the well-known IoU score. We extend the computation for a single face f_j to all the faces from $\mathcal{F}$, and denote by $\gamma/\Gamma \in \mathbb{R}^{|\mathcal{F}|}$ the complete IoU score distribution.

We adopt a thresholding strategy partially inspired from [18] and set an adaptive threshold t based on statistical quantile consideration: faces with a lower IoU score than $t = Q_\tau(\gamma/\Gamma)$ are pruned from $\mathbf{M}$ to give a refined mesh $\mathbf{M}_r$.

Given all these considerations, two different predictions can be made on the final rendered mask:

$$\begin{cases} \hat{\boldsymbol{\alpha}}[p_i] = 1 - \prod_{j=1}^{|\mathcal{F}|}(1 - D_j[p_i]) \\ \hat{\boldsymbol{\alpha}}_r[p_i] = 1 - \prod_{j=1}^{|\mathcal{F} \setminus \mathcal{F}_p|}(1 - D_j[p_i]) \end{cases} \tag{5}$$

While $\hat{\alpha}$ to the original predicted alpha mask (without any faces pruned), $\hat{\alpha}_r$ refers to the refined predicted silhouette, with $\mathcal{F}_p = \{f_p \in \mathcal{F} | \gamma_p / \Gamma_p < t\}$.

4   Experiments

Dataset. We extensively tested our approach on ShapeNetCore [25]. In line with the work from TMN [18], our experiments are thus limited to the topologically challenging "chair" class from [25]. It contains 6774 different chairs, with 1356 instances in the testing set.

Metrics. We evaluate our method through both qualitative and quantitative considerations. We use the 2D IoU metric to assess how well the refined mesh produced by our module better matches the ground truth alpha mask compared to the topologically non-refined mesh. We also use 3D metrics with the Chamfer Distance (CD), F-Score and METRO distance to evaluate our method. The METRO criterion was introduced in [3] and reconsidered in Thibault Groueix *et al.*'s AtlasNet [6] work. Its use is motivated by its consideration for mesh connectivity contrary to the CD or F-score metric that only reason onto 3D point clouds distribution.

3D Mesh Generation Network. Our refinement module can be integrated into any image-based 3D reconstruction pipeline and is thus agnostic to the network responsible for producing the 3D mesh. We chose to work with the meshes generated by [18]. Since we only want to focus on face-pruning considerations, we only retrain the ResNet18 encoder and the first stage of their 3D mesh reconstruction architecture, referred to as *SubNet-1* in [18] and abbreviated as TMN in this section. The TMN architecture thus consists of a deformation network and a learnt topological modification module. It is worth mentioning the TMN [18] architecture has been trained and used for inference with the provided ground truth labels and rendered images from 3D-R2N2 [2]. We called "Baseline" the deformation network preceding the topology modification network [18]. The genus-0 3D mesh produced by the Baseline network comes from a 3D sphere template with 2562 vertices.

PyTorch3D Renderer. We use the PyTorch3D [20] differentiable renderer and set K=30 and $\sigma = 5.10^{-7}$ to get the alpha mask as sharp as possible. All the 2D alpha masks, size 224×224, were obtained with the PyTorch3D renderer and have been centred. Similarly to what [2,12,26] did for the rendering silhouette masks, we considered 24 views per meshes with a fixed camera distance $d_{camera} = 2.732$ m and an elevation angle set to $30°$. The azimuth angle varies by $15°$ increment, from $0°$ to $345°$. All the meshes predicted by TMN [18] were normalised in the same way as ShapeNetCore [25].

We both present qualitative and quantitative results of our pruning-based method through 2D and 3D evaluation considerations. We demonstrate how effective our strategy can be by only leveraging 2D alpha masks and the renderer modularity.

4.1 Topological Refinement Evaluation - Qualitative Results

We first seek to highlight to what extent we can detect irrelevant faces on the 3D mesh, i.e. those that might be pruned during rendering. Figure 2 depicts the wrongly rendered faces (considered as is by our method) compared to the ground-truth alpha mask on three different chairs. Based on these 2D silhouette considerations, we achieve visually more appealing results than [18].

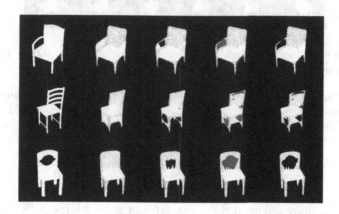

Fig. 2. Silhouette based comparison on several instance from the ShapeNetCore test set. *Faces rendered onto red regions should be pruned on 3D mesh surface -* $\tau = \mathbf{0.05}$ *-* From left to right: Ground-Truth, Baseline, TMN [18], Ours with highlighted faces to prune, Ours final result. (Color figure online)

Figure 3 somehow extends the later observation through 6 different viewpoints from the same chair instance. In this example, the TMN pruning module failed to detect some faces to discard. It produced the same mesh as the baseline one, while our method successfully pruned the faces that have been rendered the worst, according to the ground truth alpha mask. Pruned faces on each view are independent of the other viewpoints.

Even the viewpoint associated with a tricky azimuth angle as the one depicted in the last column of Fig. 3 is informative enough for our module to remove the relevant faces during rendering.

4.2 2D and 3D-Based Quantitative Evaluation

We compare the performances of our method through different thresholds τ in Table 1 with the meshes produced by the Baseline network and TMN [18]. From the 1356 inferred meshes in the ShapeNetCore [25] test set, we manually selected 50 highly challenging meshes (from a topological perspective) and rendered them through 24 different camera viewpoints with the PyTorch3D renderer. The intrinsic F-score threshold was set to 0.001. A total number of

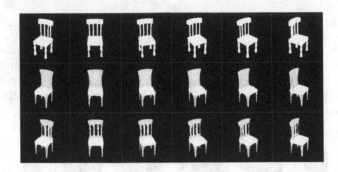

Fig. 3. Rendered silhouette mask results on 6 viewpoints - $\tau = \mathbf{0.05}$ - From top to bottom: Ground-Truth, TMN [18], Ours.

Table 1. 2D and 3D-based metric scores comparison with the Baseline and TMN [18] - *Presented results were averaged over the 50 instance from our manually curated test set and over the 24 different viewpoints for the 3D metrics.*

Method	2D IoU ↑	CD ↓	F-Score ↑	METRO ↓
Baseline	0.660	6.602	53.27	1.419
TMN [18]	0.681	**6.328**	**54.23**	**1.293**
Ours $\tau = 0.01$	0.747	6.541	53.39	1.418
Ours $\tau = 0.03$	0.755	6.539	53.39	1.417
Ours $\tau = 0.05$	0.763	6.540	53.34	1.417
Ours $\tau = 0.1$	**0.778**	6.551	53.27	1.416
Ours $\tau = 0.15$	0.771	6.548	53.26	1.416

N=10.000 points have been uniformly sampled over the different meshes' surfaces to compute the 3D metrics.

Our method outperforms the learned topology modification network from TMN [18] according to Table 1 when compared using the 2D IoU score. It is worth re-mentioning that presented results for TMN [18] come from the first learned topological modification network. They thus do not consider the topological refinement from the *SubNet-2* and *SubNet-3* networks. Whereas none of our configurations (with different τ values) overperforms TMN [18] on 3D metrics, we stress two points:

1. Topologically refined mesh by our method always get better results than the ones produced by the Baseline.
2. Our face-pruning strategy only relies on a single 2D alpha mask and does not require any form of 3D-supervised compared to [18].

Since the method we designed only relies on 2D considerations, the camera viewpoint we considered to perform the topological refinement must influence the different evaluation metrics. We show in Fig. 4 to which extent the camera pose affects both the 2D IoU and the CD scores.

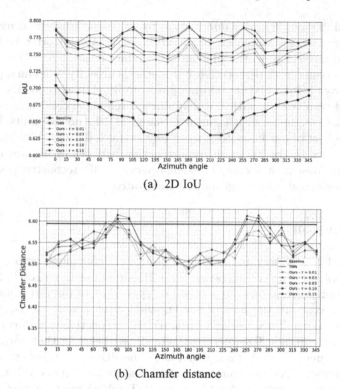

(a) 2D IoU

(b) Chamfer distance

Fig. 4. Camera viewpoint influence over the 2D IoU (top, (a)) and Chamfer distance (bottom, (b) scores.

Azimuth angles around the symmetrical pair $\{90°, 270°\}$ are more challenging since there are not as informative as the viewpoints close to 180°. Indeed, our method struggles to get better results than the Baseline in these cases. Our test set is imbalanced because it only contains more instances with topologically complex back parts to refine than with armrests. Our method thus slightly performs worse than the Baseline around both 90° and 270° angles as chairs' back complex structures are invisible from these viewpoints.

Finally, we also quantitatively confirm the intuited impact of τ during the rendering process on the 2D IoU score: the higher τ is, the larger the number of faces we discarded.

5   Limitations and Further Work

Our method shows encouraging results in 3D meshes topological refinement through 2D alpha mask considerations but has few remaining limitations. Firstly regarding the thresholding approach we used to prune whether or not a face on the 3D mesh surface. While we require to set a fixed hyperparameter - τ - in our method as [18] did, we align on [16] claims and emphasise the absolute need to rely on local 2D and 3D prior information to propose a clever and more robust thresholding strategy. Moreover, our module might also incorrectly behave on the rendered faces close to the silhouette boundary edges.

From a broader work perspective, our method currently relies on alpha masks and thus leaves behind texture information from RGB images. While impressive 3D textured results exist with UV mapping on self-supervised image-based 3D reconstruction methods with genus-0 meshes [11,19], no attempts have been made to the best of our knowledge to go beyond such 0 order. Finally, since our work is agnostic to the 3D mesh reconstruction network, a natural next move would be the design of a complete self-supervised 3D reconstruction pipeline with our topological refinement module integrated.

6   Conclusion

We proposed a new way to perform topological refinement onto a 3D mesh surface by only getting consideration for a 2D alpha mask. PyTorch3D [20] ras-terization framework allows our method to spot faces to discard from the mesh at almost no cost. To the best of our knowledge, no attempt exist in our line of work since both TMN [18] and Total3D [16] respectively perform faces and edges pruning through 3D-supervised neural networks. In that way, our work introduced a new research path to address the 3D mesh topology refinement issue. The agnostic design of our method allows any self-supervised image-based 3D reconstruction pipeline - based on the PyTorch3D renderer framework - to leverage the work we presented in this paper to reconstruct topologically com-plex meshes. We obtained consistent and competitive results from a topological perspective compared to the 3D-based pruning strategy from [18].

References

1. Chen, W., et al.: Learning to predict 3D objects with an interpolation-based dif-ferentiable renderer. In: NeurIPS (2019)
2. Choy, C.B., Xu, D., Gwak, J.Y., Chen, K., Savarese, S.: 3D-R2N2: a unified app-roach for single and multi-view 3D object reconstruction. In: Leibe, B., Matas, J., Sebe, N., Welling, M. (eds.) ECCV 2016. LNCS, vol. 9912, pp. 628–644. Springer, Cham (2016). https://doi.org/10.1007/978-3-319-46484-8_38
3. Cignoni, P., Rocchini, C., Scopigno, R.: Metro: measuring error on simplified sur-faces. Comput. Graph. Forum 17, 167–174 (1998)
4. Deng, Y., Yang, J., Xu, S., Chen, D., Jia, Y., Tong, X.: Accurate 3D face reconstruc-tion with weakly-supervised learning: from single image to image set. In: CVPRW (2019)
5. Girdhar, R., Fouhey, D.F., Rodriguez, M., Gupta, A.: Learning a predictable and generative vector representation for objects. In: Leibe, B., Matas, J., Sebe, N., Welling, M. (eds.) ECCV 2016. LNCS, vol. 9910, pp. 484–499. Springer, Cham (2016). https://doi.org/10.1007/978-3-319-46466-4_29
6. Groueix, T., Fisher, M., Kim, V.G., Russell, B., Aubry, M.: AtlasNet: a Papier-Mâché approach to learning 3D surface generation. In: CVPR (2018)

7. Henderson, P., Tsiminaki, V., Lampert, C.: Leveraging 2D data to learn textured 3D mesh generation. In: CVPR (2020)
8. Jiang, Y., Ji, D., Han, Z., Zwicker, M.: SDFDiff: differentiable rendering of signed distance fields for 3D shape optimization. In: CVPR (2020)
9. Kanazawa, A., Tulsiani, S., Efros, A.A., Malik, J.: Learning category-specific mesh reconstruction from image collections. In: ECCV (2018)
10. Kato, H., Ushiku, Y., Harada, T.: Neural 3D mesh renderer. In: CVPR (2018)
11. Li, X., et al.: Self-supervised single-view 3D reconstruction via semantic consistency. In: Vedaldi, A., Bischof, H., Brox, T., Frahm, J.-M. (eds.) ECCV 2020. LNCS, vol. 12359, pp. 677–693. Springer, Cham (2020). https://doi.org/10.1007/978-3-030-58568-6_40
12. Liu, S., Li, T., Chen, W., Li, H.: Soft rasterizer: a differentiable renderer for image-based 3D reasoning. In: ICCV (2019)
13. Liu, S., Saito, S., Chen, W., Li, H.: Learning to infer implicit surface without 3D supervision. In: NIPS (2019)
14. Longuet-Higgins, H.C.: A computer algorithm for reconstructing a scene from two projections. Nature **293**, 133–135 (1981)
15. Loper, M.M., Black, M.J.: OpenDR: an approximate differentiable renderer. In: Fleet, D., Pajdla, T., Schiele, B., Tuytelaars, T. (eds.) ECCV 2014. LNCS, vol. 8695, pp. 154–169. Springer, Cham (2014). https://doi.org/10.1007/978-3-319-10584-0_11
16. Nie, Y., Han, X., Guo, S., Zheng, Y., Chang, J., Zhang, J.J.: Total3DUnderstanding: joint layout, object pose and mesh reconstruction for indoor scenes from a single image. In: CVPR (2020)
17. Niemeyer, M., Mescheder, L., Oechsle, M., Geiger, A.: Differentiable volumetric rendering: learning implicit 3D representations without 3D supervision. In: CVPR (2020)
18. Pan, J., Han, X., Chen, W., Tang, J., Jia, K.: Deep mesh reconstruction from single RGB images via topology modification networks. In: ICCV (2019)
19. Pavllo, D., Spinks, G., Hofmann, T., Moens, M.F., Lucchi, A.: Convolutional generation of textured 3D meshes. In: NeurIPS (2020)
20. Ravi, N., et al.: Accelerating 3D deep learning with Pytorch3D. arXiv:2007.08501 (2020)
21. Saito, S., Simon, T., Saragih, J., Joo, H.: PIFuHD: multi-level pixel-aligned implicit function for high-resolution 3D human digitization. In: CVPR (2020)
22. Smith, E.J., Fujimoto, S., Romero, A., Meger, D.: Geometrics: exploiting geometric structure for graph-encoded objects. In: ICML (2019)
23. Sun, X., et al.: Pix3D: dataset and methods for single-image 3D shape modeling. In: CVPR (2018)
24. Wang, N., Zhang, Y., Li, Z., Fu, Y., Liu, W., Jiang, Y.G.: Pixel2Mesh: generating 3D mesh models from single RGB images. In: ECCV (2018)
25. Chang, A.X., et al.: ShapeNet: an information-rich 3D model repository. CoRR (2015)
26. Yan, X., Yang, J., Yumer, E., Guo, Y., Lee, H.: Perspective transformer nets: learning single-view 3D object reconstruction without 3D supervision. In: NIPS (2016)
27. Yang, B., Rosa, S., Markham, A., Trigoni, N., Wen, H.: Dense 3D object reconstruction from a single depth view. In: TPAMI (2018)

ST: Biomedical Imaging Techniques for Cancer Detection, Diagnosis and Management

ConnectedUNets++: Mass Segmentation from Whole Mammographic Images

Prithul Sarker$^{(\boxtimes)}$, Sushmita Sarker, George Bebis, and Alireza Tavakkoli

Department of Computer Science and Engineering, University of Nevada, Reno, USA
{prithulsarker,sushmita}@nevada.unr.edu

Abstract. Deep learning has made a breakthrough in medical image segmentation in recent years due to its ability to extract high-level features without the need for prior knowledge. In this context, UNet is one of the most advanced medical image segmentation models, with promising results in mammography. Despite its excellent overall performance in segmenting multimodal medical images, the traditional U-Net structure appears to be inadequate in various ways. There are certain U-Net design modifications, such as MultiResUNet, Connected-UNets and AU-Net, that have improved overall performance in areas where the conventional U-Net architecture appears to be deficient. Following the success of UNet and its variants, we have presented two enhanced versions of the Connected-UNets architecture: ConnectedUNets+ and ConnectedUNets++. In ConnectedUNets+, we have replaced the simple skip connections of Connected-UNets architecture with residual skip connections, while in ConnectedUNets++, we have modified the encoder decoder structure along with employing residual skip connections. We have evaluated our proposed architectures on two publicly available datasets, the Curated Breast Imaging Subset of Digital Database for Screening Mammography (CBIS-DDSM) and INbreast.

Keywords: Convolutional Neural Network · Mammogram · Semantic segmentation · U-Net · ConnectedU-Nets · MultiResUNet

1 Introduction

Breast cancer is the most frequent type of cancer that causes death in women, with 44,130 instances reported in the United States in 2021 [1]. The need for frequent mammography screening has been stressed in many studies in order to reduce mortality rates by finding breast malignancies before they spread to other normal tissues and healthy organs. A mammogram is an X-ray image of the breast to record changes in the tissue. The disease is typically identified by the presence of abnormal masses and microcalcifications in mammograms [2,3]. Radiologists examine a high number of mammograms on a daily basis looking for abnormal lesions and assessing the location, shape, and type of any suspicious

---

Prithul Sarker and Sushmita Sarker have equal contribution and are co-first authors.

© The Author(s), under exclusive license to Springer Nature Switzerland AG 2022
G. Bebis et al. (Eds.): ISVC 2022, LNCS 13598, pp. 419–430, 2022.
https://doi.org/10.1007/978-3-031-20713-6_32

area in the breast. This is an important procedure which requires high precision and accuracy, however, it is still costly and prone to errors since detecting these regions is challenging as their pixel intensities often coincide with normal tissue.

Deep learning advances [4], especially Convolutional Neural Networks (CNN) [5], have shown a lot of promise in addressing these issues. Despite being a game-changer in computer vision, CNN architectures have a key drawback: they require an enormous amount of training data. In order to solve this problem, U-Net [6] is introduced which is built on a simple encoder-decoder network with multiple sets of CNN. Even with a limited quantity of labeled training data, U-Net has demonstrated tremendous promise in segmenting breast masses, to the point where it has become the de-facto standard in medical image segmentation [7]. In light of the success of U-Net, various U-Net versions, such as Connected-UNets [8] and AU-Net [9], have been proposed. These variations have demonstrated promising results but appear to be inefficient in terms of fully recovering the region of interest in a given image.

In this work, we have proposed and experimented with two enhanced versions of the Connected-UNets architecture. Although the proposed networks share an architectural similarity, they are designed for different use cases which are crucial in real-world scenario. The proposed architectures take the entire mammogram image as input and perform mass segmentation along with mass boundary extraction. The main contributions of our work include:

1. We have proposed ConnectedUNets+ and ConnectedUNets++, two novel and improved versions of the Connected-UNets, by utilizing residual skip connections and enhanced encoder-decoder in order to achieve better convergence.
2. We have assessed the proposed architectures using full mammogram images in contrast to the baseline model which operates on cropped images of correctly detected and classified masses by an object detection model.
3. We have experimented using all the images from two publicly available datasets, the Curated Breast Imaging Subset of Digital Database for Screening Mammography (CBIS-DDSM) [10] and INbreast [11] for segmenting the region of interest (ROI) of breast mass tumors.

To the best of our knowledge, our paper is the first to address the shortcomings of other papers' methodologies and to conduct an unbiased comparison. We applied the same loss function, optimizer, and image size to all architectures to maintain objectivity. Additionally, to ensure a fair and accurate comparison, we used full mammograms as input for all the models and adopted a comparable preprocessing approach.

2 Related Works

U-Net [6], a deep learning network having an encoder-decoder architecture, is among the most prominent deep neural networks commonly employed in medical image segmentation. The network has a symmetric architecture, with an encoder which extracts spatial information from the image and a decoder which constructs the segmentation map from the encoded data. The encoder and decoder are linked by a series of skip connections which are the most innovative component of the U-Net architecture since they enable the network to recover spatial data that has been lost due to pooling procedures. Abdelhafiz et al. [12] used a vanilla U-Net model to segment mass lesions in whole mammograms. To segment suspicious regions in mammograms, Ravitha Rajalakshmi et al. [13] presented a deeply supervised U-Net model (DS U-Net) combined with a dense Conditional Random Field (CRF). Li et al. [14] proposed a Conditional Residual U-Net, named CRUNet, to improve the performance of the basic U-Net for breast mass segmentation.

Though U-Net is among the most popular and successful deep learning models for biomedical image segmentation, several improvements are still possible. Specifically, the concatenation of encoder and decoder features reveals a significant semantic gap despite the preservation of dispersed spatial features, which is a shortcoming of the simple skip connections. To deal with this issue, Ibtehaz et al. [15] proposed the MultiResUNet architecture by incorporating some convolutional layers along with shortcut connections in U-Net. Instead of simply concatenating the feature maps from the encoder stage to the decoder stage, they first pass them through a chain of convolutional layers and then concatenate them with the decoder features, which makes learning substantially easier. This idea is inspired from the image-to-image conversion using convolutional neural networks [16], where pooling layers are not favorable for the loss of information. MultiResUNet has shown excellent results on different biomedical images, however, the authors did not experiment with mammograms.

Based on the U-Net architecture, Baccouche et al. [8] proposed an improved architecture that connects two simple U-Nets, called Connected-UNets. In addition to the original idea of the U-Net architecture, which includes skip connections between the encoder and decoder networks, it cascades a second U-Net and adds skip connections between the decoder of the first U-Net and the encoder of the second U-Net. The key idea was to recovering fine-grained characteristics lost in U-Net's encoding process. However, the authors first used YOLO [17] to detect the location of masses in mammograms, and then applied their method to segment only correctly localized masses. Such an approach is not optimum in practical settings where it is desirable to simultaneously localize and segment masses in whole mammograms rather than processing cropped mammograms.

Several modifications of the U-Net architecture have also been proposed by incorporating an attention mechanism, which has shown to be extremely effective in medical image segmentation. Oktay et al. [18] proposed a new attention U-Net by adding an attention gate into the conventional U-Net. This enhanced the accuracy of the predictions. However, they didn't evaluate their model for breast mass segmentation. Similarly, Li et al. [19] built an attention dense U-Net for breast mass segmentation, which was compared to U-Net [6], Attention U-Net [18], and DenseNet [20]. In another study by Sun et al. [9], an attention-guided dense upsampling network, called AUNet, was built for breast mass segmentation in full mammograms. The major drawback of the papers mentioned above is they did not use all of the images available in the CBIS-DDSM dataset for experimentation (i.e., they only used a portion of the images in the training and test sets). As a result, higher scores were reported in their studies.

In this paper, we propose ConnectedUNets+ and ConnectedUNets++, two enhanced versions of the Connected-UNets and Connected-ResUNets architectures by focusing on the limitations of the aforementioned architectures. An important contribution of our work is that we compared the proposed architectures with previously reported works under identical conditions. Moreover, we did not employ any object detection models for mass localization; instead, we conducted all of our experiments using whole mammograms.

3   Methodology

3.1   Architecture

We have used Connected-UNets [8] as our baseline model because of its architectural elegance and performance. Even though, at first glance, ConnectedUNets+ and ConnectedUNets++ may merely seem a logical extension of Connected-UNets, the introduction of residual skip connections between the encoder and decoder is essential for successful segmentation. This not only improves the metric scores but also bridges the semantic barrier between the encoder-decoder features. The most crucial distinction is that ConnectedUNets+ and ConnectedUNets++ have been designed to enable mass segmentation from full mammograms rather than cropped mammograms. Figure 1a shows an overview of our proposed ConnectedUNets++ architecture. Please take note that we have not included a separate illustration for the ConnectedUNets+ since both the architectures are identical with the exception of the encoder-decoder block, which has been maintained standard like the baseline model. For both the models, we have replaced the simple skip connections of Connected-UNets with more optimal residual skip connections between encoder and decoder and between the UNets as well. However, for the ConnectedUNets++ architecture, we have also modified the encoder-decoder block by including three 3×3 convolutions and one residual connection followed by an activation layer ReLU (Rectified Linear Unit) and a batch normalization (BN) layer as shown in Fig. 1b. Specifically, the residual skip connections consist of four 3×3 convolutions where each of them is accompanied by one 1×1 convolution. The architecture of the residual skip connection is shown in Fig. 1c. The number of convolution blocks decreases in the deeper layer of the network as the semantic gap between encoder and decoder decreases due to getting closer to the bottleneck. Table 1 shows the number of filters used in each of the residual skip connections for different layers.

As mentioned by Ibtehaz et al. [15] by adding these residual path connections, the proposed architectures are more immune to perturbations, and outliers. They also help to obtain better results in less time and fewer epochs. Additionally, we have used Atrous Spatial Pyramid Pooling (ASPP) blocks to preserve the same bottleneck structure for both architectures as Connected-UNets. The architectural details of the encoder, decoder and ASPP blocks are described in Table 2.

On the encoder side, each encoder block's output is subjected to a maximum pooling operation before the features are forwarded to the next encoder, and the output of the last encoder passes through an ASPP block before being fetched to the first decoder. Each decoder block is made up of a 2×2 transposed convolution unit that up-samples the preceding block's features before concatenating them with the encoder features received by the residual skip connection; and these features are then fetched to the decoder above. A second U-Net is connected via

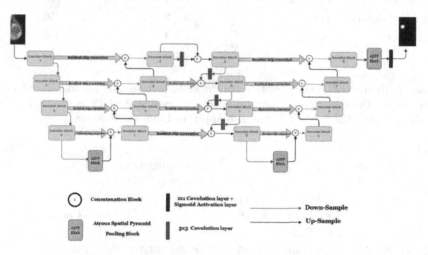

(a) Proposed architecture of ConnectedUNets++

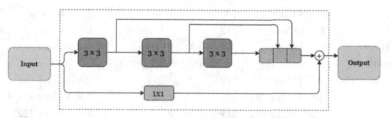

(b) Architecture of encoder and decoder blocks

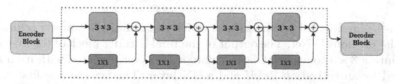

(c) Architecture of residual skip connections

Fig. 1. Detailed ConnectedUNets++ architecture

Table 1. ConnectedUNets++ and ConnectedUNets+ architecture details in terms of residual skip connections. These specifics apply to both architectures.

Residual skip connection	No. of conv. layer	Conv. layer kernel size	No of filters
Residual skip connection	4	3×3	32
01/08	4	1×1	32
Residual skip connection	3	3×3	64
02/05/09	3	1×1	64
Residual skip connection	2	3×3	128
03/06/10	2	1×1	128
Residual skip connection	1	3×3	256
04/07/11	1	1×1	256

Table 2. ConnectedUNets++ architecture details in terms of encoder-decoder and ASPP block. Dilation rate of convolution layers in ASPP block is shown in corresponding braces. ASPP block details also apply to ConnectedUNets+.

Block	Layer	Filters	Block	Layer	Filters
Encoder (01/05) Decoder (04/08)	3×3 Conv.	8	Encoder (02/06) Decoder (03/07)	3×3 Conv.	17
	3×3 Conv.	17		3×3 Conv.	35
	3×3 Conv.	26		3×3 Conv.	53
	1×1 Conv.	51		1×1 Conv.	105
Encoder (03/07) Decoder (02/06)	3×3 Conv.	35	Encoder (04/08) Decoder (01/05)	3×3 Conv.	71
	3×3 Conv.	71		3×3 Conv.	142
	3×3 Conv.	106		3×3 Conv.	213
	1×1 Conv.	212		1×1 Conv.	426
ASPP Block (Bottleneck)	3×3 Conv.	512	ASPP Block (Output Layer)	3×3 Conv.	32
	3×3 Conv.(6)	512		3×3 Conv.(6)	32
	3×3 Conv.(8)	512		3×3 Conv.(8)	32
	3×3 Conv.(12)	512		3×3 Conv.(12)	32
	1×1 Conv.	512		1×1 Conv.	32

a new set of residual skip connections, which are utilized to transfer information from the previous U-Net. The output of the final decoder block of the first U-Net is fed into a 3×3 convolution layer before it gets concatenated with itself again, followed by an activation ReLU and a BN layer. This acts as the first encoder block's input to the second U-Net. The output of the max pooling operations of each of the three encoder blocks is fed into a 3×3 convolution layer and then concatenated with the output of the preceding decoder block of the first U-Net.

The ASPP block receives the output features of the second U-Net's last encoder block; the remaining blocks are the same as discussed in the first U-Net. Finally, the predicted segmentation mask is generated by passing the output of the last decoder to another ASPP block followed by a 1×1 convolution layer and a sigmoid activation layer. In contrast to the work presented in the Connected-UNets paper [8], our work considers a full-fledged mammographic image as input instead of only a ROI since it typically fails to detect micro masses present in the image. The ROI extracted segmentation does not help in the real life scenario because the detection and localization of the mask has to be done using a different neural network or manually.

3.2 Dataset Preprocessing and Experimental Setup

We evaluated the proposed architecture on two publicly available datasets, CBIS-DDSM [10] and INbreast [11]. CBIS-DDSM contains 2478 mammography images from 1249 women and included both craniocaudal (CC) and mediolateral oblique (MLO) views for most of the exams of which 1231 cases contain single or multiple breast masses. This dataset includes real-world mammograms with background artifacts, poor contrast, corners, borders, and different orientations. To address these issues, we have applied several preprocessing steps which include border cropping to tackle the white border or corner problem, normalizing pixel values to the interval 0 to 1, eliminating background artifacts, and finally, applying CLAHE for contrast enhancement. This improves the mammogram's fine details, textures, and features that would otherwise be challenging for the model to learn. To preprocess the ground truth masks, we discarded the same amount of the borders to get rid of any artifacts and used appropriate padding to make the masks square. In the case of the CBIS-DDSM dataset, after preprocessing and fusing multiple masks of the same image, we split the 1231 images in the training set using an 85:15 ratio for training and validation (i.e., 1046 and 185 images, respectively). The test dataset had 359 images.

INbreast dataset was built with full-field digital mammograms and has a total of 115 cases which include both masses and calcifications. In total, the dataset has only 107 images of breasts with masses. We have used 69 images for training, 17 images for validation, and 21 images for testing. For preprocessing, we have solely applied CLAHE both on the mammograms and the ROIs.

In all of the experiments, adam [21] optimizer is used with an initial learning rate of 0.0001. Batch size of 16 is used during training and testing. We have experimented with input size of 224×224 and 256×256. The best score for all the architectures was obtained with the 224×224 input size, which is reported in the results section. Most of the papers mentioned in the related work section use a mixture of Dice and IOU loss. The primary motivation for directly using this loss is to maximize those metrics. However, this gives no information about convergence. So, to remove confusion regarding the convergence, the loss function used here is binary crossentropy which is the standard loss function for image segmentation task.

3.3   Evaluation Metrics

In semantic segmentation, the region of interest typically occupies a small area of the entire image. Therefore, metrics like precision and recall are inadequate and often lead to a false sense of superiority, inflated by the perfection of detecting the background. To evaluate our approach, we have considered four metrics in our experiments: Dice score (F1 score), Jaccard Index (IoU Score), accuracy and Hausdorff distance (H). Even though the Dice score (Eq. 1) and Jaccard index (Eq. 2) are two widely used metrics for semantic segmentation, they are biased towards large masses. The Hausdorff distance (Eq. 3) is an unbiased metric that treats all objects equally independently of their size. It measures the maximum deviation along the boundary between the ground truth and predictions.

$$Dice\ score(A, B) = \frac{2 \times Area\ of\ Intersection(A, B)}{Area\ of(A) + Area\ of(B)} = \frac{2 \times (A \cap B)}{A + B} \quad (1)$$

$$IoU\ score(A, B) = \frac{Area\ of\ Intersection(A, B)}{Area\ of\ Union(A, B)} = \frac{A \cap B}{A \cup B} \quad (2)$$

$$H = max(h(GT, pred), h(pred, GT)) \quad (3)$$

4   Experimental Results and Discussion

To assess the performance, all models have been run for 300 and 400 epochs for the CBIS-DDSM and INbreast datasets, respectively with early stopping and ReduceLROnPlateau callback function. Table 3 shows the comparison of the proposed architectures' results with some state-of-the-art methods on the CBIS-DDSM dataset. As it can be observed, ConnectedUNets++ consistently outperforms the baseline model Connected-UNets and Connected-ResUNets along with other models used for mass segmentation. ConncetedUNets+ performed better than Connected-UNets on the test dataset even though the only difference between them is the residual skip connections.

As seen in Table 3, the number of parameters of our proposed methods is higher than the number of parameters of the baseline architectures since we used residual skip connections between encoders and decoders as well as between the two U-Nets. Furthermore, all of the architectures performed better on the training and validation sets, but performed poorly on the test set. In particular, the architectures fail to detect any mass from some of the images in the test set, thus giving an output of no ROI and reducing the metric values. We speculate that this is due to the inferior and substandard quality of the scanned images. In Table 4, we compared our proposed architecture with the baseline model by using individual cases from the CBIS-DDSM test dataset considering various thresholds for different metrics. As shown, the proposed architecture was able to predict more cases for each threshold with respect to Connected-ResUNets; however, the average score was better for the baseline architecture. Here we argue that ConnectedUNets++ has been able to correctly segment smaller masses more accurately than Connected-ResUNets.

Table 3. Comparison of the proposed architectures and state-of-the-art methods on the CBIS-DDSM dataset. Here, DS: Dice score, JI: Jaccard index, Acc.: Accuracy, Param.: No of parameters(in million).

Model name	Param.	Training			Validation			Test		
		DS	JI	Acc.	DS	JI	Acc.	DS	JI	Acc.
U-Net	7.8	0.73	0.57	99.85	0.73	0.58	99.87	0.41	0.27	99.69
MultiResUNet	7.3	0.74	0.59	99.89	0.76	0.61	99.88	0.40	0.26	**99.7**
AUNet	11.01	**0.89**	**0.81**	**99.94**	**0.90**	**0.82**	**99.94**	0.46	0.31	99.69
Connected-UNets	20.1	0.81	0.68	99.90	0.81	0.68	99.91	0.40	0.27	99.69
ConnectedUNets+ (ours)	23.5	0.78	0.64	99.88	0.77	0.63	99.89	0.44	0.30	**99.7**
Connected-ResUNets	20.7	0.84	0.73	99.91	0.84	0.72	99.92	0.47	0.32	99.69
ConnectedUNets++ (ours)	28.15	0.88	0.79	**99.94**	0.88	0.79	**99.94**	**0.48**	**0.33**	**99.7**

Table 4. Comparison of prediction on the CBIS-DDSM test dataset and correctly predicted number of cases over multiple thresholds of Dice score (DS), Jaccard index (JI) and Hausdorff distance (HD) metric between the baseline architecture and our proposed architecture. Here, NC and AS represent the number of cases and average score, respectively.

Architecture name	$DS \geq 0.45$		$DS \geq 0.65$		$JI \geq 0.35$		$JI \geq 0.55$		$HD \leq 2.75$	
	NC	AS	NC	AS	NC	AS	NC	AS	NC	AS
Connected-ResUNets	160	**0.78**	134	**0.82**	154	**0.66**	119	**0.73**	174	**1.85**
ConnectedUNets++ (ours)	**181**	0.76	**143**	0.81	**172**	0.64	**123**	0.71	**191**	1.92

Table 5. Comparison of the proposed architectures and state-of-the-art methods on INbreast dataset.

Model name	Param.	Training			Validation			Test		
		DS	JI	Acc.	DS	JI	Acc.	DS	JI	Acc.
U-Net	7.8	0.87	0.77	99.91	0.91	0.83	99.91	0.91	0.84	99.91
AUNet	11.01	0.94	0.89	99.94	0.96	0.90	99.93	0.94	0.89	99.94
Connected-UNets	22.4	0.94	0.89	**99.99**	0.97	0.95	99.95	0.97	0.94	**99.99**
ConnectedUNets+ (ours)	23.5	**0.97**	0.94	99.97	**0.98**	0.96	99.97	0.98	0.95	99.97
Connected-ResUNets	20.7	0.94	0.88	**99.99**	0.96	0.93	**99.98**	0.97	0.94	**99.99**
ConnectedUNets++ (ours)	28.15	**0.97**	**0.95**	**99.99**	**0.98**	**0.97**	**99.98**	**0.99**	**0.97**	**99.99**

In Table 5, we also compared the proposed architectures against the baseline and other models on the INbreast dataset. As it can be observed, our model performs noticeably better on the INbreast dataset. We hypothesize that this is due to the two datasets' disparate image quality. The mammograms in the CBIS-DDSM dataset have been scanned, hence the images are of poor quality. The images in the INbreast dataset, however, have been digitally enhanced, and their quality is outstanding. Due to page restrictions, we had to omit comparison of correctly predicted cases like Table 4 for the INbreast dataset.

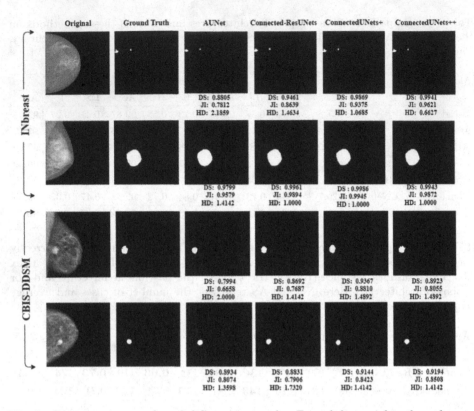

Fig. 2. Segmentation results of different networks. From left to right, the columns correspond to the input images, the ground truth labels, the segmentation results of AUNet, Connected-ResUNets, ConnectedUNets+ and ConnectedUNets++, respectively on the INbreast and CBIS-DDSM dataset.

The introduction of residual skip connections between the encoder and decoder has had a major impact on the segmentation task. The obscure and vague boundaries which other architectures fail to correctly segment (either under-segment or over-segment), are properly segmented by ConnectedUNets+ and ConnectedUNets++. Additionally, in some complex cases, because of the quality and nature of the ROIs, it becomes challenging to segment homogeneous ROIs. Even in those cases, ConnectedUNets++ exceeds other architectures in terms of Dice score, Jaccard index, and Hausdorff distance. As Hausdorff distance is highly recommended for cases with complex boundaries, our results show that the proposed architecture can predict mass boundaries more accurately. Since the boundary shape of a mass is a strong indicator of benign and malignant cases [22], the proposed architecture is more suited for mass prediction and segmentation in real-world scenarios.

Segmentation examples both for the INbreast and CBIS-DDSM datasets are shown in Fig. 2. We have compared the segmentation result of ConnectedUNets+ and ConnectedNets++ with two best-performed architectures: AUNet and Connected-ResUNets. In all the cases, the proposed architectures outperformed all other architectures and achieved almost perfect scoring regardless of the ROI's shape. Figure 2 showcases how well the models worked not just for the larger ROI (Case 2) but also for those with smaller ROI (Case 1) on INbreast dataset. The models yield similar results for CBIS-DDSM dataset as well.

5 Conclusion

We started this work by thoroughly examining the Connected-UNets architecture in order to identify potential areas for improvement. In this context, we identified certain inconsistencies between the encoder's and decoder's features. Inspired by MultiResUNet, we added some additional processing between them to make them more homogeneous. Furthermore, to give Connected-UNets the capacity to perform multi-resolutional analysis, we introduced residual blocks into the encoder and decoder architecture which resulted in ConnectedUNets++, a novel architecture that incorporates these changes. Unlike architectures previously discussed in the literature, we have used all of the available images for training and testing. For future work, we plan to conduct additional experiments to determine the ideal choice of nodes, layers, and hyperparameters. Furthermore, we would also like to assess the efficacy of our model on datasets of medical images from various modalities.

Acknowledgements. Portions of this material is based upon work supported by the Office of the Under Secretary of Defense for Research and Engineering under award number FA9550-21-1-0207.

References

1. American Chemical Society: Breast cancer facts & figures 2019–2020. Am. Cancer Soc. 1–44 (2019)
2. Elter, M., Horsch, A.: CADx of mammographic masses and clustered microcalcifications: a review. Med. Phys. **36**(6Part1), 2052–2068 (2009)
3. Jiang, Y., Nishikawa, R.M., Schmidt, R.A., Metz, C.E., Giger, M.L., Doi, K.: Improving breast cancer diagnosis with computer-aided diagnosis. Acad. Radiol. **6**(1), 22–33 (1999)
4. LeCun, Y., Bengio, Y., Hinton, G.: Deep learning. Nature **521**(7553), 436–444 (2015)
5. Zaheer, R., Shaziya, H.: GPU-based empirical evaluation of activation functions in convolutional neural networks. In: 2018 2nd International Conference on Inventive Systems and Control (ICISC), pp. 769–773. IEEE (2018)
6. Ronneberger, O., Fischer, P., Brox, T.: U-Net: convolutional networks for biomedical image segmentation. In: Navab, N., Hornegger, J., Wells, W.M., Frangi, A.F. (eds.) MICCAI 2015. LNCS, vol. 9351, pp. 234–241. Springer, Cham (2015). https://doi.org/10.1007/978-3-319-24574-4_28
7. Litjens, G., et al.: A survey on deep learning in medical image analysis. Med. Image Anal. **42**, 60–88 (2017)

8. Baccouche, A., Garcia-Zapirain, B., Castillo Olea, C., Elmaghraby, A.S.: Connected-UNets: a deep learning architecture for breast mass segmentation. NPJ Breast Cancer **7**(1), 1–12 (2021)
9. Sun, H., et al.: AUNet: attention-guided dense-upsampling networks for breast mass segmentation in whole mammograms. Phys. Medi. Biol. **65**(5), 055005 (2020)
10. Lee, R.S., Gimenez, F., Hoogi, A., Miyake, K.K., Gorovoy, M., Rubin, D.L.: A curated mammography data set for use in computer-aided detection and diagnosis research. Sci. Data **4**(1), 1–9 (2017)
11. Moreira, I.C., Amaral, I., Domingues, I., Cardoso, A., Cardoso, M.J., Cardoso, J.S.: INbreast: toward a full-field digital mammographic database. Acad. Radiol. **19**(2), 236–248 (2012)
12. Abdelhafiz, D., Bi, J., Ammar, R., Yang, C., Nabavi, S.: Convolutional neural network for automated mass segmentation in mammography. BMC Bioinform. **21**(1), 1–19 (2020)
13. Ravitha Rajalakshmi, N., Vidhyapriya, R., Elango, N., Ramesh, N.: Deeply supervised U-Net for mass segmentation in digital mammograms. Int. J. Imaging Syst. Technol. **31**(1), 59–71 (2021)
14. Li, H., Chen, D., Nailon, W.H., Davies, M.E., Laurenson, D.: Improved breast mass segmentation in mammograms with conditional residual U-Net. In: Stoyanov, D., et al. (eds.) RAMBO/BIA/TIA 2018. LNCS, vol. 11040, pp. 81–89. Springer, Cham (2018). https://doi.org/10.1007/978-3-030-00946-5_9
15. Ibtehaz, N., Rahman, M.S.: MultiResUNet: rethinking the U-Net architecture for multimodal biomedical image segmentation. Neural Netw. **121**, 74–87 (2020)
16. He, K., Zhang, X., Ren, S., Sun, J.: Deep residual learning for image recognition. In: Proceedings of the IEEE Conference on Computer Vision and Pattern Recognition, pp. 770–778 (2016)
17. Redmon, J., Divvala, S., Girshick, R., Farhadi, A.: You only look once: unified, real-time object detection. In: Proceedings of the IEEE Conference on Computer Vision and Pattern Recognition, pp. 779–788 (2016)
18. Oktay, O., et al.: Attention U-Net: learning where to look for the pancreas. arXiv preprint arXiv:1804.03999 (2018)
19. Li, S., Dong, M., Du, G., Mu, X.: Attention Dense-U-Net for automatic breast mass segmentation in digital mammogram. IEEE Access **7**, 59037–59047 (2019)
20. Hai, J., et al.: Fully convolutional DenseNet with multiscale context for automated breast tumor segmentation. J. Healthcare Eng. **2019** (2019)
21. Kingma, D.P., Ba, J.: Adam: a method for stochastic optimization. arXiv preprint arXiv:1412.6980 (2014)
22. Mahmood, T., Li, J., Pei, Y., Akhtar, F., Rehman, M.U., Wasti, S.H.: Breast lesions classifications of mammographic images using a deep convolutional neural network-based approach. PLoS ONE **17**(1), e0263126 (2022)

Severity Classification of Ulcerative Colitis in Colonoscopy Videos by Learning from Confusion

Md Farhad Mokter[1], Azeez Idris[2], JungHwan Oh[1]([⊠]), Wallapak Tavanapong[2], and Piet C. de Groen[3]

[1] Department of Computer Science and Engineering, University of North Texas, Denton, TX 76203, USA
Junghwan.Oh@unt.edu
[2] Computer Science Department, Iowa State University, Ames, IA 50011, USA
tavanapo@iastate.edu
[3] Department of Medicine, University of Minnesota, Minneapolis, MN, USA
degroen@umn.edu

Abstract. Endoscopic measurement of ulcerative colitis (UC) severity is important since endoscopic disease severity may better predict future outcomes in UC than symptoms. However, it is difficult to evaluate the endoscopic severity of UC objectively because of the non-uniform nature of endoscopic features associated with UC, and large variations in their patterns. In this paper, we propose a method to classify UC severity in colonoscopy videos by learning from confusion. The similar looking frames from the colonoscopy videos generate similar features, and the Convolutional Neural Network (CNN) model trained using these similar features is confused. Therefore, it cannot provide accurate classification. By isolating these similar frames (features), we potentially reduce model confusion. We propose a new training strategy to isolate these similar frames (features), and a CNN based method for classifying UC severity in colonoscopy videos using the new training strategy. The experiments show that the proposed method for classifying UC severity increases classification effectiveness significantly.

Keywords: CNN · Medical image classification · Ulcerative colitis severity · Learning from confusion

1 Introduction

Ulcerative colitis (UC) is a chronic inflammatory disease of the colon characterized by periods of relapses and remissions affecting more than 750,000 people in the United States [1]. As mucosal healing is a specific treatment goal in UC, the importance of endoscopic evaluation of disease activity in predicting outcomes is being increasingly recognized [2]. Disease activity in UC has been extensively evaluated using various scoring systems incorporating both clinical and endoscopic features [2]. These scoring systems have been developed to evaluate systematically the responses to treatments being

© The Author(s), under exclusive license to Springer Nature Switzerland AG 2022
G. Bebis et al. (Eds.): ISVC 2022, LNCS 13598, pp. 431–443, 2022.
https://doi.org/10.1007/978-3-031-20713-6_33

studied in UC patients [2]. Many scoring systems exist, but mainly two endoscopic score systems of mucosal inflammation are used currently in clinical practice, which are the Mayo Endoscopic Score (MES) and the Ulcerative Colitis Endoscopic Index of Severity (UCEIS) [2]. In Table 1 we compare these two scoring systems and divide the disease activity features into four different classes, Normal (Score 0), Mild (Score 1), Moderate (Score 2), and Severe (Score 3), based on their endoscopic features.

Table 1. Comparison of the Mayo Endoscopic Score (MES) and the Ulcerative Colitis Endoscopic Index of Severity (UCEIS) Features

Score	Disease activity	Features for MES	Features for UCEIS
0	Normal	No abnormality, clear vascular pattern	No abnormality, clear vascular pattern
1	Mild	Erythema, Decreased vascular pattern, Mild friability	Patchy obliteration of vascular pattern, Mucosal bleeding, Erosions
2	Moderate	Marked erythema, Absent vascular pattern, Friability, Erosions	Complete obliteration of vascular pattern, Luminal mild bleeding, Superficial ulcer
3	Severe	Absent vascular pattern, Spontaneous bleeding, Ulceration	Complete obliteration of vascular pattern, Luminal moderate or severe bleeding, Deep ulcer

Since disease severity may better predict future outcomes in UC than symptoms, UC severity measurement by endoscopy is very important [3, 4]. However, even if we have the scoring systems mentioned above, it is very difficult to evaluate the severity of UC objectively because of non-uniform nature of endoscopic findings associated with UC, and large variations in their patterns [5].

We proposed a Convolutional Neural Network (CNN) based approach evaluating the severity of UC [6]. Its accuracy was reasonable at the video level, but its frame level accuracy was very low (around 45%). We improved this CNN based approach in two ways to provide better accuracy for the classification [7]. First, we added more thorough and essential preprocessing. Second, we subdivided each class of UC severity based on visual appearance and generated more sub-classes for the classification to accommodate large variations in UC severity patterns. This method provided an improved frame-level accuracy (around 60%) to evaluate the severity of UC.

In our next work [8], we focused on one common feature in both scoring systems as seen in Table 1, which is 'vascular (predominantly vein) pattern'. In Normal and Mild disease activity, the vascular pattern is either clearly or somewhat visible, but it is either mostly or completely lost in Moderate and Severe disease activity. We proposed a CNN based method for classifying UC severity in colonoscopy videos by detecting these vascular patterns which are defined specifically as the amount of blood vessels in the video frames [8]. The proposed method for classifying UC severity by detecting these vascular patterns increased classification effectiveness by about 17% compared to our previous work [7].

What we found is that very similar looking frames belong to different classes as seen in Fig. 1. These similar looking frames generate similar features, and the CNN model trained using these similar features is confused, and the model cannot classify these frames accurately. By isolating these similar features, we potentially reduce model confusion, which allows the model to focus on additional discriminative features for each class. We propose a new training strategy to isolate these similar frames (features), and a CNN based method for classifying UC severity in colonoscopy videos using the new training strategy. For convenience, we call the proposed method as CNN_LfC (Convolutional Neural Network with Learning from Confusion).

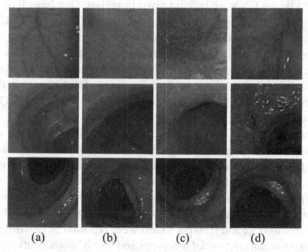

(a)   (b)   (c)   (d)

Fig. 1. Frames in Class of a) Normal, b) Mild, c) Moderate, and d) Severe.

Our contribution is that the proposed method for classifying UC severity by learning from confusion increases classification effectiveness by about 7% compared to our previous work [8]. The rest of the paper is organized as follows. Section 2 discusses the related work. Section 3 describes the proposed methodology. Section 4 shows our experimental results. Finally, Sect. 5 summarizes our concluding remarks.

2 Related Work

In this section, we discuss some recent UC related work only. A deep network for UC (DNUC) was constructed for real time analysis of endoscopic images with UC [9]. Using the annotation results provided by endoscopists, the DNUC identified patients with endoscopic remission in the prospective study. The experiment focused on classifying 4 classes of UC using UCEIS score. The training dataset includes 40,758 images from 2,012 UC patients, and the testing dataset has 4,187 images from 875 UC patients. The training and test data were collected from different periods of time, and there was no overlap between training and test datasets for the experiment. The accuracy reported was 90.1% with a kappa coefficient of 0.798.

A MES of 1, 2, or 3 was assigned to each of 777 endoscopic images. 90% of them were used to train and validate a 101-layer CNN model, and 10% were held aside as a holdout test set [10]. The model was assessed using Area Under the Curve (AUC) and some performance measures such as precision, specificity, sensitivity, positive predictive value (PPV) and negative predictive value (NPV). The final model returned AUC of 0.96 for MES 3 disease, 0.86 for MES 2 disease and 0.89 for MES 1 disease. The overall accuracy reported was 77.2% on the holdout test set.

Another neural network-based approach named "Efficient Attention Mechanism Network" (EAM-Net) was introduced, which combines the efficient channel attention network with the spatial attention module [11]. To build and splice the attention map, the features extracted by the CNN are split into two branches. One branch of these features was passed as input to the Independently Recurrent Neural Network (IndRNN), and the remaining features were pushed to the attention mechanism module. The attention module generated an attention map and highlighted target features. This method was applied on two colonoscopy image datasets containing 9,928 samples and 4,378 samples. Both datasets were classified and validated by domain experts for 4 classes with MES of 0 to 3. It was reported by the study such as accuracy of 91.6%, precision of 85.9%, recall of 85.9% and F1-score of 85.8%.

A multi-instance learning (MIL) framework was proposed in a study which focused on solving weakly labeled image samples [12]. The framework collected a small number of instances from the dataset and used a CNN with a sigmoid function to generate frame scores. A frame with maximum score was used to represent the entire video, and the MES (Ranges from 0 through 3) was obtained by thresholding. The dataset consists of 1,129,188 frames, which includes both training and test sets from 1,881 endoscopic videos. AUC scores of 0.92 and 0.90 per video were reported in two different trials.

A semi-supervised learning model was proposed for UC classification, which is using location and temporal ordering information [13]. A disentangled representation learning was applied to extract UC temporal features. Also, an objective function was introduced for order-guided learning that can capture effective features. 7,183 images were used for training and 2,052 images were used for validation. A test set of 1,027 images were used for three class classification. The model returned an accuracy of 84.5% with 77.5% precision, 73.1% recall, and F1-score of 89.9%.

In a recent study, multiple deep learning-based architectures were evaluated using a subset of Hyper-Kvasir [14]. The Hyper-kvasir dataset is a large public dataset for the gastrointestinal tract which contains 110,079 images and 374 videos from different sources with anatomical landmarks [15]. The experiment used a subset of 8,000 labeled endoscopic images with MES score of 0–3. Pre-trained models of InceptionV3 [16], ResNet50 [17], VGG19 [18] and DenseNet121 [19] were used for the experiment. All network wights were initialized with ImageNet, and grid-search over 5-fold cross validation was used for identifying best hyperparameters. The best result was reported from the DenseNet121 model with an accuracy of 87.50% and AUC of 0.90.

3 Methodology

Our proposed method for classifying UC severity in colonoscopy videos uses a new training strategy which focuses on distinguishing the features that confuse the model. Distinguishing and isolating the similar features can help the model to focus on more discriminative features, and improve model accuracy essentially. The overall procedure of the proposed method is shown in Fig. 2.

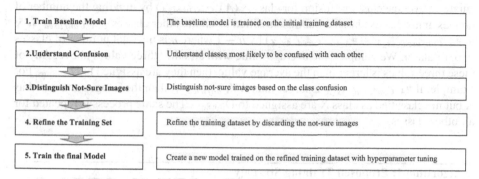

1. Train Baseline Model	The baseline model is trained on the initial training dataset
2. Understand Confusion	Understand classes most likely to be confused with each other
3. Distinguish Not-Sure Images	Distinguish not-sure images based on the class confusion
4. Refine the Training Set	Refine the training dataset by discarding the not-sure images
5. Train the final Model	Create a new model trained on the refined training dataset with hyperparameter tuning

Fig. 2. Overall procedure of the proposed method, CNN_LfC.

3.1 New Training Strategy

A baseline CNN model is trained as seen in Algorithm 1 using our initial training dataset with the colonoscopy frames classified by the domain expert to the four classes of MES discussed in Sect. 1. The baseline model was a ResNet-like [17] deep learning model with 48 layers. Each layer consists of convolution layers followed by max-pooling layers. The convolution layer has a filter size of 3 * 3 with 64 filters. We used max-pooling with stride size 2 after each convolution. 50 epochs which provided a best performance were used for training with a batch size of 30. The learning rate was set to 0.001 with the default loss function and the default setting for the *Adam* optimizer. We used Softmax function for classification. No dropout was used throughout the training.

Algorithm 1 explains the new training strategy to generate the final model. We divide our dataset into the initial training dataset (D_{train}) and testing dataset (D_{test}). The baseline model f_1 is trained using the initial training dataset (D_{train}) as seen in Step 1. The baseline model f_1 is evaluated using all images in D_{train} as seen in Step 2. During the evaluation, we can find some images that belong to one class but assigned to another class. We refer these images as "$D_{misclassified}$" images for convenience. We use the algorithm 2 to select the not-sure images ($D_{notSure}$) from the misclassified images ($D_{misclassified}$). $D_{notSure}$ is a subset of $D_{misclassified}$, which has the misclassified images with majority. After all not-sure images are distinguished, they are discarded from the initial training dataset (D_{train}). We refer this remaining training dataset as $D_{refined}$. The final model is trained on $D_{refined}$, in which it is trained with the intention of performing better than the baseline model because it is using a refined dataset. The refined dataset generated using Step 3 and Step

4 contains fewer confusing samples, therefore yielding more discriminative features for the final model.

Algorithm 2 distinguishes the not-sure images ($D_{notSure}$) from the misclassified images ($D_{misclassified}$). In $D_{misclassified}$, there are some images that belong to one class (i.e., A) but assigned to another class (i.e., X, Y, or Z). We calculate the number of images annotated as A but misclassified as class X ($\#_{A\_Confused\_As\_X}$), the number of images annotated as A but misclassified as class Y ($\#_{A\_Confused\_As\_Y}$), and the number of images annotated as A but misclassified as class Z ($\#_{A\_Confused\_As\_Z}$). . We also calculate an average class confusion for class A ($AV_{Confused\_A}$) by dividing the number of images annotated as class A, but misclassified as all the other classes ($\#_{A\_Confused\_As\_X} + \#_{A\_Confused\_As\_Y} + \#_{A\_Confused\_As\_Z}$) by $n-1$ where n is the total number of classes in our dataset. We compare the average value with all other three values above. Any of these three values is larger than the average value, then they are assigned to $D_{notSure}$. For example, if $\#_{A\_Confused\_As\_X}$ is larger than $AV_{Confused\_A}$, then the images annotated as A but misclassified as class X are assigned to $D_{notSure}$. The same process is repeated for all other classes.

Algorithm 1: Proposed Training Strategy

Input:	Dataset $D = \{D_{train}, D_{test}\}$ with n classes,
	$\mathfrak{f}_1$: Baseline CNN model,
Output:	Model $\mathfrak{f}_2$ trained on $D_{refined}$

1. Train $\mathfrak{f}_1$ on D_{train}
2. Evaluate $\mathfrak{f}_1$ using all images in D_{train}. The result is $D_{misclassified}$, a set of images misclassified by $\mathfrak{f}_1$.
3. Generate $D_{notSure}$ using Algorithm 2 with $D_{misclassified}$.
4. $D_{refined} = D_{train} - D_{notSure}$
5. Train $\mathfrak{f}_2$ on $D_{refined}$
6. Tune the hyperparameters of $\mathfrak{f}_2$

3.2   Refine the Training Dataset and Train Final Model

We refine the training dataset by distinguishing and isolating all not-sure images as mentioned above. Our hypothesis is that, class confusion is created by the images of one class that is confused with other classes. The proposed training strategy aims to separate these images to reduce the class-confusion for the model. A new refined dataset $D_{refined}$ is created by separating the not-sure images from the D_{train}. A new model f_2 is created by training on the refined dataset. The number of confused samples is reduced, which helps the model to learn more discriminative features. This allows the model to lower the misclassification by capturing more representative features for the target classes. Our final model f_2 consists of five convolutional blocks. The first block consists of 64 filters of 3 * 3 size. The second block contains 128 filters of 3 * 3 size. The third block has three convolution layers with 128 filter of same size 3 * 3, and it is followed by the fourth and fifth convolution blocks. Both fourth and fifth blocks contain four convolutional layers in total. Each of these two blocks has 512 filters of the same size. These five blocks are separated by the max-pooling layer. The final two layers are fully connected layers with 2,048 neurons for each layer.

To ensure optimum parameters for the better accuracy, we performed hyperparameter tuning as seen in [20] for our final model f_2. We also applied the grid search [21] over a range of hyperparameters to obtain the best set of hyperparameter values. We performed grid search over the range of values for each hyperparameter. For the batch size, the values were 16, 32, 64, and 128. The values for the learning rate were 0.1, 0.02, 0.001, and 0.002. The values of epochs were 10, 20, 30, 40, and 50. The model performed best with a 93% of training accuracy with the following set of hyperparameters: the batch size of 64, learning rate of 0.001, and the default *Adam* optimizer. To avoid the image translation issues, we applied the image augmentation in the final model. The augmentation consists of horizontal and vertical flipping, 180° rotation and image sheering-zooming (30%), and these augmentations were applied randomly. Early stopping conditions were applied to save the best model after every 10 epochs.

Algorithm 2: Not-sure Image Determination

Input:	$D_{misclassified}$.
	$\#_{All\_Confused\_A}$: Number of images annotated as class A, but misclassified as all the other classes.
	n : Number of classes in the dataset $D_{misclassified}$.

Notations:

$LC_{Confused\_A}$: List of classes most confused as class A

$\#_{All\_Confused}$: Number of images annotated as one class, but misclassified as other classes; this variable is set to zero, initially.

$\#_{A\_Confused\_As\_B}$: Number of images annotated as A but misclassified as class B

$\#_{Most\_Confused\_As\_A}$: Number of images annotated as A, but misclassified as classes in $LC_{Confused\_A}$

$AV_{Confused\_A}$: Average confusion of class A

Output:	$D_{notSure}$: Set of images in the not-sure class.

1. **foreach** class A:
2.   Empty $LC_{Confused\_A}$, $\#_{Most\_Confused\_As\_A}$
3. $$AV_{Confused\_A} = \frac{\#_{All\_Confused\_A}}{n-1}$$
4.   **foreach** class $X \neq A$
5.   Compute $\#_{A\_Confused\_As\_X}$
6.   **if** $\#_{A\_Confused\_As\_X} > AV_{Confused\_A}$
7.   Add class X to $LC_{Confused\_A}$
8. $\#_{All_{Confused}} += \#_{A_{Confused_{As_X}}}$
9. $\#_{Most\_Confused\_As\_A} += \#_{A\_Confused\_As\_X}$
10. **Assign all images in** $Most\_Confused\_As\_A$ **to the not-sure class**

---

4   Experimental Results

In this section, we discuss the datasets used for the experiments and the performance evaluation of the proposed method. The experiments were implemented in a Linux environment using NVIDIA GTX 1650 4 GB GPU on a system of 32 GB RAM and core-i7 8th generation with 3.20 GHz processor. Keras, a python package, was used as the framework for all the networks.

4.1   Testing and Comparison

For the experiments, we used the same datasets that we used in our previous work [6–8] for a fair comparison. To train our baseline model, we used 52,674 frames which were obtained from 135 videos from four different classes. In order to maintain the class balance, we ensured the number of samples for each as similar as possible. The details of our initial training dataset for the baseline model are given in Table 2.

After the baseline model was trained, the confusion is calculated as discussed in Sect. 3. The confusion log for the training data was obtained and used for distinguishing the not-sure class. The proposed training method isolates the confusing frames to the "not-sure" class and retains the remaining samples in their respective classes. After the "not-sure" frames are moved to the target directory, all frames from the remaining classes were collected. We refer this remaining dataset as a refined dataset because all confusing frames are eliminated from the initial dataset. Since the refined dataset contains less confusing frames, it yields more representative and discriminative features for corresponding classes. To train the final model, we ensured the refined training dataset was roughly class balanced. A detail of the refined dataset is given in Table 3.

Table 2. Details of initial dataset for training baseline CNN model.

Classes	Video clips	Frames
Normal	35	12,725
Mild	51	15,490
Moderate	30	14,027
Severe	19	10,432
Total	**135**	**52,674**

Table 3. Details of refined dataset for training final CNN model.

Classes	Video clips	Frames
Normal	35	9,856
Mild	51	10,248
Moderate	30	10,789
Severe	19	9,289
Total	**135**	**40,182**

The final CNN model was trained using the refined dataset. We tuned the hyperparameter values of the final model to ensure the best performance. To evaluate the performance of the final fine-tuned model hyperparameters, we used the same test dataset we used in our previous work [6–8] for a fair comparison. It contains 14,925 samples from four UC severity classes. These frames were extracted from 43 endoscopic videos and labelled by the domain experts. The test dataset was kept intact and was not used for any training and validation purposes. Table 4 shows the details of the test dataset.

We tested the final model with the test dataset and observed the model performance. To measure the performance, we used the accuracy metric for a comparison. Accuracy is

Table 4. Details of dataset for testing.

Classes	Video clips	Frames
Normal	12	3,623
Mild	12	4,400
Moderate	13	3,061
Severe	06	3,841
Total	**43**	**14,925**

defined as the proportion of correct predictions to all predictions for multiclass classifications. We compared the final model with our previous work [7, 8] to see the performance improvement using the same dataset. The proposed model outperformed our previous work [8] by an improvement of 7%. The proposed model showed remarkable improvement in classification for individual classes. Table 5 shows the comparison of proposed method with previous models.

Table 5. Comparisons of per-frame classification accuracy on test dataset.

Methods	UCS-AlexNet [9]	VCNN 1+2+3 [10]	Proposed method CNN_LfC
Normal	63.2	81.2	87.23
Mild	61.4	74.6	85.96
Moderate	45.7	78.4	83.50
Severe	72.3	80.1	88.01
Average	**61.5**	**78.4**	**85.18**

The proposed method can classify normal and mild frames at an accuracy of 87.23% and 85.96%, respectively. The UCS AlexNet [7] provided only 63.2% and 61.4% for the same classes. Our previous work in [8] is a patch-based approach where each frame is divided into 64 patches and the patches were fed into a model for classification. It showed an average accuracy of 78.4% whereas the proposed method outperformed this method by an increase of 6.75%. The direct performance comparison between other existing methods and the proposed method is not reasonable because the experiments were performed in different datasets. Due to the nature of our dataset, we focus more on improvement compared with our previous work.

4.2 Severity Scores

For UC classes, the domain experts manually graded a video clip's intensity using her/his own subjective scale: 0 for normal, 1 for mild, 2 for moderate, and 3 for severe. In our work, we automatically assign a severity score for the entire clip based on the class label given to each frame in a video clip. We determine the severity score S_V, for a particular video clip by averaging the class labels across all frames.

$S_V = \frac{\sum_{i=1}^{n} C_i}{n}$, where n is a total number of frames, and C_i is a class label (such as 0 for normal, 1 for mild, 2 for moderate, and 3 for severe) assigned to frame i of a given video clip.

We calculated the severity scores for the test dataset in Table 4 using the equation above. The results are shown in Table 6. The third and fourth columns show the severity scores generated from our previous work, UCS-AlexNet [7]) and VCNN 1+2+3 [8], respectively. The fifth column shows the severity scores generated from the proposed method (CNN_LfC). All severity scores generated from the proposed method are closer to our domain expert's manual evaluations (the second column) compared to those from our previous work.

To calculate how much they are closer, we calculated two Pearson correlation coefficients (PCC) by class level (Normal, Mild, Moderate and Severe) for the entire set of video clips in the test dataset in Table 4. The first and the second ones are between the severity scores generated from our domain expert's manual evaluations (the second column) and those generated from our previous work [7, 8]. The third one is between the severity scores generated from our domain expert's manual evaluations and those generated from the proposed method. These three Pearson correlation coefficients are 0.94, 0.96, and 0.97 respectively as seen in Table 6. Also, we calculated two Pearson correlation coefficients by frame level using all testing frames in Table 4 using the same way used for the class level. These three Pearson correlation coefficients are 0.80, 0.86, and 0.91 respectively as seen in Table 6. These PCCs indicate that the proposed method's prediction is closer to the domain's expert classification than the prediction by our previous work. One reason is that the proposed method provides better frame-level accuracies as seen in Table 5.

Table 6. Comparison of average severity scores and pearson correlation co-efficient.

Methods	Manual evaluation	UCS-AlexNet [9]	VCNN 1+2+3 [10]	Proposed method CNN_LfC
Normal	0	0.44	0.27	0.23
Mild	1	1.09	0.95	0.94
Moderate	2	2.42	2.09	2.11
Severe	3	2.68	2.75	2.87
PCC by Class		0.94	0.96	0.97
PCC by Frame		**0.80**	**0.86**	**0.91**

5   Concluding Remarks

Since the CNN that we implemented in this paper is not of a recurrent architecture, we can explore some CNN models using the interpretation methods recently reported in

[22–25]. These methods are shown to be quite effective for non-recurrent deep models. The current results may be sufficient for use in clinical practice. However, when used in clinical practice, we will have to calculate segmental as well as whole colon UC scores in order to distinguish a mostly normal colon with severe proctitis from mild pan-colitis which both may have a similar whole colon UC score.

Conflict of Interest and Acknowledgments. Tavanapong and Oh have equity interest and management roles in EndoMetric Corp. Dr. de Groen serves on the Scientific Advisory Board of EndoMetric Corp. This work is partially supported by the NIH Grant No. 1R01DK106130-01A1. Findings, opinions, and conclusions expressed in this paper do not necessarily reflect the view of the funding agency.

References

1. U.S. National Library of Medicine. Ulcerative colitis. https://ghr.nlm.nih.gov/condition/ulcerative-colitis. Accessed June 2022
2. Xie, T., et al.: Ulcerative colitis endoscopic index of severity (UCEIS) versus mayo endoscopic score (MES) in guiding the need for colectomy in patients with acute severe colitis. Gastroenterol. Rep. **6**(1), 38–44 (2018)
3. Kappelman, M.D., Rifas-Shiman, S.L., Kleinman, K., et al.: The prevalence and geographic distribution of Crohn's disease and ulcerative colitis in the United States. Clin. Gastroenterol. Hepatol. **5**(12), 1424–1429 (2007)
4. Rutter, M., Saunders, B., et al.: Severity of inflammation is a risk factor for colorectal neoplasia in ulcerative colitis. Gastroenterology **126**(2), 451–459 (2004)
5. Nosato, H., Sakanashi, H., Takahashi, E., Murakawa, M.: An objective evaluation method of ulcerative colitis with optical colonoscopy images based on higher order local auto-correlation features. In: 2014 IEEE 11th International Symposium on Biomedical Imaging (ISBI), pp. 89–92. IEEE (2014)
6. Alammari, A., Islam, A.R., Oh, J., Tavanapong, W., Wong, J., De Groen, P. C.: Classification of ulcerative colitis severity in colonoscopy videos using CNN. In: Proceedings of the 9th International Conference on Information Management and Engineering, Barcelona, Spain, pp. 139–144 (2017)
7. Tejaswini, S.V.L.L., Mittal, B., Oh, J., Tavanapong, W., Wong, J., de Groen, P.C.: Enhanced approach for classification of ulcerative colitis severity in colonoscopy videos using CNN. In: Bebis, G., et al. (eds.) ISVC 2019. LNCS, vol. 11845, pp. 25–37. Springer, Cham (2019). https://doi.org/10.1007/978-3-030-33723-0_3
8. Mokter, M.F., Oh, J., Tavanapong, W., Wong, J., de Groen, P.C.: Classification of ulcerative colitis severity in colonoscopy videos using vascular pattern detection. In: Liu, M., Yan, P., Lian, C., Cao, X. (eds.) MLMI 2020. LNCS, vol. 12436, pp. 552–562. Springer, Cham (2020). https://doi.org/10.1007/978-3-030-59861-7_56
9. Takenaka, K., et al.: Development and validation of a deep neural network for accurate evaluation of endoscopic images from patients with ulcerative colitis. Gastroenterology **158**(8), 2150–2157 (2020)
10. Bhambhvani, H.P., Zamora, A.: Deep learning enabled classification of Mayo endoscopic subscore in patients with ulcerative colitis. Eur. J. Gastroenterol. Hepatol. **33**(5), 645–649 (2021)
11. Luo, X., Zhang, J., Li, Z., Yang, R.: Diagnosis of ulcerative colitis from endoscopic images based on deep learning. Biomed. Signal Process. Control **73**, 103443 (2022)

12. Schwab, E., et al.: Automatic estimation of ulcerative colitis severity from endoscopy videos using ordinal multi-instance learning. Comput. Methods Biomech. Biomed. Eng. Imaging Vis. **10**(4), 425–433 (2022)

13. Harada, S., Bise, R., Hayashi, H., Tanaka, K., Uchida, S.: Order-guided disentangled representation learning for ulcerative colitis classification with limited labels. In: de Bruijne, M., et al. (eds.) MICCAI 2021. LNCS, vol. 12902, pp. 471–480. Springer, Cham (2021). https://doi.org/10.1007/978-3-030-87196-3_44

14. Sutton, R.T., Zaïane, O.R., Goebel, R., Baumgart, D.C.: Artificial intelligence enabled automated diagnosis and grading of ulcerative colitis endoscopy images. Sci. Rep. **12**(1), 1–10 (2022)

15. Borgli, H., et al.: HyperKvasir, a comprehensive multi-class image and video dataset for gastrointestinal endoscopy. Sci. Data **7**(1), 1–14 (2020)

16. Wang, C., et al.: Pulmonary image classification based on inception-v3 transfer learning model. IEEE Access **7**, 146533–146541 (2019)

17. Sarwinda, D., Paradisa, R.H., Bustamam, A., Anggia, P.: Deep learning in image classification using residual network (ResNet) variants for detection of colorectal cancer. Procedia Comput. Sci. **179**, 423–431 (2021)

18. Mascarenhas, S., Agarwal, M.: A comparison between VGG16, VGG19 and ResNet50 architecture frameworks for Image Classification. In: 2021 International Conference on Disruptive Technologies for Multi-Disciplinary Research and Applications (CENTCON), vol. 1, pp. 96–99. IEEE, November 2021

19. Dubey, N., Bhagat, E., Rana, S., Pathak, K.: A novel approach to detect plant disease using DenseNet-121 neural network. In: Zhang, Y.D., Senjyu, T., So-In, C., Joshi, A. (eds.) Smart Trends in Computing and Communications. LNNS, vol. 396, pp. 63–74. Springer, Singapore (2023). https://doi.org/10.1007/978-981-16-9967-2_7

20. Liao, L., Li, H., Shang, W., Ma, L.: An empirical study of the impact of hyperparameter tuning and model optimization on the performance properties of deep neural networks. ACM Trans. Softw. Eng. Methodol. (TOSEM) **31**(3), 1–40 (2022)

21. Liu, R., Krishnan, S., Elmore, A.J., Franklin, M.J.: Understanding and optimizing packed neural network training for hyper-parameter tuning. In: Proceedings of the Fifth Workshop on Data Management for End-To-End Machine Learning, pp. 1–11 (2021)

22. Salahuddin, Z., Woodruff, H.C., Chatterjee, A., Lambin, P.: Transparency of deep neural networks for medical image analysis: a review of interpretability methods. Comput. Biol. Med. **140**, 105111 (2022)

23. Cheng, J., et al.: ResGANet: residual group attention network for medical image classification and segmentation. Med. Image Anal. **76**, 102313 (2022)

24. Xu, J., Pan, Y., Pan, X., Hoi, S., Yi, Z., Xu, Z.: RegNet: self-regulated network for image classification. IEEE Trans. Neural Netw. Learn. Syst. (2022)

25. Mao, J., et al.: Pseudo-labeling generative adversarial networks for medical image classification. Comput. Biol. Med. **147**, 105729 (2022)

Detection and Classification of Lung Disease Using Deep Learning Architecture from X-ray Images

Anwesh Kabiraj[1] (ID), Tanushree Meena[1] (ID), Pailla Balakrishna Reddy[2] (ID), and Sudipta Roy[1(✉)] (ID)

[1] Artificial Intelligence and Data Science, Jio Institute, Navi Mumbai 410206, India
{anwesh.Kabiraj,tanushree.meena,
sudipta1.roy}@jioinstitute.edu.in
[2] Reliance Jio - Artificial Intelligence Centre of Excellence (AICoE), Hyderabad, India
balakrishna.pailla@ril.com

Abstract. The chest X-ray is among the most widely used diagnostic imaging for diagnosing many lung and bone-related diseases. Recent advances in deep learning have shown many good performances in disease identification from chest X-rays. But stability and class imbalance are yet to be addressed. In this study, we proposed a CX-Ultranet (Chest X-ray Ultranet) to classify and identify thirteen thoracic lung diseases from chest X-rays by utilizing a multiclass cross-entropy loss function on a compound scaling framework using EfficientNet as a baseline. The CX-Ultra net achieves 88% average prediction accuracy on NIH Chest X-ray Dataset. It takes ≈ 30% less time than pre-existing state-of-the-art models. The proposed CX-Ultra net gives higher average accuracy and efficiently handles the class imbalance issue. The training time in terms of Floating-Point Operations Per Second is significantly less, thus setting a new threshold in disease diagnosis from chest X-rays.

Keywords: Chest X-ray · Disease detection · Thoracic disease · Medical imaging

1 Introduction

For many decades, chest X-ray radiography (CXR) has been a central focus of imaging modalities, and it is still the most commonly used radiological scan. According to the Report of 2021 X-ray DR/CR Market Outlook, 126.8 million CXR scans were performed in the United States alone in 2021 [1]. In the last three years, CXR images increased exponentially due to the COVID-19 around the world. Another reason for the high demand for CXR images is their low radiation dose and cost-effectiveness and reasonable sensitivity to a broad range of pathologies. The CXR is also used to study for screening, diagnosis, and management of a wide range of diseases and health conditions. Therefore, the deep learning (DL) method is highly beneficial for achieving high accuracy with limited time, especially in India, where the ratio of doctors to patients is 1: 100,000. The

G. Bebis et al. (Eds.): ISVC 2022, LNCS 13598, pp. 444–455, 2022.
https://doi.org/10.1007/978-3-031-20713-6_34

complete centralized cloud-based automatic analytical tool will help the people staying in remote and rural areas. A lot of research focusing on the detection of single disease from the chest x ray has been done. However, detecting multiple disease from a single chest Xray is challenging task. Also, network stability and class-imbalance issues are not addressed. In this study we have proposed CX-Ultranet which can detect thirteen thoracic diseases with a stable network and can handle the class imbalance problem.

2 Literature Review

As an emerging technology deep learning has proved its remarkable strength in the field of medical imaging such as disease detection and classification. Researchers are trying their best to implement deep learning to detect diseases from a chest x-ray focusing on different aspects. In the automatic detection of multiple diseases from a chest x-ray, major challenges faced are the presence of unnecessary objects in the chest x-ray and second is the reduced size due to the preprocessing process. In order to overcome these challenges, a segmentation based deep fusion network was developed which gives detailed information about the lung region [2].

Another major challenge is the imperfect dataset because of the domain and label discrepancies. To tackle this problem [3] developed a model for multi-class thoracic disease classification. A similar work [4] for 14 common thoracic disease detection with a supervised multi-label classification framework based on deep convolutional neural networks (CNNs) was implemented using the CheXpert dataset and achieved AUC as 0.940.

Another study for automatic detection of covid from chest x-ray using a deep learning model was performed by [5]. A similar work [6], an automated covid screening system was developed to detect the infected patients using a hierarchical approach to segregate 3 classes. A considerable amount of work has been carried out, but the key limit persists in multi-disease classification, network stability and addressing the problem of class imbalance. The goal of most researchers is to detect one disease. Furthermore, for many image datasets, there is a higher possibility of negative data than positive data. A deep neural net is already large when trained using images, which add to the computational complexity when combined with large amounts of data. This eliminates the need to evaluate negative data for training purposes, as well as the entire process of feature extraction and training to the model, which makes the neural net heavier.

In a convolutional neural network, we also use the concepts of channel shuffling and compound scaling. A similar channel shuffling strategy for image classification was published in Shuffle NASNets [7], which demonstrated a 10% improvement in accuracy on the CIFAR-10 dataset. The exact settings of hyperparameters were optimised using the Grid Search Algorithm [8] to identify the ideal trade-off condition between FLOPS, efficiency, and accuracy. We also developed a more advanced multi-class cross-entropy loss function that we used in conjunction with the underlying CX-Ultranet to achieve standard accuracy with cutting-edge true positive and false-positive rates. When deploying a deep neural architecture on large datasets, a loss function becomes critical. To produce correct findings, both compound scaling and the loss function continuously monitor how much the model is missing. As a result, it continuously increases the CX-learning Ultranet's over time.

3 Methodology

3.1 Dataset Description

In this study, we used two chest X-rays datasets provided by the National Institute of Health (NIH) [12] and University of California San Diego, Guangzhou Women and Children's Medical Center (Mendeley Data) [13]. The NIH dataset consists of one hundred twelve thousand one hundred twenty images with the size 1024 × 1024 and corresponding 13 pathologies labelled those data collected from 30,805 unique patients. A total of 13 diseases, namely Cardiomegaly, Cardiomegaly Emphysema, Cardiomegaly Effusion, Hernia, Infiltration, Mass, Nodule, Atelectasis, Pneumothorax, Pleural Thickening, Pneumonia, Fibrosis, and Edema, are considered. The 2D chest X-rays are taken as input and processed for image augmentation. Then we send the image as input to the neural network trained on various diseases. The model is then tested to detect disease present in a chest X-ray out of the training dataset, and the corresponding results are displayed. The Mendeley dataset consist of thousands of Optical Coherence Tomography (OCT) and Chest X-Ray Images and is used for testing our model. The dataset contains two folders namely train and test, we directly used CX-Ultranet with its pre-trained weights from NIH Dataset on the test folder to test the performance of our model. The test folder contains 390 Pneumonia chest X-rays and 234 healthy chest X-rays.

3.2 Data Processing

In order to prevent data leakage, duplicate is removed. To get a normalized data, we performed data augmentation. For data augmentation, we used Image data generator class form keras library. Horizontal flipping is used for centreline extraction and disease related to symmetrical position. For lower computational complexities image size is kept at 320 × 320. The entire dataset is split into 1:1 for train and test. Around ≈ 50,000 images were used for training. The other half is used for testing.

3.3 Class Imbalance Problem

On performing exploratory data analysis, we find that most of the data belong to the negative class rather than the positive class. The contribution of the positive class becomes significantly lower than the negative class.

The Weighted Loss Function for Multiclass Cross-Entropy: The loss function is modified by replacing the y_i by the weight factor of the positive class, i.e., $weight_{positive}$ and $(1 - y_i)$ includes the weighted average of the negative class, which is $weight_{negative}$. So, the final weighted multiclass Cross-Entropy takes the form of

$$CI_{ce}^w(u) = -\big(w_p v \log(g(u)) + w_n(1 - v)\log(1 - g(u))\big) \tag{1}$$

where CI represents class imbalance Cross entropy. g(u) is the output of the model and x_i are the input features, and v are the labels i.e., the probability of it being positive (containing the disease) or negative (not including the disease). Table 1 shows the comparison of different methods to solve class imbalance problem with the proposed method with respect to time taken and accuracy on the NIH dataset.

Table 1. Comparison of different class imbalance method.

Method	Time taken to train CX-UltraNet	Remarks	Accuracy
Weighted Multi-Class Cross-Entropy	**18407 s**	**Proposed most efficient solution for solving the class imbalance**	**86.47%–92.60%**
Synthetic Minority Oversampling Technique (SMOTE)	32485 s	Creates synthetic data for the minority class due to oversampling technique, and increases the training set size	77.48%–82.98%
Ensembled Techniques – Bootstrap Aggregation	25836 s	Same test case being chosen redundantly due to relies on random replacement of data in the training set	69.53%–73.82%

3.4 Compound Scaling and Reduction Cells in CX-Ultranet

When very high-resolution images are used by the complex model, an increase in the network depth is very essential. Scaling up any component of the model such as width, depth, or resolution should result in improve the accuracy of the model. However, the accuracy improved for complex models does not rise that much at a later point of time and is slow in comparison to the initial increase at the beginning of the model.

Floating Point Operations Per Second (FP) of a regular CNN

$$FP \propto d, \omega^2, \text{ and } \gamma^2 \tag{2}$$

where $d = depth$ of the network, $\omega = Width$ of the network, and $\gamma = resolution$ of the network.

Compound Scaling Method: The compound scaling based technique is used to obtain the most optimal solution with the optimized trade-off among the accuracy and time taken.

$$depth(d) = a^\delta \quad width(\omega) = b^\delta \quad resolution(\gamma) = c^\delta \tag{3}$$

where, δ User specified coefficient controlling the resources are available for model scaling.

$$FP \propto (a.b^2.c^2)^\phi \tag{4}$$

where a, b and c specify how to assign these extra resources to network width, depth, and resolution, determined by a small grid search. Now we constrain the value of $(a.b^2.c^2)$ ≈ 2, Hence,

$$FP \propto (2)^\phi \tag{5}$$

Compound Scaling: For model scaling, we use a similar approach [7]. We fix the value of $\varphi = 1$. In order to find the values of a, b, *and* c we used simple grid-search algorithm [8], which leads to the values as, $a = 1.2$, $b = 1.1$ *and* $c = 1.14$. The same values also hold for $(a.b^2.c^2) \approx 2$. By fixing the values of a, b, *and* c, we can enhance the value of φ (Compound Coefficient), which improves the model accuracy. In order to get the best results with the least value of φ and F of the corresponding model, we optimize the product of the Model's Accuracy to the time taken by the model.

$$OG = Accuracy_{(Model)} \times FP_{(Model)} \tag{6}$$

We try to maximize our optimization goal (OG) based on the two variables (Hyper-parameter for controlling trade-offs between Accuracy and FP) in the least scaling possible.

3.5 Implementing Reduction Cells

Our main focus is to make our model very efficient in terms of time and computational complexity. We use the concept of ShuffleNet [6] and FractalNets [9]. The layers in the architecture only receive half of the channel as input while the other half is skipped which adds more skip connections to the model. The model hence created is not trained with any identity function; however, channel widths are kept equal, which reduces memory access cost. Skip connections help reduce the large group convolutions that are very frequent in bigger models with deeper network architecture. The schematic diagram of CX-Ultranet shows convolution layers with different channel widths and the cross-entropy loss function (see Fig. 1). Most of the convolutions are kept at 3×3 for finer detection as for diseases observations might be very minute. We kept the loss function layer before the compound scaling network so that only optimized feature maps are passed to the network. The compound scaling method benefits from this because if error from the CNN is not minimized then the same also gets compounded depending upon the value of δ from Eq. (4). The global and local reduction cells are more focused on decreasing the training time.

The skip connections formed with the pooling layer is because of channel shuffling. We have also used the learning rate scheduler from Keras Library [10]. Start and Max parameters are kept at 0.000002 and 0.0001, respectively. The learning rate is kept at 0.0001, and no AmsGRAD is used. We have used Adam optimizers [11] to push the model's accuracy further and stabilize the model in the long run.

The model successfully predicts multiple diseases from among thirteen thoracic diseases which utilizes the new weighted multi-class cross-entropy loss function. Our method can also give the percentage probability of different diseases (Fig. 4 B). The anomalies in the chest X-Ray are localized using the Growing seed algorithm in 3D U-Net [14]. We attained a similar training accuracy of nearly around 95%. We have also utilized the learning weights to build attention maps and GRAD-CAM-based visualizations. Because this is a multiclass detection and classification model, we utilized it to identify more diseases coupled with X-Rays. Usually, the medical professionals only focus on the highlighted disease instead of focusing on what additional medical disorders they are overlooking.

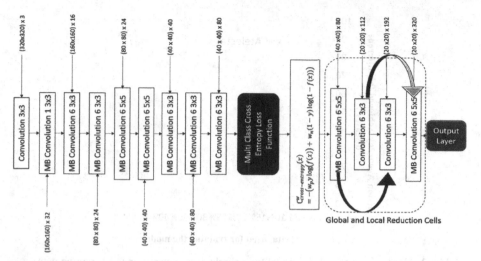

Fig. 1. The schematic flow includes the baseline network, cross-entropy loss function and reduction cells

4 Results

To check the stability of the model we plot the learning curve of the model. The model is trained by taking a subset of the data. For testing, we used a separate dataset which was not included in the overall training of the model. The amount of data taken each time is increased by 5% in the subsequent rounds, and every time it shows an improvement in accuracy. The value of loss function and trained weights are not reset in every round as some data becomes typical for every round. At the beginning of the model, we find a very high learning rate which signifies the fact that the classes are perfectly balanced. As a result, the model learns rapidly, as shown in Fig. 2. After achieving approximately 70% accuracy, the model achieves saturation point, which is very near to the highest accuracy attained by the latest state of the art model. With the cumulative impact of the loss function, learning rate scheduler, multiclass cross-entropy and Adam optimizer, accuracy of the model reaches to the 85–90% region. These play a vital role as the value of the loss function is not reset every time, and it learns by how much the model fails for the cumulative addition of new data.

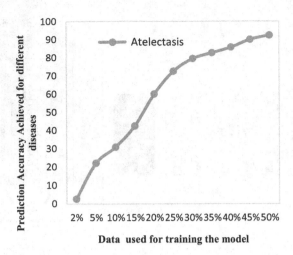

Fig. 2. The learning rate of the model for a single disease based on % of training data.

Our model learns equally from both the classes. Figure 3 shows that the class imbalance issue is resolved and there is no biasness towards a particular class.

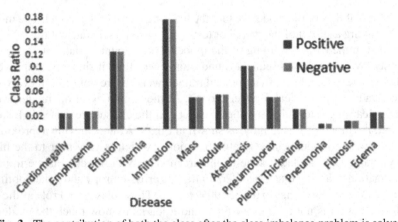

Fig. 3. The contribution of both the class after the class imbalance problem is solved.

The visualization of multiclass disease and % of disease in single chest X-ray is shown in Fig. 3. The disease with the highest % value (here Pneumothorax) is considered a primary disease of the patient. The other diseases like atelectasis and pneumothorax are the ones which the model also predicts. For better understanding, broad visualization and heat map are also shown in Fig. 4.

We have repeated the same for other thirteen diseases namely Cardiomegaly, Emphysema, Effusion, Hernia, Infiltration, Mass, Nodule, Atelectasis, Pleural Thickening, Pneumonia, Fibrosis, and Edema (like Fig. 4). An average of 88% accuracy is achieved; the highest accuracy is 92% in Atelectasis disease and the lowest at 84% in infiltration. The mean ± standard deviation (SD), maximum, and minimum test accuracy of all 13

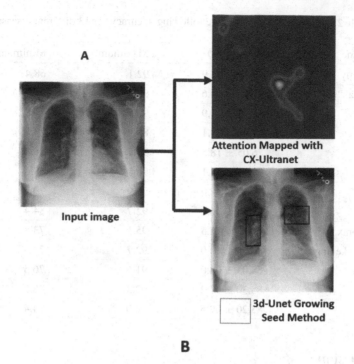

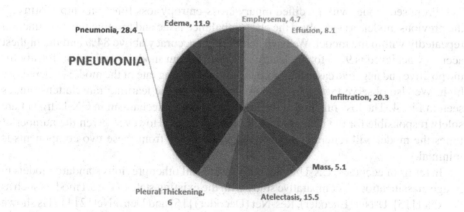

Fig. 4. The various disease predicted using the CX-Ultra net. A) The input chest X-ray and corresponding heat map and disease localization, and B) The classified anomaly where the primary disease is Pneumothorax, and the Percentage of other diseases is shown

diseases are shown in Table 2. Low SD reflect the consistency of the results and accuracy of CX-Ultranet.

Table 2. CX-Ultranet achieved the following accuracy for 13 different diseases.

Disease name	Mean ± SD	Maximum	Minimum
Cardiomegaly	80.20 ± 12.9	92.1	68.4
Emphysema	82.95 ± 10.6	92.7	73.2
Effusion	82.85 ± 11.9	93.9	71.8
Hernia	81.80 ± 09.1	89.9	73.7
Infiltration	76.05 ± 18.5	93.7	58.4
Mass	79.65 ± 12.1	90.7	68.6
Nodule	87.30 ± 08.0	94.9	79.7
Atelectasis	88.55 ± 06.0	92.7	84.4
Pneumothorax	84.45 ± 11.5	95.1	73.8
Pleural-Thickening	82.65 ± 10.9	92.7	72.6
Pneumonia	84.05 ± 08.0	91.6	76.5
Fibrosis	85.30 ± 07.2	92.3	78.3
Edema	83.20 ± 09.5	92.0	74.4

5   Discussion

The Proposed model with modified binary cross-entropy loss function outperforms all the previous models as we solved the class imbalance issue and training the loss function repeatedly within the model. We have achieved an accuracy above 84% and the highest accuracy achieved is 92% for Atelectasis disease. As our model is trained uniformly for the positive and negative cases therefore the initial learning rate of the model is incredibly high. We also observe that in the 25% to 35% region, the learning rate flattens out, as seen in Fig. 4. The loss function and compound scaling mechanism in CX-Ultra net are solely responsible for the increased prediction accuracy. However, given the number of times the model will reiterate, the increase in accuracy from these two components is minimal.

In terms of accuracy, CX-Ultranet outperforms all other previous standard models in image classification. A comparative study with the existing state of the art models such as AlexNet [15], U-Net (Encoder), Res-Net (Decoder) [16] and DenseNet121 [17] is shown in Table 3. DenseNet121 is widely known for its classification application in medical imaging. The U-Net (Encoder) Res-Net (Decoder) model is a double CNN network and challenges our model in terms of prediction accuracy. However, since we proposed a dual-channel CNN framework, it quickly falls off in computational complexity. Table 3 shows the time taken by the same is much higher than our CX-Ultranet.

In order to test the performance and applicability of our model we tested our model on any entirely different dataset which was not used for the training purpose. We tested our model for a single disease pneumonia to test the reproducibility of the model and found that our model is performing very well for the unseen data as well. We evaluated

Table 3. Accuracy metric of CX-Ultranet and five other comparative models.

Type of model	AlexNet	VGGNet	U–Net (Enc) ResNet (Dec)	DenseNET121	Efficientnet	CX-Ultranet
Cardiomegally	61.0	65.6	79.6	83.6	78.3	**88.2**
Emphysema	58.0	51.3	82.8	85.9	79.6	**89.7**
Effusion	65.0	53.6	82.1	85.0	86.6	**88.4**
Hernia	47.0	67.1	79.0	82.3	81.3	**87.2**
Infiltration	62.0	51.9	78.0	72.0	81.0	**84.4**
Mass	58.6	57.6	81.0	76.4	82.9	**86.6**
Nodule	67.3	58.2	82.0	62.6	80.3	**85.3**
Atelectasis	61.2	63.7	89.0	74.4	79.0	**92.6**
Pneumothhorax	51.4	55.3	87.5	84.1	78.0	**89.6**
Pleural thickening	68.1	59.8	87.2	74.5	84.2	**88.6**
Pneumonia	72.5	64.3	82.0	66.7	78.0	**87.3**
Fibrosis	59.4	66.1	83.4	70.6	73.6	**87.3**
Edema	53.6	51.3	88.4	84.6	81.0	**88.7**
Time taken (sec)	31678	27545	34041	29967	23446	**18407**

our model on different parameters like precision, recall and F1 score. The values of different parameters are shown in Table 4.

Table 4. Accuracy metric of CX-Ultranet on Mendeley data.

Disease name	Precision	Recall	F1-Score	Support
Pneumonia	0.93	0.96	0.94	390
Healthy Xray	0.92	0.88	0.90	234

6 Conclusion

In this paper, we proposed a novel system CX-ULTRA NET to fast and effectively detect multiple thoracic diseases from a single radiographic image. We demonstrated that deep learning algorithm can provide precise and timely solutions to the automation for medical image analysis. To deal with the stability and learning rate of the model over the large dataset, we present a novel multiclass cross-entropy loss function with an optimizer function. Also, the issue of class imbalance is resolved. The proposed system gives better results on comparison with the state-of-the-art model. It can also assist the experts quickly detect the multiple thoracic diseases. Extensive experiments on the NIH dataset confirmed the efficacy of our proposed system, thus achieving 84%–92% accuracy for multiple diseases, outperforming other methods in disease detection tasks.

Acknowledgement. This research work was supported by the RFIER-Jio Institute "CVMI-Computer Vision in Medical Imaging" research project fund under the "AI for ALL" research center.

References

1. IMV Medical Information Division, 2021 X-ray DR CR Market Outlook Report. https://imv info.com/product/2021-x-ray-dr-cr-market-outlook-report/. Accessed 4 May 2022
2. Liu, H., Wang, L., Nan, Y., Jin, F., Wang, Q., Jiantao, P.: SDFN: segmentation-based deep fusion network for thoracic disease classification in chest X-ray images. Comput. Med. Imaging Graph. **75**, 66–73 (2019)
3. Luo, L., et al.: Deep mining external imperfect data for chest X-ray disease screening. IEEE Trans. Med. Imaging **39**(11), 3583–3594 (2020)
4. Pham, H.H., Le, T.T., Tran, D.Q., Ngo, D.T., Nguyen, H.Q.: Interpreting chest X-rays via CNNs that exploit hierarchical disease dependencies and uncertainty labels. Neurocomputing **437**, 186–194 (2021)
5. Blain, M., et al.: Determination of disease severity in COVID-19 patients using deep learning in chest X-ray images. Diagn. Interv. Radiol. (Ankara, Turkey) **27**(1), 20–27 (2021)
6. Chandra, T.B., Verma, K., Singh, B.K., Jain, D., Netam, S.S.: Coronavirus disease (COVID-19) detection in chest X-ray images using majority voting based classifier ensemble. Expert Syst. Appl. **165**, 113909 (2021)
7. Laube, K.A., Zell, A.: ShuffleNASNets: efficient CNN models through modified efficient neural architecture search. In: 2019 International Joint Conference on Neural Networks (IJCNN), pp. 1–6, July 2019
8. Hesterman, J.Y., Caucci, L., Kupinski, M.A., Barrett, H.H., Furenlid, L.R.: Maximum-likelihood estimation with a contracting-grid search algorithm. IEEE Trans. Nucl. Sci. **57**(3), 1077–1084 (2010)
9. Larsson, G., Maire, M., Shakhnarovich, G.: FractalNet: ultra-deep neural networks without residuals. arXiv preprint arXiv:1605.07648 (2016)
10. Gulli, A., Pal, S.: Deep Learning with Keras. Packt Publishing Ltd. (2017)
11. Kingma, D.P., Ba, J.: Adam: a method for stochastic optimization. arXiv preprint arXiv:1412.6980 (2014)
12. National Institutes of Health - Clinical Center, ChestXray-NIHCC. https://nihcc.app.box.com/v/ChestXray-NIHCC/folder/36938765345. Accessed 10 Jan 2022
13. Kermany, D., Zhang, K., Goldbaum, M.: Large dataset of labeled optical coherence tomography (OCT) and chest X-ray images. Mendeley Data **3** (2018). https://doi.org/10.17632/rsc bjbr9sj.3
14. Roy, S., Meena, T., Lim, S.-J.: Demystifying supervised learning in healthcare 4.0: a new reality of transforming diagnostic medicine. Diagn. **12**(10), 2549 (2022). https://doi.org/10.3390/diagnostics12102549

15. Iandola, F.N., Han, S., Moskewicz, M.W., Ashraf, K., Dally, W.J., Keutzer, K.: SqueezeNet: AlexNet-level accuracy with 50x fewer parameters and <0.5 MB model size. arXiv preprint arXiv:1602.07360 (2016)
16. Chu, Z., Tian, T., Feng, R., Wang, L.: Sea-land segmentation with Res-UNet and fully connected CRF. In: IGARSS 2019–2019 IEEE International Geoscience and Remote Sensing Symposium, pp. 3840–3843. IEEE, July 2019
17. Sarker, L., Islam, M.M., Hannan, T., Ahmed, Z.: COVID-DenseNet: a deep learning architecture to detect COVID-19 from chest radiology images. Preprint, 2020050151 (2020)

PolypDEQ: Towards Effective Transformer-Based Deep Equilibrium Models for Colon Polyp Segmentation

Nguyen Minh Chau, Le Truong Giang, and Dinh Viet Sang[⊠]

School of Information and Communication Technology, Hanoi University of Science and Technology, Hanoi, Vietnam
sangdv@soict.hust.edu.vn

Abstract. Recent neural networks have shown impressive performance in computer vision tasks. However, these models mainly focus on designing deep architectures and strongly depend on the architectures themselves. This paper proposes a simple yet effective deep equilibrium model (DEQ) that exploits the advantages of implicit deep learning and multi-scale self-attention. In particular, our approach reduces the need for simultaneously finding multiple fixed points at different scales in Multi-scale Deep Equilibrium Models (MDEQs) to finding a unique fixed point at the highest resolution. Therefore, our method is more memory efficient and requires less computational complexity. To the best of our knowledge, this is the first attempt toward building an effective DEQ for polyp segmentation, and thus, we call the model PolypDEQ. Experiments on five popular polyp segmentation benchmarks show that our proposed method yields superior performance compared to previous MDEQ and Transformers.

Keywords: Semantic segmentation · Polyp segmentation · Implicit deep learning · Deep equilibrium models

1 Introduction

In recent years, the number of Colorectal cancer cases has rapidly increased. Accurate polyp detection and diagnosis are vital to the treatment. Therefore, computer-aided systems that can handle these tasks will greatly support doctors and medical professionals.

Semantic segmentation is one of the computer tasks that has recently received much attention from researchers. With the rise of deep learning-based methods, semantic segmentation can be formulated as a pixel-level classification problem. Most recent works in image segmentation are based on an Encoder-Decoder fashion, which consists of two main components: An Encoder typically receives an image and produces feature map(s) that are tensors containing abstract information about the image; A decoder takes the produced feature map(s) and forms a

G. Bebis et al. (Eds.): ISVC 2022, LNCS 13598, pp. 456–467, 2022.
https://doi.org/10.1007/978-3-031-20713-6_35

segmentation mask. Previous works used Fully Convolution Network (FCN) [13] for both Encoder and Decoder, such as U-Net [16] - a standard FCN network for image segmentation. With the aid of Vision Transformer (ViT), many new architectures (e.g., SegFormer) have shown promising results, with on-par performance compared to the traditional FCN architectures.

However, both approaches typically need to design explicit networks, also referred to as architectures, which require a considerable number of parameters to achieve good results. Bai et al. proposed a new class of implicit deep learning models for computer vision tasks: Multi-scale Deep Equilibrium model (or MDEQ) [3], which is proven to have superior memory efficiency and representative power compared to the above "explicit" models while having on-par performance. The proposed MDEQ model is rather simple, with only CNN layers with residual connections, and uses root-finding (equilibrium) solvers to find the equilibrium points for prediction. Inspired by MDEQ, in this paper, we propose a model based on implicit deep learning that takes advantage of multi-scale self-attention and the transformers-based architecture used in SegFormer [20], with the intention to achieve better performance compared to MDEQ. Our main contributions are:

- We propose a novel architecture called PolypDEQ that aggregates the idea of implicit deep learning and multi-scale self-attention for semantic segmentation. We facilitate the fixed point finding of the deep equilibrium models, yielding a much simpler yet effective deep equilibrium model while still maintaining a robust hierarchical representation.
- We compare the proposed PolypDEQ with the original MDEQ models and SegFormer on several public benchmark datasets for polyp segmentation to demonstrate the effectiveness of our method.

The rest of the paper is organized as follows: Sect. 2 reviews the general knowledge regarding implicit neural networks and briefly explains the two types of networks (MDEQ and SegFormer) that we took inspiration from. In Sect. 3.2, we describe the proposed network architecture in detail. Section 4 outlines our experiment settings. The results are presented and discussed in Sect. 5. Finally, we conclude the paper and discuss future works in Sect. 6.

2   Related Work

2.1   Medial Image Segmentation

In order to prevent Colorectal cancer, scanning and removing polyps are required. Colonoscopy analysis is an effective method that allows doctors to detect both location and severity of polyps. However, due to the variations in size, shape, and location of the polyps, it is still challenging to detect polyps with human eyes from colonoscopy. Many deep learning-based methods nowadays can support doctors via automatic colonoscopy analysis. More specifically, polyp segmentation using deep learning has shown promising results both in accuracy and speed. Following the success of UNet in biomedical image segmentation, several improved versions of UNet, such as UNet++ [22], ResUNet++ [12], AG-ResUNet++ [10], are introduced and yield promising results. While both methods focus on segmentation of the polyp area only, PraNet [8] focuses on both the area and boundary of polyps via Reverse Attention and achieves state-of-the-art performance. NeoUnet [14], BlazeNeo [1] utilized the lightweight HardNet backbone combined with attention mechanism and feature aggregation modules for polyp segmentation and neoplasm detection. TransFuse [21] combines the power of both CNNs and Transformers into an efficient model in sizes and inference speed with parallel structure. ColonFormer [7] uses pure Transformer architecture and achieves state-of-the-art results for polyp segmentation task. Nevertheless, these models require hand-crafted architecture design. They often contain a large number of parameters and need a large amount of memory for training and inference.

2.2   Implicit Deep Learning

Most deep learning models follow an explicit design, meaning they use explicit computational graphs, also called "architecture", for forward and backward propagation. Recently, Bai et al. [2] proposed implicit deep learning models: instead of defining a computational graph or an explicit architecture, they provide a criterion that the models must follow (e.g., the output of the network must satisfy an equation). Implicit models operate forward and backward propagation as root-finding problems (also referred to as finding equilibrium points), using Newton, and Quasi-Newton algorithms, such as Broyden and Anderson, as equilibrium solvers.

Implicit deep learning has been receiving much attention from researchers in recent years. Neural ODEs (NODEs) [6] use just one residual block in a recursive fashion and implicit solvers, which is equivalent to an infinite-depth ResNet [9]. Deep Equilibrium models (DEQs) [2] use equilibrium solvers (e.g., Broyden, Anderson) to find the equilibrium (fixed) point of a model for sequential tasks, which is equivalent to an infinite-depth network. Multi-scale Deep Equilibrium models (MDEQs) [3] take the idea of DEQs and add multi-resolution feature representations to perform computer vision tasks, etc.

3   Methodology

3.1   Multiscale Deep Equilibrium Models (MDEQs)

Multi-scale Deep Equilibrium models (MDEQs) [3], proposed by Bai et al., are a class of implicit deep learning models. It takes the core idea of DEQs, which is weight-tying: the same set of parameters can be shared across the layers of the network. An L-layer weight-tied transformation is formulated in MDEQs with parameter θ as follows:

$$z^{[i+1]} = f_\theta(z^{[i]}; x), \qquad i = 0, .., L-1 \tag{1}$$

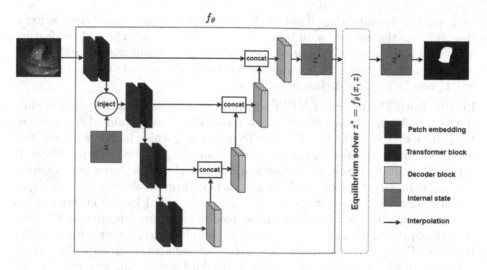

Fig. 1. Model overview.

where x is the input representation that is injected into the model at each layer, $z^{[i]}$ is the hidden state of the model at layer i, which can be a single tensor (as in DEQs) or a set of tensors at different resolutions $z = [z_1, z_2, ..., z_n]$ (n is set to 4 in the original MDEQ), hence the name Multiscale. Iterating this transformation, under certain sufficient constraints, was shown to produce a stable state z^* (an equilibrium point). Alternatively, we can formulate this iterative transformation as a root-finding problem:

$$g_\theta(z; x) := f_\theta(z; x) - z \quad \rightarrow z^* = \text{Rootfind}(g_\theta; x) \tag{2}$$

One can use Newton or Quasi-Newton solvers to solve the above equation and obtain the network's output at its infinite depth.

MDEQs use a simple design to formulate its iterative transformation f_θ. The internal state z is initialized as a set of zero-filled tensors at different scales $z = [z_1, z_2, ..., z_n]$. Each of them then goes through a sub-network that is identical in structure, which consists of a residual block that preserves the resolution at each scale to obtain the corresponding feature maps. The input image goes through a shallow CNN network to obtain the input representation, which is then injected into the highest scale only by adding in between the residual block at that scale. The feature multi-scale maps are then mixed up using a fusion network, which consists of up-sampling and down-sampling modules. The output of the transformation is a new set of tensors $z' = [z'_1, z'_2, ..., z'_n]$. MDEQs use equilibrium solvers (e.g., Anderson, Broyden) to find the equilibrium point $z^* = [z^*_1, z^*_2, ..., z^*_n]$ for all scales. Note that since the solvers are iterative, meaning we use the previous state $z^{[i]}$ at step i as input for the transformation f_θ at step $i + 1$ until convergence. It forces the tensor(s) in $z^{[i]}$ and $z^{[i+1]}$ to have the same shape (the output at each step must have the same size as the input). This is the basic rule to formulate any implicit deep models that use equilibrium solvers. One can use the output equilibrium points of MDEQ $z_1^*, z_2^*, ..., z_n^*$ as feature maps and make predictions out of them: the highest resolution map z_1^* can be used to produce masks for a segmentation task, whereas the lowest resolution one z_n^* can be used for a classification task.

Limitations: The design of MDEQs is quite simple. Its transformation module (DEQ module) f_θ consists of only Convolution blocks and Residual connections. We believe that with the aid of Vision Transformers, which has shown promising results in computer vision in general, and semantic segmentation in particular, it is possible to design an implicit deep learning model with superior performance. Moreover, in MDEQs, one needs to use an equilibrium solver to find the equilibrium points for all resolutions $z_1^*, z_2^*, ..., z_n^*$. As stated by the authors in [3], finding an equilibrium state for multiple resolution scales can improve the convergence of the equilibrium solving process itself; however, we find that it makes training MDEQ extremely slow. And since for segmentation, only the output feature map with the highest resolution is used for prediction, we argue that for this task specifically, one only needs to find the equilibrium state for the tensor with the highest resolution (z_1). Our model - PolypDEQ covers these problems of MDEQs.

3.2   SegFormer

SegFormer [20] is a class of Transformer networks for semantic segmentation, which has shown efficiency, accuracy, and robustness. Proposed by Xie et al., Seg-Former has become the baseline for many other models for the task of semantic segmentation:

SegFormer follows a typical architecture pattern of a semantic segmentation model, consisting of an Encoder module and a Decoder module. SegFormer uses Mix Transformer encoders (MiTs) to generate a set of hierarchical feature maps: it produces multi-level feature maps at different resolutions, unlike previous ViTs, which can only produce one feature map. Another difference between MiTs and the traditional ViTs is that ViTs use Positional Embedding (PE) to represent local information by a fixed-size tensor, meaning during inference, this has to be interpolated for test images whose sizes are different from the training ones; this typically results in performance drop; MiTs instead use a convolution layer in the Feed-Forward Network (FFN), instead of pure Multi-Layer Perceptron (MLP) like ViTs to create Mix-FFN. This was shown to be able to provide local information as well as allow SegFormer to adapt to new image resolutions during inference without a performance drop.

For the decoder module, SegFormer uses just a simple lightweight All-MLP decoder. It takes in the four feature maps produced by MiT Encoder, equalizes their channel dimensions using MLP, then up-samples them to the same spatial resolution and concatenates the results into a single tensor. Next, the tensor goes through an MLP layer to "mix" the information from the four source feature maps and, finally, another MLP layer to produce the prediction mask. This simple design is claimed to be sufficient enough to achieve good results. However, one can replace this All-MLP decoder with other decoder modules to achieve even better performance. For example, as will be shown in this paper, we can use a U-Net-like hierarchical decoder, which forms a U-Net-like model with a hierarchical MiT Encoder and a hierarchical Decoder and achieves superior results.

3.3 Our PolypDEQ

We propose a novel neural network architecture named PolypDEQ, which is built upon the ideas of implicit deep learning (MDEQs) and SegFormer. Figure 1 describes this overall architecture in detail.

Following the implicit deep learning approach, our central design is the iterative transformation f_θ, which can be described as follow: The input image is fed into the first MiT Encoder Block, which consists of an Overlapped Patch Embedding and a Transformer block (as in MiT encoder) to obtain a feature map. We initialize z - our internal state as a single zero-filled tensor that has the same resolution as the first input representation (or feature map) after the first MiT Encoder Block. Unlike MDEQs, which find the equilibrium state for multiple spatial resolutions (Multi-scale), we only find one equilibrium state z^* for z at a single resolution scale. We combine z and the first feature map of MiT Encoder to obtain another feature map with the same resolution. This step simulates the effect of "input representation injection" as shown in [3]. There are many strategies to combine the two tensors. This paper considers two methods: direct element-wise adding and using a simple residual block. The feature map then goes through three more MiT Encoder blocks to produce four feature maps (including the first feature map with input injection). We use a simple Hierarchical Decoder module; it resembles the traditional U-Net decoder module, which "decodes" the feature maps hierarchically from coarse to fine. At each resolution, the feature map is interpolated to match the resolution of the next larger feature map. They are concatenated and go through a convolution layer. Our decoder takes the four feature maps from our Encoder and produces a single output tensor with the same resolution as z. Normally, for explicit models, we would apply a Convolution Layer, or MLP layer, to obtain the predicted mask here (or equivalent to iterating f_θ for only one iteration); however, we take the implicit deep learning approach. Hence, we then leverage Broyden's equilibrium solver to find the equilibrium point z^* (equivalent to iterating f_θ infinitely) and then make predictions on it. Since solving for an equilibrium point is equivalent to finding the model's output at an infinite step [3], we can see this model as an infinite number of weight-tied U-Net one after another. We have experimented with two strategies: making predictions right after the first iteration of f_θ (just like an explicit model) and using the Broyden equilibrium solver to find the equilibrium state z^* and make predictions on it (implicit model). Therefore, we use both approaches for each training configuration to obtain two corresponding models: the explicit and implicit versions. The results of both approaches are compared in Sect. 5.

For our iterative transformation f_θ, which is a weight-tied U-Net, we use a similar MiT Encoder as in SegFormer. The only modification is the injection of z and the input representation, which is required for an implicit model. The SegFormer framework provides different versions of MiT Encoder, ranging from MiT-B0 to MiT-B5. They are the same in architecture, only different in size, with MiT-B0 being the smallest and MiT-B5 being the largest. Here, we use only MiT-B0 for two reasons: firstly, the process of equilibrium solving requires us to iterate through the model many times. Therefore, we cannot use a large-size network to design our f_θ. Secondly, even using a lightweight model, we show that PolypDEQ still produces comparable results to its explicit SegFormer counterparts.

We use two different strategies for the injection (combination of z and the first feature map of MiT Encoder): direct element-wise adding and leveraging a residual block. In the first strategy, we simply perform element-wise adding for the two tensors. We call this first version PolypDEQ-add. The second version, called PolypDEQ-res, uses a simple residual block to combine the two tensors. Figure 2 describes the design of our residual block used for injection. First, the internal state z goes through a simple 3×3 Convolution Layer, Group Normalization, ReLU, and a 1×1 Convolution Layer. Then we perform element-wise adding with the first feature map of MiT that we got from the input image. Finally, we use a residual connection by adding z to the result after a Group Normalization. We compare the performance of our model between the two methods in Sect. 5.

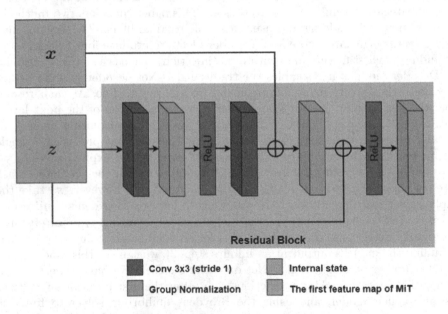

Fig. 2. Input injection using residual blocks.

4   Experiments and Discussion

4.1   Benchmark Datasets

We perform experiments with a wide range of benchmark datasets for polyp segmentation, as shown in Table 1.

Table 1. The properties of benchmark datasets.

Dataset	Train images	Test images	Resolution
Kvasir-SEG [11]	900	100	Various
CVC-ClinicDB [5]	550	62	384×288
CVC-ColonDB [18]	0	380	574×500
ETIS-Larib PolypDB [17]	0	196	1225×966
EndoScene [19]	0	60	574×500

4.2   Experiment Settings

PolypDEQ is trained in two phases: the explicit and implicit phases. For the explicit phase, we do not use equilibrium solvers (iterate f_θ only once) and train the model as an explicit model; we use AdamW optimizer, with the initial learning rate of 10^{-3}, and a linear decay learning rate scheduler. The final learning rate is 10^{-6}. We train our explicit models for 100 epochs with a batch size of 16, using a multi-scale training strategy: for each training image, we resize it to $0.25, 1, 1.25$ times the original scale before feeding it into the model. After the explicit phase, we obtain the explicit version of our model. For the implicit phase, we first load the weight obtained from training the explicit model. This is possible because the explicit and implicit versions of our model are identical in structure. The only difference is the existence of the equilibrium solver. Then, we continue training the model "explicitly" for 30 epochs before applying our equilibrium solver and training it as an implicit model for 70 epochs. We use the same training configurations as the first phase, except for the learning rate scheduler. For this phase, we first initialize the learning rate to be 10^{-3}, then linear decrease it to 10^{-6} during the first 30 epochs of training, then reset the learning rate to 5×10^{-4} and linear decrease it again to 10^{-6} for the rest of the training. After this phase, we obtain our implicit model.

We use simple Data augmentations for training PolypDEQ, with a probability of 0.5. The following augmentations are applied: Horizontal/vertical flip, random rotation, change of brightness, contrast, saturation, random cropping, and random cut-mix (cropping part of a random image and put into another image).

We evaluate models using mean Dice score (mDice) and mean Intersection over Union (mIoU).

5   Results and Discussion

5.1   Performance

Table 2 shows performance metrics for our proposed PolypDEQ, and MDEQ in both versions: implicit model and explicit model on five polyp datasets. We also compare the performance of PolypDEQ with two different injection strategies as aforementioned. Note that the models are trained on subsets of the Kvasir and CVC-ClinicDB datasets. Implicit PolypDEQ with injection using Residual Block outperforms all other models on the Kvasir and CVC-ColonDB, while implicit PolypDEQ with injection using element-wise adding outperforms others on the CVC-ClinicDB and ETIS-Larib PolypDB dataset.

Table 2. Quantitative results on benchmark datasets. Note that SegFormer-B0* below is equivalent to explicit PolypDEQ with the adding injection strategy.

Method	Mode	Kvasir		CVC-Clinic		CVC-Colon		EndoScene		ETIS	
		mDice	mIoU	mDice	mIoU	mDice	mIoU	mDice	mIoU	mDice	mIoU
MDEQ [3]	expl	0.846	0.773	0.836	0.769	0.585	0.487	0.787	0.693	0.485	0.404
MDEQ [3]	impl	0.873	0.803	0.811	0.743	0.724	0.644	0.827	0.740	0.654	0.579
Segformer-B0* [20]	expl	0.897	0.839	0.862	0.807	0.735	0.657	**0.882**	**0.803**	0.657	0.583
PolypDEQ-add	impl	0.904	0.846	**0.895**	**0.839**	0.742	0.664	0.873	0.793	**0.689**	**0.608**
PolypDEQ-res	impl	**0.905**	**0.847**	0.888	0.832	**0.742**	**0.666**	0.876	0.793	0.683	0.605

⋆ indicates that we use UNet's decoder instead of the All-MLP decoder proposed in [20]

Figure 3 shows example outputs for different models. PolypDEQ produces noticeably better segmentation than MDEQs. This shows how the MiT Encoder module has an impact on enhancing models' performance.

It is worth noticing that the models that aggregate MiT Encoder: explicit and implicit PolypDEQs outperform MDEQs by a considerable margin. Moreover, all implicit models (MDEQ-implicit, PolypDEQ-implicit) outperform their explicit versions, showing the power of implicit models: they can surpass their explicit counterparts with the same structural design and number of parameters.

5.2   Time and Space Complexity

Table 3 compares the behavior of our models and MDEQs, for both versions: implicit and explicit, in terms of time cost, memory usage, number of solver iterations, and model sizes. We record these quantities on a device with a 3.60 GHz CPU and an NVIDIA GeForce RTX 3090 GPU with 24576 MB of total memory.

We can see that both explicit and implicit versions of PolypDEQ have faster inference time as well as lower memory usage and lower numbers of parameters. However, we also notice that the number of solver iterations for PolypDEQ to find the equilibrium state is also less than MDEQs by a considerable margin. This might be due to the fact that for PolypDEQ, we only find the equilibrium state for one tensor z, as compared to multiple tensors $z = [z_1, z_2, ..., z_n]$ in MDEQs, which might also affect the time complexity.

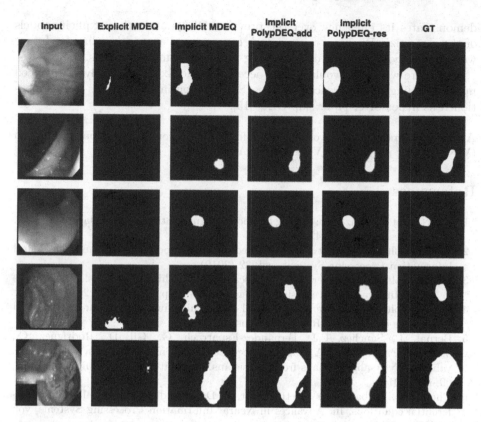

Fig. 3. Sample results from different models on the CVC-ClinicDB dataset. The first column is the sampled images, the next three columns are the prediction segmentation of the models, and the last column is the ground truth segmentation.

Table 3. Performance comparison in terms of inference time, memory usage, number of parameters, and number of solver iterations.

Model	Mode	Time (s)	MEM (MB)	# Params	# Solver iters
MDEQ [3]	explicit	0.011	2174	8949410	–
MDEQ [3]	implicit	0.774	2554	8949410	97.5
PolypDEQ-add	explicit	0.0052	2090	5525121	–
PolypDEQ-add	implicit	0.549	2292	5525121	57.5
PolypDEQ-res	explicit	0.0053	2090	5544673	–
PolypDEQ-res	implicit	0.560	2292	5544673	67.5

6   Conclusion

This paper has made the first attempt to build a deep implicit network for polyp segmentation and perhaps the first in medical image analysis. Our PolypDEQ demonstrates its efficiency over the previous DEQs and other explicit models of the same size. We hope this research can serve as a good baseline for future works in applying implicit deep learning in medical image analysis.

In future work, we would like to accelerate the fixed point solvers to speed up the training and inference processes. Some potential approaches can be mentioned as hypersolver [4] or skip DEQ [15].

Acknowledgment. This work was funded by Vingroup Innovation Foundation (VINIF) under project code VINIF.2020.DA17.

References

1. An, N.S., et al.: BlazeNeo: blazing fast polyp segmentation and neoplasm detection. IEEE Access **10**, 43669–43684 (2022)
2. Bai, S., Kolter, J.Z., Koltun, V.: Deep equilibrium models. In: Advances in Neural Information Processing Systems, vol. 32 (2019)
3. Bai, S., Koltun, V., Kolter, J.Z.: Multiscale deep equilibrium models. In: Advances in Neural Information Processing Systems, vol. 33, pp. 5238–5250 (2020)
4. Bai, S., Koltun, V., Kolter, J.Z.: Neural deep equilibrium solvers. In: International Conference on Learning Representations (2021)
5. Bernal, J., Sánchez, F.J., Fernández-Esparrach, G., Gil, D., Rodríguez, C., Vilariño, F.: WM-DOVA maps for accurate polyp highlighting in colonoscopy: validation vs. saliency maps from physicians. Comput. Med. Imaging Graph. **43**, 99–111 (2015)
6. Chen, R.T., Rubanova, Y., Bettencourt, J., Duvenaud, D.K.: Neural ordinary differential equations. In: Advances in Neural Information Processing Systems, vol. 31 (2018)
7. Duc, N.T., Oanh, N.T., Thuy, N.T., Triet, T.M., Dinh, V.S.: ColonFormer: an efficient transformer based method for colon polyp segmentation. IEEE Access **10**, 80575–80586 (2022)
8. Fan, D.-P., et al.: PraNet: parallel reverse attention network for polyp segmentation. In: Martel, A.L., et al. (eds.) MICCAI 2020. LNCS, vol. 12266, pp. 263–273. Springer, Cham (2020). https://doi.org/10.1007/978-3-030-59725-2_26
9. He, K., Zhang, X., Ren, S., Sun, J.: Deep residual learning for image recognition. In: Proceedings of the IEEE Conference on Computer Vision and Pattern Recognition, pp. 770–778 (2016)
10. Hung, N.B., Duc, N.T., Van Chien, T., Sang, D.V.: AG-ResUNet++: an improved encoder-decoder based method for polyp segmentation in colonoscopy images. In: 2021 RIVF International Conference on Computing and Communication Technologies (RIVF), pp. 1–6. IEEE (2021)
11. Jha, D., et al.: Kvasir-SEG: a segmented polyp dataset. In: Ro, Y.M., et al. (eds.) MMM 2020. LNCS, vol. 11962, pp. 451–462. Springer, Cham (2020). https://doi.org/10.1007/978-3-030-37734-2_37
12. Jha, D., et al.: ResUNet++: an advanced architecture for medical image segmentation. In: 2019 IEEE International Symposium on Multimedia (ISM), pp. 225–2255 (2019). https://doi.org/10.1109/ISM46123.2019.00049
13. Long, J., Shelhamer, E., Darrell, T.: Fully convolutional networks for semantic segmentation. In: Proceedings of the IEEE Conference on Computer Vision and Pattern Recognition, pp. 3431–3440 (2015)

14. Ngoc Lan, P., et al.: NeoUNet: towards accurate colon polyp segmentation and neo-plasm detection. In: Bebis, G., et al. (eds.) ISVC 2021. LNCS, vol. 13018, pp. 15–28. Springer, Cham (2021). https://doi.org/10.1007/978-3-030-90436-4_2

15. Pal, A., Edelman, A., Rackauckas, C.: Mixing implicit and explicit deep learning with skip DEQs and infinite time neural odes (continuous DEQs). arXiv preprint arXiv:2201.12240 (2022)

16. Ronneberger, O., Fischer, P., Brox, T.: U-Net: convolutional networks for biomed-ical image segmentation. In: Navab, N., Hornegger, J., Wells, W.M., Frangi, A.F. (eds.) MICCAI 2015. LNCS, vol. 9351, pp. 234–241. Springer, Cham (2015). https://doi.org/10.1007/978-3-319-24574-4_28

17. Silva, J., Histace, A., Romain, O., Dray, X., Granado, B.: Toward embedded detec-tion of polyps in WCE images for early diagnosis of colorectal cancer. Int. J. Com-put. Assist. Radiol. Surg. 9(2), 283–293 (2014)

18. Tajbakhsh, N., Gurudu, S.R., Liang, J.: Automated polyp detection in colonoscopy videos using shape and context information. IEEE Trans. Med. Imaging 35(2), 630–644 (2015)

19. Vázquez, D., et al.: A benchmark for endoluminal scene segmentation of colonoscopy images. J. Healthcare Eng. 2017 (2017)

20. Xie, E., Wang, W., Yu, Z., Anandkumar, A., Alvarez, J.M., Luo, P.: SegFormer: simple and efficient design for semantic segmentation with transformers. In: Advances in Neural Information Processing Systems, vol. 34, pp. 12077–12090 (2021)

21. Zhang, Y., Liu, H., Hu, Q.: TransFuse: fusing transformers and CNNs for med-ical image segmentation. In: de Bruijne, M., et al. (eds.) MICCAI 2021. LNCS, vol. 12901, pp. 14–24. Springer, Cham (2021). https://doi.org/10.1007/978-3-030-87193-2_2

22. Zhou, Z., Rahman Siddiquee, M.M., Tajbakhsh, N., Liang, J.: UNet++: a nested U-Net architecture for medical image segmentation. In: Stoyanov, D., et al. (eds.) DLMIA/ML-CDS -2018. LNCS, vol. 11045, pp. 3–11. Springer, Cham (2018). https://doi.org/10.1007/978-3-030-00889-5_1

Author Index